LYLE
ANTIQUES
PRICE GUIDE
2000

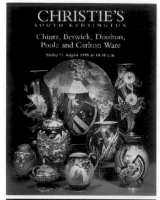
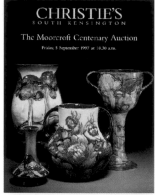

LYLE
ANTIQUES
PRICE GUIDE
2000

**COMPILED & EDITED
BY TONY CURTIS**

EBURY PRESS
LONDON

ANTIQUES PRICE GUIDE

First published in Great Britain in 1999

1 3 5 7 9 10 8 6 4 2

Ebury Press
Random House, 20 Vauxhall Bridge Road, London SW1V 2SA

Random House Australia Pty Limited
20 Alfred Street, Milsons Point, Sydney, New South Wales 2061, Australia

Random House New Zealand Limited
18 Poland Road, Glenfield, Auckland 10, New Zealand

Random House South Africa (Pty) Limited
Endulini, 5A Jubilee Road, Parktown 2193, South Africa

Random House UK Limited Reg. No. 954009

www.randomhouse.co.uk.

Papers used by Ebury Press are natural, recyclable products made from wood grown in sustainable forests.

A CIP catalogue record for this book is available from the British Library.

ISBN 0 09 186512 3

Printed and bound in Great Britain by
Butler & Tanner Ltd, Frome and London

While every care has been taken in the compiling of information contained in this volume, the publishers cannot accept liability for loss, financial or otherwise, incurred by reliance placed on the information herein.

All prices quoted in this book are obtained from a variety of auctions in various countries during the twelve months prior to publication and are converted to dollars at the rate of exchange prevailing at the time of sale. The images and the accompanying text remain the copyright of the contributing auction houses.

The publishers wish to express their thanks to the following for their involvement and assistance in the preparation of this volume:

TONY CURTIS (Editor)
EELIN McIVOR (Sub Editor)
ANNETTE CURTIS (Editorial)
CATRIONA DAY (Art Production)

ANGIE DEMARCO (Art Production)
NICKY FAIRBURN (Art Production)
PHILIP SPRINGTHORPE (Photography)
HANNAH McIVOR (Research)

INTRODUCTION

This year over 100,000 Antique Dealers and Collectors will make full and profitable use of their Lyle Antiques Price Guide. They know that only in this one volume will they find the widest possible variety of goods – illustrated, described and given a current market value to assist them to BUY RIGHT AND SELL RIGHT throughout the year of issue.

They know, too, that by building a collection of these immensely valuable volumes year by year, they will equip themselves with an unparalleled reference library of facts, figures and illustrations which, properly used, cannot fail to help them keep one step ahead of the market.

In its thirty years of publication, Lyle has gone from strength to strength and has become without doubt the pre-eminent book of reference for the antiques trade throughout the world. Each of its fact filled pages is packed with precisely the kind of profitable information the professional Dealer needs – including descriptions, illustrations and values of thousands and thousands of individual items carefully selected to give a representative picture of the current market in antiques and collectables – and remember all values are prices actually paid, based on accurate sales records in the twelve months prior to publication from the best established and most highly respected auction houses and retail outlets in Europe and America.

This is THE book for the Professional Antiques Dealer. 'The Lyle Book' – we've even heard it called 'The Dealer's Bible'.

Compiled and published afresh each year, the Lyle Antiques Price Guide is the most comprehensive up-to-date antiques price guide available. THIS COULD BE YOUR WISEST INVESTMENT OF THE YEAR!

Tony Curtis

CONTENTS

ACKNOWLEDGEMENTS

AB Stockholms Auktionsverk, Box 16256, 103 25 Stockholm, Sweden
Abbotts Auction Rooms, The Auction Rooms, Campsea Ash, Woodbridge, Suffolk
Academy Auctioneers, Northcote House, Northcote Avenue, Ealing, London W5 3UR
James Adam, 26, St Stephens Green, Dublin 2
Henry Aldridge & Son, Devizes Auction Rooms, Wine Street, Devizes SN10 1AP
Amersham Auction Rooms, 125 Station Road, Amersham, Bucks. HP7 OAH
Jean Claude Anaf, Lyon Brotteaux, 13 bis place Jules Ferry, 69456, Lyon, France
Anderson & Garland, Marlborough House, Marlborough Crescent, Newcastle upon Tyne NE1 4EE
Atlantic Antiques, Chenil House, 181–183 Kings Road, London SW3 5ED
The Auction Galleries, Mount Rd., Tweedmouth, Berwick on Tweed
Auction Team Köln, Postfach 50 11 68, D-5000 Köln 50, Germany
Auktionshaus Arnold, Bleichstr. 42, 6000 Frankfurt a/M, Germany
Bearne's, St Edmunds Court, Okehampton Street, Exeter EX4 1DU
Biddle & Webb, Ladywood Middleway, Birmingham B16 0PP
Bigwood, The Old School, Tiddington, Stratford upon Avon
Black Horse Agencies Ambrose, 149 High Street, Loughton, Essex 1G10 4LZ
Black Horse Agencies, Locke & England, 18 Guy Street, Leamington Spa
Boardman Fine Art Auctioneers, Station Road Corner, Haverhill, Suffolk CB9 0EY
JW Bollom, PO Box 78, Croydon Rd, Beckenham CR3 4BL
Bonhams, Montpelier Street, Knightsbridge, London SW7 1HH
Bonhams Chelsea, 65–69 Lots Road, London SW10 0RN
Bonhams West Country, Dowell Street, Honiton, Devon
Bosleys, 42 West Street, Marlow, Bucks SL7 1NB
Andrew Bottomley, The Coach House, Huddersfield Rd, Holmfirth, West Yorks.
Michael J. Bowman, 6 Haccombe House, Near Netherton, Newton Abbot, Devon
Bristol Auction Rooms, St John Place, Apsley Road, Clifton, Bristol BS8 2ST
British Antique Replicas, School Close, Queen Elizabeth Avenue, Burgess Hill, Sussex
Butchoff Antiques, 229–233 Westbourne Grove, London W11 2SE
Butterfield & Butterfield, 220 San Bruno Avenue , San Francisco CA 94103, USA
Butterfield & Butterfield, 7601 Sunset Boulevard, Los Angeles CA 90046, USA
Canterbury Auction Galleries, 40 Station Road West, Canterbury CT2 8AN
Central Motor Auctions, Barfield House, Britannia Road, Morley, Leeds, LS27 0HN
H.C. Chapman & Son, The Auction Mart, North Street, Scarborough.
Chapman Moore & Mugford, 8 High Street, Shaftesbury SP7 8JB
Cheffins Grain & Comins, 2 Clifton Road, Cambridge
Christie's (International) SA, 8 place de la Taconnerie, 1204 Genève, Switzerland
Christie's Monaco, S.A.M, Park Palace 98000 Monte Carlo, Monaco
Christie's Scotland, 164–166 Bath Street, Glasgow G2 4TG
Christie's South Kensington Ltd., 85 Old Brompton Road, London SW7 3LD
Christie's, 8 King Street, London SW1Y 6QT
Christie's East, 219 East 67th Street, New York, NY 10021, USA
Christie's, 502 Park Avenue, New York, NY10022, USA
Christie's, Cornelis Schuytstraat 57, 1071 JG Amsterdam, Netherlands
Christie's SA Roma, 114 Piazza Navona, 00186 Rome, Italy
Christie's Swire, 2804–6 Alexandra House, 16–20 Chater Road, Hong Kong
Christie's Australia Pty Ltd., 1 Darling Street, South Yarra, Victoria 3141, Australia
Clarke & Gammon, The Guildford Auction Rooms, Bedford Road, Guildford, GU1 4SE
Bryan Clisby, Andwells Antiques, Hartley Wintney, North Hants.
The Clock House, 75 Pound Street, Carshalton, Surrey SM5 3PG
A J Cobern, The Grosvenor Sales Rooms, 93b Eastbank Street, Southport PR8 1DG
Collins Antiques, Wheathampstead, St Albans AL4 8AP
Cooper Hirst Auctions, The Granary Saleroom, Victoria Road, Chelmsford, Essex CM2 6LH
Coppelia Antiques, Holford Lodge, Plumley, Cheshire.
The Cotswold Auction Co., Chapel Walk Saleroom, Chapel Walk, Cheltenham GL50 3DS
The Crested China Co., Station House, Driffield, E. Yorks YO25 7PY
Cundalls, The Cattle Market, 17 Market Square, Malton, N. Yorks.
The Curiosity Shop, 127 Old Street, Ludlow, Shropshire
Clifford Dann, 20/21 High Street, Lewes, Sussex
Dargate Auction Galleries, 5607 Baum Blvd., Pittsburgh PA 15206
Julian Dawson, Lewes Auction Rooms, 56 High Street, Lewes BN7 1XE
Dee & Atkinson & Harrison, The Exchange Saleroom, Driffield, Nth Humberside YO25 7LJ
Garth Denham & Assocs. Horsham Auction Galleries, Warnsham, Nr. Horsham, Sussex
Diamond Mills & Co., 117 Hamilton Road, Felixstowe, Suffolk
David Dockree Fine Art, The Redwood Suite, Clemence House, Mellor Road, Cheadle Hulme, Cheshire
Dorking Desk Shop, 41 West Street, Dorking, Surrey
William Doyle Galleries, 175 East 87th Street, New York, NY 10128, USA

Douglas Ross, Charter House, 42 Avebury Boulevard, Central Milton Keynes MK9 2HS
Dreweatt Neate, Donnington Priory, Newbury, Berks.
Dreweatt Neate, Holloways, 49 Parsons Street, Banbury
Hy. Duke & Son, 40 South Street, Dorchester, Dorset
Du Mouchelles Art Galleries Co., 409 E. Jefferson Avenue, Detroit, Michigan 48226, USA
Sala de Artes y Subastas Durán, Serrano 12, 28001 Madrid, Spain
Eldred's, Box 796, E. Dennis, MA 02641, USA
R H Ellis & Sons, 44/46 High Street, Worthing, BN11 1LL
Enchanted House, 18–24 The Roundhouse Industrial Estate, Harbour Road, Par, Cornwall
Ewbanks, Burnt Common Auction Rooms, London Road, Send, Woking GU23 7LN
Fellows & Son, Augusta House, 19 Augusta Street, Hockley, Birmingham
Fidler Taylor & Co., Crown Square, Matlock, Derbyshire DE4 3AT
Finarte, 20121 Milano, Piazzetta Bossi 4, Italy
John D Fleming & Co., The North Devon Auction Rooms, The Savory, South Molton, Devon
Four in One Promotions, PO Box 5125, Leicester LE8 9ZT
Peter Francis,19 King Street, Carmarthen, Dyfed
Fraser Pinney's, 8290 Devonshire, Montreal, Quebec, Canada H4P 2PZ
Freeman Fine Arts, 1808 Chestnut Street, Philadelphia PA19103, USA
Galerie Koller, Rämistr. 8, CH 8024 Zürich, Switzerland
Galerie Moderne, 3 rue du Parnasse, 1040 Bruxelles, Belgium
GB Antiques Centre, Lancaster Leisure Park, Wynesdale Rd, Lancaster LA1 3LA
Geering & Colyer (Black Horse Agencies) Highgate, Hawkhurst, Kent
The Goss and Crested China Co., 62 Murray Road, Horndean, Hants PO8 9JL
The Grandfather Clock Shop, Little House, Sheep Street, Stow on the Wold 9L54 1AA
Graves Son & Pilcher, Hove Auction Rooms, Hove Street, Hove, East Sussex
Greenslade Hunt, Magdalene House, Church Square, Taunton, Somerset, TA1 1SB
Hampton's Fine Art, 93 High Street, Godalming, Surrey
Hanseatisches Auktionshaus für Historica, Neuer Wall 57, 2000 Hamburg 36, Germany
William Hardie Ltd., 141 West Regent Street, Glasgow G2 2SG
Andrew Hartley Fine Arts, Victoria Hall, Little Lane, Ilkely
Hastings Antiques Centre, 59–61 Norman Road, St Leonards on Sea, East Sussex
Hauswedell & Nolte, D-2000 Hamburg 13, Pöseldorfer Weg 1, Germany
Giles Haywood, The Auction House, St John's Road, Stourbridge, West Midlands, DY8 1EW
Muir Hewitt, Halifax Antiques Centre, Queens Road/Gibbet Street, Halifax HX1 4LR
Hobbs Parker, New Ashford Market, Monument Way, Orbital Park, Ashford TN24 0HB
Holloways, 49 Parsons Street, Banbury OX16 8PF
Hotel de Ventes Horta, 390 Chaussée de Waterloo (Ma Campagne), 1060 Bruxelles, Belgium
Hubbard Antiques, 16 St Margarets Green, Ipswich IP4 2BS
Jackson's, 2229 Lincoln Street, Cedar Falls, Iowa 50613, USA.
Jacobs & Hunt, Lavant Street, Petersfield, Hants. GU33 3EF
P Herholdt Jensens Auktioner, Rundforbivej 188, 2850 Nerum, Denmark
Kennedy & Wolfenden, 218 Lisburn Road, Belfast BT9 6GD
G A Key, Aylsham Saleroom, Palmers Lane, Aylsham, Norfolk, NR11 6EH
George Kidner, The Old School, The Square, Pennington, Lymington, Hants SO41 8GN
Kunsthaus am Museum, Drususgasse 1–5, 5000 Köln 1, Germany
Kunsthaus Lempertz, Neumarkt 3, 5000 Köln 1, Germany
Lambert & Foster (County Group), The Auction Sales Room, 102 High Street, Tenterden, Kent
W.H. Lane & Son, 64 Morrab Road, Penzance, Cornwall, TR18 8AB
Langlois Ltd., Westaway Rooms, Don Street, St Helier, Channel Islands
Lawrence Butler Fine Art Salerooms, Marine Walk, Hythe, Kent, CT21 5AJ
Lawrence Fine Art, South Street, Crewkerne, Somerset TA18 8AB
Lawrence's Fine Art Auctioneers, Norfolk House, 80 High Street, Bletchingley, Surrey
David Lay, The Penzance Auction House, Alverton, Penzance, Cornwall TA18 4KE
Gordon Litherland, 26 Stapenhill Road, Burton on Trent
Lloyd International Auctions, 118 Putney Bridge Road, London SW15 2NQ
Brian Loomes, Calf Haugh Farm, Pateley Bridge, North Yorks
Lots Road Chelsea Auction Galleries, 71 Lots Road, Chelsea, London SW10 0RN
R K Lucas & Son, Tithe Exchange, 9 Victoria Place, Haverfordwest, SA61 2JX
Duncan McAlpine, Stateside Comics plc, 125 East Barnet Road, London EN4 8RF
McCartneys, Portcullis Salerooms, Ludlow, Shropshire
John Mann, Bruntshielbog, Canonbie, Dumfries DG14 0RY
Christopher Matthews, 23 Mount Street, Harrogate HG2 8DG
John Maxwell, 133a Woodford Road, Wilmslow, Cheshire
May & Son, 18 Bridge Street, Andover, Hants
Morphets, 4–6 Albert Street, Harrogate, North Yorks HG1 1JL
Neales, The Nottingham Saleroom, 192 Mansfield Road, Nottingham NG1 3HU
D M Nesbit & Co, 7 Clarendon Road, Southsea, Hants PO5 2ED
Newark Antiques Centre, Regent House, Lombard House, Newark, Notts.

John Nicholson, Longfield, Midhurst Road, Fernhurst GU27 3HA
Occleshaw Antiques Centre, The Old Major Cinema, 11 Mansfield Road, Edwinstowe, Notts. NG21 9NL
The Old Brigade, 10a Harborough Rd, Kingsthorpe, Northampton NN1 7AZ
The Old Cinema, 157 Tower Bridge Rd, London SE1 3LW
Old Mill Antiques Centre, Mill Street, Low Town, Bridgnorth, Shropshire
Onslow's, The Depot, 2 Michael Road, London, SW6 2AD
Outhwaite & Litherland, Kingsley Galleries, Fontenoy Street, Liverpool, Merseyside L3 2BE
Pendulum of Mayfair, 51 Maddox Street, London W1
Phillips Manchester, Trinity House, 114 Northenden Road, Sale, Manchester M33 3HD
Phillips Son & Neale SA, 10 rue des Chaudronniers, 1204 Genève, Switzerland
Phillips West Two, 10 Salem Road, London W2 4BL
Phillips, 11 Bayle Parade, Folkestone, Kent CT20 1SQ
Phillips, 49 London Road, Sevenoaks, Kent TN13 1UU
Phillips, 65 George Street, Edinburgh EH2 2JL
Phillips, Blenstock House, 7 Blenheim Street, New Bond Street, London W1Y 0AS
Phillips Marleybone, Hayes Place, Lisson Grove, London NW1 6UA
Phillips, New House, 150 Christleton Road, Chester CH3 5TD
Andrew Pickford, 42 St Andrew Street, Hertford SG14 1JA
Pieces of Time, 1–7 Davies Mews, Unit 17–19, London W17 1AR
Pooley & Rogers, Regent Auction Rooms, Abbey Street, Penzance
Harry Ray & Co, Lloyds Bank Chambers, Welshpool, Montgomery SY21 7RR
Peter M Raw, Thornfield, Hurdle Way, Compton Down, Winchester, Hants SC21 2AN
Remmey Galleries, 30 Maple Street, Summit, NJ 07901
Rennie's, 1 Agincourt Street, Monmouth
Riddetts, 26 Richmond Hill, Bournemouth
Ritchie's, 429 Richmond Street East, Toronto, Canada M5A 1R1
Derek Roberts Antiques, 24–25 Shipbourne Road, Tonbridge, Kent TN10 3DN
Romsey Auction Rooms, 56 The Hundred, Romsey, Hants 5051 8BX
Russell, Baldwin & Bright, The Fine Art Saleroom, Ryelands Road, Leominster HR6 8JG
St. James Antiques Market, 197 Piccadilly, London W1V OLL
Schrager Auction Galleries, 2915 N Sherman Boulevard, PO Box 10390, Milwaukee WI 53210, USA
Selkirk's, 4166 Olive Street, St Louis, Missouri 63108, USA
Skinner Inc., Bolton Gallery, Route 117, Bolton MA, USA
Allan Smith, Amity Cottage 162 Beechcroft Rd. Upper Stratton, Swindon, Wilts.
Soccer Nostalgia, Albion Chambers, Birchington, Kent CT7 9DN
Sotheby's, 34–35 New Bond Street, London W1A 2AA
Sotheby's, 1334 York Avenue, New York NY 10021
Sotheby's, 112 George Street, Edinburgh EH2 2LH
Sotheby's, Summers Place, Billingshurst, West Sussex RH14 9AD
Sotheby's, Monaco, BP 45, 98001 Monte Carlo
Southgate Auction Rooms, 55 High Street, Southgate, London N14 6LD
Spink & Son Ltd., 5–7 King Street, St James's, London SW1Y 6QS
Michael Stainer Ltd., St Andrews Auction Rooms, Wolverton Rd, Boscombe, Bournemouth BH7 6HT
Michael Stanton, 7 Rowood Drive, Solihull, West Midlands B92 9LT
Street Jewellery, 5 Runnymede Road, Ponteland, Northumbria NE20 9HE
Stride & Son, Southdown House, St John's Street, Chichester, Sussex
G E Sworder & Son, 14 Cambridge Road, Stansted Mountfitchet, Essex CM24 8BZ
Taviner's of Bristol, Prewett Street, Redcliffe, Bristol BS1 6PB
Tennants, Harmby Road, Leyburn, Yorkshire
Thomson Roddick & Laurie, 24 Lowther Street, Carlisle
Thomson Roddick & Laurie, 60 Whitesands, Dumfries
Thimbleby & Shorland, 31 Gt Knollys Street, Reading RG1 7HU
Tool Shop Auctions, 78 High Street, Needham Market, Suffolk IP6 8AW
Truro Auction Centre, City Wharf, Malpas Rd., Truro TR1 1QH
Venator & Hanstein, Cäcilienstr. 48, 5000 Köln 1, Germany
T Vennett Smith, 11 Nottingham Road, Gotham, Nottingham NG11 0HE
Garth Vincent, The Old Manor House, Allington, nr. Grantham, Lincs. NG32 2DH
Wallis & Wallis, West Street Auction Galleries, West Street, Lewes, E. Sussex BN7 2NJ
Walter's 1 Mint Lane, Lincoln LN1 1UD
Wells Cundall Nationwide Anglia, Staffordshire House, 27 Flowergate, Whitby YO21 3AX
West Street Antiques, 63 West Street, Dorking, Surrey
Whitworths, 32–34 Wood Street, Huddersfield HD1 1DX
A J Williams, 607 Sixth Avenue, Central Business Park, Hengrove, Bristol BS14 9BZ
Peter Wilson, Victoria Gallery, Market Street, Nantwich, Cheshire CW5 5DG
Wintertons Ltd., Lichfield Auction Centre, Fradley Park, Lichfield, Staffs WS13 8NF
Woltons, 6 Whiting Street, Bury St Edmunds, Suffolk 1P33 1PB
Woolley & Wallis, The Castle Auction Mart, Salisbury, Wilts SP1 3SU
Worthing Auction Galleries, 31 Chatsworth Road, Worthing, W. Sussex BN11 1LY

ANTIQUES PRICE GUIDE

For many of us, the approaching millennium is going to be a time to take stock of just where we are and where we're going. It's maybe a good opportunity too, to consider just where the antiques market is at present, how it's changed over the last years, and where it seems to be heading in the year 2000.

A measured degree of evolution has always been inevitable, even desirable, but as in so many other fields, the pace of change in the last few years has become quite vertiginous. Fifty, even forty, years ago, trading in and collecting antiques was the province of a relatively small percentage of the population. The classic image of the collector, someone of educated taste and fairly easy circumstances who could afford to indulge their passion for equally traditional items such as 18th century furniture, Meissen china, or Scottish Provincial silver, was more or less accurate. One bought from a trusted dealer, or at auction, and everyone knew their place in the great scheme of things. The other type of collectors - and there has always been the other type of collectors, whether schoolboys hoarding their comics or housewives collecting pretty figurines - bought the items from a retailer because they liked them, and the thought that they might be amassing something which one day would bring them a small fortune, never entered their heads.

Even thirty years ago, when the first Lyle Antiques Price Guide was published, this was still largely the case.

Then 21 years ago, came the first Antiques Roadshow, an unabashedly populist television programme which brought antiques into all our living rooms with the sight of people just like us bringing in things from homes just like ours and being told that they were worth untold sums. Needless to say, we very seldom saw the other 99 out a hundred people who, in equal hope and expectation, presented their treasures only to be told they were worthless tat. Gobsmacked delight makes good television, drooping disappointment does not. The process of educating the masses into the mysteries of the antiques world had begun.

Human nature being what it is, the idea quickly caught on. The Antiques Roadshow spawned a host of other programmes designed to wake people up to what might be lurking in their garages and attics, as did countless attendant publications, of which Lyle themselves have brought out not a few.

So the public were up for it and ready to have their fortunes made. The only trouble was, there wasn't enough good 18th century furniture and Meissen china to go round, and what there was was well beyond what most of these newly aware and eager collectors could afford. It's one thing to find out that Auntie Maisie's old vase in which you have dumped the daffodils for the last umpteen springs is in fact a 16th century Ming: it's quite something else to go out and buy another half dozen of the same to start a collection.

So what was to be done? We were being told that collecting is fun, collecting is lucrative, but what to collect? What in fact happened was that suddenly traditional antiques were joined by a posse of new boys on the block, in the form of what now became known as 'collectables'. The comics you hoarded as a schoolboy, the pretty china figurines, began to take their places alongside the old stalwarts at auction and in the marketplace. Nor did they remain the poor relations for long. When a baseball card fetches $500,000, a teddy bear £50,000 or a typewriter £12,000, we're right back up there, in monetary terms, with the Ming vase. The difference being that you can still buy another baseball card for $10, a perfectly respectable Steiff teddy for £200, and an old typewriter for £30. There is suddenly a level playing field for everyone, and much more of a chance that your sharp eyes could spot the winner that the next man has missed.

So, as we go into a new millennium, collectables have joined antiques in the auction houses and at the specialist dealers, and far, far more people are involved in the collecting business than ever before.

Whether this is a universal blessing is open to debate. In the past two weeks I have spoken with two highly respected dealers, specialists of long standing, who are quitting the trade. What was striking was the fact that their reasons for doing so were identical. People had become too greedy; they had seen or heard of a collectable fetching a large sum of money. They had something similar and could not understand why a dealer would not pay the same sum for theirs. Finding that no one would, they hung on to it. If buying, they would shop around and finally buy from whoever would take 50p less than the next man

Both dealers had become demoralised with the constant struggle of finding items to buy at a price where they could sell them again and make a reasonable profit, and with timewasters wanting offers for pieces which they had no intention of selling.

The auction houses, too, are often finding difficulty in putting together worth while sales. In the case of furniture, leaving the top end of the market apart for the moment, there are fewer vendors parting with the quality material which is all that is really in demand at the moment. The fact that we are approaching the millennium may have a bearing on this too, inasmuch as some twenty or even ten years ago deceased estates were coming on the market which had belonged to single women, those who did not marry because of the shortage of young men following the First World War. This supply has now all but dried up, and many of those who are now dying off set up house following the Second World War and furnished accordingly.

A late gothic period oak aumbry, with linen fold side panels and a series of carved and pierced single plank doors, some later additions, 4ft.5in. wide.
(Wilkinsons) £9,500 $15,200

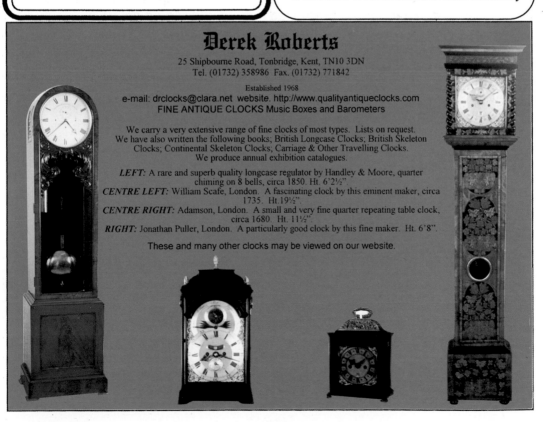

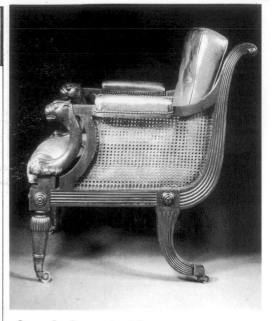

One of a fine pair of Regency mahogany caned bergères, in the manner of George Smith, circa 1810, the reeded scrolled top rail continuing to padded arms and lion monopodia end supports.
(Bonhams)   (Two)   £90,000 $144,000

A fine Regency pollard oak and ebony inlaid breakfast table, in the manner of Gillows, circa 1825, the circular top with egg and dart moulded edge and inlaid with a border of entwined vine leaves, 83½in. diameter. (Bonhams)   £125,000 $200,000

If you can get it, what *is* selling well is oak, possibly as a direct result of the dwindling supply of attractive 18th century mahogany furniture. At Tennants of Leyburn in November a Victorian oak sideboard designed by Bruce Talbert made £34,000 against a modest estimate of £2,500-$4,000. This was a latish piece, and with a designer and manufacturer label, but all British vernacular oak seems to be selling well. At Wilkinson's in Doncaster in December a late Gothic period oak aumbry went for £9,500, while at Sotheby's Summers Place a William and Mary period gateleg table attracted a bid of £8,000.

Not only oak, but all quality English furniture is selling well. At the very top end, Sotheby's in August offered the Marot table, a small marble-topped side table from William & Mary's decorations for Hampton Court, which fetched £300,000. Christie's, on the other hand drew a bid of £850,000 for a pair of gilt gessoed side tables attributed to Benjamin Goodison. The trend for quality pieces continued through the year, Bonhams selling, in April 1999, a pair of Regency mahogany caned bergeres for £90,000, and huge ebony inlaid and pollard oak veneered Regency table with a diameter of almost 7ft. for £125,000.

Last year we highlighted the popularity of the walnut commode. Now, as the millennium approaches, we are told that our social arrangements are changing and that for the first time since records began, unmarried people will be in the majority in our society. How fitting, then, that our 'item of furniture of the year' should this time be the bachelor chest! Mind you, walnut is still the favoured wood. At the start of the year under review, in June 1998, the Canterbury

One of a pair of George II gilt gesso side tables, attributed to Benjamin Goodison, each with a pounced ground, the rectangular top with re-entrant corners and gadrooned edge, 59¾in. wide. (Christie's) (Two)   *£850,000 $1,385,500*

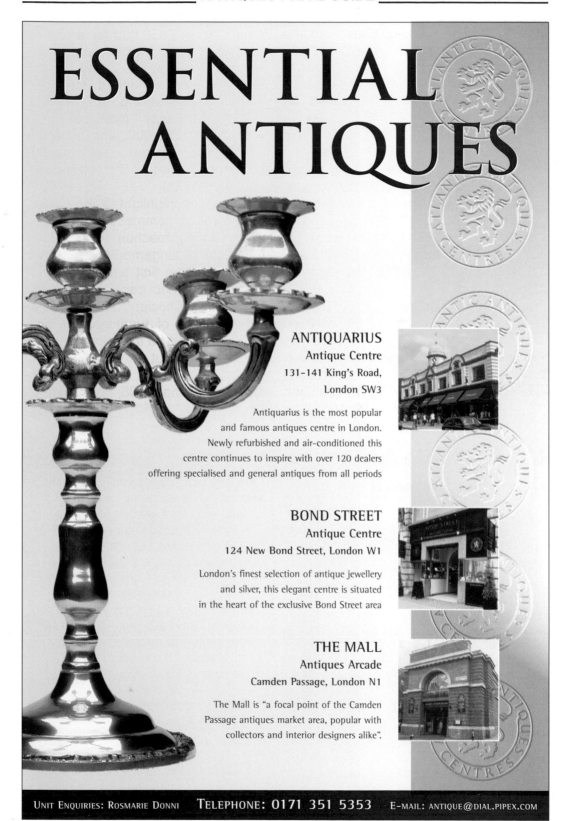

A 19th century walnut and inlaid credenza, circa 1875, with three-quarter brass gallery. (Dockree's)
£4,700 $7,520

One of a set of eight early Victorian dining chairs with shaped backs, on turned and leafage carved tapering supports. (Russell Baldwin & Bright) (Eight)
£2,900 $4,640

Auction Galleries sold a very dilapidated George II example in its unrestored condition. It had been kept for many years by the vendors under a dustsheet in their cellar (a prime candidate for the Antiques Roadshow), but it had its small size (just 2ft. 9in.) on its side, and against an estimate of just £800-£1,200, it fetched £18,500! Wilkinson's followed suit in September with a William & Mary example which was again just 2ft. 10in. wide and had an unusual six-drawer arrangement. It fetched £26,000.

An early 18th century bachelor's walnut chest, top and drawer fronts with herring-bone bandings, lacking feet and with later handles, needing extensive restoration, 31in. wide. (Canterbury) £18,500 $29,600

Phillips of Knowle got in on the act a week or two later when a Queen Anne walnut example led their sale at £23,500. Americans in particular, it seems, just can't get enough of these eligible bachelors.

But if you can't get enough desirable material to sell, what are you to do? One answer is to go elsewhere, and where closer than Ireland, where you can take advantage of a favourable pound/punt exchange rate. However, the private buyer is a real force to be reckoned with there, and dealers are far from having it all their own way. At James Adam's dispersion of the contents of Sybil Connolly's Dublin residence in November, the trade had a particularly hard time of it, though one dealer did make off with one of the top lots, an 18th century mahogany serving table for £16,400.

The other alternative is to widen the goalposts to include 20th century furniture. As we move out of the century it is clear that this has become a major new collecting field. Nor are we talking just Mies van der Rohe and other icons of the 1920s and 30s, who will soon be earning their antiques status. 20th Century Design is now just as likely to include gems from the 60s, 70s and even 80s. Both Bonhams and Sothebys hosted sales in the first three months of 1999. The hammer total at Bonhams was over £126,000, and at Sotheby's £504,000. The two were not strictly comparable, however, as Sothebys had moved back the 1935 cut-off barrier to include pieces by such as the Wiener Werkstätte, Christopher Dresser and Voysey. Later pieces performed well at both sales, however, Bonhams attracting a bid of £5,500 for Gaetano Pesce's 1980 Dahlia III polyurethane anthropomorphic chair, and Sotheby's selling a Boomerang desk and chair by Maurice Calka, dating from around 1969 for £21,000.

Maurice Calka for Leleu Deshay, 'Boomerang' desk and swivel chair, designed 1969, white plastic, the desk of biomorphic form, 180cm. wide. (Sotheby's) £21,000 $33,600

A Royal Winton breakfast tea set in the Victorian Rose pattern, comprising teapot, milk jug, cup, sugar bowl and toast rack on tray.
(Russell, Baldwin & Bright)

£540 $864

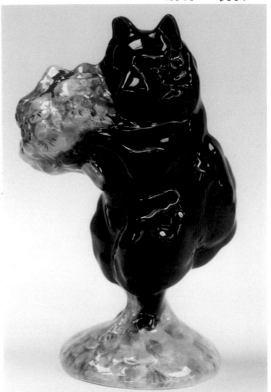

Beswick Beatrix Potter figure Duchess with Flowers, (first version), 3¾in. high, introduced 1955, gold oval backstamp.
(Ewbank)   £1,750 $2,905

In ceramics, as in furniture, there has been a marked rise in the fortunes of the home produced article, as against its Continental counterparts. In Christie's November sale an unrecorded blue and white London Delft tankard, dating from 1638 fetched £74,000 while the top lot in the Raison collection of early Worcester, a 7in. high coffee pot, decorated with pheasants on rocks, fetched £28,000. There were almost as many English as Continental pieces on sale there, while over at Sotheby's a couple of weeks later, the Continental entry far outnumbered the home-grown, largely due to a single owner collection of Meissen. Even with such a small British entry, and most of that concentrated at the lower end, three of the top ten lots still turned out to be home-produced, among them a Minton majolica vase by Albert Carrier Belleuse, which made £18,000. Just how selective buyers of Continental ceramics, and Meissen in particular, are being at present is strikingly demonstrated in the fact that only 47% of the Continental entry at that sale got away.

An unrecorded documentary inscribed and dated London delft tankard, 1638, probably Pickleherring Quay Pottery, Southwark, 5½in. high. (Christie's) £74,000 $120,620

Oriental ceramics scored one spectacular success in the Provinces in May, when a pair of slightly damaged Qianlong hawks of circa 1740 sold at Woolley and Wallis for an amazing £250,000, against an estimate of £40,000-60,000. The fact that there were still six dealers in the bidding at £100,000 shows how sought after they were. On the other hand, even the Orient seems to be buying British at the moment - at Bonhams in November a new Japanese museum paid £16,000 and £14,000 for two Hans Coper vases, and at Christie's South Kensington, another Japanese buyer paid £6,500 for a Leach pagoda shaped covered dish and £3,500 for a Leach 'Tree of Life' bottle vase.

A Worcester baluster coffee pot and cover, circa 1754, painted in a delicate famille rose palette each side with two Asiatic pheasants among pierced blue rockwork, 7in. high. (Christie's) £28,000 $44,800

A cream Staffordshire double bust of the Kaiser, as himself and the devil, titled 'Which'll he be?', sold to raise funds for disabled servicemen.
(Academy)   £200 $320

'Harmony in Four Parts, a Hummel group of four child carol singers.
(Jackson's)   £722 $1,155

An 18th century majolica figure of a dog with balls on his collar, seated in front of an urn.
(Academy)   £490 $784

A pair of large Chinese models of hawks, Qianlong, circa 1740, 20.5in. high (damaged).
(Woolley & Wallis) £250,000 $400,000

Now we mentioned at the beginning of this introduction all these housewives collecting pretty figurines, and one of the biggest manufacturers of these, Doulton, is enjoying something of a boom just now. Following the amazing £19,000 achieved at Phillips for the character jug The Maori last year, in November, new records for figurines were achieved when Phillips sold the prestige figure Jester for £12,000, while a few days earlier Bonhams achieved £11,000 for Lady with Blackamoor.

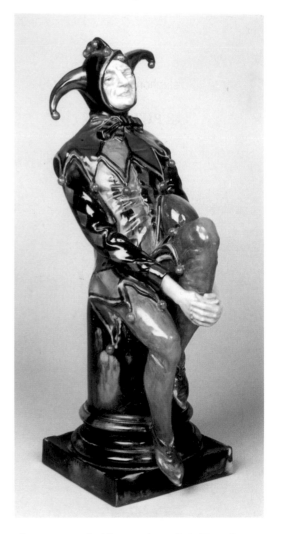

A stoneware 'Sack' form by Hans Coper, the off-white oval form rising to straight pointed shoulders, circa 1970, 6¾in. high.
(Bonhams)   £16,000 $25,600

An unrecorded large size pilot Royal Doulton Jester figure, 15¾in. high, Charles Noke, probably circa 1915.
(Phillips)   £12,000 $19,200

Doulton's nursery china too is becoming highly sought after, in particular pre-war Bunnykins items. A humble eggcup, for example, sold at Phillips for £1,500. Not a bad return on something which you might have been reliably expected to drop from your high chair!

It is just this sort of item which is becoming so sought after in the new world of collectable ceramics. Another, even less likely favourite, is one of Beswick's Beatrix Potter figures, Duchess with Flowers. Retailed in the 50s and 60s for a few shillings, and thought at one stage to be quite rare, this little black creature now regularly fetches over £1,600 at auction. The fact that in the wake of early successes they now seem to trot out of the woodwork fairly regularly, has as yet not depressed the price. One recently went as high as £1,750 at Ewbank in Surrey while Tennants of Leyburn continued the trend in their Spring catalogue sale in April, selling another for £2,170.

Shelley china of all sorts is gaining an enthusiastic following among collectors at present, and continuing the nursery theme, one of their Mabel Lucie Attwell figures, Going Ta-ta, sold for £1,550 at Louis Taylor in December.

One of a pair of Satsuma pottery vases of faceted tapering form, painted with figures on a terrace reserved on a gilded deep blue ground, late 19th century, 7½in. high. (Andrew Hartley) (Two)   £260 $416

The 20th century has become Big League in the last few years when it comes to Decorative Arts Sales. The heading embraces the widest possible spectrum of items, from china, through bronze, silver, glass and furniture. Very generally speaking, the further back you go, the bigger the names and the bigger the prices. Like good wines, perhaps, appreciation of Mackintosh, Ruhlmann, Gallé, Tiffany, and the like, takes time to mature. Take for example the pair of patinated bronze Art Deco snake door handles by Edgar Brandt which fetched £72,000 when they were auctioned by Sotheby's in April 1999.

In December, both Christie's and Sotheby's in New York each devoted a sale exclusively to the works of Tiffany, while Christie's East and Phillips both included a significant number of his pieces in their Decorative Arts sales. In all, some 530 Tiffany items came under the hammer in a very short period. Not only did this not prove to be a glut, but records crashed left, right and centre.

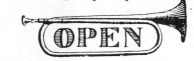

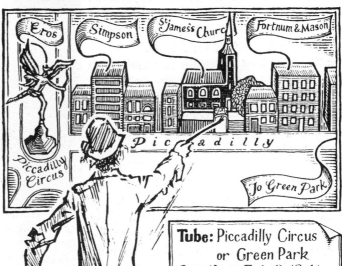
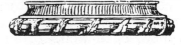

A unique Tiffany Peacock centrepiece lamp, six ruffled favrile glass bowls set into its base.
(Phillips)   £1,030,000 $1,700,000

At Christie's a Magnolia floor lamp achieved an amazing $1.6 million (£969,970), a record for this design. As one of only two known examples, this was obviously a rarity, as was the Poppy filigree floor lamp which, at $550,000 (£333,335) topped the bidding at Sotheby's. Phillips, however went even better and clocked up $1.7million (£1.03m.) for a Peacock centrepiece lamp, the second highest price ever paid for any Tiffany lamp. At Christie's, a Peony table lamp played a suitably supporting role at $680,000 (£412,120), while at Christie's East a Wisteria table lamp, despite some damage, sold for more than three times its estimate at $380,000 (£230,305). Apart from small Favrile lily lamps, which did not move particularly well, collectors, it seems, just can't get enough of Tiffany - a significant number apparently own 30, even 50 or more lamps by the master. These items, and those by the likes of Mackintosh, Lalique and so on are acknowledged works of art by master craftsmen, yet even they are subject to the vicissitudes of taste and fashion. French Art Glass has been in the doldrums lately, especially since the Japanese have largely quit the market. At Christie's in November a unique Gallé vase which moreover bore a dedication to Louis Majorelle, and with an impeccable provenance, only made £72,000, against an estimate of £80-120,000.

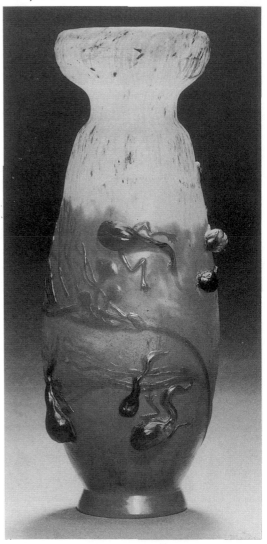

Emile Gallé, a rare and important vase 'Les Têtards', dedicated to Louis Majorelle, 1900, clear glass , the body applied in amethyst, dichroic green/amber and blue amber with seven tadpoles, 9in. high.
(Sotheby's)   £72,000 $115,200

Having soared so high, such items inevitably have further to fall, but one wonders about the megabucks now paid for other things which do not have such obvious intrinsic worth in terms of craftsmanship, and are even more vulnerable to the dictates of what's hot and what's not. One can only marvel at the ongoing popularity of Clarice Cliff, for example, and all these pieces which once graced the shelves of Woolworths and now fetch thousands. A conical coffee service painted with the Appliqué Orange Lucerne pattern led the bidding at Christie's South Ken. sale of the Daniel Brodie Hogg collection in February, when it sold for £9,000. The next week saw a new auction record for Carltonware, when, also at Christie's, a 1937 Rainbow Fan vase achieved £5,500.

Appliqué Orange Lucerne, a Clarice Cliff Bizarre conical coffee set for four, painted in colours, coffee pot 20cm. high.
(Christie's) £9,000 $14,400

So what's the secret? Perhaps it's because, for the average punter, they're so accessible, not just in terms of being something which the layman can appreciate, but also because they're something that we all just might have tucked away. Not perhaps that ultra-desirable coffee set, or that unusual vase, but we have a dish, or a bowl, and it *is* Carltonware or Clarice Cliff, and you just never know........

Apart from accessibility, the other thing that can get us going about latter day collectables is the nostalgia factor. Perhaps nowhere does that play a stronger role than when it comes to toys. The 1980s saw a high water mark in toy sales, and since then, with the odd exception, prices have fallen back. This means that toy sales can often be uneasy events, with vendors who have bought high, trying to recoup their outlay, resulting in high reserves and equally high unsold ratios. However, here, as elsewhere, aficionados remain willing to dig deep to purchase the very best. In this field, the cream of craftsmanship, is seen for example in Victorian dolls' houses, these wonderfully detailed and intricate reproductions of contemporary interiors. At Christie's South Kensington in October it was one such, made for Edith Palgrave of Yarmouth in 1865-6, which fetched the top bid of £9,000, while in December, Bonhams were favoured with a commission to sell the famous Vivien Greene collection.

Vivien Greene was the wife of novelist Graham, and the acknowledged 'doyenne of the English doll's house' in her own right. When, at the age of 94, she decided to sell off her collection, it was to expected that enthusiasts from all over the world would come flocking to the dispersal. Swiss, Germans and Americans were among the most prominent buyers, though Japanese and domestic buyers were also well represented. It was, moreover, private buyers who made off with the houses themselves, with furnishings divided fairly equally between them and the trade. The most expensive lot was an

early unfurnished model, Quantock Oak, an English Palladian oak house dating from 1730-40, which was bid up on the telephone to £20,000.

At a much lower level, there is still a healthy demand for model trains and cars, such as Schuco, Lehmann and even the humble Dinky. If they come still with their box, that of course increases their value considerably.

Few, however, would climb to the heights seen in May 1999 when Bill Bertoia Auctions in Philadelphia sold no less than four major toy collections, comprising 1342 lots in all, for an all time record total of $1.92 million (£1.2m). American toys, from the Bob Lyons collection understandably performed well, an Ives clockwork tin wagon from the 1870s reached $22,000 (£13,750).

But Europeans were also very well represented in the other collections on offer, attracting the two top prices of the entire sale. $26,000 (£16,250) was paid for a German clockwork tinplate scull, while a Lehmann Boxer toy, based on the Chinese secret society of the 1900s, did scarcely less well at $25,000.

'Quantock Oak' English, circa 1730-40, a grand Palladian oak house, the interior with fine features such as parquet floor, built-in furniture and a set of portrait prints. (Bonhams) £20,000 $32,000

An early 20th century wooden rocking horse on frame, retailed through Harrods, 82cm. high. (Wintertons) £350 $560

A fine and rare Märklin first series battleship 'Brandenburg', German, circa 1905, the hand painted tinplate boat with clockwork motor, on original wheeled base with key, 34½in. long.
(Sotheby's) £31,050 $49,600

A fine Mickey Mouse tinplate mechanical bank, German, early 1930s, probably Selhumer & Strauss, on pulling his ear his tongue flicks out to receive the coin, 7in, high. (Sotheby's) £13,225 $21,130

This was pretty heady stuff, until Sotheby's in London, in May 1999, went even better, attracting a bid of £31,050 for a Märklin first series battleship 'Brandenburg', dating from 1905. They also set a new record for a money bank (very collectable these days, incidentally, especially American mechanical examples.) This one again was German, however, tinplate and mechanical, dating from the 1930s and in the form of Mickey Mouse. It sold to a dealer for all of £13,225!

Should we then carefully preserve all the Made in China plastic examples which we now bestow on our children? Certainly it is hard to think of these ever fetching even what we paid for them. But then again, with tinplate Japanese robots from the 60s now regularly selling for four figures, and the cult of the Barbie doll and Action Man, to say nothing of Star Wars, poised to take off, who can say? Second guessing the future, is, at the end of the day, what the world of collectables is all about.

Finally, it is likely that the coming of the millennium is going to have a subtle effect on the way we consider items from the relatively recent past. In traditional parlance, an antique has to be something which is over 100 years old, i.e. something, now, which dates from the 18-umptetums. However, as we all know, items dating from up to the 1930s, and in some cases from much later, are already being avidly collected. As we stand at 1999, these may still seem of comparatively recent origin, but once we get used to the idea of being in 2000+, I bet we quickly start looking at anything from 19-something as really quite ancient. It will be interesting to see, in the coming months, just what an effect a change of millennium has on our mind set, and even more interesting to see how buying and selling antiques and collectables settles down in a new era.

ANTIQUES PRICE GUIDE 2000

The Lyle Antiques Price Guide is compiled and published with completely fresh information annually, enabling you to begin each new year with an up-to-date knowledge of the current trends, together with the verified values of antiques of all descriptions.

We have endeavoured to obtain a balance between the more expensive collector's items and those which, although not in their true sense antiques, are handled daily by the antiques trade.

The illustrations and prices in the following sections have been arranged to make it easy for the reader to assess the period and value of all items with speed.

You will find illustrations for almost every category of antique and curio, together with a corresponding price collated during the last twelve months, from the auction rooms and retail outlets of the major trading countries.

When dealing with the more popular trade pieces, in some instances, a calculation of an average price has been estimated from the varying accounts researched.

As regards prices, when 'one of a pair' is given in the description the price quoted is for a pair and so that we can make maximum use of the available space it is generally considered that one illustration is sufficient.

It will be noted that in some descriptions taken directly from sales catalogues originating from many different countries, terms such as bureau, secretary and davenport are used in a broader sense than is customary, but in all cases the term used is self explanatory.

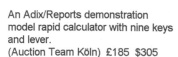

An Adix/Reports demonstration model rapid calculator with nine keys and lever.
(Auction Team Köln) £185 $305

A Russian Original Odhner drum adding machine, with 9-place insertion, 13-place answer, circa 1900.
(Auction Team Köln) £146 $232

A Doppel-Brunsviga 13ZK combination calculator for scientific calculations, 1932.
(Auction Team Köln) £336 $534

A Mercedes Euclid Model 16 manual four-function calculator by Christel Hamann, Berlin, 1927.
(Auction Team Köln) £264 $420

A Scribola 10-place German adding machine with chain drive and print-out, 1922.
(Auction Team Köln) £156 $257

A tinplate toy calculator for multiplication.
(Auction Team Köln) £41 $65

A Thales Model MEZ cylinder calculating machine, without carry-ten facility, insertion to six places, result to 10, 1925.
(Auction Team Köln) £65 $103

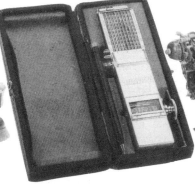

A Comptator 9-place rack adding machine by Schubert & Salzer, Chemnitz, with original case, 1908.
(Auction Team Köln) £110 £175

A Burroughs No. 9 calculating machine with 10 row keyboard and printer, circa 1900.
(Auction Team Köln) £81 $129

A Demos III Swiss four-function adding machine by Theo Muggli, Zürich, with eight place insertion 14-place result, 1923.
(Auction Team Köln) £205 $338

An Additor eight-row, full-keyboard adding machine with geared drive, by Knudsen & Bommen, Sweden, 1910.
(Auction Team Köln) £267 $441

Skeleton demonstration model of the the Vaucanson AVA four-function adding machine, French.
(Auction Team Köln) £447 $711

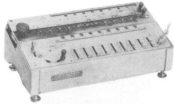

A Peerless Baby miniature step cylinder machine,with 9-place insertion, 8-place conversion and 12-place result, German, 1904.
(Auction Team Köln) £488 $776

A very early Berolina four-function adding machine by Ernst Schuster, Berlin, with sliding crank and turned wooden handle, 1901.
(Auction Team Köln) £328 $541

A Golden Gem seven-place chain adding machine, with carry-ten facility, with leather case and 8-page instructions in English, 1904.
(Auction Team Köln) £89 $141

A Facit Model 1 drum wheel calculator, Swedish, 1918.
(Auction Team Köln) £183 $291

A demonstration model Brunsviga Model A four-function calculator, 1899.
(Auction Team Köln) £493 $813

A very rare Adma manual 10-place full-keyboard calculating machine, with long side handle, German, 1919.
(Auction Team Köln) £144 $238

A black Curta Type II miniature four-function cylinder calculator by Kurt Herzstark, Vienna, 1948.
(Auction Team Köln) £406 $645

A Wales printing calculator, with ten-place keyboard, 1903.
(Auction Team Köln) £114 $181

Adix three-place adding machine with geared drive and 9 keys, by Pallweber & Bordt, Mannheim, 1903.
(Auction Team Köln) £264 $420

A rare Chateau miniature step-wheel calculating machine, with 9-place insertion and 13-place result, French, circa 1909.
(Auction Team Köln) £252 $400

A Multifix Norwegian barrel calculator, with original instructions, one of only a few models produced, circa 1950.
(Auction Team Köln) £398 $636

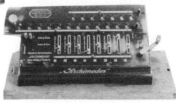

An Archimedes Model B German cylinder adding machine by Reinhold Pöthig, Saxony, with original wooden case, 1906.
(Auction Team Köln) £534 $881

An Answer Game tin calculating robot, a rare first edition without cancelling lever, partly restored, circa 1963.
(Auction Team Köln) £397 $635

The Brical round calculator for addition in British currency, with peg entry, in elegant velvet case, with pegs, 1905.
(Auction Team Köln) £314 $502

A Brunsviga Model J rare manual four-function claculator by Grimme, Natalis & Co. Brunswick, with fixed insertion lever and two unusual eight-place conversion functions, 1908.
(Auction Team Köln) £502 $804

An American Adding & Listing Machine No. 1, manual adding machine, with seven-place input and results to eight places, 1912.
(Auction Team Köln) £418 $670

A grey-black Curta Type II miniature four-function cylinder calculator, produced in Liechtenstein, with original metal box and instruction booklet, 1948.
(Auction Team Köln) £712 $1,138

A German Orga barrel adding machine with push-lever entry, which immobilises durlng the calculation process, by Bing-Werke AG, 1921.
(Auction Team Köln) £921 $1,473

An Adix 3-place adding machine with nine keys, by Pallweber & Bordt, Mannheim, with unusual number shackle, in original velvet case, 1903.
(Auction Team Köln) £356 $569

Consul the Educated Monkey, a popular tinplate toy calculator by the Educational Toy Manufacturing co., Springfield MA, 1918.
(Auction Team Köln) £92 $147

Bürk's Kollektor adding machine, a manual single-figure machine by the Württemberg clock manufacturers Bürk Söhne, with four selection dials 1,3,4, and 5, 1910.
(Auction Team Köln)
£2,863 $4,581

A 19th century alabaster and bronze bust of a young lady, signed *Kuchler*, on green marble base, 5¼in. high.
(Andrew Hartley) £250 $413

Alabaster compôte and fruit, with sixteen pieces of polychrome decorated fruit, compôte 4½in. high, 12in. diameter.
(Skinner) £718 $1,150

Bossons painted plaster study of two koalas perched on a branch, impressed marks, 8½in.
(G.A. Key) £15 $24

A Regency plaster bust of William Pitt the Younger, after a model by Joseph Nollekens, the black painted bust inscribed to the reverse *PUB.D BY F. GALLIANI January 20, 1809*, 16in. high.
(Christie's) £977 $1,563

A pair of black painted plaster figures, mid 19th century, in the Antique manner, the male and female figures with classical drapery, 30in. high.
(Christie's) £1,150 $1,840

A sculpted alabaster group of The Rape of Proserpine, 19th century, on integral square base and waisted square-section plinth, 12in. high overall.
(Christie's) £253 $405

Late 19th century carved alabaster head and shoulder bust of a young lady, signed *Nelson* (possibly Antoine Nelson), 25in. high.
(Lawrences) £900 $1,449

A large stone figure of a frog, 20th century, 21in. high.
(Sotheby's) £1,897 $3,162

A Continental carved alabaster plaque depicting The Last Supper, with traces of gilt, probably 17th century, 11.5 x 9.5cm.
(Bearne's) £780 $1,248

An early Navajo pictorial rug, woven in two shades of brown, red, green, cream and orange wool, with a central circular motif with lightning bolts and feather motifs, 85 x 51¼in. (Christie's) £2,208 $3,680

A pair of Sioux beaded and quilled hide moccasins, rawhide sole, uppers fully quilled with a yellow and blue cross and red ground, 11½in. long.
(Christie's) £4,140 $6,900

A Navajo rug, woven in brown and cream on a grey ground, decorated with terraced diamond motifs, four cross designs and chequered diamond patterns, 90¼ x 55in.
(Christie's) £345 $575

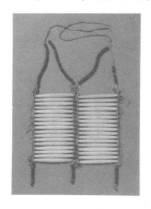

A Southern Plains breast plate, composed of two rows of tubular bone 'hairpipes' strung horizontally between hide strips, divided by a column of brass beads, 14¼in. long. (Christie's) £345 $575

A Sioux beaded hide child's vest, sinew sewn, decorated with alternating cross motifs, a pair of American flags, and American flag crests flanked by cross motifs on the front panels, 14¾in. long.
(Christie's) £3,450 $5,750

A Southern Arapaho beaded leather dispatch case, of slightly tapering rectangular form, sewn in pink, three shades of blue, green and translucent red beads against white beaded ground, 17¾in. long.
(Christie's) £966 $1,610

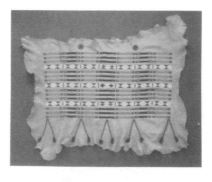

A Navajo blanket, woven in two shades of red and brown, orange, yellow and cream, decorated with five rows of linked diamonds with radiating patterns, 81 x 62in.
(Christie's) £1,380 $2,300

A Crow beaded hide child's robe by Melody Harris, slightly smoked Indian tanned deer hide with rows of beadwork across the length of hide, two rosettes at the top, 41 x 32in. (Christie's) £1,035 $1,725

A Transitional Navajo Chief's blanket, woven with an ivory ground with dark brown, blue and red dyed wool in a Second Phase pattern, 56 x 43in.
(Christie's) £1,794 $2,990

A Eastern Plateau beaded pictorial hand bag, decorated with a pair of warriors holding the reins of their horses, the warriors wearing elaborate war bonnets, 14½in. long. (Christie's)　£3,795　$6,325

A pair of Cheyenne beaded hide moccasins, each with hard soles, sinew sewn, with fully beaded uppers decorated with wide beaded bands encircling the foot and bisecting the top, 10¼in. long. (Christie's)　£1,518　$2,530

A Crow beaded hide, cloth and fringed rifle scabbard, sinew sewn with white, two shades of blue and pink beads, forming linear pattern out of bar designs, 51in. long. (Christie's)　£2,760　$4,600

A pair of woman's Apache beaded hide boots, sinew and thread sewn, with a blue, white, yellow and translucent red beaded medallion on top of the upper, 17¾in. long. (Christie's)　£5,520　$9,200

A Central Plains beaded hide and fringed war shirt, possibly Omaha, open sides and applied beaded panels with cross patterns alternating with forked designs, 62½in. wide. (Christie's)　£24,150　$40,250

A Creek beaded cloth bandolier bag, composed of narrow shoulder strap of blue wool, finely beaded, with a column of linked curvilinear designs, changing at the shoulder to a pattern of diamonds, 28¼in. long. (Christie's) £28,980 $48,300

A Navajo pictorial rug, woven in orange, green, red, yellow, cream and three shades of brown, 114 x 72in. (Christie's)　£2,208　$3,680

A Klicitat polychrome coiled bowl, coiled in cedar root with imbrication of bear grass, cedar bark and red cherry bark, 11½in. high. (Christie's)　£1,587　$2,645

A Transitional Navajo serape, woven in green, orange, cream and brown against a red wool ground with columns of linked stepped diamond motifs, 106¼ x 56½in. (Christie's)　£828　$1,380

A large Zia polychrome storage jar, thick walls painted in red and black against a creamy white slip, 22in. diameter.
(Christie's) £6,210 $10,350

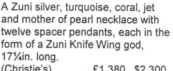

A Zuni silver, turquoise, coral, jet and mother of pearl necklace with twelve spacer pendants, each in the form of a Zuni Knife Wing god, 17¼in. long.
(Christie's) £1,380 $2,300

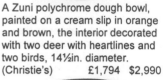

A Zuni polychrome dough bowl, painted on a cream slip in orange and brown, the interior decorated with two deer with heartlines and two birds, 14½in. diameter.
(Christie's) £1,794 $2,990

A Northern Northwest Coast bent corner storage box, probably Tlingit, with corner oriented design painted in black and red formlines, ovoids, circles, U forms and eye forms on all four sides, 14¼ x 11in.
(Christie's) £6,555 $10,925

A Navajo silver and turquoise bowguard, Ketohs, sandcast in openwork form, composed of rectangular border enclosing curvilinear details, 3½in. wide.
(Christie's) £483 $805

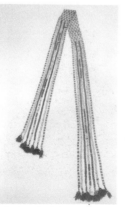

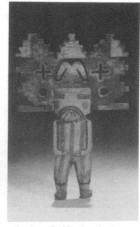

A fully beaded Creek sash, central strap and suspended tabs loom woven, the warp and weft composed of brown and black cotton twill, and beaded, 107in. long. (Christie's) £34,500 $57,500

A Southern Cheyenne girl's beaded hide dress, open sided yoke painted in yellow, a row of dentalia pendants accented with red and orange basket beads, 50½in. long.
(Christie's) £22,080 $36,800

An important early Hopi polychrome cottonwood Kachina doll, representing a dancing Shalako Mana, surmounted by an elaborate openwork tableta headdress, 11¼in. high. £64,200 $107,000
(Christie's)

A Sioux beaded hide knife sheath, painted with red pigment on the front , the curving section sinew sewn in green, 14¼in. long.
(Christie's)   £1,656 $2,760

A Haida bentwood box, the sides with relief carving showing stylised upside down faces with ovals and U forms at bottom, 9½. long.
(Christie's)   £4,485 $7,475

A Northern Plains pipe tomahawk, wood handle of rounded form with dark brown patina and accented with brass tacks, 19½in. long.
(Christie's)   £4,830 $8,050

A Tlingit beaded hide doll, wearing a fringed buckskin costume with a row of yellow and green beads at legs, an eagle figure in blue, white, yellow and red beads on chest, 13in. long. (Christie's) £345 $575

A Crow beaded hide blanket strip and robe, by Janice Little Light, fully beaded blanket strip with four panels in dark blue, pink, red yellow, and green beads forming diamonds and triangles, 80½ x 54½in. (Christie's) £2,070 $3,450

A rare Prairie parflèche cylinder, of heavy buffalo hide and tapering form with a seam down one side, painted in green, red and black outline against a rich brown colour, 23½in. long.
(Christie's)   £7,590 $12,650

A Zuni polychrome pottery drum, thick walls painted in red and brown on a light brown slip, decorated with a segmented serrated band, 22¾in. diameter.
(Christie's)   £5,865 $9,775

A Crow beaded hide saddle, constructed with an openwork wood tree covered in hide darkened in reddish pigment, with exaggerated high pommel and cantel, 14¼in. high. (Christie's)   £3,105 $5,175

A Nootka twined pictorial hat, finely woven in cedarbark with a pictorial band including four hunters in canoes pursuing four large whales, 11in. diameter.
(Christie's)   £1,518 $2,530

A Mills Silent War Eagle one-arm bandit by the Mills Novelty Co., Chicago, blue, gold and red aluminium and wood case, 65cm. high, 1931. (Auction Team Köln) £1,088 $1,741

Gaming wheel, America, late 19th/early 20th century, original paint, 32½in. high., 22in. diameter. (Skinner) £104 $172

An American Art Deco Little Duke slot machine by the O.D. Jennings Co., Chicago, with aluminium and wood casing, circa 1931. (Auction Team Köln) £1,130 $1,808

A rare pinball machine, Le Douze, by Bussoz, France. The object is to gain twelve points with just two balls, silver metal mounted wooden case, 1895. (Auction Team Köln) £1,089 $1,742

A Sun Chief Tic-Tac-Toe one arm bandit by Jennings & Co., Chicago, for the Swedish market, with wooden sides, front and upper part of silvered cast metal and brass Indian head, circa 1960. (Auction Team Köln) £1,130 $1,809

An Allwin de Luxe games machine by Jentzsch & Meerz, Leipzig, for the British market, with slot for 1d., wooden case with metal mounts, circa 1920. (Auction Team Köln) £544 $871

A wooden-cased amusement machine, with eight coin channels, for 20mm diameter coins, 1920, 76cm. high. (Auction Team Köln) £209 $334

A Mills Front OK Mint vendor, combination dispenser and amusement machine, with wood and aluminium casing, 1925, 65cm. high. (Auction Team Köln) £1,004 $1,607

A Dewag German amusement machine from the Jupiter range, white metal mounted wooden case, 75cm. high, circa 1930. (Auction Team Köln) £376 $602

A Victorian stuffed fox and rabbit in original ebonised glazed case by J. Morley, Bird and Animal Preserver, King Street, Scarborough, 38in. wide. (Dee Atkinson & Harrison) £300 $480

A cased display of flamingos, late 19th century, in a naturalistic setting, 5ft.1¾in. wide. (Sotheby's) £2,760 $4,609

A cased badger carrying a young rabbit, against a dusky sky and naturalistic surroundings, 67.5 x 90.5cm. (Wintertons) £180 $297

A 19th century stuffed young male lion, head and shoulders only, in glazed case, 30¼in. wide. (Andrew Hartley) £250 $400

A stuffed kakapo (Strigops habroptilus), in glazed case with egg and foliage, 61.5cm. high x 58cm. wide. (Bristol) £760 $1,254

A cased display of a fox cub, late 19th century, the cub on a naturalistic rocky base ornamented with foliage, 3ft.6in. wide. (Sotheby's) £690 $1,152

A cased display of stuffed foxes, a ferret, a mink and other vermin, late 19th century, in a naturalistic setting, 3ft.4in.wide. (Sotheby's) £920 $1,536

A cased display of a white pheasant and a partridge, late 19th century, in naturalistic setting, 2ft.7½in. wide. (Sotheby's) £690 $1,152

A scarce japanned salmon fly reservoir, six japanned lift-out trays; two each of 32, 40 and 50 clips, the box with leather carry handle. (Bonham's) £750 $1,222

A Hardy The 'Carry All' japanned artificial minnow and flight case, with large compartmented drawer to bottom, the top with lift out tray. (Bonham's) £320 $521

A leather fly wallet, the tooled burgundy cover with brass fastening clips and embossed with *Earl of Sefton* to one side and *Trout Flies* to the other. (Bonham's) £280 $450

A very rare Eaton & Deller nickel-silver serrated spoon, circa 1915, the 2½in. bait shaped with five swimming vanes to each side. (Bonhams) £600 $978

A scarce Gregory glass-eyed Norwich spoon, circa 1900, retaining much of original finish, stamped *Gregory*, 2½in. (Bonhams) £320 $522

A scarce Gregory nickel-silver bait, circa 1900, 1½in. stamped *Gregory to* one fin. (Bonhams) £450 $734

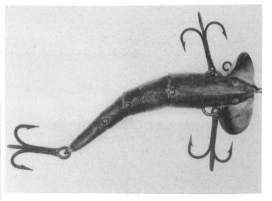

A scarce 1¼in. nickel-silver bait attributed to Gregory, circa 1900, stamped *Patent* to one fin and in excellent condition for age. (Bonhams) £190 $310

A very rare Gregory brass flexible jointed 'Cleopatra' bait, circa 1890, stamped *Gregory* to fin, 3¾in. (Bonhams) £2,200 $3,586

A Gregory glass-eyed 'Clipper' Bait, approximately 2½in. long, stamped *Gregory* and complete with trace and in good condition for age. (Bonhams) £280 $456

A Williams glass-eyed 'Clipper' Bait, probably made by Gregory, approximately 3½in. in length, stamped *F.T. Williams & Co.* and complete with trace and in good condition for age. (Bonhams) £400 $652

A Farlows 'Fario Club' #5/6, 8ft.5in. impregnated built cane Trout Fly Rod, two piece, staggered ferrule, complete with stopper in maker's bag and in good condition. (Bonhams) £130 $212

A Hardy The 'J.J.H Triumph' #6, 8ft.9in. built cane Trout Fly Rod, two piece complete with stopper in maker's bag and in good condition. (Bonhams) £160 $261

A scarce and early Hardy 8ft.4in. whole cane sea rod, circa 1893, numbered *47240*, two piece with large snake eyelets and brass roller tip ring, this stamped *Rd. No. 214522*, complete in maker's bag. (Bonhams) £65 $106

A rare J.S Sharpe 'Scottie V11' special build seven section 9ft. built cane Trout Fly Rod, built 1930-32 only, two piece, brass lockfast ferrule, complete in maker's bag. (Bonhams) £150 $244

A Hardy The 'Marvel' 7ft. 6in. built cane brook trout rod, numbered H6854, three piece with spare tip, suction ferrules, complete with alloy stoppers in maker's bag. (Bonhams) £600 $978

A B. James & Son 'Richard Walker MK. IV Avon' 10ft. built cane coarse fishing rod, two piece, agate lined tip and butt rings, professionally re-whipped. (Bonhams) £130 $212

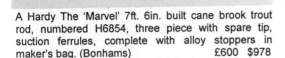

A 'Hardy Graphite' #9/10, 9ft. Trout Fly Rod, two piece in maker's bag and rod tube together with a Hardy 'Graphite De-luxe' #7/8, 10½ft. Trout Fly Rod, two-piece in bag. (Bonhams) £140 $228

An R. Chapman & Co. 'The Peter Stone Ledgerstrike' 10ft. built cane coarse fishing rod, agate lined tip and butt rings with stand-off bridge intermediates, complete in maker's bag. (Bonhams) £130 $212

A very rare Farlow's 'Lee Wulff Ultimate' #574, 5ft. 10¼in. built cane Trout Fly Rod, one piece and only weighing an incredible 1¾oz., and the prototype for the 'Lee Wulff Ultimate', made by Harold Sharpe, with a Farlow's 'Sapphire' 3⅛in. alloy Trout Fly Reel. (Bonhams) £450 $733

A J.S Sharpe 'Eighty-Eight' #5-6, 8ft.8in. impregnated built cane Trout Fly Rod, two piece. 5¼oz., staggered suction ferrule, complete with stopper in maker's bag and in unused condition. Made in February 1969. (Bonhams) £180 $293

A rare J.S Sharpe 'Royal Tribute' #5-6, 8ft.7in. impregnated built cane Trout Fly Rod, 5¼oz., two piece, staggered suction ferrule, the whips in H.R.H. Prince of Wales' racing colours. Also the prototype of the 'Royal Tribute' Rod. (Bonhams) £450 $734

A Hardy The 'Hollolight' 10ft. built cane Trout Fly Rod, numbered H33119, three piece, suction ferrules, in maker's bag and in good condition, together with a Hardy The 'Marquis' #6 alloy Trout Fly Reel, (Bonhams) £240 $391

An unnamed Hardy 5ft.9in. built cane Brook Trout Rod, numbered A80637, two piece, complete in leather-covered alloy rod tube. (Bonhams) £260 $424

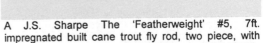

A J.S. Sharpe The 'Featherweight' #5, 7ft. impregnated built cane trout fly rod, two piece, with chromed stopper in bag. (Bonhams) £100 $163

A trout by Cooper in scarce wrap around case, the fish mounted in a setting of reeds and grasses, gilt inscription *Lough Melvin, April 1897, 9lbs.* Case 34½ x 15½in. (Bonhams)   £1,000 $1,630

A fine salmon, mounted in a setting of grasses and fern, *Salmon. 36lb. 8oz. Caught by M. Lock, River Tay, Sept. 8th 1958.* Case 49¾ x 20½in. (Bonhams)   £1,100 $1,793

A fine brown trout by Cooper, with original receipt, the fish mounted in a setting of ferns and grasses, inscription *2lb. Trout, River Bain. 1954.* (Bonhams)   £1,200 $1,956

A fine roach by Cooper, mounted in a setting of realistically modelled flowing weeds, with gilt inscription *Burgate Manor, 10th Nov: 1945. 2lbs. 4 ozs.*, case 20 x 11½in. (Bonhams)   £850 $1,388

A roach by J. Cooper & Sons, mounted in a setting of reeds and grasses in a gilt lined bowfront case inscribed *Roach – caught by C. Gill, October 8th 1904. Wgt. 2lbs. 4½ozs*, case 20¾ x 13¼in. (Bonhams)   £600 $975

Five perch by Cooper, mounted in a setting of reeds and grasses against a blue background in a flatfront case with Cooper label to interior, case 37½ x 26¾in. (Bonhams)   £500 $896

A Ferox brown trout attributed to Malloch, mounted in a picture frame case with inscription *8lbs. 5ozs. Trout. Caught by Albert Stirling, Loch Ba Argyllshire.* Backboard 32¾ x 12¾in. (Bonhams)   £300 $489

A fine carved wood cock salmon caught by J.S Sharpe, painted with a naturalistic palette and mounted to backboard with details *46½lbs. caught by J.S Sharpe at the Cruives, River Don, 19th October 1929.* (Bonhams)   £7,500 $12,225

A pike by W.F. Homer, mounted in a setting of reeds and grasses in a gilt lined bowfront case inscribed *Pike, caught by T.H. Johns on 3rd Dec. 1916*, case 37 x 15¾in. (Bonhams) £700 $1,141

A pike by P.J. Horton, mounted in a setting of reeds and grasses against a light blue background, inscription *Pike. Taken by T. W Yates at Halton. Feb 23rd 1928. Wgt. 20½lbs.* Case 46½ x 17½in. (Bonhams) £850 $1,385

A chub by Cooper, in a gilt lined bow front case with card to interior inscribed *Chub. Presented by our President to the Oldbury Piscatorials – 1905 – Weight 5½lbs.* Case 27¼ x 14³/₈in. (Bonhams) £1,000 $1,630

A fine roach by Cooper, mounted in a setting of fern and grasses, with plaque to interior *Roach. 2lbs. 4ozs. 1 drm. Caught by H.H Warwich in Hinksey Stream. 14th Dec. 1951,* case 11½in. (Bonhams) £650 $1,060

A fine roach by Homer in wrap around case, the fish against a typical blue and reed painted background, inscription to glass *Roach. 2lb 6ozs. Caught by B. Partridge. River Severn. 27 October 1935.*,case 21 x 13½in. (Bonhams) £800 $1,304

A common bream attributed to Cooper, mounted in a setting of fern and grasses, *Bream 5lbs. 3ozs. 2drms. Caught by H.H Warwick. Trout Inn Water. 4th December 1953.* Case 26 x 16½in. (Bonhams) £480 $782

A carved wood cock salmon by C. Farlow & Co. Ltd, painted with a naturalistic palette and mounted to backboard with inscription *Caught C.W Puleston in Atholl Hotel Water. Length 4ft., September 28th 1910.* Board 53³/₈ x 16½ins. (Bonhams) £2,000 $3,260

A pike, being a rare and early example of fish taxidermy, in a flatfronted case with label *This Pike 3ft. 6in. long, 21lbs. ½ in weight, was caught by one Geo: Everitt of Caister Castle, in the 79 years of his age with a baited hook, but of a piece of water situated on the farm call'd the Say; Nov 13th 1839.* Case 45¼ x 12¼in. (Bonhams) £280 $456

57

A very rare Milwards The 'Brownie' sidecasting reel, circa 1921, with 3½in. walnut drum, alloy hinged foot/spine rotating through 90 degrees for cast and retrieve positions. (Bonham's) £400 $652

A rare Illingworth No. 1 2nd series threadline casting reel in case, two flier arm model, twin ivorine handles, original red felt lined reel case. (Bonham's)   £680 $1,108

An Edward Vom Hofe 'Restigouche' 6/0 salmon fly reel, ebonite with nickel-silver rims, check adjuster to backplate. (Bonham's) £750 $1,222

A scarce Eaton & Dellar 2½in. brass crankwind reel, with dark horn handle to curved crank, raised constant check housing, triple pillared cage. (Bonham's)   £320 $522

A scarce 'Clockmakers' brass winch, late 18th century, triple steel 'peg' fastened pillars, steel drum and serpentine crank with turned wood handle. (Bonham's)   £500 $896

A scarce Rubin Heatons The 'Silent Reel', circa 1895, brass with ventilated fret work drum, brass lineguard, counterweighted horn handle and brake to foot acting as a silent check. (Bonham's)   £180 $293

A scarce Hardy The 'Super Silex' 3¼in. narrow drum multiplying bait casting reel, with ivorine on/off rim lever for engaging/disengaging the gears. (Bonhams)   £500 $815

A late 19th century G. Little & Co. 3¼in. brass crankwind winch, with anti-foul rim, horn handle, triple pillared cage and engraved to faceplate. (Bonhams)   £240 $391

A 3½in. all brass Hardy 'Perfect', circa 1894, with brass ball bearings in open ball race, bridged rim tension regulator with Turk's head locking nut.(Bonhams) £820 $1,336

A fine and rare Illingworth No.1 2nd series Threadline Casting Reel in original leather case, two flier arm model, twin ivorine handles.
(Bonhams)   £700 $1,141

An Allcock's 'Tunny Reel', manufactured under licence by A. Mitchell Henry of London, the drum 7in. wide with elaborate brake mechanism.
(Bonhams)   £850 $1,385

A scarce J. Bernard & Son 4in. brass crankwind salmon winch, with anti-foul rim, raised constant check housing, four raised pillars.
(Bonhams)   £300 $489

A Hardy brass faced 'Perfect' 4¼in. wide drum fly reel, with early check, brass bearings, bridged rim tension regulator with Turk's head locking nut, ivorine handle.
(Bonham's)   £380 $619

An extremely rare and possibly unique 6in. C. Farlow & Co. Patent lever salmon reel, late 19th century, with six pillared cage, brass patent lever adjustable check to backplate.
(Bonham's)   £450 $734

A Go-ite 'The Real Reel' 5½in. alloy skeletal fly reel, with maker's brass plaquette to alloy foot/line guard, central alloy drum tensioner and twin alloy handles.
(Bonham's)   £160 $261

A rare 3¾in. brass crankwind multiplying reel, with off-set counterbalanced serpentine crank arm and triple pillared cage.
(Bonhams)   £220 $359

An Allcock Aerial 'Popular' 3½in. alloy Centrepin Reel, with brass on/off check button, brass foot, twin Xylonite handles, circa 1930.
(Bonhams)   £240 $391

An unusual 2¾in. ivory Platewind Reel, with brass 'frogback' style foot, probably a one off craftsman/enthusiasts reel, 20th century. (Bonhams) £170 $277

An Etruscan bronze situla of bucket form, with twin handles terminating with pointed knops, circa 4th century B.C., 7in. high.
(Bonhams)   £700 $1,120

A grey-burnished Anglo-Saxon pottery urn, the upper body elaborately decorated with four horizontal elliptical pinched-out projections, circa 6th century A.D., 4¾in. high. (Bonhams) £450 $720

A Persian pottery rhyton styled as a lower leg pierced at the toe, with a handle at the back, early 1st Millennium B.C., 9½in.
(Bonhams)   £600 $960

A marble head of a Roman Emperor, possibly Vespasian, 11in. high and a marble bust set on a reel-shaped socle, 15in. high.
(Bonhams)   £900 $1,440

A Red-Figure bell krater decorated with added yellow and white to show on side A: a naked male youth seated on drapery holding a thyrsus in his left hand, later 4th century B.C., 11in. high.
(Bonhams)   £1,600 $2,560

An Egyptian wooden kneeling figure, with bag wig, red painted body and white kilt, Middle Kingdom, circa 20th century B.C., 4¾in. (Bonhams)   £280 $448

A large Etruscan hollow terracotta head of a female, her centrally parted wavy hair held in a simple headdress, circa 4th century B.C., 9½in. (Bonhams) £1,700 $2,720

A Roman aubergine glass storage jar, with globular body, mould blown with twisted striations, circa 3rd–4th century A.D., 3⅜in. high.
(Bonhams)   £580 $928

A Hellenistic marble bust of a female wearing a necklace, her hair bound in a fillet, 3rd–2nd century B.C., 9¾in.
(Bonhams)   £1,300 $2,080

A large terracotta stylised 'Tel Halaf' figure, of a female, her arms held under her exaggerated breasts, 6th–5th century B.C., 6¾in.
(Bonhams) £1,500 $2,400

An Attic Red-Figure pyxis, the lid, covering the full depth of the bowl, the top decorated with added white, circa 420–400 B.C., 3½in. high.
(Bonhams) £2,200 $3,520

A Hellenistic hollow biscuit-coloured terracotta head of a female wearing an elaborate headdress, 3rd–2nd century B.C., 6in.
(Bonhams) £750 $1,200

An Egyptian fragment from a limestone relief, showing hieroglyphs in sunk relief including the mouth, Old Kingdom or Late Period, 8⅝ x 5⅝in.
(Bonhams) £800 $1,280

A Roman marble Head of the goddess Venus, her centrally parted hair bound in a fillet and flowing out to either side, 1st–2nd century A.D., 4½in.
(Bonhams) £300 $480

A North African red slipware amphoriskos with moulded decoration of a wild boar and a male carrying an ?animal over his shoulder, 3rd century A.D., 6½in.
(Bonhams) £400 $640

A Hellenistic hollow terracotta group showing a draped standing female figure wearing a diadem clasping a standing male figure, circa 1st century, B.C., 5⅝in.
(Bonhams) £350 $560

The upper portion of an Egyptian wooden sarcophagus lid, polychrome painted with a black and cream striped wig, Late Period - Ptolemaic, 20¼in. high.
(Bonhams) £2,600 $4,160

A Roman blue glass stemmed cup, the flared sides decorated with zig-zag decoration in applied thick turquoise with manganese trailed glass, circa 4th century A.D., 3¾in.
(Bonhams) £750 $1,200

A Luristan bronze axehead with crescentic blade, collared shaft-hole and bulging butt, 7th–6th century B.C., 6¼in. long.
(Bonhams) £320 $512

A Mesopotamian terracotta plaque, depicting in relief a walking lion with heavy mane, early 2nd Millennium B.C., 3½ x 2½in.
(Bonhams) £260 $416

A Palaeolithic brown chert pointed handaxe, with broad butt, Grand Presigny, 6¼in. long.
(Bonhams) £280 $448

A Roman marble Head of Apollo, his hair dressed in neat curls and bound in a fillet, the back uncarved, 1st century B.C./A.D., 2½in.
(Bonhams) £350 $560

A large Attic Red-Figure bell krater decorated with added white to show on side A: the naked Ariadne seated on her drapery facing the figure of Cupid, circa 370–360 B.C., 16⅝in. high.
(Bonhams) £3,200 $5,120

An Egyptian limestone relief fragment, with part of a hieroglyphic inscription remaining, Late Period, after 500 B.C., 11⅜in.
(Bonhams) £500 $800

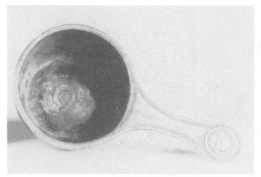

A large Syrian terracotta double-headed idol, with stylised bird-like features, an applied necklet around the necks and arms, 2nd Millennium B.C., 7¼in.
(Bonhams) £380 $608

A Roman bronze cooking vessel, the deep, rounded bowl with incised encircling lines below the rim, 2nd–3rd century A.D., 3¾in. high.
(Bonhams) £1,000 $1,600

A Roman hollow bronze appliqué styled as the bust of Minerva wearing the scaled aegis, 3rd–4th century A.D., 4½in.
(Bonhams) £500 $800

A white slipware vessel in the form of a bird, on three feet, with a wishbone handle on the back and rectangular aperture beside it, Cypriot/Phrygian, 1st Millennium B.C., 6¼in. (Bonhams) £400 $640

A Roman hollow bronze bust of a male with tightly curled hair, the eyes pierced, 2nd–3rd century A.D., 2¾in. (Bonhams) £280 $448

An Egyptian bronze and gessoed wood ibis, sacred to the god Thoth, Late Period, after 500 B.C., 3½in. (Bonhams) £500 $800

An Attic Black-Figure lekythos, enlivened with crimson and incisions to show a Dionysiac scene, circa 500–475 B.C., 7½in. (Bonhams) £950 $1,520

An Apulian Red-Figure pelike with Heraklean-knot handles, Greek South Italy, circa 330–310 B.C., 16in. (Bonhams) £3,000 $4,800

A Roman bronze figure of Herakles, naked except for the Nemean lion skin draped over his outstretched left arm, 1st–2nd century A.D., 4¼in. (Bonhams) £650 $1,040

A large South Arabian alabaster head of a male, deeply recessed under the brows, with a straight nose, 1st–2nd century A.D., 8³⁄₈in. (Bonhams) £1,400 $2,240

An Apulian Xenon ware kylix, the added red slip decoration showing a central stylised palmette on the tondo, circa 4th century B.C., 2in. high. (Bonhams) £300 $480

A black granite male head, wearing a baggy wig, 25th–30th dynasty, 4in. (Bonhams) £2,100 $3,360

An unusual Continental .177in. break action air rifle, 35¾ overall, round barrel 18½in. with octagonal breech, short fat air cylinder, the barrel remotely released by cocking 'hammer'.
(Wallis & Wallis)   £400 $640

A scarce .22in. Egyptian Hakim military training underlever air rifle, 45in. overall, barrel 19½in. with skull and crossbones mark at breech, sliding ratchet rearsight, automatic tap opening when cocked.
(Wallis & Wallis)   £260 $416

A scarce .177in. 'Lincoln' air pistol, 11½in. overall, barrel 9in., break action, of all metal construction, the top flat stamped *Lincoln,* the frame stamped *Patt No 181277.* (Wallis & Wallis)   £210 $336

A scarce pre war .22in. straight grip Webley 'Senior' air pistol, number S2210, chequered black grips with W & S logo, rear chamber plug stamped *Not to be Removed*, adjustable rearsight.
(Wallis & Wallis)   £190 $304

An unusual Continental .177in. break action air rifle, 35¾in. overall, round barrel 18¼in. with octagonal breech improved on the top flat with harpoon gun trade mark. (Wallis & Wallis)   £400 $644

A good .22in. Webley Service air rifle Mark II (third series) 41¾in. overall, barrel 26in. push button barrel release, improved folding peepsight fitting into recess to rear of air port.
(Wallis & Wallis)   £560 $896

A scarce 6mm (.25in.) smooth bore Oscar Will Bugelspanner air gun, 40½in. overall, tip down barrel 19½in. released by thumb catch on right of fore end, walnut stock with chequered wrist and cheek piece.
(Wallis & Wallis)   £220 $352

64

A Moro cuirass from the Philippines, made from black buffalo horn segments linked by butted brass mail rings. (Wallis & Wallis) £375 $619

French Carabinier's cuirass, 1842 dated example, breastplate of heavy polished brass mounted onto steel with brass studs to the front. (Bosleys) £400 $640

A rare set of Italian Great War body armour made of five metal plate panels to cover the chest, each plate secured by two webbing straps. (Bosleys) £600 $960

A North Indian mail shirt (zirih), 18th/early 19th century, formed of small butted rings of iron and brass arranged to form an alternating pattern of repeated chevrons. (Sotheby's) £575 $840

A North Italian etched back-plate, circa 1580, probably Milanese, formed with a narrow waist-flange and shaped both for the shoulder blades and for the hollow of the back, 14in. high. (Sotheby's) £2,990 $4,784

A Moro cuirass made from brass plates and brass links, thick butted brass links, plain border engraved plates, some shaped edges to four rows of verticle back plates. (Wallis & Wallis) £420 $672

Royal Horse Guards officer's cuirass, comprising both front and back nickel silver plates complete with gilt brass shoulder scales. (Bosleys) £1,400 $2,240

A fine Indian mail and lamellar shirt, 17th century, formed of rows of large riveted iron rings alternating with rows of butted rings. (Sotheby's) £575 $840

A breast-plate, circa 1600, probably Italian, formed in one piece in the late 'peascod' fashion, with a prominent waist-flange, 17½in.high. (Sotheby's) £1,380 $2,208

Great War Wilkinson private purchase body armour, to cover the breast, shoulders and back, constructed with 12 rows of interlocking steel plates with cream cotton cover. (Bosleys) £320 $512

An 18th century Indian gold damascened body armour Char Aina, two colour gold damascened floral and geometric borders. Associated Muslim breastplate. (Wallis & Wallis) £500 $800

A good 19th century Indo Persian chain mail shirt, of butted links and decorative lines and diamond shapes made from brass links, short sleeves, open front, vandyked collar of six points. (Wallis & Wallis) £250 $400

A Tosei Gusoku, Edo Period (18th century), heavy sixty-four plate russet iron koshozan hoshibachi helmet, the shikoro of kiritsuke kozane, laced with monogara kebiki odoshi. (Christie's) £8,625 $14,059

19th century Mahdist mail shirt, pull over style, with long sleeves and vented skirt, broad collar and single plastron to the front. (Bosleys) £180 $288

A composite armour, helmet Momoyama Period (16th century), armour Edo Period (mid-18th century), the thirty-two plate russet iron suji bachi kosho zan form helmet signed *Yoshimichi*. (Christie's) £6,325 $10,310

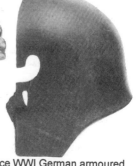

A good heavy 17th century Indian mail and lamellar shirt of good quality 11.10kg, mail of alternate rows of solid and riveted links of assorted sizes. (Wallis & Wallis) £800 $1,280

Two North German gauntlets, third quarter of the 16th century, nearly forming a pair, each with long flared pointed cuff with short inner plate, 40.8cm. and 39.4cm. (Sotheby's) £977 $1,563

A scarce WWI German armoured steel plate for attaching to the M1916 steel helmet, some field grey painted finish, stamped inside *R15*. (Wallis & Wallis) £150 $241

An unusual South Indian axe, head with 6½in. cutting edge, inlaid with copper and brass discs, shaped socket, on its brightly painted wooden haft. (Wallis & Wallis)   £180 $289

A 17th century polearm halberd, 92½in., crescent blade 7in. with truncated points, pierced with pellets and V, repeated on back blade and struck with maker's mark *OP*. On later wooden haft. (Wallis & Wallis)   £340 $544

A good 19th century Philippines Igorot axe, head 12in. including back spike with 5in. cutting edge, on its iron mounted wooden haft. (Wallis & Wallis)   £170 $273

A late 19th century Chinese polearm, 90in., foliate chiselled crescent head 8½in. with waisted top blade, turned brass ferrule, on its black painted bamboo haft. (Wallis & Wallis)   £100 $160

A late 19th century Zulu axe, 25in., shaped haft with woven brass and steel wire bindings, iron blade with geometric incised decoration. (Wallis & Wallis)   £150 $241

A good Sudanese Madhist throwing knife, 26¼in. incorporating two integral crescent heads and curved projections, etched overall with Islamic inscriptions in crocodile skin covered grip. (Wallis & Wallis)   £310 $499

A 19th century Chinese ritual axe, 29in., scroll chiselled crescent blade 4½in, emanates from the mouth of a brass dragon, chiselled and engraved, cabochon turquoise eyes, orange stone pommel. (Wallis & Wallis)   £150 $240

A 17th century axe head, 18in., of elongated form deeply struck with three sets of maker's initials *FC* within squares above stars and toothed crescents, integral socket. (Wallis & Wallis)   £120 $192

A good NCO's white metal badge of the R Gloucester Hussars.
(Wallis & Wallis)   £40 $66

A good NCO's white metal arm badge of the Northumberland Hussars.
(Wallis & Wallis)   £70 $115

A good NCO's cast silver plated arm badge of the Surrey Yeomanry.
(Wallis & Wallis)   £80 $132

90th Punjabis 1903-22 pagri badge, a good die struck white metal example. Crowned quoit encircling a Burmese Dragon.
(Bosleys)   £25 $40

King's Colonials officer's slouch hat badge, a very fine and scarce gilt die struck example comprising the full arms of the Prince of Wales resting on a scroll.
(Bosleys)   £220 $350

Army Physical Training Corps car badge, a post 1953 chrome and enamel example. Chrome laurel wreath surmounted by a crown.
(Bosleys)   £41 $65

A scarce cast giltmetal piper's badge of 603 (City of Edinburgh) Bomber squadron, RAF.
(Wallis & Wallis)   £90 $148

A good scarce NCO's white metal arm badge of the 6th (Inniskilling) Dragoons.
(Wallis & Wallis)   £105 $168

TOP TIP

Always check for markings on a gun, and NEVER attempt to clean a gun if the markings are not immediately visible.

Markings fall into two basic types:
(a) maker's name, which can usually be found on the top of the barrel and/or on the lock/action
(b) proof marks, which are usually off centre near the breech (the back of the barrel).

Garth Vincent

A Warrant Officer's silver forage cap badge of the Scots Guards, hallmarked Edinburgh 1916, gilt centre. (Wallis & Wallis) £85 $140

106th (Bombay Light Infantry) officer's forage cap badge, pre 1881 example, bullion strung bugle with *106* between the strings. (Bosleys) £220 $352

A good scarce WWI officer's bronze cap badge of the Dumfriesshire Volunteer Regt. (Wallis & Wallis) £100 $164

An officer's forage cap badge of The Dorsetshire Regt, not hall-marked, and a Worcester valise badge with leather backing. (Wallis & Wallis) £70 $112

A scarce officer's cap badge of the 11th (Lonsdale) Bn, The Border Regt, tablet on back marked *Sterling*. (Wallis & Wallis) £200 $320

A good NCO's silver plated forage cap badge of the Coldstream Guards, blue and red enamelled centre. (Wallis & Wallis) £50 $80

A scarce WWI white metal cap badge of the Loyal Manx Volunteer Corps, and pair white metal LMVC shoulder titles. (Wallis & Wallis) £140 $224

An OR's white metal cap badge of the 2nd Vol Bn The Wiltshire Regt. (Wallis & Wallis) £150 $248

West Riding officer's forage cap badge, post 1881 bullion example comprising the Duke of Wellington's crest on a black ground. (Bosleys) £100 $160

A good scarce OR's white metal glengarry badge of the 4th Vol Bn The R Scots.
(Wallis & Wallis)   £160 $264

A scarce WWII plastic glengarry badge of The Highland Regt.
(Wallis & Wallis)   £95 $159

A good OR's white metal glengarry badge of the 1st Argyll Highland Rifle Vols.
(Wallis & Wallis)   £140 $231

7th (Clackmannanshire & Kinross) VB Argyll & Sutherland Highlanders officer's glengarry badge. An 1887-11908 unmarked silver example by Marshall & Sons, 87 George St. Edinburgh.
(Bosleys)   £320 $512

106th (Bombay Light Infantry) OR's glengarry badge, 1874-81 example, brass curled bugle surmounted by a crown all on a laurel wreath, *106* within the curl. (Bosleys) £140 $224

Royal Hereford Militia glengarry badge, a good scarce white metal OR's example circa 1874-81. Crowned strap inscribed *Herefordshire Militia*.
(Bosleys)   £90 $143

Highland Borderers Light Infantry Militia glengarry badge, a good 1873-1881 OR's example, white metal strap inscribed *Highland Borderers*. (Bosleys) £240 $383

An OR's white metal glengarry badge of the 1st Vol Bn The Highland Light Infantry, with 'JR Gaunt, London' tablet on back.
(Wallis & Wallis)   £65 $107

Gordon Highlanders officer's silver glengarry badge, hallmarked *London 1917*, ivy wreath bearing the legend *Bydand* across the base. (Bosleys)   £140 $223

A scarce Victorian officer's silver plated helmet plate of Charterhouse School Cadet Corps, formed in 1873. (Wallis & Wallis) £170 $280

A good Victorian Australian officer's gilt helmet plate of the Victoria Defence Forces.
(Wallis & Wallis) £100 $160

A good Victorian other ranks' white metal helmet plate of the 10th Lancashire Rifle Volunteers.
(Wallis & Wallis) £70 $113

3rd City of London Rifle Vols. officer's helmet plate, 1902-08 example, gilt eight pointed star, the topmost point displaced by a crown, mounted on the star a silver laurel wreath. (Bosleys) £200 $319

Hanoverian heavy cavalry silver helmet plate, officer's example by Joseph Angel of London hallmarked *(London) 1818* almost identical to that worn on the 'Roman' pattern helmet by British heavy cavalry. (Bosleys) £280 $446

Northamptonshire Regiment officer's helmet plate, 1881-1901 example, gilt eight pointed star, the topmost ray displaced by a crown; mounted on the star, a gilt laurel wreath. (Bosleys) £260 $414

TOP TIPS

Once you have discovered and succeeded in purchasing your prize item, it pays to seek specialist advice on preservation. Ironic as it may seem, many items which were designed to resist the rigours of battle are not similarly proof against the ravages of time.
As in most collecting fields, condition is of the utmost importance, and in this case, spit and polish is no longer necessarily the best medicine!

(Bosley's)

A Russian Crimean period other ranks brass helmet plate of the 34th Regt., and a brass helmet (?) scroll inscribed in Cyrillic script.
(Wallis & Wallis) £130 $209

Wiltshire Regiment officer's helmet plate, a good 1881-1901 example, gilt eight pointed star, the topmost point displaced by a crown.
(Bosleys) £155 $247

6th West Suffolk Rifle Volunteers Corps helmet plate, a good 1880-1887 example comprising a brass Maltese cross surmounted by a crown. (Bosleys)   £90 $143

Kent Volunteer Artillery helmet plate, a scarce 1878-1901 OR's example, white metal Royal Arms. (Bosleys)   £140 $223

A scarce officer's silver plated helmetplate, 1902–08, of the 1st Cheshire Rifle Volunteers, crown officially altered from Victorian. (Wallis & Wallis)   £230 $368

16th Foot (Bedfordshire) officer's helmet plate, 1878-1881 example, gilt eight pointed star, the topmost ray displaced by a crown; a gilt laurel wreath mounted on a star. (Bosleys)   £360 $574

A Crimean War period Russian brass helmet plate, in the form of the Imperial Eagle, numeral 5 affixed to brass plate scroll. Wallis & Wallis)   £105 $169

1st VB East Lancashire Regiment helmet plate, a fine 1889-1901 OR's example. The topmost point displaced by a crown; within circlet *East Lancashire 1st Volr. Battn.*, the Sphinx resting on a tablet inscribed *Egypt.*(Bosleys) £80 $128

Royal West Kent Regiment officer's helmet plate, a fine post 1902 example comprising a gilt eight pointed star, the topmost point displaced by a crown. (Bosleys)   £240 $383

A Victorian officer's gilt and silver plated helmet plate of the Royal 1st Devon Yeomanry Cavalry, *VR* within Garter on crowned wreaths and title scrolls. (Wallis & Wallis)   £200 $320

4th VB Devonshire Regiment officer's helmet plate, 1902–08 example, silvered metal eight pointed star, the topmost point displaced by a crown. (Bosleys)   £340 $542

23rd Pioneers silver officer's pouch belt plate, a fine and scarce example by J & Co. (Jennens) hallmarked Birmingham 1902. (Bosleys) £180 $287

A Victorian officer's silver plated pouch belt badge of the 1st Vol Bn The Kings Own (R Lancaster Regt), with backing plate. (Wallis & Wallis) £80 $128

19th Surrey Rifles pouch belt plate, a good die struck white metal example comprising a wreath, half of laurel, half of palm, surmounted by a crown. (Bosleys) £38 $60

West Kent Rifles officer's pouch belt plate, a fine silvered example comprising a Maltese cross surmounted by a crown, lions between the arms. (Bosleys) £85 $135

7th Gurkha Rifles Officer's pouch belt plate, a good post 1953 silvered example. Laurel wreath surmounted by a crown which rests on a tablet inscribed *Ctesiphon*. (Bosleys) £50 $79

8th (Scottish) VB Liverpool Regt. pouch belt plate, by F & S (Firmin & Son) hallmarked Birmingham1902 comprising an oval silver thistle wreath surmounted by a Crown. (Bosleys) £400 $640

First Surrey Rifles officer's pouch belt plate, a good pre 1891 example, gilt wreath, half laurel half palm, surmounted by a crown. (Bosleys) £140 $223

A good officer's silver pouch belt badge of the Kent Rifle Volunteers, hall marked London 1863. (Wallis & Wallis) £105 $173

1st Suffolk Rifle Volunteers officer's pouch belt plate, a fine silvered example comprising a Maltese cross surmounted by a crown. (Bosleys) £75 $119

A good officer's cast puggaree badge of The 74th (Highlanders) Regt, brooch pin, not hallmarked. (Wallis & Wallis) £100 $165

A scarce WWII cast brass puggaree badge of the Malayan Peoples Army, blackened hollows, integral lugs. (Wallis & Wallis) £30 $50

A die struck brass puggaree badge of the 13th Madras Infantry, brooch pin. (Wallis & Wallis) £35 $58

A Victorian officer's puggaree badge of The King's Own Light Infantry, crowned KOLI monogram, brooch pin. (Wallis & Wallis) £60 $99

A good officer's cast Indian silver puggaree badge of the 2nd Punjab Regt., flat with nicely detailed design. (Wallis & Wallis) £70 $113

A good die struck white metal puggaree badge of the 90th Punjabis. (Wallis & Wallis) £35 $56

SLOUCH HAT

British African Sqn. King's Colonials officer's slouch hat badge, a very fine and scarce gilt die cast example. Two loops to reverse. (Bosleys) £180 $287

British Asian Sqn. King's Colonials officer's slouch hat badge, a very fine and scarce gilt die cast example. Two loops to reverse. (Bosleys) £130 $207

Australasian Sqn. King's Colonials officer's slouch hat badge, a very fine and scarce gilt die cast example. Two loops to reverse. (Bosleys) £130 $207

14th Light Dragoons officer's shako plate, a fine and scarce pre 1861 example. Cast gilt Maltese cross surmounted by a crown. (Bosleys) £400 $638

An officer's silver plated shako badge of the Staffordshire Rifle Vols. (Wallis & Wallis) £160 $264

Royal Marine Light Infantry officer's shako plate, a very fine and scarce 1866-78 example. Gilt eight pointed star. (Bosleys) £340 $542

2nd Admin. Bn. Forfar or Angus Rifle Vols. shako plate, a good 1864-82 OR's example. Die struck white metal Thistle star bearing circlet inscribed *In defence* with Crest of Scotland to centre. (Bosleys) £150 $239

28th Foot (N. Gloucestershire) officer's shako plate, rare Georgian example circa 1816-1829. Scalloped gilt plate surmounted by a crown, bearing pierced honours *Waterloo* top, *Peninsula* bottom, *Egypt* left and *Barossa* right. (Bosleys) £700 $1,116

13th Foot (1st Somerset) OR's shako plate, a good 1869-78 example. Brass laurel wreath surmounted by a crown; within the wreath the Garter. (Bosleys) £45 $72

50th Foot (Queen's Own) officer's shako plate, 1861-69 example. Gilt eight pointed star, the topmost point displaced by a Crown. (Bosleys) £150 $240

88th Foot (Connaught Rangers) OR's shako plate, a good scarce 1869-78 example. Brass laurel wreath surmounted by a crown. (Bosleys) £240 $383

Northamptonshire & Rutland Militia officer's shako plate, 1861-69 example, below the bottom scroll, the Horseshoe of Rutland. (Bosleys) £400 $640

A Waterloo relic. Georgian other rank's rectangular brass shoulder belt plate of The 73rd Regiment, with cut corners.
(Wallis & Wallis) £1,200 $1,920

46th Foot (S.Devon) Georgian belt plate, hallmarked Birmingham 1812, rectangular die struck plate.
(Bosleys)   £1,000 $1,600

49th Foot (Hertfordshire) officer's shoulder belt plate, 1843-55 example, seeded gilt rectangular plate with raised burnished edges.
(Bosleys)   £309 $480

A good rare pre-1855 officer's gilt and silver plated rectangular shoulder belt plate of the Jamaica Militia, bearing crown over the arms of the Colony.
(Wallis & Wallis)   £675 $1,087

West Suffolk local militia officer's shoulder belt plate, hallmarked 1809, oval burnished silver plate engraved crown strap inscribed *West Suffolk Local Militia*.
(Bosleys)   £650 $1,036

1st or East Devon Militia officer's shoulder belt plate, a very fine and rare George III example hallmarked 1803, burnished silver rectangular plate mounted with gilt crowned garter. (Bosleys)   £700 $1,116

57th (W. Middlesex Foot OR's shoulder belt plate, pre 1855 example. Brass rectangular plate bearing crowned laurel wreath with 57 to the centre.
(Bosleys)   £140 $224

Durham Militia officer's shoulder belt plate, circa 1852, burnished silver rectangular plate mounted with cut silver eight pointed star.
(Bosleys)   £475 $757

12th (Suffolk) Foot officer's shoulder belt plate, 1843-55 example comprising a burnished gilt rectangular plate mounted with silver crowned laurel wreath.
(Bosleys)   £460 $734

A 1907 SMLE bayonet, blade marked crown ER issue marks for 1908, hooked fighting quillon, pommel stamped *5 Cav R 284*, in its steel mounted leather scabbard. (Wallis & Wallis)   £100 $160

A Martini Henry artillery carbine 1879 pattern bayonet, saw backed blade 25½in., issue marks, diced black leather grips, steel knucklebow, in its steel mounted leather scabbard. (Wallis & Wallis)   £180 $288

A Nazi police dress bayonet, by F W Holler, plated blade 13in., German silver mounts, staghorn grips, eagle's head pommel, police badge to grip, in its black leather scabbard. (Wallis & Wallis)   £105 $168

A 1907 SMLE bayonet, blade issue marks for 1913, hooked fighting quillon, pommel stamped *4 N Stf 1251* in its steel mounted leather scabbard. (Wallis & Wallis)   £120 $192

Switzerland Vitriol sawbacked bayonet M1878, a good example with 18.75in. sawback blade, stamped *SAC Nissan*, the hilt is with steel crossguard and two piece chequered wooden grip. (Bosley's)   £75 $119

A late 17th century plug bayonet, broad tapered shallow diamond section blade 9in., brass crosspiece with swollen finials, fruitwood grip, brass ferrule and pommel. (Wallis & Wallis)   £180 $289

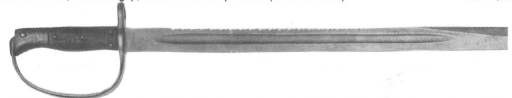

A Martini Henry artillery carbine 1879 pattern bayonet, saw back blade 25½in., blade stamped crown, VR various issue stamps, steel knucklebow, diced black leather grips. (Wallis & Wallis)   £145 $232

A Nazi police dress bayonet, by Carl Eickhorn, plated blade 11½in., German silver hilt with staghorn grips, eagle's head pommel, quillon stamped *S An 148*, in its black leather scabbard.
(Wallis & Wallis)   £110 $176

A Nazi Police dress bayonet, by E & F Horster, plated blade 12¾in., plated German silver mounts, eagle's head pommel, staghorn grips with police emblem, in its brown leather scabbard. (Wallis & Wallis)   £220 $352

Dutch 1940s Mannlicher sword bayonet, with 19in. blade, two piece wooden grip with steel rivets. Complete with original polished brown leather scabbard and belt frog. (Bosley's)   £120 $191

An 1898 Mauser Pioneer bayonet, saw backed blade 20½in., by C G Haenel Suhl, issue mark for 1906, lined wood grips, in all metal scabbard. (Wallis & Wallis)   £180 $288

A 1907 SMLE bayonet, blade marked with crown ER issue mark for 1909 etc., with hooked fighting quillon in 1st type scabbard. (Wallis & Wallis)   £125 $200

Danish Model 1889 Krag Jorgensen bayonet, forged from a single piece of steel, with maker's details of Alex Copel Solingen, pressed leather grips to the hilt. (Bosley's)   £55 $88

A Nazi carbine length police dress bayonet, trade mark of Zeitler, plated blade 9¼in.,grey metal mounts and stylised eagle's head pommel with traces of plating.
(Wallis & Wallis)   £270 $432

A scarce French M1890 Gendarmerie bayonet, blade 20½in., German silver hilt, hooked quillons, in its steel scabbard. (Wallis & Wallis)   £155 $256

A Nazi police dress bayonet by E & F Horster, plated blade 13in., German silver hilt, eagle's head pommel, staghorn grips, police emblems, in its German silver mounted black leather scabbard.
(Wallis & Wallis)   £190 $304

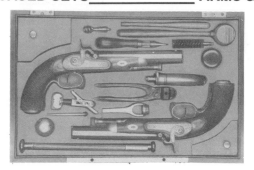

A pair of Continental percussion rifled target pistols signed John Donaghy, Amsterdam, Liège proof, mid-19th century, with octagonal sighted etched twist barrels with polygroove rifled bores, engraved breeches and tangs. (Sotheby's)   £1,380 $2,208

A pair of percussion box-lock belt pistols signed *Owen Powell, High St., Sheffield*, circa 1845-50, each with signed browned twist octagonal sighted barrel, case-hardened breech engraved with scrolling foliage, 8½in. (Sotheby's)   £1,725 $2,760

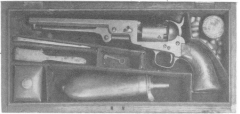

A six shot .36in. Colt Model 1851 single action Navy percussion revolver, 13in. overall, barrel 7½in. with London address, number *15788* on all parts, faint traces of naval scene on cylinder. (Wallis & Wallis)   £1,200 $1,920

A good six shot 100 bore self cocking bar hammer percussion pepperbox revolver, by Cogswell, London, 7½in. overall, barrels 3in. with London proofs, scroll engraved German silver frame, finely chequered rounded walnut butt with vacant escutcheon. (Wallis & Wallis)   £850 $1,360

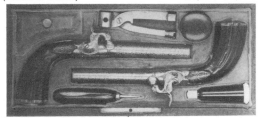

A pair of Liègois percussion pocket pistols, circa 1840-50, with sighted etched twist turn-off barrels, engraved rounded box-lock actions with side hammers, the opposing sides formed with a raised oval flat inlaid with gold scrollwork, 7½in. (Sotheby's)   £632 $1,011

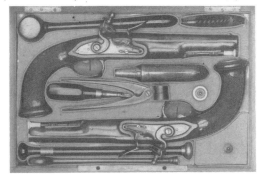

A pair of French flintlock officer's pistols, early 19th century, with sighted tapering barrels with case-hardened tangs, plain case-hardened locks with strongly bevelled edges, figured walnut full stocks, chequered butts, 12¾in. (Sotheby's)   £4,830 $7,728

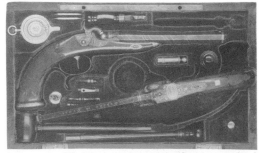

A fine pair of Bohemian percussion rifled target pistols by Lebeda in Praze, circa 1835, with swamped octagonal sighted browned twist barrels rifled with seven deep grooves, chiselled with a stylised bird's head in relief on both sides at the breech, 14½in. (Sotheby's)   £6,325 $10,120

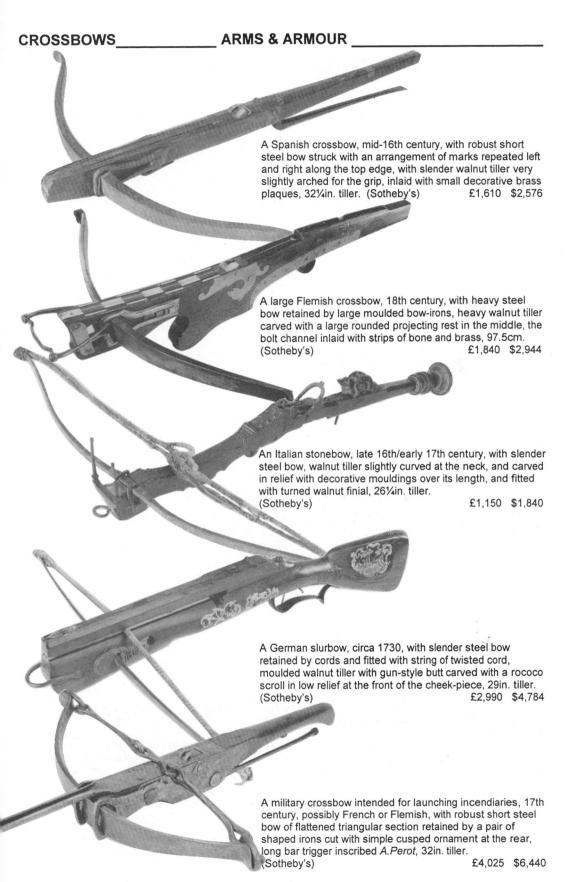

A Spanish crossbow, mid-16th century, with robust short steel bow struck with an arrangement of marks repeated left and right along the top edge, with slender walnut tiller very slightly arched for the grip, inlaid with small decorative brass plaques, 32¼in. tiller. (Sotheby's) £1,610 $2,576

A large Flemish crossbow, 18th century, with heavy steel bow retained by large moulded bow-irons, heavy walnut tiller carved with a large rounded projecting rest in the middle, the bolt channel inlaid with strips of bone and brass, 97.5cm. (Sotheby's) £1,840 $2,944

An Italian stonebow, late 16th/early 17th century, with slender steel bow, walnut tiller slightly curved at the neck, and carved in relief with decorative mouldings over its length, and fitted with turned walnut finial, 26¼in. tiller. (Sotheby's) £1,150 $1,840

A German slurbow, circa 1730, with slender steel bow retained by cords and fitted with string of twisted cord, moulded walnut tiller with gun-style butt carved with a rococo scroll in low relief at the front of the cheek-piece, 29in. tiller. (Sotheby's) £2,990 $4,784

A military crossbow intended for launching incendiaries, 17th century, possibly French or Flemish, with robust short steel bow of flattened triangular section retained by a pair of shaped irons cut with simple cusped ornament at the rear, long bar trigger inscribed *A.Perot*, 32in. tiller. (Sotheby's) £4,025 $6,440

A good 19th century Sudanese Mahdist double dagger Haladie, 23in., tapered blades 9¼in. with shaped edges, etched with repeated Arabic inscriptions on both sides. One piece shaped ivory grip, with its velvet covered wooden sheaths. (Wallis & Wallis) £175 $289

An unusual 17th century chiselled steel katar, 15¾in. single fullered watered steel blade 8½in. chiselled with raised fleurettes, scalloped stepped forte, shaped hilt. (Wallis & Wallis) £190 $313

A gold mounted Arab dagger jambiya, curved double edged blade 5½in. with raised rib. Hilt and sheath covered with gold foil, the front with elaborate wire and granulation work. (Wallis & Wallis) £250 $400

An unusual Muslim dagger Pulouar, broad double edged blade with circular swollen forte 15¼in., silver damascened on both sides with a pair of birds and foliage, panel fullers, raised ribs. (Wallis & Wallis) £140 $224

A good quality 19th century Indian katar from the Hindu Kutch, 15¾in., watered blade 8½in. with thickened point and raised rib. Hilt entirely covered with silver gilt foil engraved with repeated floral and foliate designs. (Wallis & Wallis) £370 $592

An Indian dagger, Mughal, circa 18th century, with curving steel blade, the hilt with a jade grip, terminating in a gilded ram's head, the body delicately incised with scrolling foliate vine and stylised fur. (Sotheby's) £4,209 $6,900

A 19th century Indian agate hilted dagger khanjar, slightly curved double edged blade 9¾in. with twin fullers and swollen point. One piece agate hilt carved with finger grips and foliate band to pommel. (Wallis & Wallis) £700 $1,120

An Italian Fascist 1937 pattern MVSN leader's dagger, plated blade 7½in., in its black painted metal sheath with brass mounts and chape. (Wallis & Wallis) £250 $400

A large late 19th century Turkish silver mounted dagger bichaq, 'T' section blade, 11½in., one piece ivory hilt, pommel surmounted by red glass (stone?) in silver mount. (Wallis & Wallis)   £250 $402

An unusual Muslim dagger pulouar, broad recurved double edged blade 15in. with large roundel at forte silver damascened with tiger and palm tree, thickened tip, steel hilt. (Wallis & Wallis)   £140 $225

A Victorian romantic dagger stiletto, tapered bifullered blade 4½in. silvered copper hilt in the form of a standing child holding bowl, scroll decorated sheath. (Wallis & Wallis)   £80 $128

A good 19th century silver mounted Indian kukri, swollen single edged blade 12in., silver ferrule, one piece ivory hilt. In its black leather sheath with large silver mounts. (Wallis & Wallis)   £360 $576

An Italian Fascist Gil youth leader's 1938 model dagger, plated blade, grey metal hilt mounts, brass fasces inset in black grip panel. (Wallis & Wallis)   £360 $579

A good Sudanese Mahdist double dagger Haladie, 23½in overall, curved double edged blades 9½in. etched with Islamic inscriptions, foliage and roundels containing lion. (Wallis & Wallis)   £120 $192

A good 19th century Indian dagger pesh kabz, 15½in., T section curved single edged blade 10¾in., swollen armour piercing tip, finely polished and etched with watered pattern. Steel gripstrap, four piece jade pommel and ferrules. (Wallis & Wallis)   £320 $512

A good Indian gold damascened twin bladed katar, 18in., bifurcated Zulfikar blade 12in. with serrated edges, gold damascened in four cartouches with Islamic inscriptions dated AH 1215 (=1800 AD). Steel hilt. (Wallis & Wallis)   £625 $1,000

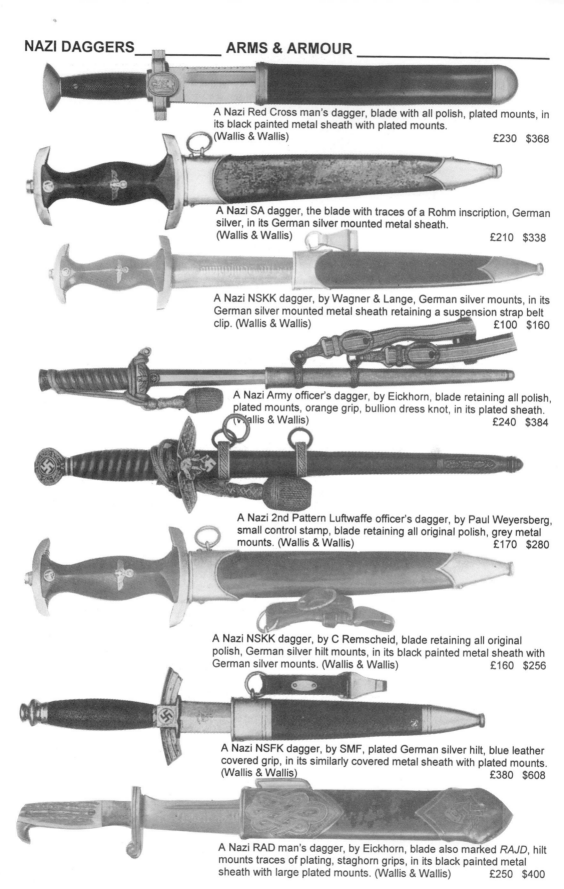

A Nazi Red Cross man's dagger, blade with all polish, plated mounts, in its black painted metal sheath with plated mounts. (Wallis & Wallis)

£230 $368

A Nazi SA dagger, the blade with traces of a Rohm inscription, German silver, in its German silver mounted metal sheath. (Wallis & Wallis)

£210 $338

A Nazi NSKK dagger, by Wagner & Lange, German silver mounts, in its German silver mounted metal sheath retaining a suspension strap belt clip. (Wallis & Wallis)

£100 $160

A Nazi Army officer's dagger, by Eickhorn, blade retaining all polish, plated mounts, orange grip, bullion dress knot, in its plated sheath. (Wallis & Wallis)

£240 $384

A Nazi 2nd Pattern Luftwaffe officer's dagger, by Paul Weyersberg, small control stamp, blade retaining all original polish, grey metal mounts. (Wallis & Wallis)

£170 $280

A Nazi NSKK dagger, by C Remscheid, blade retaining all original polish, German silver hilt mounts, in its black painted metal sheath with German silver mounts. (Wallis & Wallis)

£160 $256

A Nazi NSFK dagger, by SMF, plated German silver hilt, blue leather covered grip, in its similarly covered metal sheath with plated mounts. (Wallis & Wallis)

£380 $608

A Nazi RAD man's dagger, by Eickhorn, blade also marked *RAJD*, hilt mounts traces of plating, staghorn grips, in its black painted metal sheath with large plated mounts. (Wallis & Wallis)

£250 $400

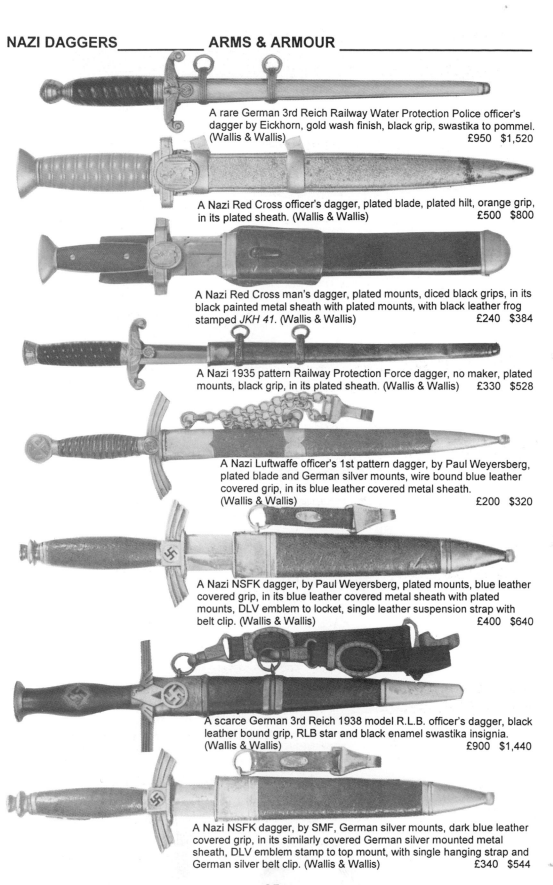

A rare German 3rd Reich Railway Water Protection Police officer's dagger by Eickhorn, gold wash finish, black grip, swastika to pommel. (Wallis & Wallis) £950 $1,520

A Nazi Red Cross officer's dagger, plated blade, plated hilt, orange grip, in its plated sheath. (Wallis & Wallis) £500 $800

A Nazi Red Cross man's dagger, plated mounts, diced black grips, in its black painted metal sheath with plated mounts, with black leather frog stamped *JKH 41*. (Wallis & Wallis) £240 $384

A Nazi 1935 pattern Railway Protection Force dagger, no maker, plated mounts, black grip, in its plated sheath. (Wallis & Wallis) £330 $528

A Nazi Luftwaffe officer's 1st pattern dagger, by Paul Weyersberg, plated blade and German silver mounts, wire bound blue leather covered grip, in its blue leather covered metal sheath. (Wallis & Wallis) £200 $320

A Nazi NSFK dagger, by Paul Weyersberg, plated mounts, blue leather covered grip, in its blue leather covered metal sheath with plated mounts, DLV emblem to locket, single leather suspension strap with belt clip. (Wallis & Wallis) £400 $640

A scarce German 3rd Reich 1938 model R.L.B. officer's dagger, black leather bound grip, RLB star and black enamel swastika insignia. (Wallis & Wallis) £900 $1,440

A Nazi NSFK dagger, by SMF, German silver mounts, dark blue leather covered grip, in its similarly covered German silver mounted metal sheath, DLV emblem stamp to top mount, with single hanging strap and German silver belt clip. (Wallis & Wallis) £340 $544

A Georgian naval officer's dirk circa 1815, blade 9in. of tapering flattened diamond section, etched with foliage, copper gilt circular petal guard, turned ivory grip.
(Wallis & Wallis)   £325 $520

An American naval dirk circa 1812-1820, curved single edged blade 12in., one piece chequered ivory grip, copper recurved crosspiece and eagles head pommel. (Wallis & Wallis)   £320 $512

A Nazi naval officer's dirk, by WKC, blade etched with sailing ship and foliage, gilt mounts, wire bound orange grip, bullion dress knot, in its hammered gilt sheath. (Wallis & Wallis)   £420 $672

A Continental naval officer's dirk circa 1810, plain tapering blade 8½in., copper crosspiece in the form of the flukes of an anchor, octagonal hilt with plain copper mounts, bone grip.
(Wallis & Wallis)   £275 $440

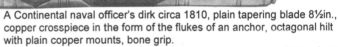

A Nazi naval officer's dirk, by Alcoso, with plain double fullered blade retaining all original polish, gilt mounts. (Wallis & Wallis)   £200 $322

A Japanese dirk Aikuchi, blade 14cm. signed *Fujiwara Kiyomitsu Kaga Province* and dated, *Made on a Lucky Day, 8th Month 3rd Year of Meiji (=1870 AD)*.Gunome hamon, muji hada, black lacquered tsuka and saya with autumn leaves and pine needles and cones.
(Wallis & Wallis)   £290 $464

A Nazi naval officer's dirk, by Eickhorn, blade retaining all original polish, etched with fouled anchor, entwined dolphins, and foliage, in its gilt sheath. (Wallis & Wallis)   £210 $346

A Georgian naval officer's dirk circa 1815, straight tapering flattened diamond section blade 9in., retaining virtually all original blued and gilt etched decoration of foliage and military trophies, oval copper gilt guard decorated with fruit, turned twist decorated ivory hilt.
(Wallis & Wallis)   £525 $840

A Georgian naval officer's dirk, shallow diamond section blade 8¼in. etched with urns and foliage. Copper hilt and sheath, oval guard with fouled anchor, swollen pommel, sheath with two hanging rings, engraved with foliage. (Wallis & Wallis) £200 $320

A Nazi naval officer's dirk, by Alcoso, etched with sailing ship and foliage, officer's name at forte *Plassmann*, gilt mounts. (Wallis & Wallis) £550 $880

A Georgian naval officer's dirk, tapering double edged blade 7¼in. of flattened diamond section, etched with foliage, small hatched cruciform copper gilt crosspiece. (Wallis & Wallis) £425 $680

A mid 19th century Continental white metal naval dirk, with pierced blade, worked white metal hilt in the form of a boat with fighting sailors, the scabbard with battle scene (possibly Dutch), 12in. long. (Dreweatt Neate) £2,000 $3,260

An Edward VIII naval officer's dirk, blade 18in. by Gieve, London, Portsmouth, brass hilt, lion head pommel, wire bound fishskin covered grip, bullion dress knot, in its brass mounted leather sheath with spring catch. (Wallis & Wallis) £150 $240

A Nazi naval officer's dirk, by WKC, plain fullered blade, gilt brass hilt mounts, brass wire bound white celluloid grip, bullion dress knot tied naval style, in its hammered brass sheath. (Wallis & Wallis) £200 $320

Georgian Naval midshipman's dirk, with double edged curved spear point blade, the hilt with a brass crossguard, with S shaped quillons. (Bosleys) £210 $336

A good German 3rd Reich naval officer's dirk by Eickhorn, etched with fouled anchor, foliage and entwined dolphins. (Wallis & Wallis) £270 $432

A silver mounted Scottish Highlander's dirk circa 1740, broad tapered single edged blade 13¾in. with twin fullers. Finely strapwork carved fruitwood hilt with silver ferrule, shoulders and circular pommel.
(Wallis & Wallis)   £1,000 $1,600

A good hallmarked silver mounted Scottish dirk, plain blade 11½in. with scallop back, corded wood hilt with silver studs, silver pommel cap and base band (hallmarked Edinburgh 1897) decorated with Celtic patterns.
(Wallis & Wallis)   £750 $1,200

A Scottish Highlander's dirk circa 1740, broad tapered bi-fullered single edged blade 13¾in., strapwork carved bog oak hilt, brass ferrule and circular brass pommel cap set with square iron nut.
(Wallis & Wallis)   £1,300 $2,080

A good Scottish silver mounted Highland dress dirk by Kirkwood circa 1880, polished single edged blade 10½in. with narrow fuller and scalloped back, roe buck horn hilt with silver pommel, in its leather covered sheath, locket stamped *R & HB Kirkwood 66 & 68 Thistle St Edinr*, companion knife and fork with pommels engraved with owner's crest. (Wallis & Wallis)   £900 $1,440

A 19th century silver mounted Highland dirk, plain scallop back, double fullered blade 11½in., wooden hilt, stepped silver pommel mounted with faceted cairngorm type stone, silver base band engraved with foliage and thistles, in its leather covered sheath with companion knife and fork, the hilts en-suite with the dirk.
(Wallis & Wallis)   £800 $1,280

A Victorian pre-1881 Scottish officer's dirk of the 93rd Highlanders, scallop back blade 11½in., by Johnston London, battle honours to Lucknow, officer's crest, motto *Per Aspera Virtus*, and initials *RSW*, corded wood hilt, decorated with brass studs, thistles, chiselled plated mounts, in its patent leather covered sheath with companion knife and fork. (Wallis & Wallis)   £1,050 $1,680

An early 18th century Scottish Highlander's dirk, straight single edged blade 14½in. with scalloped back edge. Strapwork carved bog oak hilt with brass ferrule, shoulders and pommel engraved with concentric rings and square iron nut. (Wallis & Wallis)   £2,000 $3,200

A Victorian silver mounted officer's Highland dress dirk of the 1st Lanarkshire Militia, fullered blade 12in. with scalloped back edge, forte etched *Maxsted & Son, Carlton St, Regent St, London*. Silver mounts chiselled with thistles in relief, foiled faceted cairngorm stone pommels. (Wallis & Wallis)   £1,000 $1,600

A Turkish flintlock blunderbuss of presentation quality, early 19th century, with three-stage barrel belled towards the muzzle, and a French over-and-under tap-action flintlock travelling pistol, late 18th century, the first 82.2cm. (Sotheby's) £7,475 $11,880

A 10 bore East India Co, military flintlock musket, 54½in. overall, barrel 39in., with London proofs and small EIC heart stamp at breech, also bearing Jaipur Arsenal stamps. (Wallis & Wallis) £475 $760

A flintlock blunderbuss signed *Whaley, Lynn*, late 18th century, with brass barrel formed in four stages, strongly moulded and belled at the muzzle, and fitted with spring bayonet above, 31¼in. (Sotheby's) £1,380 $2,208

A .70in. Baker's Patent Volunteer Flintlock Rifle by T Richards, 46in., barrel 30½in. Fullstocked, slightly rounded lock engraved *Theops Richards* in script. Regulation brass mounts, ramrod and bayonet bar. (Wallis & Wallis) £2,700 $4,320

An Ottoman Balkan miquelet-lock musket (dzeferdar), Herzegovina or Montenegro, 19th century, with earlier sighted tapering reeded barrel inlaid with silver scrollwork at the muzzle and enclosing a series of spurious silver-lined marks at the breech, 46¼in. barrel. (Sotheby's) £1,035 $1,656

A brass barrelled flintlock blunderbuss by Hampton, fitted with spring bayonet circa 1820, 28½in., flared barrel 12in. Birmingham proved, engraved *London*. Fullstocked, roller bearing frizzen spring. (Wallis & Wallis) £1,400 $2,240

A brass barrelled flintlock blunderbuss with spring bayonet by Reddell & Bate circa 1810, 31½in., part octagonal 3 stage barrel 15½in., Tower proved. Fullstocked, stepped bolted lock script engraved *Reddell & Bate*. (Wallis & Wallis) £950 $1,520

A rare 10 bore post 1777 military flintlock musket probably for the American Revolutionary War, made up from parts and intended for Sea Service as a 'Wartime Expedient', overall length 54½in. barrel 38¾in., Tower military proved. Fullstocked, regulation Land Pattern lock. (Wallis & Wallis) £1,700 $2,720

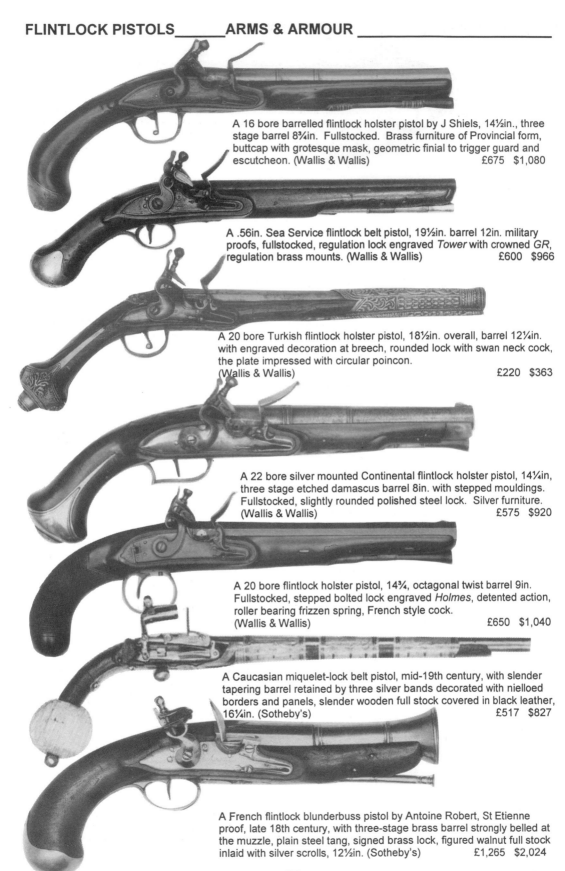

A 16 bore barrelled flintlock holster pistol by J Shiels, 14½in., three stage barrel 8¾in. Fullstocked. Brass furniture of Provincial form, buttcap with grotesque mask, geometric finial to trigger guard and escutcheon. (Wallis & Wallis) £675 $1,080

A .56in. Sea Service flintlock belt pistol, 19½in. barrel 12in. military proofs, fullstocked, regulation lock engraved *Tower* with crowned *GR*, regulation brass mounts. (Wallis & Wallis) £600 $966

A 20 bore Turkish flintlock holster pistol, 18½in. overall, barrel 12¼in. with engraved decoration at breech, rounded lock with swan neck cock, the plate impressed with circular poincon. (Wallis & Wallis) £220 $363

A 22 bore silver mounted Continental flintlock holster pistol, 14¼in, three stage etched damascus barrel 8in. with stepped mouldings. Fullstocked, slightly rounded polished steel lock. Silver furniture. (Wallis & Wallis) £575 $920

A 20 bore flintlock holster pistol, 14¾, octagonal twist barrel 9in. Fullstocked, stepped bolted lock engraved *Holmes*, detented action, roller bearing frizzen spring, French style cock. (Wallis & Wallis) £650 $1,040

A Caucasian miquelet-lock belt pistol, mid-19th century, with slender tapering barrel retained by three silver bands decorated with nielloed borders and panels, slender wooden full stock covered in black leather, 16¼in. (Sotheby's) £517 $827

A French flintlock blunderbuss pistol by Antoine Robert, St Etienne proof, late 18th century, with three-stage brass barrel strongly belled at the muzzle, plain steel tang, signed brass lock, figured walnut full stock inlaid with silver scrolls, 12½in. (Sotheby's) £1,265 $2,024

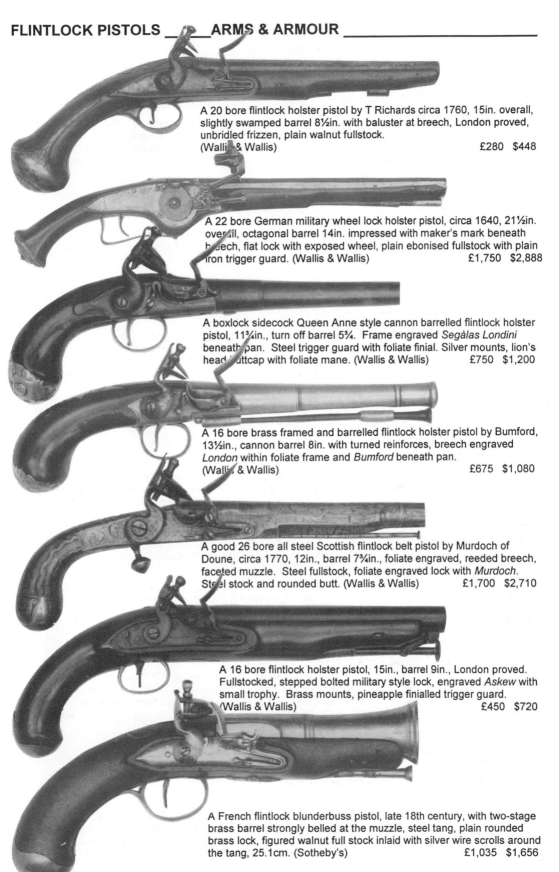

A 20 bore flintlock holster pistol by T Richards circa 1760, 15in. overall, slightly swamped barrel 8½in. with baluster at breech, London proved, unbridled frizzen, plain walnut fullstock. (Wallis & Wallis) £280 $448

A 22 bore German military wheel lock holster pistol, circa 1640, 21½in. overall, octagonal barrel 14in. impressed with maker's mark beneath breech, flat lock with exposed wheel, plain ebonised fullstock with plain iron trigger guard. (Wallis & Wallis) £1,750 $2,888

A boxlock sidecock Queen Anne style cannon barrelled flintlock holster pistol, 11¾in., turn off barrel 5¾. Frame engraved *Segàlas Londini* beneath pan. Steel trigger guard with foliate finial. Silver mounts, lion's head buttcap with foliate mane. (Wallis & Wallis) £750 $1,200

A 16 bore brass framed and barrelled flintlock holster pistol by Bumford, 13½in., cannon barrel 8in. with turned reinforces, breech engraved *London* within foliate frame and *Bumford* beneath pan. (Wallis & Wallis) £675 $1,080

A good 26 bore all steel Scottish flintlock belt pistol by Murdoch of Doune, circa 1770, 12in., barrel 7¾in., foliate engraved, reeded breech, faceted muzzle. Steel fullstock, foliate engraved lock with *Murdoch*. Steel stock and rounded butt. (Wallis & Wallis) £1,700 $2,710

A 16 bore flintlock holster pistol, 15in., barrel 9in., London proved. Fullstocked, stepped bolted military style lock, engraved *Askew* with small trophy. Brass mounts, pineapple finialled trigger guard. (Wallis & Wallis) £450 $720

A French flintlock blunderbuss pistol, late 18th century, with two-stage brass barrel strongly belled at the muzzle, steel tang, plain rounded brass lock, figured walnut full stock inlaid with silver wire scrolls around the tang, 25.1cm. (Sotheby's) £1,035 $1,656

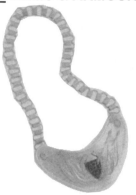

Cambridge Militia Georgian officer's gorget, burnished silver crescent with raised rim, engraved to the centre, the Royal Arms with *GR* above. (Bosleys) £620 $988

NS Reichskriegerbund standard bearer's gorget, pattern introduced 1938, polished aluminium plate with raised edges mounted with gilt oak wreath set on a trophy of flags. (Bosleys) £200 $320

A Georgian officer's universal pattern copper gilt gorget, engraved with crowned GR within laurel spray. (Wallis & Wallis) £70 $112

Foot Guards Georgian Officer's gorget, a fine and scarce example circa 1815 by R. Johnston, 68 St. James's Street, London. Gilt gorget mounted with the Royal Arms in silver.
(Bosleys) £950 $1,515

A Nazi Kornett der S.A. standard bearer's gorget, plated finish, NSDAP badge, plated hanging chains. (Wallis & Wallis) £140 $224

A good Georgian officer's universal pattern copper gilt gorget, engraved with crown and GR cypher within sprays of laurel.
(Wallis & Wallis) £140 $224

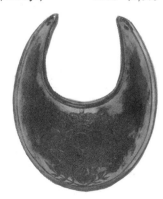

BUYER BEWARE

Once you have established what type of arms or militaria you want to collect, it is vitally important that you find a reliable source of material, for, as in other fields, there are plenty of fakers and forgers offering spurious items.

It is worthwhile building up a good relationship with a selection of reputable dealers and salerooms, always ensuring you obtain a full receipt with description and date of manufacture.

(Bosley's)

Royal Marines Georgian officer's gorget, post 1803 example, Plain burnished gilt on copper crescent engraved with Hanoverian Royal Arms. (Bosleys) £640 $1,024

Georgian officer's gorget, 1796-1830 Universal Pattern. Gilt on copper crescent engraved with crowned *GR* cypher within a wreath of laurels. (Bosleys) £220 $350

A 19th century Japanese helmet kabuto, signed *Nobutada Saku*, 32 plate bowl, black lacquered, copper te-hen kanemono and crest holder, black lacquered mempo.
(Wallis & Wallis)   £1,600 $2,576

A Victorian officer's helmet of the 2nd Dragoon Guards (Queen's Bays), brass skull with traces of gilt, ear to ear wreath.
(Wallis & Wallis)   £1,100 $1,760

A fireman's brass helmet of 'Merryweather' pattern, the moulded comb embossed with a dragon, standard embossed badge to front, 10¾in. high.
(Canterbury)   £360 $594

17th Lancers officer's lance cap. 1901-10 example, skull of black patent leather with the upper portion of white melton cloth ornamented with gold gimp cord.
(Bosleys)   £5,000 $8,000

RAF Type E partial pressure flying helmet, adopted by the Royal Air Force during the 1960s and used by pilots to the Mach 2 Lightning fighter. (Bosleys)   £700 $1,120

Duke of Lancaster's Own Yeomanry trooper's helmet, introduced 1857, black japanned, mounted with helmet plate of a large wreath half laurel, half oak.
(Bosleys)   £400 $640

A cuirassier helmet, circa 1630, probably German, with two-piece skull joined by a low comb pierced at the apex for fitting a crest, 11¼in. high. (Sotheby's)   £3,450 $5,520

London Rifle Brigade officer's shako, of green melton cloth with patent leather peak and band.
(Bosleys)   £275 $440

A fireman's brass helmet, dragons embossed to comb, helmet plate with letters *D R F B*, leather backed brass chinchains, leather lining.
(Wallis & Wallis)   £370 $610

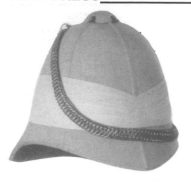

Boer War period officer's foreign service white helmet, with a seven fold wrapped pagri.
(Bosleys)   £380 $606

An Imperial German artilleryman's Pickelhaube, grey metal helmet plate and mounts, both cockades.
(Wallis & Wallis)   £140 $225

A Fire Chief's silver plated helmet, dragons embossed to comb, fire fighting devices to helmet plate.
(Wallis & Wallis)   £500 $800

A leather fireman's helmet with metal comb and brass lion's head ornament to each side, eight pointed star and arms to front, circa 1910.
(Auction Team Köln) £100 $160

A Fascist's black boat shaped mutz with tassels and Fascist symbol in bullion, from Mussolini's villa (with photograph of Captain Beck wearing it on the balcony of Villa Carpena) (H. C. Chapman)
    £2,300 $3,795

Royal Flying Corps leather helmet and face mask, rare example of a private purchase face mask, retaining original leather and elasticated straps.
(Bosleys)   £280 $446

TOP TIPS

Due to the military need for documentation (as often as not in triplicate!) there are plenty of records that allow us to chart the individual career of an officer or regiment. This allows us to touch some of the most important moments in history, yet the field remains to many undervalued and neglected. Many items start from only a few pounds and even some of the most historic pieces can still be bought for under £10,000, so there is still the chance of finding that bargain!   (Bosley's)

A rare German etched close helmet for the field, Augsburg, circa 1550, with one-piece skull rising to a comb with deeply notched crest.
(Sotheby's)   £14,950 $23,920

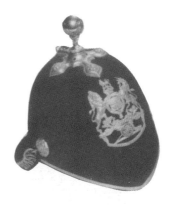

A late Victorian Royal Artillery officer's black serge helmet with gilt metal mounts and badge, chain link chin strap 10½in. high.
(Canterbury)   £320 $528

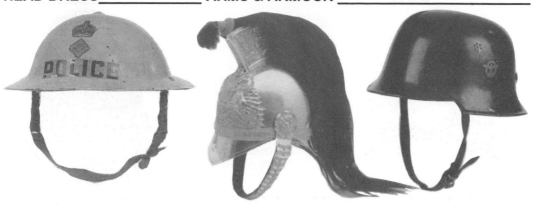

Grimsby Borough Police Chief Superintendents' steel helmet, a rare WWII Period Civil Defence Police 'Tommy' style helmet. (Bosleys) £140 $224

A fine 1843–47 pattern heavy cavalry officer's helmet of the 3rd or Prince of Wales Dragoon Guards, complete with black horsehair mane. (Bearne's) £10,800 $17,280

World War Two period Police double decal helmet, retaining National decal of the swastika and the police decal. (Bosleys) £90 $144

An English funerary close helmet, late 17th century, with two-piece skull joined by rivets along a roped medial comb pierced for the attachment of a funerary crest, 15in. high. (Sotheby's) £1,035 $1,656

A North Italian etched comb morion, mid-16th century, formed in one piece with a hemispherical skull rising to a boldly roped medial comb bordered by a pair of roped ribs, 9¼in. high. (Sotheby's) £2,300 $3,680

A composite close helmet, last quarter of the 16th century, Flemish or French, with one-piece skull rising to a high roped comb enclosed on either side by a pair of flutes, 13in. high. (Sotheby's) £2,645 $4,232

An early 20th century Prussian Picklelhaube helmet, with spike, eagle badge, and chin strap. (Dreweatt Neate) £480 $782

A scarce Vietnam period helicopter crew bone dome, green body with single tinted visor and boom microphone. (Bosleys) £160 $255

A Volunteer Fire Chief's silver plated helmet, comb embossed with dragons, brass applied lettering *Dunlop V.F.B.* (Wallis & Wallis) £900 $1,440

Royal Marine officer's Wolseley pattern foreign service helmet, khaki inter war period example, with eight fold pagri and leather edging. (Bosleys)   £180 $288

Royal Artillery Territorial 1902 OR's pattern cap, General Service buttons and correct thin leather chinstrap. (Bosleys)   £120 $192

Child's Nazi period steel helmet, modelled on the Great War pattern, green painted finish to the skull, retaining both decals. (Bosleys)   £140 $224

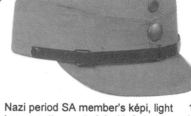

A Nazi Luftwaffe NCO's peaked cap, (flak section), scarlet piping, metal badges patent leather chinstrap. (Wallis & Wallis)   £180 $288

Nazi period SA member's képi, light brown cotton material with faded lighter tan panel to the body. (Bosleys)   £350 $560

15th (Bourne) Lincoln Rifle Volunteers other rank's shako, body of dark blue cross stitched cloth, black patent leather peak. (Bosleys)   £320 $512

An Imperial Prussian Infantry Reservists NCO's Pickelhaube, brass helmet plate, spike and mounts, leather backed brass chinscales. (Wallis & Wallis) £360 $576

A Belgian officer's lance cap of the 2nd Lancers, black patent leather skull, primrose sides and top, gilt lace band to narrow waist. (Wallis & Wallis)   £900 $1,440

An Imperial Prussian Cuirassier helmet, steel skull and spike, grey metal helmet plate, both cockades, leather lining and chinstrap. (Wallis & Wallis)   £370 $592

12th (East Suffolk) Foot Officer's 1869-78 shako, dark blue melton cloth body and crown, with patent leather peak. (Bosleys)   £430 $686

A Civil War period lobster tailed 'Dutch Pot', one piece skull embossed with eight raised radial ribs. (Wallis & Wallis) £850 $1,360

6th West York Rifle Volunteers officer's shako, senior officer's example circa 1880 by Cater & Co. Dark blue melton cloth body and crown. (Bosleys)   £750 $1,200

A Prussian officer's peaked forage cap, field grey cloth with scarlet cap band and piping to the welt.
(Bosleys)   £110 $176

Boer War period officer's field service cap, unusual private purchase example which can be worn folded as a field service cap, or unfolded to form a hat with wide brim. Khaki cotton, date *1899*.
(Bosleys)   £150 $240

A rare WWI Austrian M1916 pattern Berndorfer steel helmet with protecting front plate attached, triple leather pad liner.
(Wallis & Wallis)   £1,000 $1,610

A rare pre Great War Austrian officer's shako, black melton cloth body, with patent leather crown and peak. To the front, a gilt metal Imperial Austrian eagle plate.
(Bosleys)   £150 $240

Bavarian officer's Mütze contained in original box, field grey crown and upper body, with light blue band and white piping.
(Bosleys)   £240 $384

An 'A' pattern 'East of Malta' flying helmet, commonly used in the inter war years by RAF aircrew on the North West Frontier etc.
(Bosleys)   £460 $736

An Imperial German infantryman's Pickelhaube of the State of Mecklenberg Schwerin, grey finish to helmet plate, spike and mounts. (Wallis & Wallis)   £185 $296

A cabasset, circa 1600, formed in one piece, 'pear stalk' finial to crown, brass rosettes around base. (Wallis & Wallis)   £220 $354

An Imperial German OR's Pickelhaube of a Railway Regiment Battalion, helmet plate silvered spike, German silver mounts. (Wallis & Wallis)   £270 $445

A good Imperial Prussian infantryman's ersatz (pressed tin) Pickelhaube, black painted skull, lacquered brass helmet plate, brass spike and mounts. (Wallis & Wallis)   £340 $561

RAF WWII flying helmet, 2nd pattern C type. G type oxygen mask size medium, complete with mike and rubber tube. (Bosleys)   £330 $515

An Imperial German infantryman's Pickelhaube of the Saxon Duchies, brass helmet plate with silvered states badge affixed, dress spike and mounts. (Wallis & Wallis)   £350 $563

TOP TIPS

Wherever possible buy an item bearing the name of its original owner. A uniform will often have a tailor's label with the owner's name or a sword may have it etched on the blade. You can then start to research its history.

This is especially important to Orders and Medals, where diligent research can often enhance their value.   Many collectors set great store by the history behind the piece.
(Bosley's)

An Imperial Prussian Guard infantryman's Pickelhaube, grey metal helmet plate and mounts, both cockades, leather lining and chinstrap.
(Wallis & Wallis)   £220 $352

A fireman's brass helmet, dragons embossed to comb, leather backed brass chin chains, studs to neck guard, leather lining.
(Wallis & Wallis)   £310 $512

A scarce fireman's white metal helmet by Merryweather, complete with graduated chinchain and maker's plaque beneath back peak.
(Wallis & Wallis)　　　£280　$450

An Imperial German Wurttemberg Jäger reservist OR's black leather shako, gilt helmet plate with Landwehr cross, cloth cockade.
(Wallis & Wallis)　　　£240　$396

A pattern 1871 4th Dragoon Guards helmet, white horse hair plume, badge damaged.
(Russell, Baldwin & Bright)
£640　$1,062

An Imperial Prussian infantryman's ersatz (pressed tin) Pickelhaube, olive painted skull, brass helmet plate and spike, leather lining and chinstrap.
(Wallis & Wallis)　　　£160　$257

A Japanese helmet kabuto, Edo period, tall two plate bowl black lacquered with ornamental gilt lacquered devices, four lame laced and lacquered shikaro.
(Wallis & Wallis)　　£1,800　$2,898

An Imperial Prussian infantryman's ersatz (pressed felt) Pickelhaube, grey metal helmet plate, spike and mounts, leather lining and chinstrap.
(Wallis & Wallis)　　　£170　$280

A fire Chief's plated helmet, dragons embossed to comb, fire fighting devices to helmet plate leather backed chinchains, cloth lining. (Wallis & Wallis) £430　$710

Metropolitan Police constable's helmet, a scarce early six panel example with blackened rose boss to point of crown.
(Bosleys)　　　　　£200　$319

An Imperial Saxony infantryman's Pickelhaube, grey metal helmet plate and mounts, leather lining and chinstrap.
(Wallis & Wallis)　　　£190　$304

A very unusual late 19th century Scandinavian knife, single edged blade 5in. with roped back edge, one piece stag horn hilt 5¾in., pommel carved with moustacheod face, grip carved with mountainous scenes, in its horn sheath with white metal mounts. (Wallis & Wallis)   £70 $115

Great War Robbins punch knife & Dutch Commando knife WWII, the private purchase knife has a flat blade with double fuller, alloy grip. (Bosleys)   £250 $400

A fine Bowie knife by Gilbert Brothers, Eclipse, Sheffield, circa 1860-80, with spear point double-edged blade, German silver guard of slender oval form, moulded German silver ferrule, 15cm. blade. (Sotheby's)   £517 $827

A French WWI trench knife, spear point blade 6¼in. marked *Astier Prodon Thiers*, flat steel crosspiece, wooden hilt, in its sheath with belt loop.   £140 $231

A 19th century German hunting knife, plain, slightly curved single edged blade 9in., heavy steel mounted hilt, short plain crosspiece, small fluted shell guard, staghorn grip, hounds head pommel, in its steel mounted leather sheath. (Wallis & Wallis)   £180 $288

WWI period Belgian trench knife, double edged eight inch tapered blade stamped with the maker's details. Large oval steel guard and one piece wooden grip. Complete with original steel scabbard. (Bosleys)   £100 $160

A Victorian Bowie knife for the American market, clipped back blade 8½in. stamped with crown VR, *G & J Oxley Sheffield* at forte and *G & Oxley Texas Rangers Knife* within banners. Pewter cutlery style hilt with oval guard and acanthus scrolls. (Wallis & Wallis) £460 $736

A rare 1st pattern Fairbairn Sykes fighting knife, nickel grip with chequered design, the pattern indicating the second type, with recurved cross guard, contained in original dark brown leather scabbard with nickel plated chape. (Bosleys) £300 $480

A Bowie knife by G. Wostenholm & Son, Washington Works, Sheffield, England, late 19th century, with clipped point single-edged blade, one side signed in full along the back and stamped *I*XL* on the ricasso, German silver oval guard, 15cm. (Sotheby's) £322 $515

The Ashantee War Medal 1873-74, engraved *R. TURNER, SHIP'S CORPE. H.M.S. SIMOON.* (Bearne's) £130 $214

Suffolk Regiment Military Provost Staff Corps group of five: QSA four clasps 'Cape Colony' 'Orange Free State' Transvaal' 'South Africa 1902', BWM, Victory Medal, Defence Medal, Army Long Service Good Conduct Medal. (Bosleys) £180 $288

The Waterloo Medal, with Peninsula bar clasp, impressed *Jos. Ingea.* 15th or King's Reg. Hussars. (Bearne's) £375 $619

The Distinguished Service Cross, George V, engraved on reverse – *Lieut. J. Isdale. R.N.R. North Sea, Nov. 18th 1917* (cased). (Bearne's) £280 $462

Four: Crimea 1854, 1 bar Sebastopol (engraved *No 3702 W Chambers 71st Hd Lt Infy*), Indian Mutiny 1857; IGS 1854 1 bar and Turkish Crimea Sardinian issue. (Wallis & Wallis) £260 $429

Distinguished Flying Medal, George VI (with Ind.Imp'. in legend), engraved – 1606466 F/Sgt A.W. Knapp, R.A.F. (Bearne's) £410 $676

MGS 1793, 4 bars Barrosa, Cuidad Rodrigo, Pyrenees, Orthes. (David Powell 95th Foot). (Wallis & Wallis) £825 $1,320

Suffolk Regiment group of four, comprising 1914/15 Star, British War Medal, Victory Medal and and Shanghai Municipal Council Emergency Medal 1937. (Bosleys) £180 $287

Natal Rebellion medal, with bar 1906, (Tpr K A Phipson, Natal Carabineers). (Wallis & Wallis) £85 $140

South Atlantic Medal with rosette, (24402129 Cpl R J Stevens RAOC).
(Wallis & Wallis)   £110 $176

Four: Crimea 1 bar Sebastopol, China 1857 2 bars T Forts 1860, Pekin 1860, Army LS & GC, Turkish Crimea British Issue.
(Wallis & Wallis)   £290 $479

East and West Africa Medal, 1 bar Benin 1897 (J Gibson Ord HMS Theseus).
(Wallis & Wallis)   £95 $152

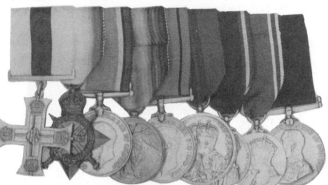

The New Zealand Medal 1865 to 1866, impressed *Adam Crawford, 4th BATn. MILITy. TRn.*
(Bearne's)   £180 $297

Nine: MC Geo V issue, reverse engraved *L J Peck 2nd Lancers, Nov 20th 1917,* 1914-15 star, BMW, Victory, Defence medal, Delhi Durbar 1911 in silver, 1935 Jubilee, 1937 Coronation, Vol Force LS Geo V Issue.(Wallis & Wallis) £430 $710

The Punjab Campaign Medal 1848-49, with Goojerat and Chilianwala bars, impressed *Geo.Colley, 61st. Foot.* (Bearne's)   £210 $346

Prussian 1870 Iron Cross, a scarce 2nd Class breast badge. Black iron Maltese cross set within a silver rim. (Bosleys)   £80 $128

Five: S. Africa 1877-79, bar 1879, QSA 3 bars, KSA both date bars, Army LS & GC Victorian issue, Austria Franz Joseph medal 'Der Tapferkeit', engraved *RSMJL Barry King's Dragoon Guards 2nd Dec 1898.* (Wallis & Wallis) £550 $886

The Indian Mutiny Medal 1857-58, with Lucknow bar, impressed *WHEELER RUDOLPH TIMOTHY, R1.H. ART.*
(Bearne's)   £180 $297

103

Sutlej medal 1864 for Sobraon (contemporarily impressed *John Winstanley 1st Dragoon Guards*). (Wallis & Wallis)   £370 $610

Suffolk Regt casualty Military Medal family group, comprising Military Medal George V, British War Medal and Victory Medal. Accompanied by a small portrait photograph of the recipient. (Bosleys) £440 $702

Royal Bristol Volunteers silver medal 1814. Obverse arms of Bristol with *Royal Bristol Volunteers* around, *In Danger Ready* below. (Wallis & Wallis)   £85 $136

1st Dragoons 'Order of Merit' 1816, a silver cross pattee with a French eagle in the centre, the arms of the cross marked *Merit, Peninsula*. The reverse engraved *B Crumsty 1816*. 55 x 44mm. (Wallis & Wallis)   £1,250 $2,000

Machine Gun Corps Military Cross group of six, awarded to Captain Albert Edward Miller formerly of the 2nd Battalion London Regiment. (Bosleys)   £450 $718

37th Bengal Light Infantry 1895 India General Service Medal, two clasps *Relief of Chitral 1895*, *Punjab Frontier 1897-98*. (Bosleys)   £60 $96

The Gulf Medal, with bar 16 Jan to 28 Feb 1991 (24851559 Pte G C Kew, RAMC), Unc, in box of issue. (Wallis & Wallis)   £95 $152

RNAS / Machine Gun Corps Military Cross group of four: Military Cross 1914 / 15 Star, British War Medal & Victory Medal (Lieut). (Bosleys)   £520 $832

Imperial Russian Order of St. Anne, a fine gilt and enamel 4th Class military breast badge with swords. (Bosleys)   £500 $797

ZAR Boer War Medal, a scarce gunmetal example, the obverse bearing the head of Kruger within the legend. (Bosleys)   £50 $80

1st Cambridge Regiment Distinguished Conduct Medal, Group of five: DCM (Pte.)1914/15 Star, BWM, Victory Medal (Pte)., Territorial Efficiency Medal. (Bosleys)   £1,300 $2,080

12th (East Suffolk) Foot Afghanistan Medal, awarded to 707 Pte. L. Casey 1/12th Regt. Single clasp *Ali Musjid*. (Bosleys)   £120 $191

Household Brigade Masonic jewel, silver gilt and enamelled Founder's breast jewel by Thomas Simms of Little Britain hallmarked Birmingham 1898. (Bosleys)   £100 $159

Imperial German group of 5: Iron Cross 2nd class; Prussian Order of the Red Eagle 4th Class; Prussian officer's 25 Year service gilt cross; Wilhelm 1st Centennial Medal; and Hamburg enamelled cross of Merit. (Wallis & Wallis)   £85 $136

Liverpool Shipwreck and Humane Society's Marine Medal, a good silver example diameter 38mm. The rim is engraved with details, dated *1886*. (Bosleys)   £125 $199

Durham Light Infantry Egypt 1882 undated Medal, awarded to 1843 Pte. J. Walsh 2/Durh. L.I. GC. (Bosleys)   £60 $96

1st Life Guards group of four medals, comprising: 1914 Star, British War Medal, Victory Medal, Army Long Service Good Conduct Medal. (Bosleys)   £280 $448

Ashantee Medal 1874, no bar, (1992 Pte M Hazel, 2 Bn 23. R W Fus, 1873-4) (Wallis & Wallis)   £130 $208

A Norwegian 6.5mm Krag Jorgensen Model 1894/1910 bolt action military rifle, 50¼in. overall, barrel 30in., number 31, the breech marked *Steyr 1896*, pale walnut fullstock. (Wallis & Wallis)   £610 $976

A good German 7.9mm Gew 88 bolt action military rifle, 49in. overall, barrel 29in., number 6317Z, the breech marked *Steyr 1890*, walnut fullstock. (Wallis & Wallis)   £400 $640

A good .450in. Westley Richards monkey tail breech loading percussion carbine, 41½in., barrel 25in. to hinge. Birmingham proved, stamped *Whitworth Patent*, platinum lined leaf sights. Lift up tail. Full stocked, bolted lock detented action. (Wallis & Wallis)   £550 $880

An 8mm Portuguese Gueddes M 1885 underlever SS military rifle, by Steyr, 1886, 48in. overall, barrel 32½in., the frame bearing cypher of Luiz I, walnut fullstock with two barrel bands, (Wallis & Wallis)   £525 $840

A good 8mm Mannlicher model 1886 straight pull bolt action box magazine military rifle, 50½in. overall, barrel 30in., Steyr logo at breech, adjustable ratchet rearsight, walnut fullstock. (Wallis & Wallis)   £350 $560

A .52in. rimfire Starr Patent breech loading carbine, 38in., barrel 21in. with hinged rearsight. Halfstocked, trigger guard linked to falling breech block. Spring retained barrel band, steel buttcap, steel lanyard ring to side of frame. (Wallis & Wallis)   £530 $848

A steel barrelled percussion blunderbuss by Moore, London, fitted with spring bayonet, 29in., half octagonal flared rebrowned twist barrel 14in. Fullstocked, steel mounts foliate engraved, chequered small, brass tipped wooden ramrod. (Wallis & Wallis)   £750 $1,200

A .577/450 Martini Henry Mark IV SS military rifle, 49in. overall, barrel 33½in. with military proofs and modern Birmingham proofs, walnut fullstock with Rawal Pindi Arsenal mark and dated *1908*. (Wallis & Wallis)   £380 $608

An unusual 10 bore Irish back action percussion martial style musket, 49in., barrel 32in., fullstocked, lock engraved *Kavanagh Dublin*, hammer screw with 2 small holes in lieu of a slot. (Wallis & Wallis)   £380 $608

An 8mm Mauser Model 1896 bolt action military rifle, 48½ overall, barrel 29in., by Ludwig Loewe & Co, Berlin, walnut fullstock with sling swivels. (Wallis & Wallis)   £250 $400

A .577in. Snider Mark III3 band military rifle, 54in. overall, barrel 36½in, the lock marked with crowned VR and *BSA Co 1871*, walnut fullstock. (Wallis & Wallis)   £400 $640

A French 11mm Model 1874 Gras bolt action SS military rifle, 51½ overall, barrel 23½in., the receiver engraved *Manufacture d'Armes St. Etienne*, walnut fullstock with ordnance stamp on butt. (Wallis & Wallis)   £150 $240

An 11mm Dutch Beaumont bolt action box magazine military rifle, 52½in. overall, barrel 32½in. dated *1874* at breech, the receiver stamped *P Stevens, Maastricht*, the butt plate tang dated *1890*, walnut fullstock. (Wallis & Wallis)   £280 $448

A good .50in. Sharps breech loading percussion carbine No 10793, 38in., barrel 21½in. stamped *Sharps Rifle Manufg Co Hartford Conn*, ladder rearsight. Halfstocked, back action lock, with pellet priming device. Falling breech linked to hinged trigger guard. (Wallis & Wallis)   £2,100 $3,360

An 11mm Egyptian Remington rolling block SS military rifle, 50½in. overall, barrel 35in. Remington address and patent dates on frame tang, walnut fullstock, with letter dated 1914 stating that it was picked up on the battlefield of Omdurman. (Wallis & Wallis)   £425 $680

A 12 bore double barrelled pinfire sporting gun by J Bourne, 46in., damascus barrels 30in, patent foresight engraved *T Gilbert Patent*. Rotary action underlever opening foliate engraved locks and frame. (Wallis & Wallis)   £520 $832

A French 12 bore converted Model 1822 military percussion musket, 55½in. overall, barrel 40½in., stamped *1822* on breech tang and *1833* at breech, the lock engraved *Mre Rle de Chatellerault*, walnut fullstocked. (Wallis & Wallis)   £190 $304

A 7.92mm Mauser Model 1896 bolt action carbine, 37½in. overall, barrel 18in., number 1132, by Ludw Loewe & Co, Berlin, walnut fullstock. (Wallis & Wallis)   £160 $256

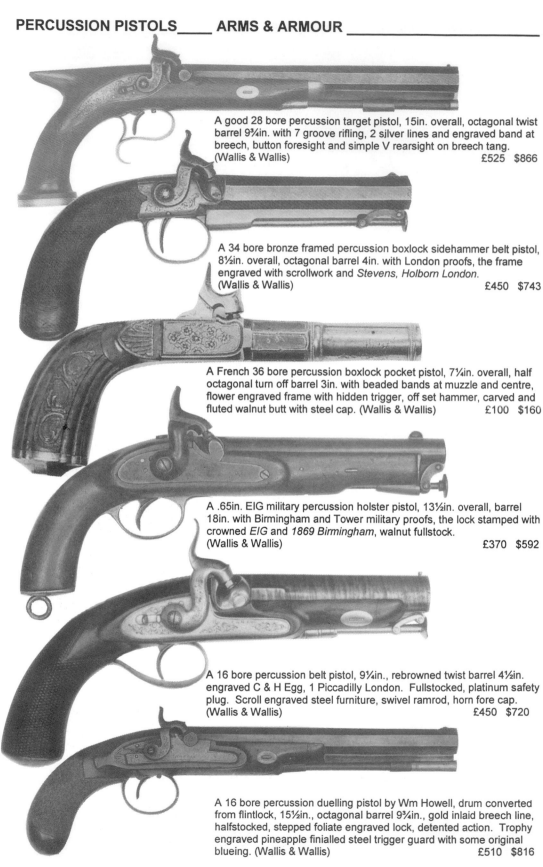

A good 28 bore percussion target pistol, 15in. overall, octagonal twist barrel 9¾in. with 7 groove rifling, 2 silver lines and engraved band at breech, button foresight and simple V rearsight on breech tang. (Wallis & Wallis)   £525 $866

A 34 bore bronze framed percussion boxlock sidehammer belt pistol, 8½in. overall, octagonal barrel 4in. with London proofs, the frame engraved with scrollwork and *Stevens, Holborn London*. (Wallis & Wallis)   £450 $743

A French 36 bore percussion boxlock pocket pistol, 7¼in. overall, half octagonal turn off barrel 3in. with beaded bands at muzzle and centre, flower engraved frame with hidden trigger, off set hammer, carved and fluted walnut butt with steel cap. (Wallis & Wallis)   £100 $160

A .65in. EIG military percussion holster pistol, 13½in. overall, barrel 18in. with Birmingham and Tower military proofs, the lock stamped with crowned *EIG* and *1869 Birmingham*, walnut fullstock. (Wallis & Wallis)   £370 $592

A 16 bore percussion belt pistol, 9¼in., rebrowned twist barrel 4½in. engraved C & H Egg, 1 Piccadilly London. Fullstocked, platinum safety plug. Scroll engraved steel furniture, swivel ramrod, horn fore cap. (Wallis & Wallis)   £450 $720

A 16 bore percussion duelling pistol by Wm Howell, drum converted from flintlock, 15½in., octagonal barrel 9¾in., gold inlaid breech line, halfstocked, stepped foliate engraved lock, detented action. Trophy engraved pineapple finialled steel trigger guard with some original blueing. (Wallis & Wallis)   £510 $816

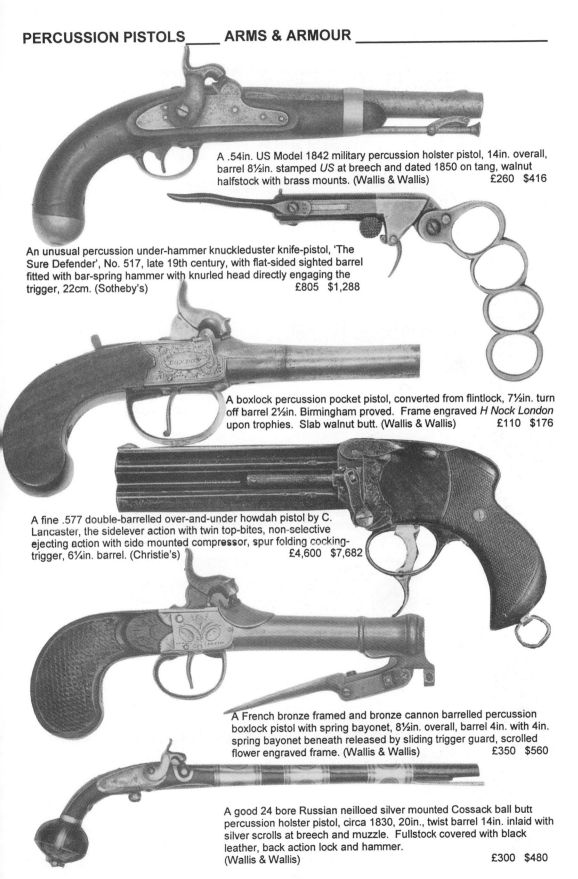

A .54in. US Model 1842 military percussion holster pistol, 14in. overall, barrel 8½in. stamped *US* at breech and dated 1850 on tang, walnut halfstock with brass mounts. (Wallis & Wallis)   £260 $416

An unusual percussion under-hammer knuckleduster knife-pistol, 'The Sure Defender', No. 517, late 19th century, with flat-sided sighted barrel fitted with bar-spring hammer with knurled head directly engaging the trigger, 22cm. (Sotheby's)   £805 $1,288

A boxlock percussion pocket pistol, converted from flintlock, 7½in. turn off barrel 2½in. Birmingham proved. Frame engraved *H Nock London* upon trophies. Slab walnut butt. (Wallis & Wallis)   £110 $176

A fine .577 double-barrelled over-and-under howdah pistol by C. Lancaster, the sidelever action with twin top-bites, non-selective ejecting action with side mounted compressor, spur folding cocking-trigger, 6¼in. barrel. (Christie's)   £4,600 $7,682

A French bronze framed and bronze cannon barrelled percussion boxlock pistol with spring bayonet, 8½in. overall, barrel 4in. with 4in. spring bayonet beneath released by sliding trigger guard, scrolled flower engraved frame. (Wallis & Wallis)   £350 $560

A good 24 bore Russian neilloed silver mounted Cossack ball butt percussion holster pistol, circa 1830, 20in., twist barrel 14in. inlaid with silver scrolls at breech and muzzle. Fullstock covered with black leather, back action lock and hammer. (Wallis & Wallis)   £300 $480

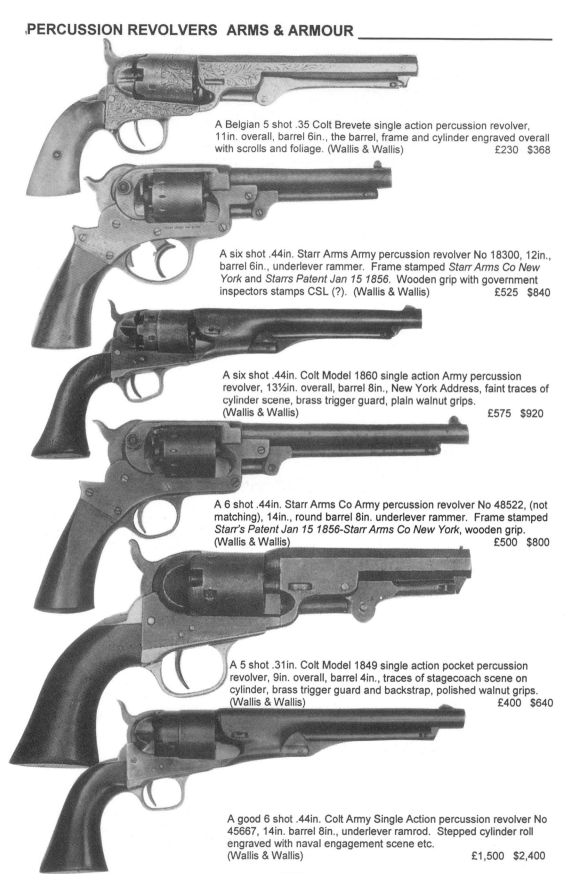

A Belgian 5 shot .35 Colt Brevete single action percussion revolver, 11in. overall, barrel 6in., the barrel, frame and cylinder engraved overall with scrolls and foliage. (Wallis & Wallis) £230 $368

A six shot .44in. Starr Arms Army percussion revolver No 18300, 12in., barrel 6in., underlever rammer. Frame stamped *Starr Arms Co New York* and *Starrs Patent Jan 15 1856*. Wooden grip with government inspectors stamps CSL (?). (Wallis & Wallis) £525 $840

A six shot .44in. Colt Model 1860 single action Army percussion revolver, 13½in. overall, barrel 8in., New York Address, faint traces of cylinder scene, brass trigger guard, plain walnut grips. (Wallis & Wallis) £575 $920

A 6 shot .44in. Starr Arms Co Army percussion revolver No 48522, (not matching), 14in., round barrel 8in. underlever rammer. Frame stamped *Starr's Patent Jan 15 1856-Starr Arms Co New York*, wooden grip. (Wallis & Wallis) £500 $800

A 5 shot .31in. Colt Model 1849 single action pocket percussion revolver, 9in. overall, barrel 4in., traces of stagecoach scene on cylinder, brass trigger guard and backstrap, polished walnut grips. (Wallis & Wallis) £400 $640

A good 6 shot .44in. Colt Army Single Action percussion revolver No 45667, 14in. barrel 8in., underlever ramrod. Stepped cylinder roll engraved with naval engagement scene etc. (Wallis & Wallis) £1,500 $2,400

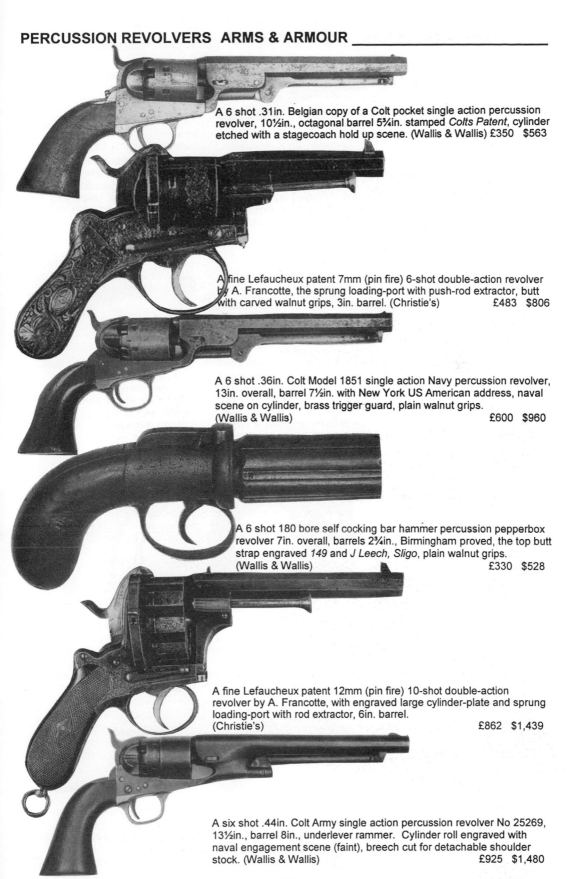

A 6 shot .31in. Belgian copy of a Colt pocket single action percussion revolver, 10½in., octagonal barrel 5¾in. stamped *Colts Patent*, cylinder etched with a stagecoach hold up scene. (Wallis & Wallis) £350 $563

A fine Lefaucheux patent 7mm (pin fire) 6-shot double-action revolver by A. Francotte, the sprung loading-port with push-rod extractor, butt with carved walnut grips, 3in. barrel. (Christie's)   £483 $806

A 6 shot .36in. Colt Model 1851 single action Navy percussion revolver, 13in. overall, barrel 7½in. with New York US American address, naval scene on cylinder, brass trigger guard, plain walnut grips. (Wallis & Wallis)   £600 $960

A 6 shot 180 bore self cocking bar hammer percussion pepperbox revolver 7in. overall, barrels 2¾in., Birmingham proved, the top butt strap engraved *149* and *J Leech, Sligo*, plain walnut grips. (Wallis & Wallis)   £330 $528

A fine Lefaucheux patent 12mm (pin fire) 10-shot double-action revolver by A. Francotte, with engraved large cylinder-plate and sprung loading-port with rod extractor, 6in. barrel. (Christie's)   £862 $1,439

A six shot .44in. Colt Army single action percussion revolver No 25269, 13½in., barrel 8in., underlever rammer. Cylinder roll engraved with naval engagement scene (faint), breech cut for detachable shoulder stock. (Wallis & Wallis)   £925 $1,480

A fine engraved powderhorn, signed *Thomas Norton*, dated *1796*, engraved with a hunt scene, 24in. long. (Sotheby's) £1,754 $2,875

An engraved powderhorn, engraved by Prince Hamblen, (1759–1836), Massachusetts Line, dated *1780*, tapering conical and engraved at the butt-end in a band of variously sized buildings, 16⁷⁄₈in. long. (Christie's) £3,312 $5,520

Engraved powder horn, 18th century, decorated with a map of a fort and the roads leading to it, and a stag hunt scene, 10½in. long. (Skinner) £1,693 $2,760

A bag shaped copper powder flask, 6in. overall, bag shaped body, top stamped *James Dixon & Sons Sheffield*: and *Colts Pocket Flask*, nozzle graduated from 2/8 to 4/8 (sic) drams. (Wallis & Wallis) £450 $720

A large German engraved cowhorn powder-flask, early 17th century, with curved flattened body, the inner face decorated with a pattern of concentric circles, the edges decorated with panels of cabling, 37cm. (Sotheby's) £460 $736

A leather covered powder flask, 9in., graduated patent safety charger, stamped *G & JW Hawksley, Patent*, from 60-100 grains with spring steel nozzle cap. (Wallis & Wallis) £260 $416

An Indian painted carved wooden powder flask, 7½in., carved as a mythical beast with a lady issuing from its mouth, holding a vase. (Wallis & Wallis) £100 $160

A late 17th century flattened Scottish cowhorn powder horn, 8¾in., body engraved with floral spray in geometric fashion emanating from a cylindrical vase. (Bosleys) £400 $640

An embossed copper powder flask, 4¾in. body embossed with a revolver. Common brass top engraved *XVII*, fixed nozzle. (Wallis & Wallis) £110 $176

A flattened Scottish cow horn powder horn dated *1692*, 11½in. front engraved with Celtic strapwork and geometric ornament with *RD 1692*. (Bosleys) £1,000 $1,600

An American copper pistol flask, 4in. similar to R755, embossed with US eagle, shield, crossed pistols, stars and *E Pluribus Unum*. (Wallis & Wallis) £160 $256

10th Prince of Wales Own Hussars officer's sabretache, scarlet cloth face edged with two inch gold lace of regimental pattern.
(Bosleys)   £650 $1,037

A Victorian officer's full dress sabretache of The Royal Artillery.
(Wallis & Wallis)   £220 $354

Saxon Hussar officer's parade sabretache, possibly of the 18th Hussars, red morocco body, the face of light blue cloth with gold lace edge. (Bosleys) £300 $480

A Victorian officer's full dress embroidered sabretache of The 3rd (Kings Own) Hussars, scarlet cloth bearing crown/VR/badge and 11 battle honours.
(Wallis & Wallis)   £350 $563

A Victorian officer's full dress embroidered sabretache of the 7th The Queen's Own Hussars, circa 1865, scarlet cloth, embroidered Guelphic crown over QO monogram.
(Wallis & Wallis)   £450 $720

A Victorian RA officer's full dress sabretache, gilt metal crown, bullion thread embroidered, gilt lace border, together with its black leather cover.
(Wallis & Wallis)   £450 $720

Cromarty Artillery Volunteers sabretache, pre 1901 officer's example. Dark blue melton cloth ground, silver embroidered Royal Arms. (Bosleys)   £370 $592

Northumberland Hussars officer's sabretache, circa 1877-1900. The green cloth face edged with two inch silver lace.
(Bosleys)   £825 $1,320

3rd (King's Own) Hussars officer's sabretache, late 19th century example, the red morocco lined scarlet cloth face edged with gold lace. (Bosleys)   £700 $1,120

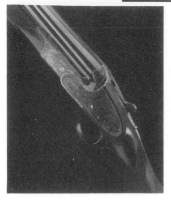

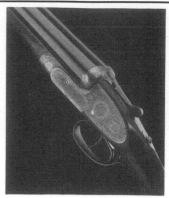

A fine 12-bore (2¾in) selective single-trigger over-and-under sidelock ejector gun by Boss, with two sets of interchangeable game and trap barrels.
(Christie's) £36,700 $60,188

A pair of 16-bore hammer guns by J. Dickson, toplever, non-rebounding sidelocks, percussion fences, best foliate-scroll engraving, boldly-figured stocks with butt-plates, 28in. barrels.
(Christie's) £3,450 $5,761

A fine 12-bore sidelock ejector gun by W.J. Jeffrey, pinless lockplates, best bouquet and scroll engraving with much hardening-colour, well-figured stock with butt-plate, 29in. barrels. (Christie's) £4,600 $7,682

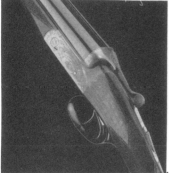

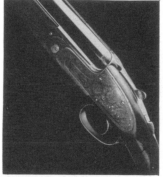

A lightweight 12-bore (2in) boxlock ejector gun by W.J. Jeffery, scroll-back action-body, full foliate scroll engraving with much hardening-colour, highly-figured stock with extension, cast-on for the left shoulder, 26in. barrels.
(Christie's) £2,760 $4,609

A fine 12-bore (2¾in) single-trigger over-and-under sidelock ejector gun by J. Purdey, with two sets of interchangeable barrels, Purdey patent single trigger, hold-open toplever, 28in. barrels and 26in. barrels.
(Christie's) £27,600 $46,092

A rare Charles Gordon 8-bore double-barrelled hammer smooth-bore shot-and-ball gun by J. Dickson, Jones patent rotary-underlever, carved serpentine fences, rebounding backlocks, 28in. barrels.
(Christie's) £2,300 $3,841

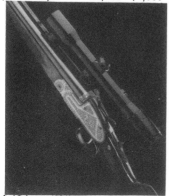

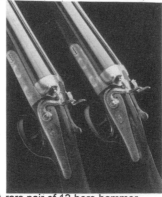

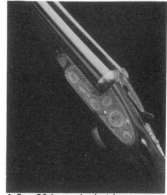

A 12-bore (2¾in) : 7 x 65Rmm sidelock ejector drilling by J. Kuchenreuter, the breech-ends mounted with a Zeiss 'Diavari-D' 1,5-6x telescopic-sight, 25½in. barrels.
(Christie's) £5,980 $9,986

A rare pair of 12-bore hammer ejector guns by J. Purdey, toplever, rebounding, backlocks with dolphin hammers, percussion fences, engraving, bright finish, boldly-figured stocks, 28in. barrels.
(Christie's) £13,800 $23,046

A fine 20-bore single-trigger sidelock ejector gun by Boss, the Boss patent single-trigger with rolled-edge triggerguard, standard easy-opening action, gold-inlaid cocking-indicators, 28in. barrels.
(Christie's) £19,550 $32,062

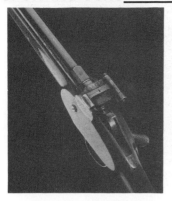

A fine Soper 1868 patent .450 self-acting side-hinged-block hammer sporting carbine, the sidelever action with rotating breech-block and self-cocking action, 28in. barrel. (Christie's)   £5,750 $9,602

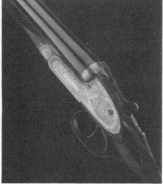

A fine 28-bore (2¾in) sidelock ejector gun by H. Atkin, the maker's name gold-inlaid in gothic script on the sides of the lockplates, well-figured replacement stock, 28in. barrel.
(Christie's)   £10,350 $16,974

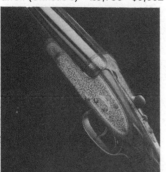

A 7mm double barrelled hammerless Royal sidelock non-ejector rifle, rounded bar, bolted automatic safe, gold-inlaid cocking indicators, best bold foliate-scroll engraving, bright finish, 24in. barrels.
(Christie's)   £10,350 $17,284

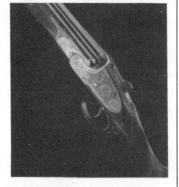

A rare .410 (3in) over-and-under sidelock ejector gun by Boss, hold-open toplever, rolled-edge triggerguard, best bouquet and scroll engraving with some hardening colour, 26in. barrel.
(Christie's)   £58,700 $96,268

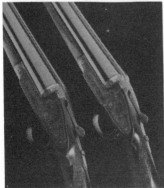

A pair of 12-bore single-trigger sidelock ejector guns by J. Rigby, 'Class B', non-selective single-triggers, optional ejector non-ejector action, dipped-edge lockplates, 28in. barrels.
(Christie's)   £4,025 $6,722

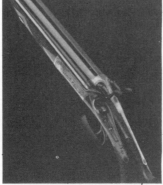

A J.D. Dougall 'lock-fast' patent .500, hammer rifle by J.D. Dougall, the patent slide-and-tilt action with bolted sidelever, non-rebounding backlocks with bolted dolphin hammers, 25½in. barrel.
(Christie's)   £1,150 $1,920

TOP TIPS

If you are interested in a gun, it's important to know what you have. Running through this check list will help.

1. How long is it? If it is more than 60cm. it is likely to be a rifle, shotgun or musket.
2. Does it open? If by moving a lever near the stock or pulling back a bolt the gun opens, then it is probably a shotgun or a firearm requiring a licence. Seek advice from the police or an expert. Some such guns do not require a licence, but age is no exemption.
If a gun barrel does not open at the breech then it is possibly a muzzle loader.
3. Does it have two barrels? If so, it is almost certainly a shotgun.
4. How does it fire? Most guns have a hammer which is pulled back to cock it and is released when the trigger is pulled. Without removing the hammer (old guns were often left loaded, so beware!) look carefully. Does it strike a pin or have a pin attached to it? If so it is centre fire and almost certainly requires a licence. Does it have a raised ridge down the centre of the face of the hammer? If so, it is rimfire and possibly requires a licence. Does the hammer strike a hollow nipple? If so, it is percussion. Does the hammer have an adjustable jaw at the top? If so it is flintlock.
5. How long is it? If less than 60cm. it is almost certainly a pistol. If it has a revolving cylinder, it is a revolver.
6. Does the wooden grip extend the whole length of the gun? (Is it full or half-stocked?)

Garth Vincent

An early wavy bladed sword tulwar, probably Tanjore Arsenal, broad wavy blade 30½in., with scalloped serrated edges, swollen rounded tip. Hilt chiselled with foliage and fish. (Wallis & Wallis)   £280 $448

A Victorian 1821 pattern light cavalry officer's undress sword, blade 34½in. by Henry Wilkinson, Pall Mall, etched with crown, *VR* foliage, and *J C L K* 15th Kings Hussars, plain steel scabbard. (Wallis & Wallis)   £190 $304

A Nazi Luftwaffe officer's sword, by Paul Weyersberg, inspection stamp, blade 30in., plated mounts, wire bound navy blue leather covered grip, in its navy blue leather covered metal scabbard. (Wallis & Wallis)   £290 $464

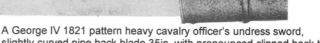

A George IV 1821 pattern heavy cavalry officer's undress sword, slightly curved pipe back blade 35in. with pronounced clipped back tip, by Andrews Pall Mall, Warranted. (Wallis & Wallis)   £290 $464

An early Assam Garo two handed sword dao, 32in. broad swollen double edged blade 21in., shaped swollen forte, slender quillons with hairy hide windings, swollen angled pommel.   £110 $176

A Georgian officer's mameluke sabre circa 1825, plain curved blade 31in. with pronounced clip back tip, copper hilt, traces of gilding, crosspiece with central Talisman emblem, ivory grips with twin rosettes. (Wallis & Wallis)   £1,000 $1,600

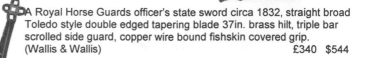

A Royal Horse Guards officer's state sword circa 1832, straight broad Toledo style double edged tapering blade 37in. brass hilt, triple bar scrolled side guard, copper wire bound fishskin covered grip. (Wallis & Wallis)   £340 $544

A well made Scottish Highland two handed sword claymore in mid 16th century style, 57½in., broad double edged blade 42¼in., half length broad fuller flanked by two narrow fullers. Thick down turned quillons with quatrefoil finials around pierced square, integral long langets. (Wallis & Wallis)   £2,100 $3,360

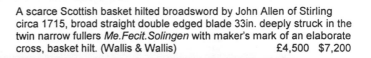

A scarce Scottish basket hilted broadsword by John Allen of Stirling circa 1715, broad straight double edged blade 33in. deeply struck in the twin narrow fullers *Me.Fecit.Solingen* with maker's mark of an elaborate cross, basket hilt. (Wallis & Wallis)   £4,500 $7,200

A Scottish basket hilted broadsword circa 1740, double edged blade 32½in., almost full length triple fullers with traces of *Andria Farara* in central fullers, steel basket guard of traditional form with unusual cylindrical pommel divided into segments.
(Wallis & Wallis)   £1,150 $1,840

A composite medieval sword, partly 15th century, with short blade of flattened diamond section gradually changing to hollow-ground section towards the base, globular pommel formed with a raised fluted lateral girdle, 25¼in. blade. (Sotheby's)   £4,025 $6,440

A good 17th century Spanish rapier, blade 37¼in. deeply stamped *X Fransisco X Ruys X N X Toledo X*. Large guards partly fluted, partly struck with granular ground and foliate chiselled. Fluted knucklebow and recurved swollen quillons. (Wallis & Wallis)   £2,100 $3,360

An unusual Scottish basket hilted broadsword circa 1720, broad straight double edged blade 33¾in., deeply struck *I TL I TL I* in the short fullers, basket hilt with panels supported by saltires, pierced with hearts and pellets. (Wallis & Wallis)   £1,500 $2,400

A Victorian officer's mameluke sabre of the 11th (Prince Albert's Own) Hussars, circa 1860, curved, clipped back blade 32in., by Hawkes & Co, London, Manufacturers to the Queen, etched with crown, VR, XI Hussars Sphinx, Egypt, battle honours in scrolls to Sevastopol.
(Wallis & Wallis)   £1,100 $1,760

A Victorian 1821 pattern light cavalry officer's undress sword, awarded for the Best Man At Arms in the Bengal Army 1871-2 by a VC Winner of the Indian Mutiny, blade 34in., by Henry Wilkinson, Pall Mall.
(Wallis & Wallis)   £800 $1,280

A Georgian 1803 pattern Grenadier Company officer's sword, curved blade 31in., maker in scrolls *Hunt & Potter*, etched with crown GR 1801-16 Royal Arms and foliage, the lower section frost etched with military trophies, copper gilt hilt, slotted guard.
(Wallis & Wallis)   £1,300 $2,080

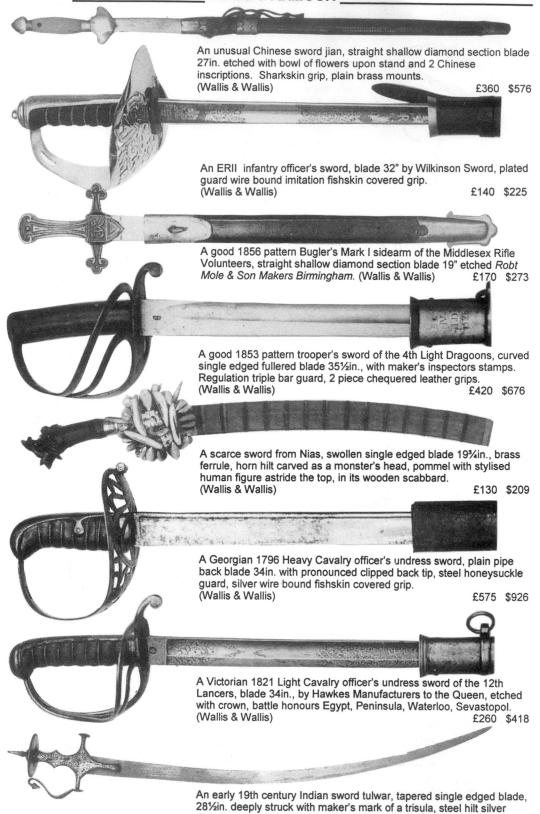

An unusual Chinese sword jian, straight shallow diamond section blade 27in. etched with bowl of flowers upon stand and 2 Chinese inscriptions. Sharkskin grip, plain brass mounts. (Wallis & Wallis) £360 $576

An ERII infantry officer's sword, blade 32" by Wilkinson Sword, plated guard wire bound imitation fishskin covered grip. (Wallis & Wallis) £140 $225

A good 1856 pattern Bugler's Mark I sidearm of the Middlesex Rifle Volunteers, straight shallow diamond section blade 19" etched *Robt Mole & Son Makers Birmingham.* (Wallis & Wallis) £170 $273

A good 1853 pattern trooper's sword of the 4th Light Dragoons, curved single edged fullered blade 35½in., with maker's inspectors stamps. Regulation triple bar guard, 2 piece chequered leather grips. (Wallis & Wallis) £420 $676

A scarce sword from Nias, swollen single edged blade 19¾in., brass ferrule, horn hilt carved as a monster's head, pommel with stylised human figure astride the top, in its wooden scabbard. (Wallis & Wallis) £130 $209

A Georgian 1796 Heavy Cavalry officer's undress sword, plain pipe back blade 34in. with pronounced clipped back tip, steel honeysuckle guard, silver wire bound fishskin covered grip. (Wallis & Wallis) £575 $926

A Victorian 1821 Light Cavalry officer's undress sword of the 12th Lancers, blade 34in., by Hawkes Manufacturers to the Queen, etched with crown, battle honours Egypt, Peninsula, Waterloo, Sevastopol. (Wallis & Wallis) £260 $418

An early 19th century Indian sword tulwar, tapered single edged blade, 28½in. deeply struck with maker's mark of a trisula, steel hilt silver dasmascened with flowers and foliage. (Wallis & Wallis) £160 $257

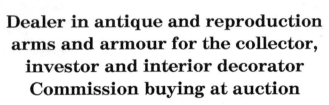

An 1889 Prussian Infantry officer's sword, plain, double fullered blade 29in. by ACS, copper gilt folding side guard, wire bound black grip, with WRII cypher. (Wallis & Wallis) £200 $320

An unusual early S Indian shortsword, possibly Malabar, broad trifullered single edged blade 19in. foliate chiselled brass mounted hilt with 4 piece ivory grips. Brass inlaid geometric gripstrap, pommel with shaped finial and applied rosettes. (Wallis & Wallis) £180 $297

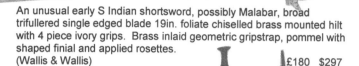

A 19th century Indian Hindu sword kora, 'elephant ear' shaped blade 22½in. chiselled with various Hindu divinities, tigers attacking elephant, mounted horseman, foliage and calligraphic cartouche. (Wallis & Wallis) £115 $184

A late Victorian hallmarked silver mounted Eastern style sabre made for Admiral Woods Pasha, curved blade 32in. by Henry Wilkinson Pall Mall, etched within foliate scroll patterns with gold wash background, the hilt of solid hallmarked silver gilt, in its solid silver gilt scabbard. (Wallis & Wallis) £1,800 $2,880

An interesting 19th century mameluke sabre presented to an officer in the 16th Lancers by an officer killed at the Battle of Aliwal, 1846, mounted with curved Indian blade, 33in. inlaid with small brass armourer's mark, English gilt crosspiece and grip strap. (Wallis & Wallis) £3,100 $4,960

Highland Light Infantry officer's sword, pre 1901 example, the blade is with double fuller and etched decoration of a crowned entwined VR cypher, basket with buff leather lining, with scarlet outer and blue silk edging. (Bosley's) £450 $718

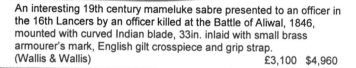

A 19th century Indian sword sossum patta, swollen single edged blade 19in. with 'T' section fluted back edge, retaining traces of silver damascened ornament at forte. Steel hilt of traditional form, silver damascened overall with flowers and foliage. (Wallis & Wallis) £160 $256

An Imperial German artillery officer's sword, curved plated blade 31½in, etched with mounted officer, crossed cannon, horse's head and foliage, and Regt *Field Art Regt V Scharnhorst (1 Hannov) No 10* and battle honours Peninsula Waterloo Gohrde. (Wallis & Wallis) £210 $336

An interesting Japanese shortsword wakizashi, blade 51.6cms, signed *Noshu Noju Harima No Daijo Fujiwara No Kanetaka*, dated *1674AD*, pierced circular iron tsuba chiselled with ho ho bird above fruiting ivy. (Wallis & Wallis) £750 $1,207

A good Dyak head hunter's sword Mandau, swollen single edged blade 18in. with maker's stamp. One piece stag horn hilt carved with stylised skull, jaws and entwined scrollwork with tufts of red, black and white hair. (Wallis & Wallis) £150 $240

A massive Chinese Boxer period executioner's two handed sword, 36½in., broad curved slightly swollen blade 22 x 3½in. (max). Brass guard and ferrule, woven fabric bound grip and ring pommel, in its brown leather scabbard. (Wallis & Wallis) £320 $512

A fine Japanese cloisonné mounted tachi with a 17th century blade 70.5cm., signed *Munenaga*, the hilt, tsuba and scabbard decorated with flowers, foliage, dragons and birds, 105cm. overall. (Bearne's) £3,000 $4,950

A large Chinese Boxer Rising period two handed executioner's sword, broad glaive shaped blade 24in., with twin fullers. Thick bronze oval guard and ferrule turned hardwood grip. (Wallis & Wallis) £150 $240

A good quality Indian sword tulwar, broad blade 28in. chiselled on both sides with assorted fighting animals, engraved with Islamic inscription and maker's cartouche dated 1225 AH(1810 AD), and applied with large silver device chiselled as a female divinity. (Wallis & Wallis) £525 $840

A Victorian officer's mameluke sabre of the 11th (Prince Albert's Own) Hussars circa 1850, curved, clipped backed blade 31in. by Andrews 9 Pall Mall, Battle honours to Bhurtpore, copper gilt hilt, crosspiece with scrolled patterns and central silver Sphinx and Egypt badge. (Wallis & Wallis) £1,250 $2,000

Indian kukri of massive form, a mid 19th century example, with heavy blade and Kora style steel hilt. Blade length 18in. (Bosley's) £75 $119

A Georgian painted wooden truncheon, by Parker of Holborn, painted with 1801-1816 Royal Arms, 18in.
(Wallis & Wallis)   £150 $240

A Victorian painted wooden truncheon, black background, painted in gold and colours with crown, white rose,
and *WRC*, 15½in. . (Wallis & Wallis)   £220 $352

A William IV painted wooden truncheon, painted with *WR* Royal Arms, *1836*, and coat of arms with motto.
(Wallis & Wallis)   £240 $384

A Victorian special constable's painted wooden truncheon, painted in gold and colours, with crown, VR, Hull SC,
plain wood grip, 16in. (Wallis & Wallis)   £110 $176

A polished wood 19th century life preserver, turned wooden globe head with barrel base, secured to turned
wood baluster haft by thick leather cord, 17in. (Wallis & Wallis)   £65 $104

A Victorian painted wooden truncheon, black painted background painted in gold and colours.
(Wallis & Wallis)   £140 $224

A William IV painted wooden truncheon, painted in gold *WR IV*, blue painted body, swelling grip, 14in.
(Wallis & Wallis)   £120 $192

A Victorian painted wooden truncheon, painted in gold and colours with crown, *VR* in Garter belt and *MS*, turned
wood grip, 12in. (Wallis & Wallis)   £220 $352

A Victorian painted tipstaff, rounded head, painted in gold and colours with crown, *VR Borough of Stamford
1837*, turned wooden grip, 10in. (Wallis & Wallis)   £310 $496

A Victorian painted wood truncheon, black painted, painted in gold and colours with crown, *VR* and in green with
numeral *4*. 11½in. (Wallis & Wallis)   £250 $400

122

A Victorian painted wood police truncheon, painted in gold and colours with Royal Arms and *Staffordshire Constaby*, turned grip, 16in. (Wallis & Wallis)   £150 $240

A Victorian painted truncheon, black painted body, painted in gold and colours with crown, VR, turned wood grip, 14in. (Wallis & Wallis)   £140 $224

A Victorian painted wooden truncheon of the Naval police, surmounted by carved wood crown, 13in. (Wallis & Wallis)   £350 $560

A George III weighted painted wooden truncheon, head painted in gilt and black *GIIIR*, 15in. (Wallis & Wallis)   £300 $480

A 19th century wooden life preserver, polished pear shaped head, brass base band, secured to pear shaped polished wooden haft with chain link, 18in. (Wallis & Wallis)   £40 $64

A Georgian painted wooden truncheon, painted crown, GR in gilt and colours, above arms of Newcastle-upon-Tyne, turned wood grip, 15in. (Wallis & Wallis)   £220 $352

A Georgian black painted wooden truncheon, painted in gold and colours with crown, GR, stepped swelling top, 14in. (Wallis & Wallis)   £100 $160

A Victorian Railway Police black painted wooden truncheon, painted in gold and colours with crown, *G M R 17*, 21½in. (Wallis & Wallis)   £300 $480

A 19th century wooden life preserver, pear shaped polished head, affixed by cord to rounded haft, 19in. (Wallis & Wallis)   £50 $80

A William IV black painted wooden truncheon, painted in gilt and colours with crown, WR IV, 11½in. (Wallis & Wallis)   £210 $336

Leeds Rifles bandsman's tunic. A rare example of the Rifle pattern tunic with black horn buttons. Dark green fine cloth.
(Bosleys) £100 $160

91st (Princess Louise's Argyle Highlanders) shell jacket, a scarce Crimea War period example attributed to Lieutenant James Michael Allen. (Bosleys) £500 $800

Irish Guards Colour Sergeant's tunic, a good scarce Elizabeth II example of scarlet cloth with dark blue facings to cuffs and epaulettes.
(Bosleys) £220 $352

Royal Flying Corps OR's 'Maternity' tunic, a rare example of the plastron fronted tunic. To each sleeve, full Royal Flying Corps embroidered titles.
(Bosleys) £700 $1,120

An officer's full dress scarlet coatee, circa 1807, of the Western Battalion Stirlingshire Volunteers, together with matching pair white buckskin breeches.
(Wallis & Wallis) £800 $1,280

RAF Inter-War period officer's full dress tunic. Bullion post 1918 pilot's wings to left breast. The shoulder straps embroidered with bullion eagle device surmounted by a Crown. (Bosleys) £200 $320

A Captains's uniform, circa 1865, of the 8th Lancashire Artillery Volunteers, comprising: full dress blue tunic, mess jacket, pill box hat. (Wallis & Wallis)   £850 $1,360

6th Inniskilling Dragoons officer's tunic, of scarlet melton cloth, with white facing to the collar and cuffs. (Bosleys)   £525 $840

Women's Timber Corps work coat, heavy cotton light khaki work coat with open pockets to the waist. On the lapel is a plastic Timber Corps badge. (Bosleys)   £275 $440

Lincolnshire Regiment officer's uniform, of scarlet melton cloth with white facings to the collar and cuffs, each decorated with gold lace of regimental pattern. (Bosleys)   £270 $432

A rare 1942 dated Indian made 44th Indian Airborne Division WW2 battledress, 1937 pattern, to each sleeve a printed Indian Pegasus badge and Sergeant's chevrons. (Bosleys)   £250 $400

A good collection of uniforms worn by Major Stephen Noel Furness of the London Irish Regiment including a Patrol pattern tunic of dark green, Service dress uniform with overalls. (Bosleys)   £250 $400

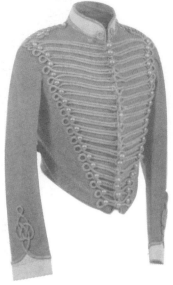

Cambridge Regiment WWI Other Rank's uniform, a rare 1902 pattern attributed example worn by Sjt G. Branch, to each sleeve Sergeant's private purchase chevrons.
(Bosleys)   £480 $765

Westmorland & Cumberland Yeomanry officer's tunic, scarlet melton cloth with white facings to the cuff and collar. (Bosleys)
£300 $478

Royal Marine Light Infantry Colour Sgt's tunic. Post 1902, scarlet cloth with dark blue facings to the collar and cuffs with brass regimental pattern buttons. Accompanied by a Colour Sergeant's sash.
(Bosleys)   £200 $319

A scarce post 1902 senior NCO's full dress scarlet tunic of The King's own Royal Lancaster Regt., shoulder straps gilt bullion embroidered *Lancaster*.
(Wallis & Wallis)   £50 $80

Scottish Volunteer officer's tunic, bearing silvered buttons of the pattern used by the 1st Sutherland Highlanders Volunteers.
(Bosleys)   £210 $335

A good 2nd Lieutenant's full dress scarlet tunic of The Duke of Cambridge's Own (Middlesex Regiment), together with shoulder sash and tassels, pair overalls, pair Wellington boots.
(Wallis & Wallis)   £200 $320

Irish Guards drum major's tunic, superfine scarlet cloth with dark blue facings to the cuff and collar. Eight double loops of gold bullion lace of Guards pattern, post 1953 anodised buttons.
(Bosleys)   £800 $1,276

Westmorland & Cumberland Yeomanry officer's rare patrol pattern tunic. Black melton cloth with Persian lamb wool facings to the cuff and collar.
(Bosleys)   £310 $494

Royal Flying Corps officer's tunic. A rare example of the officer's maternity pattern wrap over tunic, the collar with original bronze regimental pattern collar badges.
(Bosleys)   £550 $877

A good interesting uniform, circa 1908, of Colour Sergeant CJ Rofe, 5th Bn. The Buffs, with associated shooting items.
(Wallis & Wallis)   £500 $805

Sherwood Foresters officer's tunic, a good Field officer's transitional example of the 1880 pattern tunic with rounded collar.
(Bosleys)   £160 $255

A Victorian complete uniform of Col T E J Lloyd, Commanding Officer's 3rd Bn. The Duke of Cornwall's Light Infantry.
(Wallis & Wallis)   £650 $1,046

Womens Transport Service FANY battledress blouse, ATS pattern, to each sleeve FANY embroidered titles, Scottish Command formation badges and sergeant chevrons. (Bosleys) £70 $112

Argyllshire Volunteers Local Militia officer's coatee, Napoleonic example of an officer's short tail coatee. Scarlet woollen cloth, with yellow facings to the cuffs and collar. (Bosleys) £1,200 $1,920

Seaforth Highlanders officer's scarlet doublet, melton cloth with buff coloured facings to the collar and cuffs. (Bosleys) £280 $448

West Essex Yeomanry officer's tunic, a rare late 19th century example of the short pattern tunic, of dark blue melton cloth, with scarlet facings to the cuffs and collar. (Bosleys) £680 $1,088

Royal Marine Combined Operations Battledress uniform, a rare Second World War example worn by Lt F.R. Sillitoe of 41 Commando. (Bosleys) £250 $400

17th Lancers trooper's plastron tunic, a scarce post 1902 example of dark blue woollen cloth with white plastron to the front. (Bosleys) £190 $304

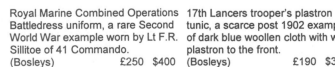

A US WWI other ranks' khaki
service dress jacket, bronzed
buttons and one collar disc.
(Wallis & Wallis)   £20 $32

Royal Devonshire Yeomanry
Artillery officer's uniform, scarlet
melton cloth, with dark blue facings
to the collar. (Bosleys) £480 $768

Eton Volunteer Rifle Corps shako
and uniform. Victorian example.
Shako of a light grey cloth.
(Bosleys)   £550 $880

Indian Army Supply and Transport
Corps officer's uniforms and
accoutrements, rare Edward VII
period example of the officer's
dress uniform.
(Bosleys)   £700 $1,120

Royal Horse Artillery Field Officer's
tunic, a rare pre 1902 example of
the Eton style tunic. Dark blue
melton cloth with scarlet facings to
the collar. (Bosleys)   £520 $832

An important Imperial Russian
Crimean War period coatee,
believed to have been worn by a
trooper of the Chevalier Guard
Regiment. (Bosleys) £700 $1,120

A late 19th century Chinese polearm 97in., trident head with wavy outer spikes, square section central spike, octagonal steel mount, turned brass ferrule, on its black painted bamboo haft. £140 $224

A late 19th century Chinese polearm 93in., foliate chiselled glaive shaped head 19in. issues from a brass dragon's head, on its black painted bamboo haft. (Wallis & Wallis) £170 $192

A late 17th century Italian polearm partizan, 73½in., broadhead 11½in. with raised central rib, swollen base, tapered octagonal socket. On its brass studded red silk covered octagonal haft. (Wallis & Wallis) £230 $368

An unusual 19th century African weapon, possibly Sudanese, 19¾in., blade 13½in. with swollen tip, curved lateral projections, large warthog tusk hilt, with leather and crocodile skin binding, good patina. (Wallis & Wallis) £140 $225

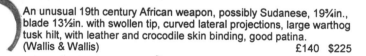

A double-flue whale harpoon, impressed *C. Linn & Co.,* probably British, dated *1852*, with wood pole and original roping, 8ft.4in. long. (Sotheby's) £3,332 $5,462

A rare Spanish elbow-length parrying gauntlet combined with a dagger blade, second half of the 17th century, for the left arm, the gauntlet formed in two parts articulated by a short strap, 95.5cm. (Sotheby's) £2,300 $3,680

An early 17th century polearm partizan, probably Italian, 89in., broad tapered double edged head 22in., with raised central rib, the base upturned at both edges, swollen octagonal socket. On later brass studded oak haft. (Wallis & Wallis) £390 $624

An early Nayar temple sword, 35in. broad blade 27¾in. with shallow central ridge, shaped foot to tip. Elaborate brass hilt with pierced blade reinforce, guard with reinforced edge, brass grip, multi section 'jingling' pommel. (Wallis & Wallis) £170 $272

Bob Kane, a 7.5 x 9 original signed blue ink sketch of Batman.
(Vennett-Smith)   £160 $256

Pope John Paul II, signed colour 6 x 4, 5th Sept. 1996, head and shoulders.
(Vennett-Smith)   £220 $352

Friz Freleng, signed original pencil sketch of Tweety's head, 4 x 6.
(Vennett-Smith)   £140 $224

James I, James VI of Scotland, fine large signed document, 25th Sept. 1604, being a Royal Warrant instructing Sir Richard Smith Knight and Treasurer to pay one thousand pounds to Sir Robert Lee.
(Vennett-Smith)   £760 $1,216

Pablo Picasso, a 10 x 13 coloured print, entitled *Jacqueline II*, signed in pencil, with certificate of authenticity from the National Art Guild (USA), June 1988.
(Vennett-Smith)   £410 $656

Winston S. Churchill, hardback edition of My Early Life, reprint 1958, signed in full to half title page, with old age signature.
(Vennett-Smith)   £540 $869

Good signed black & white photograph of Hitler seated in Party Uniform, signed across the image with ink autograph inscription *Adolf Hitler Berchtesgaden An 5/Septr 1936.*
(Wallis & Wallis)   £1,300 $2,080

Diana Princess of Wales, leather hardback limited edition of the catalogue of the sale of dresses from the collection of Diana Princess of Wales, by Christie's.
(Vennett-Smith)   £8,800 $14,080

Edward VII, a very fine signed 7 x 11in., as King, three quarter length standing in overcoat with top hat and cane, 1904.
(Vennett-Smith)   £300 $489

Pope John Paul II, signed colour 4 x 6in, 19th Oct. 1996, head and shoulders with hands clasped.
(Vennett-Smith) £180 $289

Apollo 11, signed colour 10 x 8in. by Neil Armstrong, Buzz Aldrin and Michael Collins, individually, threequarter length seated together in space suits.
(Vennett-Smith) £860 $1,385

Dwight D. Eisenhower, signed 8 x 10in., head and shoulders in military uniform.
(Vennett-Smith) £230 $375

Ethel Christie, typed signed letters and autographed signed letter, all to her family in Sheffield, 1943–44, each from 10 Rillington Place, with various references to Reg and his health.
(Vennett-Smith) £1,200 $1,932

George VI and Queen Elizabeth (the Queen Mother), a good pair of signed 30 x 22in. photographs, each head and shoulders, the King in uniform and the Queen in ceremonial dress, signed and dated *1943*. (Vennett-Smith) £400 $652

Edward VIII, a rare typed letter signed *Edward R.I.* as King, one page, Buckingham Palace, no date, to Lt. W.A.G. Burns of the 3rd Battalion, Coldstream Guards.
(Vennett-Smith) £600 $978

Salvador Dali, signed 8½ x 11in. bookweight photo, close-up portrait of the artist with the words *My secret life* across his forehead.
(Vennett-Smith) £105 $171

Albert Einstein, signed sepia piece from magazine photo, 3½ x ½in., laid down above 9½ x 5½in. magazine photo, 1954.
(Vennett-Smith) £190 $309

Louis Armstrong, early signed and inscribed sepia 8 x 10in., 20th August 1933, half-length with trumpet.
(Vennett-Smith) £190 $309

Roy Lichtenstein, signed postcard of one of his works.
(Vennett-Smith) £92 $149

Elizabeth II, signed 11½ x 10½in., to mount, full-length seated amongst Commonwealth Leaders 1977, pencil annotation to reverse.
(Vennett-Smith) £420 $685

Andy Warhol, signed postcard, with initials, head and shoulders.
(Vennett-Smith) £120 $193

Diana Princess of Wales, a souvenir programme for the Wales Festival of Remembrance, St David's Hall Cardiff, 5th Nov. 1994, signed by Diana.
(Vennett-Smith) £1,900 $3,097

Framed autographed signed letter: Dickens, Charles (1812–1870), dated 11 February 1841, to 'Maclise', signed 'Boz', one octavo page, framed with a print of Dickens, 11 x 13in. overall.
(Eldred's) £550 $880

Harry Houdini, signed postcard, *sincerely yours Houdini* , three quarter length standing with autograph signed note to reverse, dated *2nd February 1920*.
(Vennett-Smith) £900 $1,467

Wallis Duchess of Windsor, signed sepia 4¾ x 6¾in. Wallis Windsor, half-length wearing large hat, probably in Bahamas.
(Vennett-Smith) £170 $277

George Bernard Shaw, signed 7½ x 5½in., half-length seated at desk with microphone, photo by the BBC. (Vennett-Smith) £360 $587

Winston S. Churchill, signed 5 x 7in. bookweight reproduction of artist's impression of Churchill, signed in full.
(Vennett-Smith) £405 $660

Moe Howard, Three Stooges, signed and inscribed 4 x 5, by Howard for all three. (Vennett-Smith)   £50 $80

Rudolph Nureyev, signed postcard, half-length wearing costume. (Vennett-Smith)   £50 $80

Andy Warhol, signed 4 x 6 reproduction of his painting of Elvis Presley, overmounted in green, framed and glazed. (Vennett-Smith)   £190 $304

Robert Baden Powell, signed commemorative colour postcard with additional B.P. rhyme in another hand celebrating the relief of Mafeking. (Vennett-Smith)   £110 $17

Napoleon Bonaparte, excellent large document signed Napoleon at base, on vellum, Madrid, 21st Dec. 1808, in French. (Vennett-Smith)   £1,550 $2,480

Sarah Bernhardt, signed postcard, head and shoulders, photo by Reutlinger, *1895-1914* written to top. (Vennett-Smith)   £75 $120

Edward VIII & George VI, an excellent signed 6 x 4 sepia photo, 'Edward & Albert', showing the two young princes standing alongside each other wearing kilts, 1907. (Vennett-Smith)   £520 $832

George S. Patton, typed signed letter, one page, 25th May 1945, on Third United States Army HQ headed notepaper, to Capt. P.S. Paterson. (Vennett-Smith)   £560 $896

Wallis Duchess of Windsor, signed 4 x 7 bodyweight photo, removed from book, signed to lower white border, overmounted in ivory. (Vennett-Smith)   £100 $160

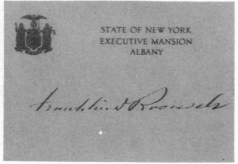

Montgomery of Alamein, signed 5 x 6, half-length standing in fur-lined jacket. (Vennett-Smith) £70 $112

Franklin D. Roosevelt, signed State of New York Executive Mansion Albany crested card. (Vennett-Smith) £135 $216

Neil Armstrong, signed and inscribed in colour 8 x 10, half-length in spacesuit. (Vennett-Smith) £180 $288

Marvin Hagler, copy of The Ring magazine, Sept. 1990, signed to colour front cover, head and shoulders. (Vennett-Smith) £55 $88

Harry Houdini, signed and inscribed sepia 6 x 8in, green, in original white oval mount, 10 x 12. (Vennett-Smith) £820 $1,312

Muhammad Ali, Sports Illustrated Magazine, 25th April 1988, signed in silver by Ali to front cover photo. (Vennett-Smith) £100 $160

Prince Philip, a large 19 x 25 photo, three quarter length standing in uniform, signed to mount and dated 1953, photo by Baron. (Vennett-Smith) £210 $336

Rupert Brooke, large signed piece, 6½ x 5½in., with additional note and date, 'Original M.S.S. 1912–13', overmounted in light brown and grey alongside photo. (Vennett-Smith) £450 $724

George Bernard Shaw, a very fine signed cabinet photo, half-length by Alfred Ellis & Walery of Baker Street. (Vennett-Smith) £720 $1,159

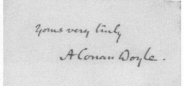

Napoleon Bonaparte, signed piece, *Bonaparte*, cut from an official document and mounted, 4 x 2in. (Vennett-Smith) £340 $547

Winston S. Churchill, signed piece, 2¼ x ¾in. laid down to album page (dated *1910*). (Vennett-Smith) £300 $489

Arthur Conan Doyle, signature and three additional words in his hand on the reverse of his calling card, 3 x 1½in. (Vennett-Smith) £170 $277

Queen Elizabeth, The Queen Mother, signed 8 x 8½in. to lower mount, three quarter length seated in ceremonial dress, 1975. (Vennett-Smith) £310 $505

Graham Greene, signed 8 x 10in. bookweight photo, head and shoulders with hand on chin. (Vennett-Smith) £80 $128

Diana, Princess of Wales, signed and inscribed 5 x 4¾in. to mount, pictured with Princes William and Harry 1995. (Vennett-Smith) £2,250 $3,667

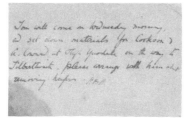

Beatrix Potter, autograph signed letter, on two separate correspondence cards, to her farm manager Tom Stoddart. (Vennett-Smith) £350 $570

Queen Victoria, being a signed cheque, partially printed and completed in another hand, made payable to W. Ray for 50 pounds, 23rd October 1840, drawn on Coutts. (Vennett-Smith) £310 $505

Cole Porter, signed card, 4.5 x 3in. (Vennett-Smith) £115 $188

Apollo XIII, three individual colour 7 x 9in. made-up plaques, each featuring portraits, mission badge etc., signed by Jack Swigert (rare), Fred Haise and James Lovell. (Vennett-Smith) £340 $554

Enrico Caruso, signed ink caricature, head and shoulders profile on album page, 4½ x 7in. (Vennet-Smith) £400 $644

T. E. Lawrence autograph letter signed, T. E. Shaw, one page, RAF Cattewater, Plymouth, 21st May 1929, to Mr Bain, asking him to send a list of five books. (Vennett-Smith) £1,300 $2,119

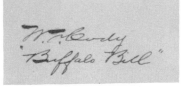

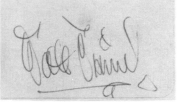

William Cody, small signed card, *W. Cody Buffalo Bill*, 3 x 1½in. (Vennett-Smith) £270 $435

Andy Warhol, signed green card, 5 x 3in. (Vennett-Smith) £90 $145

Walt Disney, small signed piece, in green, 3 x 2in., laid down. (Vennett-Smith) £360 $587

Mikhail Gorbachov, signed 5 x 7in. bodyweight photo, in recent years, head & shoulders. (Vennett-Smith) £140 $225

Cosmonauts, a rare signed colour 12 x 9½in., by both Valentina Tereshkova and Valery Bykobsky individually (husband and wife), half-length in close pose wearing uniforms. (Vennett-Smith) £170 $274

Rudolph Nureyev, signed 8 x 12in. magazine photo from a programme, three, three quarter length in costume. (Vennett-Smith) £55 $89

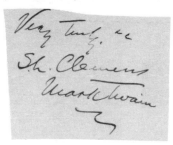

Mark Twain, signed piece, in both forms, *S.L. Clemens, Mark Twain,* in purple, 3¼ x 2½in., cut from end of letter. (Vennett-Smith) £280 $450

Henry Ford, signed piece, 4 x 1½in., laid down to album page beneath printed heading from notepaper. (Vennett-Smith) £210 $342

Buddy Holly, signed album page, still in autograph album, containing 56 signatures, 5 x 4in., inc. Bill Haley, John Gilpin, Anton Dolin, Gigli. (Vennett-Smith) £480 $773

Mahatma Gandhi, autograph, signed quotation in Hindi, although the quote in English, 22nd Feb. 1928, on reverse of postcard with affixed newspaper photo. (Vennett-Smith) £320 $515

Anna Pavlova, signed postcard, head and shoulders in costume. (Vennett-Smith) £70 $113

Florence Nightingale, signed piece in ink, removed from the end of letter, with six additional words, 4 x 2in., together with a hardback edition of Notes of Lectures by John Croft. (Vennett-Smith) £130 $209

Salvador Dali, signed 8½ x 12in. bookweight photo, half-length painting the head of his wife Gala. (Vennett-Smith) £80 $128

Edward VIII, signed sepia 8½ x 11in., as Prince of Wales, three quarter length standing in naval uniform, 1913. (Vennett-Smith) £180 $293

Muhammad Ali, signed 8 x 5½in. bookweight photo, three quarter length in boxing pose, overmounted in ivory. (Vennett-Smith) £130 $209

Josephine Baker, a good signed and inscribed sepia 7 x 9½, with first name only, half-length in French uniform, 1946. (Vennett-Smith) £290 $467

James I, (James VI of Scotland), signed document, one page, folio, 15th March 1600, signed at conclusion, with several counter signatures and good attached red wax seal. (Vennett-Smith) £700 $1,127

George VI, and Queen Elizabeth, a fine signed 8 x 11½in., by both individually to lower mount, 1937, full-length standing in coronation robes with the two princesses. (Vennett-Smith) £420 $684

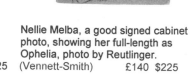

Enrico Caruso, signed cabinet photo, three quarter length in costume, London, 1907, photo by Alfred Ellis & Walery of Baker Street. (Vennett-Smith) £300 $483

Prince Charles & Princess Diana, signed 4 x 5in., colour photo, by both individually, full-length standing, each holding the infant princes. (Vennett-Smith) £2,500 $4,025

Nellie Melba, a good signed cabinet photo, showing her full-length as Ophelia, photo by Reutlinger. (Vennett-Smith) £140 $225

ANDY WARHOL

Andy Warhol, signed and inscribed 8 x 10in., head and shoulders. (Vennett-Smith)　　　£80　$130

Princess Margaret, signed 6 x 8in., head and shoulders in tiara, photo by Lord Snowdon. (Vennett-Smith)　　　£130　$211

Roy Lichtenstein, signed postcard of one of his works, girl with ball. (Vennett-Smith)　　　£80　$129

Pablo Picasso, signed print of one of his paintings 'Femme III', 7½ x 10½, overmounted in cream, together with a certificate of authenticity from The National Art Guild of America. (Vennett-Smith).　　　£620　$998

King George V and Queen Mary, pair of 9½ x 13in. photos, each half-length, the King in Army uniform, the Queen in ceremonial dress, each dated by hand *1916*. (Vennett-Smith)　　　£210　$342

An early 19th century mahogany cased wheel barometer and thermometer by Cetti & Co., 39in. high. (Canterbury) £720 $1,188

A 19th century mahogany cased wheel barometer and thermometer by Della Bella of Manchester, 42in. high. (Canterbury) £600 $990

Ciceri & Pini, Edinburgh, a Victorian papier mâché wheel barometer, 100cm. (Bearne's) £620 $1,023

A 19th century mahogany cased clock barometer and thermometer by Sweet of London, 42in. high. (Canterbury)£1,150 $1,897

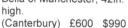

An early Victorian mother of pearl inlaid rosewood wheel barometer, mid 19th century, dial signed *W. GILBERT & SON BELFAST*, 45in. high. (Christie's) £747 $1,195

A 19th century 'Black Forest' stick barometer, the ivory dial with twin vernier scales, the stained wood case with mercury thermometer, 124cm. (Bearne's) £500 $825

An early Victorian rosewood wheel barometer, mid 19th century, dial signed *D. FAGIOLI & SON*, 46½in. high. (Christie's) £575 $920

An 18th century stick barometer by W & S Jones, Holburn, London, in mahogany case, 36½in. high. (Andrew Hartley) £1,300 $2,184

140

An early 19th century mahogany wheel barometer by Php. Bianchi, Lane End, 97cm. (Bearne's)   £300 $499

Late Georgian satinwood wheel barometer, early 19th century, signed F. *Amadio & Son, London*, 42½in. high. (Skinner) £1,286 $2,070

J. Springer, Bristol, a George III mahogany stick barometer, boxwood and ebony strung. (Dreweatt Neate) £1,600 $2,608

An English inlaid mahogany banjo barometer, Piotti, Hull, 19th century, 38½in. high. (Sotheby's) £828 $1,380

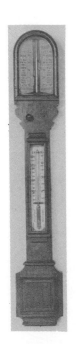

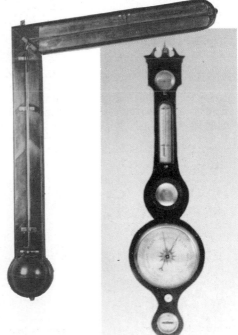

An Edwardian golden oak stick barometer, with top white enamel register and mercurial thermometer, 98cm. (Bristol)   £500 $820

An unusual, early Victorian papiermâché wheel barometer and thermometer, the shaped 'banjo' case inlaid with mother-of-pearl, 100cm. (Bearne's) £860 $1,419

A Regency mahogany angle barometer, first quarter 19th century, signed *TORRE FECIT*, 33in. high. (Christie's) £1,150 $1,840

A George III mahogany veneered wall barometer, inscribed *Ellis Exeter*, 97cm. (Bearne's)   £370 $592

Splintwork apple basket, 19th century, 16½in. diameter. (Eldred's) £62 $99

Large woven splint field basket, American 20th century, the open circular basket with round bottom and openwork hand holds, 9½in. high, 17¼in. diameter. (Sotheby's) £140 $230

Miniature melon basket, 19th century, 2½in. diameter. (Eldred's) £150 $247

Blue painted splint basket, America, 19th century, of circular form with banded rim and base and shaped wooden fixed handle, 13¼in. high, 13in. diameter. (Skinner) £836 $1,380

A George III mahogany linen basket, the back with a baluster rail between turned uprights with a hinged top above caned sides, 18¾in. wide. (Christie's) £1,955 $3,128

Splint pitcher-form basket, America, 19th century, with banded rim and base and ash handle, 7¾in. high, 4½in. diameter. (Skinner) £522 $862

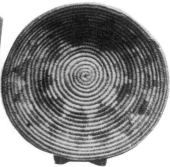

Nantucket basket, early 19th century, 13¾in. diameter. (Skinner) £790 $1,265

Arts and Crafts wastebasket, copper and leather decoration, 12½in. high. (Skinner) £52 $86

Navajo Indian wedding basket, with star motif, diameter 13½in. (Eldred's) £154 $247

A pair of large Venetian style blackamoors, of recent manufacture, each turbanned figure clad in gilt and polychrome decorated robes and bearing a torchere, 90in. tall. (Christie's) £13,800 $22,080

A pair of Italian ebonised and polychrome-painted blackamoor five-light candelabra, 19th century, each with pierced strapwork candelabra branches, 41½in. high. (Christie's) £8,050 $12,880

A pair of polychrome and giltwood blackamoor figures, 20th century, each shown holding a dish to the front, on waisted octagonal plinths, 73in. high. (Christie's) £16,100 $26,082

A polychrome and giltwood blackamoor figure, late 19th/early 20th century, the crouching figure seated on a draped plinth and supporting a shell above his shoulders, 39in. high. (Christie's) £5,980 $9,688

A pair of reproduction carved wood kneeling blackamoor stands, gilded and painted, the square tops and bases with cream marbling, 34in. (Woolley & Wallis) £1,150 $1,851

A Venetian carved hardwood blackamoor table, the kneeling boy draping himself in a cloth, his arm raised to form support, 18in. high. (Dreweatt Neate) £1,700 $2,805

A pair of parcel-gilt and polychrome-decorated blackamoor figures, each standing on a model of a half gondola carrying in its left hand a torch, 30in. high. (Christie's) £3,450 $5,520

A pair of Venetian polychrome-painted blackamoor torchères, one 18th century, the other of later date, each holding a spirally gadrooned cornucopia, wearing a feather hat, 50in. and 49in. high. (Christie's) £4,715 $7,544

A pair of late 19th century Venetian blackamoors, the richly decorated carved wood and gesso figures of two Negro boys holding detachable scallop trays, 175cm. high. (Christie's) £5,100 $8,160

A large bluejohn veneered circular table top, 20th century, 40in. diameter.
(Christie's)　　£14,950　$23,920

A bluejohn and black and white urn, part 19th century, the oviform body with domed top, on a waisted socle and square stepped plinth, 11½in. high. (Christie's)　　£920　$1,472

A 19th century bluejohn tazza, the round bowl with moulded rim on plain stem, round foot and square slate base, 6in. diameter.
(Dreweatt Neate)　　£880　$1,434

A bluejohn urn, the tapering ovoid body with gilt bronze floral finial and waisted socle with laurel border, 20in high.
(Christie's)　　£3,220　$5,152

A pair of bluejohn candlesticks, 20th century, of waisted tapering form with turned circular bases and silvered metal mounts, 5¾in. high.
(Christie's)　　£805　$1,288

A bluejohn goblet, 20th century, the semi-circular bowl on a reeded stem and spreading circular foot, 7in. high.
(Christie's)　　£3,450　$5,520

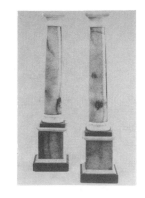
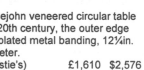

A pair of bluejohn veneered obelisks, 20th century, of typical form, the square stepped plinths with black and white marble galleries, 12¼in. high.
(Christie's)　　£3,450　$5,520

A bluejohn veneered circular table top, 20th century, the outer edge with plated metal banding, 12¼in. diameter.
(Christie's)　　£1,610　$2,576

A pair of 19th century marble and blue john columns, the flared stems raised on stepped square sectioned plinths, each 38.5cm. high.
(Phillips)　　£2,900　$4,756

The Cricketers' Almanack, for the year 1864... containing the Laws of Cricket, as revised by the Marylebone Club (John Wisden's Cricketers' Almanack...) 1864 (-1875), The First Twelve Volumes of 'Wisden'.
(Sotheby's)   £22,425 $36,553

Greco (Gioachino) The Royall Game of Chesse-Play. Sometimes the Recreation of the late King, with many of the Nobility. First edition, small 8vo, for Henry Herringman, 1656. (Sotheby's) £1,265 $2,062

Nineteen Blackie & Sons and Blackie books with covers designed by Charles Rennie Mackintosh, a Red Letter Library book with similar cover and seven 'The Modern Carpenter & Cabinet Maker'.
(Christie's)   £483 $724

Brook, James, Sir, Rajah of Sarawak (1803-1868), Narrative of Events in Borneo and Celebes, London, 1848, two volumes, First edition, 8vo, half calf, with plates, charts, and maps.
(Skinner)   £288 $460

Maclure, Robert, The Discovery of the North-West Passage, London, 1856, First edition, 8vo, half calf, with folding coloured map and four lithographs.
(Skinner)   £467 $747

Extremely rare 1930 Lakeside Press edition of Moby Dick, three volumes in an aluminium slipcase, limited edition of 1000; the so-called 'Moby Dick in a Can' edition.
(Sotheby's)   £3,332 $5,462

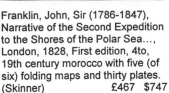

Franklin, John, Sir (1786-1847), Narrative of the Second Expedition to the Shores of the Polar Sea..., London, 1828, First edition, 4to, 19th century morocco with five (of six) folding maps and thirty plates.
(Skinner)   £467 $747

Carver, Jonathan (1732-1780), Travels Through the Interior Parts of North America, 1766-1768, London, 1781, 8vo, half calf, the expanded third edition, with two folding maps and five plates.
(Skinner)   £1,581 $2,530

Du Chaillu, Paul Belloni (1831-1903), Explorations and Adventures in Equatorial Africa, London, 1861, First English edition, 8vo, half calf, with twenty-two plates and fold out map. (Skinner)   £144 $230

A large bronze figure of Hercules and the Cyrenian Stag after the antique, raised on oval base, unsigned, 30½in. wide.
(Andrew Hartley) £1,500 $2,475

A bronze figure, 'The water carrier', a female figure balancing a jar on her head, 4ft.3½in. high, cast by the Singer Foundry, Frome.
(Woolley & Wallis) £1,750 $2,818

A pair of Victorian gilt metal six light candelabra, on foliate scrolled supports issuing from an urn with lion mask ring handles, 34in. high.
(Andrew Hartley) £600 $960

A Japanese bronze large vase, circa 1900, formed as rope-tied leaves, on lily pad and tendril base supports, 60cm.
(Bristol) £900 $1,440

A pair of 19th century bronze Marly style horses after Coustou, 57cm. high. (Wintertons) £1,050 $1,732

A 19th century bronze figure of Napoleon astride Marengo, unsigned, on oblong base, 17in. high.
(Andrew Hartley) £950 $1,520

A Russian patinated bronze group of a mounted cattle drover, late 19th/early 20th century, attributed to A. Gratchev, the peasant modelled reining in his mount, 12in. wide.
(Christie's) £368 $588

A pair of ormolu candlesticks, 19th century, of Louis XV style, each with foliate scrolled nozzle and foliate-wrapped baluster shaft, 13¼in. high.
(Christie's) £2,070 $3,436

After P.J. Mêne 'Valet de Chasse de Louis XV et Sa Harde', bronze figure group, height 63.5cm. x 72cm. wide.
(Wintertons) £3,000 $4,950

Pointer with rabbit, circa 1890, signed *J. Moigniez*, bronze with light to medium brown patination. (Skinner)   £1,725 $2,875

A late 19th century French bronze figure of a female muse, draped and holding a Roman lamp and seated on a stool, inscribed *Pfeiffer*, 14in. (Dreweatt Neate) £680 $1,108

A good late 19th century Japanese bronze figure of an Indian elephant and her calf, 10¼in. and 5¼in. high. (Canterbury)   £740 $1,221

A French bronzed spelter figure after Moreau of a standing fisherman carrying baskets of fish, on turned base, 28in. high. (Canterbury)   £260 $429

A pair of bronze Empire tazze, the gadrooned dishes with beaded rim and foliate scroll handles, on red marble square plinths, 14½in. high. (Andrew Hartley) £2,000 $3,200

A bronze figure of Milo of Croton, cleaving a tree with his bare hands, after Edmé Dumont, mid 19th century French, 14½in. high. (Andrew Hartley)   £800 $1,320

French bronze seated neoclassical female figure, late 19th century, 12½in. long. (Skinner) £607 $978

A 19th century Japanese squat baluster vase, cast in high relief with a procession of elephants, 38cm. high. (Wintertons)   £800 $1,320

A pair of 19th century gilt bronze candelabra. (Dockree's)   £320 $528

A 19th century bronze bust of Alexander of Macedonia, with inscription, 53cm.
(Bearne's)   £900 $1,440

A French animalier bronze model of a tiger, 19th century, after Antoine-Louis Barye, shown snarling and crouching on a rocky outcrop, signed *Barye*, 13½in. long.
(Christie's)   £1,265 $2,049

Etienne Henry Dumaige (French, 1830–1888), bust of Daphnis, bronze with light brown patination, red socle, 20in. high.
(Skinner)   £1,242 $2,070

A French bronze figure La Verité Méconnue, late 19th century, after a model by Aimé Jules Dalou (1838–1902), the nude lady shown on a rock with her head lowered to her knees, 5¾in. high.
(Christie's)   £1,725 $2,795

A large bronze and inlaid vase, with an impressed mark *kiritsu kosho kaisha and kako*, Meiji period, 19th century, decorated with peonies and silver stylised butterflies, 10½in. high.
(Christie's)   £24,150 $39,365

An archaic bronze tripod libation wine vessel, jue, late Shang dynasty, the body cast with a leiwen band between simple raised lines and set to one side with an ox-head handle, 8in. high.
(Christie's)   £3,680 $5,998

A Japanese bronze tripod koro and domed cover, with shishi finial and mythical fish handles, decorated with a band of fruiting vines, 22in. high. (Christie's)   £1,265 $2,049

An archaic bronze tripod vessel, ding, late Shang dynasty, the shallow bowl cast around the sides with a taotie band divided by six small projecting flanges, 6in. high.
(Christie's)   £26,450 $43,114

A French bronze group of an amorino and a setter, last quarter 19th century, the youth holding aloft a gamebird, 12½in. wide.
(Christie's)   £1,495 $2,422

French Art Nouveau small bronze ewer, signed *P. Loiseau-Rousseau*, the high looped handle moulded with foliage.
(Skinner) £89 $144

An impressive large model of an elephant with tigers, signed *Dai Nippon Genryusai Seiyazo*, Meiji period, the two tigers attacking the elephant, approx. 100 x 103cm. incl. base.
(Christie's) £9,200 $14,996

Jules André Meliodow (French, b. 1867), Rapture of Nymph and Satyr, 20th century, stamped *Louchet* on foot, part gilt and patinated bronze vase, 7in. high.
(Skinner) £655 $1,092

A large lacquered gilt-bronze seated figure of a King, 17th century, the figure cast seated wearing elaborately embroidered multi-layered robes, 33in. high.
(Christie's) £19,550 $31,867

A pair of large bronze vases, 19th century, decorated with Chinese children playing and with a crane flying over bamboos, each approx. 17¾in. high.
(Christie's) £14,950 $24,369

An archaic style bronze koro, signed *Ikkokusai Mitsutaka*, 19th century, decorated in iroe hirazogan and takazogan with four roundels depicting birds, 9¼in. high.
(Christie's) £29,900 $48,737

A set of six large gilt-bronze wall appliqués, French, each with a central espagnolette upholding five leaf-cast scrolling candlearms, 225cm. high.
(Sotheby's) £67,500 $111,375

A Regency bronze and marble inkwell, the hinged scallop-shell, enclosing a removable glass well, pierced sand-well and semi-circular well, 6in. high.
(Christie's) £2,875 $4,686

Danseuse à la pomme. by Jean Léon Gérôme, French (1824–1904) the patinated, gilded bronze and tinted marble figure in Grecian dress, 67cm. high.
(Sotheby's) £56,500 $93,225

A good pair of 19th century French bronze and gilt brass two-light candelabra in the form of a putto and figure of Pan in the style of Clodion (1738-1814), 16½in. high.
(Canterbury)   £1,250 $2,063

Leon Noel Delagrange, a patinated bronze figure of a page carrying a casket, on marble base, signed, 19in. high.
(George Kidner)   £1,200 $1,980

A French bronze model of a whippet, cast from a model by Antoine-Louis Barye, 19th century, with one forepaw raised and head down, 12½in. wide.
(Christie's)   £1,380 $2,235

Franz Bergman, Austrian cold painted and gilt bronze figure of an Arabian dancer with skirt lifting to reveal naked body, 7¾in. high.
(Canterbury)   £390 $644

A bronze reduction of the Warwick vase, 19th century, the beaded and lappeted lip above a vine-trail issuing from a pair of entwined vine handles, 14¼in. diameter.
(Christie's)   £2,300 $3,818

A late 19th century French gilt-bronze figure of Juno in flowing robes and holding a crown and shield, 66cm.
(Bearne's)   £1,450 $2,395

A fine and large archaic bronze tripod censer, ding, middle Western Zhou dynasty, the rounded body cast with a band of confronted stylised dragons, 14¼in. high.
(Christie's)   £25,300 $41,239

Ferdinand Preiss (1882-1943), a silvered bronze figure of a young girl with curly hair standing in front of her hoop, 12¼in. high.
(Canterbury)   £1,250 $2,062

A bronze model of a hippopotamus, first half 19th century, mounted on a marmo giallo plinth, the bronze 6⁵/₁₆in. long.
(Christie's)   £1,725 $2,795

A 19th century bronze figure of Narcissus after the Neapolitan antique, on circular base, 24¾in. (Andrew Hartley) £1,500 $2,400

C.Valton, bronze figure of a recumbent lioness on rough hewn stone base, 8in. (Ewbank) £980 $1,617

A French bronze figure of a naked lady in classical stance balancing ball on forearm, 36in. high. (Russell Baldwin & Bright) £1,800 $2,970

A late 19th century bronzed spelter pair of dancing maidens, L'Univers par Guillemin, the girls holding aloft a scroll branch supporting a 5in. diameter terrestrial globe by J. Forest, Paris, 25½in. high. (Christie's) £862 $1,405

A pair of Chinese gilt bronze models of seated lohans, dressed in long robes covering the heads, decorated with birds among flowering lotus, 6in. high. (Christie's) £1,610 $2,608

A fine silver-inlaid archaistic bronze ewer and hinged cover, Ming/early Qing dynasty, the large globular pear-shaped body applied with a raised band inlaid with leafy scrolls, 13½in. high. (Christie's) £13,800 $22,494

Franz Bergman, Austrian cold painted and gilt bronze figure of an Arabian dancer, her swirling skirt opening to reveal her naked body, 10¾in. high, *Namgreb* mark. (Canterbury) £1,350 $2,227

A fine 19th century bronze figure group of two horses and a hound on a rockwork base, raised on a veined marble plinth, 14in. high. (Russell Baldwin & Bright) £2,500 $4,125

After A. Keller, a bronze figure of a nude lady in pose on circular base with signature on a brown marble column, 16in. high. (Russell Baldwin & Bright) £400 $660

A brass bound mahogany bucket, possibly Irish, 19th century, of cylindrical form with two brass bands and loop handle, 14in. high. (Christie's) £1,035 $1,656

A pair of George III mahogany and brass bound peat buckets, each with ribbed tapering body and brass carrying handle, 18in. high. (H. C. Chapman) £9,600 $15,840

A Dutch brass bound kettle stand, 19th century, of coopered construction, with a copper liner and loop handle, 14in. high. (Christie's) £920 $1,472

A brass bound mahogany bucket, 19th century, of cylindrical form, with a tin liner and lions mask ring handles, on paw feet, 15½in. diameter. (Christie's) £805 $1,288

A pair of mahogany plate buckets, early 19th century, of coopered brass band form with brass carrying handles. (Sotheby's) £8,050 $13,443

An Irish George III brass-bound mahogany bucket, of ribbed circular tapering form with a brass carrying handle, and metal liner, 16½in. high. (Christie's) £3,680 $6,108

A Dutch brass bound mahogany kettle stand, 19th century, the ribbed body of tapering cylindrical form, with loop handle and liner, 13in. high. (Christie's) £1,092 $1,747

A matched pair of Irish George III mahogany brass-bound buckets, each with handle, scrolling attachment, inset metal liner and ribbed tapering sides, 16¾ and 16½in. high. (Christie's) £10,350 $17,181

An Irish George IV brass-bound mahogany bucket, of tapering circular form with hinged and part rope-twist loop carrying-handle, 19in. high. (Christie's) £4,370 $7,254

A French mahogany musical vanity box, circa 1840, in the form of a miniature piano, the top inlaid with a mock keyboard in ebony and ivory, 12in. wide. (Christie's) £850 $1,360

An Anglo Indian porcupine quill veneered workbox, early 19th century, the lobed horn finial above panels of alternating ivory and horn veneers, 8½in. wide.
(Christie's) £4,140 $6,624

A George III tortoiseshell veneered tea caddy of octagonal form with concave panels to the angles, with ivory banding and finial, 11cm. wide. (Christie's) £2,760 $4,416

Ebonised and lacquered jewellery cabinet with painted and mother of pearl panel.
(Jacobs & Hunt) £580 $957

A good pair of George III mahogany knife boxes, circa 1790, with canted tops and waved fronts outlined with barber's pole stringing, 8½in.
(Christie's) £3,000 $4,800

An oak letterbox, 20th century, fitted with aperture and cupboard door, inscribed *Post Office Letterbox*, with further inscriptions, 19½in. wide.
(Christie's) £920 $1,472

An early Victorian mother of pearl and tortoiseshell veneered tea caddy, of pagoda form, the geometric panels of mother of pearl inlaid with stylised foliate tortoiseshell, 8in. wide.
(Christie's) £5,520 $8,832

A George III ivory veneered tea caddy, late 18th century, of polygonal form, strung in horn, the front with silver plaque, incised with a monogram, 6in. wide.
(Christie's) £2,300 $3,680

An early Victorian papier mâché tea caddy, circa 1845, with serpentine moulded front, the top painted with a peacock and flowers, 7¾in. wide.
(Christie's) £1,725 $2,760

A rare Japanese black lacquered casket, 1630–50, the pagoda shaped hinged top with a sliding panel revealing a well, 17in. wide. (Sotheby's)   £7,475 $12,483

Red painted carved cherry pipe box, Connecticut River Valley, late 18th/early 19th century, with metal lined interior, 19½in. high. (Skinner)   £3,594 $5,750

A George III lacquer tea caddy with Staffordshire enamel canisters, circa 1770, with brass loop handle to the cover, 7¾in. wide. (Christie's)   £2,990 $4,784

A George III satinwood and marquetry inlaid tea caddy, circa 1780, the cover with brass loop handle rising from a boxwood inlaid bats' wing patera, 5½in. wide. (Christie's)   £747 $1,195

A George III fruitwood tea caddy, late 18th century, modelled as a pear, with oval steel escutcheon, drilled to underside, 6in. high. (Christie's)   £3,565 $5,704

An early 19th century rosewood combined work, jewel and writing chest, inlaid with mother-of-pearl, the two front doors leather lined and opening to reveal a dummy drawer. (David Lay)   £420 $676

A Victorian tortoiseshell and pewter-strung tea caddy, mid 19th century, of polygonal bombé form with conforming pagoda cover, 7½in. wide. (Christie's)   £2,070 $3,312

Black painted one-drawer pipe box, New England, 18th century, old black paint, 21⅝ in. high. (Skinner)   £2,116 $3,450

A fine and rare inlaid whale ivory and lemon wood miniature chest, probably American, mid 19th century, the rectangular chest with hinged lid opening to deep well, 6¾ x 12¾in. (Sotheby's) £3,507 $5,750

A fine and rare inlaid whale ivory and fruitwood sewing box, signed *T. Nickerson*, probably American, mid 19th century, 5 x 9½in.
(Sotheby's)   £9,821 $16,100

A George III mahogany knife urn, circa 1790, with acorn finial and barber's pole stringing, 23½in. high.
(Christie's)   £1,400 $2,240

A Victorian tortoiseshell and mother-of-pearl inlaid tea caddy, mid 19th century, with pewter stringing.
(Christie's)   £1,955 $3,128

A William IV tortoiseshell and pewter-strung tea caddy, second quarter 19th century, the slightly domed cover with silver-plated ball finial, 6½in. wide.
(Christie's)   £2,185 $3,496

A good pair of George III inlaid mahogany knife urns, last quarter 18th century, each with a turned finial above a domed lid and a swag-inlaid frieze, 28in. high.
(Sotheby's)   £5,175 $8,625

A shagreen-veneered and ivory mounted and strung tea caddy, circa 1929, of curved octagonal outline and with conforming ivory finial, 5½in. diameter.
(Christie's)   £2,530 $4,048

A George II brass-mounted walnut tea-caddy, inlaid overall with boxwood and ebony chequer-banding, the stepped rectangular top, with foliate-wrapped handle, 11in. wide.
(Christie's)   £5,980 $9,807

A George III mahogany candlebox, circa 1790, with shell inlaid canted top above a front inlaid with an urn of flowers on a plinth base, 6¾in. wide. (Christie's)   £580 $928

An Italian pietre dure inlaid black marble tea caddy, second half 19th century, inlaid to each side and cover with geometric designs of specimen marbles, 11in. wide.
(Christie's)   £2,530 $4,080

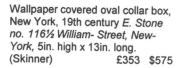

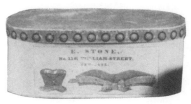

Wallpaper covered oval collar box, New York, 19th century *E. Stone no. 116½ William- Street, New-York,* 5in. high x 13in. long. (Skinner) £353 $575

A Spanish silver-mounted casket, second half 17th century, the exterior covered in green velvet, on later lion's paw feet, 12½in. high. (Christie's) £1,150 $1,909

Paint decorated poplar document box, America, 19th century, with lidded till, decorated with ochre paint on a red ground, gilt lettering *GWS,* 18in. wide. (Skinner) £719 $1,150

19th century Eastern rosewood dressing stand/compendium, the lifting lid enclosing mirror with two opening compartments below, profusely inlaid in the Shibayama manner. (G.A. Key) £180 $288

Italian ebony and pietra dura jewellery casket, of shaped octagonal form and inset with foliate and insect panels, 13¹/₈in. long. (Skinner) £1,071 $1,725

A Victorian tortoiseshell and pewter-strung giant tea caddy, mid 19th century of bombé form with stepped rising cover, 12¼in. wide. (Christie's) £4,600 $7,360

Victorian brass mounted walnut tea caddy, 19th century, with domed top and openwork foliate mounts, 9in. long. (Skinner) £429 $690

Paris Universal Exhibition 1867, a pietre dure, bronze and gilt-bronze casket by Auguste Klein, Austrian, circa 1870, 48cm. wide. (Sotheby's) £45,500 $75,075

A Regency burr walnut tea caddy, circa 1820, of bombé sarcophagus form, the top inset with a panel of 17th century ivory and ebony foliate inlay, 10in. (Christie's) £260 $416

A kingwood and ebony jardinière of serpentine oblong form with gilt metal mounts, inset with porcelain plaques, 14¼in. wide. (Andrew Hartley) £600 $1,010

A 19th century tortoiseshell tea caddy of oblong form with pewter stringing and mother of pearl floral inlay, 6¾in. wide. (Andrew Hartley) £720 $1,210

A 19th century walnut writing slope, with applied pierced brass mounts, hinged top opening to reveal fitted interior, 14in. wide. (Andrew Hartley) £210 $336

An Edwardian painted satinwood writing slope, early 20th century, with brass carrying handles, with drawer to one side, 14¾in. wide. (Christie's)   £1,610 $2,576

An Anglo-Indian stained horn work box, second quarter 19th century, with bowed and fluted sides, 13¼in. wide. (Christie's)   £920 $1,472

A Victorian papier-mâché rectangular work box inlaid with mother-of-pearl and painted with flowers and gilding, 34cm. (Bearne's)   £370 $592

An Edwardian tortoiseshell and silver-mounted leather-bound stationery casket, circa 1906, the curved cover and front with panels of tortoiseshell within reeded and ribbon-tied border mounts, 12¼in. wide. (Christie's)   £920 $1,472

Mahogany and flame birch veneer inlaid box, possibly Boston, Massachusetts, early 19th century, with shield-form escutcheon, 10⅝in. wide. (Skinner) £458 $748

A George III mahogany and tulipwood banded tea caddy, circa 1780, of rectangular form with cavetto top, the front inlaid with a shell patera and stylised flowering stems, 10¼in. (Christie's)   £1,400 $2,240

A fine and rare inlaid abalone shell and baleen ditty box, probably American, mid 19th century, with fitted lid inlaid with diamonds of contrasting wood, 3¼ x 6¾in. (Sotheby's)   £1,754 $2,875

A Victorian burr-walnut dressing box with silver-mounted fittings, circa 1859, of rectangular outline with ebony banding, 12¼in. wide. (Christie's)   £862 $1,379

Oval inlaid satinwood veneer tea caddy, England or America, early 19th century, the interior with mahogany divider and lids with turned ivory knobs, 7⅝in. wide. (Skinner)   £790 $1,265

A 19th century rosewood tea caddy of oblong tapering form, with satinwood edging, canted hinged lid, 7½in. wide. (Andrew Hartley)   £70 $112

A 19th century papier mâché jewellery box, of waisted oblong form painted with gilt arabesques, 9in. wide. (Andrew Hartley)   £180 $288

A Tunbridge ware inlaid walnut box, of oblong form, the domed lid featuring a country house within a floral border, 8½in. wide. (Andrew Hartley)   £480 $796

A George III tortoiseshell rectangular two-division tea caddy, the top and front veneered in figured shell, and inlaid with pewter stringings, 5¾in. high. (Canterbury) £1,400 $2,310

A 19th century flame mahogany tea caddy in the form of a serpentine front sideboard, with hinged lid enclosing two mixing bowls and central well, width 42cm. (Bristol) £560 $924

An early 19th century curl work paper tea caddy of hexagonal form, with an inset painted panel of a girl holding a garland of flowers, 18.5cm. wide. (Phillips) £580 $951

A 19th century coromandel writing box, hinged lid revealing fitted interior and hinged slope with mother o' pearl and brass marquetry inlay, 10½in. wide. (Andrew Hartley) £150 $240

Italian inlaid lap desk, third quarter 19th century, the front sliding writing surface inlaid with depiction of the prize medal for the 1862 London International Exhibition, 20in. wide. (Skinner) £11,429 $18,400

Liquor chest, England, late 18th century, the two-handled iron mounted oak chest opens to reveal a compartmented interior, 17⅝in. wide. (Skinner) £279 $460

A late George III blonde tortoiseshell rectangular single tea caddy with slight shaped top inlaid with pewter stringings and on turned ivory bun feet, 4¾ x 3¼ x 4¼in. (Canterbury) £640 $1,056

Bird's-eye maple and inlaid walnut tiered, one drawer, sewing box, America, mid-19th century, 9½in. wide. (Skinner) £228 $373

BUYER BEWARE

The collector who learns to recognise applewood and pearwood among other woods, will not be deceived by whitewood fakes when it comes to buying tea caddies made in the form of apples in applewood or pears in pearwood.

Knowing one's woods is a useful body of knowledge which furniture buyers in particular would do well to copy.

(Ewbank)

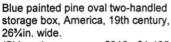

Blue painted pine oval two-handled storage box, America, 19th century, 26¾in. wide.
(Skinner)　　　　£918　$1,495

Wallpaper covered hat box, America, 19th century, decorated with birds amidst foliage and an architectural view, 16¾in. long.
(Skinner)　　　　£295　$488

A good 19th century Tunbridge Ware rectangular tea caddy, probably by Henry Hollamby, the slightly domed lid inlaid with view of Eridge Castle, 14in. wide, circa 1860. (Canterbury)　£720　$1,188

A Victorian oak and brass mounted hall letter box, in the form of a panelled outside door, 13in. high.
(George Kidner)　£1,100　$1,815

Pair of George III inlaid mahogany knife boxes, 19th century, of typical form, inlaid with shells, with fitted interior, 14¾in. high.
(Skinner)　　　£1,587　$2,645

A Victorian patent oak letter box of hexagonal section, the pagoda top carved with acanthus and with a bud finial, 23in. with associated wall bracket.
(David Lay)　　　£3,900 $6,240

A George III satinwood tea caddy of oblong from with crossbanding and string inlay, hinged lid revealing fitted interior with two compartments and a glass bowl, 12in. wide.
(Andrew Hartley)　　£240　$384

An Edwardian walnut writing slope/stationery box, the well-fitted interior with ivory ruler, maroon leather blotter, inset falls, two inkwells, pen rest and stationery racks, 42.5cm. wide.
(Bristol)　　　　£400　$656

A rare and unusual Victorian mahogany tea caddy, circa 1840, in the form of a miniature pedestal sideboard, the galleried back above a frieze with a drawer and mock cupboards, 13in. wide.
(Christie's)　　£2,400 . $3,840

Leica IIIg no. 968655 chrome, with Leitz Elmar f/2.8 5cm. lens no. 161878 and Leicameter.
(Christie's)   £977 $1,592

Silver Ticka camera, Houghtons Ltd., London; rollfilm, the body and fittings hallmarked London 1907, with lens cover, in fitted plush-lined case. (Christie's)   £2,300 $3,680

Exakta no. 786431, Ihagee, Germany; with rectangular magnifier, and an Ihagee Exaktar Anastigmat f/3.5 5.4cm. lens no. 786431. (Christie's) £143 $228

R.B. Cycle Graphic camera, Folmer & Schwing Division, Rochester, NY; 4 x 5 inch, with Rapid Rectalinear lens, double darkslides, and film pack adapter.
(Christie's)   £322 $515

Nikon F2S no. 7332411, black, with DP-2 photomic head, a Nikon Nikkor f/1.8 50mm. lens no. 1818470. (Christie's) £414 $675

Le Photo-Revolver no. 413, E. Krauss, Paris, with rollfilm back and a Krauss/Zeiss Tessar 4cm. f/4.5 lens no. 132816, in maker's purse.
(Christie's)   £2,760 $4,499

Epifoka aerial camera, Vrsofot, Czechoslovakia; 120-rollfilm, metal-body, with Voigtländer Skopar f/4.5 7.5cm. lens in a Compur-Rapid shutter. (Christie's)   £517 $827

Kodak Bantam Special no. 26635, Eastman Kodak Co., Rochester, NY; with a Kodak Ektar f/2 45mm. lens no. EC2514.
(Christie's)   £299 $478

Mecaflex no. A333, Seroa Anastigmat 40mm. f/3.5 lens.
(Christie's)   £575 $937

Panophic 140 camera, Panon
Camera Co., Japan; 120-rollfilm,
with a f/2.8 50mm. lens no. 37214,
in maker's ever ready case.
(Christie's) £920 $1,472

Ticka camera, Houghtons Ltd.,
London, nickel-metal body, with
lens cover, in maker's box.
(Christie's) £184 $299

Polaroid stereo camera, Italian;
35mm., with a pair of Galileo Eliog
f/3.5 4cm. lenses nos.1001 and
1002. (Christie's) £632 $1,011

Hand and stand camera, Germany;
9 x 12cm., wood-body, lacquered-
brass fittings, blue-cloth with
bellows, retailer's label *F. Ludolf
Wllhausen, Hannover, Königstr 3.*
(Christie's) £402 $643

Tropical Deckrullo no. F15181,
Contessa Nettel, Germany, 9 x
12cm, with a Carl Zeiss, Jena
Tessar f/4.5 16.5cm. lens no.
460787.
(Christie's) £253 $412

Tropical Adoro camera, Contessa-
Nettel, Germany, 9 x 12cm.,
polished teak body, and a Carl
Zeiss, Jena Tessar f/4.5 15cm. lens
no. 443335.
(Christie's) £207 $337

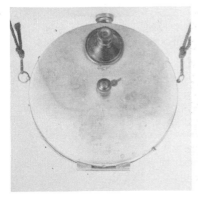

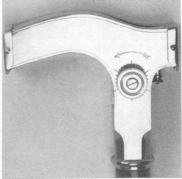

Ben Akiba walking stick camera,
replica; the nickel-plated metal
body with shutter, lens, five film
spools and wood cane holding ten
film spools.
(Christie's) £4,600 $7,360

No. 1 Vest camera, no. 12150 C.P.
Stirn, Berlin, 4cm. diameter, nickel-
metal body, with lens.
(Christie's) £805 $1,312

Minicord TLR no. 5143, C.P. Goerz,
Wien, 16mm., black body panels,
with a Goerz Helgor f/2 2.5cm. lens
no. 5319. (Christie's) £126 $205

Leica IIIf no. 531443, chrome, black-dial, with a Leitz Elmar 5cm. f/2.8 lens no. 1549468, in maker's ever ready case.
(Christie's) £437 $699

Matchbox camera, Eastman Kodak Co., Rochester, NY; metal-body with United States War Department identity card with photograph.
(Christie's) £2,990 $4,784

Busch Verascope F40 no. 2247100, Richard, Paris, with a pair of Berthiot f/3.5 40mm. lenses nos. 993284 and 993308 in maker's ever ready case. (Christie's) £299 $487

Leica M2 no. 935118, chrome, button-rewind, with a Leica-Meter MC and a Leitz Elmar 5cm. f/2.8 lens no. 1495953.
(Christie's) £1,150 $1,840

Nikon SP no. 6206765 chrome, the rewind knob engraved *E P,* and with a Nippon Kogaku Nikkor-S f/1.4 5cm. lens no. 412137.
(Christie's) £1,035 $1,687

Leica IIIb no. 331424, chrome, with a screw-fit adapted Schneider Retina-Xenon f/2.8 5cm. lens no. 1681858 in a Compur-Rapid shutter. (Christie's) £368 $588

Karma-Flex, Karl Arnold, Germany, with a Hermagis Hellor f/4.5 60mm. lens no. 256106.
(Christie's) £253 $412

Lucidograph no. 362598, Blair Camera Co., Boston, 4 x 5in. mahogany body with brass fittings and black bellows.
(Christie's) £862 $1,405

Ford's Tom Thumb camera no. 744, Max Juruik, USA, 2½ x 2½in., nickelled-metal body, lens and darkslides.
(Christie's) £4,600 $7,498

Leica IIIf no. 694873 chrome, red-scale, delayed-timer, with a Leitz Elmar f/3.5 5cm. lens no. 1198118, in maker's ever ready case.
(Christie's) £483 $787

Leica Ic no. 455848, (converted to If) with a Leitz Super-Angulon f/4 21mm. lens no. 1646310 and lens hood. (Christie's) £977 $1,563

Prototype camera, Zeiss Ikon, Germany; the top plate engraved *vk 12*, with a Zeiss Novar-Anastigmat f/3.5 4.5cm. lens.
(Christie's) £483 $773

Prototype Stereo camera, French; 16mm., with a pair of Berthiot Stellor f/3.5 lenses nos. 152803 and 149234.
(Christie's) £368 $588

Leica IIIf no. 632235, chrome, red-scale, delayed-timer, with a Leitz Summitar f/2 5cm. lens no. 859734.
(Christie's) £345 $562

Kodak Ektra no. 4617, with a Kodak Ektra f/1.9 50mm. lens no. EY552, a Kodak Ektar f/3.5 90mm. lens no. EC618. (Christie's) £920 $1,499

Leica IIIg no. 879273, chrome, with a Leitz Summaron 3.5cm. f/3.5 lens no. 1308966, in maker's ever ready case. (Christie's) £1,265 $2,024

Petie vanity set, W. Kunik, Germany; comprising a 16mm. Petie camera in a brown-enamel vanity case with powder compact, lipstick holder and film holder.
(Christie's) £552 $883

Tessina 35 no. 565103, Concava S.A., Switzerland, with a 25mm. f/2.8 lens and a Tessina top-mounted lightmeter, in maker's case. (Christie's) £402 $655

New Academy camera, Marion & Co., London, 2 x 2in. wood body, brass fittings, the top section with removable waist-level finder with label. (Christie's) £4,830 $7,873

Daguerreotype camera, Charles Chevalier, Paris, 9 x 12cm., walnut body, brass fittings, sliding-box, removable focusing screen.
(Christie's) £9,775 $15,933

Deardorff View no. 281, L.F. Deardorff & Sons, Chicago, 5 x 7in., mahogany body, nickel-plated fittings and black leather bellows.
(Christie's) £299 $487

The King's Own De Luxe model, London Stereoscopic Co., London, rollfilm, with polished teak body, inset brass binding.
(Christie's) £1,495 $2,437

Alpa 9d no. 50242, chrome with an Angènieux Retrofocus f/3.5 28mm. lens no. 789934.
(Christie's) £805 $1,312

Invincibel camera, H. Mader, Württemberg, Germany, 5 x 7in., metal folding camera, red leather bellows.
(Christie's) £690 $1,125

A Photo-Marine II underwater camera case for screw Leicas by R.G. Lewis, England, aluminium with hammered and painted finish.
(Auction Team Köln) £237 $379

A Marlboro 70 pocket camera, boxed.
(Auction Team Köln) £125 $200

A wooden and nickel mounted Ernemann Stereo Bob IV camera, with dark red bellows, with Goerz-Dagon 6,8/90 lens, for 94mm. film and plates.
(Auction Team Köln) £473 $758

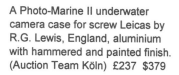

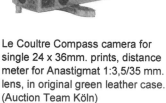

A KGB secret camera, hidden in a brown leather briefcase, the brass closure with a slit through which the camera operates, with cassette, in original case.
(Auction Team Köln)
£1,340 $2,144

A Zeiss Ikon Stuttgart Contarex accessory kit, including lenses, filters, cassettes, folding camera, in black leather case, post 1959.
(Auction Team Köln)
£1,981 $3,170

Le Coultre Compass camera for single 24 x 36mm. prints, distance meter for Anastigmat 1:3,5/35 mm. lens, in original green leather case.
(Auction Team Köln)
£1,381 $2,210

Asahi Pentax 6x7and accessories, with two Takumar lenses, with prismatic insert, and two original filters, in large case.
(Auction Team Köln)
£1,120 $1,792

A Contessa-Nessel Ergo secret camera in telescope form for 4.5 x 6cm. film, with Tessar 1:4,5,5 cm. lens, 90° viewfinder, with original case and two cassettes.
(Auction Team Köln)
£1,636 $2,618

A rare Foton viewfinder camera by Bell & Howell, with wind up mechanism and interchangeable optics, produced in very small numbers between 1948 and 1950.
(Auction Team Köln)
£1,172 $1,875

Cyclops combined binocular/camera, Toko Photo Co., Japan, with a Telesigmar f/4.5 35mm. lens no. 20160.
(Christie's) £437 $712

Leica M2-R no. 1249755, chrome, with a Leitz Summicron f/2 50mm. lens no. 1950813 with close-focusing optical finder in maker's box. (Christie's) £1,150 $1,875

Prominent no. D966311, pre-war, Voigtländer Heliar f/4.5 10.5cm. lens no. 890985.
(Christie's) £598 $957

A Sola camera by Schatz & Söhne, for 13 x 18mm on 16mm unperforated film, with wind-up motor, used by the German Secret Service during the Second World War, 1938.
(Auction Team Köln)
£2,240 $3,584

A Voigtländer 'original' replica all metal camera No. 84, with authentic four-lens Petzval System objective, with cassette and colour manual.
(Auction Team Köln)
£1,884 $3,015

A Stirn brass secret camera, for four 6cm diameter prints on a 162mm. round plate, in original leather case.
(Auction Team Köln)
£2,303 $3,684

A dark green leather covered wooden Fingerprint camera, with dual fold, the back part with a removable matt plate, with built in electric illuminator and voltmeter.
(Auction Team Köln) £56 $89

A transparent Canon T90 demonstration model camera, signed by the designer Luigi Colani, February 1986.
(Auction Team Köln)
£1,465 $2,344

A Carl Zeiss Sonnar 2/85 black lens nr. 3336792, with original box, cover and filter.(Auction Team Köln)
£1,163 $1,860

A Royal Mail Postage Stamp camera by W. Butcher & Son, London, for 15 19 x 23mm. prints on a 3¼ x 4¼in. plate, 1907-15. (Auction Team Köln)
£1,884 $3,015

Korona Panoramic View camera, Gundlach Manhattan Optical Co., Rochester, NY, 8 x 20in., with a Turner-Reich 24in. lens no. 150166. (Christie's) £977 $1,592

An Ernemann Ermanox Reflex camera for 4.5 x 6cm., with Ernostar 1:1,8/10,5cm. lens, in original case with three new silver cassettes. (Auction Team Köln)
£1,766 $2,825

A Globus walnut studio camera by Ernemann, Dresden, adjustable height and angle, on axle stands, circa 1920. (Auction Team Köln) £502 $804

Nikon F no. 645003, chrome, photomic head, a Nippon Kogaku Nikkor- Auto f/1.4 5.8cm. lens no. 166732. (Christie's) £575 $920

A Norita Model I wooden and brass mounted camera by Naert, Brussels, on trestle stand with castors, with angle adjustment, circa 1920, 184cm. high. (Auction Team Köln)
£1,421 $2,274

A Rollei prototype W0000 of the 2,8 GX camera, made for the 75 anniversary of Rollei in 1995, in white leather case and with Seiko closure, in wooden box. (Auction Team Köln)
£2,596 $4,153

Pentax 6 x 7 SLR no. 4042588, Asahi Optical Co., Japan, 120-rollfilm, with a Takumar/6 x 7 f/2.4 105mm. lens, and a Takumar/6 x 7 f/4.5 75mm. lens. (Christie's) £552 $899

A Carl Zeiss, Jena Sonnar 2,8/180 lens for a Contarex, up to 1.5m, with Voigtländer UV filter and Zeiss Ikon Voigtländer cover. (Auction Team Köln)
£1,249 $1,999

A '75 Years of Rollei' Rolleiflex limited edition camera, with gold mountings and black and brown snakeskin case, with Planar 2,8/80 lens, with certificate and in original packing.
(Auction Team Köln)
£1,989 $3,182

Kodak Duo 620 Series II no. 335095K, Kodak A.G., Germany, with rangefinder and a Kodak Anastigmat f/3.5 7.5cm. lens no.1518688.
(Christie's)   £253 $412

Zeiss Ikon Stereotar C accessories, Stereotar C 1:3,5/35mm lens, Contameter 439, 432/5 viewfinder and 50, 30 and 20 Proxars, in original leather case.
(Auction Team Köln)
£1,508 $2,412

Rolleiflex T no. 2103451, 120-rollfilm, grey, with a Heidosmat f/2.8 75mm. viewing lens no. 2478655 and a Carl Zeiss Tessar f/3.5 75mm. taking lens.
(Christie's)   £207 $337

Compass II no. 1230, Le Coultre et Cie, Switzerland with a CCL3B Anastigmat f/3.5 35mm. lens with film back. (Christie's) £1,150 $1,874

A pre-war Voigtländer Prominent camera for 6x9 on 120 film with photometer and light meter and original instructions.
(Auction Team Köln) £947 $1,516

A Hasselblad 503 CX 50th Anniversary Camera, special edition with blue leather and gilt cover, in mint condition and in original box, 1991.
(Auction Team Köln)
£3,618 $5,789

Royal Mail copying camera no. 35, W. Butcher & Sons., London, quarter-plate, wood body, brass fittings, and fifteen lenses.
(Christie's)   £747 $1,217

Vega camera, Vega S.A., Switzerland, 9 x 12cm., leather-covered wood body, red bellows and guillotine shutter.
(Christie's)   £632 $1,030

American carousel horse, possibly by Looff, traces of original paint, 42½in. long.
(Eldred's)   £1,600 $2,640

A carved and painted pine carousel pig, attributed to Gustav Denzel, Philadelphia, third quarter 19th century, 57in. long.
(Sotheby's)   £3,156 $5,175

A carved and painted carousel prancer, possibly Stein and Goldstein, early 20th century, 59in. high. (Christie's)   £4,830 $8,050

A carved and painted carousel prancer, attributed to Muller Dentzel, Philadelphia, late 19th century, carved in the Philadelphia style, 55in. high.
(Christie's)   £3,450 $5,750

Carved carousel horse, attributed to C. W. Parker Co., Abilene, Kansas, late 19th/early 20th century, the running horse with raised head, 53in. high. (Skinner) £2,335 $3,737

A fine carved and painted carousel horse, American, early 20th century, painted white with pink, yellow and green star-decorated saddle and bridle, 55in. long.
(Sotheby's)   £2,806 $4,600

A carved and painted wood carousel figure of a jumper horse, stamped #37, *C.W. Parker, Leavenworth, Kansas*, circa 1917, 37in. high x 69in. long.
(Sotheby's)   £9,375 $15,000

A carved and painted carousel jumper, attributed to Charles I.D. Looff (active 1875–1918), Brooklyn, New York, late 19th-early 20th century, 58in. wide.
(Christie's)   £8,970 $14,950

A carved and painted pine carousel horse, American, late 19th century, the black-painted horse with red and yellow bridle, saddle blanket and eagle-carved saddle, 61in. long. (Sotheby's) £6,250 $10,000

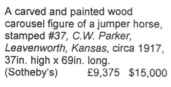

A Heriz carpet, Northwest Persia, first quarter 20th century, 19ft. x 11ft.1in.
(Sotheby's)　　£9,821　$16,100

A Donegal carpet, possibly designed by Gavin Morton, circa 1900, central olive green field with geometric design in gold within broad border, 144 x 204in.
(Christie's)　　£10,925　$17,480

A Heriz carpet, Northwest Persia, early 20th century, new fringes, approx. 12ft. x 8ft.9in.
(Sotheby's)　　£11,224　$18,400

A Donegal carpet, the design attributed to Gavin Morton and G.K. Robertson, circa 1900, deep salmon field with willow trees and branches detailed in cornflower blue and moss green, 193 x 146in.
(Christie's)　　£5,750　$9,200

A large Aubusson carpet, circa 1880, the pale rose field with diagonal rows of raspberry red quatrefoil flowerheads around a cusped six lobed ivory medallion, 20ft.10in. x 18ft.5in.
(Christie's)　　£6,325　$10,500

A Donegal carpet, designed by Gavin Morton and G.K. Robertson, circa 1900, the red field with formalised floral design incorporating stylised trees and branches in cornflower blue, green and mustard, 156 x 192in.
(Christie's)　　£13,800　$22,080

A Tabriz carpet of garden design, the deep indigo field with multicoloured rectangular panels containing polychrome pictorial scenes, 16ft. 3in. x 11ft. 6in.
(Christie's)　　£3,450　$5,589

A shaped European pile carpet, probably Wilton, England, circa 1940, of arched form, the lower square panel with golden fanlight spandrels around a mint-green roundel, 21ft. 5in. x 11ft. 7in.
(Christie's)　　£18,400　$30,544

A Heriz carpet, North West Persia, the brick red field of flowering plants centred by an indigo flowerhead medallion, 11ft.5in. x 8ft.6in.
(Phillips)　　£1,500　$2,460

1965 Mercedes-Benz 230SL Roadster with hardtop, silver grey with tan interior and black hood, engine: six cylinders in-line single overhead camshaft, 2300cc, Bosch fuel injection, 150bhp at 5600rpm; gearbox: manual four-speed with synchromesh. Left hand drive. (Christie's) £6,834 $11,344

1966 Jaguar E-type series 1 4.2 Roadster, black with tan leather interior, engine: six cylinders in line, twin overhead camshafts, 4235cc, 265bhp at 5400rpm; Gearbox: manual four-speed synchromesh; Brakes: servo assisted discs all round; centre-lock wire wheels. Left hand drive. (Christie's) £25,451 $42,249

1973 Jaguar E-Type series III Roadster, primrose yellow with black leather interior, engine: V12, single overhead camshaft, 5343cc. 272bhp at 5850rpm, Gearbox: manual four-speed, suspension: independent all round, Brakes: power assisted vented disc all round. Left hand drive. (Christie's) £17,910 $29,731

1954 MG TF Midget 1250 Sports Two Seater, red with black leather interior, beige hood and sidescreens, engine, four cylinders in line, pushrod overhead valves, 1250cc, 58bhp at 5500rpm, gearbox: manual four-speed with synchromesh, brakes: four-wheel hydraulically operated drum. Right hand drive. (Christie's) £9,426 $15,647

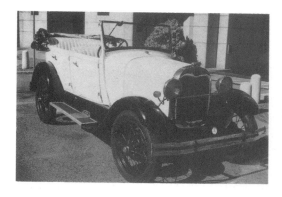

1929 Ford Model A four seat Phaeton Tourer, white with black wings, white interior and black hood, engine: four cylinder in-line L-head sidevalve, 200.5cu ins. (3200cc), 40bhp at 2,200rpm; gearbox: manual three speed; brakes: cable operated drum. Right hand drive. (Christie's) £5,656 $9,389

1991 Ferrari 348 TB, red, with magnolia leather interior, engine: all aluminium V-eight, double overhead camshafts to each bank, four valves per cylinder, 3405cc, gearbox: five-speed manual; steering: rack and pinion. Left hand drive. (Christie's) £25,451 $42,249

1968 Bizzarrini 5300 Strada, metallic green with beige leather interior, engine: Chevrolet Corvette 327 cu V8, 5359cc, 355bhp at 5800rpm, gearbox: four-speed manual by Borg-Warner, suspension: independent front and de Dion type rear axle. Left hand drive. (Christie's)   £44,262 $73,474

1953 Fiat 500C Belvedere estate car, green with red interior, engine: four cylinder, 570cc overhead valves, 16.5bhp at 4,400rpm; gearbox: manual four speed; suspension: independent with transverse half elliptic leaf spring and wishbones, brakes: four-wheel hydraulic. Left hand drive. (Christie's) £5,184 $8,605

1926 Bentley 6½ litre short chassis drophead Coupé, coachwork by H.J. Mullliner, pale olive-green with garnet wings and claret leather interior, engine: straight six, 6597cc, 24 valves, overhead camshaft driven by triple-throw eccentrics, gearbox: manual four speed. Right hand drive.
(Christie's)   £220,082 $365,336

1978 Mercedes-Benz 600 Pullman limousine, silver-grey with blue interior, leather in the front and velours in the rear, engine: 90° V8, single overhead camshaft per bank, Bosch fuel injection, 6332cc, 300bhp; at 4100rpm; gearbox: four speed automatic; brakes: front and rear servo-assisted discs. Left hand drive. (Christie's)   £35,246 $58,508

1970 Ford Mustang Coupé, red with red leatherette interior, engine: 90° V8 289ci (4728cc), gearbox: automatic; suspension: independent front by unequal length arms and vertical coil spring, semi-elliptic springs to rear live axle, telescope dampers: brakes hydraulic drum all round. (Christie's)   £282 $468

1954 Austin Healey 100/4 Two-Seater Sports, red with black leather interior, engine: four cylinder in line, pushrod overhead valve, 2660cc, clutch: single plate; gearbox: BN2 four speed with syncromesh; disc front, drum rear. Left hand drive.
(Christie's)   £21,209 $35,207

1963 Ford Thunderbird Sport Roadster, mauve with mauve and white interior. Engine: overhead valves, 360ci., 330bhp at 5,000rpm; Gearbox: automatic; Brakes: four wheel drum. Left hand drive. (Christie's) £20,700 $34,500

1957 Ford Thunderbird convertible with removable hardtop, white with blue and white interior. Engine: V8, overhead valve, 312 cu. in., 198bhp at 4,400rpm; Gearbox: Fordomatic 3-speed; brakes: four wheel drum. Left hand drive. (Christie's) £21,390 $35,650

1979 Aston Martin V8, metallic brown with biscuit leather interior, engine: V8, twin overhead camshafts, four twin-choke Weber carburettors, 350bhp; gearbox: three speed automatic; Steering: power assisted rack and pinion; brakes: power assisted four-wheel discs. Left hand drive. (Christie's) £19,795 $32,860

1956 Mercedes-Benz 300 SL Gullwing, slate grey with red leather interior and red leather fitted luggage. Engine: six cylinder, in-line, 2,996cc., 240bhp at 6,100rpm; Gearbox: 4-speed manual; Brakes: hydraulic drum. Left hand drive. (Christie's) £146,700 $244,500

1966 Fiat 1500 two seater cabriolet, red with black hard top and black leatherette interior, engine: four cylinders in line, pushrod overhead valves, 1481cc, 72bhp at 5200rpm; gearbox: manual four-speed all synchromesh; brakes: power assisted, hydraulically operated disc to front, drum to rear. Left hand drive. (Christie's) £2,357 $3,913

1973 Jaguar XJ6 4.2 four-door saloon, Bordeaux red with beige leather interior, engine: straight six cylinder, twin overhead camshafts, 4235cc, transmission: four-speed manual; suspension: fully independent by wishbones and coil springs; brakes: power assisted four-wheel discs. Left hand drive. (Christie's) £848 $1,408

1952 Alfa Romeo 1900 C Sprint Coupé, coachwork by touring, red with tan leather interior, engine: four cylinders in line, 1844cc, gearbox: five speed synchromesh; brakes: hydraulic drum. Left hand drive. (Christie's) £30,635 $50,854

1938 Packard 1605 Super Eight Sedanca de Ville, coachwork by Barker. Engine: L-head straight eight, 360ci., 135bhp at 3,200rpm; Gearbox: 3-speed; Bendix hydraulic four wheel drum. Left hand drive. (Christie's) £64,200 $107,000

1955 Mercedes-Benz 300 S Roadster, white with red leather interior. Engine: six cylinder, 2,996cc, 150bhp at 5,000rpm; Gearbox: 4-speed manual; Suspension: front, independent with coil springs, brakes: hydraulic drums. Left hand drive. (Christie's) £84,000 $140,000

1957 Jaguar XKSS Sports two-seater, British racing green with tan leather upholstery. Engine: six cylinders, twin overhead camshaft, 3,442cc. Gearbox: 4-speed manual; Brakes: four-wheel disc. Right hand drive. (Christie's) £608,700 $1,014,500

1962 Maserati 3500GT Coupe, coachwork by Touring, maroon with tan leather interior. Engine: 101 Series six cylinder, twin overhead camshaft, 3,485cc, Gearbox: 5-speed ZF manual; Brakes: four-wheel servo-assisted discs. Left hand drive. (Christie's) £19,320 $32,200

1941 Ford Super Deluxe Woody Station Wagon, body by Ford Iron Mountain, Cayuga blue, Honduras mahogany panels, Michigan hard maple stiles, ash roof slats with tan leather interior. Engine: V8 flathead, 221ci, 96bhp at 3,800rpm; Brakes: drums all round. Left hand drive. (Christie's) £46,380 $77,300

1939 Jensen model H straight eight dual Cowl Sports Tourer, coachwork by Jensen, two-tone red with tan leather upholstery. Engine: eight cylinder in line, 4.2 litres giving 120bhp at 3,500rpm; Gearbox: 3-speed manual with dual speed rear axle; Brakes: four-wheel drum. Right hand drive. (Christie's) £60,900 $101,500

1931 Cadillac model 452 V16 Madame X Imperial (Faux) Cabriolet, coachwork by Fleetwood, dark blue with black fenders and running gear with black leather interior in the front and broadcloth in the rear compartment. Engine: V16, 165bhp at 3,400rpm; Brakes: four wheel drum. Left hand drive. (Christie's) £70,800 $118,000

1953 Chrysler Ghia, coachwork by Ghia, Candy apple Red with tan leather upholstery. Engine: hemispherical head V8, 180bhp at 4,000rpm; Gearbox: PowerFlite automatic; Brakes: four wheel drums. (Christie's) £87,300 $145,500

1955 Jaguar XK 140 MC fixed head Coupe, Royal Battleship grey with red leather interior. Engine: six cylinder, twin overhead camshafts, 3,442cc. Brakes: four wheel drum. Left hand drive. (Christie's) £37,800 $63,000

1934 Lancia Augusta four door Sedan, hunter green with biscuit cloth interior. Engine: narrow-angle V4, 1196cc., 35bhp at 4,000rpm; Gearbox: 4-speed manual with freewheeling; Brakes: four wheel drum. Right hand drive. (Christie's)   £5,520 $9,200

1994 McLaren F1, black with cream leather seats and brown carpets, engine: V12 BMW, double overhead camshaft, 6064cc, 627bhp at 7,500rpm; gearbox: six-speed manual; brakes: ventilated discs.   Central steering. (Christie's)   £452,074 $750,443

1950 Jaguar XK 120 Roadster, silver and French grey with duotone blue leather interior. Engine: six cylinder in-line, double overhead camshaft, 3,422cc, 160bhp at 5,250rpm; Gearbox: 4-speed manual; Brakes: hydraulic four wheel drum. Left hand drive. (Christie's)   £31,050 $51,750

1929 Dupont Model G Speedster, coachwork by Merrimac, grey body and fenders with silver wheels, black leather interior. Engine: straight eight Continental 12K, L-head, duPont modified, 322ci., 140bhp at 3,600rpm. Left hand drive. (Christie's)   £159,900 $266,500

1957 Chrysler 300-C Convertible, cloud white with saddle leather interior. Engine: hemispherical head V8, 392ci., 375bhp at 5,200rpm; Gearbox: pushbutton 3-speed torqueflite automatic; Brakes: power assisted drums. Left hand drive. (Christie's)   £33,120 $55,200

1933 Rolls-Royce Phantom II Woody Estate Wagon, coachwork by Bohman & Schwartz. Engine: six cylinder, iron cylinder head, overhead valves, 7,668cc; Gearbox: 4-speed manual; Brakes: four wheel internal expanding servo-assisted drum. Right hand drive. (Christie's)   £93,900 $156,500

1949 Willys Jeepster Phaeton, red over cream with beige vinyl and red piping. engine: in-line four cylinder, L-head, 69bhp at 4,000rpm; Gearbox: 3-speed manual with overdrive; Brakes: drum. Left hand drive. (Christie's)   £11,040 $18,400

1968 Fiat Dino 2000 Spider, coachwork by Pinin Farina, red with beige leather interior, engine: V-6 Ferrari, double-overhead camshafts per bank, 1987cc, gearbox: five-speed manual; brakes: discs all round. Left hand drive. (Christie's)   £15,082 $25,036

CARS

1989 Porsche 959, champagne metallic with maroon and grey leather interior, engine: flat-six cylinder, double overhead camshaft, 2,849cc, 450bhp at 6,500rpm: gearbox: six speed manual, permanent four-wheel drive; brakes: power-assisted self-ventilated discs, ABS. Left hand drive.
(Christie's)   £125,410 $208,180

1930 Duesenberg Model J Dual Cowl Phaeton, coachwork by the Walter Murphy Co., dark blue with red leather interior. Engine: straight-eight with twin overhead camshafts, 265bhp at 4,200rpm; Gearbox: 3-speed. Left hand drive.
(Christie's)   £430,500 $717,500

1925 Rolls-Royce 20 HP Salamanca, coachwork by Kellner of Paris, maroon with brown leather interior. Engine: six cylinder in-line, pushrod overhead valve, 3127cc; Brakes: servo-assisted, mechanically operated four wheel drum. Right hand drive.
(Christie's)   £23,460 $39,100

1932 Lincoln KB coupe, coachwork by Dietrich. Engine: V12, 448ci., 150bhp at 3,400rpm; Gearbox: 3-speed manual; Brakes: four wheel drum. Left hand drive. (Christie's)   £41,100 $68,500

1960 Messerschmitt KR-200 Cabriolet, red with red interior. Engine: Fichtel & Sachs single cylinder, two stroke, 198cc; Gearbox: 4-forward speeds, electric reverse; Direct handlebar steering.
(Christie's)   £8,280 $13,800

1977 Mercedes-Benz 450 SLC Coupé, silver grey with black leather interior, Engine: in line V8, single overhead camshaft, Bosch K-Selectronic fuel injection, 4520cc 217bhp at 5000rpm; gearbox: three speed automatic. (Christie's)   £1,791 $2,973

1933 Lincoln Model KA Convertible Roadster, coachwork by Murray, dark blue and olive with black fenders and black leather interior. Engine: V12, overhead valve; Gearbox: 3-speed manual; Brakes: four wheel drum. Left hand drive.
(Christie's)   £74,100 $123,500

175

An Empire style gilt and bronze patinated ceiling light, early 20th century, the circular frosted shade with anthemion clasped terminal and conforming frieze, 18in. high. (Christie's)　£1,035　$1,677

A French gilt bronze plafonnier, early 20th century, early 20th century, the octagonal tapering shade inset with frosted glass panels (later associated), 22⁷/₈in. (Christie's)　£4,830　$7,728

Tiffany bronze and leaded turtleback ceiling lamp, unusual scalloped beaded rim on fiery golden green translucent leaded favrile glass shade, 16in. high. (Skinner)　£3,622　$6,037

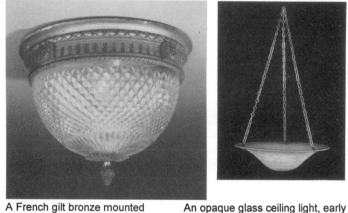

An Edwardian gilt and bronze patinated ceiling light, by Farraday and Son, the circlet with writhen border and winged angel mounts, 24in. diameter. (Christie's)　£1,265　$2,049

A French gilt bronze mounted plafonnier, early 20th century, the hobnail domed shade with stiff-leaf and berried terminal, suspended from a circlet, 12in. diameter. (Christie's)　£2,300　$3,680

An opaque glass ceiling light, early 20th century, the domed underside with pâte-sur-pâte style foliate decoration and running scrolls, 23½in. diameter. (Christie's)　£1,495　$2,422

A gilt bronze and glass plafonnier, early 20th century, the star cut spherical part-frosted shade with cone terminal, 24in. diameter. (Christie's)　£3,910　$6,334

Bronze figural bat ceiling light with Austrian Art Glass shade, full-bodied flying bat suspended from bronze chains and ceiling mount, drop 29in. (Skinner) £3,450　$5,750

Bronze and turtleback glass hanging lamp, dark patina and framework of blown-in iridescent glass with round gold turtleback tile at centre drop, shade 9½in. diameter. (Skinner) £1,380　$2,300

A Regency eight-branch chandelier, the tiered brass frame hung throughout with elongated prismatic drops, approximately 80cm. diam.
(Bearne's)   £3,100 $4,960

A Regency bronze hanging lamp, of cruciform design, the underside cast with central radiating spray, within palmettes to the four branches, 21¾in. wide.
(Christie's)   £3,680 $5,888

A gilt bronze twelve branch chandelier, early 20th century, with four pairs of bifurcating branches about a circular well, 28in. high.
(Christie's)   £1,840 $2,980

One of a pair of early 20th century 'Black Forest' carved oak chandeliers, each in the form of a ring, one surmounted by two courting couples in rural dress, 60cm. diameter.
(Bearne's) (Two) £1,200 $1,920

A French bronze and beaded glass chandelier, early 20th century, the domed shade of graduated faceted beads with cone terminal, 32in. high. (Christie's) £2,185 $3,496

One of a pair of Continental gilt brass twelve light chandeliers, early 20th century, of inverted trumpet shape, the trifurcating down scrolling branches applied with leafy mounts, 51in. high.
(Christie's) (Two)   £5,175 $8,280

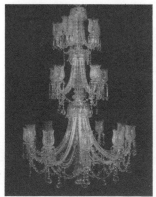

A Muller Fres hanging lamp, the black patinated metal frame cast with stylised foliate motifs, suspended with three frosted glass bell shades and central globe shade, approx. 68cm. high overall.
(Christie's)   £460 $743

A George V cut glass electrolier, by F & C. Osler, circa 1914, the faceted up-scrolling arms arranged in three tiers totalling twenty lights supporting tulip-shaped shades, 165in. high.
(Christie's)   £73,000 $116,800

A 19th century majolica and gilt-metal six branch gasolier, the branches with gryphons and scrolls having central baluster majolica column and bowl, diameter 36in.
(Russell, Baldwin & Bright)
                    £2,300 $3,818

An eight branch gilt metal and glass chandelier, part late 18th century adapted, the branches with glass spire finials, 38in. high.
(Christie's)   £1,380 $2,236

A Dutch brass chandelier, the baluster shaft below fixing ring issuing eight scrolling branches with grotesque beasts, 31in. high.
(Christie's)   £3,680 $6,108

A gilt bronze six light chandelier, early 20th century, the bifurcating naturalistic branches issuing from a conforming foliate column, 28in. high. (Christie's) £2,530 $4,099

A bronze twenty four light chandelier, early 20th century, of inverted trumpet outline, the lower tiered frame pierced and cast with interlinking scrolls and foliate motifs, 60in. high.
(Christie's)   £4,600 $7,360

A gilt bronze and beadwork chandelier, early 20th century, the spherical frame with floral garlands, hung with strings of graduated faceted beads, 34in. high.
(Christie's)   £1,380 $2,208

An early Victorian gilt bronze six branch argand chandelier, with branches radiating about the cast circlet with bell flower swags below a conforming openwork tiered cresting, 25in. diameter.
(Christie's)   £7,475 $11,960

A George IV ormolu and cut-glass twelve-light chandelier, with five graduating tiers, each with a fleur-de-lys crown above lozenge-cut rectangular drops, 57in. high.
(Christie's)   £17,250 $28,290

A William IV or early Victorian cut glass eight light chandelier, of inverted trumpet outline, hung with tiers of faceted pendants and beads, 48in. high.
(Christie's)   £3,220 $5,152

A Swedish ormolu and clear and blue cut glass six-light chandelier, the pierced coronet with scrolling ribbon-twist branches suspending swags of droplets, 34in. high.
(Christie's)   £5,175 $8,590

A brass framed rock crystal eight light chandelier, 20th century, the frame of open cartouche outline, with outset spire finials, 35in. high.
(Christie's) £2,530 $4,099

An eight light cut glass chandelier, fitted for electricity, with slice cut ovoid sconces above petalline drip pans, circa 1930, 109cm.
(Tennants) £2,400 $3,840

A gilt bronze twelve light chandelier, early 20th century, of naturalistic form, the branches issuing from a circular well, 34in. high.
(Christie's) £1,380 $2,208

A Swedish ormolu and cobalt blue tinted glass nine light chandelier, circa 1860, on a circular frame, intersected by faceted clear glass spike finials and outspreading leafy mounts, 64in. high.
(Christie's) £6,900 $11,040

A glass twelve light chandelier, 20th century, with scroll branches in two registers about a baluster column, 51in. high.
(Christie's) £2,875 $4,658

A cut glass twelve light chandelier, basically second half 19th century, the S scroll tiered branches supporting petal-cut drip pans, hung with faceted pendants and chains of graduated beads, 55in. high.
(Christie's) £4,025 $6,440

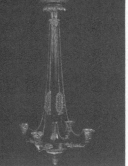

A Restauration style gilt and bronze patinated four branch electrolier, early 20th century, the leaf wrapped cornucopia shaped branches hung with chains, 33in. high.
(Christie's) £1,265 $2,024

A Régence style silvered bronze chandelier, 20th century, with six scroll branches about a circular well and incised knopped baluster column, 23½in. diameter.
(Christie's) £862 $1,396

A George III cut-glass six-light chandelier, with baluster stem, issuing six serpentine branches terminating in star-shaped drip pans, 41in. high.
(Christie's) £9,200 $15,088

Phipps & Wynne custom-made dry sink, with painted shorebird decoration, 32in. high, 32in. long.
(Eldred's)   £241 $385

Two Bennington flint enamel pitchers, 1849–58, the first of alternate rib pattern, the second of tapering panel design, both with 1849 mark, 8¹/8 and 12½in. high.
(Skinner)   £348 $575

Lincoln Presidential pattern porcelain soup plate, retailed by J. W. Boteler & Bro., Washington, circa 1877 or 1884, 9½in. diameter.
(Skinner)   £494 $805

Incised cobalt decorated salt glazed stoneware jug, New York, circa 1810–16, the ovoid form is decorated with a figure of a girl bent over peering between her legs, 17in. high.
(Skinner)   £6,272 $10,350

A pair of gilt and enamelled-decorated porcelain urns, attributed to Tucker and Hemphill China Factory (active 1826-1838), Philadelphia, 1827-1928, 11in. high. (Christie's) £8,625 $13,800

A rare American Porcelain Manufacturing Company pitcher, Gloucester, New Jersey, 1854-57, moulded on either side with a boy kneeling in front of another seated on the gilt-dashed pale blue ground, 6¼in. high.
(Sotheby's)   £701 $1,150

American majolica pitcher, 19th century blue body with floral decoration and cat-form handle, 10in. high.
(Eldred's)   £481 $770

Incised cobalt decorated salt glazed stoneware double jug, attributed to Stedman & Seymour, New Haven or Hartford, Connecticut, circa 1830, 10⁵/8in. high.
(Skinner)   £10,454   £17,250

Sarreguemines Pottery face pitcher, 8½in. high. (Eldred's)   £137 $220

An Arita jar, late 17th century, decorated in various coloured enamels and gilt on underglaze blue with a ho-o bird in flight, 17½in. high.
(Christie's)   £1,380 $2,249

An Arita blue and white vase and cover, late 17th century, decorated with a ho-o bird perched on a rock and another in flight, 21in. high.
(Christie's)   £3,680 $5,998

An Arita sake bottle, late 17th century, decorated with brown diagonal enamelled bands, with a handle formed as a branch, 8¼in. high. (Christie's)   £1,610 $2,624

BERLIN

Berlin porcelain plaque of the Annunciation, Germany, late 19th century, enamel decorated rectangular form, 17 x 21in.
(Skinner)   £4,830 $8,050

A Berlin teacup and saucer, with pink and gilt scroll edge borders, painted with vignettes of garden birds in branches, circa 1772.
(Tennants)   £700 $1,148

Berlin porcelain plaque depicting the three Muses of Time, Germany, early 20th century, of rectangular form and handpainted in enamel colours, 7½ x 9⅞in.
(Skinner)   £1,932 $3,220

BESWICK

Beswick figure of 'Simpkin', brown back stamp, 3½in.
(G.A. Key)   £350 $581

Beswick Beatrix Potter figure 'Tommy Brock', 3½in. high, introduced 1955, gold oval back stamp. (Ewbank)   £220 $365

Beswick Beatrix Potter figure 'Duchess' (first version) 3¾in. high, introduced 1955, gold oval back stamp. (Ewbank)   £1,750 $2,905

181

A Böttger porcelain green-ground beaker (Bechertasse), the porcelain circa 1715, the decoration probably later, with a yellow entwined handle. (Christie's) £656 $1,093

A pair of Böttger red-stoneware square sake bottles, circa 1715, typically formed, supported by stepped bases, 8in. and 7⅞in. high. (Christie's) £8,280 $13,800

A Böttger red-stoneware bust of Vitellius, circa 1715, perhaps modelled by P. Heermann, turned slightly to his left, 4in. high. (Christie's) £6,210 $10,350

A Böttger porcelain Goldchinesen coffee pot and cover, the porcelain circa 1718, gilt slightly later at Augsburg by Bartolomeus Seuter, the mounts by Elias Adam, 8¼in. high. (Christie's) £11,730 $19,550

A Böttger red stoneware hexagonal baluster teacaddy, circa 1715, each recessed panel moulded in low relief with birds of paradise in flight or perched among branches, 12.4cm. high. (Christie's) £5,000 $8,000

A Böttger silver-gilt mounted chinoiserie baluster coffee-pot and domed cover, circa 1725, with a short curved spout and scroll handle, painted by J G Höroldt, 8⅝in. high overall. (Christie's) £8,280 $13,827

A Böttger porcelain white figure of a seated pagoda, circa 1715, the laughing pagoda seated with his right hand resting on his raised right knee, 4in. high. (Christie's) £6,900 $11,500

A Böttger porcelain two-handled beaker and a saucer, circa 1715, the moulded gadrooned section enriched alternately in gilt and a lustrous pink. (Christie's) £2,760 $4,600

A Böttger porcelain flower-encrusted beaker vase, circa 1720, the decoration slightly later, applied with flowering branches of puce and iron-red blossoms, 6¾in. high. (Christie's) £27,600 $46,000

A Bow transfer-printed octagonal soup bowl, printed in dark purple after Robert Hancock with 'L'Amour', within three landscape vignettes below a purple-line rim, circa 1760, 22.5cm. wide. (Christie's) £1,035 $1,656

A rare Bow model of a tawny owl, perched upon a tree stump with an applied pink flower and leaves between the feet, circa 1755, 8½in. (Woolley & Wallis)£15,500 $25,730

Two Bow figures of cherubs, each with floral headware and garlands and holding baskets of flowers, circa 1760, 13cm. (Tennants) £320 $525

BRANNAM

A Brannam, Barum jar jardinière, the cream ground incised with peacock and foliage, and dated *1892*, 33.5cm. (Bristol) £250 $413

A C.H. Brannam Pottery flower holder, in the form of a boat, a fierce mask moulded in the prow, 37.5cm. long, inscribed and dated *1904*. (Bearne's) £220 $365

A Brannam, Barum spherical vase, with central wide neck and three subsidiaries, incised with swimming ducks, on green ground, no.419, 20cm. (Bristol) £75 $124

BRISTOL

A Bristol Delft blue and white pierced circular basket, circa 1760, the centre painted with an urn of flowers and foliage, 10in. wide. (Christie's) £1,200 $1,920

A Bristol baluster shaped sparrow beak jug, with reeded loop handle, painted in famille rose palette with European flowers and leaves, 3¼in. high, circa 1770. (Dreweatt Neate) £230 $380

A Bristol delft blue and white chinoiserie plate, probably Temple Back, painted with a Chinaman seated beneath a tree fanning himself, 22cm. diameter. (Christie's) £287 $459

An early 19th century blue and white pottery mug with flattened loop handle and depicting an Arcadian scene with figures in the foreground, 4¾in. high.
(Andrew Hartley)   £150 $252

A blue and white coffee can, with slightly flared base, painted with the jumping boy pattern, probably Chaffers Liverpool, circa 1758, 6.5cm.
(Tennants)   £1,500 $2,460

An early 19th century creamware masonic jug inscribed _Jonathan Lambert 1828_, over an equestrian portrait of George III, 4½in. high.
(Andrew Hartley)   £70 $118

A Salopian blue and white cabbage leaf jug with mask-head spout, the moulded body printed with the 'Fisherman' pattern, 24cm. high.
(Bearne's)   £360 $576

A pair of Staffordshire pottery figures, of the Prince of Wales and the Princess Royal, each sitting on a pony, 24cm. high.
(Bearne's)   £740 $1,221

Shorters large majolica style jug, modelled as a barrel and moulded with elaborate hunting scenes, decorated in colours on a washed blue ground, printed mark, 9in.
(G.A. Key)   £90 $144

A yellow glazed earthenware jug, printed with _Faith, Hope_ and _Charity_, perhaps Sunderland, circa 1820, 16cm.
(Tennants)   £350 $574

A large copper lustre jug, printed and painted below the spout with a coat-of-arms, and figures, inscribed below _God Speed the Plough_, a verse on either side, 23cm. high.
(Bearne's)   £540 $891

A 19th century slipware 'Cricket' mug inscribed _Fred Lee Champion 1885_, in yellow and brown slip, possibly Yorkshire, 4¼in. high.
(Andrew Hartley)   £190 $319

Charlotte Rhead (Crown Ducal) small baluster vase, deep blue speckled rim and decorated below with panel of stylised foliage, signed 7in. (G.A. Key)　£100　$160

A pair of Jackfield type tea urns and covers, painted and gilt with trailing leaves, circa 1900, 35cm. high. (Christie's)　£115　$184

A ceramic 'Leech' jar and cover, the white ground baluster jar with dark blue and gilt handles and label, 20th century, 41cm. (Bristol)　£130　$208

Enoch Wood ironstone historical blue water pitcher, early 19th century, 'Landing of Gen. Layfayette at Castle Garden, August 1820', 9½in. high. (Du Mouchelles)　£406　$650

A garniture of three 19th century Alcock porcelain vases, the reverse painted with floral sprays within gilded borders, tallest 12¼in. high. (Andrew Hartley)　£340　$571

An English porcelain Imari ice pail, liner and cover, probably Coalport, of typical form with gilt scroll handles and loop finial, circa 1800, 25cm. high. (Christie's)　£517　$827

A late 18th century earthenware baluster jug, painted in ochre, green and blue with exotic birds/landscapes, titled *Thomas Wolverstone 1797*, 16cm. high. (Wintertons)　£480　$792

A pair of Vauxhall blue-ground vases, circa 1760, the overglaze decoration perhaps slightly later, each of inverted pear shape, brightly painted perhaps in the atelier of James Giles, 5in. high. (Christie's)　£4,140　$6,914

A transfer printed Victoria and Albert marriage jug, with Union flowers border, with the date *1845* and flanked by two Farmers Arms verses, 21cm. (Tennants)　£600　$984

Rose medallion wash basin and pitcher, China, 19th century, basin 16in. diameter, pitcher 13¾in. high. (Skinner)   £383 $632

Blue and white Canton bidet, with landscape design on interior and a floral design on the exterior with rain and cloud border, 23½in. long. (Eldred's)   £1,400 $2,310

Blue and white Canton handled serving dish, in jui form with landscape design and butterfly handle, 10½in. long. (Eldred's)   £350 $577

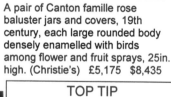

A famille rose Canton enamel yellow-ground double-gourd vase, Qianlong seal mark and of the period, the lower body enamelled with two shaped cartouches enclosing roses and butterflies, 6½in. high. (Christie's)   £6,900 $11,247

A Chinese Export Canton enamel and gilt hand mirror, 18th century, the oval mirror surrounded by a foliate border and above a scrolling foliate support, 11½in. high. (Christie's)   £4,025 $6,681

A pair of Canton famille rose baluster jars and covers, 19th century, each large rounded body densely enamelled with birds among flower and fruit sprays, 25in. high. (Christie's)   £5,175 $8,435

A matched pair of Chinese famille rose Canton enamel wine-ewers, Qianlong (1736-96), decorated overall in pink, green, black, blue, yellow and white foliate scrolls and flowers, 11½in. high. (Christie's)   £6,325 $10,499

A massive Canton famille rose celadon-ground punchbowl, early 19th century, enamelled and gilt to the centre and sides with panels enclosing figures at leisure in terraced pavilion settings, 22¾in. diameter. (Christie's)   £3,105 $5,061

Capodimonte porcelain group of two perched cockerels, painted in colours, 20th century, 19in. (Aylsham) £420 $697

Pair of Capodimonte painted porcelain urns, 19th century, each with lion finial, the body decorated with a band of classical sea-gods and nymphs, 16½in. high. (Skinner) £1,438 $2,300

A Capodimonte group of a gallant and companion, the porcelain circa 1755, perhaps decorated at Buen Retiro, modelled by Giuseppe Gricci, 8½in. high. (Christie's) £4,370 $7,297

CARLTON WARE

'Devil's Copse', a Carltonware dish, printed and painted in colours and gilt on a deep blue ground, 22cm. diameter. (Christie's) £57 $91

A pair of Carltonware vases of ovoid form, decorated with vines and flowers, enamelled in colours on a powder blue ground, 10½in. high. (H. C. Chapman) £240 $396

'Jagged Bouquet', a Carltonware baluster vase, printed in colours and gilt on a matt green ground, 25cm. high. (Christie's) £862 $1,379

CASTEL DURANTE

A Castel Durante wet-drug jar with short yellow spout and wide strap handle, named for *S. ABSINTII*, circa 1570, 21cm. high. (Christie's) £3,000 $4,800

A Castel Durante foliage-moulded lobed crespina, circa 1560, painted in the workshop of Andrea da Negroponte with Moses receiving the Tablets and the Israelites worshipping the Golden Calf, 9¼in. diam. (Christie's) £5,980 $9,986

A maiolica albarello, decorated with grotesques, with inscription *S. di rapi*, late 16th/early 17th century Castel Durante, 16cm. (Finarte) £1,497 $2,396

A Castelli dated shallow bowl, 1727, painted with the Virgin of Loreto and the Christ child appearing among clouds before the Holy House of Loreto in a rocky bay, 17.5cm. diameter.
(Christie's)   £1,955 $3,128

Two Castelli oval plaques, first quarter of the 18th century, painted in the Grue workshop, the first with the Flight into Egypt, the other with the interior of a barber's shop, 11½in. wide.
(Christie's)   £3,000 $4,800

A Castelli plate, early 18th century, painted with an extensive river landscape with fortified buildings among trees, 9½in.
(Christie's)   £920 $1,472

CAUGHLEY

A Caughley blue and white cabbage leaf-moulded mask jug printed with the 'Fisherman' pattern, the interior with cell pattern border, 15cm. high. (Christie's) £552 $883

A Caughley ink-pot and a well of drum form with a spreading foot, the surface with a large central well within four apertures, painted with insects and sprigs of flowers, both circa 1785, 9.2cm. diameter.
(Christie's)   £805 $1,288

A Caughley blue and white mug, printed with the 'Parrot pecking fruit' pattern, C mark in blue, circa 1775, 11.5cm.
(Tennants)   £260 $426

CHANTILLY

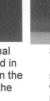

A Chantilly melon tureen and cover, circa 1750, red hunting horn mark, the naturally modelled fruit with green stalk handle with moulded double leaf foliage terminal, 10in. wide. (Christie's) £25,300 $40,480

A Chantilly porcelain octagonal beaker and saucer, decorated in typical vivid enamel colours in the Kakiemon style, circa 1735, the saucer 12.5cm.
(Tennants)   £1,700 $2,788

Seventeen Chantilly plates, circa 1755-60, painted with a bouquet, scattered flowers and an insect within a lobed osier moulded border, 9¾in. diameter.
(Christie's)   £1,500 $2,400

A Charlotte Rhead gallery plate, with stylised flower motifs with vacant cartouche, 31cm. (Locke & England) £200 $429

A Bursley Ltd. toilet set, probably decorated by Charlotte Rhead, tubelined with large flowers and leaves in pale and dark blue. (Woolley & Wallis) £280 $448

A Charlotte Rhead art gallery plate in red, green spiral design, with centre flower motif, rope twist border, 36cm., signed and numbered *4957*. (Locke & England) £280 $462

CHELSEA

A Chelsea teabowl and a Meissen saucer, circa 1755 and 1745, painted with Holzschnitt Blumen, the teabowl with a sunflower, carnation and insects. (Christie's) £828 $1,383

A Chelsea figure of a woman emblematic of 'Smell', circa 1758, from a set of The Senses, wearing a headdress and flowered robe, 24.5cm. (Sotheby's) £1,610 $2,576

A Chelsea 'Hans Sloane' botanical plate, circa 1755, red anchor mark, painted with a spray of flowering broad bean, flowers, butterflies and a 11in. diameter. (Christie's) £2,875 $4,801

CHELSEA KERAMIC

Chelsea Pottery U.S., dolphin with mask plate, possible H.C.R. signature in border, impressed *C.P.U.S.* mark, 10in. diameter. (Skinner) £3,795 $6,325

Chelsea Keramic Art Works terracotta vase, Chelsea, Massachusetts, circa 1880, classical urn form with two applied leaf form handles, 5¾in. high. (Skinner) £250 $400

Chelsea Pottery U.S. Tulip on raised upside down dolphin, impressed *C.P.U.S.* marks, 10in. diameter. (Skinner) £3,105 $5,175

A Chinese armorial saucer dish, the cavetto boldly painted with the coat of arms for Banks, 27.5cm. diameter, Transitional.
(Bearne's)　　　£1,150　$1,897

A Chinese porcelain small tea bowl and saucer, the saucer and bowl exterior delicately painted with pairs of lilac winged parrots, Yongzheng/Qianlong, circa 1740, the saucer 9cm diameter.
(Tennants)　　　£240　$384

18th century Chinese octagonal plate, probably Nanking, typically decorated in underglazed blue with scene of figures, pagodas etc., 9in.
(G.A. Key)　　　　£40　$64

Blue and white garden seat, China, 19th century, chrysanthemum and bird design, 18¼in. high.
(Skinner)　　　£682　$1,092

A set of three 'famille-rose' figures of Immortals, Qing Dynasty, Guangxu (1875–1908), one holding a ruyi sceptre, another a child and the third Shoulao a staff, 24¼in.
(Sotheby's)　　　£3,220　$5,377

ALL IS NOT (QUITE) LOST

A small Chinese vase smashed by the Kobe earthquake of 1995 fetched £2,200 at Woolley & Wallis in December 1998. The Kangxi piece had formed part of the world famous Baur Collection, part of which was on loan in Japan when the earthquake struck.

With an ovoid body and flaring neck, the base moulded with petals, the peach bloom chrysanthemum vase measured 8.25in. When in perfect condition, i.e. pre-earthquake, its insurance value measured £150,000!!

Rose medallion wash basin, China, 19th century, on hardwood stand, 16¹/₈in. diameter.
(Skinner)　　　£790　$1,265

Chinese blue and white fan-shaped box and cover decorated with dragons and flowers, 3½in. high.
(Ewbank)　　　£3,200　$5,280

Pair of rose medallion baluster-form vases, circa 1900, 12in. high.
(Eldred's)　　　£350　$577

A Chinese glazed biscuit figure of a horse, with an amber body, a dark brown mane and tail, 7¹⁵/₁₆in.
(Sotheby's)   £385 $632

A Chinese European-decorated beaker and saucer, the porcelain Kangxi, circa 1700, the decoration circa 1730 and by Ignaz Preissler.
(Christie's)   £6,210 $10,350

A Chinese blue and white bowl and cover, painted inside and out with flowering plants within diaper bands, late 17th/early 18th century, 23cm. diameter.
(Bearne's)   £480 $792

A Chinese porcelain tea cup, depicting merchants on a quayside near moored trade vessels, the porcelain circa 1740/50, 6.5cm.
(Tennants)   £80 $128

Pair of rose Mandarin ku-form vases, China, first half 19th century, with raised acanthus leaf ribbing and gilt archaic dragon design, 12³/₈in. high.
(Skinner)   £2,084 $3,335

A Chinese copper-red and cobalt-blue decorated stag-form jardinière, early 19th century, the sacred deer reclining with his head turned to one side, 11½in. wide.
(Christie's)   £5,175 $8,625

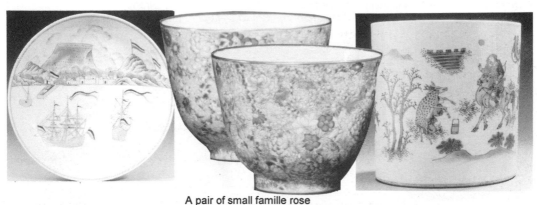

A very rare 'Table Mountain' saucer dish, 18th century, enamelled with a coastal view of Cape Town with the Table Mountain in the background, 6¼in. diameter.
(Christie's)   £14,950 $24,369

A pair of small famille rose 'millefiore' bowls, Jiaqing seal mark and of the period, overall finely enamelled to the exterior with a profusion of flowers and leaves, 3¹/₈in. diameter.
(Christie's)   £3,450 $5,624

A Transitional blue and white brushpot, bitong, mid 17th century, painted around the sides with a continuous landscape scene with a hunter on horseback, 7½in. high.
(Christie's)   £4,830 $7,873

A pair of massive Chinese Export blue and white circular tureens and covers, 1790–1810, each tureen painted on the front and reverse with a beribboned vase, 15 and 15¼in. high.
(Sotheby's)   £12,627 $20,700

A pair of Chinese Export shield-shaped urns 1810–20, each moulded on the front and reverse with a gilt-edged oval panel, 14⅞in. high. (Sotheby's)   £4,209 $6,900

A Chinese Export 'Tobacco Leaf' pattern oval platter, 1770–80, painted with a green centred rose and yellow tobacco blossom, 14¾in. long.
(Sotheby's)   £9,120 $14,950

A pair of Chinese Export famille rose octagonal plates, circa 1740, each painted with a boy peeking through a window at a man wearing only his hat and shirt, 8⅜ and 8½in. wide. (Sotheby's) £1,052 $1,725

A Chinese Export figure of a cockerel, late 18th/early 19th century, with shaded iron-red plumage and gilt-heightened wings 13⅝in. high.
(Sotheby's)   £2,981 $4,887

A Chinese Export Armorial oval soup tureen, cover and stand, 1730–40, each piece painted with the arms of Clifford below a helmet, 12½ and 12⅝in. long.
(Sotheby's)   £1,052 $1,725

A graduated set of three Chinese Export crested leaf-shaped dishes, 1810–20, each painted in the centre with an iron-red lion's head crest below a brown banderole, 5⁷/₁₆, 6½ and 7⁷/₁₆in. long.
(Sotheby's)   £1,122 $1,840

A Chinese Export famille rose teapot stand and 'Mandarin Palette' teapot and cover, circa 1740 and 1785, the stand applied in the centre with a blue-centred rose chrysanthemum sprig, 5⅝in. high.
(Sotheby's)   £632 $1,036

A Chinese Export octagonal plate, 1785–95, painted in sepia and shades of brown in the centre with tiny figures, 9⁵/₁₆in. wide. (Sotheby's) £421 $690

A pair of Chinese Export famille rose large baluster-form jars and covers, circa 1750, each painted on the front with rose, iron-red and gilt peonies, 16⁷/₈in. high. (Sotheby's) £10,523 $17,250

A fine Chinese Export famille rose saucer dish, circa 1730, painted in shades of pink, green, turquoise-green, yellow and white, 8¾in. diam. (Sotheby's) £3,507 $5,750

A rare pair of Chinese Export white-glazed tree and figure groups, early 19th century, each modelled as a Chinese lady holding a branch of flowering prunus, 15¹/₁₆ and 14⁵/₈in. high. (Sotheby's) £4,209 $6,900

A Chinese Export Armorial hexagonal tea caddy and cover, circa 1740, painted on the front in rose, blue white and gold with the arms of Gore, 5in. high. (Sotheby's) £842 $1,380

A pair of Chinese Export silver-shape candlesticks, 1765–75, each with an octagonal candle nozzle decorated with an iron-red-edged blue enamel trelliswork border, 7³/₈ and 7½in. high. (Sotheby's) £3,157 $5,175

A Chinese Export barrel-shaped toddy jug, circa 1785, the body moulded with horizontal ribs, affixed with a ribbed strap handle, 9¹/₁₆in. high. (Sotheby's) £1,052 $1,725

A pair of Chinese Export turquoise-ground small garden seats, 19th century, painted on the front, reverse and top with green and yellow crickets, 12⁵/₈in. high. (Sotheby's) £4,209 $6,900

A Chinese Export urn and cover, circa 1785, the U-shaped body affixed at the sides with reeded entwined strap handles, 9⁵/₈in. high. (Sotheby's) £596 $977

A Chinese Export circular écuelle and cover, 1760–70, the bowl painted on the front and reverse with four small insects flitting around a beribboned bouquet, 7³/8in. wide.
(Sotheby's) £561 $920

An unusual Chinese Export cider jug, circa 1805, the front with a roundel containing an elaborate circular cypher formed of floral-decorated gilt script initials, 8½in. high. (Christie's) £503 $805

A Chinese Export armorial platter, dated 24 January 1791, with the arms of Chadwick quarterly of six suspended from a purple bow with gilt husk swag, 16in. wide.
(Christie's) £1,725 $2,760

An unusual Chinese exportware cistern and cover, Qing Dynasty, Qianlong (1736–1795), painted in the famille rose palette with five figures in a landscape, 24in.
(Sotheby's) £4,830 $8,066

A pair of Chinese Export porcelain armorial toddy jugs and covers, circa 1785, each of barrel form with a reeded entwined-strap handle, 11½in. high.
(Sotheby's) £2,932 $4,887

A Chinese Export American market shipping teabowl and saucer, circa 1785, with a war ship flying the American flag and a interlaced gilt script monogram CWFER, 5½in. diameter.
(Christie's) £2,875 $4,600

A Chinese Export porcelain two-handled oval soup tureen, cover and stand, circa 1790, painted in underglaze blue, floral finial above moulded leaves, 13¾ and 14¾in. long. (Sotheby's) £3,508 $5,750

A Chinese Export famille rose soup tureen and cover, circa 1750, each side with sacred deer in a fenced garden, and cranes, 11in. wide over handles. (Christie's) £3,953 $6,325

HISTORICAL FACTS

Many items of Chinese porcelain bear the marks of the reigning Emperor on their base. However, such marks do not always reflect the true period of manufacture, and were often put on much later pieces as an honorific or a gesture of respect to a long deceased Emperor. While there was no original intention to deceive, in later years these spurious marks can and have been passed off as an indication of age.
Cotswold Auction Company

A Clarice Cliff pottery plate of Biarritz form, brightly painted overall with the blue version of the 'Autumn Balloon Trees' pattern, 22.8cm. wide. (Bearne's)　£1,050　$1,680

A Clarice Cliff three piece condiment set, with graded orange and yellow banding and painted with orange and red trees with black trunks, circa 1935, 8.5cm. (Tennants)　£320　$525

A Clarice Cliff Bizarre pottery plate painted with 'Pine Grove' pattern on yellow line banded ground within orange and black rim, 9¾in. wide. (Andrew Hartley)　£120　$202

Clarice Cliff two handled balustered vase, the quatrefoil spreading rim applied with two handles, moulded at the bases with rosettes, 12in. (G.A. Key)　£115　$184

A Clarice Cliff Bizarre Pottery tea for two, of Trieste shape painted in orange Capri pattern. (Andrew Hartley)　£1,300　$2,080

A Clarice Cliff Newport Pottery figure of Friar Tuck, 21cm. high. (Wintertons)　£200　$330

A Clarice Cliff 'Fantasque' jug, of bellied form, moulded with two flower heads and stalks and a dimpled effect, early 1930s, 18cm. (Tennants)　£280　$459

A Clarice Cliff Fantasque Bizarre 'Gibraltar' pattern vase of mushroom shape, painted in colours, 5½in. high. (Canterbury)　£620　$992

A Clarice Cliff small cauldron, with two angular handles and three feet, painted with the 'Trees and a House' pattern, 1930, 7cm. (Tennants) £340 $558

A rare Clarice Cliff posy holder decorated with the 'Carpet' pattern in red/orange, black and grey. (David Lay) £450 $724

A Clarice Cliff bizarre 'Fantasque' single-handled Lotus jug, in the 'Fruit' pattern. (Bristol) £520 $858

A Clarice Cliff 'Autumn Crocus' pattern tea service, comprising; twelve cups, twelve saucers, twelve tea plates, two bread and butter plates, milk jug and sugar basin, 1931-1933, and a cream linen tea cloth worked with the same pattern and four matching napkins. (Canterbury) £1,150 $1,897

Clarice Cliff Newport Fantasque Bizarre baluster vase, painted with the 'Secrets' design, brown roofed cottages and tree with green and yellow foliage in the foreground, shape No. 360, 7½in.
(G.A. Key) £650 $1,040

A Clarice Cliff coffee set, of daffodil shape and painted with the 'Canterbury bells' pattern, circa 1933, the coffee pot 17cm.
(Tennants) £1,450 $2,378

A Clarice Cliff sugar caster, decorated with the 'My Garden' pattern, with streaked yellow and brown colouring, the base moulded and coloured with flower heads, 14cm. (Tennants) £200 $328

A Coalport china figure 'Sarah', figure of the year only available in 1994, 8¼in.
(H. C. Chapman)   £80 $133

A pair of 19th century Coalport baluster vases, one with panel of Kinnaird House, the other Abbey Church St. Albans, 11in. high.
(Dee Atkinson & Harrison)
                      £900 $1,485

A Coalport figure 'Summer Days', from the Ladies in Fashion series, 8¼in. (H. C. Chapman)   £80 $133

COPELAND

A Copeland majolica 'Lotus' jug, with square mouth and moulded with panels of lotus blooms and foliage, July 1887, 19cm.
(Tennants)   £1,400 $2,240

A pair of Copeland porcelain fruit dishes, painted with floral swags on gilded cream ground with pink and blue jewelled batwing motifs, 11in. wide. (Andrew Hartley) £380 $638

A Copeland Parian figure of a girl with tambourine, etched mark *Marshall fec't* and *Cheverton Sculpt*, 45cm. high.
(Wintertons)   £360 $594

COPELAND SPODE

Copeland late Spode platter, with polychrome floral decoration, 21in. long. (Eldred's)   £300 $495

Pair of Copeland Spode porcelain figural compotes, late 19th century, each with reticulated dish and putti form standard, 10in. high.
(Skinner)   £786 $1,265

Copeland late Spode milk pitcher, early 20th century, in green with brown banding and white golfing decoration, 6¼in. high.
(Eldred's)   £206 $330

A Copenhagen (Royal Danish Porcelain Manufactory) figure of a boy emblematic of Fire, circa 1782, in yellow-edged red coat, striped waistcoat and breeches, 3¹/₈in. high. (Christie's)   £207 $345

A Copenhagen topographical cabinet-plate, circa 1835, painted with a view, named in black script on the reverse, of Frederiksborg castle seen across water, 8in. diameter. (Christie's) £1,200 $1,920

Copenhagen bust of a woman, designed by Johannes Hedegaarf, Denmark, mid-20th century, brown bisque form with glossy glazed scarf, 13¾in. high.
(Skinner)   £188 $300

CREAMWARE

A creamware Masonic frog mug, printed in black with figures and Masonic symbols, with verse, the interior with a black agate glazed frog, early 19th century, 12cm.
(Tennants)   £220 $360

An English creamware pierced and fluted oval bowl, the well painted with rustic figures of a man and woman in a landscape, circa 1780, 33.5cm. wide.
(Christie's)   £690 $1,104

An English creamware 'Platt Menage', the two-tiered centrepiece surmounted with a tulip above two graduated tiers each radiating four shell-moulded bowls, circa 1785, 27cm. high.
(Christie's)   £1,092 $1,747

A William Greatbatch creamware teapot and cover, moulded with the 'Fruit basket', pattern, enriched in green, yellow, pale-manganese and grey/blue glazes, circa 1775, 11.5cm. high.(Christie's) £500 $800

A creamware salad bowl, possibly Yorkshire, the fluted and lobed circular bowl with a shaped rim, supported by a domed foot, circa 1785, 31.5cm. diameter.
(Christie's)   £1,150 $1,840

A Staffordshire creamware oviform teapot and cover, with pierced globular finial, painted in colours with an exotic bird perched on a branch, circa 1775, 15.5cm. high.
(Christie's)   £1,035 $1,656

Blackpool Ferris wheel. £24 $38

Arcadian Submarine. £36 $58

Grafton First and Last House.
£36 $58

Carlton, Tommy in his dugout.
£85 $136

Willow, Hamsfell Hospice. £65 $104

Victoria Submarine. £36 $58

Arcadian Field Glasses. £36 $58

English Cat. £26 $42

Arcadian Tommy and his
machine gun. £75 $120

(The Crested China Company)

199

Three Davenport porcelain plates, the shaped borders moulded with flowers, the centres brightly painted in polychrome enamels with flowers, 9in.
(Woolley & Wallis)   £100 $160

A Davenport part service, 19th century, green transfer printed with a classical river landscape, impressed and printed marks.
(Bonhams)   £300 $480

A 19th century Davenport dessert service comprising; comport, two-handled oval dish, four dishes, 12 plates, 9in. diameter, painted with central landscapes.
(Russell Baldwin & Bright)
                        £1,400 $2,310

DE MORGAN

A large William De Morgan Iznik vase, ovoid with knopped cylindrical neck, applied with strap handles, decorated in the 'Damascus' manner, 49cm. high.
(Christie's)   £7,475 $11,212

A William De Morgan plate, by Charles Passenger, painted with a galleon at sail, in shades of ruby and copper lustre on a white ground, 25cm. diameter.
(Christie's)   £1,725 $2,760

A William De Morgan Persian vase, twin-handled form, painted with repeating winged serpent motif, in blue and green on a white ground, 22cm. high.
(Christie's)   £2,070 $3,105

DEDHAM

Dedham Pottery Fish Pattern plate, scalloped edge, blue stamp, 9in. diameter. (Skinner) £2,415 $4,025

Dedham Pottery Rabbit Pattern pitcher, blue registered stamp, 6¼in. high x 7in. wide.
(Skinner)   £345 $575

Dedham Pottery snipe plate, blue stamp, 10in. diameter.
(Skinner)   £2,932 $4,887

Dedham Pottery Rabbit Pattern
mug, blue stamp, 5in. high x 5½in.
wide. (Skinner)　　£276　$460

Dedham Pottery Fairbanks House
plate, blue registered stamp, two
impressed rabbits, 8½in. diameter.
(Skinner)　　　£1,035　$1,725

Dedham Pottery Azalea Pattern
pitcher, blue stamp, 5in. high x 4in.
wide. (Skinner)　　£207　$345

Dedham Pottery crab decorated
plate, blue stamp, one impressed
rabbit, 10in. diameter.
(Skinner)　　£655　$1,092

Dedham Pottery cream pitcher, in
Night and Morning pattern, 4¾in.
high. (Eldred's)　　£166　$275

Dedham Pottery Golden Gate plate,
signed H.C.R., blue stamp, M.
Shephard, 10in. diameter.
(Skinner)　　£1,587　$2,645

Dedham Pottery Horse Chestnut
Pattern plate, rebus for Maud
Davenport, raised design, blue
stamp, 8½in. diameter.
(Skinner)　　　£86　$143

Dedham Pottery Oriental
Landscape decoration plate, blue
registered stamp, Ned Devlin,
8/20/34, 8½in. diameter.
(Skinner)　　£1,794　$2,990

Dedham Pottery Butterfly with
Flower Pattern plate, blue
registered mark, two impressed
rabbits, 9½in. diameter.
(Skinner)　　£655　$1,092

A London delft blue and white royal portrait plate, circa 1705, the centre with a half-length portrait of Queen Anne wearing her crown and coronation robes, flanked by the letters *A R*, 8⁵/₈in. diam.
(Christie's) £4,600 $7,682

A rare pair of Chinese Export stag's head wall ornaments, early 19th century, the young bucks modelled turned slightly towards each other, 15½in. high.
(Christie's) £51,000 $85,000

A Bristol delft sponged blue and white plate, circa 1740, the centre with Cupid standing on a fence flanked by grasses, 9¾in. diam.
(Christie's) £1,150 $1,920

Two English Delft wall-pockets, circa 1760, one of Liverpool facture, each of cornucopia form, painted in blue with a bird perched in flowering branches, 8½in. high.
(Christie's) £2,898 $4,830

A pair of Dutch Delft models of recumbent horses, 18th century, each spotted blue and white horse with manganese mane and tail, 4in. wide. (Christie's) £8,280 $13,800

A Bristol delft two-handled blue and white vase, circa 1730, of campana form with scroll handles, painted with an exotic bird perched on a tree-stump, 9½in. high.
(Christie's) £4,025 $6,723

A London Delft tulip and carnation charger, circa 1670–85, painted in blue and white and enriched in yellow, green and manganese with tulip and carnations, 12⁷/₈in. diameter. (Christie's) £3,450 $5,750

A pair of Dutch Delft blue and white models of seated hounds, 18th century, each with spotted marking and wearing a manganese collar, 4⁷/₈in. high.
(Christie's) £3,450 $5,750

A Bristol delft Adam and Eve blue-dash charger, circa 1720, painted in blue, green, yellow and iron-red with the Tree of Knowledge at the centre, 13in. diameter.
(Christie's) £2,875 $4,801

A pair of Dutch (De Blompot) Delft blue and white tobacco jars and brass covers, mid-18th century, of oviform, labelled '*N°=4*' and '*N°=5*' within elaborate cartouches, the covers later, 10¼in. high.
(Christie's) £3,450 $5,750

A Dutch delft blue and white shaped oval plaque, circa 1750, painted with St. Peter's denial of Christ, with Christ flanked by St. Peter and a Roman guard, 9⅝in. wide. (Christie's) £1,495 $2,496

A pair of Dutch delft blue and white octagonal ovoid vases and covers, mid-18th century, each painted on the front with peonies and bamboo issuing from pierced rocks, 13⅛in. high. (Sotheby's) £966 $1,610

DERBY

A Derby figure of John Wilkes, circa 1765–70, standing beside a gilt titled pedestal and holding the Bill of Rights, 12⅜in.
(Sotheby's) £2,070 $3,457

Three Derby figures emblematic of 'Europe', 'Africa' and 'Asia', circa 1770, from a set of Four Quarters of The Globe, each approximately 10⅛in. (Sotheby's) £1,840 $3,073

A Derby figure of James Quinn as Sir John Falstaff, circa 1770–80, the portly knight modelled standing and holding a shield, 12¼in.
(Sotheby's) £575 $960

A Derby dog head whistle, modelled as a pointer-like hound with black and white markings, 19th century, 5cm.
(Tennants) £420 $689

A pair of Derby chaffinches, circa 1760, each with pale-green, blue, purple and pale-yellow plumage, perched astride tree-stumps, 4⅝in. and 4½in. high.
(Christie's) £1,092 $1,823

A pair of Derby figures of Milton and Shakespeare, circa 1765-70, each modelled standing, wearing a puce-lined cloak over gilt edged white attire, each approximately 11¼in.
(Sotheby's) £2,185 $3,649

A Doccia coffee cup with bracket handle, painted in colours with a maiden reclining upon a rock before trees, circa 1770.
(Christie's) £207 $331

A Doccia armorial shaped oval dish from the Marchese Marana service, 1750, the central accollée arms of Marana and Isola surrounded by purple scrolls centred below by a grotesque mask, 12¼in. wide.
(Christie's) £10,350 $17,284

A Doccia teabowl and saucer painted with loose sprays of stylised flowers, circa 1765.
(Christie's) £287 $459

DOUCAI

A Doucai bowl with widely flaring sides and short foot, painted to the interior with a central roundel of the Three Friends issuing from rockwork, 8in. diameter, 17th century. (Christie's) £600 $960

A small Doucai jar, Tian mark, 18th century, painted and decorated in yellow and red enamels to the sides with mythical beasts striding over crested waves, 4¾in. high.
(Christie's) £3,450 $5,624

A Doucai baluster vase with short neck, painted with a band of writhing dragons chasing flaming pearls amongst cloud scrolls, 4¼in. high, Kangxi.
(Christie's) £1,200 $1,920

A Doucai flaring footed bowl decorated with phoenix and writhing dragons chasing flaming pearls, 15.5cm. diameter, underglaze blue Qianlong seal mark and of the period. (Christie's) £500 $800

A pair of Doucai saucer dishes decorated with boys at play in fenced, riverside gardens among pine, bamboo and rockwork, 15cm. diameter, underglaze blue Yongzheng six character marks.
(Christie's) £200 $320

A Doucai bowl with decorated with birds and ducks in flight and swimming among lotus issuing from a river, 7½in. diameter, underglaze blue Yongzheng six character mark.
(Christie's) £1,200 $1,920

A pair of Doucai saucer dishes decorated with birds and ducks among lotus issuing from a river within borders of stylised characters, 6¼in. diameter.
(Christie's) £1,000 $1,600

Doulton Burslem two handled oval dish, printed in blue with the 'Norfolk' pattern printed and impressed marks, circa 1895–96, 12in. (G.A. Key) £135 $216

'Bulldog in Union Jack', a Royal Doulton seated bulldog, painted in colours, printed factory marks (small chip to paw), 21cm. diameter. (Christie's) £207 $330

Royal Doulton ashtray, modelled as 'Old Charley' printed mark and no. D5599, 3½in. (G.A Key) £90 $149

Rare Doulton Lambeth milk pitcher, three panels depicting raised white golfing decoration on a tan ground, 8½in. high. (Eldred's) £567 $907

A Royal Doulton figure 'Patricia', HN3365, 8½in. (figure of the year issued 1993 only). (H. C. Chapman) £100 $160

'The McCallum', a rare Royal Doulton Kingsware character jug, modelled in relief, covered in a green and brown glaze, 17cm. high. (Christie's) £1,035 $1,656

A vase painted on either side with a stylised plant in shades of green, by Mark Marshall, circa 1895, 8¼in. high. £700 $1,120

A pair of covered vases by Florence Barlow, with upright handles, c.m., 1878, 7¾in. high. £1,450 $2,320

A jug by Rosina Brown, the shaded green ground with incised scrolls, circa 1892, 7¼in. high. £320 $512

A Royal Doulton Chang stoneware vase by Charles Noke and Harry Nixon, the short neck applied with a dragon in high relief, 7¾in. high. (Andrew Hartley) £2,600 $4,368

A Royal Doulton figure entitled 'Fair Lady', green dress, HN2193, height 7¼in. (H. C. Chapman) £42 $69

A Doulton Lambeth stoneware mug, by Hannah Barlow, of tapered form with incised decoration of cattle, sheep and a donkey, 1876, 13.5cm. (Tennants) £450 $738

A Doulton & Watt's stoneware two-handled filter, circa 1850, the gently flaring cylindrical body applied on the front with a royal crest, 16½in. high. (Sotheby's) £456 $747

A Royal Doulton figure 'Mary', HN3375, 8½in. (issued 1992 only), designer N. Pedley. (H. C. Chapman) £155 $257

A Royal Doulton International Collectors Club character jug, 'Punch and Judy' modelled by Stanley James Taylor, 1993, D6946, limited edition. (H. C. Chapman) £155 $256

Royal Doulton Lambeth barrel-formed tobacco jar, the cover and body elaborately moulded with rosettes, swags and scrolls, by Nellie Garbitt, 5½in. (G.A. Key) £55 $88

Champion Benign of Picardy, a Royal Doulton figure. (Academy Auctioneers) £240 $384

Royal Doulton 'The Dickens Jug', mask moulded spout and the whole heavily moulded and decorated in colours with characters, by C.J. Noke, 10½in. (G.A. Key) £700 $1,162

Royal Doulton character jug, 'Clown', white hair model, painted in colours, circa 1951/55, 7½in.
(G.A. Key)   £420 $697

A pair of Doulton stoneware vases, probably by Eliza Simmance, applied and painted with an encircling foliate band, 25.5cm. high. (Bearne's)   £360 $594

A Queen Elizabeth II Coronation loving cup, by Doulton, No. 998 of 1000, decoration in low relief, printed marks, 27cm. high.
(Wintertons)   £290 $478

A pair of George Tinworth Doulton Lambeth unglazed tiles, 'The Angels and the Women in the Tomb' and 'In Gethsemane', both impressed *1899*, each approximately 8¾in. square.
(Academy Auctioneers)
£660 $1,056

A Doulton Lambeth vase, by Hannah Barlow, incised with a band of sheep in pasture, circa 1900, 29cm.
(Tennants)   £600 $984

A Royal Doulton figure 'Amy', HN3316, 8in. (figure of the year issued 1991 only).
(H. C. Chapman) £260 $432

Royal Doulton figure 'Sunshine Girl' designed by L. Harradine, 5in. high., issued 1929-1938.
(G. E. Sworder)   £2,800 $4,620

A Royal Doulton figure 'Julia', HN2705, 7½in., discontinued 1990.
(H. C. Chapman)   £110 $183

One of six Dresden porcelain Operatic plates, Germany, early 20th century, handpainted borders with continuous scenes from Wagnerian operas, 10in. diameter. (Skinner) (Six) £552 $920

A pair of Dresden porcelain bon bon dishes, each scrolled base surmounted by a cherub with hammer and anvil and bellows, 10¾in. high.
(H. C. Chapman) £360 $594

Dresden covered punch bowl and stand, Germany, 19th century, the bodies enamel decorated with titled figures depicting the 'Punch Society', bowl diameter 11¾in. (Skinner) £17,143 $27,600

A pair of late 19th century Dresden porcelain figures, both in 18th century dress painted with flowers, she holding a rose, he dancing by an architectural plinth, 23in. high. (Dreweatt Neate) £1,800 $2,880

Pair of German porcelain magenta ground covered urns, late 19th century, probably Helene Wolfsohn of Dresden, each painted with reserves of battle scenes, 13in. high. (Skinner) £1,071 $1,725

A pair of 'Dresden' porcelain jars with foliate handles, covers and stands, each piece painted with alternate panels of figures in gardens and flowers on a yellow ground, 52cm. high, late 19th century. (Bearne's) £1,100 $1,826

A pair of 'Dresden' porcelain jars and covers, each ovoid body painted with alternate panels of figures in gardens and flowers on a pink ground, 37.5cm. high, late 19th century. (Bearne's) £760 $1,261

A Dresden yellow-ground flask shaped vase, painted with exotic birds within gilt panels of scrolling leaves, late 19th century, 48.5cm. high. (Christie's) £402 $643

Pair of Dresden porcelain potpourri urns, 20th century, each painted on both sides with harbour scenes, 16½in. high.
(Skinner) £1,429 $2,300

A Continental abstract glazed pottery bowl with stylised bronze leaf and berry mounts, signed *L. Dage ? & Val.*
(Academy Auctioneers)
£180 $288

A Bohemian opaque flask, stopper and stand, mid-19th century, overlaid in pale-green and cut with bands, stylised leaves and the stand with a ropetwist border, 10¾in. high. (Christie's) £437 $729

Pirkenhammer hors d'oeuvres dish/crudité dish, comprising five sections with a central quatrefoil bowl, circa 1870, 12in.
(G.A. Key)   £135 $224

Continental majolica circular covered cheese dish and stand, moulded with berry and fruit designs and the cover applied with a pineapple finial, 9in.
(Aylsham)   £90 $149

Plaue porcelain centre piece, encrusted with flowers, the base applied with putti figures, on scrolled foot, painted in colours, circa late 19th century, 13½in.
(Aylsham)   £560 $930

A pair of late 19th century Continental pottery figures, in 18th century dress, he playing a flute, she a lute, raised on rustic bases, 38½in. high.
(Andrew Hartley) £1,600 $2,688

A life-size pottery standing figure of a pug dog, mid 19th century.
(Academy Auctioneers)
£680 $1,088

A 19th century Continental porcelain group depicting an allegorical female figure in flowing floral dress holding flowers, 12¾in. high. (Andrew Hartley) £380 $638

A large majolica pedestal ewer, probably Portuguese, the spout in the form of a fish, 40.5cm. high.
(Bearne's)   £600 $960

A fine and rare famille rose armorial teabowl and saucer, circa 1730, the bowl enamelled primarily in rose, green and yellow to one side with a coat-of-arms, the bowl 6.7cm. the saucer 10.5cm. diameter.
(Christie's)   £16,100 $26,726

A pair of 18th century famille rose vases of tapering form, painted with garden scenes with figures, 9in. high. (Andrew Hartley)   £200 $336

A fine famille rose armorial plate for the Portuguese market, circa 1765, brightly enamelled at the centre with fruit, vegetables, fish, game and poultry around a ribboned harvest wreath, 9in. diameter.
(Christie's)   £14,950 $24,817

FOLEY

A Foley 'Intarsio' biscuit barrel, decorated with a broad band of squire and toper figures seated with jugs and two cats at their feet, circa 1900, 18cm.
(Tennants)   £300 $492

A Foley 'Intarsio' bowl, decorated with a continuous frieze of various fish against waves on a green ground, circa 1900, 19cm.
(Tennants)   £450 $738

A Foley 'Intarsio' vase, of tapered cylindrical form, decorated with a repeated band of three medieval maidens against a cloudy sky, circa 1900, 28cm.
(Tennants)   £400 $656

FRANKENTHAL

A Frankenthal figure of a hurdy-gurdy player, circa 1759, modelled by J.F. Lücke, in yellow cape, brown jacket and green breeches, 6in. high.
(Christie's)   £897 $1,495

A Frankenthal group of a shepherd and a shepherdess, circa 1770, modelled by K.G. Lücke, the shepherdess standing holding a basket of eggs, her companion reclines on rockwork, 7½in. wide.
(Christie's)   £3,312 $5,520

A Frankenthal group of pastoral lovers, modelled by Johan Wilhelm Lanz, the gentleman gazes towards the lady, circa 1756, 15.5cm.
(Tennants)   £1,600 $2,624

A tin glazed charger, primitively painted in underglaze blue and yellow with an oversized bird on a branch, French or Low Countries, circa 1700, 34cm.
(Tennants) £300 $492

A gilt metal and bisque group, French, circa 1890, modelled with two sleeping children, on a canapé, 44cm. wide.
(Sotheby's) £6,325 $10,436

'Toilette of Venus': a French ormolu mounted and biscuit porcelain group of Venus and attendants, last quarter 19th century, after a Sèvres original, 14¾in.
(Sotheby's) £2,875 $4,801

A large French biscuit porcelain figure group, circa 1860–1870, after a Sèvres original, modelled as three classical female figures carrying infants and cherubs, 11½in.
(Sotheby's) £460 $768

A French Art Deco pottery vase, enamelled in blue, black, white and brown with two stylised naked female figures within leafy trees, 31cm. high.
(Christie's) £500 $808

'Triumph of Bacchus': a French biscuit porcelain figural centrepiece late 19th century, after a Sèvres original, 13½in.
(Sotheby's) £1,380 $2,305

Pair of pâte sur pâte decorated porcelain portrait vases, France, late 19th century, each with gilt banded and foliate borders and central relief of birds within a landscape, 13in. high.
(Skinner) £571 $920

A rare French faience seau probably circa 1765, in Marseilles style, painted with trailing flowers in petit feu, 9½in. diameter.
(Sotheby's) £345 $576

Two French biscuit porcelain groups, 19th century, after Sèvres originals, each group with an arrangement of scantily clad female figures holding an infant child, 10½in. (Sotheby's) £1,265 $2,113

Fulper Pottery vase, cylindrical form with green crystalline glaze, incised vertical mark, 10in. high.
(Skinner) £207 $345

Fulper Pottery bowl, blue high glaze on green ground, incised horizontal mark, 9½in. wide.
(Skinner) £138 $230

Fulper Pottery vase, blue crystalline flambé glaze on a sea green ground translating to a famille rose glaze, 9½in. high.
(Skinner) £224 $373

FÜRSTENBURG

A Fürstenberg gold-mounted oval portrait snuff-box, circa 1760, the exterior painted with lovers in landscape vignettes after Watteau, 3¼in. wide.
(Christie's) £6,900 $11,523

A pair of Fürstenberg two-handled turquoise-ground ice-pails, circa 1790, painted in puce camaïeu with a shepherdess playing a flute in a meadow and with gallants and companions at discussion, 14.6cm. high. (Christie's) £2,500 $4,000

A Fürstenberg porcelain tea cup and saucer, both pieces moulded with three gatherings of fruiting vine and strawberries, circa 1760, the tea cup 5cm.
(Tennants) £1,400 $2,240

GALLÉ

A Gallé faience basket, modelled as a young oriental girl wearing traditional costume decorated with birds and flowers, painted marks, 18.5cm. high.
(Christie's) £1,000 $1,600

A Gallé pottery vase, incised with a partially draped female soldier and simple scrolls and curls, on a brown ground, circa 1900, 31.5cm.
(Tennants) £600 $984

Gallé Art Pottery figural pitcher, swirled surface painted underglaze with pansy decoration enhanced by gold accents, 9in. high.
(Skinner) £759 $1,265

A Gardner porcelain figure of a peasant cobbler, modelled seated at work, on rectangular base, mid 19th century, 16cm. high.
(Christie's)   £207 $331

A pair of Gardner figures of peasant dancers, circa 1830, in brown and blue on green scroll-moulded bases, 8¾in.
(Sotheby's)   £1,265 $2,113

A Gardner figure of a cobbler modelled seated repairing a shoe, on rectangular base, printed and impressed iron-red mark, 13cm. high, mid 19th century.
(Christie's)   £225 $360

GEORGE JONES

Five George Jones porcelain plates painted to the centres with fish and signed *W. Birbeck*, within a blue and gilt ground, first quarter 20th century, 26cm. diameter.
(Christie's)   £575 $920

A George Jones majolica quatrefoil two-handled dish moulded with strawberry leaves and blossom on a cobalt-blue ground, registration lozenge for 1869, 27.5cm. long.
(Christie's)   £517 $858

A George Jones majolica tête à tête set, decorated with the 'apple blossom' pattern on a turquoise and basket weave ground, lozenge for 29 April 1873, the teapot 15.5cm.
(Tennants)   £2,000 $3,280

GERMAN

A Gmunder Keramic terracotta figure, modelled as a seated Scots terrier, with a mottled black and white coat, 21.5cm. high.
(Christie's)   £196 $317

A German faience dish, of circular fluted silver shape, painted in blue and yellow with an equestrian figure, early 18th century, 34cm.
(Tennants)   £250 $410

German porcelain busts of children, male and female, blue wheel mark under glaze, 11in. high.
(Du Mouchelles)   £469 $750

A Goldscheider figure of a dancer, 1930s, designed by J. Lorenzl, polychrome glazed earthenware figure, in a short skirt with long drapes decorated with orchid blossoms, 16½in. (Sotheby's) £1,092 $1,813

A pair of Goldscheider pottery figures, modelled as a young peasant boy and girl, he stands with hands in pockets of his shorts, 48cm. high. (Christie's) £138 $223

A Goldscheider polychrome pottery figure, cast from a model by Dakon, of a young blonde beauty wearing floral lace dress with green sleeves, 32cm. high. (Christie's) £632 $1,020

GRUEBY

Grueby faience Art Pottery vase, Boston, circa 1900, swollen lobed body with everted rim, matte mustard yellow glaze, 6in. high. (Skinner) £3,125 $5,000

Grueby Pottery trivet, landscape decoration under a matte green, blue, cream, and brown glaze, initialled *M.D.*, 6 x 6in. (Skinner) £1,380 $2,300

Important Grueby Pottery vase, globular form with rolled rim, seven broad leaf-forms with negative space in relief, 11in. high. (Skinner) £15,180 $25,300

HAN

A fine large Sichuan Pottery saddled horse, Han Dynasty, standing in playfully attentive position, a detachable saddle placed over the arched back, 57in. high. (Christie's) £26,450 $42,320

A rare pair of massive Sichuan pottery hunting mastiffs, Han dynasty, each modelled seated on its haunches with curled-up tail behind, each 38in. high. (Christie's) £34,500 $56,235

A brown-glazed pottery recumbent hunting hound, Eastern Han dynasty, modelled with a long neck and raised head with alert expression, 17¾in. wide. (Christie's) £8,050 $13,122

An Hirado vase and cover, Edo period, 19th century, decorated in underglaze blue with a band of key-fret design to the neck, approx. 11¼in. high.
(Christie's)   £1,150 $1,875

A Hirado white glazed model of a cockerel with its tail feathers raised and head turned slightly to the left, 19th century, 20.4cm. high.
(Christie's)   £500 $800

A Hirado brushpot modelled with a snarling tiger standing on rockwork before a writhing dragon among bamboo, 7½in. high, 19th century.
(Sotheby's)   £800 $1,328

HÖCHST

A Höchst figure of a poultry vendor, circa 1750-53, black *IZ* mark for Johannes Zeschinger, modelled by Simon Feilner, wearing a black cap tied with a white headscarf, 15.5cm. high. (Christie's)   £1,000 $1,600

A Höchst figure group of 'The Disturbed Slumber', circa 1770, modelled by J.P. Melchior, modelled as a boy tickling the nose of a sleeping girl, 7½in. wide.
(Christie's)   £4,485 $7,475

A Höchst coffee pot and cover, with an ovoid body, a dog's head spout above a face mask, the handle modelled as a snake, circa 1775, 9.75in.
(Woolley & Wallis)   £250 $400

A Höchst figure of a gardener, circa 1755, in black hat, green-edged white jacket and iron-red breeches, 4in. high.
(Christie's)   £1,104 $1,840

A pair of Höchst figures of a youth and companion, circa 1770, modelled by J.P. Melchior, he feeding a squirrel, she standing before a rock, 6¼in. and 7in. high.
(Christie's)   £1,092 $1,823

A Höchst figure of a putto, circa 1750, possibly from a set of the Seasons, in loose drapes and enriched in a pale palette, 3¼in. high. (Christie's)   £345 $575

An Imari charger, Japanese, 19th century, painted with a phoenix and two lotus leaves within radiating borders of kirin, 18in. diameter. (Sotheby's)   £977 $1,632

An Imari condiment group, late 17th/early 18th century, the centre of the dish with a flared column decorated in iron red enamel and gilt, 10in. diameter. (Christie's)   £3,680 $5,998

An Imari charger, Japanese, late 17th/early 18th century, painted with three ladies in a garden within a deep foliate border, 18¼in. diameter.(Sotheby's) £1,955 $3,265

An ormolu-mounted Imari vase and cover, the porcelain 17th century and the mounts late 19th century, decorated overall in blue, green, orange and gilt with flowers, 22½in. high. (Christie's)   £5,980 $9,927

A rare large Imari dish, late 17th century, decorated gilt on underglaze blue, the centre with karako playing with an ox, 15¾in. diameter. (Christie's)   £6,900 $11,247

An Imari ovoid jar and domed cover, 19th century, painted and heavily gilt with shaped panels of ho-o in flights among clouds, 16¾in. high. (Christie's)   £437 $708

A pair of 19th century Japanese porcelain Imari chargers, the central reserve depicting flowers on a terrace, embellished in gilt, 13in. wide. (Andrew Hartley)   £740 $1,243

Japanese Imari jardinière, the reeded body painted with garden scenes in fan shape panels, 32cm. high. (Bearne's)   £880 $1,452

An Imari charger, late 17th/early 18th century, painted with a jardinière of pomegranates and flowers within a foliate border, 16½in. diameter. (Sotheby's)   £1,955 $3,265

An Italian maiolica bust of a boy in the Della Robbia style, painted in ochre-blue and cream glazes, painted cockerel mark, late 19th century, 29cm. high. (Christie's) £500 $800

An Italian (Le Nove) coffee-cup and saucer, circa 1770, iron-red star marks, finely painted with equestrian figures in capriccio landscapes reserved within gilt and pink seeded bands. (Christie's) £1,035 $1,725

An Essevi figure of a woman in front of a looking glass, 1930s, designed by Sandro Vacchetti, polychrome glazed earthenware, on an oval peach mirrored glass base, 48.5cm. (Sotheby's) £1,725 $2,863

Italian maiolica ewer, late 19th century, polychrome decorated with figures slaying a dragon to one side, mark for Cantigalli of Florence, 13¼in. high. (Skinner) £357 $575

Two Italian maiolica wet drug jars, probably Montelupo, with ovoid bodies, green and yellow handles modelled as fish, 17th/18th century, 13in. (Woolley & Wallis) £2,200 $3,652

Italian majolica two-handled vase, late 19th century, with scrolled snake handles and painted oval reserves of cherubs on a blue-green foliate ground, 22½in. high. (Skinner) £750 $1,200

Italian maiolica flask, 19th century, polychrome decorated battle scene and village landscape, mark for Cantigalli of Florence, 11in. high. (Skinner) £357 $575

A Montelupo dish, circa 1650, boldly painted with a musketeer wearing a plumed hat and striped clothing, 12⅞in. diameter. (Christie's) £2,760 $4,609

Italian majolica two-handled vase, late 19th century, with armorial oval reserve, the ground with cherubs and scrolled foliage, 16in. high. (Skinner) £466 $747

One of a pair of Jacob Petit flower-encrusted ewers of baluster form, with gilt scroll spout and handle, the lower section with a strapwork band, circa 1850, 40.5cm. high. (Christie's) (Two) £1,500 $2,400

A Paris (Jacob Petit) blue-ground baluster vase, circa 1845, blue *J.P.* mark, with richly gilt corn-cob and foliage handles and a flared convoluted lip, 20in. high. (Christie's) £2,000 $3,200

A near pair of porcelain vases by Jacob Petit, late 19th century, profusely painted with birds and sprays of summer flowers applied with mask handles, 70cm. high. (Sotheby's) £29,900 $48,737

JAPANESE

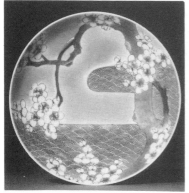

A Nabeshima dish, late 17th century, decorated in iron red enamel on underglaze blue and celadon with a blossoming cherry tree by a stylised shore, 8⅛in. diameter. (Christie's) £47,700 $77,751

A Haniwa standing figure, Tumulus period, (250–552 AD), the columnar figure of a female shaman standing with outstretched hands, 35⅝in. high. (Christie's) £11,500 $18,745

A Japanese ovoid jar with everted rim, decorated in underglaze blue, white and olive green enamels with two men standing among rockwork beneath a tree, 35cm. high, late 19th century. (Christie's) £400 $664

KPM

Large KPM painted porcelain figural group, late 19th century, depicting a peasant couple with an infant, 12in. high. (Skinner) £232 $374

A German oblong porcelain plaque painted with Judith holding the head of Holofernes, 10¼ x 8in., in gilt frame. (Andrew Hartley) £950 $1,568

KPM painted porcelain figural group, 19th century, depicting two bacchantes and a goat, 8in. long. (Skinner) £107 $173

A Kakiemon square dish, Fuku mark, Edo period (late 17th century), decorated in iron-red, green, blue, yellow and black enamels and gilt on underglaze blue with a cockerel and a hen, 8in. wide. (Christie's)   £3,450 $5,796

A Kakiemon jar and cover, late 17th century, decorated in iron red, yellow, green and blue enamels on underglaze blue with peonies, cherry blossom and chrysanthemums, 10in. high. (Christie's)   £18,400 $29,992

A rare Kakiemon ewer, Edo period (late 17th century), decorated in iron-red, yellow, black, blue and green enamels with a flowering branch and scattered plum blossom and peony, 18.1cm. high. (Christie's)   £16,675 $28,014

KANGXI

A fine blue and white saucer-dish, Kangxi six-character mark and of the period, painted to the central roundel with a boy holding a scrolling branch, 16³/₈in. diameter. (Christie's)   £3,680 $5,998

A very fine garniture of three blue and white baluster jars and covers, Kangxi, each painted in brilliant cobalt-blue with petal-shaped panels in three registers, each approximately 22in. high. (Christie's)   £29,900 $48,737

A pair of Sancai-glazed laughing boys, hehe erxian, Kangxi, each modelled standing casually on a raised rockwork pedestal, 6½in. high. (Christie's) £3,220 $5,249

KINKOZAN

A Kinkozan pierced and moulded vase, impressed and sealed Kinkozan zo, sealed Fuzan, Meiji period (late 19th century), 12¼in. high. (Christie's)   £10,925 $18,354

A Kinkozan koro and cover, decorated in various coloured enamels and gilt with two panels, signed, late 19th century, 20cm. high. (Christie's) £2,000 $3,200

Tapered Kinkozan vase, signed Nippon Kinkozan Keizan Ga, Meiji period, decorated in various coloured enamels and gilt on a blue ground, 6⁷/₈in. high. (Christie's)   £2,645 $4,311

219

A Kloster Veilsdorf figure salt modelled by L. D. Heyd, with a figure of a seated lady, flanked by two white basket salts, 11.5cm. (Phillips) £500 $800

A Kloster-Veilsdorf figure of Pantaloon, circa 1764–65, modelled by W. Neu, in a black snood, cape and orange suit with a white belt, 6¹/₈in high. (Christie's) £16,560 $27,600

A Kloster-Veilsdorf figure of a man, circa 1765, wearing a black tricorn hat, loose white shirt, pale-red breeches and black buckled shoes, 4¼in. high. (Christie's) £1,200 $1,920

KUTANI

A Japanese Kutani cylindrical box and cover, in four sections, decorated with panels of crane and minogame, Meiji, 1868-1912, 10in. (Woolley & Wallis) £250 $400

A Kutani shaped square dish, late 17th /early 18th century, decorated with figures standing beside a waterfall beneath a pine, 7⁵/₈in. diameter. (Christie's) £29,900 $48,737

A large Kutani ovoid jar and domed cover, 19th century, painted and gilt with a wide band of cockerels and other birds, 19¾in. (Christie's) £1,667 $2,700

LEEDS

A Leeds creamware tea canister of octagonal shape, 12.5cm. high, incised no. 25. (Phillips) £1,500 $2,400

An 18th century Leeds creamware bullet shaped teapot and cover, painted in manganese, russet and ochre with a musician seated in a landscape, height 15cm. (Wintertons) £440 $726

A Leeds Pottery circular plaque moulded to the centre with the bust of Sir Henry Irving, on a blue ground, circa 1905, 28.5cm. diameter. (Christie's) £600 $900

A Limbach figure of a fisherman leaning against a tree-stump, one bare foot raised, holding a large fish in his arms, circa 1770, 14cm. high. (Christie's)   £725 $1,160

Four Limbach figures emblematic of the Seasons, each modelled as a gallant, two with puce and one with sepia crossed L Marks, circa 1775, 15.5-17cm. high. (Christie's)   £5,000 $8,000

A Limbach figure emblematic of Winter, circa 1770, in white cap, yellow bodice, fur-lined orange jacket, $6^5/8$in. high. (Christie's)   £345 $575

LINTHORPE

A Linthorpe jug, designed by Dr. Christopher Dresser, humped shape with vertical spout and carved handle, 18cm. high. (Christie's)   £650 $1,040

A Linthorpe Pottery plaque, in the form of a shield, possibly designed by Christopher Dresser, the central boss moulded with a head, surrounded by the rays of the sun, 42cm. diameter. (Bearne's)   £340 $564

A Linthorpe teapot, the design attributed to Dr. C. Dresser, 21.3cm. high. (Christie's)   £250 $400

LIVERPOOL

Antique English oversize Liverpool pitcher, circa 1798, one side with polychrome transfer decoration of a vessel flying an American flag, reverse with Masonic emblems, 12in. high. (Eldred's)   £9,625 $15,400

Liverpool pitcher, England, early 19th century, transfer decorated with *Washington in Glory America in Tears*, $8^7/8$in. high. (Skinner)   £1,394 $2,300

Liverpool jug, early 19th century, transfer decorated with the Proscribed Patriots of America, a three-masted ship flying the American flag and a spread eagle, 9¾in. high. (Skinner) £1,058 $1,725

A pair of Longwy pottery plaques, each centre brightly decorated with birds in landscapes within a border of colourful patterns, 31.7cm. diameter. (Bearne's) £400 $660

Longwy Primavera Pottery centre bowl, France, circa 1930, broad flared form with cream crackle glaze, interior decorated with stylised flowers and grapes, 15in. diameter. (Skinner) £375 $600

Longwy Pottery charger, black deer designs on deep blue glaze, incised *Longwy, Atelier, Primavera*, 15in. diameter. (Skinner) £379 $632

LUDWIGSBURG

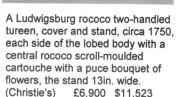

A Ludwigsburg group of dancers, circa 1765, modelled by Joseph Nees, with a dancer and companion pirouetting, 6⁵/₁₆in high. (Christie's) £759 $1,265

A German porcelain centrepiece group, possibly Ludwigsburg, modelled with a seated woman wearing classical robes, holding two large footed bowls, 1770, 17.5cm. high. (Christie's) £400 $640

A Ludwigsburg rococo two-handled tureen, cover and stand, circa 1750, each side of the lobed body with a central rococo scroll-moulded cartouche with a puce bouquet of flowers, the stand 13in. wide. (Christie's) £6,900 $11,523

MALING

Maling hexagonal covered jar, the whole printed in blue with scenes of Newcastle, Middlesborough etc, 5½in. (G.A. Key) £145 $240

Maling teapot, 1930s, with grapevine decoration. (Muir Hewitt) £40 $60

Maling plate with floral decoration, 10in. diameter. (Muir Hewitt) £200 $300

Unusual Marblehead Pottery tile, incised and relief image of an Egyptian figure under a vibrant blue-green glaze, 7½in. high. 4½in. wide. (Skinner) £276 $460

Marblehead Pottery ship tile, decorated with ship in colours of blue, green, brown, and creamy white, impressed logo, 4½in. square. (Skinner) £276 $460

Decorated Marblehead Pottery vase, Marblehead, Massachusetts, circa 1905, decorated with repeating stylised trees, black trunks and blue leaves over grey ground, initialled by Hannah Tutt, 3⅝in. (Skinner) £1,509 $2,415

MASONS

A Mason's Ironstone blue-ground hexagonal vase and pierced cover with dragon handles and dragon finial, circa 1820, 63cm. high. (Christie's) £977 $1,563

A Mason's Ironstone hexagonal section tureen and cover, decorated in polychrome with vases of flowers, leaves and scrolls, gilded details, circa 1815-25, 35cm. (Woolley & Wallis) £420 $672

A large Mason's Ironstone blue-ground and gilt ewer or 'Noble Vase', with scrolling foliate spout, the fluted and broad shoulder applied with two putti, circa 1825, 68cm. high. (Christie's) £1,265 $2,024

A Mason's Ironstone china jug and cover, of hydra shape with twig handle and Imari pattern, 25cm. (Bristol) £270 $445

A 19th century Masons Ironstone vase, hand painted in Imari colours with gilt scroll handles on circular foot, 6½in. high. (Dee Atkinson & Harrison) £280 $462

A Mason's Ironstone china cylindrical mug, with snake handle and an Imari pattern, 12.5cm. (Bristol) £145 $239

A Meissen teabowl and a saucer, circa 1722, painted by J.G. Mehlhorn, the teabowl painted with a lady in a garden by a fountain.
(Christie's)   £2,622 $4,370

A Meissen model of a dove, circa 1735, modelled to the right, its incised grey feathers enriched in green, blue and iron-red, with dark hood, 11in. high.
(Christie's)   £7,590 $12,650

A Meissen Resedagrünen-ground hot-milk jug and cover, circa 1740, of baluster form with mask beak spout and rocaille-moulded wishbone handle, 6½in.
(Christie's)   £1,932 $3,220

A Meissen monkey ewer and cover (Affenkanne), circa 1750, incised *M* to the underside, modelled as a seated monkey wearing a puce tasselled fez, the tail as the handle, 7½in. high.
(Christie's)   £5,175 $8,625

A pair of Meissen male and female Pagoda figures, second half 19th century, each seated cross-legged wearing loose floral robes, their heads and hands articulated, 7in.
(Sotheby's)   £7,130 $11,907

A Meissen figure of a linen salesman, circa 1742–45, modelled by J.J. Kändler, in black hat and lilac coat carrying a pannier containing two packages, 7³⁄₈in. high. (Christie's)   £4,140 $6,900

A Meissen Hausmalerei teabowl and acanthus-moulded saucer, circa 1720, decorated circa 1735 in Bayreuth at the J.F. Metzsch workshop.
(Christie's)   £11,040 $18,400

A Meissen giltmetal-mounted rectangular snuff-box, circa 1750, the interior of the cover finely stippled with a gallant and companion, 3¼in. wide.
(Christie's)   £4,140 $6,914

A Meissen group of a shepherd and shepherdess, circa 1760, modelled after Boucher, with a shepherd leaning forward to garland his companion with flowers, 5¾in. high.
(Christie's)   £2,990 $4,993

A Meissen model of a cat, circa 1745, modelled by J.J. Kändler, seated to the right, pawing a rat grasped between its jaws, 7in. high. (Christie's)   £7,590 $12,650

A Meissen figure of an articulated nodding magot, circa 1740, by J.J. Kändler, the seated pagoda figure, in black skull-cap, iron-red kerchief, yellow-lined robe, 8in. high. (Christie's)   £11,730 $19,550

A Meissen figure of Harlequin, circa 1740, modelled by J.J. Kändler, in tricorne hat, blue tunic incised with scrolls, 5in. high. (Christie's)   £1,587 $2,645

A Meissen figure of a fish seller, circa 1745, modelled by P. Reinicke and J.J. Kändler, in white kerchief, yellow bodice and grey skirt, 5½in. high. (Christie's)   £3,105 $5,175

A pair of Meissen models of guinea-fowl, circa 1745, modelled by J.J. Kändler, modelled to the left and right standing astride reeds, 6½in. high. (Christie's)   £10,350 $17,250

A Meissen figure of a mapseller, circa 1745, modelled by J.J. Kändler, in black hat, red-lined blue frock-coat, 6½in. high. (Christie's)   £2,990 $4,993

A Meissen model of a partridge (Stehendes Rebhuhn), circa 1750, modelled by J.J. Kändler, with iron-red and brown plumage standing amidst grasses, 6in. high. (Christie's)   £3,450 $5,750

A pair of Meissen figures of dancing children, circa 1750, she in puce-edged white dress, 4¾in. high. (Christie's)   £2,300 $3,841

A Meissen bowl and cover, circa 1730, blue Caduceus mark, painted with shrubs issuing from stylised rockwork within a diaper pattern band, 7¼in. diameter. (Christie's)   £3,795 $6,325

A Meissen gold-mounted rectangular snuff-box, circa 1750, each facet painted with Holzschnitt Blumen and ombrierte insects, 2¾in. wide.
(Christie's)   £8,050 $13,443

A Meissen squirrel teapot, circa 1735, modelled by J.J. Kändler, as a squirrel nibbling an acorn, a green bow-tied collar around its neck, 6in. high. (Christie's)   £1,932 $3,220

A Meissen 'celadon' ground teapot, with a pale blue ground reserved with two gilt edged quatre-lobed panels painted in Kakiemon style, circa 1735, 16.5cm.
(Tennants)   £700 $1,148

A Meissen figure of a dancing girl in Turkish dress, circa 1740, modelled by P. Reinicke, wearing a pink and gilt headdress, flowered pink-lined robe, 5¾in. high.
(Christie's)   £1,840 $3,073

A pair of Meissen groups of a pen and two cygnets, circa 1745, modelled by J.J. Kändler and P. Reinicke, with black and iron-red beaks, black webbed feet and incised plumage, approx. 5¹/₈in. high. (Christie's) £6,325 $10,563

A Meissen large baluster vase and cover, circa 1735, painted in the Kakiemon style with exotic birds among branches of flowering peony and prunus growing behind a fence, 21¾in. high.
(Christie's)   £12,420 $20,700

An early Meissen pagoda figure, as a seated Chinaman with distinct fixed grin and holding a tea bowl and saucer in his right hand, circa 1730, 11cm.
(Tennants)   £2,500 $4,000

A Meissen chinoiserie beaker and saucer, circa 1725, painted in the manner of J.G. Höroldt, the beaker with an Oriental in a long-sleeved black robe.
(Christie's)   £3,220 $5,377

A Marcolini Meissen coffee can and saucer, the can with two oval reserves vividly painted with birds in an open country landscape, circa 1790.
(Tennants)   £1,500 $2,400

A Meissen saucer, painted in the manner of Christian Friedrich Heroldt, 12cm.
(Tennants)   £580 $928

A Meissen teapot and cover, circa 1725, of squat form with everted spout rising from the mask terminal, 5½in. high.
(Christie's)   £5,520 $9,200

A Meissen porcelain milk jug, painted in enamels on both sides with battle scenes of hussars and cavalrymen, circa 1745, 12.5cm.
(Tennants)   £850 $1,360

A Meissen two-handled beaker and saucer, the porcelain circa 1728 and 1730, painted in puce camaïeu with European and Turkish merchants.
(Christie's)   £2,990 $4,993

A pair of Meissen 'Schneeballen' vases, circa 1880, of thistle form with applied flowers, green foliage, parrots and hoopoes, 47cm. high.
(Sotheby's)   £7,475 $12,184

A Meissen model of a snarling marten, circa 1734–35, modelled by J.J. Kändler, the animal rearing up over a tree-stump with mushrooms and ferns growing at its base, 15¼in. high.
(Christie's)   £34,500 $57,500

A gilt-metal mounted Meissen bombé snuff box and cover, circa 1740, painted with several views of gallants and companions promenading in the gardens of an Italian palazzo, 2⅞in. wide.
(Christie's)   £24,150 $40,250

A Meissen group of the Spanish lovers, circa 1741, modelled by J.J. Kändler, he in an iron-red jacket with purple rosettes, she in puce hat with yellow bow and a plume, 7in. high.
(Christie's)   £8,625 $14,404

A pewter-mounted Meissen fluted barrel-shaped jug, circa 1730, painted in chocolate and chased with chinoiseries above Gitterwerk, the later pewter hinged lid dated 1760, 3¾in. high overall.
(Christie's)   £1,311 $2,185

A Meissen Goldchinesen two-handled beaker and saucer, circa 1720, gilt at Augsburg, with Chinoiserie vignettes based on those in the Schulz Codex.
(Christie's) £2,208 $3,680

Two Meissen models of pugs, circa 1745, modelled by J.J. Kändler, seated to the left and right, with black muzzles and fine brown and black markings, 4½in. high.
(Christie's) £3,105 $5,175

Meissen porcelain nodder, 19th century, laughing Chinese figure depicted sitting with legs crossed, movable weighted head and hands, hand-painted, 5¾in. high.
(Du Mouchelles) £1,562 $2,500

Meissen porcelain mantel clock, late 19th century, the elaborate foliate modelled case mounted with the four Seasons, 22½in. high.
(Skinner) £4,286 $6,900

A pair of Meissen teabowls and saucers, with gilt edged ozier moulded borders and painted with assorted fruit, nuts and legumes, circa 1745.
(Tennants) £1,100 $1,804

Meissen porcelain figural group, Germany, 20th century, enamel and gilt decorated with three figures gathering flowers and picking fruit , 10in. high. (Skinner) £759 $1,265

A Meissen porcelain écuelle cover and stand, each piece painted with alternate panels of figures and buildings in landscapes and blue scroll panels, 15.5cm. high.
(Bearne's) £520 $858

A Meissen hot milk jug and cover, with ozier moulded decoration and bud knop, mid 18th century, 13cm.
(Tennants) £1,050 $1,680

Meissen cherub figure group, Germany, late 19th/early 20th century, depicting three cherubs surrounding an easel as one paints, 7¼in. high. (Skinner) £571 $2,530

A Meissen blue and white tea caddy, painted with the fisherman pattern in rounded panels, circa 1725, 10.5cm.
(Tennants) £900 $1,440

A Meissen Hausmaler saucer, the decoration attributed to Joseph Philipp Dannhofer, with a Manchu in a garden setting, the porcelain circa 1740 or earlier, 12.6cm.
(Tennants) £400 $640

A Meissen rectangular tea caddy, circa 1730, blue crossed swords and Dreher's mark, painted by J.E. Städler, painted with Chinese figures in gardens, 4¹/₈in. high.
(Christie's) £621 $1,035

A Meissen large figure of a jay perched on an oak tree stump and naturalistically painted in coloured enamels, on rockwork base, 15½in. high.
(Dreweatt Neate) £650 $1,073

A pair of Meissen models of swans, circa 1745, modelled by J.J. Kändler and P. Reinicke, modelled to the left and right with incised plumage, 10½in. high.
(Christie's) £16,560 $27,600

A Meissen porcelain figure of a woman gardener, after an original by Michel Victor Acier, standing by an urn with a basket of flowers, 19.3cm. high.
(Bearne's) £340 $561

Meissen-type porcelain figure group, Germany late 19th/early 20th century, depicting six figures modelled in various stages of gardening, 11½in. high.
(Skinner) £607 $978

A Meissen tea cup and saucer, the wishbone handled tea cup and saucer centrally painted with ladies and gentlemen promenading in wooded countryside, circa 1750, 12.3cm.
(Tennants) £1,000 $1,600

Meissen allegorical figure group, Germany, late 19th/early 20th century, depicting females and child supporting a net filled with sea creatures and a child merman, 12¾in. high.
(Skinner) £929 $1,495

A fine large late Ming blue and white kraak porselein dish, Wanli, painted in a strong cobalt blue 51cm. diameter.
(Christie's) £9,200 $15,272

A fine late Ming blue and white kraak porselein jar, Wanli, the rounded sides painted with four shaped panels enclosing flower, bird and rock compositions, 13¾in. high. (Christie's) £9,200 $15,272

A large early Ming blue and white deep dish, yongle, painted centrally with a large peony scroll roundel below a band of floral scroll at the well, 16¹/₈in. diameter.
(Christie's) £13,800 $22,494

A fine late Ming blue and white oviform jar, second quarter 17th century, painted around the wide central band around the body with four oval cartouches with scenes depicting scholars and their attendants, 22in. high.
(Christie's) £12,000 $19,920

A pair of late Ming blue and white octagonal baluster jars and covers, early 17th century, each softly lobed vase painted around the upper section of the body with scattered flower-sprays below a ruyi-lappet collar, 14¼in. high.
(Christie's) £3,450 $5,727

A late Ming blue and white kraak porselein jar, Wanli, the heavily potted sides freely painted with a continuous scene with a pair of peacocks in flight, 14in. high.
(Christie's) £7,475 $12,408

A rare documentary Ming Sancai tripod censer, dated 26th year of Jiajing (AD 1547) and of the period, the bulbous body elaborately modelled in relief with two confronted dragons, 15in. high.
(Christie's) £7,475 $12,184

A pair of green-glazed Buddhistic lions, Ming dynasty, energetically modelled with their heads turned to the left and right, one with its paw resting on a lion cub, 15½in. high.
(Christie's) £1,380 $2,249

A late Ming blue and white 'Kraak porselein' jar and cover, Wanli, heavily potted and painted with four panels of flower sprays, 19¾in. high.
(Christie's) £8,050 $13,122

Mintons oval large platter, the centre printed in blue with the 'Chinese Marine' pattern, within a blue floral border, early 19th century, 20½in.
(Aylsham)   £350 $581

A Minton earthenware large tazza, painted by William S Coleman, with Leda and the Swan, between orchids and prunus blossom, 34cm. diameter.
(Christie's)   £3,680 $5,888

A Minton majolica butter tub and cover, the recumbent goat knop with grey colouring and white and brown streaked back, 1870, 13.5cm.
(Tennants)   £600 $984

A Mintons pottery 'Henri Deux' salt by Charles Toft, the shallow circular bowl applied with masks and shells on arched octagonal base enclosing a figure, 5¼in. high.
(Andrew Hartley)   £1,000 $1,680

A pair of Minton vases painted with lilac blossom on a pale green ground by J. Hackley, signed, gilded rims, circa 1891-1902, 25cm.
(Wintertons)   £500 $800

A Minton porcelain figure of a man in finely painted costume sitting on a wicker seat, circa 1830, 13.5cm. high. (Bearne's)   £340 $561

A Minton majolica cornucopia vase, emblematic of Autumn, modelled as a putto seated with his arms around a bundle of corn above an upturned basket of grapes, year cypher for 1872, 28.5cm. high.
(Christie's)   £2,760 $4,582

A Minton majolica jug, modelled in high relief with peasant figures dancing and carousing by a seated man, date code for 1861.
(Bearne's)   £480 $768

A Moorcroft vase, of shouldered form, tube-lined with 'Pansies', on a deep blue ground, 1930s, 17.5cm. (Tennants) £400 $656

A Moorcroft 'Anemone' jardinière, tube-lined and coloured with a band of open and closed blooms on a blue ground, 16cm. (Tennants) £650 $1,066

A large Moorcroft Macintyre Pottery bottle vase decorated with brown chrysanthemum design on a pale green wash ground, 31.7cm. high. (Bearne's) £3,400 $5,610

A pair of Moorcroft Macintyre Florian ware vases, of balloon shape, tube-lined with blue poppies, circa 1902, 29cm. (Tennants) £3,700 $6,068

Moorcroft pottery round jar decorated with pomegranate on a dark blue ground with screw top cover, 7in. diameter. (Ewbank) £580 $957

A pair of Moorcroft 'Cornflower' vases, of baluster form, painted and tube-lined on a white ground, signature and date *1914*, 31cm. (Tennants) £3,500 $5,740

A Moorcroft 'Poppy' vase, of baluster form, tube-lined and painted with three flower heads in pink and purple, circa 1930, 18.5cm. (Tennants) £420 $689

A pair of Moorcroft Macintyre circular plaques, painted and tube-lined with poppies and cornflowers on an ivory ground, circa 1900–10, 27cm. (Tennants) £3,400 $5,576

A Moorcroft 'Anemone' lamp base, tube-lined and painted with four open and three closed flower heads in tones of pink and blue, circa 1930, 32cm. (Tennants) £850 $1,394

A Morrisware vase, designed by George Cartlidge, of cylindrical form with knopped neck painted with stylised cornflowers, 31cm. high. (Christie's)   £1,725 $2,588

A Morrisware footed vase, designed by George Cartlidge, painted with poppies, in shades of pink and blue on a green ground, 17cm. high. (Christie's)   £1,150 $1,725

A large S. Hancock & Sons Morrisware baluster vase, decorated with mauve and inky blue thistles on a greeny yellow ground, 32.9cm. high.
(Christie's)   £1,250 $2,000

NEWCOMB

Newcomb Pottery vase, decorated with three trees in Spanish moss with a large moon, 6in. high. (Skinner)   £552 $920

Fine Newcomb College high glaze mug, decorated by Amelie Roman, thrown by Joseph Meyer, depicting five rabbits running and seated in the woods, 4in. high. (Skinner)   £2,587 $4,313

Exceptional Newcomb College carved matte vase, decorated by Anna Frances Simpson, thrown by Jonathan Hunt, depicting five live oaks with Spanish moss and a finely detailed landscape, 5¼in. high. (Skinner)   £2,760 $4,600

NEWHALL

A Newhall type coffee pot, painted with two bouquets and floral sprigs below a wavy dot line and garland border, circa 1790, 23cm. (Tennants)   £320 $525

A New Hall part tea and coffee service painted with pattern of gilt scrolls on an orange band, painted pattern numbers, circa 1810. (Christie's)   £632 $1,011

A late 18th century New Hall porcelain cream jug, helmet shaped with pattern No 241 depicting a floral spray, 4½in. high. (Andrew Hartley)   £85 $143

A Robinson & Leadbeater Parian porcelain bust of Benjamin Disraeli, Conservative Prime Minister, 38.5cm. high.
(Bearne's)   £270 $445

A Parian porcelain figure of a wood nymph with deer, after an original model by Charles Bell Birch, 50.5cm. high. (Bearne's)   £1,050 $1,732

A Parian bust of Clytie after an original by C. Delpech, probably Copeland, 35cm. high.
(Bearne's)   £320 $528

PARIS

A pair of Paris porcelain Schneeballen vases, late 19th century, in the white, of pear form, applied with flowerheads, fruiting branches and birds, 11in.
(Sotheby's)   £862 $1,440

A pair of Paris two-handled krater vases, circa 1825, decorated by Feuillet, the neck painted with continuous Italianate landscapes, 13¼in. high.
(Christie's)   £4,830 $8,050

A pair of Paris gold-ground two-handled vases, circa 1815, painted in colours with mythological scenes, 21¾in. high.
(Christie's)   £8,970 $14,950

A fine pair of platinum ground porcelain vases, Paris, dated 1878, the bodies painted with flowering cacti, exotic birds and butterflies, 56cm. high.
(Sotheby's)   £26,450 $43,642

A Paris cabinet plate, the centre painted with an equestrian huntsman with hunting horn in a river landscape, circa 1820, 23cm. diameter. (Christie's) £200 $320

A pair of Paris two-handled amphora vases, circa 1850, the black bodies each with classical figures, 17in. high.
(Christie's)   £4,025 $6,721

A Yorkshire pearlware figure of a spotted horse, standing four square, with turned head and black, green, blue and claret colouring, 19th century, 43cm.
(Tennants)   £8,500 $13,940

A pearlware blue and white baluster coffee pot and cover, perhaps Swansea, printed with the 'Long Bridge' pattern below brown line rims, circa 1810, 29cm. high.
(Christie's)   £207 $331

An early 19th century pearlware puzzle jug, the pierced neck above an ovoid body transfer printed in underglaze blue with foliage, circa 1820, 19cm. high. (Cheffins Grain & Comins)   £600 $960

PENNINGTON

A Penningtons Liverpool creamware sparrow beak jug painted & printed with floral sprays and banding, in blue and iron red, 3½in. high.
(Andrew Hartley)   £55 $92

A Penningtons Liverpool creamware teapot of globular form, painted and printed with floral sprays and banding, in blue and iron red, 8in. wide.
(Andrew Hartley)   £150 $252

A Liverpool porcelain 'Chelsea ewer' cream-jug, probably Seth Pennington's factory, spirally fluted and moulded with a band of leaves, 3in. high, circa 1780-90.
(Christie's)   £250 $400

PILKINGTON

A Pilkington Lancastrian vase, compressed ovoid form, by Richard Joyce, painted with a band of fish to the shoulder, 1918, 12cm. high.
(Christie's)   £253 $380

A Pilkington Lancastrian vase, by Charles Cundall, ovoid with cylindrical neck, painted with panels of fritillary and daisy flowers, datemark 1911, 19cm. high.
(Christie's)   £200 $320

A Pilkington Lancastrian bowl by William S Mycock, the well painted with a stylised flower, the rim with maple leaves, datemark 1930, 27.5cm. diameter.
(Christie's)   £103 $165

A Poole Pottery Studio charger painted with an abstract plant design in green, orange and black on an orange ground, 13½in. wide. (Andrew Hartley) £210 $353

A Poole pottery Portuguese Stripe vase, shouldered form painted with alternating panels of blue and pink, blue and yellow stripes, 15cm. high. (Christie's) £69 $110

'Night and Day', a Poole Studio dish by Tony Morris, painted with an Aztec 'Sun-face' above reflected image, in shades of blue and orange. (Christie's) £1,035 $1,656

A Poole pottery vase, by Hilda Trim, painted with geometric flowers and foliage in shades of yellow, grey and black on a white ground, 16.5cm. high. (Christie's) £253 $405

'The Love Birds', a Poole pottery figure group, modelled by Harry Brown, on oval base covered in a green, blue and brown Picotee glaze, 20cm. high. (Christie's) £149 $238

A Poole Atlantis vase, thrown by Jennie Haigh, shouldered form painted with simple brushstroke motif, in shades of green on a mottled brown ground, 17cm. high. (Christie's) £115 $184

PUB JUGS

An Old Rarity Scotch Whisky jug by Highland China, 4in. high. (Gordon Litherland) £35 $56

A Seagrams Grand National jug 'Royal Athlete', by Seton Pottery, 1995, in a limited edition of 6,000, 5¾in. high. (Gordon Litherland) £60 $96

A Macbeth Scotch Whisky jug by Lord Nelson Pottery, 1972, in a limited edition of 500, 6¾in. high. (Gordon Litherland) £120 $192

A blue and white oblong octagonal soup-tureen, cover and stand, Qianlong, finely painted with leafy lotus and peony sprays 15in. wide. (Christie's) £2,645 $4,391

A Ming-style yellow-ground blue and white dish, Qianlong seal mark and of the period, 21.2cm. diameter. (Christie's) £4,500 $7,200

A pair of famille rose models of cockerels, Qianlong, each standing proudly astride an earth-coloured rock, 9¾in. high. (Christie's) £6,325 $10,310

A fine and rare blue and white hexagonal vase, Qianlong seal mark and of the period, painted in a deep cobalt-blue with a variety of fruiting and flowering sprays between geometric scrolling leaf designs, 26in. high. (Christie's) £62,000 $101,060

A pair of famille rose models of cranes, Qianlong, each modelled standing with raised neck, before a gnarled prunus tree, 9in. high. (Christie's) £14,950 $24,369

A fine blue and white bottle vase, yuhuchunping, Qianlong seal mark and of the period, painted in a rich cobalt blue Imitating 'heaping and piling' around the sides with plantain, bamboo and rockwork, 11⅜in. high. (Christie's) £16,100 $26,243

A rare gilt-decorated celadon-ground Tibetan-style ewer, Qianlong seal mark and of the period, the globular body with a monster mask issuing an S-shaped spout, 8in. high. (Christie's) £2,530 $4,124

A pair of blue and white turquoise-ground vases and covers, late Qianlong, the flattened sides with shaped panels painted with ladies seated on rockwork beside grazing sheep before a lakescape, 17½in. high. (Christie's) £7,475 $12,408

Quimper faience charger, France, circa 1930, polychrome decorated with floral banded borders and central landscape, 18in. diameter. (Skinner) £643 $1,035

Quimper pottery teapot and cover with a snake handle and spout, 7in. (Woolley & Wallis) £150 $240

Quimper circular balustered covered two handled soup tureen and four soup bowls, all decorated with typical stylised foliage in puce, green and blue, tureen 10in., bowls 9in. (G.A. Key) £32 $53

REDWARE

A glazed redware flower pot and saucer, Pennsylvania, 19th century, cylindrical tapering, with double ruffled rim, 9in. high. (Christie's) £1,300 $2,080

A very rare pair of figural redware lions, attributed to John Bell, Waynesboro, Pennsylvania, mid-19th century, 6½in. high. (Sotheby's) £5,963 $9,775

Slip decorated Redware pottery flower pot, America, mid-19th century, yellow slip decoration *1864* within two wavy lines, attributed to Harvey Brooks, Goshen, Connecticut, diameter 5³/₈in. (Skinner) £791 $1,265

ROBJ

A Robj pottery tobacco jar and cover, each side modelled with a stylised Aztec mask, under a celadon green glaze, 24cm. high. (Christie's) £253 $409

A Robj pottery figure, modelled as a stylised negro drum player, wearing white and black suit, 16.5cm. high. (Christie's) £300 $480

A Robj decanter and stopper, modelled as three stylised sailors standing back to back, wearing blue and white uniforms, 27.5cm. high. (Christie's) £400 $640

A Rockingham porcelain shoe inkwell, with tied bow and matt blue colouring with gilt edging, 1830–42, 12.5cm.
(Tennants)   £450 $738

A garniture of three Rockingham stork handled vases, painted with floral sprays, 1830–42, 37cm and 27.5cm.
(Tennants)   £3,800 $6,232

A Rockingham porcelain inkstand, the rectangular stand with twin handles and flower encrusted edging, 1830–42, 31cm.
(Tennants)   £3,200 $5,248

A Rockingham porcelain figure of John Liston as 'Lubin Log', carrying a hat box, umbrella, bag and a coat, circa 1830, 18cm.
(Tennants)   £720 $1,181

A 19th century Rockingham pattern tea set decorated in green and gilt, teapot, sugar basin and cover and milk jug. (Dee Atkinson & Harrison)
                              £170 $280

A Rockingham porcelain figure of a milkmaid, modelled carrying a pail in one hand, 1826–30, 18.5cm.
(Tennants)   £1,700 $2,788

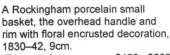

A Rockingham porcelain small basket, the overhead handle and rim with floral encrusted decoration, 1830–42, 9cm.
(Tennants)   £420 $689

A pair of Rockingham porcelain vases, each painted on one side with a colourful bouquet of flowers on a gold decorated deep blue ground, 25.7cm. high.
(Bearne's)   £2,300 $3,680

A Rockingham porcelain trumpet vase, of flared form, painted with a floral panel, 1826–30, 11cm.
(Tennants)   £420 $689

Rookwood vellum glaze scenic plaque, 1913, landscape of lake, trees, and distant mountains in colours of blue, ivory, and pink, 8in. high. (Skinner) £1,587 $2,645

Large Rookwood Pottery modelled matte glaze vase, 1910, decorated by William Ernst Hentschel, raised flower under a mottled matte green and rose glaze, 10in. high. (Skinner) £518 $863

Fine Rookwood Pottery tile, decorated with recessed design of sailing ship under a dark green, tobacco brown and red matte glaze, tile 8in. square. (Skinner) £518 $863

ROSENTHAL

Rosenthal white glazed figure group, modelled as nude female riding the back of an ostrich, 18in. high. (Skinner) £552 $920

A Rosenthal porcelain figure group, modelled as three Bacchanalian revellers, with two bare-breasted maidens, walking forward either side of a partially naked drunken male, 20cm. high. (Christie's) £287 $463

A Rosenthal figural clock, 1920s, white-glazed porcelain, with pink, yellow and green highlights surmounted by a stylised female nude, flanked by a small boy blowing a trumpet, 14in. (Sotheby's) £1,265 $2,100

ROYAL COPENHAGEN

A Royal Copenhagen model of Adam and Eve, both are kneeling amidst a heap of fruit while the fair skinned Eve offers black Adam an apple, 5.5in. (Woolley & Wallis) £310 $496

Twelve Royal Copenhagen 'Flora Danica' plates, Denmark, 20th century, each with raised panelled border and enamel decorated botanical design, 10in. diameter. (Skinner) £4,714 $7,590

A Royal Copenhagen figure, modelled by Carl-Johan Bonnesen, of a clown linking arms with two grey bears who dance alongside him, 29.5cm. high. (Christie's) £977 $1,578

A pair of Royal Dux classical figurines, she holding an urn on her right shoulder and he carrying a basket on his left shoulder, 14in. high. (Dee Atkinson & Harrison) £700 $1,120

A Royal Dux figure of the Shepherd Boy David, standing semi nude about to cast a stone, signed *P Aichels*, 24¼in. high. (Andrew Hartley) £300 $504

A pair of colourful Royal Dux figures, both wearing court costume, he playing a violin, 59cm. high. (Bearne's) £1,550 $2,557

An Art Deco Royal Dux figural ashtray, reputedly modelled on Greta Garbo. (Academy Auctioneers) £170 $272

A pair of Royal Dux figures in conversation, she holding an open fan, 44.5cm. high. (Bearne's) £1,450 $2,392

A Royal Dux Godiva like group, of a naked young woman riding side saddle, 46.5cm. high. (Bearne's) £900 $1,485

A Royal Dux porcelain model of an Indian elephant, its mahout in pink and green costume with gold slippers 27cm. high. (Bearne's) £270 $445

A Royal Dux porcelain figure of a goatherd, the young man wearing a bearskin over his tunic standing with a goat at his side, 52cm. high. (Bearne's) £460 $736

A Royal Dux figure group modelled as two seated hounds, oval base, applied pink triangle mark, 25cm. high. (Wintertons) £650 $1,073

RUSKIN   CHINA

A Ruskin high-fired stoneware vase, baluster form with everted rim, pitted mint green and sang de boeuf spots running to lavender base rim, 1905, 17cm. high.
(Christie's)   £1,725 $2,760

A Ruskin high-fired egg-shell stoneware bowl, with dark mottled red glaze clouding to green and purple towards the foot, 21cm. diameter.
(Christie's)   £1,500 $2,400

An unusual Ruskin stoneware vase, slender, shouldered form, incised with vertical linear decoration, covered in a blue lustre glaze, 1923, 31.5cm. high.
(Christie's)   £977 $1,563

RUSSIAN

A Michaelevsky figure of a soldier, circa 1845, leaning on a tree-stump, curling his moustache, 10¾in.
(Sotheby's)   £805 $1,344

A tazza from The Kremlin Service, the centres of the saucer-shaped dish with the Imperial eagle, 7½in.
(Sotheby's)   £2,415 $4,033

A rare pair of Imperial porcelain figures of Ottoman Janissaries, period of Catherine II, circa 1770, modelled after J.J. Kaendler, 6in.
(Sotheby's)   £4,600 $7,682

SAMSON

A large pair of Samson famille rose baluster jars and domed covers, 19th century, painted with continuous bands of peacocks and butterflies, 27½in. high.
(Christie's)   £4,025 $6,520

A fine Samson and gilt-bronze pot pourri vase, Paris, circa 1870, of hexagonal form, the cover with a foliate finial, 41cm. high.
(Sotheby's)   £4,830 $7,969

A large pair of Samson baluster vases, the domed covers with iron brown dog of Fo finials, each decorated in polychrome with exotic birds amidst bamboo and peony, late 19th century, 36.5in.
(Woolley & Wallis)   £1,900 $3,040

A Satsuma shallow bowl, the interior painted with four people in a garden, 12.6cm. diameter, signed. (Bearne's)   £840 $1,386

A Satsuma pottery koro of square tapering form, the reserves depicting figures in a garden, signed, 8in. high. (Andrew Hartley)   £230 $386

A Satsuma Pottery shallow dish, the cavetto painted with a warrior and his attendants in an extensive river landscape, 30.5cm. diameter, signed. (Bearne's)   £240 $396

A 19th century Satsuma Pottery vase, the upper part painted with birds amongst autumnal branches, signed 9in. high. (Andrew Hartley)   £900 $1,512

A pair of Satsuma ovoid vases, 19th century, moulded in relief with flowering chrysanthemums issuing from pierced rockwork, 12½in. high. (Christie's)   £1,495 $2,421

A Satsuma vase of ovoid form with short neck, boldly and brightly painted with peonies and hawthorn, 25cm. high, signed. (Bearne's)   £520 $858

Satsuma Imperial baluster vase with short everted neck, painted and gilt with a continuous band of irises and grasses, 11¾in. high. (Christie's)   £460 $736

A pair of Satsuma vases, signed *Kusubu,* Meiji period, 19th century, decorated in gilt with panels depicting temples and figures, each 7½in. high. (Christie's)   £1,725 $2,812

A Satsuma Imperial model of Guanyin, seated on a rockwork base wearing flowing robes and a high cowl and holding a ruyi sceptre in her hands, 9¼in. high. (Christie's)   £690 $1,104

Saturday Evening Girls Pottery decorated motto pitcher, Boston, Massachusetts, early 20th century, 9¾in. high.
(Skinner)   £1,143 £2,200

Two Saturday Evening Girls paperweights, sailboat and windmill design, one unmarked, one signed, 2½in. diameter.
(Skinner)   £395 $632

Saturday Evening Girls Pitcher, 1911, decorated by Sara Galner with six squirrels in black outline with a blue background on a porous cream ground, 4½in. high.
(Skinner)   £518 $863

SAVONA

An Italian tureen and cover, possibly Savona, blue painted with woodland animals and insects, 42.5cm. (Bonhams)   £300 $480

A Savona (Jacques Boselly) bottle, circa 1780, of globular form, the central sunbursts about a crowned oval medallion with the monogram *IHS*, 7½in. high.
(Christie's)   £800 $1,280

A Savona blue and white plate, painted with a woman under a stormy sky carrying a tambourine, 29.2cm. diameter, painted *G.F.* under a crown.
(Bearne's)   £240 $396

SÈVRES

A French biscuit bust of an 18th century shepherdess, Sèvres style, spurious blue interlaced L's mark, the young woman en deshabille and wearing a straw hat, 30¾in. high. (Christie's)   £2,760 $4,600

A Sèvres dark-blue-ground compressed teapot and cover, the compressed globular body painted with a band of flowers above a gilt fluted lower section, potter's date for 1840, 13.5cm. high.
(Christie's)   £1,725 $2,760

A pair of gilt-metal mounted French cobalt-blue ground vases, Sèvres style, late 19th century, of shield shape, the bracket handles with female mask terminals, 24¾in. high. (Christie's)   £2,760 $4,600

A 'Sevres' plate, painted in coloured enamels with a named view *Chateau Ambriose*, the blue ground decorated in gilt, 9½in. diameter. (Dreweatt Neate) £400 $660

A Sèvres écuelle, cover and stand, with six later painted reserves of busy harbour scenes, circa 1770, 26cm. (Tennants) £3,700 $5,920

A Sèvres dated polychrome rectangular plaque painted by Marie-Pauline Laurent, dated 1830, after the portrait by Titian of the Donna allo Specchio, 10⁷⁄₈ x 13⁵⁄₈in. (Christie's) £4,600 $7,682

A 19th century Sèvres coffee service, moulded rococo spiral fluting painted with alternating panels of flowers in natural colours and floral, husk and scroll giltwork on bleu-de-ciel, 21 pieces. (Russell Baldwin & Bright) £620 $1,023

A Sèvres biscuit porcelain figure group of a gallant and companion third quarter of 19th century, modelled seated on a bench with cupid spying from a tree behind, 12½in. (Sotheby's) £460 $768

A Sèvres cup and saucer, each piece painted by Charles-Nicolas Dodin, the elaborately gilded borders with tooled oval medallions, code for 1778, the cup 7.5cm. (Tennants) £9,500 $15,200

A pair of 'Sèvres' gilt-bronze porcelain vases, Paris, circa 1880, painted with young girls and cupids in a landscape with classical ruins, 68cm. high. (Sotheby's) £11,500 $18,975

A Shelley Pink Sweet Pea Queen Anne part service, comprising six cups, saucers and plates and a large plate; and other Sweet Pea items. (Bonhams) £250 $400

A twelve piece Shelley tea service in 'diamond pattern'. (Dockrees) £2,300 $3,680

A Shelley Queen Anne coffee pot, decorated with coral flowers; together with a coral Daisy part tea service for six, 18.5cm. (Bonhams) £300 $480

SONG

A fine black-glazed ribbed globular jar, Song dynasty, the rounded body slip decorated with a dense pattern of vertical lines creating oil-black, olive green and brown stripes, 8½in. high. (Christie's) £6,900 $11,247

A small purple-splashed Junyao bowl, and a Junyao-type saucer-dish, the bowl Song dynasty, the saucer dish probably Ming dynasty, the dish 6¼in. diameter. (Christie's) £51,000 $83,130

A fine black-glazed ribbed globular jar, Song Dynasty, the globular body with slip-applied vertical striations and wide cylindrical neck with lipped rim, 9in. high. (Christie's) £3,450 $5,727

SPODE

A garniture of three early 19th century Spode bulbous two-handled urns, each enamelled in orange, blue, green and gilt with a 'Japan' pattern, 8¼in. high, 6in. high. (Canterbury) £920 $1,518

An English porcelain dark-blue and platinum-ground two handled bowl, and stand, probably Spode, painted with a band of garden flowers, circa 1810, 19.5cm. wide. (Christie's) £1,265 $2,024

A pair of 19th century two handled oviform covered Spode vases, hand painted with a landscape panel within a radiating gilt border, 10in. high. (Dee Atkinson & Harrison) £2,000 $3,300

A pair of Staffordshire pottery equestrian spill vase groups, late 19th century, each mottled with a mare with a recumbent foal at her side, 12in. high.
(Sotheby's)   £1,122 $1,840

A Staffordshire pink lustre political jug, printed in sepia with a portrait of T.W. Beaumont M.P. for the County of Staffordshire 1826, circa 1826, 12cm.
(Tennants)   £700 $1,148

A pair of Staffordshire figural groups, second half 19th century, mottled with a boy and girl on the back of a seated billy goat, height of tallest 12¼in.
(Sotheby's)   £702 $1,150

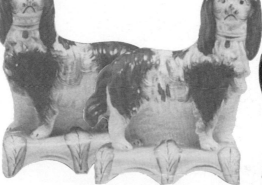

A Staffordshire 'Historical Blue' printed earthenware pitcher, circa 1825, printed in underglaze-blue, depicting the landing of General Lafayette at Castle Garden, New York, 16 August 1824, 8in. high.
(Sotheby's)   £552 $920

A pair of Staffordshire pottery figures of spaniels, second half 19th century, each moulded with a shaggy coat painted in iron red, 7¾in. high.
(Sotheby's)   £3,175 $5,175

A Staffordshire agateware baluster milk-jug and cover, circa 1750, with pinched lip and strap handle, on three lion's mask paw feet, the cover with a recumbent lion finial, 5¾in. high overall.
(Christie's)   £1,725 $2,880

A Staffordshire Gaudy Dutch pearlware large coffee pot and cover, circa 1800, with flattened flower finial, domed cover and bracket handle, 10¼in. high.
(Christie's)   £1,222 $1,955

A Staffordshire blue printed pearlware oval two handled footbath, circa 1820, the hooped vertical sides decorated with a continuous English landscape, 14½in. wide.
(Sotheby's)   £1,380 $2,305

A Victorian earthenware Christening egg, printed in black with a couple and a dog watching goldfish in a bowl, Sunderland or Staffordshire, 6.5cm.
(Tennants)   £260 $426

Staffordshire figure, a girl and dog, 10¼in. high. (Eldred's) £144 $231

Pair of 19th century Staffordshire figures of Victoria and Prince Albert, both painted in colours, naturalistic faces and body markings, 6in. (G.A. Key) £200 $320

A 19th century Staffordshire Mr Punch toby jug, 10in. high. (Dee Atkinson & Harrison) £110 $176

Staffordshire Toby jug, modelled as a seated hearty goodfellow, painted in colours, 19th century, 10in. (G.A. Key) £310 $496

Pair of late 19th century Staffordshire figures of elephants surmounted by seated figures and leopards, 7½in. high. (Lawrences) £1,000 $1,610

An early 19th century Staffordshire earthenware figure of John Wesley, depicted in white bands and black robes, 8¼in. (Andrew Hartley) £180 $302

A 19th century Staffordshire pottery male figure in Arabian dress with orange turban and pink coat, 9¼in. high. (Andrew Hartley) £200 $336

Two Staffordshire pearlware figures of dogs, probably by Enoch Wood, early 19th century, each seated on a canted rectangular cushion and base, height of tallest 7in. (Sotheby's) £2,105 $3,450

A 19th century Staffordshire pottery figure of John Wesley, depicted standing holding an open Bible, wearing blue bands, 7¼in. high. (Andrew Hartley) £100 $168

A rare Victorian Staffordshire flat back group of a seated Mr Punch and his dog, the group brightly painted, height 11¾in.
(David Lay) £480 $768

Pair of Staffordshire seated spaniels, clutching baskets of flowers in their mouths, yellow eyes, black noses, late 19th century, 8in.
(Aylsham) £1,050 $1,743

Staffordshire study of Napoleon Bonaparte reclining against an outcrop and clutching a book in his left hand, painted in colours, 19th century, 8in. (Aylsham) £110 $182

A pair of 19th century Staffordshire figures, a King and Queen on horseback, painted cobalt blue, orange, green and black, 8in. high.
(Dee Atkinson & Harrison)
£190 $304

A 19th century Staffordshire pottery figure group depicting the Vicar and Moses in black cassocks seated in a brown glazed two tier pulpit, 10in. high. (Andrew Hartley) £210 $353

Two 19th century Staffordshire bookends, in the form of seated gentlemen in blue coat and waistcoat, 7in. high.
(Dee Atkinson & Harrison)
£2,300 $3,795

HISTORICAL FACT

The Four Seasons are often represented in symbolic terms on sculpture, porcelain, embroidery and even marquetry on furniture.
Spring can be shown as a young woman holding flowers, often with garlands in her hair or holding a spade. Summer may have a sickle and be holding corn and fruit. Autumn is often associated with grapes and vine leaves, and Winter is sometimes depicted as an old man wearing a thick coat or cloak.
Cotswold Auction Company

A 19th century Staffordshire spill vase in the form of a cow being milked by a young boy seated on a stool, 8½in. high. (Dee Atkinson & Harrison) £90 $144

An assembled pair of Staffordshire pottery greyhounds, late 19th/early 20th century, possibly Kent, each with grey body and painted facial details, 12in. high.
(Skinner) £982 $1,610

A brown stoneware Bartmannkrug, Cologne or Frechen, circa 1550, of stout bulbous form, with bearded mask to neck of the body, 8½in. (Sotheby's) £920 $1,536

A 19th century reed 'stoneware' two handled cup, blue printed pastoral scene with figures before a cottage and floral border, 6in. high. (Andrew Hartley) £250 $420

Three-gallon stoneware crock, 19th century, by J. & E. Norton, cobalt blue decoration of a nightingale perched on a branch. (Eldred's) £366 $605

SUNDERLAND LUSTRE

A purple lustre jug, printed on one side with *A West View of the Iron Bridge near Sunderland*, 18cm. high. (Bearne's) £300 $495

Antique English Sunderland lustre pitcher, 'The Sailor's Farewell' on one side, martial arms flanked by flags on reverse, 8½in. high. (Eldred's) £378 $605

A large purple lustre jug, a nautical verse below the spout, printed and painted on one side with a portrait of 'The Great Australian Clipper-ship', 23cm. high. (Bearne's) £440 $726

TANG

A straw and amber-glazed pottery horse, Tang dynasty, modelled standing four-square, the raised head slightly tilted to the left, 14in. wide. (Christie's) £3,680 $5,998

Two painted pottery matrons, Tang dynasty, each modelled standing with both arms raised before the chest, one figure modelled looking to the left and wearing a loose top-knot, 14¼in. and 13¼in. high. (Christie's) £5,520 $8,998

A fine stone head of a Bodhisattva, Tang dynasty, the round face with a calm expression finely carved with a small angular nose below arched eyebrows, 17½in. high, fitted wood stand. (Christie's) £19,550 $31,867

A Tournai two-handled double-lipped sauceboat with osier-moulded border, painted in blue with scattered sprays of flowers, circa 1760, 18.5cm. wide. (Christie's) £200 $320

A Tournai blue-ground armorial écuelle, cover and stand, circa 1760, painted by Henri-Joseph Duvivier, the lobed circular écuelle with two entwined foliage loop handles, the écuelle 7¾in. wide. (Christie's) £60,900 $101,703

A Tournai (later decorated) flower-encrusted pot pourri and cover, with a turquoise and gilt caillouté ground, on rocky mound base with seated putto and hound, 18th century, 22cm. high. (Christie's) £400 $640

VAN BRIGGLE

Van Briggle pottery copper clad vase, Colorado, 5½in. high. (Skinner) £850 $1,275

A Van Briggle pottery bowl, the underside formed as a large shell, with the reclining figure of a mermaid to one side, 39cm. diameter. (Christie's) £1,000 $1,550

Fine Van Briggle pottery vase, 1904(?), cylindrical tapering form with speckled matte green glaze at shoulder graduating to smooth green glaze at base, 8½in. high. (Skinner) £448 $748

VENICE

A Venice maiolica istoriato dish, circa 1560, painted with the story of Rachel meeting Jacob at the well, 13in. diameter. (Christie's) £5,175 $8,642

A white porcelain allegorical group of Hebe and the eagle of Jupiter, Cozzi, Venice, circa 1780, 11.6cm. (Finarte) £528 $846

A Venice istoriato shallow bowl circa 1560, painted with Bathsheba scantily draped and bathing in a rectangular fountain before flower-beds in a fenced courtyard, 12¼in. diameter. (Christie's) £1,500 $2,400

A large Vienna circular wall plaque, painted by H. Stadler with Diana the Huntress, with attendant nymphs, late 19th century, 49cm.
(Tennants) £2,800 $4,592

A Vienna bacchic group emblematic of Autumn modelled with three putti and a satyr with garlands of fruiting vine, circa 1765, 23.5cm. high.
(Christie's) £253 $405

A Vienna (Du Paquier) large shaped saucer dish (Grosse Schüssel), circa 1730, painted in Schwarzlot with a vignette of Dido and Aeneas within a border, 14⅝in. diameter.
(Christie's) £11,040 $18,400

VINCENNES

A Vincennes cup and saucer, painted with three shaped panels of flower sprays divided by large green scrolls with gilt detailing, circa 1755. (Woolley & Wallis) £420 $697

A Vincennes white biscuit figure of 'Le Batelier de Saint-Cloud', circa 1755, modelled after Boucher, standing in a hat, jacket, waistcoat tied with a sash, breeches and shoes, 9¼in. high.
(Christie's) £1,380 $2,208

A Vincennes bleu lapis two-handled chocolate-cup, cover and stand (gobelet à lait et soucoupe), 1756, painted en camaieu bleu with Cupid playing a lyre, the stand 7¼in. diam. (Christie's) £12,650 $21,125

VOLKSTEDT

A pair of Volkstedt figures of a gallant and companion modelled standing facing left and right poised in dance, late 19th century, 25cm. and 24cm. high.
(Christie's) £437 $699

A Volkstedt hen tureen and cover, circa 1780, with pale-brown, dark brown, black and white plumage, 17.5cm. long.
(Christie's) £3,000 $4,800

A Volkstedt group of bird-nesters, circa 1775, modelled as a young man climbing down from the branches of a tree, 10⅜in. high.
(Christie's) £1,437 $2,399

A Wedgwood porcelain Fairyland lustre octagonal bowl, the exterior decorated with 'Castle on a Road' pattern, 7¼in. wide.
(Andrew Hartley) £1,600 $2,688

A Wedgwood earthenware vase, designed by Keith Murray, ribbed spherical form, covered in a matt green, 18cm. high.
(Christie's)   £460 $690

A Wedgwood butterfly lustre octagonal bowl, the orange lustre interior decorated with gold butterflies round a central medallion, 24.5cm. diameter.
(Bearne's)   £460 $736

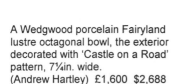

A Wedgwood black basalt hare's head stirrup-cup, the collar inscribed in iron red enamel _Success to bowl away & the merry Harriers of Newton_, circa 1785, 17cm. high.(Christie's) £920 $1,472

A pair of Wedgwood blue and white jasperware pot pourri vases and covers, with pierced circular internal fitments, each raised upon three dolphin supports, early 19th century, 5in.
(Woolley & Wallis) £1,800 $2,880

A Wedgwood earthenware vase, designed by Keith Murray, shouldered, flaring cylindrical form, incised with horizontal bands, 20cm. high. (Christie's) £345 $517

A pair of ormolu-mounted Wedgwood dark-blue jasperware urns, circa 1900, each of circular form with a fixed top, 8½in. high.
(Christie's)   £1,207 $2,003

Wedgwood 19th century copy of the Portland vase, typically moulded pâte sur pâte with mythological scenes, on a black ground, 11in.
(G.A. Key)   £450 $747

A pair of Wedgwood pearlware inverted baluster pot pourri, covers and liners, printed and painted in a bright palette with peonies and chrysanthemum, circa 1820, 40cm. high. (Christie's) £2,760 $4,416

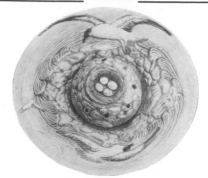

Weller Flemish-style umbrella stand, applied curling design in green, brown, and ivory, 20in. high. (Skinner)   £155 $258

Weller Glendale console bowl and flower holder, raised designs in yellow, blue, green, and brown, marked *Weller*, 15½in. diameter. (Skinner)   £414 $690

Weller Woodcraft basket vase, green and brown colours, unmarked, 9¾in. high. (Skinner)   £138 $230

Weller Pottery vase, six raised leaves under a feathered matte glaze, unsigned, 14in. high. (Skinner)   £448 $748

Weller Dickensware art pottery mantel clock, housed in elaborate pottery frame decorated with yellow pansies, 10in. high. (Skinner)   £249 $440

Weller Forest vase, raised design in colours of green and brown, marked *54*, 12in. high, 6½in. diameter. (Skinner)   £395 $632

Weller Woodcraft vase, applied squirrel and owl design in colours of brown and green, impressed *Weller*, 18½in. high. (Skinner)   £655 $1,092

Weller Pottery Etna pot, Zanesville, Ohio, high gloss glazed and decorated with low relief flowers in rose, yellow, white and green, 4½in. high. (Skinner)   £65 $100

Weller Pottery jardinière and pedestal, signed *Ferrell*, banded sunflower design in brown, green and ivory on a matte light green field, impressed *Weller*, 38½in. high. (Skinner)   £759 $1,265

A Wemyss pig, modelled seated upon its haunches and with black and white markings, early 20th century, 16cm.
(Tennants)   £1,050 $1,722

One of a pair of Wemyss chamber pots, decorated with cherries, 21.7cm.
(Bonhams) (Two)   £400 $640

A Wemyss Ware Audley bowl-on-stand, painted with cabbage roses, impressed and painted Wemyss marks, 6½in. high.
(Christie's)   £500 $800

WHIELDON

A creamware teapot and cover, the lined globular body decorated in the Whieldon manner in green and brown on a cream ground, 8½cm. high. (Bearne's) £600 $960

A Whieldon cow creamer and cover, circa 1760, 6½in. high.
(Christie's) £1,700 $2,720

A Whieldon teapot and cover, mid 18th century, of bullet form on three volute feet, moulded with a foliate cross between leaf moulded handle and spout, 43.7cm.
(Bonhams)   £500 $800

WIENER WERKSTÄTTE

A Wiener Keramik pottery figure, modelled as a young woman with ringlet hair, wearing long yellow dress, 29.5cm. high.
(Christie's)   £400 $640

Wiener Werkstätte ceramic figurine, Oriental figure with horse in colours of yellow, blue, black, and green on a white ground, 8in. wlde.
(Skinner)   £552 $920

A Weiner Keramik ceramic wall-mask, moulded as a girl's head with a hat, painted in polychrome glazes, 24cm. high.
(Christie's)   £700 $1,120

A Royal Worcester pedestal vase, mounted with grotesque, painted by E.M. Fildes with panels of roses, date code for 1920, 18.5cm. (Tennants) £520 $832

A pair of Worcester (Flight) lobed oval armorial dishes from the Duke of Clarence dessert service, 1789, each richly painted and gilded with the Duke's coat of arms, 11¹/₈in. wide. (Christie's) £9,775 $16,324

A Worcester cream jug, of upright bulbous form, with sparse floral decoration and a ladybird, circa 1770, 10.5cm. (Tennants) £220 $361

A Royal Worcester porcelain figure of a Hereford Bull 'Vern Inspiration', modelled by Doris Lindner, 1959, 6¾in. high. (Canterbury) £440 $726

A Worcester blue scale-ground vase, circa 1775, blue psuedo-Chinese seal mark, of inverted baluster form with a flared neck, painted in the manner of James Giles, 5⁷/₈in. high. (Christie's) £2,875 $4,801

A Royal Worcester porcelain figure of Percheron stallion 'Saltmarsh Silver Crest', modelled by Doris Lindner, 1966, 9½in. high. (Canterbury) £600 $990

A Worcester cabbage leaf mask jug, of typical moulded form, printed in blue, with the 'natural sprays group', workman's mark, circa 1770, 23cm. (Tennants) £280 $459

A Worcester porcelain blue and white quatrefoil tureen, cover and stand, circa 1775, the interior of the tureen and centre of the stand printed with the 'Pine Cone' pattern, 10¾in. long and 11³/₈in. (Sotheby's) £1,897 $3,162

An 18th century Worcester sparrow-beak cream jug enamelled in colours with floral sprays, 3½in. high, circa 1765. (Canterbury) £160 $264

A Worcester blue and white porcelain chesnut basket with twist handles, the interior base printed with the 'Pinecone' pattern, 25cm. wide. (Bearne's)   £520 $832

A Royal Worcester porcelain two-handled jar and cover, painted with roses in the Hadley palette, 24cm., date code for 1919. (Bearne's)   £500 $825

An 18th century Worcester teapot and cover with floral finial, the barrel shape body enamelled in colours with Chinese figures, 5in. high, circa 1765. (Canterbury)   £500 $825

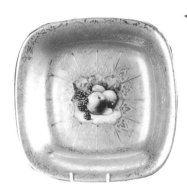

A Royal Worcester square bowl painted central still life of fruit including apples and blackberries, signed *T. Nutt*, 9¹/₅in. (Russell Baldwin & Bright)   £400 $660

A pair of Royal Worcester cylindrical vases with flared necks and footrims, enamelled in colours by J. Stinton with pheasants in a moorland landscape, 4½in. high. (Canterbury)   £500 $800

A Royal Worcester circular bowl, the centre painted by J. Stinton with a pheasant and one other bird in a country landscape, 4¼in. diameter, 1933. (Canterbury)   £140 $224

A Worcester polychrome porcelain sauce boat, the leaf moulded and spiral reeded body brightly painted with sprigs and sprays of flowers, 11cm. long. (Bearne's)   £440 $704

A Royal Worcester porcelain cylindrical vase, with pierced rim and scroll feet, painted by Harry Stinton with cattle in a misty highland landscape, 14.5cm. high, date code for 1912. (Bearne's)   £860 $1,420

A Royal Worcester porcelain figure of a dairy shorthorn bull 'Royal Event', modelled by Doris Lindner, 1966, 7½in. high, no.183 of a limited edition of 500. (Canterbury)   £460 $736

A Worcester porcelain two-handled sauce boat, the interior painted with a Chinese river landscape, flowers and diaper patterns, 19cm long. (Bearne's)　　　£500　$800

A Graingers, Worcester jar and cover, the globular body painted with chrysanthemums in the Hadley palette, circa 1880, 14cm. high. (Bearne's)　　　£520　$858

A Royal Worcester porcelain posy holder in the form of a basket supported by an apricot and ivory glazed swan with a gold decorated band around its neck, date code for 1895, 19cm. high. (Bearne's)　　　£180　$297

A Royal Worcester pot pourri jar with inner and outer pierced cover, the lower portion of the ovoid body moulded with a basket weave pattern, date code for 1903, 15cm. high. (Bearne's)　　£540　$891

A Worcester two-handled sauce tureen, cover and stand, brightly painted with a version of the 'Wheatsheaf' pattern, mid 18th century. (Bearne's) £380　$627

A Worcester lobed ovoid tea canister and domed cover, with flower knop, decorated in gilt with blue London atelier of James Giles, 6½in. circa 1770. (Dreweatt Neate)　　£370　$611

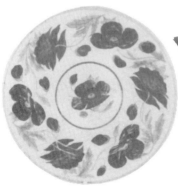

Barr Flight & Barr circular plate, painted in colours with mauve and iron red flowers and green foliage with gilded detail, early 19th century, 8in. (Aylsham)　　　£110　$183

An 18th century Worcester bullet shaped teapot and cover, painted in puce and gilt with foliate sprays and cartouches, 15cm. high. (Wintertons)　　　£300　$495

A Royal Worcester porcelain circular plaque painted by John Stinton with Highland cattle in a landscape, 4¼in. wide. (Andrew Hartley) £1,300 $2,184

Cinematographic camera, G.J. Badgley, 35mm., hand-cranked, polished wood body, film counter with a Goerz Hypar f/3.5, 3in. lens.
(Christie's) £1,840 $2,999

Cinematographic camera no. 521, U.S. cinematograph Co., Chicago, 35mm., hand-cranked, leather-covered wood body, and an Ernemann Ernon f/3.5 50mm. lens no. 32857.
(Christie's) £805 $1,312

Cinematographic camera no. 423, Ernest F. Moy, London; 35mm., wood-body, hand-cranked, with a brass bound lens and crank.
(Christie's) £1,150 $1,840

Cinematographic camera, G. Gennert, New York, 35mm., hand-cranked, polished mahogany body, Goerz Dagor, f/6.8 12.5mm. lens no. 558577, in leather case.
(Christie's) £1,265 $2,062

Universal ciné camera, Universal Camera Co., Chicago, 35mm., hand-cranked, wood body with engine-turned aluminium panels.
(Christie's) £977 $1,592

An Ol'Ywood 35mm ciné camera by Ets. Le Blay, Paris, brass mounted metal case, with Krauss-Tessar Zeiss 1:3,5/5 cm. lens.
(Auction Team Köln)
£1,292 $2,067

Cinematographic camera no. 418, Ernest F. Moy, London, 35mm., wood body, hand-cranked, with a Cooke Cinematograph f/3.5 2in. lens no. 79316.
(Christie's) £2,185 $3,561

Le Parvo cinematographic camera no. 1355, J. Debrie, Paris, 35mm, hand-cranked, polished teak body, with two 120mm., film magazines and Krauss Tessar f/3.5 50mm. lens. (Christie's) £747 $1,217

Cinematographic camera no. 1214, Pathé S.A., Paris, France, 35mm., hand-cranked, leather covered wood body, Bausch & Lomb Tessar 50mm. lens.
(Christie's) £1,092 $1,779

A George III black stained bracket clock, the dial with silvered chapter ring signed *Robt Henderson, London*, 20in. high.
(George Kidner)   £1,800 $2,988

A Queen Anne ebonised grande sonnerie bracket clock, Daniel Quare, London, circa 1700, the case with Quare's typical elaborate double-S baluster handle, 18in. high. (Christie's) £25,300 $41,998

A George III ebonised striking bracket clock, the dial and movement inscribed *Jno. Fladgate, London*, 45cm.
(Bearne's)   £1,650 $2,723

A Queen Anne ebonised small bracket timepiece, Daniel Hawthorn, first quarter 18th century, typical five ringed pillar single fusee movement with later anchor escapement, 12½in. high.
(Christie's)   £1,610 $2,673

A Charles II ebony striking bracket clock, John Fromanteel, London, late 17th century, the case with moulded flat top and large central rectangular panel centred by a gilt-metal handle, 15in. high.
(Christie's)   £6,670 $10,939

A Regency mahogany striking bracket clock, first quarter 19th century, the white-painted Roman dial with strike/silent ring in the arch and signed *DEBOIS & WHEELER*, 15¾in. high.
(Christie's)   £2,760 $4,416

A William and Mary ebonised striking bracket clock, Richard Jarratt, London, circa 1695, the case on bun feet with glazed sides, 14¾in. high.
(Christie's)   £4,370 $7,167

A George I ebony striking bracket clock, Joseph Windmills, London, first quarter, 18th century, the case with foliate cast gilt-metal handle to the inverted bell top, 9¼in. high.
(Christie's)   £4,600 $7,544

A George II gilt-metal mounted oak striking bracket clock, the case with concave moulded top surmounted by a gilt-metal basket of flowers, 15¼in. high.
(Christie's)   £1,035 $1,718

A 19th century bracket clock, 8-day striking movement, in arched rosewood case finely inlaid, 22in. high. (Russell Baldwin & Bright) £1,900 $3,135

A George III ebonised striking bracket clock, the circular cream painted Roman dial inscribed _Jno Wontner, Minories London_, 33cm. (Bearne's) £2,700 $4,459

A George III ebonised striking bracket clock, the twin fusee five-pillar movement with arched brass dial inscribed _John Hiccox, London_, 46cm. (Bearne's) £2,900 $4,785

A Regency mahogany striking bracket clock, Desbois & Wheeler, London, first quarter 19th century, the case with gilt-brass handle on a rectangular pad to the break-arch top, 14½in. high.
(Christie's) £4,370 $7,254

A William and Mary ebony bracket clock, Henry Jones, London, circa 1695, the case with foliate cast handle to the gilt-metal foliate cast basket top, 13¾in. high.
(Christie's) £2,300 $3,772

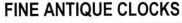

J. Jackson, Bristol, a Regency mahogany bracket clock, with eight day two train fusee movement and anchor escapement, 17in.
(Dreweatt Neate) £1,450 $2,364

A Victorian eight-day mahogany bracket clock, arched brass dial inscribed *J.L Bath. Bath*, with silvered Roman chapter ring, 53cm.
(Bearne's) £1,500 $2,475

Late 19th century mahogany bracket clock, the four corners crested with ball finials, inlaid throughout with satinwood stringing, movement by Archard of London, 19in. high. (G.A. Key) £600 $960

A Regency mahogany striking bracket clock, circa 1825, the case with stepped and chamfered top, signed on the backplate *Barrauds & Lund Cornhill LONDON*, 14¾in. high. (Christie's) £1,725 $2,760

A George IV mahogany bracket clock, twin fusee movement and anchor escapement, striking hours on a bell, brass floral marquetry, 35cm. high.
(Dreweatt Neate) £2,200 $3,586

German gilt metal mounted ebony bracket clock, late 19th century, with quarter strike, foliate mounts and pendulum adjustment in the arch, 17in. high.
(Skinner) £536 $863

A German walnut striking bracket clock, early 20th century, the twin barrel movement with ting-tang strike on two gongs, stamped on the backplate for *LENZKIRCH*, 23½in. high.
(Christie's) £805 $1,290

A Victorian mahogany and gilt-bronze mounted quarter-chiming large bracket clock, last quarter 19th century, the dial signed *BARRAUD & LUNDS 49, CORNHILL,LONDON*, 20¾in. high.
(Christie's) £2,070 $3,312

A late 18th century ebony cased 8 day bracket clock, inscribed *Henry Russell, London*, the sides with fabric backed brass, on a plinth base, 17in.
(Woolley & Wallis) £1,100 $1,771

A French brass striking and repeating carriage clock with alarm, circa 1880, signed *Charles Oudin – Palais-Royal 52 Paris Horloger De La Marine De L'Etat*, 4¾in. high. (Christie's)   £1,150 $1,840

An unusual French gilt-brass carriage clock, with petite sonnerie on a sequence of four gongs, circa 1880, the gorge case with white enamel Roman dial with Arabic five minutes, 6in. high. (Christie's)   £1,380 $2,208

A French engraved gilt-brass striking carriage clock, circa 1840, the multi-piece engraved overall with leafy scrolls, signed *Berrolla A Paris*, 5¼in. high. (Christie's)   £437 $700

A French brass carriage timepiece, circa 1895, the beaded boîte riche case with gilt mask, paste brilliant set bezel to Arabic dial with conforming circlet to ivory portrait miniature of a lady below, 4¾in. high. (Christie's)   £230 $368

A French oval carriage timepiece/aneroid barometer, by Duverdry & Bloquel, with 4.5cm. white enamel circular dials, in a brass oval case with four turned supports, 16cm. with handle raised. (Bristol)   £540 $886

A French small brass striking and repeating carriage clock with alarm, circa 1880, white enamel Roman dial with Arabic five minutes, spade hands, with signature to the centre *Henry Capt Geneve*, 10.5cm. high. (Christie's)   £1,092 $1,747

A French brass and porcelain-mounted striking and repeating carriage clock, circa 1890, with porcelain panels to the sides painted with blue and white flowers, 7½in. high. (Christie's)   £1,725 $2,760

Attractive Edwardian period ormolu carriage clock, rectangular shaped with cast scrolled feet, dated *1906*, gilt painted cream coloured dial, 4in. tall. (Aylsham)   £190 $315

A Victorian gilt-metal and lapis lazuli mounted miniature carriage timepiece, Thomas Cole, London, third quarter 19th century, the case on toupie feet, foliate engraving to sides, 2¾in. high. (Christie's)   £4,140 $6,790

An early Victorian foliate engraved gilt-metal striking giant carriage clock, Barwise, London, second quarter 19th century, the case with substantial reeded handle to the foliate engraved top, 8½in. high.
(Christie's)   £16,675 $27,680

An early Victorian rosewood three-train quarter striking giant four glass clock with chronometer escapement, Grohé, London, second quarter, 19th century, 11¼in. high.
(Christie's)   £56,500 $92,660

An Edwardian tortoiseshell and silver mounted carriage clock, London, 1909, the rectangular case with bellflower mounts to the angles and inlaid with floral swags and trophies, 2¾in. high.
(Christie's)   £1,495 $2,392

An early Victorian ebonised striking four glass clock, James McCabe, London, second quarter, 19th century, the case on gadroon-carved ogee moulded base, 9¼in. high. (Christie's)   £5,980 $9,807

A gilt-metal perpetual calendar humpback carriage timepiece, Frodsham, London, 20th century, the case on bun feet with engine turned sides and top, 6¾in.high,
(Christie's)   £5,175 $8,487

A Victorian gilt-metal striking large carriage clock, John Moore & Sons, London, third quarter 19th century, the case in the Frodsham style, 6¾in. high,
(Christie's)   £5,750 $9,430

A French repeating lever carriage clock, for Hirsbrunner & Co., Shanghai, with white enamel dial, centre seconds and alarm, corniche case, 15cm.
(Tennants)   £480 $768

A Victorian bronzed striking giant carriage clock, James McCabe, London, circa 1850, the case with typical reeded handle to the top with large bevelled glass escapement viewing aperture, 18¾in. high.
(Christie's)   £11,500 $19,090

An ebony and brass inlaid perpetual calendar giant chronometer four glass clock with equation of time, Sinclair Harding, modern, 13½in. high.
(Christie's)   £5,520 $9,053

A Victorian gilt-metal and bronze striking giant carriage clock, Payne, London, circa 1860, the case on bun feet with fluted columns, 9in. high. (Christie's) £2,300 $3,772

A Victorian gilt-metal striking giant carriage clock, James McCabe, London, third quarter 19th century, the case with brass veneered oak carcase on bun feet, 13¼in. high. (Christie's) £8,050 $13,202

A Victorian engraved gilt-brass striking chronometer carriage clock, Arnold Chas. Frodsham, circa 1850, the case by L. Lange. (Christie's) £9,200 $15,088

A French gilt-metal mounted ebonised quarter-striking travel clock, 20th century, rectangular case with foliate cast gilt-metal mounts, on toupie feet, dial with silvered Roman chapter ring and engraved centre, signed *Breguet & Fils PARIS.*(Christie's) £747 $1,195

A Victorian gilt-metal quarter striking giant travelling clock, Lund & Blockley, fourth quarter, 19th century, the case of heavy architectural form, 10½in. high. (Christie's) £54,300 $89,052

A French brass and Limoges enamel-mounted grande sonnerie carriage clock with alarm, circa 1885, plain columns and Corinthian capitals, dentil cornices, with Limoges enamel side panels, 18cm. high. (Christie's) £6,900 $11,040

A French brass striking and repeating carriage clock with alarm, the strike, repeat and alarm on one gong to the backplate, 16.5cm. (Bearne's) £760 $1,254

A Victorian striking giant bronze carriage clock, James McCabe, London, third quarter 19th century, the case on bun feet, bevelled glass to the sides and stepped top, 9in. high. (Christie's) £12,075 $19,083

A Victorian carriage clock, in a silver case decorated with gold bands with swing handle, 16cm. high, William Frederick Wright London, 1897. (Bearne's) £1,250 $2,063

Etruscan Revival marble and patinated metal three-piece clock and garniture, circa 1890, clock 20in. high. (Skinner) £517 $862

A French porcelain and gilt-bronze mounted striking mantel clock and garniture, last quarter 19th century, the urn-shaped case with flambeau urn and dove finials and rams' head mounts to the sides, 19¾in. high, and the pair of five-light candelabra en suite, 19¾in. high. (Christie's) £1,380 $2,208

A French gilt-bronze and porcelain-mounted striking mantel clock and garniture, circa 1880, the case with raised urn cresting flanked by scroll mounts, with conforming ornament to the dial with Roman chapter ring, the twin barrel movement with strike on bell, 15¾in. high, pair of side urns en suite, 12½in. high. (Christie's) £1,380 $2,208

A Louis Philippe ormolu and jasper ware clock garniture, porcelain stamped *Adams*; second quarter 19th century, the clock formed as an urn on a hollow-cornered ormolu base, 13in. high. (Christie's) £6.325 $10,373

A Louis XV style gilt and patinated striking mantel clock and garniture, last quarter 19th century, the waisted and foliate cast case surmounted by the figure of an amorino with a bunch of grapes, with quatrefoil pierced sound frets to the sides, 15in. high, and pair of three-light candelabra en suite, 11¾in. high. (Christie's) £1,725 $2,760

A green onyx and marble striking mantel clock and garniture, early 20th century in the Art Deco style, the tricoloured case of angular form symmetrically mounted with green patinated bronze figures of young women, 17¼in. high. (Christie's) £460 $736

Brass lantern clock, bell domed cover, circular silvered chapter ring, by Dickerson of Framlingham, 18th/19th century, 14in.
(G.A. Key)   £1,550 $2,480

A brass lantern clock in the late 17th century style, with silvered chapter ring and single fusee movement, 38cm.
(Bearne's)   £400 $660

A 19th century lantern-style clock, rear and top bell strike, silvered chapter ring with Roman numerals, brass case, 19cm. wide.
(Bristol)   £520 $832

A 19th century brass lantern-style clock, with silvered chapter ring named *Hen Jackson, Lavington*, in typical case with armorial cresting frets, 16cm. wide.
(Bristol)   £580 $951

A brass 'wing' lantern clock, in the 17th century style, of typical form, with steel Roman chapter ring, the centre bearing the signature *Thomas Bryan, Holbourne*,15in. high. (Christie's)   £2,000 $3,200

A Charles II brass striking lantern clock, unsigned, fourth quarter 17th century, the dial with narrow Roman chapter ring, rosette and foliate engraved centre with single steel hand, 37cm. high.
(Christie's)   £2,300 $3,818

A late 19th/early 20th century brass mantel timepiece in case of 'lantern clock' pattern, the 4in. polished brass chapter ring with leaf engraved dial centre to the French eight-day movement, 9½in. high.
(Canterbury)   £150 $240

A Victorian reproduction brass striking lantern clock, late 19th century, the case of typical form with pierced frets to the bell stand, 15in. high. (Christie's) £575 $920

A 20th century 'Coronation' lantern style clock, the single bell strike surmounted by crown, with central inscription *GR crowned 12th May 1937*, 35cm.
(Bristol)   £250 $400

An eight day mahogany long case clock, by W. Farnill, Rotherham, 1825, 234cm.
(Tennants) £1,600 $2,560

A late George III thirty hour oak longcase clock, T. Pollard, Exeter, 190cm.
(Bearne's) £680 $1,122

A George III mahogany longcase clock, George Suggate, Halesworth, fourth quarter 18th century, 7ft.4in. high.
(Christie's) £4,600 $7,636

A 19th century eight day mahogany longcase clock, dial inscribed *Rhodes Bradford*, 240cm.
(Bearne's)   £980 $1,617

A Scottish Regency mahogany longcase clock, J. Russell, Falkirk, first quarter 19th century, 7ft. high. (Christie's)
£4,370 $7,254

An early 19th century eight day mahogany longcase clock, dial inscribed *T. Wilson, Guisborough,* 235cm.
(Bearne's) £1,050 $1,733

An onyx and champlevé enamel pedestal clock, French, circa 1870, the dial with ivorene chapter ring, supported by outset columns, 127cm. high.
(Sotheby's) £3,450 $5,692

A George III mahogany longcase clock, Thomas Drew, London, fourth quarter 18th century, 7ft.1in. high.
(Christie's) £5,750 $9,545

An eight day mahogany long case clock, by Webster, Whitby, basically circa 1770, 214cm. (Tennants) £1,700 $2,720

An eight day mahogany long case clock, by Whitehurst, Derby, circa 1780, 228cm. (Tennants) £2,400 $3,840

An early 19th century eight day Provincial oak longcase clock, 205cm. (Bearne's) £760 $1,254

A good George III eight day mahogany longcase clock by Thos. Fletcher, Chester, 225cm. (Bearne's) £2,500 $4,125

A George III eight-day oak longcase clock, the twin-train movement with anchor escapement, 203cm. high. (Phillips)   £1,250 $2,000

A fine early 18th century longcase clock, dial inscribed *Robert Henderson Scarborough,* 96in. high. (Dee Atkinson & Harrison) £5,600 $9,240

An 18th century longcase clock, eight day movement by Isaac Goddard of London, 213cm. high. (Wintertons)   £1,200 $1,920

William and Mary walnut and floral marquetry longcase clock, signed *Robert Clements, London,* 7ft. 2in. high. (Lawrences)   £4,000 $6,440

A George III oak longcase clock, thirty hour movement by Thomas Noon of Ashby, 207cm. (Wintertons)£1,800 $2,970

A 19th century oak and mahogany crossbanded longcase clock, 201cm. (Wintertons) £900 $1,440

An oak and mahogany cross-banded longcase clock, late 18th or early 19th century, 79in. high. (Christie's) £805 $1,288

A mid 19th century mahogany longcase clock, eight day movement by Adams, 226cm. high. (Wintertons)£1,200 $1,980

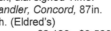

A George II walnut longcase clock, James Pyke, London, circa 1750, 8ft.2in. high. (Sotheby's) £5,290 $8,834

An eight day mahogany long case clock, by Bentley, Darlington, 231cm. (Tennants) £3,300 $5,445

American maple long case clock, dial signed *Timo. Chandler, Concord,* 87in. high. (Eldred's) £2,133 $3,520

A George III mahogany eight-day longcase clock, dial inscribed *Henry Lucas, London,* 204cm. (Bearne's) £600 $960

A fine and rare Chippendale carved and figured cherrywood tall case clock, Jacob Gorgas, Lancaster County, Pennsylvania, circa 1780, 8ft. 1in. high. (Sotheby's) £15,617 $25,300

A Federal brass-mounted figured mahogany tall case clock, William Cummens, Boston, Massachusetts, circa 1790, 7ft 11in. high. (Sotheby's) £17,537 $28,750

An eight day long case clock, signed (?) *Nock Netherton,* inlaid with marquetry and mahogany banding, circa 1840, 225cm. (Tennants) £800 $1,280

An 18th century oak longcase clock, brass dial inscribed *John Hampson.* (Russell Baldwin & Bright) £1,700 $2,805

A George III mahogany eight-day longcase clock, brass dial inscribed *Jos. Eayres, St. Neots*, 243cm. (Bearne's) £3,100 $4,960

An early 19th century eight day Provincial oak longcase clock, 235cm. (Bearne's) £1,100 $1,815

A William & Mary walnut and floral marquetry longcase clock, Thomas Johnson, London, circa 1695, 8ft.1in. (Christie's) £7,475 $12,259

An eight day long case clock, by Peter King, London, the case with chinoiseries, basically circa 1760, 264cm. (Tennants) £1,800 $2,880

A French gilt metal and porcelain mantel clock, the movement stamped *Hry Marc Paris*, 19in. high. (Andrew Hartley)   £620 $1,023

A French gilt-spelter and black slate striking mantel clock, last quarter 19th century, the drum-shaped case surmounted by a floral bouquet and flanked by the figure of a classical maiden playing a lyre, 15in. wide. (Christie's) £195 $312

A French black boulle cased mantel clock, the 8 day movement striking a bell, with an outside countwheel, 8½in. wide. (Woolley & Wallis)   £400 $644

A French gilt brass mantel clock, the bell-strike movement by J.W.C. Smith, Paris, the 5in. white Roman numeral dial in a drumhead case, 24.5cm. wide. (Bristol) £580 $928

A French gilt-metal striking mantel clock, last quarter 19th century, the case surmounted by a group of a country youth with a horse, on naturalistic base, 14¾in. high. (Christie's)   £184 $295

Papier mâché shelf timepiece, labelled *Botsford's improved patent timepiece manufactured by Coe & Co. 52 Dey Street, New York*, 11in. high. (Skinner)   £790 $1,265

A French porcelain mantel clock case, with later electric movement, the detachable top of two Turkish dancers, 25.5cm. wide. (Bristol)   £220 $360

An Empire gilt-bronze striking mantel clock, first quarter 19th century, the rectangular case incised with simulated brickwork and applied with butterfly mounts, , 14¼in. high. (Christie's) £402 $643

French baroque-style bronze mantel clock, late 19th century, works by Denière, scrolled case and base with foliate and mask mounts, 18in. high. (Skinner)   £379 $632

A Victorian sanderswood travelling timepiece with alarm, circa 1835, the dial with narrow silvered Roman chapter ring signed *Vulliamy, London*, 6¾in. high.
(Christie's)   £10,120 $16,597

A silvered, parcel-gilt and lapis lazuli mantel clock by Elkington and Co., Victorian, circa 1880, the dial with a silvered chapter ring in a drum case, 40cm. high.
(Sotheby's)   £9,775 $16,128

A Louis XV style gilt-bronze striking mantel clock, last quarter 19th century, signed *RICHOND*, the twin barrel movement with countwheel strike on bell, 17in. high.
(Christie's)   £920 $1,472

Rouen porcelain small mantel clock with circular Arabic chapter ring, moulded with scrolls, painted in colours throughout in the faience manner, late 19th/early20th century, 8½in. high.
(G.A. Key)   £140 $224

A white marble and gilt bronze mantel clock, French, late 18th century, movement signed *Louis Musson A Paris*, enamel dial signed *Foucher à Argentan*, contained in a drum with Leda and the Swan on left, fluted marble base,1ft.4in. high.
(Sotheby's)   £3,335 $5,569

Federal mahogany miniature pillar and scroll mantel clock, Eli Terry, Plymouth, Connecticut, circa 1822, the swan's neck cresting above a glazed door, 22½in. high.
(Skinner)   £4,530 $7,475

Georgian-style inlaid mahogany mantel clock, early 20th century, with French works, the stepped case inlaid with stringing and butterfly. (Skinner) £828 $1,380

A 1930s Breguet timepiece, the silvered dial with black Roman numerals and blued hands, in an Art Deco style brass case, 10cm.
(Bearne's)   £1,050 $1,733

Grignon-Meusnier a Paris, a 19th century ormolu and porcelain mantel clock, the bell-striking movement with enamel chapter ring, 38.8cm.
(Bristol)   £840 $1,377

A French gilt-metal and marble early electric skeleton clock, Paul Garnier, France, No. 168, circa 1850, on large gilt-brass columns supported on a verde antico moulded base, 24½in. high.
(Christie's) £6,325 $10,500

A modern 'Congreve' rolling ball clock in the form of a classical temple on stepped wood base, Twaites and Reed, 83cm.
(Bearne's) £900 $1,485

An early Victorian ormolu mantel timepiece, circa 1840, the silvered dial with Roman chapter ring signed *VULLIAMY LONDON*, with engine-turned centre and moon hands, 11in. high.
(Christie's) £4,600 $7,360

A Louis XVI ormolu and Meissen porcelain mantel clock, the porcelain figure modelled by Friedrich Elias Meyer, the circular enamelled dial signed *Imbert L'Ainé, Paris*, 23¾in. high.
(Christie's) £6,325 $10,499

An English Scott electric mantel timepiece, the Ever Ready Electric Specialities Co. / Herbert Scott, circa 1905, the circular white enamel Arabic dial with blued spade hands, 16¼in. high.
(Christie's) £1,610 $2,673

A 19th century mantel clock in ormolu case with porcelain panels, with striking movement by Chas Frodsham, 13½in. high.
(Russell Baldwin & Bright) £1,000 $1,650

A Continental porcelain clock case, the flower encrusted body supported on either side with man and woman, 37.5cm. high.
(Bearne's) £270 $432

A gilt-bronze mantel clock with figure of George Washington, Du Buc, Paris, circa 1805, on chased ball feet, 10½in. wide.
(Christie's) £26,910 $44,850

A late 19th century, French brass and champlevé enamel mantel clock, the eight-day movement striking on a gong, 30.5cm.
(Bearne's) £380 $627

A Louis Philippe acajou moucheté jump-hour striking table clock, Breguet No. 4726, reverse of enamel dial signed *Valah*, circa 1828, 11¼in. high.
(Christie's)   £45,500 $74,620

A Regency rosewood silver-mounted striking four-glass travelling clock, Arnold Charles Frodsham, London. 767, circa 1850, 11¼in. high.
(Christie's)   £16,100 $26,726

An Empire amboyna and ormolu mounted musical table orrery clock, Raingo a Paris, the neo-classical case in the form of a Doric rotunda, 30½in. high.
(Christie's)   £76,300 $125,132

A French gilt-metal and marble four-glass electric timepiece, Bulle, France, first quarter 20th century, the case with red veined marble base supporting the glazed gilt-metal four-glass frame with similar marble top, 14¼in. high.
(Christie's)   £2,070 $3,437

An English mahogany and brass electric mantel timepiece, Eureka Clock Co. Ltd., London, circa 1910, the movement of typical construction with massive balance wheel, 11in. high.
(Christie's)   £862 $1,430

A French gilt-bronze and enamel-mounted striking four-glass mantel clock, circa 1880, the twin barrel movement with strike on gong, stamped on the backplate for *JAPY FRÈRES*, 15¾in. high.
(Christie's)   £2,530 $4,048

A gilt metal solar and battery powered table clock, signed *Patek Philippe*, 1970s, in upright gilt metal rectangular case with applied decoration, 17.3cm. high.
(Christie's)   £1,092 $1,791

A French rouge griotte marble and gilt bronze mounted mantel clock, late 19th century, the rectangular case surmounted with a model of the Warwick vase, 18½in. high.
(Christie's)   £2,530 $4,048

A Victorian silver gothic combination mantel timepiece, movement by John Carter, case by John Samuel Hunt, hallmarked London 1840, 6¾in. high,
(Christie's)   £11,500 $18,860

An early 20th century golden oak mantel clock having a square moulded case with brass lion head, 13in high.
(H. C. Chapman)   £290 $478

An Art Nouveau mantel timepiece, the hammered and embossed copper case decorated with foliage heightened with enamel, 33cm. long. (Bearne's)   £550 $880

Classical mahogany and stencilled shelf clock, Norris North, Torrington, Connecticut, circa 1825, the flat cornice above a glazed door with eglomise tablet, 13½in. wide. (Skinner)   £2,962 $4,887

A painted marmo nero Belgio striking mantel clock, early 20th century, the French twin barrel movement wound through the rear and striking on a gong, stamped on the backplate for *Etienne Maxant Paris*, 14½in. high.
(Christie's)   £207 $331

A French gilt-spelter and alabaster mantel timepiece, late 19th century, the case with floral mounts flanked by the standing figure of a dragoon with flag and pistol, on alabaster plinth with foliate frame, 17½in. high. (Christie's)   £161 $258

A French mahogany striking mantel clock, early 20th century, Regency style, the silvered Roman dial with blued moon hands, twin train movement with strike on gong, stamped for *JAPY FRÈRES*, 11¾in. high. (Christie's)   £287 $460

A French gilt-bronze and porcelain-mounted striking mantel clock, third quarter 19th century, the twin barrel movement with countwheel strike on bell stamped for *OPPENHEIM LONDRES-PARIS*, 20in. high. (Christie's)   £287 $460

A Louis Philippe bronze and Siena marble mantel clock, circa 1840, the case modelled with the figure of a semi-naked man tethered to a fleeing stallion's back, 19¼in. wide. (Christie's)   £690 $1,104

A German walnut and marquetry inlaid striking mantel clock, early 20th century, twin barrel movement with strike on gong, stamped on the backplate *W & H Sch* for Winterhalder and Hofmeier, 14¼in. high. (Christie's)   £862 $1,380

278

Rosewood carved mantel
timepiece, J. C. Brown, Bristol,
Connecticut, mid-19th century,
ripple moulded gilt decorated
rectangular case, 8¼in. high.
(Skinner)   £1,812 $2,990

Chelsea ship's bell clock, in ship's
wheel form, bronze base, 17½in.
high, ship's wheel diameter 15in.
(Eldred's)   £1,100 $1,760

A Victorian walnut double dial table
regulator, Dent, London, circa 1851,
the case of rectangular design with
detachable viewing portal to top,
17¼in. high.
(Christie's)   £8,050 $13,202

A German carved oak striking
mantel clock, early 20th century,
the architectural case with pilasters
to the front, with retailer's signature
*Muirhead & Arthur 57, St, Vincent
St, Glasgow,* 15¼in. high.
(Christie's)   £207 $331

French black marble, brass and
ormolu mantel clock, 19th century,
surmounted by bronze finish figure
group of a woman and child, relief
brass panels, 20½in.high.
(Eldred's)   £481 $770

A German carved oak striking
mantel clock, early 20th century, ,
caryatid figures to front, twin barrel
movement with ting-tang strike on
two gongs, stamped on the
backplate *W & H Sch* for
Winterhalder and Hofmeier, 19½in.
high. (Christie's)   £517 $827

Victorian brass-mounted oak
quarter striking and chiming triple-
fusee mantel clock, circa 1880, with
five gongs and chiming on a nest of
eight bells, 21½in. high.
(Skinner)   £2,070 $3,450

A French Empire period ormolu
mantel lock, the case with a cast
figure of Orpheus playing a lyre,
dial signed *L. Mallet, H & MDD
Orleans.*
(Dreweatt Neate)   £800 $1,304

Whimsical French brass and
marble steam engine train-form
mantel clock, circa 1890, with
barometer, two thermometers and
compass, 14¼in.high.
(Skinner)   £1,380 $2,300

A Victorian gilt-metal mantel timepiece, third quarter 19th century, the case engraved overall with scrolling foliage, 7½in. high. (Christie's) £1,150 $1,886

An Art Deco shagreen and chromed metal mantel clock, the silvered metal body resting upon two stepped feet, 18.5cm high. (Christie's) £253 $409

A late 19th century bracket clock in Louis XV style, with strike/silent movement in scarlet Boullework and ormolu case, 1ft. 3in. high. (Sotheby's) £690 $1,152

A Napoleon III large and impressive gilt-bronze striking mantel clock, third quarter 19th century, the white enamel Roman chapter ring with recessed centre with visible Brocot escapement, signed *A & J Kleiser Paris*, 33in. high. (Christie's) £5,520 $8,832

A brass-inlaid mahogany eight-day Hertfordshire mantel chronometer, Thomas Mercer, St. Albans, No. 660, circa 1932, with rectangular recessed bevelled escapement viewing glass to the top, 11½in. high. (Christie's) £3,910 $6,491

A Louis Philippe gilt and silvered bronze striking mantel clock, circa 1830, the case surmounted by the figure of woman in Oriental costume with dove reclining against a pillow and holding a fan, 46cm. high. (Christie's) £805 $1,288

An Empire ormolu mantel clock, first quarter 19th century, the case surmounted by a model of a Grecian oil lamp and two books, flanked by a classical female figure seated on a stool and reading, 16in. high. (Christie's) £1,265 $2,024

A William IV satinwood small mantel timepiece, Frodsham, Gracechurch St, London; second quarter 19th century, the case with scroll pediment above a dentilled freize, 9in. high. (Christie's) £1,955 $3,245

A Second Empire ormolu and ebonised mystery timepiece, A. Cadot; second quarter 19th century, the ebonised moulded base with green velvet platform for the ormolu rectangular clock frame, 15in. high. (Christie's) £6,670 $11,072

An English great wheel skeleton timepiece, Murday/The Reason MFG Co. Ltd., circa 1915, the glass dial with back-painted Roman chapters, on circular moulded mahogany base, 13¾in. high.
(Christie's)   £3,450 $5,727

An early American gilt-metal and inlaid mahogany electric skeleton timepiece, Chester Pond, New York, circa 1875, gothic-pierced Roman chapter ring with blued steel hands, 17in. high.
(Christie's)   £1,495 $2,482

A Victorian mahogany, brass and flint glass skeleton timepiece, attributed to Edwards of Stourbridge, mid 19th century, the scrolling brass frame with six substantial tapered, 24¼in. high.
(Christie's)   £12,075 $20,045

A brass escapement model of Hardy's escapement, Sinclair Harding, modern, the movement with twin wire fusees secured by four double-screwed vase shaped pillars, 18¾in. high.
(Christie's)   £5,750 $9,430

A brass skeleton timepiece with planetary wheels, Dent, London, modern, the movement with four double-screwed pillars to the chamfered brass scroll frame, 11¾in. high.
(Christie's)   £1,610 $2,640

A year-going perpetual calendar and world time skeleton timepiece with chronometer escapement, second half, 19th century, the frame cut to a foliate design, 46.5cm. high.
(Christie's)   £16,675 $27,347

A brass grasshopper escapement model, Dent, London, modern, the movement of typical form, with five double-screwed pillars securing a pierced brass frame, 20½in. high.
(Christie's)   £3,220 $5,281

A Victorian brass skeleton timepiece with single fusee movement and anchor escapement, 31cm., on a marble base under under glass dome.
(Bearne's)   £440 $726

A Swiss early electric skeleton clock, Dr Matthaus Hipp, Neuchatel, circa 1870, the movement mounted on two extended arms from the iron backboard bracket, 24½in. (over dome). (Christie's) £6,325 $10,500

A Heals oak wall clock, the oak circular face with carved and ebonised arabic numerals, with English 18-day movement, 14in. wide. (Christie's)   £437 $655

A Coca Cola painted tin neon clock, with opaque white plastic dial and green numbers, 36cm. high, circa 1965. (Auction Team Köln)   £188 $301

A large octagonal office clock, with wooden case and 48cm. dial with Arabic numerals, circa 1900. (Auction Team Köln)   £175 $280

Rosewood grained banjo #5 timepiece, E. Howard & Co., Boston, mid 19th century, the circular moulded bezel enclosing a white painted metal dial, 28½in. high. (Skinner)   £1,481 $2,415

A Victorian carved oak wall timepiece, second half 19th century, the white-painted dial with trefoil steel hands and signed TAYLOR HAVERHILL, 15¼in. high. (Christie's)   £690 $1,104

A Régence style gilt-bronze striking cartel clock, last quarter 19th century, the twin barrel movement with countwheel strike on bell stamped for JAPY FRÈRES, 22½in. high. (Christie's)   £690 $1,104

A Regency mahogany drop-dial wall clock, the twin-fusee movement striking on a bell, dial indistinctly inscribed Stowbridge, 72cm. (Bearne's) £800 $1,320

Antique American gallery clock, Boston, circa 1835, attributed to Aaron Willard Jr., original eight-day brass weight-driven movement. (Eldred's)   £1,200 $1,980

A German ebonised wall regulator, J.D. Thies, Hamburg, movement by F. Dencker, third quarter 19th century, the case divided into two sections, 52¾in. high. (Christie's)   £7,820 $12,825

A late 18th century black and gilt painted tavern clock with painted Roman numerals and outer minute dial, 30in. x 51in. high. (Anderson & Garland)   £1,100 $1,815

Dutch brass and tin comptoise wall clock, late 18th/early 19th century, stamped dial surround decorated with farmers and horses, white enamel dial, 17in. high. (Eldred's)   £344 $550

A Victorian brass wall timepiece, second half 19th century, the single chain fusee movement with lever escapement and engraved balance cock, signed *JNO. WARNER ISLINGTON*, 7¾in. high. (Christie's)   £517 $827

Dutch Baroque-style walnut Friesland clock, 19th century, with four seasons spandrels, striking on two bells, approximately 42in. long. (Skinner)   £786 $1,265

A shop timepiece, in shaped and carved mahogany cartouche with serpentine white glass sign *Laboratory*, dial signed *John Volz, Winchmore Hill*, 41½in. wide. (Christie's)   £862 $1,379

E. Howard & Co. marble gallery clock, white marble face with black and red numerals, 44in. high. (Eldred's)   £1,994 $3,190

A parcel-ebonised and walnut-veneered quarter-chiming Vienna regulator, last quarter 19th century, the case with breakarch top with turned finials, 45in. high. (Christie's)   £1,495 $2,392

A George VI mahogany dial timepiece, second quarter 20th century, the white-painted Roman dial with Roman chapters and marked with the Royal insignia,15½in. (Christie's)   £517 $827

A Viennese ebonised Brettl-Uhr, first quarter 19th century, the white enamel dial with blued steel hands encased in a milled ormolu glazed bezel, 22¼in. high. (Christie's)   £1,840 $3,108

A French oak electric wall timepiece with slave clock, Paul Garnier/Charles Fery, first quarter 20th century, a cream painted Arabic dial with blued steel spade hands, 22½in. (master clock). (Christie's)   £1,495 $2,482

A Swedish giltwood cartel clock, third quarter 18th century, with a rectangular beaded and dentilled platform to the top with seated figure of Minerva, 28in. high. (Christie's)   £2,415 $4,008

A French oak electric wall timepiece, Bardon, Clichy, first quarter 20th century, the rectangular glazed case with moulded frame and white marble slab backboard, 19in. high. (Christie's)   £1,495 $2,482

A Biedermeier mahogany and boxwood-lined small Laterndl-Uhr, first quarter 19th century, the well-proportioned small case with architectural top, 33¼in. high. (Christie's) £12,075 $19,803

A French automaton picture clock, mid 19th century, the dial inset within a ruined tower and signed LEROY A PARIS, 35½ x 26½in. (Christie's)   £2,530 $4,048

A mid 19th century regulator wall clock, in Biedermeier style satin birch case, by Joseph Petrovits, Wien, 99cm. (Bearne's)   £740 $1,221

A French mahogany electric wall timepiece, Vaucanson, Paris, first quarter 20th century, the moulded rectangular case suspended from a white marble slab backboard, 17in. high. (Christie's)   £1,495 $2,482

A French mahogany electric dial timepiece, Bulle, 20th century, the convex moulded frame hinged to a rectangular box, 12in. diameter. (Christie's)   £109 $180

A French oak electrical wall clock, ATO, first quarter 20th century, the case with curved pediment beneath the door with three bevelled glass windows, 20½in. high. (Christie's)   £253 $420

A Regency mahogany drop-dial wall timepiece with single fusee movement and cream painted Roman dial. 58cm.
(Bearne's)   £370 $610

A Regency mahogany and brass sedan timepiece, Joseph Wilson, Stamford; first quarter 19th century, the 30-hour movement with rectangular plates and four back-pinned pillars, 6in. diameter.
(Christie's)   £1,035 $1,718

A Regency wall clock, single train fusee movement in octagonal rosewood case having brass scroll inlay and satinwood stringing, 17in. diameter. (Russell Baldwin & Bright)   £680 $1,122

A Swedish giltwood cartel clock, 19th century, the circular glazed and enamelled dial with Roman and Arabic chapters inscribed *Rob. Engström / Stockholm*, 35in. high.
(Christie's)   £2,530 $4,199

A 19th century Continental picture clock depicting a church and cottages with cattle and a river in the foreground, in gilt-gesso frame, 64 x 80cm. (Bearne's) £900 $1,485

A Louis XV-style gilt metal cartel clock, the eight-day movement striking on a bell with a circular white enamel Roman dial.
(Bearne's)   £500 $825

A French mahogany electric wall clock, Bulle, circa 1910, the glazed case with brass angles and mahogany moulded top and bottom, 16in. high.
(Christie's)   £575 $955

A 19th century dial clock, the Roman dial inscribed *J. Hill & Son, Teignmouth*, in stained wood case, 41cm. diameter.
(Bearne's)   £330 $545

A French oak electric timepiece, Electrique Brillie, first quarter 20th century, the moulded rectangular case with typical white marble backboard, 17¾in. high.
(Christie's)   £345 $573

A rare English verge with rotating enamel scene, silver champlevé dial with an aperture revealing an enamel disc in silver pair cases, signed Denton, London circa 1690.
(Pieces of Time)   £3,980 $6,567

A fine mid 17th century oval English verge made for the Turkish market, large full plate fire gilt movement with elaborate pierced and engraved pillars.
(Pieces of Time)   £6,500 $10,725

A late 19th century Swiss automaton lever with a polychrome enamel dial depicting a windmill, the sails rotating as the watch runs, circa 1870, 48mm. diameter.
(Pieces of Time)   £750 $1,200

An early 19th century English verge with finely painted polychrome enamel dial in silver pair cases, signed *J Hudson London*, hallmarked London 1812, 56mm. diameter.
(Pieces of Time)   £995 $1,592

A very rare French movement with Sully's escapement in a silver open face case, small keywind gilt movement, signed *Dubois de Perigueux a Paris*, circa 1780, 38mm. diameter.
(Pieces of Time)   £5,500 $8,800

An 18th century French verge made for the Turkish market with gilt and enamel dial in a silver consular case and repoussé protective outer, signed *Jn Leroy a Paris*, circa 1780, diameter 51mm.
(Pieces of Time)   £1,850 $2,960

A late 18th century Continental mock pendulum verge in silver and tortoiseshell pair cases, signed *Norton London*, circa 1790, diameter 67mm.
(Pieces of Time)   £1,450 $2,392

A mid 19th century Swiss independent seconds Captain's watch with dual time in an engine turned silver full hunter case, circa 1860, 53mm. diameter.
(Pieces of Time)   £1,200 $1,920

A rare late 18th century Swiss verge, the polychrome enamel centre seconds dial with flyback date, gilt open face case, circa 1790, 52mm. diameter.
(Pieces of Time) £2,250 $3,600

A late 18th century Continental calendar verge with an unusual decorative polychrome dial in a silver consular case, circa 1790, 61mm. diameter.
(Pieces of Time) £1,625 $2,600

A late 19th century Swiss lever watch with fly-back minute and hour hands in a silver gilt case, signed *Record Watch Co. J. A. Tramelan*, circa 1885, 60 x 71mm.
(Pieces of Time)   £1,650 $2,640

Gilt verge by Windmills in contemporary gilt metal consular case, deep full plate fire gilt movement with Egyptian pillars, circa 1710, 59mm. diameter.
(Pieces of Time) £1,200 $1,980

A late 19th century Swiss cylinder with Hebrew dial in silvered open face case, the cast back depicting a scholar pointing to a manuscript, diameter 48mm.
(Pieces of Time)   £330 $545

An 18th century verge repeating chaise watch, with alarum, by Ludovicus Antonius Lanzoron, Bon (sic), in gilt metal case pierced and engraved with cartouche mask and scrolls, circa 1740, 90mm.
(Tennants)   £1,200 $1,920

A slim gold Imperial Prince dress watch by Rolex with duo dial, signed brushed metal dial with subsidiary for time above the subsidiary seconds, circa 1930, diameter 42mm.
(Pieces of Time) £1,750 $2,887

A late 18th century French calendar verge with an unusual decorative dial in a silver case, signed *Humbert & Mairet*, circa 1790, 56mm. diameter.
(Pieces of Time)   £1,350 $2,160

A late 19th century Swiss lever with digital dial in a gunmetal open face case, keyless gilt plate movement with going barrel, signed *GT.*, circa 1895, 55mm. diameter.
(Pieces of Time)   £830 $1,310

A fine Swedish verge of large size in a gold consular case, full plate gilt fusee movement, signed *Iac Kock, Stockholm, 386*, circa 1760, 57mm. diameter.
(Pieces of Time)   £2,500 $4,125

An unsigned verge watch, No. 744, the movement with baluster pillars and enamel dial, in silver pair cases, Birmingham, 1808, 60mm.
(Tennants) £320 $512

A keyless lever karrusel, by Thos Russell & Son, Liverpool, No. 107221, in 18ct gold hunter case with inscribed testimonial on the cuvette, Chester, 1902, 56mm.
(Tennants) £2,400 $3,840

A watch, by Samson, the dial depicting a fisherman with boat, church and castle, in plain silver pair cases, 1790, 50mm.
(Tennants) £300 $480

A verge watch, by Jas Brickles, London, in gilt metal pair cases, the outer painted with rocks and ferns under translucent horn, circa 1790, 54mm.
(Tennants) £360 $576

A pocket chronometer by John Roger Arnold, with Arnold escapement, in silver consular case with Regency pendant, 1816, 57mm.
(Tennants) £2,600 $4,160

A verge watch, of Dutch type, by Samson, London, the dial with painted scene depicting a man o' war and pinnace upon a calm sea, 1806, 51mm.
(Tennants) £380 $608

A verge watch, by Robert Bowers, Chester, with diamond end stone, the dial painted with a windmill with revolving sails, in silver pair cases, Birmingham, 1803, 53mm.
(Tennants) £480 $768

A Turkish market verge watch, by Edward Prior, in silver pair cases, the outer with bright cut bands, 1858, within silver piqué tortoiseshell outer case, 60mm.
(Tennants) £550 $880

A verge watch, by W. Ward, Grimsby, the enamel dial painted with a ploughing scene, in silver pair cases, Birmingham, 1865, 57mm.
(Tennants) £350 $560

A cylinder watch, by Fras Perigal, London, the later gold dial in gold consular case with pearl and enamel bezels, circa 1790, 45mm. (Tennants)　　　　£360　$576

A silver paircased pocket watch, the painted white enamelled dial depicting a windmill, signed *Langford, London*. (Bearne's)　　　　£250　$330

A cylinder watch, by D & W Morice, London, the enamel dial inscribed in white upon black, in 18ct gold open face case, 1818, 52mm. (Tennants)　　　　£1,100　$1,760

A verge watch, by D Rutland, London, in gilt metal pair cases, the outer painted with the figure of a huntsman, under translucent horn, circa 1775, 49mm. (Tennants)　　　　£400　$640

An 18ct gold half hunter pocket watch, the case with blue enamelled Roman numerals, signed *Army & Navy*. (Bearne's)　　　　£190　$314

A mid 18th century verge watch, by Thos Cope, London, the movement with well pierced cock and slide plate, with later gold dial in gold pair cases, 50mm. (Tennants)　　　　£480　$768

A verge watch, by Markwick Marham Borrell, London, the enamel dial painted with a ploughing scene, '*Speed the Plough*', in silver pair cases, 1826, the outer 1841, 57mm. (Tennants)　　　　£280　$448

An 18ct gold hunter pocket watch, with keywound three-quarter plate lever movement, signed *Johnson Walker & Tolhurst, London*. (Bearne's)　　　　£200　$330

A quarter repeating cylinder watch, by Bautte, à Geneve, the bar movement with engraved silvered dial in gold open face case, circa 1835, 43mm. (Tennants)　　　　£420　$672

A Swiss lever watch in a silver and niello full hunter case depicting 'modern' inventions. signed, *Orion*, circa 1900, 48mm. diameter.
(Pieces of Time)   £3,100 $4,960

An 18ct. gold keyless hunter chronograph pocketwatch, signed *Nicole Neilsen & Co.*, 1880s, the frosted gilt three-quarter plate movement jewelled to the third, 53mm. diameter.
(Christie's)   £920 $1,472

An early 19th century Swiss verge in a gold and enamel open face case, full plate fusee movement, circa 1820, diameter 42mm.
(Pieces of Time)   £1,250 $2,062

A large 19th century English fusee lever used as the first watch on an early British railway, full plate keywind fusee movement with rear hand set, signed *Robert Bryson & Sons Edinburgh 119347*, 63mm. diameter, circa 1847.
(Pieces of Time)   £950 $1,520

A 20th century Swiss military lever in a nickel open face case and brass keep case, gilt three quarter plate keyless movement with going barrel, signed *Zenith 30 hour non Luminous Mark V*, circa 1918.
(Pieces of Time)   £485 $776

A very fine early 18th century English verge clockwatch with gold champlevé dial in gold repoussé pair cases and shagreen covered gilt metal protective outer, signed *Geo Clarke* London 203, circa 1720, 57mm. diameter.
(Pieces of Time)   £5,750 $9,200

A late 19th century Swiss Goliath lever watch with moonphase calendar in a nickel open face case, keyless gilt bar movement with going barrel, circa 1900, 66mm. diameter.
(Pieces of Time)   £1,170 $1,872

An unusual silver keyless mystery pocketwatch, unsigned, second half 19th century, the frosted gilt movement with cylinder escapement driving two glass discs 54mm. diameter.
(Christie's)   £1,495 $2,482

An American two day lever deck watch with power reserve indication in a large nickel open face case and mahogany keep box, signed *Hamilton Watch Co.*, circa 1943, 71mm. diameter.
(Pieces of Time)   £695 $1,112

Freesprung gold half hunter with black dial, signed *J.W. Benson, Rowley London,* hallmarked, London 1871, diameter 48mm. (Pieces of Time) £1,080 $1,782

A gold and enamel keyless minute repeating and automata hunter pocketwatch, signed *L. Perrot,* 1890s, the blued centre field superimposed with pink gilt automata of two smiths apparently striking the time on an anvil, 53mm. diameter. (Christie's) £2,300 $3,818

A late 19th century Swiss lever watch of eight days duration in a square silver open face case, unsigned, circa 1890, 55 x 55mm. (Pieces of Time) £500 $800

An early 18th century English quarter repeating verge in a leather gilt metal case, deep full plate fire gilt movement with gilt dust ring secured by two squared dig screws, signed *Luke Wise Reading*, circa 1710, 51mm. diameter. (Pieces of Time) £2,600 $4,160

A 20th century Swiss lever in a plain gold oval case, circular keyless gilt bar movement with going barrel, signed *Longines,* circa 1920, 40 x 59mm. (Pieces of Time) £975 $1,560

A Turkish market verge watch, by Markwick Markham Borell, in silver pair cases, the outer engraved with a basket of flowers, 1807, 48mm.
(Tennants) £400 $640

A gold purse watch with shutters, signed *Vacheron Constantin*, 1920s, contained within gold rectangular outer case engraved with geometric designs, 43 x 41mm.
(Christie's) £2,185 $3,583

A gentleman's gold World Time keyless openface pocketwatch with 24 hour indication, signed *Agassiz Watch Co.*, 1950s, 46mm. diameter.
(Christie's) £4,600 $7,544

An early 18th century English verge with silver champlevé dial in silver pair cases, deep full plate fire gilt movement with Egyptian pillars, signed *Fk Barrett y London*, circa 1710, 56mm. diameter.
(Pieces of Time) £2,650 $4,240

A fine gold, diamond and ruby keyless skeletonised dress watch, signed *Patek Philippe*, 1980s, the finely chased and skeletonised movement jewelled to the centre, 49mm. diameter.
(Christie's) £16,100 $26,726

A gold openface verge pocketwatch, signed *Iac. Kock, Stockholm*, late 18th century, the frosted gilt chain fusee movement with unusual pierced and engraved bridgecock, 57mm. diameter.
(Christie's) £1,150 $1,886

A lady's gold and enamel keyless pendant watch, signed *Tiffany*, 1890s, the chased and engraved covers with enamelled scene of a putto, 25mm. diameter.
(Christie's) £747 $1,240

A good 18ct. gold quarter repeating cylinder hunter pocketwatch, signed *Recordon* late Emery, early 1800s, the frosted gilt full plate movement with chain fusee, 54mm. diameter.
(Christie's) £1,265 $2,100

An interesting gilt perfume flask in the form of a keyless openface pocketwatch, signed *Rolex, Perpetually Yours*, 1960s, 54mm. diameter.
(Christie's) £1,380 $2,262

292

A late 18th century French dumb quarter repeating verge in a gold consular case set with a polychrome enamel portrait, signed *L Chalon a Paris 426.*, circa 1780, 45mm. diameter.
(Pieces of Time)   £3,200 $5,120

A 9 ct. gold purse watch, signed *Rolex Model Sporting Princess*, 1930s, the nickel plated extra prima chronometer movement timed to six positions, 50 x 34mm.
(Christie's)   £3,450 $5,658

A good gold openface keyless pocketwatch, *signed Patek Philippe & Co., Chronometro Gondolo,* 1910s, the frosted gilt bar movement jewelled to the centre, 56mm. diameter.
(Christie's)   £1,955 $3,206

An 18ct. gold half quarter repeating Duplex pocketwatch, signed *Grayhurst, Harvey & Co., Strand, London*, 1820s, in engine turned openface case with ribbed band, hinged back and cuvette, 56mm. diameter. (Christie's) £1,265 $2,100

A white metal pull quarter repeat and alarm coach watch, signed *Charles Baltazar a Paris,* early 18th century, the frosted gilt chain fusee movement with verge escapement, 117mm. diameter.
(Christie's)   £6,325 $10,373

A gold, enamel and seed pearl openface verge pocketwatch, signed *Roman Melly & Roux, Constance*, 1800s, the back cover with painted scene of a maiden offering fruit to Pegasus, 47mm. diameter. (Christie's) £1,035 $1,718

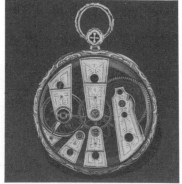

A nickel openface keyless deckwatch with power reserve indication, signed *A Lange & Söhne, Glashütte*, 1940s, 59mm. diameter.
(Christie's)   £1,150 $1,886

A most unusual gold and enamel openface cylinder dress watch with enamelled bridges, unsigned, 1820s, the blued steel top plate with floral decoration, 43mm. diameter.
(Christie's)   £1,725 $2,863

An early 19th century English verge, the unusual regulator dial with calendar indications in gilt metal pair cases, circa 1805, signed *Johnson London 876*, 59mm.
(Pieces of Time)   £995 $1,592

293

An 18 carat white gold limited edition self-winding perpetual calendar wristwatch, signed _Patek Philippe_, recent, 36mm. diameter. (Christie's)   £20,700 $34,362

A stainless steel self-winding water resistant calendar wristwatch, with 24 hour indication, signed _Rolex GMT Master_, 1960s, 40mm. diameter. (Christie's) £1,725 $2,829

A steel and gold quartz calendar wristwatch, signed _Cartier, Model Panthère_, 1980s, the matt silvered dial with Roman numerals, 37 x 25mm. (Christie's) £1,725 $2,829

A gold and steel self-winding water resistant calendar world time wristwatch, signed _Ebel,_ recent, the black dial with raised Roman numerals, date aperture, luminous gold hands, 38mm. diameter. (Christie's)   £1,150 $1,909

A gentleman's 18ct. gold self-winding perpetual calendar and moonphase wrist watch, signed _Patek Philippe_, 1980s, integral woven gold bracelet and clasp, 36mm. diameter. (Christie's)   £10,925 $17,917

A gold, steel and diamond set quartz calendar wristwatch, signed _Ebel_, 1990s, the cream dial with diamond set numerals, date aperture and luminous gold hands, 33mm. diameter. (Christie's)   £1,380 $2,263

A rectangular gold wristwatch, signed _Cartier_, 1980s, the nickel plated movement jewelled to the centre, adjusted to temperatures and three positions, 28 x 20mm. (Christie's)   £1,725 $2,829

A stainless steel self-winding water resistant chronograph wristwatch, signed _Rolex, Oyster Perpetual Chronometer Cosmograph Daytona_, 1996, 28mm. diameter. (Christie's)   £4,025 $6,681

A pink gold self-winding water resistant wristwatch with centre seconds, signed _Rolex_, the associated painted enamel dial depicting a peacock, 34mm. diameter. (Christie's) £5,520 $9,163

A stainless steel self-winding water resistant chronograph wristwatch, signed *Bulgari*, recent, the black dial with luminous indexes, 38mm. diameter. (Christie's) £2,530 $4,149

A stainless steel self-winding water resistant wristwatch, signed *Rolex Oyster Perpetual Chronometer, Bubble-Back*, 1940s, 39 x 33mm. (Christie's) £1,150 $1,886

A stainless steel self-winding water resistant calendar wristwatch with 24-hour indication, signed *Rolex, GMT Master*, 1960s, 40mm. diameter. (Christie's) £1,610 $2,640

A gentleman's white gold and diamond set wristwatch, signed *Piaget,* 1980s, the chequered dial consisting of two diamond set quarters and two onyx quarters, 31mm. square.
(Christie's) £2,645 $4,338

An 18ct pink gold reversible wristwatch with skeletonised movement, signed *Jaeger-Le Coultre*, model Reverso, recent, engine-turned brushed silvered dial, 42 x 26mm.
(Christie's) £5,750 $9,545

A lady's white gold and diamond set wristwatch, signed *Piaget,* 1980s, the nickel plated movement jewelled to the centre with gold alloy balance and three adjustments, 23 x 24mm.
(Christie's) £4,830 $7,921

An airman's self-winding water resistant chronograph wristwatch, signed *Breguet, Model Aeronavale*, recent, the black dial with luminous Arabic numerals, 40mm. diameter.
(Christie's) £2,760 $4,526

A gentleman's gold wristwatch, signed *Rolex* and *W&D*, 1920s, the nickel plated spotted movement with 15 jewels with monometallic balance, 32mm. diameter.
(Christie's) £920 $1,509

A lady's gold self-winding water resistant calendar wristwatch, signed *Rolex Oyster Perpetual Datejust*, recent, with flexible gold President bracelet, 26mm. diameter. (Christie's) £2,990 $4,904

An 18 carat gold diamond set self-winding water resistant wristwatch, signed *Omega*, recent, in circular case with diamond set bezel, 35mm. diameter.
(Christie's)   £1,150 $1,886

An 18ct. gold limited edition wristwatch, signed *Cartier*, model Cloche, 1990s, in D-shaped case with shaped crystal, cabochon winder, 33 x 25mm.
(Christie's)   £5,980 $9,927

A gold and stainless steel self-winding water resistant calendar wristwatch, signed *Rolex, Model Oyster Perpetual Date Submariner Chronometer*, recent, 40mm. diameter. (Christie's) £2,300 $3,772

A fine special edition 18ct. pink gold perpetual calendar moonphase repeating split second chronograph wristwatch, signed *International Watch Company, Model II Destriero Scafusia*, 42mm. diameter.
(Christie's)   £58,700 $96,268

A fine steel chronograph wristwatch. signed *Vacheron & Constantin*, 1950s, the matt gilt movement jewelled to the centre with monometallic balance, 33mm. diameter.
(Christie's)   £5,175 $8,487

A stainless steel self-winding water resistant calendar wristwatch, signed *Audemars Piguet*, model Royal Oak, 1990s, subsidiary dials for day and date, in typical case, 36mm. diameter.
(Christie's)   £3,220 $5,345

A fine 18ct gold perpetual calendar and moonphase self-winding wristwatch with power reserve indication, signed *Breguet*, 1980s, 36mm. diameter.
(Christie's)   £15,525 $25,461

A gold and diamond set quartz calendar wristwatch, signed *Cartier, Model Panthère*, 1980s, in typical gold case with diamond set bezel, 37 x 27mm.
(Christie's)   £4,830 $7,921

A gold self-winding calendar moonphase chronograph wristwatch, signed *Girard Perregaux, Chronometer*, recent, subsidiary dials 36mm. diameter.
(Christie's)   £1,495 $2,482

A rare 18ct. gold asymmetric wristwatch, signed _Cartier, Model Crash_, 1980s, the nickel plated movement signed _LeCoultre_ with gold alloy balance, 43 x 23mm. (Christie's)　£14,950 $24,518

A stainless steel self-winding water resistant calendar wristwatch with 24 hour indication, signed _Rolex Oyster Perpetual Date Explorer II Chronometer_, 1970s, 38mm. diameter. (Christie's) £2,530 $4,149

A gentleman's gold wristwatch, signed _Patek Philippe_, 1950s, in square case with downturned wedge-shaped lugs, snap-on back, 26mm. square. (Christie's)　£1,552 $2,545

A lady's early gold wristwatch, signed _Patek Philippe & Cie._, 1910s, the frosted gilt movement jewelled to the third with bimetallic balance and counterpoised lever escapement, 27mm. diameter. (Christie's)　£1,495 $2,451

A pink gold chronograph wristwatch with unusual chamfered lugs, signed _Vacheron & Constantin_, 1940s, the matt silvered dial with raised pink gold Arabic quarter hour marks, 36mm. diameter. (Christie's)　£7,475 $12,408

A lady's 19ct. white gold and diamond set heart shaped quartz wristwatch, signed _Piaget_, recent, the mother of pearl dial with diamond set heart shaped centre, 21 x 21mm. (Christie's)　£1,265 $2,100

An airman's steel self-winding water resistant chronograph wristwatch, signed _Breguet, Model Aeronavale_, recent, the black dial with luminous Arabic numerals, 40mm. diameter. (Christie's)　£2,760 $4,526

A lady's white gold and diamond set oval wristwatch, signed _Piaget_, 1980s, the nickel plated movement jewelled to the centre with gold alloy balance, 27 x 25mm. (Christie's)　£2,533 $4,149

A fine gold self-winding perpetual calendar wristwatch, signed _Daniel Roth, Numero 009_, recent, the nickel plated self-winding movement with pink gold rotor, 37 x 35mm. (Christie's) £9,775 $16,031

A gentleman's gold wristwatch, , signed *Patek Phillipe,* 1950s, the nickel plated bar movement jewelled to the centre with gold alloy balance, 27 x 35mm. (Christie's) £2,300 $3,818

A gold reversible quartz wristwatch, signed *Jaeger-LeCoultre, Model Reverso,* 1970s, the two tone silvered dial with Arabic numerals and blued steel hands, 39 x 22mm. (Christie's)   £2,530 $4,149

A lady's gold self-winding water resistant calendar wristwatch, *signed Rolex, Model Oyster Perpetual Datejust Chronometer,* 1990s, 26mm. diameter. (Christie's)   £2,760 $4,526

An interesting gold quartz controlled electronic calendar wristwatch, signed *IWC, DA VINCI,* 1960s, the textured gold dial with raised baton numerals, date aperture, gold hands, 38 x 35mm. (Christie's)   £1,725 $2,850

A gentleman's 18ct. white gold chronograph wristwatch, signed *Daniel Roth,* recent, the silvered and textured dial with blued steel hands and sweep centre seconds, 38 x 35mm. (Christie's)   £4,830 $7,921

A gentleman's 18ct. gold rectangular wristwatch, signed *Patek Philippe, Model Gondolo,* recent, with mechanical movement, the white dial with Arabic numerals, 33 x 25mm. (Christie's)   £3,680 $6,035

A gentleman's gold wristwatch, signed *Patek Philippe,* 1960s, the nickel plated movement jewelled to the centre with gold alloy balance, 33 x 28mm. (Christie's)   £2,300 $3,772

A lady's white gold wristwatch, signed *Piaget,* 1980s, the nickel plated movement jewelled to the centre, adjusted to five positions and temperature, 24mm. diameter. (Christie's) $805 $1,320

A gold single button chronograph wristwatch, *signed Sarda, Besancon,* 1920s, the nickel plated movement jewelled to the centre with bimetallic balance, 32mm. square. (Christie's) £1,265 $2,075

An 18ct. gold quartz chronograph wristwatch, signed *Bulgari*, 1990s, the white dial with raised gilt baton numerals, 35mm. diameter.
(Christie's) £2,070 $3,436

A lady's gold quartz wristwatch, signed *Cartier, Model Tank Chinoise*, 1980s, in typical case with cabochon winder, 27 x 21mm.
(Christie's) £1,725 $2,829

Ladies fine high yellow metal cased Rolex Oyster Perpetual Datejust Chronometer with diamond mounted face.
(Aylsham) £2,600 $4,316

A gold water resistant chronograph wristwatch, signed *Omega, Speedmaster Professional,* 1960s, the pink gilt movement jewelled to the centre with pink gold alloy balance, 40mm. diameter.
(Christie's) £3,450 $5,727

An 18ct. gold self-winding water resistant calendar wristwatch, signed *Vacheron & Constantin*, 1960s, the nickel plated self-winding movement with gold alloy balance, 35mm. diameter.
(Christie's) £2,300 $3,818

A gold self-winding and water resistant calendar wristwatch, signed *Audemars Piguet, Model Royal Oak,* 1980s, in tonneau shaped case, with octagonal bezel and back, 36mm. diameter.
(Christie's) £4,830 $8,018

A gentleman's gold wristwatch, signed *Vacheron & Constantin,* 1950s, the nickel plated movement jewelled to the centre, adjusted to temperatures, 35mm. diameter.
(Christie's) £2,070 $3,395

An 18 carat gold water resistant rectangular wristwatch, signed *Patek Philippe & Cie.,* model Gondolo, recent, with mechanical movement, Calibre 215, 38 x 30mm. (Christie's) £3,450 $5,727

A gentleman's white gold rectangular wristwatch, signed *Vacheron & Constantin,* 1980s, in tonneau case with snap on back, 35mm. diameter.
(Christie's) £1,035 $1,697

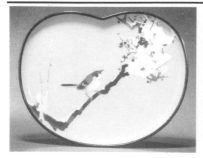

A Namikawa Sosuke kidney-shaped cloisonné tray, Meiji period, decorated in various coloured enamels, depicting a sparrow perched on a blossoming branch, 11⁵/₈in. diameter.
(Christie's)   £13,800 $22,494

A Chinese cloisonné two-handled large vase, 17th century, Hu, decorated with colourful bands of stylised flowers and foliage, 21in. high. (Sotheby's)   £702 $1,150

An Imperial cloisonné enamel model of a saddled horse, Qianlong, colourfully enamelled with elaborately decorated saddlecloth and detachable saddle, 7⁷/₈in. wide.
(Christie's)   £8,625 $14,059

A cloisonné enamel and gilt-bronze square beaker vase, fanggu, Qianlong four-character mark and of the period, pale blue ground, 11¾in. high.
(Christie's)   £3,450 $5,624

A pair of large cloisonné enamel quatrefoil jardinières, late 18th/19th century, this sides colourfully decorated with exotic birds perching on flowering lotus and chrysanthemum, 15in. wide. (Christie's)   £2,070 $3,374

A dark blue cloisonné vase, attributed to the Hayashi workshop, Meiji period, decorated in various coloured enamels with a sparrow perched on a blossoming tree, 3⁵/₈in. high.
(Christie's)   £1,610 $2,624

A fine Ando moriage cloisonné vase, with Ando Jubei mark inlaid in silver wire, Meiji period, decorated in various tones of coloured enamels, 13¾in. high.
(Christie's)   £45,500 $74,165

A rare pair of cloisonné candlesticks, Meiji period, decorated with a repeated pattern of stylised chrysanthemums and scrolling foliage, each approx. 15¼in. high.
(Christie's)   £3,450 $5,624

A cloisonné vase, with a Hayashi Kodenji mark, Meiji period, decorated in green, blue and yellow enamels on a dark blue ground with sprays of hydrangea, 3⁹/₁₆in. high.
(Christie's)   £1,610 $2,624

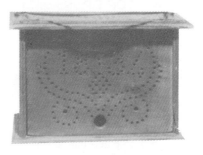

A Victorian copper helmet coal scuttle, with turned wood handles, 48cm. long.
(Bristol) £125 $205

An 18th century brass dog collar, with later padlock and key, inscribed *Mr John Bordwisell of Booth Ferry owner in Yorkshire 1721*, 14cm. diameter.
(Tennants) £850 $1,360

Antique American foot warmer, in poplar, pierced heart motif on obverse with *1834* inside, original tin burner, 10in. long.
(Eldred's) £266 $440

A pair of brass candlesticks, probably Dutch, mid-18th century, each with a circular moulded rim above a ring-turned candleholder, 4¾in. high.
(Christie's) £1,066 $1,610

A pair of brass candlesticks, 18th century, each with notched flared candlecups and baluster stems on scalloped dome bases, 7¾in. high.
(Sotheby's) £690 $1,150

A pair of baroque brass candlesticks, Continental, mid-17th century, each with a cylindrical candlesocket above a mid-drip pan, 10in. high.
(Sotheby's) £1,897 $3,162

A 19th century Dutch brass coal bucket, with swan head loop handles and fan mounts, on a flared foot, 23cm. high.
(Phillips) £380 $623

A pair of brass candlesticks, probably English, early 18th century, each with a circular moulded rim above a faceted cylindrical candle cup, 6¼in. high.
(Christie's) £2,012 $3,220

An Edwardian copper coal bucket, with chased foliate bands and swing handle, 33cm.
(Bristol) £72 $118

W.M.F.-style tray, copper border with brass handles surrounding china painted blank with irises, unmarked, 18in. wide. (Skinner)　　　　£138　$230

Arts and Crafts copper and brass vase, repoussé design, cut out handles, 17¼in. high. (Skinner)　　　　£138　$230

An Arts and Crafts copper jug of tapering form, with applied beaten copper banding with stud work, brass finial on hinged lid and brass loop handle, incised maker's mark to base, 12in. high. (Andrew Hartley)　　　　£60　$100

Pair of brass trumpet based candlesticks, probably England, second half 17th century, with sausage turnings, 7⁹/₁₆in. high. (Skinner)　　　　£8,625　$13,800

Impressive W.M.F. copper pitcher, raised foliate design, brass handle and mount, impressed diamond with bird mark, polished, 17½in. high. (Skinner)　　　　£104　$173

A rare copper tea kettle, Benjamin and/or Joseph Harbeson, Philadelphia, circa 1800, with a hinged strap handle, 11in. high. (Sotheby's)　　　　£2,279　$3,737

A pair of brass candlesticks, 18th century, each with petal-form flared candlecup and baluster stem, 7¾in. high. (Sotheby's)　　　　£3,277　$5,462

An Edwardian Burmese brass table gong with electroplated scrolled mounts on ivory supports, serpentine shape oak base, height 16½in. (H. C. Chapman) £175 $290

Impressive W.M.F. copper wall plaque, raised foliate design around a woman's portrait, impressed diamond with bird mark, polished, diameter 17in.
(Skinner)   £189 $316

A 19th century brass wall light bracket, with flower etched cranberry glass shade and fluted glass reservoir, 16in. wide.
(Andrew Hartley)   £820 $1,353

A 19th century yew jardinière, with brass ring banding and rivets, 27cm. diameter.
(Bristol)   £310 $496

A William and Mary cast brass candlestick, English or Flemish, cylindrical candle socket pierced at the side for cleaning, 7¾in. high.
(Sotheby's)   £1,052 $1,725

Onondaga copper candlesticks, attributed, hammered finish, two handles, unmarked, 9¼in. high.
(Skinner)   £258 $431

W.M.F. copper pitcher, hammered finish with incised design, good patina, diamond mark, 15½in. high.
(Skinner)   £69 $115

Arts and Crafts loving cup, brass floral work over oak, *First Prize, High Stepper, National Western Stock Show, Denver, Jan. 18–23, 1909*, 7¾in. high.
(Skinner)   £138 $230

An Edwardian brass jardinière, of cylindrical form with paw feet, embossed with foliage and various crests, 15¾in. high.
(Christie's)   £920 $1,490

A pair of Queen Anne cast brass petal-base candlesticks, English, first half 18th century, on a domed foot with shaped petal base, height of pair 8¾in.
(Sotheby's)   £1,403 $2,300

A French polychrome petit-point needlework cushion, the needlework 18th century, woven in wools, silks and with a silver thread background, approx. 28 x 21in. (Christie's)   £4,370 $7,254

A pair of Brussels tapestry cushions, the tapestry 17th century, woven in wools and silks, each depicting a youth holding a ribbon and a shield, above a quiver, 20 x 15in. (Christie's)   £4,600 $7,636

A Louis XVI Aubusson mythological tapestry cushion, woven in wools and silks, depicting a scene from La Fontaine's Fables, with a crow sitting on the back of a ram, 16in. x 18in. (Christie's)   £1,725 $2,794

A pair of French needlework cushions, late 18th/early 19th century, in wool and silk and of heart-shape, each with a vase issuing foliate sprays with flowers, 15in. long.
(Christie's)   £3,220 $5,216

A French gros and petit point needlework cushion, 18th century, in wool and silk, depicting within a C-scrolled cartouche a peasant maiden bringing a pot to a copper or iron-smith seated and working another copper pot, 20in. x 19in.
(Christie's)   £747 $1,210

A pair of English gros and petit point needlework cushions, 18th century, in wool, depicting Chinese scenes, one with a maiden playing a lute seated before a pagoda, the other with a figure seated before a horse, 20in. x 14½in.
(Christie's)   £4,370 $7,079

A French gros-point needlework cushion, late 17th/18th century, in wool, depicting numerous flowers and scrolling foliage on a blue ground, 20in. x 22in.
(Christie's)   £4,370 $7,079

A pair of Flemish tapestry cushions, second half 16th century, woven in wools and silks, each depicting two youths holding drapery centred by a flowering vase on a grotesque head, 14in. x 19in.
(Christie's)   £2,760 $4,471

A Brussels mythological tapestry cushion, second half 16th century, woven in wools and silks, depicting the story of Erichthonius, with a man bringing chalice to a maiden, 17in. x 27in.
(Christie's)   £1,955 $3,167

A very rare 18th century carved and painted limewood doll, with unusual protruding blue eyes, flared nostrils, deeply carved lips, 23in. high, circa 1770. (Christie's) £8,625 $13,713

A Käthe Kruse plastic-headed doll, with painted brown eyes and blond real hair wig, calico body, circa 1952, 52cm. high. (Auction Team Köln) £284 $455

A Kammer and Reinhardt mould 100, with painted pale blue eyes, baby's body, whitework frock and 'Baby' brooch, 18.5in. (Christie's) £437 $699

A fashionable doll probably by François Gaultier, with swivel head, blue eyes, pierced ears, fair mohair wig over cork pate and gussetted kid body, 14½in. high. (Christie's) £862 $1,379

A fine pair of early 19th century English wooden dolls, turned and painted, with inset pupilless eyes and brown wigs, dressed in contemporary outfits, 12½in. and 13in. high. (Christie's) £3,450 $5,520

A late 19th/early 20th century poupard doll, with bisque head and rotating body containing a musical box, operated by spinning the stained and turned wood handle, 40cm. (Bearne's) £680 $1,122

A Simon & Halbig biscuit character doll, open mouth with two teeth, brown real hair wig and brown sleeping eyes, 45cm. high. post 1912. (Auction Team Köln) £334 $534

A ventriloquist's dummy modelled as a boy, with jaw, eye and hand movement and dressed in contemporary green tweed suit, 33in. high. (Christie's) £253 $405

A Gebrüder Heubach character googly-eyed doll, the circular painted eyes with blue irises glancing to the right, with moulded top-knot, 9½in. (Christie's) £345 $552

A Simon & Halbig/Kammer & Reinhardt bisque headed doll, no.70, with sleeping brown eyes, open mouth and curly fair wig, 73cm. (Bristol) £1,250 $2,000

A Schildkröt 'Strampelchen' doll, the head and body marked 56, with blue sleeping glass eyes, open mouth, 1953.
(Auction Team Köln) £125 $201

A swivel head bisque doll, probably by Gaultier, with fixed blue glass eyes, closed mouth, pierced ears, blonde mohair wig, 12in. high.
(Andrew Hartley)   £600 $990

A Kestner '211' bisque-headed character doll, with sleeping brown eyes, open mouth, curly brown wig and composition body, 30cm.
(Bristol)   £190 $313

An unusual china-headed doll modelled as a child with hairband, swivel head, composition shoulder plate and lower torso with floating joints and china limbs, 9¼in. high, German, circa 1850.
(Christie's)   £1,725 $2,760

A rare 117 X doll by Kämmer & Reinhardt, bisque head with grey-blue swivel eyes, mohair wig, hard rubber hands, jointed body, 1912, 36cm. high.
(Auction Team Köln)
                          £1,423 $2,277

A Kämmer & Reinhardt china headed baby doll, open mouth with two glass teeth, blonde mohair wig, circa 1914.
(Auction Team Köln) £460 $736

BUYER BEWARE

If you are considering the purchase of a bisque headed doll, always check the part of the doll beneath the wig, which normally is a small hole in the bisque head. Often cracks can be disguised by the wig at this point and so it should be carefully inspected.

Cracks in the structure of the head are a fundamental disability, and would result in a serious downturn in the value.

Dockree's

A Kestner 211 character with brown sleeping eyes, blonde mohair over plaster pate and jointed body in cotton print frock, 14½in. high, impressed *J.D.K. 211*.
(Christie's)   £184 $294

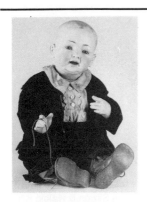

A large J D K character baby with blue sleeping eyes, painted hair and bent-limbed baby body dressed in black velvet suit, 24in. high.
(Christie's)   £632 $1,011

A Schau ins Land boy doll in the style of Käthe Kruse, with wooden head and fabric body, painted blue eyes and synthetic wig, 1950, 33cm. high.
(Auction Team Köln) £188 $301

A large child doll by J D Kestner with blue sleeping eyes, blonde mohair wig over plaster pate and jointed body, 26in. high.
(Christie's)   £862 $1,379

An Armand Marseille bisque-headed baby doll, with sleeping brown eyes, open mouth, curly blonde wig, on ball-jointed composition body, clothed, 73cm.
(Bristol)   £260 $429

An Armand Marseille bisque china head doll, with blonde wig, the kid body with composition limbs, 67cm.
(Bearne's)   £240 $396

An Armand Marseille bisque-headed baby doll, with sleeping blue eyes, open mouth, curly brown wig, on ball-jointed composition body, clothed 78cm.
(Bristol)   £210 $346

BUYER BEWARE

Another useful tip for new collectors, of dolls, say, is to make a careful list of key points as they discover them.

If they learn how to distinguish such features as known makers, untouched condition, original clothes and whether the example dates from before the First World War, for example, they will soon know when some less than scrupulous vendor is trying to feed them a line.
(Ewbank)

A Bébé Jumeau bisque head girl doll, with fixed blue glass eyes, closed mouth, jointed wood and papier mâché body with pull string voice box.
(Andrew Hartley) £2,700 $4,455

A German bisque shoulder head girl doll with blue glass sleeping eyes, blonde mohair wig, jointed kid limbs and body, bisque forearms and hands, 16in. high.
(Andrew Hartley)   £480 $792

A Bébé Gaultier, with closed mouth, pierced ears, blonde mohair wig over cork pate and jointed wood and papier mâché body, 22in. high. (Christie's) £2,530 $4,048

A Lenci boy, with felt face, brown painted side-glancing eyes, blonde mohair wig and straight-limbed felt body, 17½in. high. (Christie's) £517 $825

A large Simon & Halbig 1329 Oriental, with brown sleeping eyes, moulded brows, pierced ears, black wig and jointed body, 27in. high, 26¼in. long. (Christie's) £4,025 $6,480

A Simon & Halbig K*R child doll, with brown sleeping eyes, moulded brows, pierced ears, fair mohair wig and jointed body, 21½in. high. (Christie's) £368 $592

A Bébé Jumeau, with closed mouth, brown yeux fibres, pierced ears, blonde wig over cork pate, jointed wood and papier mâché body, 19in. high. (Christie's) £2,070 $3,312

A Schuco Tyrolean Dancing Couple, tin with plush hair and felt clothing, clockwork, the woman celluloid, post 1933. (Auction Team Köln) £133 $214

An Armand Marseille 390 doll, with blue lashed sleeping eyes, fair wig and jointed body, 23in. high, and a dolls wardrobe with mirror, 25½in. high. (Christie's) £184 $296

A Bébé Jumeau, with closed mouth, blue yeux fibres, pierced ears, blonde mohair wig over cork pate, 10in. high. (Christie's) £2,760 $4,416

A fine A. Thuillier Bébé with closed mouth, blonde mohair wig, jointed wood and papier mâché fixed wrist body, 22in. tall, circa 1879, impressed A 11 T. (Christie's) £17,250 $27,427

A Kestner mould 214, with blue lashed sleeping eyes, jointed body and white tucked frock, 22½in. high, impressed F½ 10½ JDK 214. (Christie's) £600 $960

A large Bébé Jumeau, with closed mouth, blue eyes, pierced ears, blonde mohair wig and jointed wood and papier mâché body, 24in. high. (Christie's) £920 $1,472

A Vichy smoking Chinaman automaton with composition head and eyelid, head, lower jaw and arm movements, 28in. high, circa 1890. (Christie's) £2,530 $4,023

The Callard House, a William IV wooden dolls' house of five bays and two stories, the exterior painted in dark and mid green.
(Christie's)   £10,925 $17,480

An American Gothic Revival painted wood single-storey model house, early 20th century, possibly intended as a bird house, the front with a central open door with arched pediment, 19¼in. long.
(Sotheby's)   £281 $460

An English wooden dolls' house of circa 1900, opening at both back and front to reveal four rooms with hall, staircase, landing, 38in. wide, 30in. high. (Christie's) £368 $589

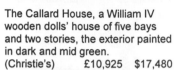

An unusual Moritz Gottschalk doll's house, of three bays and two stories with blue roof, balcony at first floor level and steps to front door with wooden rail, 14in. deep.
(Christie's)   £552 $883

A wooden box-back doll's house, of two bays and two stories, brick painted, with steps to the front door, opening at the front to reveal two rooms, 20in. high.
(Christie's)   £517 $827

A late 19th century wooden doll's house, having four rooms with fire places and central staircase to landing, on turned legs 36in. wide.
(Dee Atkinson & Harrison)
    £420 $672

A fully mechanical clockwork Mechanical Workshop, by J.I. Austen & Co., Chicago, modelled as an Art Nouveau building containing figures at various pursuits, 62cm. high, 1906.
(Auction Team Köln)£5,862 $9,379

A wooden box-back dolls' house, painted to simulate brickwork, of two bays and two stories, opening to reveal four rooms, 24in. high.
(Christie's)   £483 $773

An early Victorian warming stand of plated circular outline with a flared rim, Paul Storr, 1838, 14cm. diameter, 14oz.
(Christie's) £552 $883

Pair of wrought steel pipe tongs, *Fort W.M. Henry Capt. B Williams 1756*, with incised decoration, 17¼in. long.
(Skinner) £5,644 $9,200

A late Victorian novelty reception bell cast in the form of a tortoise or terrapin with red glass eyes, by J.B. Carrington, 1896, 16cm. long.
(Christie's) £2,760 $4,609

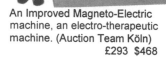

An Improved Magneto-Electric machine, an electro-therapeutic machine. (Auction Team Köln) £293 $468

A musical toilet paper dispenser, playing two melodies (including the national anthem!), by L.R. Paris
(Auction Team Köln) £293 $468

Wrought iron, whalebone and wood sugar nippers, late 18th/early 19th century, with scribe line decorated whalebone handle, 12in. long.
(Skinner) £359 $575

A red painted cast iron Siemens W250T fan, with gold painted blades and basket, circa 1930.
(Auction Team Köln) £33 $53

A Silo Coca Cola refrigerator by Wilhelm Lok & Co., Siegen, red painted with chrome mounting 55cm. high, circa 1960.
(Auction Team Köln) £418 $669

A Universal E9410 heart shaped push button toaster, which flips the frames over, with original handles and feet, 1929.
(Auction Team Köln) £272 $435

A black and green painted cast metal mangle by Alexander Werk, Berlin, with gold decoration, two cylinders with adjustable setting, circa 1900. (Auction Team Köln) £137 $220

An Art Nouveau cigarette dispenser by H. Stiles, England, in working order, 1909.
(Auction Team Köln) £502 $803

An cast iron coffee grinder by the Enterprise Mfg. Co., Philadelphia, with later-painted drawer to base, circa 1900.
(Auction Team Köln) £272 $435

Two pairs of ropework sea chest beckets, probably American, mid to late 19th century, the first of natural ropework with monkey fist knots, the second painted black on red blocks. (Sotheby's)　£315　$517

An unusual Estate 4 slice electric toaster Model 177, with synchronised swing mechanism for all four doors, 1925. (Auction Team Köln) £108 $173

A pair of Victorian grape scissors, decorated with scrolling grape vines and with textured decoration, William Hutton & Sons Ltd., London, 1894, 17cm. long. (Bearne's)　£290　$479

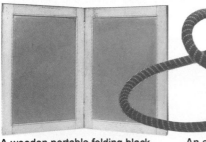

A wooden portable folding black board, probably American, 19th century, hinged at centre, 15¾ x 11½in. (Sotheby's) £245　$402

An early German cylinder vacuum cleaner on wheels, circa 1925, unattributed, with original cable. (Auction Team Köln)　£293　$468

A Victorian cast iron & brass goffering mangle, on mahogany base, 14in. wide. (Academy Auctioneers) £150　$240

An American Reading apple peeler, cast iron with table clamp, 21 x 30 x 18cm. 1878. (Auction Team Köln)　£146　$234

Unusual mechanical pin catcher, 19th century, turning a knurled knob activates a yellow bird to fetch a pin out of a red velvet covered box, 6in. wide. (Eldred's)　£133　$220

The Original Knox Fluting Machine No. 22, American pleating iron with adhesive portrait of Susan Knox, with original handle and table clamp and ten replacement cylinders, 1870. (Auction Team Köln) £795 $1,272

Enterprise #9 coffee mill, 19th century, in red and black, repainted, 28½in. high. (Eldred's)　£126　$209

A black-painted cast iron Wimshurst machine, with gold decoration, ebonised plates, 20cm. diameter. (Auction Team Köln) £75　$120

A Great Lion cast iron door stop, circa 1900, 37cm. high. (Auction Team Köln)　£158　$254

A fine Canton fan with filigree sticks, the leaf painted recto and verso with figures on terraces, their faces of ivory, their clothes of silk, hung with a silk tassel, 12in. circa 1860. (Christie's) £1,610 $2,576

A mercer's shop, a fan, the leaf painted with ladies buying silk, the ivory sticks carved and pierced and painted, English, circa 1760, 11in. (Christie's) £3,220 $5,152

Robert-Houdin, a printed fan publicising the famous conjuror, with wooden sticks, circa 1865, 9in. (Christie's) £1,610 $2,576

Dido and Aeneas, a fine fan painted in Italianate style, the ivory sticks carved and pierced with flowers, English, circa 1730, 11in. (Christie's) £7,475 $11,960

A circular handscreen, of ivory silk embroidered recto and verso in brightly coloured silks with a parrot, pheasant, butterflies and wisteria, 17in. including handle, Chinese, mid-19th century. (Christie's) £862 $1,379

Views of Macao, a fan, the leaf painted with three vignettes of Macao, with variegated sticks of white metal and gilt metal filigree enamelled in blue and green, 9in., Macao, mid-19th century. (Christie's) £4,140 $6,624

A Tessen or Japanese iron war fan, the leaf of gold and silver suns against a black ground, with iron guardsticks silvered and gilt, 11in., Japanese late 19th century. (Christie's) £1,150 $1,840

A rare 17th century fan, the kid leaf painted with tulips and other flowers, the tortoiseshell sticks slotted through the leaf, 8½in., circa 1680. (Christie's) £2,990 $4,784

A fine fan, the leaf painted with two elegant ladies in a formal garden with a gardener, the ivory sticks carved and pierced with flowers, circa 1750,10in. (Christie's) £1,495 $2,392

A fan, the leaf painted with an allegory of a proxy marriage, with a classical king, a lady and her portrait, French, circa 1770, 10in. (Christie's) £460 $736

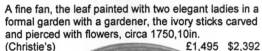

Gibraltar, a printed commemorative fan, the leaf a hand-coloured etching of the rock of Gibraltar with a fleet of French and Spanish vessels in the foreground, 11in. French for the Spanish market, mid-18th century. (Christie's) £12,650 $20,240

A Canton fan painted with an extensive landscape with two pagodas and a river, with lacquer sticks, 11in., circa 1860. (Christie's) £2,070 $3,312

Cleopatre Expirante, The Death of Cleopatra, a fan, the chickenskin leaf painted bright colours within an Etruscan border, the guardsticks backed with mother-of-pearl, 10in, Italian for the French market, circa 1810. (Christie's) £1,012 $1,619

A chinoiserie fan, painted with Chinese figures in the garden with a gazebo with mica windows, the figures with applied silk clothes, the flowers decorated with mother-of-pearl and foil, 11in., circa 1780. (Christie's) £977 $1,563

A fine Brussels point de Gaze fan with monogram *LMT*, worked with garlands of flowers, the mother of pearl sticks carved, pierced and gilt, circa 1865,11in., with Faucon box. (Christie's) £690 $1,104

A fine cabriolet fan painted with five vignette views of possibly the Canton river, the sticks lacquered in black and gold with a frieze of animals and with vines, 11in., Macao, mid-19th century. (Christie's) £5,750 $9,200

Ronald Reagan, signed colour 8 x 10in., head and shoulders. (Vennett-Smith)   £100 $160

Frank Sinatra, signed and inscribed 7½ x 9½, head and shoulders. (Vennett-Smith)   £280 $456

Fred Astaire, signed sepia postcard, head and shoulders, early. (Vennett-Smith)   £95 $152

Vivien Leigh, signed postcard, head shoulders as Scarlett O' Hara, from Gone With The Wind (German edition). (Vennett-Smith)   £340 $547

Vivien Leigh, signed postcard to lower white border, head and shoulders. (Vennett-Smith)   £130 $209

Laurel & Hardy, signed and inscribed postcard, by both Stan Laurel and Oliver Hardy, half-length in bowler hats. (Vennett-Smith)   £265 $427

Ronald Reagan, signed sepia postcard, head and shoulders. (Vennett-Smith)   £95 $155

Joan Crawford, a collection of 58 typed, signed letters, the majority signed with first name only, a few in full, most one page, 1950s–70s. (Vennett-Smith)   £550 $885

Silence of the Lambs, signed 8 x 10in., by Jodie Foster, Anthony Hopkins, Scott Glenn, individually. (Vennett-Smith)   £160 $257

Orson Welles, signed sepia postcard, head and shoulders. (Vennett-Smith) £130 $209

Richard Burton, signed and inscribed 8 x 10in. (Vennett-Smith) £70 $114

Boris Karloff, signed 5 x 7in., half-length with silhouette background. (Vennett-Smith) £190 $309

Frank Sinatra, signed postcard, three quarter length, 1950s, in green. (Vennet-Smith) £300 $483

Shirley Temple, signed sepia 6 x 7in., bodyweight photo, half-length, signed as child. (Vennett-Smith) £160 $257

Marlon Brando, signed postcard, head and shoulders, surname light and partially in darker portion. (Vennett-Smith) £140 $225

Joan Blondell, signed 8 x 10in., half length from Blondie Johnson. (Vennett-Smith) £55 $89

Conchita Supervia, signed sepia postcard, three quarter length standing, extremely rare. (Vennett-Smith) £130 $211

Julia Roberts, signed colour 8 x 10in., full-length in red dress on garden swing. (Vennett-Smith) £75 $120

Charles Chaplin, signed sepia 7 x 9½in., early, photo by Witzel of Los Angeles. (Vennett-Smith)£350 $570

Laurel and Hardy, signed and inscribed, 5 x 3½in., by both Stan Laurel and Oliver Hardy, half-length in candid pose. (Vennett-Smith) £160 $257

Beatrice Dalle, signed colour 8 x 10in., head and shoulders. (Vennett-Smith) £35 $57

Alfred Hitchcock, signed and inscribed sepia 8 x 10in., half-length with Vistavision Camera in background. (Vennett-Smith) £280 $456

Titanic, signed colour 10 x 8in., by Leonardo Di Caprio, Kate Winslet and director James Cameron, standing together on the set of Titanic. (Vennett-Smith) £310 $499

Grace Kelly, signed colour 4 x 6in. postcard, as Princess of Monaco, three quarter length standing behind chair. (Vennett-Smith) £120 $193

Mel Gibson, signed colour 8 x 10in., three quarter length from Braveheart, in silver. (Vennett-Smith) £110 $177

Eastwood & Russo, signed 10 x 8in., by both Clint Eastwood and René Russo, from In The Line of Fire. (Vennett-Smith) £80 $128

Stallone and Shire, signed 8 x 10in., by Sylvester Stallone and Talia Shire, half-length from Rocky. (Vennett-Smith) £65 $106

Audrey Hepburn, signed postcard, head and shoulders, early. (Vennett-Smith) £120 $196

Stephen Spielberg, signed colour 8 x 10, head and shoulders with arms folded. (Vennett-Smith) £60 $96

Lili Damita, signed and inscribed 8 x 10in. head and shoulders. (Vennett-Smith) £60 $96

Kelly & Charisse, signed 8 x 10in. by Gene Kelly and Cyd Charisse, individually, full-length dancing together. (Vennett-Smith) £130 $209

Charles Chaplin, signed sepia 8 x 10, head and shoulders 1936, in darker portion but legible. (Vennett-Smith) £450 $720

W.C. Fields, a good signed and inscribed sepia 10 x 13in. of Fields seated three quarter length in costume as a schoolboy, inscribed *To the baby Fay Adler*. (Vennett-Smith) £480 $782

Harrison Ford, signed colour 8 x 10in., three quarter length in costume as Indiana Jones. (Vennett-Smith) £130 $209

Helen Morgan, signed and inscribed sepia 8 x 10, head and shoulders. (Vennett-Smith) £45 $72

Hedy Lamarr, signed 10 x 8in., head and shoulders, modern reproduction signed in later years. (Vennett-Smith) £60 $97

Harpo Marx, signed sepia postcard, half length at piano.
(Vennett-Smith)　　£130　$208

Power & Novak, signed 10 x 8 still by Tyrone Power (slightly weaker) and Kim Novak (first name only).
(Vennett-Smith)　　£90　$144

Vivien Leigh, signed postcard, in turquoise, head and shoulders.
(Vennett-Smith)　　£115　$184

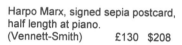

Marx Brothers, signed album page, 3 x 4½in. in red, by Harpo, Chico, Zeppo and Groucho, each with full name also signed by Reginald Tate. (Vennett-Smith)　£370　$603

Steven Spielberg, signed 10 x 8, half-length on the set of Schindler's List, alongside Liam Neeson.
(Vennett-Smith)　　£150　$240

Alfred Hitchcock, an excellent large signed and inscribed self-caricature on 11 x 14 white board, rare in this large size.
(Vennett-Smith)　　£460　$736

Bela Lugosi, signed postcard, in red, head and shoulders as Dracula, scarce.
(Vennett-Smith)　　£410　$656

Titanic, signed colour 10 x 8, by both Leonardo Di Caprio and Kate Winslet individually, full-length seated on deck of the Titanic.
(Vennett-Smith)　　£120　$192

Grace Kelly, signed 8 x 10, head and shoulders, Grace de Monaco, in later years.
(Vennett-Smith)　　£95　$152

Nicole Kidman, signed colour 8 x 10, half-length in period costume. (Vennett-Smith) £40 $64

Indiana Jones, signed colour 10 x 18, by Harrison Ford and Kate Capshaw (1989), from Indiana Jones. (Vennett-Smith) £95 $152

Frank Sinatra, signed 5 x 7, head and shoulders, first name only. (Vennett-Smith) £75 $120

Errol Flynn, an excellent signed 8 x 10, inscribed to a make-up man who worked with Flynn on his TV series Errol Flynn Theatre 1957. (Vennett-Smith) £430 $688

Grease, signed colour 10 x 8, by both John Travolta and Olivia Newton John, in a scene from Grease. (Vennett-Smith) £190 $304

John Wayne, a full-length black and white publicity photograph of subject signed and inscribed in green ink *To Jim, Good Luck, John Wayne*, 10 x 8in. framed. (Christie's) £483 $773

Ingmar Bergman, signed 8 x 10, head and shoulders, signed in later years. (Vennett-Smith) £62 $99

Baywatch, signed colour 10 x 8 cast photo, 9 signatures including Yasmin Bleeth, Gena Lee Nolin etc., with certificate of authenticity. (Vennett-Smith) £80 $128

Laurel and Hardy, signed postcard, by both Stan Laurel and Oliver Hardy. (Vennett-Smith) £230 $308

Richard Burton, signed postcard, head and shoulders, early (Vennett-Smith) £95 $152

Ingrid Bergman, signed 8.5 x 6, half-length alongside Bogart in Casablanca, modern reproduction signed in later years. (Vennett-Smith) £160 $256

Sabu, signed and inscribed 8 x 10, head and shoulders as Little Toomai, from The Elephant Boy. (Vennett-Smith) £130 $208

Orson Welles, signed postcard, head and shoulders from Moby Dick. (Vennett-Smith) £130 $208

Laurel and Hardy, signed 8.5 x 5.5, by both Stan Laurel and Oliver Hardy, together with similar photos of Stewart Granger and Jean Simmons, Yvonne Arnaud, Anna Neagle. (Vennett-Smith) £260 $416

Basil Rathbone, signed postcard, three quarter length holding two dogs. (Vennett-Smith) £100 $163

Margaret Rutherford, signed postcard, head and shoulders leaning on chair. (Vennett-Smith) £95 $152

Orson Welles, signed 10 x 8, half-length from a scene from A Crack In The Mirror, signed in later years. (Vennett-Smith) £85 $136

Pickford & Fairbanks Snr. signed sepia 7 x 9, by both Mary Pickford and Douglas Fairbanks Snr, 1924. (Vennett-Smith) £110 $176

Singin' In The Rain, 1952, M.G.M., U.S. one-sheet, 41 x 27in., linen backed. (Christie's) £1,150 $1,897

Pinky, 1949, T.C.F., British quad, 30 x 40in. (Christie's) £126 $207

Gigi, 1958, M.G.M., U.S. one-sheet, 41 x 27in., linen backed. (Christie's) £299 $493

Tarzan The Mighty, 1928, Universal, U.S. one-sheet, 41 x 27in., linen backed. (Christie's) £3,220 $5,313

Rock Around The Clock, 1956, Columbia, British quad, 30 x 40in linen backed. (Christie's) £207 $341

Double Indemnity, 1944, Paramount, U.S. one-sheet, 41 x 27in., paper backed. (Christie's) £2,530 $4,175

Green For Danger, 1946, Rank, U.S. one-sheet, 41 x 27in., linen backed. (Christie's) £632 $1,042

Felix The Cat, 1955, Italian, 19 x 27in., linen backed. (Christie's) £230 $379

Grease, 1978, Paramount, U.S. one-sheet, 41 x 27in., linen backed. (Christie's) £207 $341

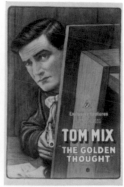

Chang, 1927, Paramount, U.S., one-sheet, 41 x 27in., linen backed. (Christie's) £632 $1,042

Get Carter, 1971, M.G.M., British quad, 30 x 40in. (Christie's) £253 $417

The Golden Thought, 1916, Selig, U.S., one-sheet, 41 x 27in. (Christie's) £1,380 $2,277

Roma Citta Aperta/Roma Open City, 1945, Minerva, Italian, Aldo Fabrizzi style, 39 x 27in., linen backed, (B). Art by Anselmo Ballester (1897-1974) (unsigned). (Christie's) £2,070 $3,415

The Incredible Shrinking Man, 1957, Universal, U.S. half-sheet, 22 x 28in. Art by Reynold Brown. (Christie's) £368 $607

The Phantom Of The Opera/Il Fantasma Dell'Opera, 1943, Universal, Italian four-foglio, 79 x 55in., linen backed. Art by F. Carfagni. (Christie's) £3,680 $6,072

Africa Speaks, 1930s, Mascot, U.S. one-sheet, 41 x 27in. (Christie's) £207 $341

Lifeboat, 1944, T.C.F., U.S. half-sheet, 22 x 28in. paper backed. (Christie's) £862 $1,422

Gone With The Wind, 1939, M.G.M., U.S. window card, 22 x 14in. (Christie's) £1,150 $1,897

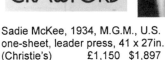

Sadie McKee, 1934, M.G.M., U.S. one-sheet, leader press, 41 x 27in. (Christie's)   £1,150 $1,897

Goldfinger, 1964, U.A., British quad, 30 x 40in. (Christie's)   £1,035 $1,707

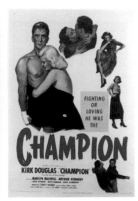

Champion, 1949, U.A., U.S. one-sheet, 41 x 27in., linen backed. (Christie's)   £276 $455

The Invisible Man, 1933, Universal, U.S. one-sheet, 41 x 27in., linen backed. This is the first time an example of this poster has appeared at auction. (Christie's)   £36,700 $60,555

Belle Of The Nineties, 1934, Paramount, U.S. half-sheet, 22 x 28in., linen backed, signed in black ink *Mae West*. (Christie's)   £253 $417

The Bride Of Frankenstein/La Fiancée De Frankenstein, 1935, Universal, French, 23 x 15½in., linen backed. Art by Constantine Belinsky. (Christie's) £2,300 $3,795

City Lights, 1931, U.A., U.S. window card, 22 x 14in. (Christie's)   £1,725 $2,846

Funny Face, 1957, Paramount, U.S. half-sheet, 22 x 28in., paper backed. (Christie's) £402 $663

Rebecca/La Prima Moglie, 1940, Selznick, Italian, 39 x 27in., paper backed. (Christie's) £483 $796

Tom Mix, 1930s Universal Studios
personality poster, Belgian, 30 x
23in. linen backed.
(Christie's)   £172 $283

As You Desire Me/Comme Tu Me
Veux, 1931, M.G.M., Belgian, 32 x
24in., linen backed.
(Christie's)   £1,380 $2,277

Modern Times/Les Temps
Modernes, 1936, U.A., Belgian, 29
x 23in., linen backed.
(Christie's)   £1,150 $1,897

Bulldog Drummond, 1929, U.A.,
insert, 36 x 14in.
(Christie's)   £1,265 $2,087

Rear Window, 1954, Paramount,
U.S. half-sheet style A, 22 x 28in.
(Christie's)   £805 $1,328

Lolita, 1962, M.G.M., U.S. three-
sheet, 81 x 40in., linen backed.
(Christie's)   £690 $1,138

The Wages Of Fear, 1955,
Filmsonor, British double crown, 30
x 20in., linen backed. Art by Eric
Pulford. (Christie's)   £345 $569

The Lavender Hill Mob, 1951,
Ealing, British six-sheet, 76 x 76in.,
linen backed.
(Christie's)   £2,990 $4,933

Scram!/Les Deux Vagabonds,
1932, M.G.M., Belgian, 30 x 23in.
linen backed.
(Christie's)   £460 $759

Paramount Paragraphics, 1936, Paramount, U.S. one-sheet, 41 x 27in., paper backed.
(Christie's) £322 $531

Spione/Les Espions (Spies), 1928, UFA/Fritz Lang, Belgian, 30 x 23in., linen backed.
(Christie's) £1,380 $2,277

The Blue Angel/Der Blaue Engel, 1940s re-release, German, 33 x 23½in., linen backed. Art by Bonné.
(Christie's) £517 $853

Vertigo, 1958, Paramount, U.S. 60 x 40in. unfolded, Art by Saul Bass (b.1920-1996).
(Christie's) £3,220 $5,313

Thunderball, 1965, U.A., British quad, 30 x 40in., unfolded.
(Christie's) £500 $825

The Godfather, 1972, Paramount, Australian one-sheet, 40 x 27in., linen backed.
(Christie's) £345 $570

It's A Wonderful Life/La Vie Est Belle, 1946, R.K.O., French, 63 x 47in., linen backed.
(Christie's) £1,610 $2,656

Broadway, 1929, Universal, Belgian, 33 x 24in., linen backed, unfolded.
(Christie's) £2,415 $3,984

The Man From Utah, 1934, Lone Star, U.S. one-sheet, 41 x 27in. linen backed.
(Christie's) £632 $1,042

The Kiss/Le Baiser, 1929, M.G.M.,
Belgian, 32 x 24in. linen backed.
(Christie's)   £1,035 $1,707

Titanic, 1953, T.C.F., Belgian, 14½
x 11½in., linen backed.
(Christie's)   £161 $265

Psycho, 1960, Paramount, U.S.
one-sheet, 41 x 27in., linen backed.
(Christie's)   £632 $1, 042

The Bride Of Frankenstein, 1935, Universal, U.S. snipe, 14 x 28in., paper backed.
(Christie's)   £3,680 $6,072

Breakfast At Tiffany's, 1961,
Paramount, Japanese, 29 x 20in.,
linen backed, unfolded.
(Christie's)   £1,265 $2,087

Les Enfants du Paradis, 1946,
Pathé, French two-panel, 63 x
94in., linen backed.
(Christie's)   £1,840 $3,036

The Man Who Knew Too Much,
1956, Paramount, U.S. 40 x 30in.,
linen backed, unfolded.
(Christie's)   £368 $607

Jane Eyre, 1943, T.C.F., U.S. one-sheet, 41 x 27in., linen backed. (Christie's) £230 $379

From Russia With Love, 1963, U.A., Japanese, 28 x 20in., unfolded. (Christie's) £460 $759

Zazie Dans Le Metro, 1960, Pathé, French, 23 x 15½in., linen backed. (Christie's) £28 $46

Broadway Melody/Broadways Melodi, 1929, M.G.M., Swedish, 39 x 27in., unfolded. Art by Eric Rohmann (1891-1949). (Christie's) £632 $1,042

Rebel Without A Cause/Gioventu Bruciata, 1955, Warner Bros., Italian two-foglio, 55 x 39in., linen backed, Art by Luigi Martinati (1893-1984). (Christie's) £1,092 $1,801

The Devil Is A Woman/La Femme Et Le Pantin, 1935, Paramount, Belgian, 30 x 23in., linen backed. This is the only known copy of this poster. (Christie's) £2,185 $3,605

La Dolce Vita, 1960, Cineriz, Italian four-foglio, 79 x 55in., linen backed. Art by Georgio Olivetti. (Christie's) £4,025 $6,641

ZouZou, 1934, Belgian, 30 x 23in. linen backed. (Christie's) £2,530 $4,174

Laura, 1944, T.C.F., French, 47 x 31½in. linen backed, Art by Boris Grinsson (b.1907). (Christie's) £805 $1,328

With Byrd At The South Pole, 1929, Paramount, U.S., one-sheet, 41 x 27in. (Christie's) £805 $1,328

Batman, 1966, T.C.F., British quad, 30 x 40in. (Christie's) £517 $853

Gaslight, 1944, M.G.M., U.S. one-sheet, 41 x 27in. linen backed. (Christie's) £368 $607

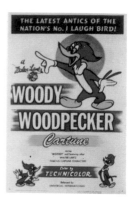

The Invisible Ray/Den Osynliga Stralen, 1936, Universal, Swedish, 39 x 27in. Art by Fuchs. (Christie's) £690 $1,138

The Blue Lamp, 1949, Ealing, British half-sheet, 22 x 28in., linen backed. (Christie's) £460 $759

Woody Woodpecker, 1950, Universal, U.S. one-sheet, 41 x 27in., linen backed. (Christie's) £517 $853

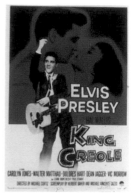

The Invisible Man Returns, 1940, Universal, U.S. one-sheet, 41 x 27in. (Christie's) £2,530 $4,175

Thunderbirds Are Go, 1967, M.G.M., British quad, 30 x 40in. (Christie's) £977 $1,612

King Creole, 1958, Paramount, U.S. one-sheet, 41 x 27in., linen backed. (Christie's) £345 $569

A pair of Napoleon III gilt bronze chenets, circa 1860, modelled with the figures of semi-naked children, the bases cast with rocaille ornament, 16¼in high.
(Christie's)　　　£3,220　$5,152

A pair of gilt-bronze chenets, Paris, circa 1890, in the Louis XVI style, each cast with an urn applied with swags of vine leaves, 47cm. wide.
(Sotheby's)　　　£2,530　$4,048

A pair of French bronze chenets, the imbricated plinths inset with a balustraded gallery and surmounted by patinated models of a recumbent lion and lioness, 18½in. wide.
(Christie's)　　　£2,185　$3,496

A pair of Louis XV style bronze chenets, late 19th century, the pierced naturalistic bases surmounted with figures of Neptune and Proserpine respectively, re-gilt, 14½in. wide.
(Christie's)　　　£1,725　$2,760

A pair of large Napoleon III bronze chenets, with sphere finials on tapering spires with term mounts, 43½in. high.
(Christie's)　　　£2,875　$4,600

A pair of French bronze chenets, late 19th/early 20th century, the pierced standards of scrolling naturalistic form, on shaped plinths with ovolo fluting, 16¾in. high.
(Christie's)　　　£2,530　$4,048

A pair of Empire style bronze chenets, late 19th century, with foliate clasped ovoid finials above balustrade galleries flanked by lion masks, 13¼in. high.
(Christie's)　　　£920　$1,472

A pair of Regency black-painted cast-iron firedogs, after a design by Thomas Hope, each in the form of a griffin on a moulded plinth base, 26¼in. high.
(Christie's)　　　£7,475　$12,100

A pair of French gilt bronze chenets, late 19th century, in the Régence taste, the uprights modelled as stylised floral urns, on spreading bases, 14in. high.
(Christie's)　　　£862　$1,379

A pair of French bronze chenets, late 19th century, in the chinoiserie taste, each modelled with a snarling dragon, seated on their haunches, 12¾in. high.
(Christie's)   £4,600 $7,544

A pair of second Empire bronze chenets, circa 1860, modelled as crossed fruiting cornucopiae, 13½in. wide.
(Christie's)   £920 $1,508

A pair of Victorian cast iron and brass andirons, circa 1890, in the manner of Christopher Dresser, the uprights with conical-shaped intersections, 22½in. high.
(Christie's)   £690 $1,132

A pair of French wrought iron andirons, 19th century, the square section and part writhen uprights applied with scrolling mounts below bulbous writhen knop surmounts, 32½in. high.
(Christie's)   £1,725 $2,760

A pair of 19th century brass andirons, each with knopped urn finials on a lobed sphere and spreading scrolling plinth, each 73cm. high.
(Phillips)   £1,700 $2,788

A pair of Victorian brass andirons, circa 1880, with twin handled fluted urn surmounts above draped platforms and splayed hairy hoof feet, 17½in. high.
(Christie's)   £483 $792

A pair of French Louis XV style ormolu chenets, late 19th century, modelled with berried scrolling acanthus ornament, 15½in. wide.
(Christie's)   £4,600 $7,544

A pair of brass andirons, late 19th century, in the Low Countries 17th century style, the bulbous knopped standards on scrolling bases, 20in. high. (Christie's)   £1,955 $3,128

A pair of brass andirons, possibly New York, circa 1785, each with a spiral-turned finial above a double faceted diamond knob, 24½in. high.
(Christie's)   £9,660 $16,100

A pair of Louis XV-style bronze and ormolu chenets, second half 19th century, mounted with bronze figures of an Oriental lady and gentleman respectively, 11in. high. (Christie's) £1,265 $2,024

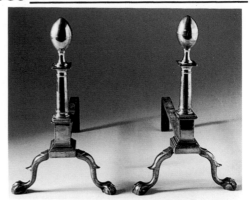

A pair of Chippendale engraved bell-metal andirons, Massachusetts, probably Boston, circa 1795, each with a lemon form finial above a bright-cut decorated wafer, 20in. high. (Sotheby's) £5,175 $8,625

A pair of ormolu and patinated bronze chenets, 19th century, after a design attributed to Lambert-Sigisbert-Adam Slodtz, of Louis XV style, each with a figure of Neptune, 16in. high. (Christie's) £5,750 $9,430

A pair of bronze and gilt-bronze chenets, 19th century, each in the form of a recumbent lion on a plinth base, 34cm. wide. (Sotheby's) £2,415 $3,936

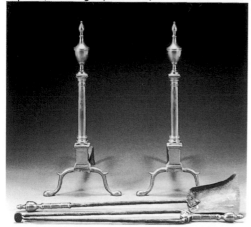

A pair of Federal brass andirons and matching tools, stamped *Richard Wittingham* (working circa 1813), New York, first quarter 19th century, 26in. high. (Christie's) £5,750 $9,200

A set of brass and iron firetools, American, 1800–20, comprising a pair of andirons, a shovel, poker and tongs, together with a bowed brass rail and iron wire fire fender. (Christie's) £11,730 $19,550

A cast iron and brass mounted fire grate, 20th century, the bowed and railed basket above a pierced fret of stylised foliate ornament, 23½in. wide. (Christie's) £483 $772

A late Victorian cast iron and brass mounted fire grate, by Thomas Elsley, the sloping railed basket with canted angles, flanked by baluster knopped standards, 42in. wide. (Christie's) £5,750 $9,200

A George III style polished steel fire gate, early 20th century, the rectangular railed basket above a lattice pierced fret, 29in. (Christie's) £1,610 $2,576

A cast iron and brass mounted fire grate, early 20th century, the serpentine fronted and railed basket above a pierced fret, elaborately pierced and cast with scrolling foliate ornament, 31in. wide. (Christie's) £4,600 $7,360

A Continental brass and steel firegrate, late 19th century, the serpentine railed basket above a swept apron, cast in relief with central scallop motif within pomegranates and griffons, 36½in. wide. (Christie's) £633 $1,012

A George III style steel and brass fire grate, early 20th century, the serpentine railed front with double column uprights surmounted by elongated urn-shaped finials, 34½in. wide. (Christie's) £2,990 $4,784

A cast iron and brass fire grate, 20th century, in the George III style, the serpentine railed front above a pierced fret, applied with paterae mounts, 22½in. wide. (Christie's) £460 $754

A George III style wrought iron and brass fire grate, late 19th century, the serpentine railed front with pierced fret centred by a shield device flanked by lions rampant, 37¾in. wide. (Christie's) £3,450 $5,520

A cast iron and brass mounted fire grate, early 20th century, the railed rectangular basket flanked by square knopped standards with spherical finials, 40½in. wide. (Christie's) £1,840 $2,944

A George IV polished steel fire grate, the bowed and railed basket above a Greek key pierced fret and conforming flanges terminating in applied phoenix heads, 34¼in. wide. (Christie's) £10,350 $16,560

A late Victorian Aesthetic Movement cast iron and brass mounted fire grate, circa 1890, of architectural outline, the pierced standards surmounted by orb-shaped finials, 46in. wide. (Christie's) £3,450 $5,520

A cast iron and brass fronted grate of Adam design, the serpentine front with four bold turned brass urn finials engraved with Neo Classical ornament, 33 x 31in. wide. (Canterbury) £1,550 $2,480

A Regency cast iron fire grate, circa 1810, the rectangular railed basket surmounted by campana-shaped finials to the top-rail, the backplate boldly cast with scrolling foliate ornament, 36½in. wide. (Christie's) £1,035 $1,697

A George III style steel and brass fire grate, circa 1900, the railed front above a pierced fret incised with a basket of flowers within mythical beasts, 28¼in. wide. (Christie's) £1,035 $1,656

A cast iron and brass fire grate, early 20th century, in the Adam Revival style, the serpentine railed front above a pierced fret, the tapering standards with flambeau urn finials, 31in. wide. (Christie's) £1,495 $2,452

A 19th century cast iron Gothic fire grate, the elaborate backplate cast with ogival arched recessed panels with crocketted spires, 1840, 101cm. wide. (Tennants) £3,600 $5,760

An Arts and Crafts wrought iron and brass mounted fire grate, late 19th or early 20th century, the bowed and railed basket flanked by panels of pierced scroll work, applied with fleur de lis mounts, 53½in. wide, overall. (Christie's) £8,050 $13,202

A polished steel fire grate, 20th century, in the Adam taste, the serpentine railed front with flambeau urn finials, 29¾in. wide. (Christie's) £1,035 $1,697

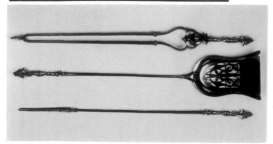

A set of three mid Victorian polished steel and brass fire irons, the writhen grips with foliate pommels, on part-faceted shafts, 30in. (Christie's) £805 $1,304

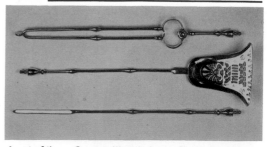

A set of three George III style brass fire irons, with urn pommels on knopped shafts, the flared shovel with pierced stylised foliage, 30in. (Christie's) £920 $1,490

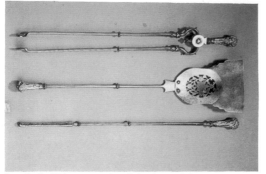

A set of gilt brass and polished steel fire irons, circa 1830, the gilt grips and pommels cast as a floral bouquet, on cylindrical shafts with knopped intersections, 28½in. (Christie's) £1,610 $2,576

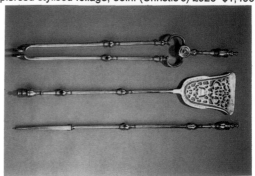

A set of George III style brass fire irons, late 19th/early 20th century, the foliate engraved urn-shaped pommels on cylindrical shafts with baluster intersections, 28¾in. (Christie's) £978 $1,564

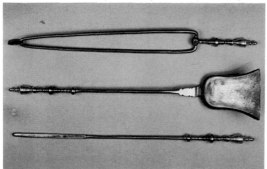

A set of three Dutch steel fire irons, 19th century, with brass urn finials and knopped baluster grips, on plain cylindrical shafts, with flared shovel, 26¼in. (Christie's) £862 $1,379

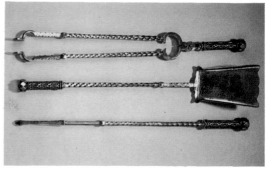

A set of three Victorian polished steel fire irons, with faceted pommels and grips boldly cast with a lattice pattern, on writhen shafts, 31in. (Christie's) £1,955 $3,128

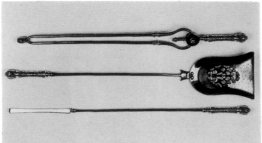

A set of three mid Victorian polished steel and brass fire irons, with foliate cast grips on plain cylindrical shafts, the tulip-shaped shovel with a pierced oval, 30½in. (Christie's) £483 $782

A set of three polished steel fire irons, circa 1800, with knopped urn finials on cylindrical shafts with baluster intersections, 31¼in. (Christie's) £920 $1,472

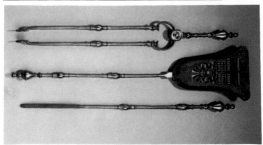

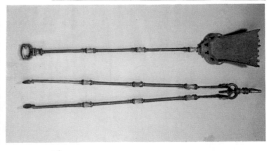

A set of George III steel fire irons, circa 1790, with urn finials and shafts with baluster intersections, 30½in. (Christie's) £1,495 $2,392

A pair of Restauration ormolu mounted steel fire irons, with ring handles cast as conjoined dolphins, 34½in. (Christie's) £690 $1,104

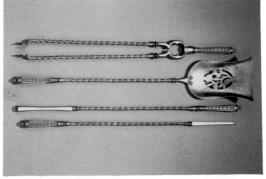

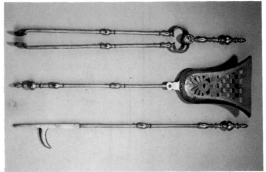

A set of four gilt brass and polished steel fire irons, second half 19th century, the pommels with stiff-leaf borders on tapering square section grips, 31¼in. (Christie's) £2,300 $3,680

A set of George III style steel fire irons, late 19th or early 20th century, with knopped pommels and acorn finials, the cylindrical shafts with baluster intersections, 33¼in. (Christie's) £1,093 $1,748

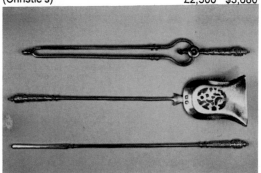

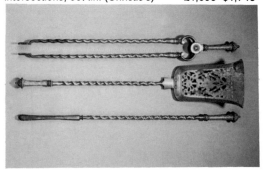

A set of three Victorian brass and steel fire irons, the grips cast with foliate panels, on cylindrical shafts, the tulip-shaped shovel with pierced oval, 28¼in. (Christie's) £1,093 $1,748

A set of three brass and steel fire irons, second half 19th century, the brass beaded grips cast with entwined lattice work, 30½in. (Christie's) £978 $1,564

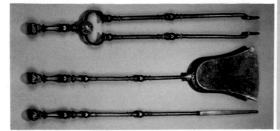

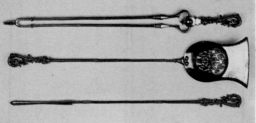

A set of three George III steel fire-irons, comprising a pair of tongs, a poker and a shovel, each with foliage-clasped bulbous finial and a ring-turned slender baluster stem, 28in. long. (Christie's) £483 $802

A set of three William IV polished steel and brass fire irons with scrolling foliate grips and plain cylindrical shafts, the tulip-shaped shovel with pierced oval, 30½in. (Christie's) £1,495 $2,422

A late Victorian carved walnut chimney piece, circa 1890, the shelf with dentil moulding above the relief carved frieze with scrolling foliage, the jambs with anthemion friezes above fluted pilasters, 72in. wide. (Christie's) £3,450 $5,658

A Continental rosso Verona and white marble chimneypiece, 19th century, the shelf above a frieze with recumbent sphinx and egg and dart border, the jambs with quiver crested tapering pilasters, 59in. wide. (Christie's) £6,325 $10,373

A Victorian statuary marble chimneypiece, third quarter 19th century, the inverted plain jambs on stepped plinths, supporting the panelled frieze, centred by an integral tablet, carved in high relief with a finch amidst foliage, 81½in. wide. (Christie's) £10,350 $16,974

A Victorian black painted cast iron chimneypiece, with lozenge date mark for 1865, the scrolling jambs applied with fruiting swag mounts flanking the arched opening with multiple borders of foliate, tongue and beaded ornament, 61½in. wide, overall. (Christie's) £1,840 $3,017

A French white marble chimneypiece, late 19th century, the volute moulded jambs surmounted with stiff-leaf carved caps, flanking the beaded and panelled frieze, 53½in. wide. (Christie's) £2,875 $4,715

A William IV brass chimneypiece, circa 1835, with convex bosses surmounting the reed moulded jambs and flanking the conforming frieze, lacking shelf, 53½in. wide, overall. (Christie's) £5,750 $9,430

A carved pine fire surround, with dentilled cornice, the frieze centred by a tablet carved with a basket of fruit and flowers and flanked by swags, 192 x 153cm. overall. (Tennants) £2,860 $4,719

An impressive carved stone fire surround in the 17th century manner, the frieze with putti, classical figures and a cartouche surrounded by scrolling foliage, 184cm.wide. (Bearne's) £12,600 $20,160

A George III cream-painted carved pine chimneypiece, supplied to Aske Hall under the direction of John Carr of York, the breakfront moulded cavetto cornice with ribbon and rosette band, 60 x 71in. (Christie's) £9,775 $16,031

A George III white painted carved pine chimneypiece, supplied to Aske Hall under the direction of John Carr of York, the moulded rectangular breakfront shelf above a cavetto-moulded cornice, 60½ x 68½in. (Christie's) £18,400 $30,176

A fine carved Carrara marble chimney piece, French, circa 1860, the shaped moulded mantel above a frieze centred by a cabochon flanked by scrolling foliage and flower heads, supported by female terms, 190cm. wide. (Sotheby's) £34,500 $56,925

A George III white-painted carved pine chimneypiece, supplied to Aske Hall under the direction of John Carr of York, the double breakfront moulded shelf above a lappeted and egg-and-dart moulded cornice, 60 x 70½in. (Christie's) £12,650 $20,746

A French and bronze patinated fender, second half 19th century, with twin flambeau urn standards on claw feet, 45in. (Christie's) £2,300 $3,726

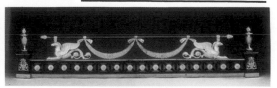

An Empire style parcel gilt bronze fender, mid19th century, the cylindrical rail with berried terminals suspending acorn leaf swags flanked by two griffins, 60in. wide. (Christie's) £3,450 $5,520

An Edwardian brass club fender, of rectangular form, the railed front applied with urn-shaped relief mounts in the neo-classical taste, 55½in. wide. (Christie's) £4,025 $6,601

A Louis Philippe bronze fender, mid 19th century, the cylindrical rail with foliate intersection above a rectangular plinth, the raised ends with winged torchere mounts, 43½in. wide. (Christie's) £2,070 $3,312

An early Victorian gilt bronze bowed fender, the moulded plinth mounted with cherubs hunting panthers, amidst foliate scrolls, the standards with cherubs within arches; and a pair of French firedogs, late 19th century, 41in. wide. (Christie's) £3,105 $4,968

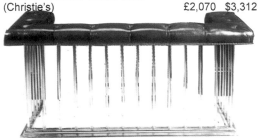

A brass club fender, early 20th century, of rectangular form, the railed front with moulded plinth, supporting a later buttoned leather upholstered seat, 65½in. wide, overall. (Christie's) £2,070 $3,395

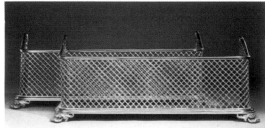

A fine pair of William IV brass fenders, circa 1835, of rectangular outline, inset with cast panels of pierced lattice ornament, 55½in. wide. (Christie's) £9,200 $14,720

A brass club fender, 20th century, the padded seat rail on plain cylindrical uprights, with a curved central section and raised plinth, 73in. wide. (Christie's) £4,370 $6,992

A gilt bronze fender, late 19th century, the standards modelled with cherubs on shaped plinths and toupie feet, the rail with beaded border, 46in. (Christie's) £1,725 $2,795

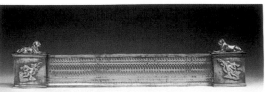

A Regency brass fender, circa 1820, of inverted breakfront form, the uprights surmounted by models of recumbent lions, 39½in. wide. (Christie's) £690 $1,104

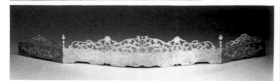

A steel and brass fender, late 19th/early 20th century, in the George III style, of serpentine form with folding end panels, 58in. extended. (Christie's) £690 $1,104

A George III serpentine brass fender, the pierced front decorated with roundels, 174cm. (Bearne's) £1,250 $2,063

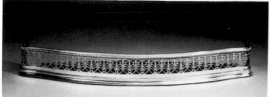

A Regency silver plated brass fender, the serpentine frieze with pierced anthemions below a beaded border, with moulded plinth, the silver worn, 46in. wide. (Christie's) £2,300 $3,680

A French bronze fender, late 19th century, the pierced adjustable rail flanked by urns with berried finials and acorn swags, re-gilt, 46in. wide. (Christie's) £2,530 $4,048

A Napoleon III bronze adjustable fender, circa 1860, the uprights modelled as winged lions, on stepped plinths of scrolling outline, cast with foliate galleries, flanking the moulded frieze, centred by a loop handle, 53in. wide, extended. (Christie's) £4,830 $7,921

A Louis XVI-style gilt bronze patinated fender, late 19th century, the twin urn standards with gadrooned bodies issuing urn swags, on shaped plinths with pierced friezes and tasseled aprons, the adjustable rail with scrolling foliage, 48in. (Christie's) £2,185 $3,540

A pair of early Victorian Gothic Revival cast iron fenders, circa 1850, of rectangular form, the frieze pierced with quatrefoil motifs, the angles with projecting turreted uprights, 47½in. wide. (Christie's) £1,495 $2,451

A French gilt and bronze patinated fender, late 19th century, the pierced tapering standards with lion mask rings and foliate clasped cone finials, 46in. (Christie's) £1,150 $1,863

A Regency brass serpentine fronted fender, circa 1820, the frieze pierced with S scrolls adossée, intersected by foliate motifs, on a stepped plinth, 44½in. wide. (Christie's) £633 $1,012

A French parcel gilt bronze fender, mid19th century, the cylindrical rail supported by boldly cast foliate capped claw feet above a rectangular plinth 45in. wide. (Christie's) £1,150 $1,840

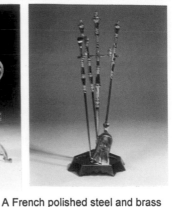

A Victorian brass coal scuttle, circa 1880, of helmet-shape, the swing handle with ebony grip, on tripod feet, 17½in. high.
(Christie's)　　　　£483　$792

A late Victorian cast iron and brass mounted fire grate, circa 1880, in the Gothic Revival taste, the rectangular railed basket supported on free-standing tapering andirons, 48in. wide.
(Christie's)　　　£3,450　$5,658

A French polished steel and brass companion stand, 19th century, the twin faceted knopped stand issuing from a triform base, 31in. high.
(Christie's)　　　£1,092　$1,769

A late William IV sheet iron and brass mounted coal box, circa 1840, the stepped cover inset with sloping mirrored panels cut and etched with trailing vines, 24½in. wide. (Christie's)　£1,500　$2,460

Rare Gustav Stickley fireplace set, attributed, shovel, poker, brush, tongs, and stand, 33in. high.
(Skinner)　　　£3,278　$5,463

A Dutch brass and copper log bin, 19th century, of drum-shape, the sides applied with repoussé lion and serpent and, foliate mounts, 19½in. wide.
(Christie's)　　　£805　$1,320

A late George IV or early William IV japanned sheet iron coal box, circa 1830, the green ground decorated with panels of flowers, 20in. high.
(Christie's)　　　£2,300　$3,772

A Dutch brass coal scuttle, late 19th century, of barrel shape, the hinged cover to the end embossed with flowers, 16½in. high.
(Christie's)　　　£322　$528

A pair of Charles X ebonised wood and ormolu mounted fire bellows, the mounts pierced and cast with Gothic tracery, with a stained wood stand, the bellows 14½in. long.
(Christie's)　　　£518　$827

A Régence style bronze firescreen, second half 19th century, the mesh ground with a lion mask mount within a pierced foliate cast frame, 29½in. high.
(Christie's) £1,725 $2829

A Victorian brass coal scuttle, circa 1880, of helmet-shape, the hinged concave cover embossed in the Adam taste with a fan patera motif, 19in. high.
(Christie's) £920 $1,509

A Victorian West Midlands japanned metal coal box, circa 1850, the black ground painted and heightened in gilt with exotic birds and trailing foliate ornament, 17½in. wide. (Christie's) £3,680 $6,035

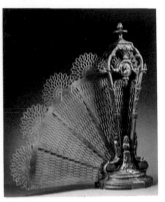

A Louis XV style gilt-bronze and wire mesh firescreen, late 19th or early 20th century, of cartouche outline and modelled with foliate scrolls, 32¼in. wide.
(Christie's) £1,495 $2,392

A Continental polished steel fireplace garniture, late 19th or early 20th century, comprising: a pair of spit dogs, a connecting spit rail, and a set of three fire irons; and associated steel fender frieze rail. The fire dogs 22½in. high.
(Christie's) £920 $1,472

A French bronze folding fan fire screen, late 19th or early 20th century, the screen pierced with geometric ornament, the tapering frame cast with foliate decoration, 44in. wide, extended.
(Christie's) £1,840 $3,018

A pair of late Victorian lacquered wood and leather bellows, circa 1890, the pale green ground painted and heightened in gilt in the chinoiserie taste, 23¾in. long.
(Christie's) £920 $1,508

A Dutch brass coal or log bin, late 19th century, of drum-shape, the sides applied with lion mask ring handles, 16¼in. diameter.
(Christie's) £460 $754

An Edwardian brass coal scuttle, the hinged cover embossed with a foliate patera, with turned handle and waisted foot, 18½in. high.
(Christie's) £1,955 $3,167

A fine paint decorated pine bucket, Joseph Long Lehn, Elizabeth Township, Lancaster County, 1880–92.
(Sotheby's)　　£2,760　$4,600

A French wrought iron firescreen, early 20th century, of rectangular form with curved top, the centre as a flowering urn, 43½in. wide.
(Christie's)　　£1,265　$2,024

An Edwardian polished brass coal scuttle, early 20th century, the oval body and cover with urn finial, on four paw feet with circular stretcher, 26½in. high.
(Christie's)　　£1,150　$1,840

A French bronze firescreen, 20th century, the mesh ground with putti mount, within a pierced scrolling frame, re-gilt, 28in. wide.
(Christie's)　　£1,035　$1,656

A painted leather ceremonial fire bucket, signed *Wm. Caban, Franklin Fire Society*, probably New England, late 18th century, 12in. high. (Sotheby's)　£3,507　$5,750

A French bronze firescreen, 20th century, the rectangular frame with flambeau torchère uprights and floral garland loop handle, 26in. high. (Christie's)　　£1,725　$2,760

A George IV bronzed, cast-iron, brass and parcel-gilt telescopic fire-screen, the tripartite base with acanthus-wrapped legs, 63in. high, extended.
(Christie's)　　£5,520　$9,053

A French bronze and brass fan firescreen, early 20th century, the tapering frame with twin lions flanking a heraldic shield, with further pierced foliage, 30in. high.
(Christie's)　　£1,000　$1,600

A French bronze firescreen, early 20th century, the frame of chinoiserie style, with winged mythical beast handle and mesh ground, 25in. wide.
(Christie's)　　£1,380　$2,208

A George III brass-mounted mahogany plate-bucket, of cylindrical form with pierced vertical sides and lion-mask carrying handles, 14½in. high.
(Christie's) £2,530 $4,100

A brass coal bin, 20th century, of cylindrical form with beaded bands of pierced ovolo decoration and lion's mask ring handles, 30.8cm. diameter. (Christie's) £253 $404

A French bronze firescreen, early 20th century, the pierced foliate border with arabesques, the mesh ground with a suspended urn, 32in. wide. (Christie's) £1,495 $2,392

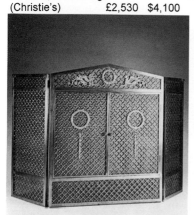

An Empire style gilt-brass and bronze folding firescreen, mid 20th century, the rectangular frame with twin lattice work mesh doors with laurel wreath mounts, 43in. high.
(Christie's) £1,000 $1,600

An oval gilt bronze firescreen, late 19th century, the ribbon tied laurel cast border with a floral bouquet to the mesh ground, 19 x 29½in.
(Christie's) £1,265 $2,049

A Napoleon III gilt-bronze and tôle peinte coal basket, circa 1870, of rectangular form, with rounded underside, the ochre ground end panels painted with ribbon-suspended baskets of fruit, 19in. wide. (Christie's) £1,092 $1,747

A French giltwood and tapestry firescreen, by Charles Bernel, Paris, dated *1914*, the feather-carved frame with scroll cartouche crest flanked by floral chains, 47½in. high.
(Christie's) £1,725 $2,760

A mahogany and brass bound coal bin, late 19th/early 20th century, of navette form, the shaped oval top with tin liner above a ring-bound body, 19in. wide.
(Christie's) £500 $810

A late Regency or William IV japanned metal and cast iron purdonium, circa 1830, of rectangular form, with rounded underside, the black ground heightened in gilt, 18½in. wide.
(Christie's) £920 $1,472

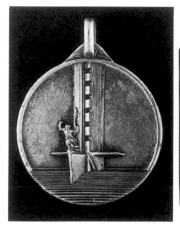

Gibson, Alfred & Pickford, William: Association Football & The Men Who Made It, four volumes, published by The Caxton Publishing Company, London.
(Christie's)   £598 $987

F.A. Cup final, match programme, 25/4/31.
(Christie's)   £241 $398

F.A. Cup final, match programme, 27/4/29.
(Christie's)   £310 $512

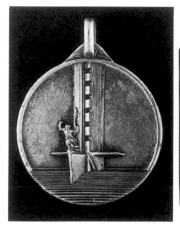

A South American silver World Cup, 1930, medal, unmarked, the obverse cast with a view of the tower at the Centenary Stadium, Montevideo, Uruguay.
(Christie's)   £5,750 $9,488

A blue Scottish Football League v. Football League shirt, No.9, inscribed *S.F.L. v. F.L., 1956-57*, gained by Tommy Thompson as a swap with the Scottish striker Willie Bauld, 1957.
(Christie's)   £1,265 $2,087

A 9ct gold medal, the reverse inscribed *The Football Association Challenge Cup, Runners-up, 1951, Blackpool F.C. 0, Newcastle United F.C. 2, H. Johnston (Capt.)*.
(Christie's)   £1,150 $1,897

A green and gold South African XI shirt, with v-neck collar, gained by Tommy Thompson as a swap after a match played by Preston North End against a South African XI in 1958.
(Christie's)   £322 $531

A Continental gold World Cup 1970 medal, the obverse inscribed *F.I.F.A.*, the reverse inscribed *Campeonato Mundial de Futbol Copa Jules Rimet, Mexico 1970*.
(Christie's)   £4,600 $7,590

George Cohen, a blue, red and white France World Cup 1966 shirt, No.18, with embroidered cloth badge, inscribed *France, Coupe du Monde 1966*.
(Christie's)   £2,415 $3,985

George Cohen, a red, black and yellow Belgium shirt, No.2, with cloth badge.
(Christie's)   £368 $607

Billy Wright, a blue England World Cup 1958 International cap v. U.S.S.R.
(Christie's)   £3,220 $5,313

A blue Yugoslavia International shirt, No.9, with v-neck collar and embroidered cloth badge.
(Christie's)   £517 $853

A 15ct gold F.A. Cup winner's medal, the obverse inscribed *1895*, the reverse inscribed *The Football Association, Winners, Aston Villa, R. Chatt,* with ring suspension.
(Christie's)   £3,335 $5,503

A white Northern Ireland International shirt, No.10, with v-neck collar and embroidered badge, inscribed *Northern Ireland, Irish Football Association, F.I.F.A. World Cup, Mexico 1986.*
(Christie's)   £460 $759

A 9ct gold medal, the obverse inscribed *Scottish Football League* the reverse inscribed *Won by Celtic F.C., 1925–26, P. Connolly,* with ring suspension.
(Christie's)   £2,070 $3,415

Tom Finney, a green Republic of Ireland International shirt, No.11, with button-up white collar and embroidered cloth badge.
(Christie's)   £368 $607

George Male, a 14ct gold F.A. Cup winner's medal, the reverse inscribed *The Football Association,* with ring suspension, in original fitted case.
(Christie's)   £4,600 $7,590

A yellow England goalkeeper's International shirt, No.1, with button-up collar and embroidered cloth badge.
(Christie's)   £598 $986

World Cup 1966, a red England long-sleeved shirt, No.7, with embroidered badge.
(Christie's)   £2,645 $4,364

A red Arsenal F.C. Cup Final shirt, 1931-32, inscribed *A.F.C. 1932*, the collar bearing a rectangular label embroidered *Presented To A Good Sportsman By Tom Webster*.
(Christie's)   £2,875 $4,744

Jeff Hall, a red England International shirt, No.2, with v-neck collar and embroidered cloth badge.
(Christie's)   £977 $1,612

F.A. Cup final, match programme, 27/4/35.
(Christie's)   £448 $739

Paul Price, a red and blue Barcelona shirt, No.11, with embroidered cloth badge, inscribed *F.C.B.*, and a programme from the match.
(Christie's)   £460 $759

F.A. Cup final, match programme, 23/4/32.
(Christie's)   £310 $512

A white Santos shirt, No.11, circa 1970, bearing numerous autographs including Pele, Pepe, Orlando, Antonio etc and inscribed *To Rangers*.
(Christie's)   £345 $569

Jeff Hall, a yellow and green Brazil International shirt, No.11, with v-neck collar and embroidered cloth badge.
(Christie's)   £1,092 $1,802

Allan Morton, a white Football League v Scottish League shirt, 1923–24, with lace-up collar and embroidered cloth badge, inscribed *F.L., Scottish Match, 1923–24*.
(Christie's)   £322 $531

Jeff Hall, a white satin Birmingham City F.A. Cup final shirt, 1956, No.2, inscribed *Wembley, B.C.F.C., 1956*, and a pair of dark blue satin shorts.
(Christie's) £2,300 $3,795

A red England shirt, No.9, with embroidered badge, together with a letter autographed by Roy Reyland.
(Christie's) £460 $759

Gordon Banks, an autographed yellow England 1970 World Cup International goalkeeping jersey, Umbro, Aztec.
(Sotheby's) £1,207 $1,979

George Cohen, a white and black West Germany World Cup final 1966 shirt, No.11, with circular cloth badge, inscribed *Deutscher Fussball Bund*.
(Christie's) £1,955 $3,226

World Cup 1966, a colour photocard depicting the victorious England team, autographed by all eleven players, creased, in common mount, framed and glazed, 18¾ x 16in. overall.
(Christie's) £1,782 $2,940

A white England International shirt, No. 6, with embroidered cloth badge; and a black and white photograph of Bobby and Tina Moore, inscribed *Best Wishes and thank you for all your help, Bobby Moore*.
(Christie's) £2,300 $3,795

A white wool England International jersey, Kinch & Lack, circa 1925, long-sleeved with button-up cuffs and collar and embroidered badge.
(Sotheby's) £517 $848

A green Northern Ireland shirt, No. 11, with v-neck collar and embroidered cloth badge, inscribed *Irish Football Association*; and a photograph of George Best.
(Christie's) £805 $1,328

A white Manchester United short-sleeved shirt, No.9, with v-neck collar and embroidered cloth badge, inscribed *U.E.F.A Cup 1984-85*.
(Christie's) £345 $569

Jack Nicholls, a green Wales v. England and Ireland International cap, 1924.
(Christie's) £345 $569

A bronze figure of a footballer, his right leg raised kicking a football, on octagonal marble base, 11¾in. high, overall.
(Christie's) £977 $1,612

Jeff Hall, a blue England v Germany International cap, 1956.
(Christie's) £667 $1,100

A 9ct. gold and enamel medal, the obverse inscribed *The Football League v. Scotland,* the reverse with inscription erased, with ring suspension.
(Christie's) £287 $474

A 9ct gold and blue enamel medal, the obverse inscribed *South Wales & Monmouthshire F'ball Assocn.,* the reverse inscribed *Senior Cup, Winners, 1913–14, J. Evans.*
(Christie's) £207 $342

A 9ct gold and enamel medal, the obverse inscribed *S.F.L., 1912–13,* the reverse inscribed *Southern Football League, Champions Div. II, Cardiff City, J. Evans.*
(Christie's) £437 $721

Jack Evans, a 9ct gold and enamel medal, the obverse inscribed *Cardiff City A.F.C., Season 1920–21.*
(Christie's) £552 $911

A blue England v. Wales International cap, 1948-49, the interior with rectangular white label inscribed in ink *Billy Wright.*
(Christie's) £1,150 $1,898

A 9ct gold and enamel medal, the reverse inscribed *Charity Cup, Won by Celtic F.C., J. Crum, 1935-36,* with ring suspension.
(Christie's) £747 $1,233

A red Wales International cap, 1980–81, which represents seven appearances by Paul Price for Wales in 1980–81.
(Christie's)   £460 $759

A red Russia International shirt, No.11, with button-up collar, the front initialled *CCCP*.
(Christie's)   £598 $986

A blue England v. Sweden International cap, 1947-48, the interior with a rectangular white label inscribed in ink *Billy Wright*.
(Christie's)   £1,092 $1,802

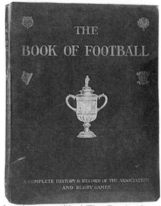

A 9ct gold and enamel medal, the obverse inscribed *Canon League Division Winners*, the reverse inscribed *Season 1983–84*, with ring suspension.
(Christie's)   £322 $531

A volume entitled The Book of Football, A Complete History and Record of the Association and Rugby Games, printed by The Amalgamated Press Limited, London 1906, with original green boards.
(Christie's)   £483 $797

A 9ct gold and enamel medal, the obverse inscribed *Northampton Hospital Shield*, the reverse inscribed *Arsenal, Winners, 1932, G.C. Male*.
(Christie's)   £299 $493

A 9ct gold and enamel medal, the obverse inscribed *Lancashire Football Association, 1900–1*, the reverse inscribed *Winners, Blackburn Rovers F.C., H Morgan*.
(Christie's)   £805 $1,328

A 15ct gold medal, the obverse cast with the Division 1 Championship Trophy and inscribed *League Winners, 1902-1903*, the reverse inscribed *W.F.C., F. Spiksley*.
(Christie's)   £5,750 $9,488

A 15ct gold and enamel medal, the obverse inscribed *Glasgow Cup, 1893–94* and bearing the club crest of Rangers F.C., the reverse inscribed *J. Steele*.
(Christie's)   £632 $1,043

The claret and blue Burnley FC jersey worn by William Watson in the 1914 F.A. Cup final, long-sleeved with crew-neck collar. (Sotheby's)   £3,450 $5,623

The official French Football Association pennant for the France v. England International match, played in Paris, 22nd May 1949, 76cm. high. (Sotheby's)   £460 $749

Ray Wilson: a red England No.3 1966 World Cup final International jersey, long-sleeved with crew-neck collar and embroidered 'three lions' badge. (Sotheby's)   £3,680 $5,998

George Best: a green Northern Ireland No.10 International jersey, short-sleeved with v-neck collar and embroidered cloth badge. (Sotheby's)   £1,035 $1,687

A 15ct. gold medal, the obverse inscribed *1914*, the reverse inscribed *English Cup, Winners, Burnley F.C., R.W. Sewell, presented by King George V*, with ring suspension. (Sotheby's)   £3,450 $5,623

Carlos Alberto: a yellow Brazil No.5 International jersey, short-sleeved with crew-neck collar, trimmed in green, with embroidered badge. (Sotheby's)   £1,495 $2,436

The official Yugoslav Football Association pennant for the Yugoslavia v. England International match, played at Belgrade, 18th May 1939, 61cm. (Sotheby's)   £862 $1,405

Dave Mackay: a blue Scotland No.6 International jersey, short-sleeved with v-neck collar and embroidered badge. (Sotheby's)   £552 $899

The official Belgian Football Association pennant for the Belgium v. England International match, played at Brussels, 21st September 1947. (Sotheby's)   £414 $674

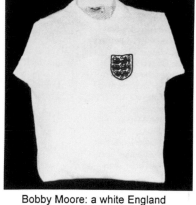

Michael Owen: a white England No.20 1998 World Cup finals International jersey, short-sleeved with button-up collar. (Sotheby's) £2,415 $3,936

Bobby Moore: a white England No.6 International jersey, airtex, long-sleeved with crew-neck collar and embroidered 'three lions' badge. (Sotheby's) £3,450 $5,623

Teddy Sheringham: a white England No.10 1998 World Cup finals International jersey, the reverse inscribed *Sheringham*. (Sotheby's)   £747 $1,217

The red England No.21 International jersey worn by Roger Hunt in the World Cup final at Wembley, 30th July 1966, together with a letter of authenticity from the German internationalist Wolfgang Weber. (Sotheby's) £17,250 $28,117

The official United States Football Association pennant for the U.S.A. v England International match played at Los Angeles, 28th May 1959, the blue felt pennant with yellow match inscription and fringe, 73cm. (Sotheby's)   £368 $599

Gordon Banks: a yellow England International goalkeeping jersey, long-sleeved with crew-neck collar and embroidered 'three-lions' badge inscribed *Centenary Year, 1863-1963*. (Sotheby's)   £1,035 $1,687

The official Hungarian Football Association pennant for the England v. Hungary International, played at Highbury, 2nd December 1936. (Sotheby's)   £805 $1,312

A 9ct. gold medal, the obverse inscribed *The Football League, Champions, Division 1*, the reverse inscribed *Winners, Burnley F.C., W. Watson, 1920-21*. (Sotheby's)   £2,300 $3,749

Bobby Moore, a claret and blue West Ham United No.6 jersey, Bukta, circa 1959–60 season, short-sleeved with v-neck collar and embroidered 'Hammers' badge. (Sotheby's)   £1,380 $2,263

Paul Price, a blue France International shirt No.7, with embroidered badge, inscribed *F.F.F.*, and a programme from the match. (Christie's)　£345　$569

George Cohen, a blue England World Cup 1966 International cap, embroidered *Uruguay, Mexico, France, Argentina, Portugal* and *West Germany*. (Christie's)　£11,500　$18,975

Pele, colour machine print, autographed in green chalk by Pele, backed on linen 37¼ x 28¼in. (Christie's)　£517　$853

The White England No. 10 International jersey worn by Gary Lineker in his last appearance for England, in the European Championship finals, v. Sweden in the Råsunda Stadium, Solna, 17th June 1992, Umbro. (Sotheby's)　£690　$1,132

A 9ct gold medal, the reverse inscribed *The Football Association Challenge Cup, Winners, 1953, Blackpool F.C., H. Johnston (Capt.)*. (Christie's) £5,750　$9,488

A green and white Hibernian shirt, No. 11, autographed by George Best; a pair of white Hibernian shorts, similarly autographed; and a photograph of George Best wearing a similar strip. (Christie's)　£1,840　$3,036

The blue Cardiff City FC jersey worn by Joe Nicholson in the F.A. Cup final at Wembley, 25th April 1925, Welsh Sports Ltd, Church Street, Cardiff. (Sotheby's)　£2,300　$3,772

A blue Scotland International shirt, No.7, the reverse inscribed *Dalglish*, and a programme from the match. (Christie's)　£1,380　$2,277

Frank Brennan, a green Northern Ireland No. 5 International jersey, Bukta, circa 1953–54, long-sleeved with tie-up collar and embroidered badge. (Sotheby's)　£287　$471

F.A. Cup final match programme, Chelsea v. Sheffield United, at Old Trafford, Manchester, 24th April 1915. (Sotheby's) £6,900 $11,316

A Staffordshire pottery teapot, the detachable lid surmounted by a finial formed as the F.A. Cup, the handle formed as a footballer, 6in. high. (Christie's)   £368 $607

F.A. Cup final match programme, Aston Villa v. Huddersfield Town, 24th April 1920. (Sotheby's)   £1,035 $1,687

A plastic ice bucket formed as a football, inscribed *World Cup England 1966*, and bearing the autographs of the eleven England World Cup-winning side and manager Alf Ramsay, 11¾in. high. (Christie's)   £414 $683

A sheet of blue Hendon Hall Hotel paper bearing the 22 England World Cup 1966 team/squad autographs; and a Hendon Hall Hotel envelope addressed to the vendor. (Christie's)   £1,265 $2,087

Richard Beck, F.A. Cup Final, London Underground, lithograph in brown and black, 1937, printed by The Baynard Press, framed and glazed, 40 x 25in. (Christie's)   £575 $949

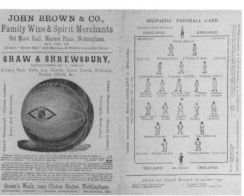

A Newcastle United v. Manchester United match programme, 3rd April 1915. (Sotheby's)   £595 $976

A Richard's football match card for the England v. Ireland International match, played at Trent Bridge, Nottingham, 20th February 1897, four-sides with illustrated team line-ups. (Sotheby's)   £4,600 $7,498

Manchester United v. Woolwich Arsenal match programme, 23rd November 1907. (Sotheby's)   £1,667 $2,734

Bill Shankly's red and white trimmed Liverpool FC track suit, Umbro, 1973.
(Sotheby's)   £690 $1,132

A pair of painted spelter figures of footballers, circa 1910, both players painted in the colours of Swindon Town FC, mounted on a common wooden base, 9in. long.
(Sotheby's)   £345 $566

Ian Callaghan, a white and red trimmed Liverpool FC No. 7 away jersey, Umbro, 1967, long-sleeved with crew-neck collar and embroidered badge.
(Sotheby's)   £632 $1,036

A rare poster produced for the 1966 World Cup Replay, with blue lettering on a white ground, framed and glazed, 31 x 20¾in. overall.
(Christie's)   £977 $1,612

Paul Cannell, a black and white striped Newcastle United FC, No.12, 1976 Football League Cup final jersey, Umbro.
(Sotheby's)   £690 $1,132

Scottish Cup final, match programme, 18/4/36.
(Christie's)   £345 $573

Manchester City v. Manchester United match programme, 12th October 1918.
(Sotheby's)   £805 $1,320

Billy Wright, a blue England v. Italy International cap, 1952–53, sold together with photograph of Billy Wright presenting the cap to the current vendor.
(Sotheby's)   £1,035 $1,697

Manchester City v. Manchester United F.A. Cup semi-final match programme, played at Sheffield United, 27th March 1926.
(Sotheby's)   £1,667 $2,734

A sepia-toned black and white photograph of Abercorn football club, 1895-96, the mount with team legend, in original moulded oak frame, the image 10½ x 14½in. (Christie's)　　　　£368　$607

The silver referee's whistle used by Mr. W.P. Harper of Stourbridge in the 1932 F.A. Cup final at Wembley, with ring suspension and inscribed, in case, 4.5cm. long. (Sotheby's)　　　£1,150　$1,886

A Newton Heath (Lancashire and Yorkshire Railway) Cricket & Football Club member's ticket, season 1890–91, Samuel Blomely printers, Manchester, 1890. (Sotheby's)　　　£1,380　$2,263

Allan Ball, a white England No.7 1966 World Cup tournament International jersey, Umbro, long-sleeved with crew-neck collar and embroidered 'three lions' badge. (Sotheby's)　　　£2,875　$4,715

Monty Fresco MBE (photographer), an autographed black and white photograph of Vinnie Jones 'squeezing' Paul Gascoigne, the image 40 x 51cm., autographed by both players.(Sotheby's) £322 $528

Erwin Vandenbergh; a red Belgium 1982 World Cup finals No. 9 International jersey, short sleeved with v-neck collar, trimmed in red, yellow and black. (Christie's)　　　　£149　$242

Rare Manchester United v. Wolverhampton Wanderers, postponed match programme, 8th February 1958. (Sotheby's)　　　£4,600　$7,360

George Best, a Northern Ireland v. Scotland International cap, 1967–68. (Sotheby's)　　£3,450　$5,658

A FIFA Coupe du Monde 1938 colour postcard, signed and dated *Joe Bridge '37*. (Sotheby's)　　　　£230　$374

Nayim: a white Tottenham Hotspur No.14 1991 F.A. Cup final jersey, together with a colour photograph of Nayim.
(Sotheby's)   £920 $1,499

A programme and souvenir of the 1906 F. A. Cup final in the form of a fine-paper square napkin, with central monochrome block print of the Everton and Newcastle United sides, 14in. square.
(Sotheby's)   £506 $824

Zbigniew Boniek: a red Poland 1982 World Cup finals No.20 International jersey, short-sleeved with v-neck collar.
(Sotheby's)   £322 $524

Steve Archibald: a blue Scotland 1982 World Cup finals No.18 International jersey, short-sleeved with v-neck collar, trimmed in white.
(Sotheby's)   £230 $374

Gary Lineker: an autographed yellow Everton FC No.8 away jersey, season 1985-86, autographed by Gary Lineker and sixteen other Everton players.
(Sotheby's)   £460 $749

A Walsall Town Swifts v. Preston North End match card, friendly, played at The Chuckery 27th October 1890.
(Sotheby's)   £517 $842

A Russian promotional match poster for Dynamo Moscow v. Arsenal, 5th October 1954, printed in colour, published in Moscow, September 1954, 38½ x 26in.
(Sotheby's)   £368 $599

The green and white hooped Celtic jersey worn by George McCluskey in the 1979-80 Scottish Cup final, short-sleeved with v-neck collar with embroidered badge.
(Sotheby's)   £690 $1,124

Airdrieonians v. Aberdeen, match card, 23/9/05; a coloured postcard depicting Airdrieonians; and a small quantity of newspaper cuttings relating to Rombach.
(Christie's)   £402 $663

F.A. Cup final match programme, Blackburn Rovers v. Huddersfield Town, 21st April 1928.
(Sotheby's)   £782 $1,274

Kenny Dalglish: a red Liverpool No.7 jersey, short-sleeved with v-neck collar and embroidered badge.
(Sotheby's)   £747 $1,217

F. A. Cup final match programme, Aston Villa v. Newcastle United, 26th April 1924.
(Sotheby's)   £2,185 $3,561

Phil Parkes: a green Queen's Park Rangers goalkeeping jersey, together with an autographed Phil Parkes Testimonial dinner menu, Royal Lancaster Hotel, 23rd September 1990.
(Sotheby's)   £172 $280

A Walsall Town Swifts v. Accrington match card, friendly, played at The Chuckery 17th November 1890, Accrington were one of the twelve original members of the Football League, but resigned from the League in 1893. This match represents the only known programme for Accrington.
(Sotheby's)   £575 $937

The official Romanian Football Association pennant for the Romania v. England International match played in Bucharest on 24th May 1939, framed and glazed, overall 69 x 61cm.
(Sotheby's)   £805 $1,312

Aron Winter: an Orange Holland 1988 European Championship final No. 5 International jersey, short-sleeved with v-neck collar, trimmed in white, with applied badge.
(Sotheby's)   £299 $487

An autographed Bobby Moore display including printed colour photograph of the England 1966 World Cup winning side, autographed by all eleven players and Alf Ramsey, overall 54 x 66cm.
(Sotheby's)   £1,380 $2,249

Steve Wooddin: a white New Zealand 1982 World Cup finals No.9 International jersey, short-sleeved with v-neck collar, trimmed in black, with embroidered badge.
(Sotheby's)   £207 $337

The red and white Arsenal FC No.3 jersey worn by Lionel Smith in the 1952 F.A. Cup final, long-sleeved with button-up collar.
(Sotheby's)   £2,300 $3,749

Stoke City v. Glasgow Rangers, souvenir programme in aid of The Holditch Colliery Disaster Relief Fund, 19/10/37, the centre autographed by most of the players.
(Christie's)   £264 $435

A green and red England v Italy International cap, 1934–35.
(Christie's)   £1,035 $1,708

A green painted spelter figure of a footballer, modelled as a player volleying a football, mounted on a marble base, 8in.
(Sotheby's)   £138 $224

A bound volume of Wolverhampton Wanderers match programmes, season 1929-30, comprising 38 match programmes.
(Sotheby's)   £920 $1,499

A painted metal alloy 'Flick-a-Penny' football figure, 1950s, with spring-loaded kicking action for flicking a coin, mounted on a green base with turned wooden handle, 9½in. (Sotheby's)   £345 $562

F.A. Cup final, match programme, 25/4/25.
(Christie's)   £805 $1,328

Arsenal v. Liverpool F. A. Cup final replay programme, Hillsborough, 11th May 1971, this rare programme was produced in case the 1971 final needed to be settled by a replay. Arsenal won in extra-time at Wembley and the programme was therefore not required. (Sotheby's)   £368 $599

F.A. Cup final match programme, Sheffield United v. Cardiff City, 25th April 1925.
(Sotheby's)   £977 $1,592

A Surridge Sterling leather football, autographed by the Manchester United squad, circa 1968, including Nobby Stiles, George Best.
(Christie's)   £276 $455

The Busby Babes: an autographed B.E.A. Manchester-Dusseldorf flight card, 20th November 1956, the inside autographed by seventeen members of the Manchester United party. (Sotheby's) £1,380 $2,249

A children's warming plate, the white glazed pottery plate depicting Teddy Bears playing football and other sports, mounted within a metal hot water vessel, diameter, 8in. (Sotheby's)   £149 $242

A white England v. Ireland International Cap, 1909, from the England v. Ireland match played at Valley Parade, Bradford, on the 13th February 1909.
(Sotheby's)   £690 $1,124

A 1966 Jules Rimet Cup flag Porter Bros Ltd Kings Dock Mill, Liverpool circa 1966, complete with original rope for flying, 54 x 108in.
(Sotheby's)   £805 $1,320

Colin Veitch, a white England v. Ireland International Cap, 1906.
(Sotheby's)   £460 $754

Patsy Gallagher, a green Irish Free State v. Spain International cap, 1931.
(Christie's)   £690 $1,138

An autographed colour photograph, 'The Hand of God', autographed by Peter Shilton, seen attempting to punch the ball, 10 x 12in.
(Sotheby's)   £253 $415

Walter Boyes, a purple England v. Wales International cap, 1938-39, sold together with ephemera relating to the career of Walter Boyes.
(Sotheby's)   £862 $1,414

A Sadler's Art Deco novelty teapot, in the form of a leather football, the handle modelled as a player in claret and blue hoops taking a throw-in, 6in. high.
(Sotheby's)   £218 $355

Fédération Française de Football Association, Coupe du Monde 1938, Official World Cup Revue, published by Kossuth, Paris, oblong 8vo. (Sotheby's)   £2,760 $4,498

A good metal alloy group of two footballers, finely modelled as two players challenging for possession of the ball, 6½in. high.
(Sotheby's)   £862 $1,405

F.A. Cup final match programme, Newcastle United v. Aston Villa, 26th April 1924, pictorial colour covers preserved.
(Sotheby's)   £1,495 $2,452

A French Art Deco style table lamp, in the form of a spelter footballer in shooting position, besides the pink moulded glass shade, on marble base, 9½in. long.
(Sotheby's)   £460 $749

A bound volume of 22 Manchester United home match programmes, season 1936–37.
(Sotheby's)   £5,520 $9,053

An Italian 17th century carved and gilded frame, with foliage at outer edge; ogee moulding strapwork, 14.9 x 19 x 8.9cm.
(Christie's)   £1,035 $1,656

A Siennese carved and gilded tabernacle frame, 16th century, the entablature with dentilled architrave and cornices, 53.4 x 41.9 x 25.4cm.
(Christie's)   £5,175 $8,250

An Italian carved, gilded and painted cassetta frame, 16th/17th century, with cavetto to the outer edge, astragal, 74 x 58.2 x 13.3cm.
(Christie's)   £3,220 $5,152

A Spanish late 17th or early 18th century carved, gilded and painted frame, the shaped and pierced outer edge with scallop shells, flowers, foliage, rocaille work, and tools at the corners, 13½ x 9½ x 8½in. (Christie's)   £2,070 $3,312

A French Louis XV carved and gilded swept frame, the pierced corners and centres of the swept scotia with rocaille cartouches with scalloped shell motifs on a punched ground, 35½ x 28½ x 4¼in.
(Christie's)   £5,520 $8,832

A Provincial Italian carved, painted and gilded tabernacle frame, 16th century, the cresting with scrolled volutes flanking a central cartouche depicting a bird, 48.9 x 38.1cm.
(Christie's)   £6,900 $11,040

An English carved and gilded frame, in the Louis XIV style, possibly 18th century, with foliate outer edge, outer scotia, 23½ x 13¼ x 6⁷/₈in.
(Christie's)   £920 $1,472

A Dutch style tortoiseshell frame, with various ripple and wave mouldings to the outer edge, 9 x 7¼ x 2in. (Christie's)   £632 $10,111

An Italian carved, silvered and painted frame, 17th century, astragal to the outer edge, the centres of the plate with winged cherub masks, 69.8 x 50.8 x 11.5cm. (Christie's) £2,070 $3,312

A French Louis XIV carved and gilded frame, with foliate reverse ogee moulding at outer edge, outer scotia, 22.5 x 16.8 x 7.6cm. (Christie's) £2,760 $4,416

A French gilt composition swept frame in the Louis XV style, mounted in a shadow box, with scallop shells and scrolling foliage at the corners, 19.7 x 13.7 x 10.8cm. (Christie's) £632 $1,011

A French carved and gilded Louis XIV frame, with continuous schematised foliage on a hatched ground to the outside edge, 64.1 x 50.2 x 9.8cm. (Christie's) £1,840 $2,944

A French Louis XIV carved and gilded frame, with foliate outer edge, outer cavetto; the acanthus corners of the ogee flanked by scrolling foliage, 59.4 x 39.4 x 12.7cm. (Christie's) £4,370 $6,992

An Italian carved, pierced and gilded frame, 18th century, the pierced outer edge with a continuous course of stylised foliage, a second course of imbricated fruits and nuts, 109.3 x 88.3 x 19cm. (Christie's) £3,910 $6,256

A Venetian early 16th century carved, gilded and painted tabernacle frame, the cresting with an urn at centre flanked by scrolling foliage in low relief on blue ground, overall size 64 x 38½in. (Christie's) £9,200 $14,720

An Italian 17th century carved and gilded reverse profile frame, with foliate ogee at outer edge, 130.5 x 86 x 18cm. (Christie's) £2,530 $4,048

A French Regence carved and gilded frame, with dentilled outer edge; outer scotia; the corners of the ogee with anthemia flanked by scrolling foliage, 35¾ x 28⅜ x 5⅛in. (Christie's) £1,955 $3,128

A French Louis XIV carved and partly décapé frame, with egg-and-spool at outer edge, outer scotia, 43.5 x 28.5 x 12cm. (Christie's) £1,380 $2,208

A good Southern French late 17th/early 18th century carved and gilded frame, with ogee sight, scotia, and panels to the cushion-moulded top edge, 80.6 x 67.3 x 8.3cm. (Bonhams) £2,000 $3,200

An English 19th century gilt composition frame, the raised astragal with imbricated laurel leaves tied at corners and centres, 13³/₈ x 9 x 4¼in.
(Christie's) £322 $515

An Italian 17th century gilt reverse profile frame, the reverse ogee moulding with incised scrolling foliage on a punched ground, 47.9 x 38.1 x 13cm.
(Christie's) £1,265 $2,024

A Spanish 16th or 17th century painted and gilded reverse cassetta frame, with various mouldings at outer and raised inner edges, 13 x 8.8 x 8.6cm.
(Christie's) £632 $1,011

An Italian late 16th century painted tabernacle frame, the cornice with various mouldings above a frieze with painted scrolling foliage, 17 x 16 x 13in.
(Christie's) £3,220 $5,152

A French Louis XIV carved and gilded top arched drawing frame, the pierced corners of the ovolo with stylised fleur-de-lys, 14½ x 10½ x 2in.
(Christie's) £632 $1,011

A pair of French 19th century gilt composition frame, the oval corners of the torus with bead course at sight edge, 27½ x 22¾ x 1½in.
(Christie's) £805 $1,288

An Italian 17th century carved and gilded tondo frame, with ogee moulding at outer edge, outer scotia, diameter 79 x 12.3cm.
(Christie's) £2,185 $3,496

A Spanish 17th century ebonised and partly gilded reverse profile frame, with ogee and taenia mouldings at outer edge, 28.2 x 21 x 10.2cm. (Christie's) £460 $736

Late Victorian mahogany half-tester bedstead complete with mattress and curtain drapes.
(Jacobs & Hunt) £1,300 $2,145

A painted iron cradle, 20th century, the boat shaped and canopied cradle hung from a scrolled trestle end support, 3ft. 9¼in. long.
(Sotheby's) £316 $528

A Federal turned maple and stained poplar and pine bedstead, American, probably Pennsylvania, circa 1830, with four acorn finials above turned supports, 4ft.4in. wide. (Sotheby's) £631 $1,035

A fine George III mahogany four-poster tester bedstead, third quarter 18th century, each foot post with cluster-columns above faceted balusters, 4ft.7in. wide.
(Sotheby's) £2,455 $4,025

A late George III polychrome-painted four poster bed, with baluster front posts joined by a square stretcher to the front and a three piece cornice, 6ft.2½in. wide.
(Christie's) £18,400 $30,544

A rare stained pine and maple folding three-quarter bedstead, New England, second half 18th century, the three-quarter tester on arched supports, 4ft.8in. wide.
(Sotheby's) £2,105 $3,450

A rare Chippendale carved and inlaid mahogany four post bedstead, Charleston, South Carolina, circa 1780, overall width 5ft.8in.
(Sotheby's) £25,955 $42,550

A mahogany four poster bed, part 18th century, comprising a pair of fluted mahogany posts and a shaped cornice and a box base and cross pieces, 5ft.4in. wide.
(Sotheby's) £3,450 $5,762

A Federal figured maple bedstead, probably Pennsylvania, circa 1820, the serpentine tester above turned supports.
(Sotheby's) £2,806 $4,600

Classical carved mahogany tall post bed, Massachusetts, circa 1825–35, with scrolled mahogany headboard flanked by reeded, carved and ring turned posts, 59in. wide x 81in. deep.
(Skinner)   £4,233 $6,900

A rare Louis XVI steel campaign bed, circa 1770, the arched headboard with inset supports, the posts with faceted balusters.
(Sotheby's)   £6,664 $10,925

A Lombard walnut cradle, 18th century, the foot-end with an open handle and strapwork decoration surmounted by square finials, 37½in. wide.
(Christie's)   £1,150 $1,909

A brass and pressed brass four-poster bed, late 19th/early 20th century, with reeded and flower-headed moulded finials and cylindrical drape rails, 82in. wide.
(Christie's)   £1,380 $2,208

A Chinese hardwood and mother-of-pearl inlaid opium bed, late 19th century, profusely decorated and carved, depicting birds in foliate surroundings with mother-of-pearl inlaid panels, 79in. deep.
(Christie's)   £3,335 $5,336

A French walnut four poster bed, 19th century, in the Renaissance style, carved with gadrooned, egg and dart and foliate mouldings, masks and figures, 64in. wide.
(Christie's) £7,820 $12,512

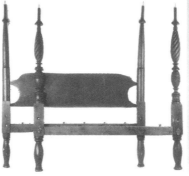

An early 19th century mahogany and brass mounted cradle, spindled hood, the two end poles on square legs. (Academy Auctioneers)
          £590 $944

Painted and turned tall post bed, New England, circa 1820, the turned and tapering headposts flanking a shaped headboard, with accompanying tester, 60½in. wide. x 79in. long.
(Skinner)   £847 $1,380

A mahogany four-post double bedstead, the cornice carved with C-scrolls and foliage, 153cm. wide, the posts 18th century.
(Bearne's)   £6,800 $10,880

Enchanted House

The Traditional Bedstead Company

When only the best will do.....

USUAL DELIVERY 3 TO 4 WEEKS

WORLDWIDE DELIVERIES ARRANGED

MANUFACTURERS OF SOME OF THE FINEST
VICTORIAN STYLE ANTIQUE REPLICA CAST
METAL BEDSTEADS IN THE WORLD

Made in the U.K. the old fashioned way

All our bedsteads are handmade at our own foundry in Cornwall to the highest calibre using only the finest materials, just like in the Victorian era.

We manufacture traditional authentic designs in the same way Victorian craftsmen used to, thus producing your bedstead which not only has an everlasting guarantee, but will remain part of our heritage which is sought all over the world today.

OVER 100 DIFFERENT BED DESIGNS
FROM 3' TO 6' AND OVER 1,000 BEDS IN STOCK
4 POSTERS • HALF TESTERS • TRADITIONAL

18 - 24 The Roundhouse Industrial Estate
Harbour Road
Par
Cornwall
PL24 2BB

SPECIALIST
COMMISSIONS
UNDERTAKEN

OUR
CAPABILITIES
ARE ENDLESS

☎ **(01726) 812213 Fax (01726) 816477**

A companion pair of Victorian mahogany bookcases, each with moulded cornice and a pair of arched glazed doors, both 42in. wide. (Canterbury) £2,800 $4,480

A Regency mahogany two stage bookcase, with rosewood crossbanding, the shelved upper part with scrolled surmount, 36¼in. wide.
(Andrew Hartley)   £1,800 $3,024

A Regency mahogany breakfront bookcase, with small cornice and plain frieze over four astragal glazed doors, having four panelled doors below, on a plinth base, 248 x 51 x 248cm.
(Tennants)   £16,500 $27,225

Regency mahogany bookcase/cabinet, early 19th century, rectangular moulded cornice over two glazed doors enclosing shelves, 36in. wide.
(Skinner)   £1,500 $2,415

A large mahogany break-front bookcase with dentil cornice above three pairs of glazed panel doors, three pairs of fielded panel doors below, 166in. wide.   (Anderson & Garland)   £9,000 $14,850

A Victorian walnut bookcase of narrow proportions, with a moulded cornice above three adjustable open shelves, 37½in. wide.
(Christie's)   £2,415 $3,864

An early Victorian mahogany inverted breakfront bookcase with moulded cornice over three arched glazed doors, 72in. wide.
(Andrew Hartley)   £2,500 $4,000

An Edwardian mahogany and marquetry revolving bookcase, the satinwood crossbanded top inlaid with arabesques and foliage, 20in. square. (Christie's) £805 $1,288

A Victorian mahogany breakfront bookcase, with moulded cornice, three arched glazed doors with carved capitals, 62in. wide.
(Andrew Hartley) £6,000 $9,600

L.& J.G. Stickley three-door
bookcase, no. 647, nine stationary
shelves, through keys and tenons,
original finish, 72in. wide.
(Skinner)   £10,350 $17,250

A Victorian mahogany bookcase
with moulded cornice over two
arched glazed doors, 49in. wide.
(Andrew Hartley) £1,400 $2,352

A mahogany breakfront bookcase,
early 20th century, the foliate
carved and moulded cornice above
four astragal glazed doors, 98in.
wide. (Christie's) £3,105 $4,968

A Classical mahogany bookcase
cabinet, Mid-Atlantic States,
possibly Baltimore, circa 1825, in
three parts.
(Sotheby's)   £2,455 $4,025

A mahogany breakfront bookcase
by Robson & Sons, Newcastle, with
a dentil cornice above two pairs of
glazed panel doors enclosing
adjustable shelves, 117in. wide.
(Anderson & Garland)
                    £4,800 $7,920

A late Regency mahogany and
brass inlaid bookcase cabinet, the
pedimented cornice with central
brass scrollwork roundel and brass
lining, 155cm. wide.
(Phillips)   £3,000 $4,800

L. & J.G. Stickley two-door
bookcase, No. 643, attributed,
sixteen individual panes of glass,
keys and tenons, 35½in. wide.
(Skinner)   £3,278 $5,463

An Edwardian mahogany revolving
bookcase, boxwood and ebony
strung, the moulded square top with
satinwood banding, 46.5cm. wide.
(Phillips)   £800 $1,280

An early 19th century mahogany
bookcase cabinet, the moulded
cornice above a pair of glazed
doors, 127.5 cm. wide.
(Phillips)   £1,750 $2,800

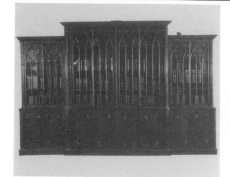

A George IV mahogany breakfront bookcase, the moulded cushion cornice above a pair of Gothic-arched and spandrel-glazed doors, 153½in. wide.
(Christie's)   £13,800 $22,632

Fine Gustav Stickley single door bookcase, sixteen panes, through tenons, original hardware with deep patina, original finish, 35in. wide.
(Skinner)   £2,933 $4,888

A George III mahogany breakfront bookcase, the moulded rectangular broken pediment above a fluted frieze interspersed with paterae and centred by an urn, 107½in. wide.
(Christie's)   £14,375 $23,431

A pair of Regency plum-pudding mahogany upright bookcases, attributed to William Trotter, each with a scrolled pediment carved with foliage above a Gothic-arched frieze, 23in. wide and 23½in. wide.
(Christie's)   £51,000 $84,660

A Regency ormolu-mounted rosewood and parcel-gilt bookcase, the later lobed breakfront black fossil marble top above a frieze centred by laurel-wreath sprays and flower-head paterae, 45½in. wide.
(Christie's)   £10.925 $18,135

An Edwardian mahogany tabletop revolving bookcase with parquetry banding, the moulded edged square top inlaid with marquetry batwing roundel, 12¾in. wide.
(Andrew Hartley)   £290 $478

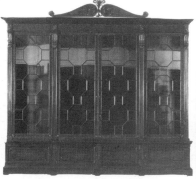

A pair of George III oak bookcases, each with moulded cornice with a fluted frieze, above a glazed door enclosing four shelves, 26in. wide.
(Christie's)   £5,750 $9,372

One of a pair of large mahogany bookcases, 19th century, each with central double-scroll cresting edged with fluting and centred with paterae, 167in. wide.
(Christie's) (Two) £54,300 $90,138

A George III mahogany breakfront secrétaire bookcase, later line inlaid, 82in. wide.
(Christie's)   £16,100 $26,082

A Regency mahogany bookcase, the tapering moulded cornice above a plain frieze and a pair of arched glazed hinged doors, 124in. wide. (Christie's) £12,075 $20,044

A George IV mahogany bookcase, circa 1825, the inverted moulded breakfront cornice above a pair of arched astragal glazed cupboard doors, 64in. wide. (Christie's) £4,000 $6,400

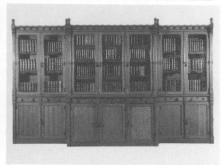

A mid-Victorian oak and ebonised breakfront bookcase, chamfered overall, the castellated and cavetto-moulded cornice with lappeted squared finials, 163in. wide. (Christie's) £13,800 $22,632

A Regency brass-mounted mahogany breakfront bookcase, inlaid overall with ebony lines and stars, the stepped moulded top above a frieze and a pair of glazed doors, 81in. wide. (Christie's) £13,800 $22,908

A George III mahogany breakfront bookcase, attributed to Wright and Elrick, the stepped dentil cornice previously with pierced angle-brackets above a single glazed door, 57in. wide. (Christie's) £111,500 $182,860

A Victorian mahogany and gilt-bronze breakfront bookcase, circa 1880, with two pairs of glazed doors interposed by outset fluted columns, 213cm. wide. (Sotheby's) £11,500 $18,975

A George III mahogany breakfront secrétaire-bookcase, inlaid overall with ebony lines, the arched moulded cornice with central raised circular panel, 97in. wide. (Christie's) £28,750 $46,862

A small mahogany bookcase by Henry Dasson, Paris, circa 1892, with a shaped grey marble top within a moulded cast border, 85cm. wide. (Sotheby's) £5,175 $8,538

A Regency brass-mounted rosewood open bookcase, the moulded cornice above a panelled frieze applied with rosettes and pierced stylised foliate mounts, 77in. wide. (Christie's) £8,050 $13,121

A mahogany bureau bookcase, George III, circa 1760, in the manner of Thomas Chippendale, the top with a pierced swan-neck pediment with carved paterae ornament, 3ft.8in. wide.
(Sotheby's)   £19,550 $32,648

A fine and rare Chippendale carved and highly figured 'plum pudding' mahogany block-front bonnet-top secretary bookcase, Boston, Massachusetts, circa 1760, 42in. wide. (Sotheby's) £26,910 $44,850

A Colonial rosewood bureau bookcase, the dentil-moulded broken arched pediment around a circular plinth with a further dentil-moulded cornice, 46in. wide.
(Christie's)   £5,520 $8,832

An Edwardian mahogany and inlaid bureau bookcase, the upper section surmounted by a broken arch pediment and enclosed by a pair of astragal glazed doors, 39½in. wide.
(George Kidner)   £1,700 $2,805

A German walnut, fruitwood ebonised and parquetry roll-top bureau cabinet, late 18th century/early 19th century, the arched and stepped cornice above two doors with a central star motif in an octagonal panel, 47in. wide.
(Christie's)   £7,475 $12,408

An early 18th century walnut bureau bookcase, the upper twin arched section enclosed by a pair of glazed doors, 40¼in. wide.
(George Kidner)   £5,800 $9,570

A North Italian rosewood, walnut, Karelian-birch and ebonised bureau cabinet, mid 18th century, inlaid overall with chevron banding and pewter cartouche, 42½in. wide.
(Christie's)   £28,750 $47,725

An early George III oak bureau cabinet, circa 1760, the concave moulded cornice above a pair of arched panelled doors enclosing a compartmented interior, 40in. wide.
(Bonhams)   £4,400 $7,040

A George I walnut double-domed bureau-cabinet, crossbanded overall, the double-domed cornice with later finials above a pair of later mirror-backed doors, 39½in.
(Christie's)   £17,250 $28,117

A late George III mahogany bureau bookcase, with dentil cornice, quarter-veneered frieze, two thirteen-pane astragal-glazed doors, 111cm. wide.
(Bearne's)   £2,200 $3,520

A Chippendale carved and figured walnut secretary bookcase, Pennsylvania, circa 1770, in two parts, on ogee bracket feet, width of desk 41in.
(Sotheby's)   £12,627 $20,700

A George II Provincial oak bureau cabinet with a cavetto cornice, two fielded panel doors enclosing shelves, 100.5cm. wide.
(Bearne's)   £1,900 $3,040

A green, red and gilt-japanned bureau-cabinet, early 18th century, Spanish, decorated overall with chinoiserie landscapes with birds, animals, flowers and foliage, 47½in. wide. (Christie's) £26,450 $43,378

A Queen Anne green and gilt-japanned bureau cabinet, the double-domed pediment flanked by later finials above a pair of arched later mirror-panelled doors, 39½in. wide.
(Christie's)   £69,700 $115,702

A Chippendale carved and figured cherrywood secretary bookcase, Connecticut, circa 1780, in three parts; the removable dentil-moulded upper section with pitched pediment, 38in. wide.
(Sotheby's)   £22,770 $37,950

A Queen Anne walnut bureau cabinet, crossbanded overall, the moulded rectangular cornice, above a pair of engraved mirrored doors, 34½in. wide.
(Christie's)   £45,500 $75,530

A North Italian green-painted and parcel-gilt bureau cabinet, decorated overall with Arcadian ruins, vistas and with trophies, 75in. wide. (Christie's) £37,800 $62,748

A fine and rare Queen Anne carved and inlaid cherrywood bonnet-top secretary bookcase, Connecticut, 1750–70, in two parts; the swan's-neck pediment above raised panel 'tombstone' doors, 36in. wide.
(Sotheby's)   £17,940 $29,900

A Queen Anne oak bureau, early 18th century, the hinged fall enclosing two drawers centred by a panelled cupboard door, 30in. wide. (Bonhams) £500 $800

A Chippendale carved and figured mahogany reverse-serpentine slant-front desk, Massachusetts, circa 1780, 42in. wide. (Sotheby's) £5,963 $9775

A Queen Anne oak and laburnum crossbanded bureau, circa 1710, the fall enclosing a fitted interior of drawers and pigeon holes over a well, 35¼in. wide. (Bonhams) £1,700 $2,720

Queen Anne maple slant lid desk, probably Northern Maine, 18th century, the interior of valanced compartments above small drawers, 35½in. wide. (Skinner) £3,175 $5,175

A Scandinavian mahogany, rosewood and inlaid cylinder bureau, a garland inlaid front enclosing three drawers and a forward sliding lined writing surface, 34½in. wide. (Christie's) £2,415 $3,864

Chippendale curly maple slant-lid desk, Massachusetts or New Hampshire, late 18th century, with small drawers above a central opening flanked by valanced small compartments, 36in. wide. (Skinner) £2,046 $3,335

A Chippendale figured maple slant-front desk, Southern New England, 1780-1800, the hinged lid opening to a fitted interior, 36in. wide. (Sotheby's) £2,242 $3,737

Queen Anne style two-part lady's desk, by F. Valentino of Dennis, MA., in cherry with slant lid and fitted interior, three drawers below, 35in. wide. (Eldred's) £447 $715

A Chippendale figured walnut slant front desk, Pennsylvania, circa 1780, the hinged lid opening to an interior with a prospect door, 38½in. wide. (Sotheby's) £2,981 $4,887

A Queen Anne burr-yew and yew-wood bureau, feather-banded to the front, the rectangular top above a hinged slope, 39in. wide.
(Christie's)   £9,775 $16,226

A fine and rare Queen Anne figured walnut slant-front desk, Philadelphia, circa 1770, the case with four graduated long drawers on ogee bracket feet, 39in. wide.
(Sotheby's)   £4,911 $8,050

A George I walnut bureau, inlaid overall with cross and feather-banding, the writing-slope enclosing a fitted interior, 39in. wide.
(Christie's)   £14,950 $24,817

A George III mahogany bureau, the hinged writing-slope enclosing nine short drawers and six pigeon-holes, above a frieze drawer and a serpentine kneehole drawer, 43¼in. wide. (Christie's) £4,600 $7,636

A small Italian polychrome painted bureau, early 20th century, of bombé outline, decorated throughout with flowers and foliage, 31in. wide.
(Christie's)   £1,265 $1,379

A George III mahogany bureau, the rectangular top above a hinged slope enclosing a green baize-lined writing surface, and fitted interior, 46in. wide.
(Christie's)   £2,185 $3,561

A good Chippendale carved mahogany slant-front desk, Rhode Island, circa 1780, on a moulded base and ogee bracket feet, 38in. wide. (Sotheby's) £5,612 $9,200

Chippendale mahogany carved reverse serpentine slant lid desk, Massachusetts, 18th century, opens to a two-stepped interior of valanced compartments and small drawers, 42in. wide.
(Skinner)   £3,175 $5,175

A tulipwood and cube parquetry bureau à cylindre, 18th century and later, on cabriole legs headed with foliate decoration, 38½in. wide.
(Christie's)   £5,175 $8,384

An early 18th century walnut bureau with feather banding having fitted interior above two short and two long drawers, 2ft.7in. wide. (Russell Baldwin & Bright)
£1,450 $2,392

A George III mahogany bureau, the inlaid slope with good fitted interior, four graduated drawers with pierced brass handles, 99cm. wide. (Bristol) £1,600 $2,560

An early George III Provincial oak bureau, the sloping flap enclosing pigeon holes and small drawers, 95cm. wide.(Bearne's) £980 $1,617

A fine North Italian walnut bureau, Verona, circa 1740, the rectangular inlaid top above an inset, strapwork inlaid and laburnum crossbanded fall, 40½in. wide. (Christie's) £7,200 $11,520

A Queen Anne walnut desk-on-frame, Philadelphia, 1740–60, in two sections: the upper with a rectangular top above a thumbmoulded slant-lid, 33in. wide. (Christie's) £45,720 $76,200

An 18th century North Italian walnut crossbanded and inlaid bureau, the sloping fall with a slide and central panel enclosing a fitted interior, 114cm. wide. (Phillips) £11,000 $18,040

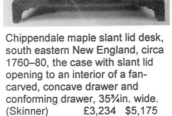

A Louis XVI Provincial walnut cylinder bureau, decorated with lines, chequer bandings and fluting, the cylinder fall enclosing a fitted interior, 45in. wide. (Christie's) £2,875 $4,658

Chippendale maple slant lid desk, south eastern New England, circa 1760–80, the case with slant lid opening to an interior of a fan-carved, concave drawer and conforming drawer, 35¾in. wide. (Skinner) £3,234 $5,175

Chippendale mahogany oxbow inlaid slant lid desk, Newport, Rhode Island, circa 1780–1810, a reverse serpentine case of cockbeaded graduated drawers, 40in. wide. (Skinner) £8,625 $13,800

A fine antique figured walnut and crossbanded bureau, the fall front opening to reveal fitted interior with drawers and pigeon holes, 2ft. 6in. (Academy) £6,600 $10,890

A burr-walnut bureau-on-stand, 20th century, feather-banded to the top and front, the rectangular sloping fall-flap enclosing a fitted interior, 32¾in. wide. (Christie's) £5,175 $8,590

A Georgian mahogany bureau, with fitted interior, four graduated drawers with later turned handles, on bracket feet, 91½in. wide. (Bristol) £1,200 $1,920

A George I walnut bureau, the top and front inlaid with feather-banding, on a moulded plinth base with shaped bracket feet, 38in. wide. (Christie's) £16,100 $26,404

A Louis XV ormolu-mounted black and gold lacquer bureau en pente, by Jaques Dubois, decorated overall with Chinese garden landscapes with pagodas and baskets of flowers, 25½in. wide. (Christie's) £14,950 $24,817

A William and Mary inlaid burl walnut slant-front bureau, circa 1700, the moulded slant-front opening to a fitted interior, 37in. wide. (Sotheby's) £7,717 $12,650

A Chippendale maple slant-front desk, possibly Salem, 1760–80, the rectangular top above a thumbmoulded slant-lid enclosing a compartmented interior, 38in. wide. (Christie's) £2,208 $3,680

A North Italian walnut parquetry inlaid bureau, circa 1740, the fall enclosing four short drawers centred by a recess, 46¾in. wide. (Christie's) £7,200 $11,520

Chippendale walnut slant lid desk, Delaware River Valley, circa 1770, the slant lid opens to an interior of central prospect door with recessed thumb-moulded tombstone panel. (Skinner) £15,333 $25,300

A Regency black and gilt-japanned side cabinet, the shaped top with serpentine sides above a frieze decorated with anthemion and stars, central pair of trellis and silk-backed doors, 46in. wide.
(Christie's)   £3,680 $5,998

An Art Deco burr-walnut cocktail cabinet, 44½in. wide extended, including a green and clear glass silver overlaid cocktail set.
(Christie's)   £2,530 $3,795

A Victorian walnut breakfront side cabinet with string and marquetry inlay and gilt metal mounts, 60in. wide.
(Andrew Hartley)   £2,300 $3,680

A George III gilt-decorated black japanned brass-mounted cabinet on later stand, the rectangular cabinet decorated with chinoiseries, 40½in. wide. (Sotheby's)   £1,263 $2,070

A pair of French ebonised and brass inlaid serpentine side cabinets, late 19th/early 20th century, applied with gilt metal mounts and decorated with panels of meandering foliage and strap-work, 42in. wide.
(Christie's)   £3,220 $5,152

A George III mahogany Estate cabinet, the moulded cornice above a pair of cut-cornered panelled cupboard doors, 51in. wide.
(Christie's)   £3,450 $5,520

A 19th century English burr thuya side cabinet, ebonised, crossbanded and string inlaid, with porcelain and gilt metal mounts, 49½in. wide.
(Andrew Hartley)   £3,000 $4,800

A Victorian figured walnut and floral-marquetry breakfront side cabinet, the rectangular top with canted angles and a moulded edge above an inlaid frieze, 74in. wide.
(Christie's)   £2,415 $3,864

A Victorian metal mounted figured walnut side cabinet, the painted shaped marble top above porcelain mounted door flanked by glazed sides.
(Academy Auctioneers)
                   £2,600 $4,160

A George II padouk, mahogany and parquetry cabinet-on-stand, attributed to Wright & Elrick, chequer-banded overall in greenheart and fruitwood, 35½in. wide. (Christie's) £33,350 $54,694

A pair of George III pedestal side cabinets, each with a moulded rectangular concave-fronted top above a spreading concave-moulded frieze, 26¾in. wide. (Christie's) £8,625 $14,317

A mahogany 'estate' cabinet in the George III manner by James Shoolbred & Co. with panelled doors, on a shaped plinth base, 103cm. wide. (Bearne's) £920 $1,518

19th century walnut cabinet with a single glazed door, glazed sides, the base with a cupboard, 40in. wide. (Ewbank) £2,100 $3,465

A pair of parcel-gilt and kingwood side cabinets, circa 1860, each with a white marble top within a gadrooned border, 97cm. wide. (Sotheby's) £15,525 $25,616

A 19th century Dutch marquetry cabinet on stand, inlaid with vases of flowers and scrolling foliage, on tapering square legs and bun feet, 97cm. wide. (Tennants) £1,500 $2,400

A pair of gilt-bronze, kingwood and marquetry meubles d'appui, Paris, circa 1870, each with a serpentine marble top above frieze and a panelled door, 98cm. wide. (Sotheby's) £14,375 $23,431

A late George III black and gilt-japanned and polychrome-decorated cabinet on stand, decorated overall with foliate and flowering sprays and geometrical borders, 18¾in. wide. (Christie's) £9,200 $15,088

A Victorian burr walnut side cabinet cross-banded in kingwood and satinwood stringing with arched raised mirror back, 6ft.6in. wide. (Russell Baldwin & Bright) £4,800 $7,920

Italian neoclassical-style painted parcel gilt side cabinet, early 20th century, shaped moulded top over conforming case, 55in. wide. (Skinner) £2,322 $3,738

An Asprey Art Deco oak cocktail cabinet, the hinged divided top with an architectural surmount, revealing a fully fitted interior, 32½in. wide. (Christie's) £1,610 $2,576

A 19th century breakfront side cabinet, veneered in burr figured walnut, having ebonised mouldings, 5ft.5½in. wide. (Woolley & Wallis) £1,600 $2,656

A late 19th century burr walnut music cabinet, with a pair of boxwood floral inlaid doors enclosing fitted interior and pull out writing slope, on plinth and bracket feet, 24in. (Dreweatt Neate) £1,950 $3,218

A 17th century Provincial German oak cabinet, moulded cornice, decorated frieze with incised date *Anno 1774*, two shallow carved side sections, two twin panel doors with raised bosses, panelled front, 168cm. wide. (Locke & England) £1,100 $1,815

A William and Mary olivewood, oyster veneered and crossbanded cabinet on later stand, the upper part with a moulded cornice and cushion frieze drawer, fitted with ten drawers about a central cupboard, 105cm. wide. (Phillips) £7,000 $11,480

Antique American cabinet, in maple with two drawers over two doors, 39In. wide. (Eldred's) £619 $990

A Victorian inlaid rosewood side cabinet base, 54½in. (Dockree's) £300 $495

A late Victorian mahogany music cabinet with galleried top and mirror back above a glazed fall front door, 18in. wide. (Christie's) £414 $662

William and Mary style oysterwood veneer cabinet, late 19th century, rectangular moulded cornice over two pairs of short drawers above a cabinet door, 52in. wide.
(Skinner)   £2,679 $4,313

A Regency mahogany tea cabinet-on-stand, the hinged rectangular top crossbanded in rosewood, with cushion moulded frieze, 39in. wide.
(Christie's)   £11,500 $19,090

A Dutch late 18th century mahogany side cabinet, inlaid with neoclassical urns and ribbon tied tassels, with bands of chequer stringing, 4ft.3in.
(Woolley & Wallis) £1,500 $2,490

Indo-Portuguese hardwood marquetry and bone inlaid cabinet on chest, probably Goa, 19th century, the top section with twelve drawers, 44in. wide.
(Skinner)   £12,143 $19,550

A French ebonised scarlet tortoiseshell and brass-inlaid side cabinet, the sepentine-shaped top above an inlaid frieze between paterae mounted corners, 44½in. wide. (Christie's) £1,495 $2,392

A late 19th century French cabinet, shaped marble top, the front filled with a single door painted with a scene depicting a courting couple, 99cm. wide.
(Wintertons)   £1,400 $2,296

An early Victorian rosewood veneered breakfront side cabinet, the top with a block moulded edge and mirror back, 5ft.3in. wide.
(Woolley & Wallis) £3,200 $5,412

A late 19th century inlaid rosewood music cabinet, with single glazed and panelled door, on straight supports, 54cm. wide.
(Bristol)   £250 $413

A mid-Victorian pietra-dura mounted figured-walnut, ebonised and parcel-gilt side cabinet, on a moulded plinth base, 76¼in. wide.
(Christie's)   £52,100 $85,444

A Napoleon III ebony-veneered and gilt-metal mounted side cabinet, with a black marble top, on shaped bracket feet, 35¾in. wide.
(Christie's) £2,070 $3,353

An Algraphone lacquer gramophone cabinet, of console format in Chinese Chippendale style with lacquer-work on a black ground, 45in. wide.
(Christie's) £316 $505

An ash cabinet, Danisn, 19th century, the moulded and shaped cornice above a frieze drawer, 3ft.5in. wide.
(Sotheby's) £1,150 $1,920

A black-lacquered and gilt cabinet, English, circa 1840, decorated in the Chinese manner with figures and landscapes, in two parts, 3ft.2½in. wide,
(Sotheby's) £1,610 $2,689

Two Italian walnut side cabinets, 19th century, each decorated with foliate carvings, carved uprights and projecting corbels, 30in. wide and 31in. wide.
(Christie's) £8,050 $13,041

A William IV rosewood side cabinet, applied with gilt metal mounts, the raised shelved superstructure with a pierced three-quarter gallery, 41½in. wide.
(Christie's) £2,530 $4,099

A Queen Anne brass-mounted black and gilt-japanned cabinet-on-stand, decorated overall with bold Chinoiserie landscapes with figures, birds and buildings, 43in. wide.
(Christie's) £9,775 $15,933

A fine and rare figured and inlaid walnut punched-tin pie safe, Rich Family, Wythe County, Virginia, 1770–1820, 4ft.5in. wide.
(Sotheby's) £3,507 $5,750

A brass-bound polychrome and gilt-japanned cabinet-on-stand, the cabinet decorated overall with Oriental courtly figures, pagodas, foliage and birds, 44½in. wide.
(Christie's) £2,185 $3,496

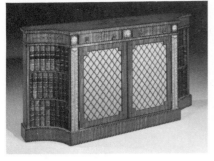

A satinwood and penwork side cabinet, late 20th century, of broken outline, decorated with ebonised lines, 60in. wide.
(Christie's)   £11,500 $18,400

Arts and Crafts liquor cabinet, lift top, slag glass doors, brass feet, original finish, 24in. wide.
(Skinner)   £483 $805

A Victorian walnut breakfront side cabinet, applied with gilt-metal mounts and inlaid with meandering floral lines and trails, 79in. wide.
(Christie's)   £5,175 $8,280

A Regency brass-inlaid calamander cabinet-on-stand, the rectangular top above a pair of panelled doors enclosing six drawers, on a later rosewood stand, 28in. wide.
(Christie's)   £2,300 $3,749

A near pair of walnut and gilt-bronze library cabinets, Paris, circa 1880, the leather-inset top within a moulded cast border, 74cm. wide.
(Sotheby's)   £16,100 $26,565

A mid-Victorian Gothic Revival walnut cabinet, the rectangular top above a pair of astragal doors, each with gothic tracery and quatrefoil carved decoration, 29in. wide.
(Christie's)   £552 $828

An ebonised scarlet tortoiseshell and brass inlaid side cabinet, late 19th century, the rectangular top and frieze with applied foliate ormolu mounts, 58in. wide.
(Christie's)   £1,150 $1,840

A walnut cabinet, French, 16th century, the moulded cornice and banded and scroll painted frieze above two conforming fielded panelled doors, 4ft. 5in. wide.
(Sotheby's)   £7,475 $12,483

A good Victorian satinwood side cabinet, circa 1880, the shelf superstructure with a pierced three quarter brass gallery above a mirrored back, 36in. wide.
(Christie's)   £2,700 $4,320

Stained cherry tilt-top stand, Connecticut, late 18th century, with a dished top above a ring-turned swelled pedestal, 20¼in.
(Skinner)   £1,995 $3,220

A very fine and rare Chippendale carved and figured walnut bird cage candlestand, Philadelphia, circa 1770, 24¼in. diameter.
(Sotheby's)   £106,790 $173,000

Federal cherry inlaid and birch tilt-top candlestand, New England, circa 1800, the oval tilting top with central inlaid star, 19¾in. wide.
(Skinner)   £847 $1,380

A Queen Anne walnut candlestand, Newport, 1730–1760, the circular dished top above a tapering ring-turned pedestal, 15¾in. diameter.
(Christie's)   £4,485 $7,475

Cherry and maple candlestand, south eastern New England, late 18th century, the circular top on a vase and ring turned post and tripod base, 12in. diameter.
(Skinner)   £646 $1,035

A good Queen Anne walnut tilt-top candlestand, Philadelphia, circa 1760, the circular dished top tilting above a flaring standard and ball-turned support, 20in. diameter.
(Sotheby's)   £4,560 $7,475

Federal painted and decorated candlestand, New England, early 19th century, the octagonal shaped top outlined in black and decorated with a chequerboard, 29in. high.
(Skinner)   £7,760 $12,650

A Federal walnut candlestand, Philadelphia, late 18th century, on a tripartite base with cabriole legs and slipper feet, 18¼in. diameter.
(Christie's)   £11,040 $18,400

A red-painted pine candlestand, New Mexico, probably Penasco, circa 1880, the square top with moulded edge above a turned flaring standard, 17¼in. wide.
(Sotheby's)   £631 $1,035

A mid 19th century coromandel and mahogany canterbury with foliate-carved scrolling divisions, a drawer below, 57cm wide.
(Bearne's)   £1,300 $2,080

A George IV mahogany canterbury, the gadrooned moulded rectangular top with three pierced supports above a panelled drawer, 31½in. wide. (Christie's) £3,450 $5,623

A Regency mahogany canterbury, of rectangular outline having four divided sections, with ring turned supports, 48cm. wide.
(Phillips)   £780 $1,248

A mahogany canterbury, early 19th century, with four slatted compartments with central carrying handle between block and turned finial-capped uprights, 19in. wide.
(Christie's)   £1,840 $2,944

A late George III mahogany canterbury, the incurved divided top above a single frieze drawer, on ring-turned legs, 17¾in. wide.
(Christie's)   £2,208 $3,680

A late Regency mahogany four division canterbury, the slatted open compartments with a carrying handle and single drawer below, 19in. wide.
(Christie's)   £2,070 $3,312

A walnut canterbury cabinet, 19th century, the four division top with pierced fret-carved sides and spiral-turned supports, 29in. wide.
(Christie's)   £1,610 $2,576

A Victorian rosewood two-division canterbury with twin pierced side panels, spiral turned corner pillars, 20in. (Canterbury) £800 $1,320

A Federal turned rosewood canterbury, New York or Philadelphia, circa 1810, of rectangular form with four ball finials and a tri-partite section, 16in. wide. (Sotheby's) £1,052 $1,725

A fine and rare Chippendale carved and figured mahogany corner chair, Boston, Massachusetts, circa 1770, the shaped crest above a concave arm. (Sotheby's) £24,150 $40,250

A fine and very rare Queen Anne carved and figured walnut corner chair, New York, 1750–70, concave arm with dramatically scrolled terminals.
(Sotheby's)   £16,560 $27,600

Maple roundabout chair, New England, late 18th century, with a shaped crest above the scrolled arm on turned arm supports.
(Skinner)   £683 $1,093

Queen Anne maple roundabout commode chair, New England, the shaped crest above the scrolled arm, shaped splat, moulded seat, and frontal cabriole leg.
(Skinner)   £1,294 $2,070

William and Mary painted roundabout chair, New England, 18th century, the shaped backrest anad chamfered crest ending in scrolled handholds.
(Skinner)   £846 $1,380

A Chippendale walnut corner-chair, mid-Atlantic States, late 18th century, the moulded crestrail above a shaped arm continuing to outscrolled handholds.
(Christie's)   £2,622 $4,370

An Arts and Crafts stained beechwood corner seat, the curved top rail above slatted back and sides, with caned seat on turned tapering uprights.
(Christie's)   £172 $258

A Queen Anne carved and figured mahogany corner chair, English or Irish, 1710–40, the shaped crest above a concave arm with outscrolled terminals.
(Sotheby's)   £2,932 $4,887

A rare Chippendale carved mahogany corner chair, New York, circa 1760, the reverse-scrolling crest above a concave arm with outscrolled terminals.
(Sotheby's)   £5,520 $9,200

A set of four yew wood and ash Windsor chairs, the hooped stick backs with a central pierced splat raised on turned legs.
(Tennants)   £4,800 $7,680

Pair of Chinese export side chairs, mid-19th century, in rosewood with pierced medallion backs depicting fruit, flowers and vines, cabriole legs, cane seats.
(Eldred's)   £584 $935

An early Victorian rosewood child's chair, in Carolean Revival style, the needlework panel back with scrolls and a leaf cresting.
(Woolley & Wallis)   £220 $354

Two maple and oak plain top chairs with doubled nailed leathers, 1707–25, Massachusetts, the finial topped baluster and ring-turned stiles flank the leather covered back.
(Skinner)   £5,031 $8,050

Two of a set of six early-Victorian oak side chairs, each with a pierced confronting C-scroll and lozenge geometric rectangular back flanked by spirally-turned uprights.
(Christie's) (Six)   £3,450 $5,623

A pair of George II mahogany side chairs, attributed to William Hallett, on cabriole legs headed by a pendant-hung shell and gadrooned angle-brackets.
(Christie's)   £45,500 $74,620

One of a pair of Anglo-Indian ivory-inlaid padouk side chairs, mid 18th century, Vizagapatam, inlaid overall with line-inlaid ivory of scrolling flowers and foliage.
(Christie's) (Two) £41,000 $67,240

A pair of George III painted mahogany hall chairs, the spoon-shaped pierced back with dipped crest and recessed circular centre section.
(Sotheby's)   £5,261 $8,625

One of a set of six Regency brass inlaid rosewood dining chairs with rail backs with fancy arabesques, on grained sabre legs, now upholstered with floral gros point seats. (Graves Son & Pilcher)
(Six) £2,450 $4,043

A pair of J & J Kohn Fledermaus chairs, designed by Josef Hoffman, circa 1907, each with curved top rail above open back and padded seat. (Christie's)   £747 $1,120

A pair of Victorian rosewood high-back side chairs, each with turned finials and part-upholstered backs. (Christie's)   £299 $478

Gio Ponti for Cassina, 'Superleggera' chair (699), 1957, light black wooden frame, fine cane, 32¾in. high. (Sotheby's)   £1,035 $1,676

A pair of walnut chaises, 20th century, in the Louis XV style, each with a padded cartouche-shaped back with a cabochon rocaille and foliate cresting. (Christie's)   £299 $484

One of a set of six William IV rosewood dining chairs, each with bowed toprail, lotus-carved crossbars and uprights. (Bearne's) (Six) £1,850 $2,960

A carved pine territorial side chair, probably Pueblo origin, New Mexico, 1910-1940, the shaped sunburst and chip-carved crest flanked by chip-carved stiles. (Sotheby's)   £526 $862

A fine and rare pair of Chippendale carved mahogany side chairs, Portsmouth, New Hampshire, circa 1780, each with a shaped C-scroll carved crest with leaf-carved ears. (Sotheby's)   £5,679 $9,200

A joined oak child's side chair, Derbyshire, mid 17th century, the straight top rail surmounted by finials above a feather carved frieze. (Bonhams)   £800 $1,280

Stickley Brothers style hall chair, worn original finish, 27½in. high. (Skinner) £138 $230

Pair of painted and decorated side chairs, New Jersey or Philadelphia, circa 1825, with curving crests above a curving splat. (Skinner) £776 $1,265

A Chinese Export padouk side chair, mid-18th century, carved overall in relief with foliate scrolls, the pierced back above a padded drop-in seat. (Christie's) £11,500 $19,090

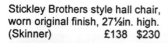

One of a set of four George III white-painted and parcel-gilt side chairs, the back flanked by detached fluted and spirally-fluted columns, on fluted turned tapering legs. (Christie's) (Four) £9,200 $15,272

Two of a set of twelve mahogany dining chairs, late 19/early 20th century, including a pair of armchairs, each with a shield-shaped back with a pierced wheat-ear decorated vase splat. (Christie's) (Twelve) £5,175 $8,384

A fine Chippendale carved walnut side chair with fluted stiles, Philadelphia, circa 1760, the serpentine crest with central cabochon-, ruffle-, and volute-carved device. (Sotheby's) £21,296 $34,500

Tapio Wirkkala for Asko, chair, circa 1955, decorative laminated birch of an angular slice through the year rings of the tree. (Sotheby's) £3,220 $5,216

Two of a set of six early Victorian oak hall chairs, each back carved with a scallop shell above scrolled supports. (Christie's) (Six) £3,450 $5,589

A rare and early turned pine side chair, New Mexico, circa 1780, the horizontal crest above three ring-turned backrests, plank seat below. (Sotheby's) £3,332 $5,462

387

Two of a set of twelve late 19th century mahogany dining chairs of Chippendale style, each with shaped scroll and leaf carved top rail, pierced vase splat. (Dreweatt Neate) (Twelve) £9,800 $16,170

A fine and rare pair of Chippendale carved mahogany side chairs, New York, circa 1770, each with a shaped ruffle-, leaf-, and C-scroll-carved crest. (Sotheby's) £41,100 $68,500

A pair of George III mahogany side chairs, each with pierced circular back with central patera radiating leaves and joined by swags, on scrolling channelled stiles.(Christie's) £3,220 $5,248

A pair of late Federal carved mahogany side-chairs, New York, 1815—1825, each with carved and inlaid tablet crest above a pierced carved splat centring a roundel. (Christie's) £4,830 $8,050

Two of a set of eight Regency brass-inlaid grained beech dining-chairs, including two armchairs, each with scrolled cresting and tablet back. (Christie's) (Eight) £5,520 $8,997

Two from a set of eight Hepplewhite mahogany dining chairs. (Christopher Matthews) (Eight) £3,200 $5,280

Two of a set of four George III mahogany dining chairs including one carver, of Sheraton style, the reeded bar and ball back with straight crest.
(Andrew Hartley)   (Four)   £700 $1,120

Two of a set of six George III mahogany dining-chairs, each with tapering pierced back with cabochon-linked spindles. (Christie's)   (Six)   £5,520 $9,163

A pair of George II figured walnut open armchairs, each with a solid vase-shaped splat between serpentine uprights, above a padded drop-in seat.
(Christie's)   £194,000 $322,040

Two of a set of nine George III mahogany dining-chairs, including one open armchair, each with triple-arched toprail above a pierced tapering rectangular splat. (Christie's)   (Nine)   £44,400 $73,704

A pair of George III mahogany side chairs, on square chamfered beaded legs carved with geometrical blind fretwork. (Christie's)   £19,550 $32,453

Two of a set of twelve Regency mahogany dining chairs, including two carvers, each with reeded swag backs. (Phillips) (Twelve)   £7,000 $11,200

One of a 19th century set of six ash and elm dining chairs, with arched crest, vase shaped splat.
(Andrew Hartley)
(Six) £1,700 $2,856

Two of a set of eight Regency mahogany dining chairs including two carvers, with ebony stringing, deep curved crest rail. (Andrew Hartley) (Eight) £4,600 $7,360

One of a set of four Victorian walnut dining chairs, the buckle back with carved splat and turned finials.
(Andrew Hartley)
(Four) £750 $1,200

One of a matched pair of William and Mary walnut side chairs, circa 1690, the double 'S' scroll top rail above a conforming splat centred by twin oval caned panels.
(Bonhams) (Two) £900 $1,440

Three of a Harlequin set of ten oak spindle back dining chairs including two carvers.
(Academy) (Ten) £3,400 $5,610

One of a set of six Victorian rosewood balloon back dining chairs, with leaf carved crest, cabriole legs and peg feet.
(Andrew Hartley)
(Six) £1,800 $2,880

One of a set of nine early Victorian rosewood bar back dining chairs, the top rail with carved C scroll brackets, turned fluted tapering front legs and sabre back legs.
(Dreweatt Neate) (Nine)
£3,800 $6,270

Two of a set of six early 19th century mahogany dining chairs in the Hepplewhite style, the arched backs with pierced vase splats with foliate ornament.
(Phillips) (Six) £1,800 $2,952

One of a set of six Regency mahogany dining chairs with arched curved rail and cable bar back.
(Andrew Hartley)
(Six) £2,500 $4,000

Two of a set of six George IV mahogany bar back dining chairs, each with reeded top rail, pierced S scroll carved back rest.
(Dreweatt Neate) (Six)
£1,600 $2,640

Crooked-back walnut side chair, probably England or Continental, the pierced crest above an upholstered back and seat.
(Skinner)   £458 $748

Two of a set of ten George III mahogany dining chairs including carvers, with arched crest, moulded uprights, pierced waisted splat.
(Andrew Hartley)
(Ten) £5,800 $9,744

A Chippendale mahogany side-chair, the serpentine crestrail with scrolled ears centring a carved shell with volutes above a solid vasiform splat.
(Christie's)   £2,760 $4,600

A pair of George III mahogany open armchairs, each with waved toprail above a pierced Gothic vertical splat and a padded rectangular seat. (Christie's) £5,175 $8,590

One of a set of four George III mahogany dining chairs with shaped crest rail, pierced and waisted interlacing splat.
(Andrew Hartley)
(Four) £1,500 $2,520

Two of a set of eight 19th century mahogany ladder back dining chairs, in the George III manner, each with four scroll carved and pierced rails.
(Phillips) (Eight) £3,300 $5,280

Chippendale mahogany carved side chair, Massachusetts, circa 1780, the shaped crest rail with carved terminals above the pierced splat.
(Skinner)   £1,058 $1,725

Two of a set of seven Regency mahogany bar back dining chairs, reeded backs with three vertical splats, including one carver.
(Wintertons) (Seven) £1,000 £1,650

Two of a set of six Regency mahogany dining chairs, with panelled toprails and carved mid rails.
(George Kidner)   (Six)   £1,600 $2,656

Two of a set of four William IV rosewood side chairs, with scrolled palmette carved open buckle backs.
(Woolley & Wallis)   (Four)   £1,150 $1,909

Two of a set of eight Georgian style ladderback mahogany dining chairs, including two carvers, each with four pierced rails centred by an anthemion.
(Phillips)   (Eight)   £2,200 $3,520

Two of a set of eight Regency simulated rosewood dining chairs, each with scrolling uprights leading into sabre legs, with arched turned and reeded top bar.
(Phillips)   (Eight)   £2,100 $3,360

Two of a set of seven 18th century Portuguese walnut dining chairs, the vase shaped splats carved with foliage, on cabriole front legs.
(Dreweatt Neate)   (Seven)   £3,500 $5,705

Two of a set of six Victorian mahogany buckle back dining chairs.
(Academy Auctioneers) (Six)   £1,250 $2,000

Two of a set of four early 19th century side chairs, in faded rosewood with moulded rails and scroll open backs.
(Woolley & Wallis)   (Four)   £460 $741

Two of a late 19th century set of twelve mahogany dining chairs, with pierced slat backs.
(Bristol)   £3,000 $4,950

Two of a set of eight oak ladderback chairs, including two armchairs, each with five graduated shaped bars between turned uprights.
(Phillips)   (Eight)   £1,000 $1,600

Two of a set of six Regency grained beech side chairs, the open backs with a scrolling ribbed horizontal splat.
(Woolley & Wallis)   (Six)   £1,400 $2,324

Two George III style paint-decorated maple side chairs, circa 1930, rectangular back with painted tablet, upholstered seat, 33½in. high.
(Skinner)   £429 $690

Two of eight mid Victorian balloon back dining chairs, the moulded top rails above a scroll carved midrail and upholstered seats.
(Phillips)   (Eight)   £2,500 $4,000

One of a set of six George IV mahogany dining chairs with plain cresting rails and pierced and carved mid rails. (Anderson & Garland)   (Six) £3,300 $5,445

Two of a set of seven plus two arm Victorian oak dining chairs with broad cresting rails and carved scrolling mid-rails.   (Anderson & Garland)   (Nine) £860 $1,419

One of a set of six Victorian fruitwood bobbin-turned dining chairs each with knob finials and turned supports with spindles. (Christie's)   (Six) £805 $1,288

A mid-Victorian Gothic Revival pitch-pine side chair, with crenellated top rail above panel back and seat.
(Christie's)   £92 $138

A fine and rare set of four Federal carved mahogany shield-back dining chairs, attributed to John Carlile & Sons, Providence, Rhode Island, 1789–1801.
(Sotheby's)   £23,851 $39,100

One of a pair of French fruitwood high-back side chairs, late 19th century, each with pierced foliate-carved top-rail between turned finials. (Christie's) (Two) £115 $184

One of a pair of Chippendale carved walnut side chairs, Pennsylvania, circa 1760, each with a ruffle-, leaf-, and volute-carved crest centred by reverse-scrolling moulded ears. (Sotheby's) (Two) £9,660 $16,100

Two orange and blue painted pine plank-seat side chairs, Taos, New Mexico, circa 1850, the projecting moulded stiles with stepped finish centring a diamond-pierced stepped crest. (Sotheby's) £10,873 $17,825

A rare Queen Anne carved walnut slipper chair, Pennsylvania, circa 1750, the shaped crest with outscrolled ears above a figured vasiform splat.
(Sotheby's)   £3,277 $5,462

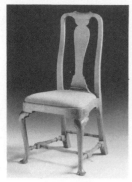

A Queen Anne turned maple compass-seat side chair, Boston, Massachusetts, 1730-1750, with a yoke-form crest above a vasiform splat compass-seat.
(Sotheby's)   £1,596 $2,587

A pair of Dutch walnut and marquetry side chairs, each inlaid overall with flowers, the double vase-shaped splat flanked by scrolling uprights.
(Christie's)   £4,025 $6,560

A fine and rare Queen Anne carved and figured walnut compass-seat side chair, Philadelphia, circa 1760, the projecting volute-and-shell-carved crest, above a volute carved splat. (Sotheby's) £11,040 $18,400

A Charles II oak bobbin turned side chair, circa 1680, with a solid seat, baluster legs and stretchers.
(Bonhams)   £360 $576

A set of six Federal grain-painted and polychrome-decorated plank seat side chairs, probably West Chester County, Pennsylvania, circa 1815.
(Sotheby's)   £1,952 $3,162

One of a set of six Victorian rosewood balloon-back dining chairs, each waisted back with a horizontal splat above a serpentine fronted upholstered seat.
(Christie's)   (Six)   £736 $1,177

A Queen Anne walnut side-chair, Boston, 1740-60, the arched crestrail centring a lobed and scalloped shell above a solid vasiform splat.
(Christie's)   £5,520 $9,200

Two of a set of twelve Regency mahogany dining chairs, stamped by James Winter, 101 Wardour Street, Soho, London, comprising two open armchairs and ten side chairs. (Christie's)
(Twelve)   £31,050 $50,611

A fine and rare carved pine 'Cochiti-style' side chair, Territorial, circa 1840, the stepped finials above moulded stiles with corn husk decoration.
(Sotheby's)   £4,209 $6,900

An 18th century oak and elm lambing chair, the panelled back with straight crest inscribed with the date 1775.
(Andrew Hartley)   £1,250 $2,000

A pair of 19th-century giltwood framed fauteuils, of Louis XV style, the upholstered panel backs enclosed within moulded and flower carved frames.
(Phillips)   £1,400 $2,240

A Gordon Russell walnut open armchair, with adjustable padded back and seat on square section uprights, circa 1938.
(Andrew Hartley)   £240 $384

A 19th century mahogany framed Raeburn chair, the rectangular upholstered back and seat with padded elbow rests.
(Phillips)   £580 $928

A pair of side chairs circa 1860, each with padded turkey-work covers above a tassel fringe, on turned legs.
(Sotheby's)   £4,140 $6,831

One of a pair of Victorian walnut framed armchairs, in the Louis XV style, each with channelled frame, on scrolled supports.
(Andrew Hartley)
            (Two) £850 $1,360

A mahogany framed library chair, by Whytock and Reid, Edinburgh, outscrolled arms with carved scrolling terminals.
(Phillips)   £1,450 $2,320

Pair of Louis XVI style beechwood and upholstered fauteuils, 19th century, each with gros point and petit point depicting garden scenes and animals, 34in. high.
(Skinner)   £1,357 $2,185

Victorian rosewood elbow chair, splayed scrolled back, slightly splayed arms, raised on foliate moulded uprights, mid 19th century.
(G.A. Key)   £500 $800

A leather upholstered engraved pine armchair, attributed to Thomas Molesworth, Shoshone Furniture Company, Cody, Wyoming, circa 1935. (Sotheby's) £1,242 $2,012

A pair of mahogany fauteuils, Restauration, each with a padded back within a moulded frame punctuated with rosettes. (Sotheby's) £10,925 $17,808

A Régence beechwood fauteuil, the arched cane panel back with shaped padded arm supports and stuffover seat. (Phillips) £650 $1,066

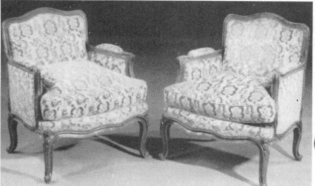

One of a pair of 19th century French mahogany open armchairs of Empire design with scroll backs, scroll arms with leaf capped terminals. (Canterbury) £540 $864

A pair of French beechwood chaises, 18th century, each with a channelled frame, with an arched top-rail and padded arms. (Christie's) £1,380 $2,208

A Victorian walnut framed spoonback parlour chair with leaf and scroll carved crest, on cabriole legs and china castors. (Andrew Hartley) £550 $880

A 19th century mahogany framed Raeburn armchair, the serpentine upholstered back and seat enclosed by downswept open arms. (Phillips) £380 $608

A pair of George III giltwood open armchairs, the frame channelled overall, the backscrolled framed back with acanthus and on downswept supports. (Christie's) $5,750 $9,545

A Chinese-Export bamboo armchair, early 19th century, the square back and arms with pierced geometrical patterns above a caned seat. (Christie's) £1,150 $1,874

One of a pair of French pale blue painted bergères, late 19th century, each with a carved padded back and part-padded arms above a bowed seat.
(Christie's) (Two)   £805 $1,288

Martin Eisler for Forma, adjustable chair, 1959, black tubular metal and wire rod frame, brass feet.
(Sotheby's)   £2,990 $4,845

A mahogany library armchair, early 19th century, the tapered caned back with part-upholstered downscrolled arms and close-nailed padded seat.
(Christie's)   £977 $1,563

One of a pair of Central European mahogany and upholstered tub armchairs, late 19th century, on bulbous cabriole legs.
(Christie's) (Two) £1,380 $2,208

An early Victorian mahogany and leather-upholstered library armchair, the waisted buttoned back and outscrolled close-nailed arms above a squab cushion.
(Christie's)   £1,035 $1,656

Alvar Aalto for Finmar, cantilevered armchair, 1938–39, laminated birch, pale red cross woven webbing secured to wooden seat frame with brass tacks.
(Sotheby's)   £2,070 $3,353

One of a pair of French beech and upholstered fauteuils, each with a shaped padded back within a channelled foliate-carved surround.
(Christie's) (Two)   £632 $1,011

Ettore Sottsass for Poltronova, 'Harlow' chair, 1971, cast aluminium, orange velvet fabric.
(Sotheby's)   £667 $1,080

A Victorian mahogany upholstered open armchair with scrolled padded back, padded open arms with turned supports.
(Christie's)   £1,265 $2,024

A Victorian walnut and upholstered armchair, the padded back with a moulded incised top-rail flanked by fluted and leaf-carved stiles.
(Christie's) £920 $1,472

A pair of French walnut and upholstered bergères, each with an arched chanelled and flowerhead carved back.
(Christie's) £920 $1,472

A George III mahogany open armchair, the arms on reeded downswept supports, on square tapering panelled legs.
(Christie's) £1,725 $2,811

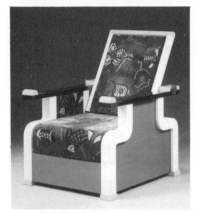

George J. Sowden for Memphis, 'Mamounia' armchair, designed 1985, no longer in production, lacquered wood, coloured plastic laminate and velvet.
(Sotheby's) £2,990 $4,844

A fine and rare Federal mahogany barrel-back lolling chair, attributed to Lemuel Church, Massachusetts, circa 1795, the rectangular crest above a concave, tapering, trapezoidal back.
(Sotheby's) £9,660 $16,100

One of a pair of late Victorian walnut and upholstered armchairs each with a shaped foliate and dolphin carved top-rail and a close-nailed padded back.
(Christie's) (Two) £805 $1,288

A late Victorian easy armchair, with buttoned back and arms, on ring-turned legs with brass castors, stamped *Howard & Sons, Berners St.* (Christie's) £1,035 $1,656

A pair of hardwood caned bergères, each with a panelled frame, the scrolled backs, arms and seat caned, with buttoned brown leather back and seat cushions.
(Christie's) £12,650 $20,619

A Napoleon III mahogany and gilt-metal mounted fauteuil, the upholstered back within a gilt-metal mounted frame.
(Christie's) £690 $1,104

A Chippendale mahogany easy-chair, the arched, canted and upholstered back flanked by shaped wings and outward scrolling arms. (Christie's) £4,140 $6,900

George III mahogany and caned reading Armchair, circa 1800, of typical form, with loose black leather cushions, adjustable ratcheted writing/reading arm. (Skinner) £2,857 $4,600

A rosewood and upholstered prie dieu chair, Victorian, circa 1860, with contemporary needlework, the back depicting a chapel interior. (Sotheby's) £644 $1,075

One of a pair of North European cream and blue painted fauteuils, each with square padded back, part padded arms with scrolled terminals. (Christie's) (Two) £920 $1,472

A pair of rosewood open armchairs, the oval padded backs with carved floral crests. (George Kidner) £800 $1,328

A Regency mahogany and caned library bergère, the channelled top-rail and arms on turned tapering legs. (Christie's) £1,265 $2,024

A Federal mahogany lolling chair, Massachusetts, circa 1800, the serpentine crest above a padded back and seat on shaped arms. (Sotheby's) £3,277 $5,462

An oak and elm 'lambing' chair, George III, late 18th century, the wing back with a canopy top, the box base with a deep drawer. (Sotheby's) £2,070 $3,457

One of a pair of caned beechwood and upholstered bergères, 20th century in the Louis XV style, each with channelled shaped padded back and part-upholstered arms. (Christie's) (Two) £1,380 $2,208

A mahogany side chair, George III, circa 1760, with an arched padded back and serpentine stuffed seat. (Sotheby's)   £977 $1,632

A walnut armchair, George II, with a straight padded back, shepherd's crook arms, on leaf carved cabriole legs with hairy claw feet. (Sotheby's)   £920 $1,536

A mahogany library bergère, early 19th century, with caned back, sides and seat, on turned reeded legs. (Christie's) £1,840 $2,944

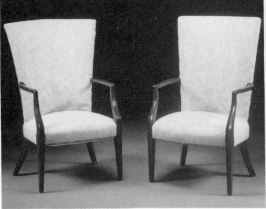

A walnut armchair, late 19th/early 20th century, the curved back and arm-rail and overscrolled terminals above a bowfronted upholstered seat. (Christie's)   £345 $552

Two similar Federal mahogany lolling chairs, attributed to Lemuel Church, Boston, 1805-10, each with bowed crestrail, curved arms above downswept moulded arm supports, 26in. wide. (Christie's)   £11,040 $18,400

A George III mahogany back-stool, circa 1760–1780, on Marlborough legs with block feet joined by H-stretchers. (Christie's)   £345 $575

A beechwood and upholstered bergère, early 19th century, the padded back and sides within a channelled ribbon-twist surround. (Christie's)   £690 $1,104

A white, blue and parcel-gilt decorated duchesse, late 19th century, the raised padded back with guilloche-carved surround and part upholstered arms, 80in. wide. (Christie's)   £862 $1,379

An oak reclining armchair, French Provincial, late 18th century, the padded down-curved arms above a deep ribbon moulded apron. (Sotheby's)   £805 $1,344

A late Victorian oak armchair, the bowed tablet top-rail carved with scrolling foliage and floral garlands.
(Christie's)   £1,380 $2,235

A pair of green and gilt-painted 'grotto' armchairs, early 20th century, each with a shell shaped back and seat, flanked by scrolled dolphin arm supports.
(Christie's)   £5,520 $8,832

A Regency mahogany library bergère, with a reeded caned back, padded arms on ring-turned tapered uprights.
(Christie's)   £4,370 $7,079

A beech and walnut fauteuil, 18th century, the cartouche-shaped padded back with a foliate toprail and rocaille cresting.
(Christie's)   £517 $838

A pair of late Victorian walnut library armchairs, decorated with ebonised mouldings and foliate carvings.
(Christie's)   £2,760 $4,471

A Venetian walnut open armchair, late 19th/early 20th century, carved with foliage, the raised scrolled back with a shield of a lion.
(Christie's)   £1,955 $3,128

A George III mahogany library armchair, the undulating top-rail above padded arms with downswept supports.
(Christie's)   £805 $1,304

A fine and very rare pair of classical carved gilt, white-painted armchairs, Baltimore or possibly Philadelphia, circa 1830.
(Sotheby's)   £15,617 $25,300

A mahogany library bergère, 19th century, with a reeded caned back, padded sides and seat with cushion.
(Christie's)   £2,530 $4,099

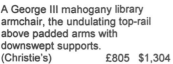

A walnut armchair, 19th century, with a padded back, arms and seat, terminals carved with lions' masks and foliage.
(Christie's) £1,380 $2,235

A pair of French cream and gilt-heightened fauteuils, mid 19th century, each with a button-down arched back, padded scroll arms and serpentine seat.
(Christie's) £3,450 $5,589

A George III mahogany library armchair, the fluted downswept arms headed by paterae, on turned, fluted tapering legs.
(Christie's) £14,950 $24,817

A Victorian porter's chair, upholstered in brass studded green leather, with an arched canopy, 67in. high.
(Christie's) £4,370 $7,079

A pair of George IV mahogany caned bergères, each with rounded, scrolled toprail centred by a stylised floral spray, each corner with a scrolled leaf.
(Christie's) £12,650 $20,999

A stained beechwood library bergère, 19th century, with a caned arched back, sides and seat with cushion, on sabre legs.
(Christie's) £2,760 $4,471

An early Victorian mahogany library armchair, with roundel arms terminals and ring-turned legs.
(Christie's) £2,070 $3,353

A pair of Victorian walnut-framed open armchairs on scroll supports continuing into moulded cabriole legs with scroll toes and castors.
(Bearne's) £2,300 $3,680

A mahogany open armchair, 19th century, the arched top-rail above padded arms with outswept arm terminals, possibly Scottish.
(Christie's) £1,035 $1,677

A late Regency carved open armchair, attributed to Gillows, the back carved with C and S scrolls enriched with acanthus leaves. (Phillips) £6,600 $10,560

A fine pair of Anglo-Indian ebony armchairs, circa 1820, each with a reeded rail filled with a shell above a caned back and reeded arms. (Sotheby's) £28,750 $46,863

A Regency mahogany bergère library armchair with reeded frame, cane panelled sides, seats and back. (Russell Baldwin & Bright) £1,700 $2,805

A French walnut bergère, early 18th century and later, the arched toprail with central rocaille motif and trailing flowers and foliage. (Christie's) £1,265 $2,099

A pair of mid-Victorian walnut tub bergères, by Gillows, each with curved padded back on ring-turned legs with beaded collars. (Christie's) £3,105 $5,061

A Louis XV beechwood bergère, the padded cartouche-shaped back and seat covered in close-nailed polychrome floral gros-point needlework. (Christie's) £2,070 $3,436

A Regency mahogany library bergère, with caned back, sides and seat, with channelled arms on baluster supports. (Christie's) £2,070 $3,353

A pair of tôle painted armchairs, Napoleon III, each with a pierced cresting cast with cabochon, foliage and leopard masks, 139cm. high. (Sotheby's) £4,830 $7,873

A George III mahogany library armchair, the serpentine padded back, arms and seat covered in associated 18th century gros and petit-point needlework. (Christie's) £8,050 $13,202

A George III small mahogany armchair, acanthus carved arm supports, above a serpentine foliate carved apron.
(Christie's)   £7,475 $12,259

A pair of George III mahogany open armchairs, the scrolled arms on channelled serpentine supports, on channelled cabriole legs.
(Christie's)   £14,375 $23,862

A Regency mahogany and parcel-gilt bergère, inlaid with brass anthemions, husks and stars.
(Christie's)   £5,175 $8,487

A Classical mahogany armchair en gondole, New York, 1820–1835, the tablet crestrail above an upholstered back, on carved scrolled legs with castors, 38¾in. high. (Christie's) £3,795 $6,325

A pair of George II mahogany library open armchairs, on cabriole legs each headed by a shell and foliage-carved angle brackets.
(Christie's)   £18,400 $30,176

A Dutch Colonial hardwood fauteuil de bureau, late 18th century, the rounded caned back and sides with scrolled arms, with channelled frame and drop-in caned seat.
(Christie's)   £2,300 $3,818

A Regency mahogany writing chair, the curved padded bar top rail and splayed uprights with lyre shaped splat with flowerheads and brass uprights.
(Phillips)   £1,300 $2,132

A pair of walnut side chairs 19th century, in George II style, each with a padded back and seat above a rail carved with foliage.
(Sotheby's)   £11,500 $18,745

A Dutch mahogany metamorphic wing armchair, mid 18th century, the channelled toprail centred by a rockwork cartouche, on cabriole legs and pad feet.
(Christie's)   £8,050 $13,363

A Victorian walnut framed spoonback easy chair with shaped and moulded show-wood frame, on cabriole front legs with scroll toes. (Canterbury) £620 $1,023

Victorian Renaissance Revival chair with matching footstool, scroll sides decorated with acanthus leaves, medallions and carved tassels, mounted on upward curving legs with casters.
(Jackson's) £172 $275

A Victorian lady's occasional chair, with rosewood spiral twist supports and terminals to the padded back rail. (Woolley & Wallis)
£260 $432

A William IV library armchair, the lyre shape front arms with a moulded scrolling show frame, terminating in fluted leaf effect scrolls. (Woolley & Wallis)
£1,500 $2,490

A George IV mahogany invalid's chair, the caned back and sides with an overscrolled top rail and downswept arms, wheels stamped _J. Ward, Leicester Square, London._ (Phillip) £850 $1,394

A mahogany framed open armchair, by Whytock and Reid, Edinburgh, the leather upholstered back and seat flanked by moulded open arms.
(Phillips) £950 $1,520

A late Victorian oak chairman's chair, the scrolled foliate carved cresting rail dated _AD1892_, on turned square section front legs. (Tennants) £1,100 $1,815

Marcel Breuer for the Isokon Furniture Company, long chair, designed 1935–36, first produced 1936, laminated wood, 50½in. (Sotheby's) £5,520 $8,942

One of a pair of 18th century French walnut hall chairs/church stalls, of panelled and angled form, with wooden seats.
(Canterbury) (Two) £960 $1,584

One of a set of ten chairs including two carvers by Robert Thompson of Kilburn, with low panel back, cow hide seat. (Andrew Hartley)
(Ten) £4,200 $7,056

Two of a set of three Regency black japanned and gilt elbow chairs, with cane seats, the scrolled crest painted with key pattern and vitruvian scroll. (Andrew Hartley)
(Three) £975 $1,560

A Queen Anne style mahogany corner-chair, the yoked crestrail above a pierced and scrolled splat over an outward scrolled arm. (Christie's) £1,104 $1,840

A Jacobean turned elmwood rush-seat armchair, in part 17th century, the curved back with a shaped crest with tiers of inset spindles.
(Sotheby's) £1,403 $2,300

Pair of Regency beechwood elbow chairs. (Christopher Matthews)
£1,450 $2,392

An 18th century mahogany elbow chair in the Chippendale style having shaped cresting rail over pierced splat. (Russell Baldwin & Bright) £740 $1,221

A Regency simulated rosewood carver, the curved top rail with incised panel above a pierced and scrolling mid rail.
(Phillips) £400 $640

A pair of early George III mahogany open armchairs, each with a waved toprail in a stylised scrolled acanthus leaf, above a pierced Gothic fretwork back.
(Christie's) £76,300 $125,132

A 19th century Anglo-Indian solid ebony armchair in the Regency manner, the back with scroll terminals and with reeded crest rail and matching conforming splat. (Canterbury) £1,050 $1,680

A George III mahogany open armchair, the pierced Gothic ladderback above a padded drop-in seat, the channelled serpentine arms on downswept supports.
(Christie's) £1,380 $2,249

A pair of Regency pollard oak, oak and ebonised open armchairs, in the manner of George Bullock, the toprail with three spheres flanked by a pair of turned finials.
(Christie's) £8,625 $14,317

A Regency painted and parcel-gilt ebonised caned armchair, circa 1810, the rectangular back with an oval caned panel, 24in. wide.
(Sotheby's) £1,403 $2,300

A Charles II walnut open armchair, the rectangular pierced back with shell and acanthus-scrolled vertical splat below a pierced conforming cresting.
(Christie's) £1,725 $2,863

A pair of solid mahogany open armchairs, late 18th/19th century, each with a shield-shaped padded back, arms and serpentine-fronted seat, the channelled back centred by a ribbon-tied cornsheaf.
(Christie's) £9,200 $14,996

A Chinese Export padouk open armchair, mid-18th century, the pierced rounded rectangular back with solid baluster splat, with shepherd's crook arms.
(Christie's) £16,100 $26,726

A mahogany armchair, early 20th century, with a pierced interlaced back and padded arms with reeded scroll arm terminals.
(Christie's) £1,955 $3,167

A pair of Dutch walnut open armchairs, late 17th century, each carved overall with scrolling acanthus and flowerheads, the shaped rectangular caned back below a pierced toprail.
(Christie's) £3,450 $5,727

An unusual early 18th century 'red walnut' armchair, the 'escutcheon' shaped moulded solid back with outswept scroll arm supports with trailing acorn leaves.
(Phillips) £2,700 $4,428

One of a set of ten late George III simulated rosewood, polychrome-painted and parcel-gilt open armchairs, attributed to John Gee. (Christie's) (Ten) £52,100 $85,444

An Anglo-Indian gold, green and red decorated solid ivory armchair, third quarter 18th century, Murshidabad, decorated overall with scrolling foliage.
(Christie's) £87,300 $143,172

A George I walnut open armchair, the vase-shaped splat flanked by scrolled uprights and shaped arms with scrolled terminals.
(Christie's) £16,100 $26,404

A George II mahogany reading chair, mid 18th century, the shaped bowed solid back continuing to outswept arms with outswept circular ends.
(Christie's) £1,900 $3,040

A pair of Anglo-Indian ivory inlaid padouk open armchairs, mid 18th century, Vizagapatam, inlaid overall with line-inlaid ivory of scrolling flowers and foliage.
(Christie's) £84,000 $137,760

One of a pair of George III white-painted and parcel-gilt armchairs, attributed to Gillows, each with fluted oval back with pierced anthemion.
(Christie's) (Two) £16,100 $26,404

A late Victorian brass-mounted oak hall stool, attributed to James Shoolbred and Company, reeded overall, the rectangular back with a pierced baluster horizontal toprail.
(Christie's) £2,530 $4,123

A Regency simulated-rosewood metamorphic library armchair, in the manner of Morgan and Sanders, the scrolled tablet back and seat covered in red leather flanked by scrolling arms and a panelled seat-rail. (Christie's) £6,900 $11,247

A rare pine armchair, New Mexico, 18th century, the horizontal reeded crest above three shaped backrests with a moulded stayrail and plank seat below.
(Sotheby's) £4,559 $7,475

A Provincial George III mahogany open armchair, the overscrolled back above a pierced splat with downscrolled arms.
(Christie's)   £402 $643

One of a pair of Old Hickory armchairs, overcoated, 25in. deep. (Skinner) (Two)   £448 $747

Arts and Crafts armchair, three vertical slats, original finish, 23½in. wide. (Skinner)   £86 $143

A Queen Anne walnut armchair, the yoked crestrail above a solid vasiform splat with outward scrolling arms.
(Christie's)   £2,760 $4,600

A North European birch rosewood-banded open armchair, late 19th/early 20th century, the square back with an X-shaped splat centred by an oval flowerhead inlaid medallion.
(Christie's)   £218 $349

A good Queen Anne carved and figured open armchair, Philadelphia, circa 1750, the serpentine crest with shell and leaf-carved ears centring a volute-ruffle and leaf-carved device.
(Sotheby's)   £12,420 $20,700

A Chippendale carved and figured walnut open armchair, Pennsylvania, circa 1770, the shaped crest with moulded ears above a heart-pierced strapwork splat. (Sotheby's) £3,508 $5,750

A Sussex beechwood armchair attributed to Morris & Co., with bobbin-turned open back above rush seat.
(Christie's)   £1,035 $1,552

An unusual George III oak reclining armchair, late 18th century, the waved top rail and pierced splat with outswept arms and adjustable iron supports.
(Bonhams) £280 $448

Painted turned wagon seat, New England, late 18th century, two pairs of arched slats joining three turned stiles, with double rush seat.
(Skinner) £682 $1,092

Grain painted sack-back Windsor, Southern New England, late 18th century, with later rosewood graining and yellow in outline.
(Skinner) £917 $1,495

A very fine turned maple rush-seat ladder-back armchair, Delaware River Valley, possibly by the Ware family of Roadstown, New Jersey, 1740–1780.
(Sotheby's) £14,725 $24,140

A George II mahogany armchair, circa 1750, the moulded back with a bolster carved crest above a pierced fan splat.
(Sotheby's) £2,185 $3,649

A Chippendale carved walnut armchair, the serpentine crestrail with scrolled ears centring a carved shell above a solid vasiform splat flanked by scrolled arms.
(Christie's) £3,105 $5,175

A Victorian cane seated commode armchair, late 19th century, with a shaped apron and turned legs.
(Sotheby's) £28 $47

A fine and very rare Chippendale carved mahogany double chairback settee, Boston, Massachusetts, circa 1770, the two part crest with moulded ears, above pierced strapwork splats, 5ft. long.
(Christie's) £13,800 $23,000

A Queen Anne walnut open armchair, the yoked crestrail above a solid vasiform splat flanked by rounded stiles with shaped arms.
(Christie's) £1,656 $2,760

Painted child's Windsor high chair, New England, 1820–30, the arrow-back chair with shaped and incised seat about the foot rest, seat 21½in. high. (Skinner) £1,764 $2,875

A Regency mahogany child's high chair on stand, English, early 19th century, the scrolled tablet crest incised with trailing vines above a pierced and anthemion-carved horizontal slat.
(Christie's) £604 $978

Painted child's rod-back Windsor high chair, New England, early 19th century, old black paint with incised tapering spindles painted gold, seat 21¾in. high.
(Skinner) £600 $978

ROCKING CHAIRS

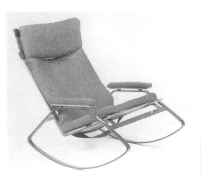

Rocker, modified shield back with crest, arms curve out from back and are supported by six bowed rib supports. (Jackson's) £69 $110

A William Plunkett Ltd 'Reigate' range rocking chair, the grey nylon-finished steel frame with red fabric cushioned back, arms and seat, circa 1966. (Bristol) £160 $256

A fine and rare painted and smoke-decorated plank-seat rocking chair, Pennsylvania, circa 1820, the horizontal crest flanked by projecting 'bamboo'-turned stiles.
(Sotheby's) £5,261 $8,625

TABLE CHAIRS

Painted pine chair table, Middle Atlantic States, the round scrubbed top above a box base on shaped feet, 45in. wide.
(Skinner) £1,975 $3,220

Painted William and Mary maple and pine chair table, south eastern New England, early 18th century, 51¼in. wide.
(Skinner) £12,937 $20,700

Painted pine chair table, New England, 19th century, the rectangular cleated top with old red painted surface tilts, 36in. wide.
(Skinner) £1,995 $3,220

George III mahogany and upholstered wing armchair, late 18th/19th century, shaped back, outscrolled arms.
(Skinner)   £966 $1,610

A Queen Anne walnut easy chair Boston, Massachusetts, 1730–50, the arched crest with ogival wings and outscrolled arms up.
(Sotheby's)   £5,865 $9,775

A Federal mahogany easy chair, Philadelphia, circa 1810, the serpentine crest flanked by ogival wings and outscrolled arms.
(Sotheby's)   £2,806 $4,600

An Irish George I walnut wing armchair, the rounded rectangular padded back, sides, outscrolled arms and seat cushion covered in associated early 18th century petit-point wool needlework.
(Christie's)   £45,500 $74,620

A mahogany humpback sofa, late 19th/early 20th century, the undulating toprail and winged sides with outswept arms above a frieze with inlaid shell and foliate carvings, 60in. wide.
(Christie's)   £2,530 $4,048

A Queen Anne mahogany easy-chair, North Shore, Massachusetts, 1740–1760, the serpentine crestrail above a canted back with shaped wings, 47in. high.
(Christie's)   £9,660 $16,100

A George I walnut wing armchair, the rectangular padded back, shaped sides, outscrolled arms and seat-cushion covered in gold foliate silk-damask.
(Christie's)   £20,125 $33,005

A Queen Anne mahogany easy-chair, Boston area, 1730–60, the shaped crestrail above an upholstered canted back flanked by shaped wings.
(Christie's)   £33,120 $55,200

A Federal cherrywood easy-chair, Massachusetts, early 19th century, the serpentine crestrail above an upholstered canted back flanked by shaped wings.
(Christie's)   £4,830 $8,050

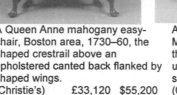

Chinese brass-bound lift-top camphor chest, 19th century, with brass carrying handles, 39in. long.
(Eldred's)   £670 $1,072

A North Italian walnut cassone, late 17th century, the hinged lid above a panelled front carved with scrolling floral designs and flanked by figural pilasters.
(Christie's)   £2,700 $4,320

Antique American canted sea chest, in pine with old green paint, strap hinges, ditty box cover replaced, original rope and leather beckets, 42in. long.
(Eldred's)   £516 $825

A 19th century black lacquered and ray skin coffer with mother o' pearl inlaid banding and copper mounts, 31in. wide.
(Andrew Hartley)   £4,600 $7,590

A William and Mary joined oak chest, Westmorland, dated 1692, the twin panelled rectangular top above an 'S' carved frieze bearing the initials *EB* and dated *1692*, 48¼in. wide.
(Bonhams)   £1,500 $2,400

Grain and fancifully painted dome top trunk, probably Vermont, early 19th century, decorated with various foliate devices in sienna paint on an ochre ground, 25¾in. wide. (Skinner)   £1,834 $2,990

A late 17th century oak coffer, with moulded edged and panelled cover, the fascia with leaf and tendril carved frieze, 27½in. high.
(Andrew Hartley)   £750 $1,200

A camphor wood sea chest, probably American, late 19th century, with hinged lid opening to an interior, with a till and single drawer, 39in. long.
(Sotheby's)   £1,263 $2,070

A rare panelled pine chest-on-legs, New Mexico, circa 1820, the rectangular panelled top opening to a well above a similarly panelled case and sides, 6ft. 4in. wide.
(Sotheby's)   £12,627 $20,700

A painted and polychrome decorated pine blanket chest, Pennsylvania, dated *1803*, the hinged rectangular top painted with flowers within arched reserves, 4ft. wide. (Sotheby's)   £5,612 $9,200

Painted and decorated pine and poplar chest over drawers, Berks County, Pennsylvania, early 19th century, the top lifts to a well above two drawers, 43½in. wide.
(Skinner)   £776 $1,265

A German oak and fruitwood casket, early 18th century, the cavetto moulded top with double locks above a panelled front overlaid with double headed eagle mounts, 21in. wide.
(Christie's)   £1,600 $2,560

Spanish Baroque iron-mounted walnut chest, slightly domed lid over an intricately carved front, 42½in. wide.
(Skinner)   £828 $1,380

A Dutch colonial teak and camphor chest on stand, circa 1830, with ebonised mouldings, the hinged top over two apron drawers, 4ft. 4½in. wide. (Sotheby's) £1,610 $2,689

An 18th century dark stained oak coffer, triple panelled hinged lid, triple panelled front, 131cm. wide.
(Wintertons)   £1,050 $1,733

An Italian 17th century cedar cassone, with contemporary carved and penwork decoration of figures, friezes and panels to the lid, 5ft.3½in. (Woolley & Wallis)
               £2,600 $4,316

A Charles II joined oak chest, circa 1770, the hinged top with moulded edge above a guilloche carved frieze and three panelled front, 54¾in. wide.
(Bonhams)   £1,100 $1,760

A joined oak chest, North Country, mid 18th century, the hinged plank top above an eight panelled front, on bracket feet, 61in. wide.
(Bonhams)   £750 $1,200

A fine painted pine blanket chest Pennsylvania, dated *1816*, ochre painted case with incised spandrels and hex signs centring an arched reserve, 4ft.4in. wide.
(Sotheby's)   £6,314 $10,350

A Victorian walnut box-stool, with a padded hinged seat and pierced fret-carved sides with a central roundel, 32¾in. wide.
(Christie's)   £1,150 $1,840

American painted lift-top blanket chest, signed *E. G. Colonna 1947 Barnstable Mass*, scrolled bracket base, 39in. long.
(Eldred's)   £433 $715

An iron mounted carved pine chest-on-legs of impressive size, probably Taos, New Mexico, 1820-1840, the hinged, cleated top fitted with cotter pin hinges and a punchwork-decorated hasp, 5ft. wide.
(Sotheby's)   £17,537 $28,750

A very rare and early chip-carved framed pine chest-on-legs, probably Velarde area, New Mexico, late 18th century, the hinged rectangular top opening to a well, 4ft. 7in. wide.
(Sotheby's)   £61,915 $101,500

A rare green-painted carved pine diminutive chest, Northern New Mexico, possibly Taos, circa 1820, the rectangular hinged top opening to a well, the case with panelled front and sides, 33in. wide.
(Sotheby's)   £21,045 $34,500

Antique American lift-top blanket chest, in pine with moulded top, one false and two real drawers with wooden pulls, scrolled apron, 38½in. wide. (Eldred's) £516 $825

Painted and decorated pine wood box, New England, 1830s, the hinged top lifts above a nailed box with old mustard paint, 29in. wide. (Skinner) £503 $805

American lift-top blanket chest, in pine with tiger maple, carving done by a man of Annisquam, Massachusetts, top carved with facing griffins, 38in. wide. (Eldred's) £566 $935

An important carved pine blanket chest, New Mexico, 18th century, the rectangular top opening to a well, carved with large rosettes and pomegranates, the front divided into seven panels. (Sotheby's) £71, 980 $118,000

Queen Anne red painted pine and maple chest over drawer, probably Massachusetts, mid 18th century, the moulded hinged top above a double arch moulded case of single drawer, 35½in. wide. (Skinner) £34,140 $54,625

A rare blue-painted pine chest-on-legs, possibly Pueblo, Taos, New Mexico, circa 1800, the hinged rectangular top opening to a well, the panelled sides carved with geometric motifs, 30½in. wide. (Sotheby's) £16,134 $26,450

A very fine and rare carved pine chest-on-legs, Velarde area, New Mexico, 18th century, the case sides with raised panels of geometric carving, 37½in. wide. (Sotheby's) £46,817 $76,750

A diminutive pine chest-on-legs, Northern New Mexico, possibly Taos area, circa 1840, the rectangular hinged top opening to a well, above a panelled front and sides, 34½in. wide. (Sotheby's) £7,716 $12,650

An important brown-painted pine chest, probably Spanish, 17/18th century, the rectangular top with moulded edge opening to a paper lined well, 44½in. wide. (Sotheby's) £3,156 $5,175

Martha Cahoon decorated cottage bureau, 19th century, in pine with floral stencilled decoration, 38½in. wide. (Eldred's)   £300 $495

A late 17th century oak chest, the cavetto moulded edge top above four long pine lined drawers with geometric and cushion moulded fronts, 3ft.2in. (Woolley & Wallis)   £1,400 $2,324

A George I walnut and burr-yew chest, the top and drawer fronts inlaid with shaped burr-yew panels within herringbone bandings, 38in. wide. (Canterbury) £4,200 $6,720

A pair of painted drawers, 20th century, each of tapering form, simulating eight stacked books with drawers fitted to each spine, each 26in. wide. (Christie's)   £2,875 $4,600

A late 18th century North Country mahogany chest, the well figured moulded edge top above two short and two long drawers, 3ft.3½in. wide. (Woolley & Wallis)   £1,600 $2,656

A William and Mary figured walnut chest of drawers, Pennsylvania, 1740–60, the rectangular moulded top above two short and three long drawers, 41in. wide. (Sotheby's)   £5,612 $9,200

An 18th century Dutch walnut and floral marquetry poudreuse, with birds and flowers heightened in ivory, the galleried undulating top with hinged sliding panel, 78cm. wide. (Phillips)   £4,800 $7,872

A Chippendale figured walnut chest of drawers, Pennsylvania, circa 1760, the rectangular moulded top above four graduated thumb-moulded long drawers, 35½in. wide. (Sotheby's) £2,455 $4,025

A late 17th century oak chest with two short and three long drawers, on later bun feet, 95cm. wide. (Bearne's)   £950 $1,567

Federal bird's-eye maple chest of drawers, Massachusetts, early 19th century, with ovolo corners and reeded columns ending in turned feet. (Skinner)   £846 $1,380

A George III mahogany chest with moulded edged top, two short over three long drawers, 33½in. wide. (Andrew Hartley)   £2,200 $3,696

A late George IV mahogany bow front chest, the reeded edge top enclosing three long graduated cock beaded drawers with turned handles, 40in.
(Dreweatt Neate)   £2,100 $3,423

A George III small mahogany serpentine chest, crossbanded to the top and front in yew-wood, the moulded rectangular top above three graduated drawers, 34¼in. wide. (Christie's) £20,700 $34,362

A good Federal inlaid walnut chest of drawers, Mid-Atlantic States, circa 1790, the rectangular moulded top above four graduated cock-beaded and line-inlaid long drawers, 41½in. wide. (Sotheby's)   £2,130 $3,450

A William and Mary style ash chest with herringbone banding, moulded edged top, four graduated drawers, 31in. wide.
(Andrew Hartley)   £975 $1,619

A George III mahogany serpentine chest, circa 1770, the moulded top above four long graduated drawers, on ogee bracket feet, 2ft. 11in. wide. (Sotheby's) £6,325 $10,563

A Queen Anne walnut and oak chest, with moulded edge top above two short and three long banded drawers, 38in. wide. (Dreweatt Neate)   £1,100 $1,793

A small George III mahogany chest, with moulded edged top, four graduated drawers, 32½in. wide. (Andrew Hartley) £2,100 $3,528

An early Victorian mahogany architect's chest, the rounded rectangular lined top with a moulded edge above two banks of four drawers, 62½in. wide. (Christie's) £1,610 $2,576

A Victorian mahogany chest of drawers, rounded corners, 48in. wide. (Dockree's) £520 $832

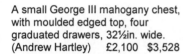

A Regency bowfront chest, of low proportions, faded mahogany veneered, on front splay french feet, 3ft. 1in. wide. (Woolley & Wallis) £2,200 $3,542

A William & Mary walnut and burr-yew chest, the plain top with wide walnut crossbanding, on later bracket feet, 40in. wide. (Canterbury) £2,300 $3,680

Painted oak, cedar and yellow pine joined chest of drawers, south eastern New England, circa 1700, the rectangular top with applied moulded edge above a case of four drawers, 37¾in. wide.
(Skinner)   £16,531 $26,450

A Victorian rosewood Wellington chest with moulded edged top over an arrangement of eight drawers with brass handles, 22 x 51½in.
(Andrew Hartley)   £2,600 $4,160

A good Chippendale cherrywood chest of drawers, Philadelphia, circa 1780, the rectangular moulded top above four graduated long drawers, width of top 40½in.
(Sotheby's)   £4,209 $6,900

Classical mahogany carved and mahogany veneer bureau, northshore Massachusetts, circa 1825, the scrolled backboard on three short drawers on projecting case, 42¾in. wide.
(Skinner)   £610 $977

A fine Queen Anne figured mahogany block-front chest of drawers, Boston, Massachusetts, circa 1760, the oblong moulded top above four graduated long drawers, width of top 36in.
(Sotheby's)   £37,800 $63,000

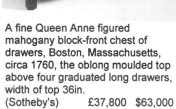

A William and Mary walnut and 'seaweed' marquetry chest, the whole inlaid with geometric reserves of scrolling foliage, 102cm. wide. (Bearne's)   £5,200 $8,320

A George IV mahogany bow fronted chest, with two short and four long drawers, on splayed bracket feet, 3ft. 6in. wide.
(Sotheby's)   £862 $1,440

TRICKS OF THE TRADE

Many pieces of 18th century cabinet furniture will have drawers whose handles have been changed at least once, often as a result of changing fashions. However, it may be that one handle broke and rather than replacing one, especially if no exact match could be found, the entire piece will have been fitted with new and larger handles to cover the original holes. The inside of the drawer front will have the holes where the original handles were fixed, and it follows that there should be corresponding holes in the drawer front.

If this is not the case then it means that the piece has been through the restorer's workshop, which usually means reveneering. Although this may have been done to enhance desirability and value, it can significantly reduce the worth of an otherwise valuable piece. Country oak chests and bureaux are the main examples found with a later walnut veneer, so examine all prospective items carefully.

Cheffins Grain & Comins

A George II walnut and burr-walnut chest, inlaid overall with feather-banding, the moulded rectangular quarter-veneered top above an inlaid brushing-slide, 29¾in. wide. (Christie's)   £25,300 $41,998

A George II mahogany small chest, the moulded rectangular top above two small drawers and four larger drawers, on shaped bracket feet, 10½in. wide. (Christie's)   £12,650 $20,746

The Sarah Slocum Chippendale mahogany block-and-shell carved chest-of-drawers, labelled by John Townsend (1732–1809), 36¾in. wide. (Christie's) £2,839,500 $4,732,500

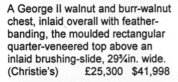

A Chippendale figured maple reverse serpentine-front chest of drawers, Massachusetts, circa 1785, the oblong top with thumbmoulded edge, 36¼in. wide at top. (Sotheby's)   £8,519 $13,800

An ash chest, basically 18th century, chevron-banded to the top and front, the moulded rectangular quarter-veneered top above a later green baize-lined slide, 29in. wide. (Christie's)   £6,900 $11,454

A burr-walnut chest, 20th century, feather-banded to the top and front, the quarter-veneered moulded rectangular top above a red velvet-lined slide and three small drawers, 31½in. wide. (Christie's)   £6,670 $11,072

An 18th century walnut veneered chest with string inlay, moulded edged quarter veneered top, 31½in. wide. (Andrew Hartley)   £4,700 $7,896

Gustav Stickley chest of drawers, No. 906, two drawers over four graduated drawers, Gustav Stickley red mark, 40in. wide. (Skinner)   £4,410 $6,900

A walnut chest of drawers, Queen Anne, circa 1705 and later with a moulded quarter-veneered top, on later bracket feet, 3ft.1½in. wide. (Sotheby's)   £1,840 $3,073

Federal cherry inlaid bowfront bureau, New England, early 19th century, with bowed tip edged in inlay above a case of four cockbeaded drawers, 38¾in. wide. (Skinner) £1,834 $2,990

A mid-Victorian Scottish mahogany chest with cushion moulded frieze drawer and three deep drawers, above three further long drawers, 51in. wide. (Christie's) £483 $773

A Regency stripped pine chest, circa 1815, with two short and three long drawers separated by simulated bamboo mouldings, 3ft. 3in. wide. (Sotheby's) £1,150 $1,920

A good Federal inlaid mahogany and birchwood bow-front chest of drawers, New England, circa 1800, the oblong top with bowed front, 37½in. wide. (Sotheby's) £5,520 $9,200

Grain painted chest of drawers, Pennsylvania, early 19th century, with a split top drawer over four graduated thumb-moulded drawers, 35¾in. wide. (Skinner) £2,469 $4,025

A fine and rare Chippendale blocked and carved cherrywood serpentine-front chest of drawers, Connecticut, circa 1780, the oblong moulded top above four graduated cockbeaded long drawers, 38in. wide. (Sotheby's) £24,840 $41,400

A Victorian mahogany bowfront chest decorated with lines and chequer-bandings, the frieze with concealed drawer, 47¹/₃in. wide. (Christie's) £552 $883

Painted blanket chest, New England, 18th century, the moulded top lifts above a well and two thumb-moulded drawers, 36in. wide. (Skinner) £1,199 $1,955

A mahogany chest, early 19th century, the rectangular top with a moulded edge above a plain frieze and three frieze drawers, 48½in. wide. (Christie's) £437 $699

A Chippendale cherrywood reverse-serpentine chest of drawers, probably Connecticut, circa 1770, the shaped oblong top with moulded lower edge, 40in. wide.
(Sotheby's)   £10,350 $17,250

A George II small mahogany and walnut D-shape chest of two short over three long drawers, on bracket feet, 74cm. wide.
(Bristol)   £3,600 $5,760

A fine Chippendale figured mahogany reverse serpentine front chest of drawers, Massachusetts, circa 1780, the oblong top above four graduated blocked long drawers, 37in. wide.
(Sotheby's)   £8,418 $13,800

A white painted serpentine chest of drawers, George III, late 18th century, the moulded serpentine top above a slide and three graduated drawers, 3ft.9¾in.
(Sotheby's)   £5,750 $9,602

A Chippendale carved cherrywood chest-of-drawers, probably New London, Connecticut, circa 1775, on bracket feet, 38¾in. wide.
(Christie's)   £5,865 $9,775

A walnut chest, mid 18th century, the rectangular top with a moulded edge above two short and three long figured graduated drawers, 38¼in. wide.
(Christie's)   £1,840 $2,944

Federal cherry bowfront bureau, New England, early 19th century, with cockbeaded graduated drawers, above a veneer cyma curved skirt, 41½in. wide.
(Skinner)   £1,764 $2,875

A rare Chippendale block-and-shell-carved cherrywood chest of drawers, attributed to Benjamin Burnham, Colchester-Norwich area, Connecticut, circa 1770, 38in. wide.
(Sotheby's)   £42,750 $71,250

A very fine Federal birchwood-inlaid mahogany bow-front chest of drawers, North Shore of New England, circa 1795, 39in. wide.
(Sotheby's)   £15,433 $25,300

A George III mahogany chest on chest, with moulded cornice, on bracket feet, 42in. wide.
(Andrew Hartley) £1,900 $3,192

A George III mahogany chest on chest, the dentil cornice above two short and three long drawers, on a three-drawer base, 103.5cm.
(Bristol)   £1,300 $2,080

A George III mahogany chest on chest with moulded and key pattern cornice, the upper section with two short over three long drawers, 40in. wide.
(Andrew Hartley)   £3,000 $4,800

BUYER BEWARE

On small chests of drawers with brushing slides in the frieze, check that these have not been part of a tallboy, the chest usually forming the upper part. There will usually be signs of bracket or other feet having been added to the base and the top part being rearranged to accommodate the slide. At the same time the whole top would need to be completely reveneered as originally there would have been no such refinement, the upper portion not having been visible.

Dockree's

A George III mahogany chest on chest, the upper section with dentil cornice and blind fret carved frieze, 44¼in. wide.
(George Kidner)   £3,000 $4,980

A George III mahogany chest on chest, with moulded and key pattern cornice, two short over three long drawers, 45in. wide.
(Andrew Hartley) £1,400 $2,240

An early 18th century burr elm, elm and crossbanded tallboy chest, in two parts, the upper part with a moulded cornice and chequer fluted inlay frieze, 107cm. wide.
(Phillips)   £2,900 $4,756

A mid 18th century walnut veneered chest on chest, chequer strung, the moulded cavetto cornice above three short over three long graduated drawers, 106cm. wide.
(Phillips)   £3,100 $4,960

A George II walnut chest on chest, circa 1740, the moulded cornice above two short and three long herringbone crossbanded graduated drawers, 40¾in. wide.
(Christie's)   £7,500 $12,000

A William and Mary walnut chest on stand, with herringbone crossbanding, moulded cornice, on bun feet, 38½in. wide.
(Andrew Hartley)   £7,000 $11,200

A scarlet lacquer cabinet and giltwood stand of Charles II design, the cabinet decorated in gilt and black with chinoiseries, cabinet 38in. wide.
(Canterbury)   £2,800 $4,620

A walnut chest on stand with oak crossbanding, on turned tapering legs, 38½in. wide, early 18th century and later.
(Andrew Hartley)   £2,600 $4,368

A walnut chest on stand, crossbanded with herringbone stringing, moulded edged top, 39¼in. wide, early 18th century and later.
(Andrew Hartley)   £4,800 $8,064

A late 17th/early 18th century walnut and chequer crossbanded chest on stand of small size, the upper part containing four long drawers crossbanded alternately with mulberry and yewwood, 74cm. wide. (Phillips)   £900 $1,476

An early 18th century walnut-veneered chest on stand outlined throughout with feather banding, on later bun feet, 105cm. wide.
(Bearne's)   £1,400 $2,310

William and Mary painted pine high chest of drawers, south eastern New England, early 18th century, the top section with flat moulded cornice, 33in. wide.
(Skinner)   £10,062 $16,100

A Queen Anne figured walnut and herringbone banded chest on stand, on six barley-twist supports with S-scroll stretchers and bun feet, 105cm. wide.
(Bristol)   £2,200 $3,608

Painted maple cherry oak and pine chest on frame, south eastern New England, early 18th century, the top with flat moulded cornice above a double arch moulded case, 35in. wide. (Skinner)   £2,012 $3,220

425

Early 19th century rosewood chiffonier, the pediment with a galleried shelf over and raised on ring turned support, 42in.
(Aylsham)   £1,450 $2,407

An early Victorian mahogany chiffonier, the superstructure with arch top and display shelf with turned supports, 28in. wide.
(Dreweatt Neate)   £1,100 $1,815

A George III mahogany chiffonier, in the manner of Gillows, inlaid overall with boxwood lines, the superstructure with moulded rectangular top above a pair of glazed doors, 43in. wide.
(Christie's)   £6,900 $11,247

A small Victorian mahogany chiffonier, the panelled S-scroll carved gallery with a shaped shelf above a cushion moulded frieze drawer, 35in. wide.
(Christie's)   £575 $920

A Regency brass-mounted black and gold-japanned chiffonier, decorated overall with floral trellis, the rectangular top with pierced gallery and rectangular marbled superstructure, 50½in. wide.
(Christie's)   £4,600 $7,498

A Regency rosewood and brass strung dwarf chiffonier, the single shelf superstucture with a pierced three-quarter gallery, 76cm. wide.
(Phillips)   £2,900 $4,756

A rosewood and parcel gilt chiffonier, early 19th century, the shelved mirrored superstructure within a three quarter gallery, 38¾in. wide.
(Christie's)   £1,840 $2,944

A late Victorian rosewood and marquetry chiffonier, the upper section with a pierced swan-neck pediment and a dentil frieze above a pair of bevelled glazed doors, 55in. wide. (Christie's) £977 $1,563

A Regency burr-elm chiffonier, the rectangular superstructure with three-quarter foliate brass gallery supported by brackets, 42½in. wide. (Christie's) £3,450 $5,727

A gilt-bronze, mahogany and marquetry commode, Paris, circa 1890, after the model by Riesener, the shaped moulded white marble top above two central drawers sans travers, 204cm. wide.
(Sotheby's)   £16,100 $26,565

A German ash, walnut and parquetry commode, mid18th century, inlaid overall with panels with roundels to the angles and crossbanded overall, 50¾in. wide.
(Christie's)   £4,600 $7,636

A Louis XVI walnut and inlaid commode, with bardiglio marble top over three short and two long drawers, 127.5cm. wide.
(Bristol)   £4,600 $7,544

A German walnut serpentine commode, 18th century, decorated with rosewood crossbanding, the later grey marble top above three drawers, 35in. wide.
(Christie's)   £2,990 $4,784

A pair of Italian walnut bombé commodes, decorated with lines and crossbanding and fitted with two drawers above a shaped apron, 24in. wide.
(Christie's)   £2,530 $4,048

A mid-18th century Dutch walnut and marquetry bombé commode inlaid throughout with urns of flowers, foliage, floral spays, birds and butterflies, 97cm. wide.
(Bearne's)   £2,600 $4,290

A mid 18th century Dutch mahogany and marquetry bombé commode, the serpentine fronted top above four concave and convex fronted drawers, 104cm. wide.
(Bearne's)   £3,400 $5,610

A Venetian giltwood and polychrome-decorated commode, second quarter 18th century, the shaped and moulded Siena marble top above two shaped and panelled long drawers, 52in. wide.
(Christie's)   £23,000 $38,180

A George III mahogany commode, retailed by Edwards and Roberts, the eared serpentine, rectangular top inlaid with later satinwood and harewood paterae, 54½in. wide.
(Christie's)   £24,150 $39,606

A parcel-gilt and green painted commode, in the manner of Bonzanigo, the shaped sarancolin moulded top above three drawers, 128cm. wide.
(Sotheby's)   £14,375 $23,431

A pair of late Louis XV tulipwood and parquetry bedside commodes, by Joseph Stocket, each with a slightly bowed and canted rectangular Brocatello marble top and brass three-quarter gallery, 15½in. wide.
(Christie's)   £9,200 $15,272

A pair of Dutch sycamore, satinwood and Chinese lacquer commodes, late 18th century, each inlaid overall with fruitwood and ebonised lines, 33in. wide. (Christie's)   £17,250 $28,635

A George III satinwood, sabicu and mahogany serpentine commode, attributed to Mayhew and Ince, crossbanded to the top and front in rosewood, 41¾in. wide.
(Christie's)   £11,500 $18,860

A Dutch walnut and marquetry bombé commode inlaid throughout with vases of flowers, scrolling foliage, floral sprays and birds, mid-18th century.
(Bearne's)   £3,200 $5,280

A pair of satinwood semi-circular commodes, in George III style, the segmentally veneered tops over ivy painted borders, above frieze drawers and doors, 2ft. 4in. wide.
(Sotheby's)   £6,670 $11,139

A pair of Italian cream-painted and parcel-gilt bedside commodes, first half 19th century, each with a waved and moulded brêche violette marble top above a door, 26¾in. wide. (Christie's)   £10,350 $17,181

A Louis XV Provincial walnut and pine serpentine commode, fitted with two drawers centred with a scroll carved cartouche, 48½in. wide. (Christie's) £2,875 $4,658

A Venetian green-painted and parcel-gilt bombé commode, mid 18th century, the shaped and moulded top above two shaped long drawers with cartouche-shaped drawer fronts, 62in. wide. (Christie's)   £23,000 $38,180

A pair of Italian walnut bedside commodes, crossbanded overall, each of bombé shape and with a shaped top above a spreading frieze, 27¾in. wide. (Christie's)   £9,200 $15,272

A pair of George II mahogany serpentine commodes, possibly by Wright and Elrick, the tops attributed to Thomas Carter the Younger, each with a Sicilian jasper-veneered white marble serpentine top, 53½in. wide. (Christie's)   £117,000 $191,880

A purpleheart and marquetry serpentine commode, George III, circa 1795, the top inlaid with a lozenge shaped panel of a fruit basket with a bird, 3ft. 11in. wide. (Sotheby's)   £8,625 $14,404

429

A gilt-bronze mounted red japanned bombé commode, in Louis XV style, the mottled red marble top above two drawers decorated with chinoiserie, 3ft. 3in. wide.
(Sotheby's)   £1,610 $2,689

A gilt-bronze mounted marquetry breakfront commode, French, 19th century, bearing the stamp of Henri-Léonard Wassmus, in Louis XVI style, 4ft. 2in. wide.
(Sotheby's)   £10,350 $17,285

A mahogany and gilt-bronze commode, French, circa 1890, of bombé form, with a shaped filetto rosso marble top above two drawers sans travers, 139cm. wide.
(Sotheby's)   £4,600 $7,590

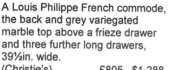

A Louis Philippe French commode, the back and grey variegated marble top above a frieze drawer and three further long drawers, 39½in. wide.
(Christie's)   £805 $1,288

A pair of Italian walnut bombé commodes, 20th century, each of serpentine outline, with a shaped frieze drawer and two further drawers below, 20in. wide.
(Christie's)   £1,380 $2,208

A George II mahogany commode, the serpentine top with gadrooned moulding above four graduated drawers, 35in. wide.
(Christie's)   £48,800 $81,008

A kingwood, marquetry and gilt-bronze commode, Paris, circa 1890, with a moulded brocatelle marble top, 144cm. wide.
(Sotheby's)   £5,750 $9,487

A rare Federal inlaid mahogany demilune commode, Boston, Massachusetts, circa 1800, with a chevron-inlaid D-shaped top,
4ft.8in. (Sotheby's) £3,332 $5,462

A French plum-pudding mahogany commode, late 18th century, of undulating outline, the top with a moulded edge and fitted with three drawers, 45½in. wide.
(Christie's)   £3,680 $5,962

A French kingwood and parquetry bombé commode, late 19th century, applied with gilt-metal mounts, inlaid with chequer and crossbandings, 47½in. wide.
(Christie's)   £4,370 $6,992

A good early Louis XV Provincial walnut commode, circa 1730, the en-arbalette front fitted with three long panel front drawers, 48in. wide. (Christie's) £4,500 $7,200

A Louis XV kingwood, crossbanded and gilt-metal mounted commode en tombeau, with mottled red marble top, 51in. wide.
(Christie's)   £9,775 $15,835

A Directoire brass-mounted mahogany commode, the rectangular grey bardiglio marble top above three long graduated drawers flanked by fluted edges, 24in. wide.
(Christie's)   £27,600 $45,816

An Italian rosewood serpentine commode, Genoese, circa 1750, the shaped and broadly crossbanded top with moulded edge above four short off centre drawers, 38in. wide.
(Christie's)   £4,000 $6,400

A Dutch marquetry inlaid mahogany bombé commode, early 19th century, the serpentine top above four long graduated drawers flanked by outset canted corners, 37½in. wide.
(Christie's)   £3,100 $4,960

A black japanned and gilt-bronze meuble d'appui, Paris, circa 1890, in the manner of Cressent, the shaped grey and red marble top above a pair of undulating doors, 158cm. wide.
(Sotheby's)   £19,550 $32,257

A gilt-bronze mounted kingwood and marquetry commode, French, 19th century, in Louis XV style, the mottled cream marble top above three long drawers, 3ft. 3in. wide.
(Sotheby's)   £2,990   £4,993

A George III mahogany serpentine commode, in the manner of Thomas Chippendale, the moulded rectangular serpentine-fronted top above a pair of concave cut-cornered panelled doors, 44¾in. wide. (Christie's) £69,700 $115,702

Antique American rabbit-ear potty chair, with grained and stencilled decoration. (Eldred's) £158 $253

A Queen Anne walnut commode stool, first quarter 18th century, the green leather-upholstered rectangular drop-in seat above deep shaped sides.
(Sotheby's)   £2,105 $3,450

A George III mahogany tray-top bedside cabinet with inlaid tambour front above a commode drawer, 53cm. wide.
(Bearne's)   £1,350 $2,227

A mahogany and marquetry tray-top bedside commode, late 18th century, later inlaid with meandering floral sprays, 22in. wide. (Christie's) £1,725 $2,794

An early Victorian mahogany step commode, with three tiers lined with gilt tooled green leather, on ring-turned legs, 19in. wide.
(Christie's)   £1,725 $2,795

A set of leather-inset mahogany bedsteps, American, possibly Baltimore, 19th century, with three leather-inset moulded treads, 17½in. wide.
(Sotheby's)   £2,280 $3,737

A Victorian mahogany commode, with cream glazed earthenware basin, lift-up tapestry cover and pull-out step, the polygonal base with upper fluted column, 18½in. high. (Christie's) £172 $275

HISTORICAL FACT

A bourdaloue is a boat-shaped chamber pot for ladies, made in various metals or ceramics. It is named after Père Bourdaloue, a preacher at the Court of Versailles in the 18th century. He was so popular that his church filled up hours before his sermons, and as ladies wanted to keep their places, they had to carry emergency accoutrements.
There is a story of a lady who had one of these items in her possession, but not knowing exactly what it was, she approached an auctioneer for guidance. Someone, apparently, had told her that it was a dish for holding sweet peas, which in a manner of speaking, was no less than the truth!
Interestingly, at that time it was quite acceptable to relieve oneself in church or even at the dining table, hence the little cupboards in sideboards for chamber pots. Once the ladies had retired, the men could sit indefinitely over their port without letting calls of nature interrupt the conversation.

Clarke & Gammon

An 18th century oak hanging corner cupboard, the upper part with moulded and dentil cornice above arched opening, 36in. wide. (Canterbury) £1,550 $2,480

A Georgian oak hanging corner cabinet with swan neck surmount over astragal glazed door, 3ft.7in. high. (Russell Baldwin & Bright) £1,140 $1,881

An 18th century North Italian marquetry bow-front corner cabinet inlaid throughout in various woods and ivory, 93cm. wide. (Bearne's) £3,300 $5,445

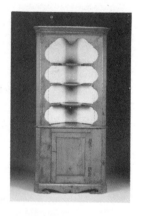

A mid 19th century Welsh oak double corner cupboard, the upper part with moulded cornice above a pair of arch glazed doors, 39in. wide. (Peter Francis) £850 $1,360

A George III mahogany hanging corner display cabinet with dentil cornice, canted corners and glazed door, 67cm. wide. (Bearne's) £820 $1,353

A Chippendale pine corner cupboard, American, 19th century, the trapezoidal moulded cornice above a conforming case with shaped frame enclosing three lobed shelves,36½in. wide. (Christie's) £1,932 $3,220

A black japanned hanging corner cupboard, Queen Anne, circa 1710, the bow front with two cupboard doors decorated with figures, birds and pavilions, 3ft.½in. wide. (Sotheby's) £1,380 $2,304

A Dutch yew wood serpentine corner bookcase, circa 1750, the arched moulded cornice centred by a scroll carved cabochon above a pair of fielded panelled doors, 48in. wide. (Christie's) £6,000 $9,600

A George III black japanned corner cupboard, the raised shaped surmount with shelf, moulded cornice, panelled door with gilt chinoiserie decoration, 22½in. wide. (Andrew Hartley) £440 $739

A George III golden oak bow fronted corner cupboard, 38in. (Dockree's) £840 $1,344

An inlaid mahogany bowfront hanging corner cupboard, American or English, circa 1795, with cove moulded cornice, 29½in. wide. (Sotheby's) £1,929 $3,162

Walnut glazed corner cupboard, probably Middle Atlantic States, circa 1790, the top section with flat moulded cornice above a cockbeaded case, 48in. wide. (Skinner) £2,613 $4,312

A George III oak floorstanding corner cupboard, moulded cornice, fitted twin panelled doors above and below, on plinth base, width 112cm.wide. (Wintertons) £1,400 $2,310

An early George III mahogany and polychrome-painted corner cupboard, the moulded cornice above a pair of panelled doors flanked by a stop-fluted angles, 46in. wide. (Christie's) £12,650 $20,999

Chippendale carved cherry glazed corner cupboard, probably Pennsylvania, early 19th century, the scrolled moulded pediment flanking a fluted keystone with flame finial, 41½in. wide. (Skinner) £5,750 $9,200

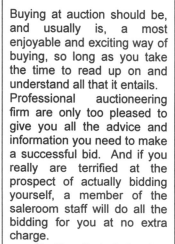

Pine glazed panelled corner cupboard, Pennsylvania area, early 19th century, the upper case with glazed doors opening to an interior, 59½in. wide. (Skinner) £1,185 $1,955

A George III mahogany standing corner cupboard, with parquetry banded inlay, moulded cornice over frieze with marquetry inlaid paterae, 40½in. wide. (Andrew Hartley) £2,200 $3,520

An early 19th century inlaid oak corner cupboard, the ogee cornice above two arched crossbanded doors, 153cm. high x 113cm. wide. (Bearne's)   £390 $644

An Edwardian mahogany, chequer-banded and inlaid corner display cabinet, with arched pediment inlaid with a patera motif, 29½in. wide. (Christie's)   £747 $1,195

A George III oak hanging corner cupboard, 40in. (Dockree's)   £660 $1,089

Antique American architectural one-piece corner cupboard in pine with old blue and red paint, moulded cornice, three shelves above two doors below, 47in. wide. (Eldred's)   £2,200 $3,520

A Federal comb-decorated ochre-painted poplar corner cupboard, Pennsylvania, circa 1830, in two parts; the upper section with a cove moulding, 4ft.2in. wide. (Sotheby's)   £5,963 $9,775

Chippendale poplar glazed corner cupboard, Pennsylvania, late 18th century/early 19th century, the glazed arched doors above a lower case of raised panel doors, 51in. wide. (Skinner)   £2,257 $3,680

A George III mahogany and marquetry bowfront corner cupboard, with a moulded cornice and frieze with oval medallions, 28in. wide. (Christie's)   £1,160 $2,576

A George III mahogany inverted breakfront corner cupboard, crossbanded with string inlay, moulded cornice, 35½in. wide. (Andrew Hartley)   £480 $768

A George III mahogany standing corner cupboard, with moulded and dentil cornice, two long panelled doors, 42½in. wide. (Andrew Hartley)   £1,600 $2,688

Antique American pie safe, single drawer below two doors with pierced tin panels, 40½in. wide. (Eldred's)   £516 $852

An oak press cupboard, 17th century, later carved, the recessed superstructure with baluster uprights, 4ft.9¾in. wide. (Sotheby's)   £1,035 $1,728

A large oak cupboard by Robson & Sons Ltd Newcastle upon Tyne, with flared cornice above a pair of arched panelled doors, on a plinth base, 72in. x 94in. high. (Anderson & Garland)   £1,550 $2,558

A joined oak press cupboard, late 17th century, the later moulded rectangular top with floral lunette carved frieze, above turned front column supports, 46in. wide. (Bonhams)   £1,900 $3,040

A Stuart oak court cupboard, late 16th/early 17th century, the canted shaped top above a cupboard door carved with a stylised lion, 44½in. wide. (Sotheby's)   £3,157 $5,175

A late 17th/early 18th century oak and ebonised cupboard on stand, the upper part with a moulded cornice and enclosed by ebony and rosewood panel doors, 121cm. wide. (Phillips)   £950 $1,558

A late 18th century oak press cupboard, the moulded cornice over two ogee panelled doors flanked by fluted quarter columns, 51½in. wide. (Andrew Hartley)   £2,400 $3,840

A good figured walnut raised panel Schrank, Pennsylvania, 1760–1800, the massive overhanging cornice above raised panel cupboard doors, 6ft.6in. wide. (Sotheby's)   £21,746 $35,650

Cherry inlaid wall cupboard, possibly Ohio, early 19th century, the flat moulded cornice above a door with flush cockbeaded panel, 19½in. wide. (Skinner)   £906 $1,495

A 19th century panelled oak bacon cupboard, the high back with single door, 118cm. wide.
(Bearne's)   £800 $1,320

A fine and rare green-painted pine Schrank, Pennsylvania, circa 1780, the rectangular overhanging cornice above panelled doors, 5ft.2in. wide.
(Sotheby's)   £7,015 $11,500

An early 19th century oak and mahogany cupboard on chest, crossbanded with string inlay, on bracket feet, 46½in. wide.
(Andrew Hartley)   £875 $1,470

An 18th century Welsh joined oak cwpwrdd deuddarn, the moulded cornice over projecting frieze with turned end pendants, 59in. wide.
(Andrew Hartley) £5,600 $8,960

Painted wall spice cupboard, probably Northern Europe, last half 18th century, the flat moulded cornice above a hinged cupboard door with moulded recessed panel, 16in. wide.
(Skinner)   £934 $1,495

A good cut-decorated panelled pine trastero, Penasco, New Mexico, circa 1850, the moulded rectangular cornice surmounted by a shaped scrolling pediment, 37½in.
(Sotheby's)   £14,731 $24,150

A Shaker pine cupboard over drawers, probably Hancock-New Lebanon area, Massachusetts, 1830–1850, case fitted with a panelled door, over five graduated long drawers, 43in. wide.
(Christie's)   £6,900 $11,500

Walnut raised panelled dovetailed spice chest, Pennsylvania, 1780-1800, the cove-moulded cornice above a raised panel hinged door, 15½in. wide.
(Skinner)   £9,061 $14,950

A glazed surface pine trastero, Aniceto Garundo, Chacon, New Mexico, circa 1870, the rectangular overhanging dentil moulded cornice above two field panelled doors, 4ft. wide. (Sotheby's)   £4,559 $7,475

437

A George III oak bacon settle with moulded cornice over three small drawers, two panelled doors below, 63½in. wide.
(Andrew Hartley)   £4,400 $7,260

Renaissance Revival rosewood marquetry and parcel-gilt credenza, New York, circa 1865-70, 71½in. long. (Skinner)   £12,857 $20,700

An antique oak deuddarn, the moulded cornice with inverted finials above two panelled doors, raised on bracket feet.
(Academy)   £4,100 $6,765

A joined oak press cupboard, Yorkshire, mid-17th century, the gadrooned canopy above a scroll carved frieze bearing the initials *H. T. M.* with acorn drop pendants above a pair of panelled cupboard doors, 57¾in. wide.
(Bonhams)   £2,400 $3,840

An important blue-green painted turned and joined pine trastero, New Mexico, circa 1780, the arched scalloped removable cornice flanked by similarly decorated sides, 24½in. wide.
(Sotheby's)   £49,837 $81,700

Red painted pine panelled cupboard, New England, early 19th century, the one-part cupboard with double raised panel upper door above a similar door, 43½in. wide.
(Skinner)   £683 $1,093

A 19th century inlaid walnut credenza, the twin D-shape open end shelves flanking twin panelled doors with gilt beading, on a plinth base, 183cm. wide.
(Bristol)   £1,500 $2,475

A rare diminutive spindle-door pine trastero, New Mexico, 1780–1800, with shaped removable cornice, flanked by stiles with stepped finials, 31in. wide.
(Sotheby's)   £36,752 $60,250

A Victorian figured walnut veneered harlequin davenport, the rising section with a pierced gilt brass gallery. (David Lay) £3,300 $5,280

A 19th century burr walnut davenport, with fitted maple interior, four true and four false drawers, 54in. wide. (Bristol) £920 $1,472

A George IV ormolu-mounted and brass-inlaid ebony davenport, the rectangular top with three-quarter pierced baluster gallery, 24in. wide. (Christie's) £5,750 $9,430

A Victorian walnut davenport, with pierced brass gallery, serpentine fronted leather inset writing slope opening to reveal fitted interior, 22in. wide.
(Andrew Hartley) £1,550 $2,480

A Victorian walnut piano-topped davenport, the rising superstructure with pierced fret-carved gallery enclosing pigeon holes and three small drawers, above a hinged top, 22¼in. wide. (Christie's) £3,220 $5,152

A Victorian walnut davenport, the raised top with hinged lid revealing fitted stationery compartment, on carved and scrolled supports, 21in. wide.
(Andrew Hartley) £1,400 $2,240

A Victorian walnut davenport, the top with a pierced fret-carved three-quarter gallery above a lined slope enclosing a bird's-eye maple interior, 23¾in. wide.
(Christie's) £1,725 $2,760

A Victorian walnut davenport, with three-quarter pierced galleried back pen compartment, leather inset slope with serpentine front, 56cm. wide.(Bristol) £1,150 $1,840

A Victorian burr walnut piano-top davenport with pop-up stationery compartment, inset writing surface, 23in. wide. (Russell Baldwin & Bright) £2,800 $4,480

An Edwardian mahogany bonheur du jour, with satinwood banding and string inlay, 24½in. wide. (Andrew Hartley) £2,000 $3,200

A French mahogany and gilt-metal mounted writing desk, early 19th century, fitted with four drawers around a leather-lined writing surface, 45½in. wide. (Christie's) £862 $1,379

Gustav Stickley desk, no. 732, (replaced veneer on front lid), 42in. high. 32in. wide, 14in. deep. (Skinner) £1,104 $1,840

A late 19th century French bureau cabinet, with painted Vernis Martin panels of young lovers in landscapes, the superstructure with gilt metal gallery and mounts, 30in. wide. (Dreweatt Neate) £1,350 $2,200

A beechwood desk and chair, the raised superstructure elaborately carved overall with various mythological representations, Continental, early 20th century 48in. wide. (Christie's) £4,370 $6,555

Federal tiger maple and mahogany inlaid desk, Massachusetts, circa 1820, the top section with cross-banded cornice board above two tambour doors, 39¼in. wide. (Skinner) £10,781 $17,250

An Arts and Crafts mahogany bureau, attributed to Liberty & Co, the raised superstructure with a pair of glazed cupboard doors, 26in. wide. (Christie's) £575 $863

A mahogany Carlton House desk, early 20th century, in the George III style, the stepped superstructure with a bank of four drawers flanked by panelled cupboard doors, 48in. wide. (Christie's) £2,530 $4,048

Stickley Brothers style desk and chair, worn finish, 33in. high, 22in. wide, 16¼in. deep. (Skinner) £207 $345

An Arts and Crafts oak writing cabinet, the rectangular top above hinged fall, opening to reveal writing surface and fitted compartments, 33in. wide. (Christie's) £862 $1,293

A 19th century carved oak writing desk, 51in. (Dockree's) £560 $896

Stickley Brothers desk, no. 6534, original finish, 46¾in. high, 30in. wide, 15¼in. deep. (Skinner) £241 $402

A French mahogany, painted and brass-inlaid bonheur du jour, the serpentine superstructure with a variegated marble top above a glazed cabinet, 34in. wide. (Christie's) £1,265 $2,024

A Secessionist-style maroon lacquered desk, the desk with fitted superstructure and trays above a flaring rectangular top inset with glass surface, and a matching armchair, 49½in. wide. (Christie's) £690 $1,035

A William and Mary burl walnut ladies writing desk, 18th/19th century, of small size, the hinged lid opening to three pigeonholes and six short drawers, 18in. wide. (Sotheby's) £1,929 $3,162

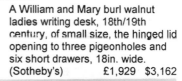

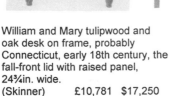

William and Mary tulipwood and oak desk on frame, probably Connecticut, early 18th century, the fall-front lid with raised panel, 24¾in. wide.
(Skinner) £10,781 $17,250

Gustav Stickley desk, no. 708, two drawers, postcard top, original finish, 39½in. wide., postcard box 12½in. wide.
(Skinner) £1,035 $1,725

A 19th century French style bonheur du jour in walnut with floral marquetry, the upper section with central mirror cupboard door and arrangement of seven drawers, 4ft. high. (Russell, Baldwin & Bright) £2,100 $3,465

An Edwardian mahogany display
cabinet with string and parquetry
inlay, moulded cornice with arch
centre, 60in. wide.
(Andrew Hartley) £1,800 $2,970

A walnut display cabinet,
Biedermeier, circa 1835, the part
ebonised moulded cornice above
four doors, the upper section
glazed, 7ft. 4in. wide.
(Sotheby's)   £5,750 $9,603

Gustav Stickley No. 815 china
cabinet, three stationary shelves,
through tenons top and bottom
sides, 41½in. wide.
(Skinner)   £8,970 $14,950

An unusual Edwardian mahogany
jade cabinet, with bevelled glass
back, sides and top, over two small
drawers, 16½in. wide.
(Dee Atkinson & Harrison)
                    £550 $907

A 19th century ebony and
boullework breakfront display
cabinet, the stepped rectangular
top above the brass bound glazed
doors, 182cm. wide.
(Phillips)   £1,850 $2,960

A fine inlaid Edwardian mahogany
display cabinet, the shaped
pediment with central floral
marquetry and swag inlay, 52½in.
wide. (Dee Atkinson & Harrison)
                    £2,800 $4,480

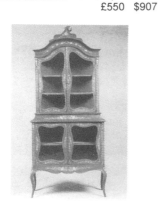

A mahogany and floral marquetry
vitrine, early 20th century, the
asymmetric scrolled cresting above
an arched frieze and a pair of
shaped glazed doors, 42½in. wide.
(Christie's)   £2,415 $3,864

A mid 19th century brass inlaid
ebonised side cabinet with chased
pierced ormolu gallery and mounts,
43½in. wide.
(Dreweatt Neate)   £900 $1,467

Sheraton Revival satinwood china
cabinet of demi-lune form with
segmental veneered top, figurative
inlaid frieze, 36in. wide.
(Lots Road Galleries)
                    £2,100 $3,465

Leavens Co. china cabinet, four shelves, original finish, 59¼in. high. (Skinner) £328 $546

A beechwood and tulipwood crossbanded vitrine table, with a quarter-veneered top above bevelled glazed sides, 27in. wide. (Christie's) £575 $920

Limbert two-door china cabinet, no. 1338, three shelves, brand mark, original finish, 46in. wide. (Skinner) £2,760 $4,600

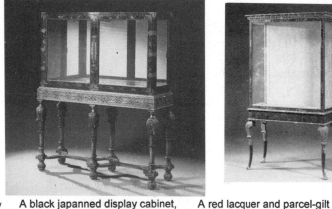

A mahogany display cabinet, early 20th century, the cavetto moulded cornice above a plain frieze above four glazed sides all with geometric astragal glazed panels, 56in. wide. (Christie's) £575 $920

A black japanned display cabinet, circa 1900, in William and Mary style, the glazed cabinet within black chinoiserie frames upon a gilt stand, 4ft.2½in. wide. (Sotheby's) £1,150 $1,920

A red lacquer and parcel-gilt chinoiserie decorated display cabinet-on-stand, the stand George I, with a foliate-carved cornice above a glazed front and sides, 43in. wide. (Christie's) £1,035 $1,656

An Oriental ebonised carved wood display cabinet, with domed top having arched foliate crest centred by a bird, 50in. wide. (Andrew Hartley) £425 $680

A Dutch walnut display cabinet, mid 18th century, the shaped cornice centred by a floral and C-scroll pedestal flanked by two similar pedestals, 61½in. wide. (Christie's) £7,475 $12,408

A 19th century mahogany and gilt bronze mounted vitrine, of Louis XVI style, the demi-lune marble top above a panelled frieze, 85.5cm. wide. (Phillips) £3,000 $4,800

Dutch baroque walnut and floral marquetry cabinet, mid-18th century, arched cornice over a conforming glazed door enclosing shelves, 40½in. wide. (Skinner) £3,795 $6,325

A French kingwood vitrine, late 19th century, of a broken bombé outline, applied with giltmetal mounts, 46in. wide. (Christie's) £4,025 $6,440

A fine gilt-bronze and boulle display cabinet, Victorian, circa 1860, with a shaped moulded pediment centred by a coat of arms above a pair of glazed doors, 163cm. wide. (Sotheby's) £36,700 $60,555

A 19th century Dutch walnut and marquetry vitrine inlaid with vases of flowers, arched moulded cornice above two conforming astragal-glazed doors and canted glazed sides, 177cm. high x 145cm. wide. (Bearne's) £3,600 $5,940

An ormolu-mounted tulipwood and parquetry vitrine-cabinet, inlaid with quarter-veneered panelling with fruitwood bands, 39½in. wide. (Christie's) £920 $1,527

An Edwardian mahogany Sheraton style display cabinet cross-banded with satinwood, serpentine front fitted glazed and panelled door, on square taper legs, 3ft.6in. wide. (Russell Baldwin & Bright) £1,420 $2,343

A satinwood, purple-heart banded and brass-mounted corner display cabinet, 19th century, decorated with boxwood stringing, the frieze inset with a gilt-metal plaque, 28in. wide. (Christie's) £3,105 $4,968

A Victorian mahogany bow fronted display cabinet, the upper section with moulded and dentil cornice, 31in. wide. (Andrew Hartley) £1,400 $2,352

An oak dresser with dentil cornice, pierced and shaped frieze and three open shelves to the upper section, 188cm. wide, 18th century and later.(Bearne's) £2,800 $4,620

A beechwood dresser, English, early 19th century, the boarded plate-rack with moulded cornice and two open shelves, 76½in. wide. (Christie's)   £1,610 $2,576

Early 19th century oak Welsh dresser, the open shelf back above a central drawer and alcove, 58in. wide. (Lawrences)   £2,600 $4,186

A joined oak enclosed dresser, North Wales, early 18th century, the plate rack with moulded cornice above three shelves and stepped sides, 70in. wide. (Bonhams)   £4,800 $7,680

A George II joined oak enclosed dresser, North Wales, circa 1750, the associated open plate rack with a waved frieze above two shelves, the base with three frieze drawers, 84¼in. wide. (Bonhams)   £4,000 $6,400

An 18th century oak enclosed dresser, the moulded cornice over pierced frieze, three moulded shelves below six spice drawers, 71in. wide. (Andrew Hartley)   £5,000 $8,000

George III oak Welsh dresser, 18th/19th century, the rectangular top section with open shelves and two cabinet doors, 61in. wide. (Skinner)   £2,857 $4,600

A joined oak enclosed dresser, early 18th century, the moulded cornice and waved frieze above two open shelves, on block feet, 64in. wide. (Bonhams)   £5,200 $8,320

A George III oak dresser, the moulded dentil cornice with pierced frieze over three shelves, fitted as plate rack, 205cm. wide. (Phillips)   £3,900 $6,240

A mahogany two tier dumb waiter, William IV, circa 1830, the two revolving sections with moulded borders, on a columnar pillar, 2ft. (Sotheby's)   £1,150 $1,920

A late Victorian mahogany oblong three tier dumb waiter, turned supports and porcelain castors, 43in. high. (H. C. Chapman)   £560 $924

A 19th century mahogany three tier dumb waiter, on plain tripod support on porcelain castors, 39½in. high. (Dreweatt Neate)   £650 $1,073

A George III mahogany three-tier dumb waiter, mid 18th century, having three graduated dished circular tiers above a ring-turned baluster stem, 23½in. diameter. (Christie's)   £1,380 $2,300

A Victorian mahogany metamorphic dumb-waiter, the rectangular extending top above a moulded middle tier and lower tier, on trestle ends, 48in. wide. (Christie's)   £4,025 $6,560

A French walnut buffet, 19th century, the grey fossil marble top above a plain frieze and baluster-turned supports, 31½in. wide. (Christie's)   £552 $883

A 19th century mahogany two tier dumb waiter, with two moulded edged circular trays over a tambour cupboard, 43½in. high. (Andrew Hartley)   £950 $1,596

A George IV mahogany three-tier waiter's stand, the adjustable platforms on standard and splayed end supports, 48in. wide. (Christie's)   £862 $1,396

A George III mahogany three-tier tripod dumb-waiter, the circular top with moulded gallery, above two graduating tiers with concave-cut divides, 45½in. high. (Christie's)   £10,925 $17,807

Cherry high chest of drawers, Chester County, Pennsylvania, late 18th century, the cornice cove moulding above a single drawer, visually divided into three, 38in. wide. (Skinner) £12,218 $19,550

A fine Queen Anne figured mahogany flat-top high chest of drawers, Rhode Island, 1740–70, in two parts, width of case 34½in. (Sotheby's) £4,910 $8,050

A Chippendale carved walnut high chest-of-drawers, Philadelphia, 1740–1750, in two sections: the upper with moulded broken swan's-neck pediment, 42½in. wide. (Christie's) £179,700 $299,500

A Queen Anne carved cherrywood high chest-of-drawers, probably Colchester, Connecticut, 1750–1780, in two sections, the upper with a moulded broken swan's-neck pediment, 39in. wide. (Christie's) £232,500 $387,500

A Queen Anne inlaid-maple diminutive flat top highboy Massachusetts, 1720–40, in two parts; the upper section with an overhanging stepped cornice, width at mid-moulding 39¼in. (Sotheby's) £6,664 $10,925

American Queen Anne mahogany bonnet top highboy, circa 1740, with moulded cornice, two small drawers flanking a fan-carved centre drawer, 36½in. wide. (Eldred's) £4,000 $6,600

A Queen Anne figured maple diminutive flat-top high chest of drawers, Massachusetts, 1730–60, on cabriole legs ending in pad feet, 36in. wide. (Sotheby's) £6,313 $10,350

A fine and rare Queen Anne carved and figured cherrywood diminutive bonnet-top high chest of drawers, Connecticut River Valley, 1750–70, 37½in. wide. (Sotheby's) £60,900 $101,500

A Queen Anne mahogany high chest of drawers, New England, 1740–1760, in two sections, cabriole legs with pad-and-disc feet, 38in. wide. (Christie's) £4,830 $8,050

447

A good George III mahogany partner's desk, circa 1780, the top with a moulded edge and later tooled red leather insert above six frieze drawers, 73½in. wide. (Christie's)   £7,500 $12,000

A William IV walnut writing desk, the rectangular top inset with a gilt tooled green leather fitted below with five drawers, 46in. wide. (Christie's)   £1,150 $1,840

A Victorian figured walnut pedestal desk, with galleried top over nine drawers about the kneehole, 154cm. wide. (Tennants)   £2,000 $3,200

A George IV inlaid mahogany kneehole desk outlined with feather banding and barber-pole stringing, 110cm. wide. (Bearne's)   £920 $1,472

A marquetry bureau-cabinet, 19th century, in four sections, decorated in various types of wood with floral and geometric designs, 41⅞in. wide. (Christie's) £12,650 $20,620

A George II walnut kneehole desk, cross and feather-banded overall, the moulded rectangular quarter-veneered top above a frieze drawer and three short drawers, 32in. wide. (Christie's)   £7,820 $12,981

An Italian Provincial inlaid walnut kneehole writing table inlaid in the Classical manner with heroic figures, mythical beasts, swags and urns, 97cm. wide. (Bearne's)   £1,800 $2,970

A late George III mahogany pedestal desk, attributed to Gillows, the rounded rectangular brown leather-lined top with reeded edge above a long fitted frieze drawer simulated as three drawers, 49¼in. wide. (Christie's) £8,625 $14,317

A George III mahogany pedestal desk, circa 1790, the leather inset rectangular top with moulded edge above an arcaded frieze, 49in. wide. (Christie's) £5,800 $9,280

A figured walnut kidney shaped desk, early 20th century, the top inset with a gilt tooled leather, above a frieze fitted with three drawers, 59in. wide.
(Christie's)   £7,130 $11,408

An Edwardian mahogany partner's pedestal desk, in the early George III style, the green leather-lined everted breakfront top with gadrooned edge, 70in. wide.
(Christie's)   £18,400 $30,544

A mahogany pedestal desk, 20th century, of recessed broken outline, with a foliate carved edge, the interlaced blind fret-carved frieze fitted with three drawers, 58in. wide. (Christie's)   £8,280 $13,248

A George I walnut kneehole desk, feather-banded to the top and front, the quarter-veneered rectangular top with re-entrant front corners, 31¾in. wide.
(Christie's)   £11,500 $19,090

A Victorian mahogany pedestal desk, the red leather-lined top above three mahogany-lined frieze drawers above a central kneehole, 59¼in. wide.
(Christie's)   £13,225 $21,953

A mahogany serpentine-fronted sideboard, early 19th century, the raised tablet centred back above a shaped top with three frieze drawers, 60in. wide.
(Christie's) £1,667 $2,667

A painted, decorated and inlaid pedestal desk, supported on two rectangular pedestals, decorated scenes from ancient Egyptian life and hieroglyphics, 60in. wide.
(Christie's) £1,150 $1,725

A rosewood grained elongated octagonal pedestal desk, late 19th/early 20th century, the shaped leather-lined top with a moulded edge and four frieze drawers, 64in. wide. (Christie's) £2,990 $4,784

A late 19th century kneehole desk, veneered in satinwood and sycamore with marquetry flowers and landscapes, 44in. wide.
(Dreweatt Neate) £3,200 $5,280

George I figured walnut and chevron line inlaid kneehole desk, the moulded top with pinched corners, 2ft. 7in. wide.
(Lawrences) £8,000 $12,880

A George II walnut kneehole desk, the crossbanded top with re-entrant corners, a long drawer above a recessed cupboard, 36in. wide.
(Dreweatt Neate) £2,600 $4,290

A Victorian mahogany pedestal desk, the rounded rectangular leather-lined top with three frieze drawers, 52in. wide.
(Christie's) £977 $1,563

German pedestal desk, late 19th/early 20th century, in figured walnut and walnut veneers, removable stepped upper section with four drawers and two doors, 56in. long. (Eldred's) £1,512 $2,420

A George III style mahogany pedestal desk with tooled leather insert to the rounded rectangular top, 138cm. wide.
(Bearne's) £1,900 $3,135

A walnut linen press, the moulded cornice with a plain frieze above a pair of fielded panel doors, 44in. wide. (Christie's) £2,070 $3,312

A George III mahogany linen press, the moulded cornice above a pair of boxwood lined panelled doors, 52in. wide. (Christie's) £1,840 $2,944

A 19th century satinwood linen press with dentil cornice over pair of solid panelled doors, 4ft 1in. wide. (Russell Baldwin & Bright) £2,550 $4,207

A Victorian mahogany linen press, the angled cornice with foliate scrolled cresting above a plain frieze and a pair of figured mahogany panelled doors, Channel Isles, 52in. wide. (Christie's)   £1,035 $1,656

A George II mahogany linen-press, the moulded rectangular cornice above a Greek-key frieze and a pair of serpentine-panelled doors, 50in. wide. (Christie's)   £11,500 $18,860

A mahogany linen press, second half of 19th century, the moulded cornice above a plain frieze and pair of panelled cupboard doors, 51¼in. wide. (Christie's)   £862 $1,379

A Regency mahogany linen press, decorated with ebonised lines, the shaped cornice applied with ebonised balls, above a pair of panelled doors, 49in. wide. (Christie's)   £1,610 $2,608

An attractive George III mahogany and boxwood strung linen press, circa 1790, the moulded cornice with a band frieze centred by patera above a pair of rosewood cross-banded oval panelled doors, 50¼in. wide. (Christie's)   £3,400 $5,440

A Victorian yellow-painted linen press, decorated with ebonised lines and simulated bamboo mouldings, 46in. wide. (Christie's)   £1,495 $2,422

A George II walnut lowboy, the quarter veneered and crossbanded top having cut corners, over five drawers, 80cm. wide.
(Tennants)   £3,000 $4,800

A George I burr-elm and walnut lowboy, the moulded rectangular quarter-veneered top crossbanded in walnut with re-entrant front corners, 29¼in. wide.
(Christie's)   £23,000 $37,720

A good Queen Anne carved walnut dressing table, Pennsylvania, circa 1750, the rectangular moulded top above three drawers, 32¾in. wide.
(Sotheby's)   £2,806 $4,600

A Queen Anne figured-maple dressing-table, mid-Atlantic States, 1740–1760, with one long thumbmoulded drawer over three short similar drawers above a shaped apron, 22¾in. wide.
(Christie's)   £5,520 $9,200

A rare Queen Anne walnut veneered lowboy, Boston, Massachusetts, circa 1740, on cabriole legs ending in pad feet, top 32in. wide.
(Sotheby's)   £30,000 $50,000

A George I walnut lowboy, cross and feather-banded to the top and front, the quarter-veneered rectangular top with re-entrant front corners, 27¾in. high.
(Christie's)   £10,350 $17,181

A Chippendale carved walnut dressingtable, the rectangular moulded top with double-cusped corners above a conforming case, 36½in. wide.
(Christie's)   £5,520 $9,200

A rare Queen Anne quarter-veneered walnut maple dressing table, Boston area, possibly Newburyport, Massachusetts, 1740–60, 30in. wide.
(Sotheby's)   £14,197 $23,000

A Chippendale carved mahogany dressing table, Philadelphia, 1745-1765, the rectangular moulded top with canted corners above a cavetto moulding, 37in. wide.
(Christie's)   £6,388 $10,350

A George III mahogany tray top bedside cupboard, later decorated with crossbanding and lines and enclosed by two doors, 17½in. wide. (Christie's) £460 $736

An unusual early George III walnut serpentine night table, circa 1760, the boxwood strung top with eared corners above a pair of serpentine cupboard doors, 20½in. wide. (Christie's) £5,500 $8,800

A George III mahogany tray-top bedside cupboard, the front fitted with a door, each side pierced with a carrying handle, 16¼in. wide. (Christie's) £862 $1,396

A Victorian maple and simulated bamboo night table, circa 1870, with a drawer and fall flap, on ring turned legs and an undertier, 2ft. 3in. wide. (Sotheby's) £575 $960

A German black and gold-japanned bedside commode, mid 18th century, the rectangular top with bowed front and three-quarter shaped gallery centred by an image of a Chinese temple, 21¼in. wide. (Christie's) £3,220 $5,345

A mahogany two door bedside cupboard, George III, circa 1780, on square tapering legs with later inlay, 1ft.7½in. wide. (Sotheby's) £805 $1,344

A satin birch cupboard, Victorian, circa 1850, the moulded drop flap top above a panelled drawer and door, 1ft. 9½in. wide. (Sotheby's) £1,035 $1,728

A George III mahogany bedside table, the three-quarter galleried bowfronted rectangular top with carrying-handles to the sides, 14in. wide. (Christie's) £1,035 $1,687

A George III mahogany tray-top bedside commode, the gallery pierced with carrying handles above a tambour shutter, 51¾in. deep. (Christie's) £1,725 $2,760

A pair of three-leaf needlework screens, the needlework early 19th century, each with three close-nailed wool and silk gros point needlework panels of polychrome flowers and foliage, each leaf 81in. x 24¼in.
(Christie's) £6,900 $11,454

An early Georgian black and gilt-japanned eight-leaf screen, in the manner of Stalker and Parker, each leaf with three panels decorated in imitation of Chinese lacquer with chinoiserie figures, each leaf 101in. x 17¾in. (Christie's) £4,140 $6,748

A Chinese Export black and gold lacquer eight-leaf screen, 19th century, each leaf depicting courtly scenes within a mountainous and watery landscape, each leaf 81 x 21½in.
(Christie's) £26,450 $43,907

An ebonised four fold Aesthetic Movement screen, English, circa 1875, each panel with varied fretwork top above open panelling below, 69²/₃in. high, 29²/₃in. wide each panel.
(Christie's) £1,500 $2,400

A painted-leather five-leaf screen, 19th century, painted with a continuous scene across the five arched leaves of a stone balustrade with a central plinth supporting an urn filled with flowers, each leaf: 84¼in. x 20in.
(Christie's) £16,100 $26,726

An Art Deco style gilt-decorated black lacquer four-fold screen decorated with incised elements depicting a pair of scantily draped maidens above waves, width of each panel 16in.
(Sotheby's) £1,754 $2,875

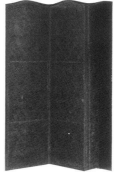

French five-panel wallpaper floor screen, early 19th century, depicting genre scenes, each panel 63¾ x 21½in.
(Skinner) £893 $1,438

A four-fold painted and embossed leather screen, 19th century, each leaf with close-nailed borders and arched top decorated with floral sprays, 92in. wide, 77½in. high.
(Christie's) £1,207 $1,931

A six-fold chinoiserie screen, 19th century, each panel decorated with roundel scenes of pavilions and figures, 10ft.7½in. wide open.
(Sotheby's) £5,175 $8,642

A Chinese Export six-leaf screen, 18th century, decorated overall with figures, pagodas, temples, rivers and bridges and the reverse with warriors, each leaf: 98in. x 18¾in. (Christie's)　£5,175　$8,435

A fine French 19th century brass firescreen with raised foliated scrolls, fitted with a mesh panel with attached brass flaming urn, 28½in. x 30in. high. (Anderson & Garland)　£800　$1,320

A pair of Regency rosewood firescreens, each with a sliding panel, with later patterned silk damask depicting exotic birds perched amongst foliage, 19½in. wide. (Christie's)　£900　$1,440

A three fold lacquer screen, by Leonor Fini, circa 1930, decorated with three dancing figures, against a black ground, 57 x 15¾in. dimensions of each panel. (Christie's)　£9,775　$15,640

'Les Roses', a wrought iron firescreen, designed by Edgar Brandt, circa 1927, circular central panel decorated with roses and leaves, within scrolls, leaves and berries, 33½ x 44in. (Christie's)　£19,550　$31,280

A two-fold screen, 20th century, framed with bamboo, depicting sixteen coloured drawings on paper of Oriental figures, 77½in. high. 65in. wide. (Christie's)　£800　$1,280

A nine fold mirrored screen, French, 1940s, ebonised wood and mirrored glass, 63¼ x 11½in. dimensions each panel. (Christie's)　£2,000　$3,200

A Newlyn style copper and iron fire screen, iron legs with scroll feet and twisted terminals supporting copper screen, set with two Ruskin blue crystalline roundels, 67cm. high. (Christie's)　£345　$518

Piero Fornasetti, 'Reflecting City' folding screen, 1955, lacquered wood, reversible brass hinges, castors, each panel 19¾in. wide. (Sotheby's)　£6,900　$11,178

A Victorian walnut and burr crossbanded secrétaire music cabinet, with a pierced three-quarter gallery, enclosed by a pair of glazed panel doors, 22¼in. wide. (Christie's)　£1,495　$2,392

A Regency mahogany secrétaire à abattant, circa 1810, in the French Empire style, the rectangular top above a frieze drawer, 35in. wide. (Christie's)　£2,000　$3,200

A French tulipwood and kingwood serpentine secrétaire semainier, late 19th century, deocrated with crossbanding and quarter veneers, 27in. wide. (Christie's)　£1,840　$2,944

An ormolu-mounted kingwood, tulipwood, amaranth and ebonised parquetry cartonnier, the rectangular top above a shaped cartonnier with ten drawers with ebonised bands, 36½in. wide. (Christie's)　£5,175　$8,590

A Queen Anne walnut crossbanded and featherstrung secrétaire cabinet, the upper part with a moulded cornice and enclosed by a pair of panel doors with ogee arched bevelled plate mirrors, 106cm. wide. (Phillips)　£16,000　$26,240

Fine and rare Gustav Stickley inlaid desk, No. 706, original dark chocolate finish with three inlaid foliate designs in exotic wood, pewter and copper inlay, 30¼in. wide. (Skinner)　£13,800　$23,000

A mahogany secrétaire chest on chest, George III, circa 1780, the dentil cornice over two short and three long rosewood banded and boxwood strung drawers, 3ft. 9in. wide. (Sotheby's) £2,990　$4,993

A Louis XV/XV1 Transitional kingwood and marquetry secrétaire à abattant by Nicolas-Alexandre Lapie, with a brèche d'alep marble top, 32¼in. wide. (Christie's)　£8,625　$13,973

A satin birch secrétaire, Biedermeier, circa 1825, the ebonised moulded oblong top with flattened triangular pedimented moulding, 3ft. 7½in. wide. (Sotheby's)　£5,520　$9,218

A late George III rosewood-veneered cylinder bureau with a galleried shelf on brass column supports, 66cm. wide.
(Bearne's)   £7,500 $12,000

An unusual oyster walnut and copper-bound chest, circa 1700 and later, the fall flap enclosing an arrangement of drawers and compartments, 2ft. 11in. wide.
(Sotheby's)   £1,150 $1,920

A kingwood and walnut escritoire, Northern European, early 18th century, the top with two drawers above the flap enclosing a fully fitted interior, 3ft.11in. wide.
(Sotheby's)   £2,990 $4,993

A fine George III rosewood grained and brass mounted secrétaire cabinet, attributed to John Maclean, circa 1800, the superstructure with three open shelves flanked by brass trellis work sides and turned brass supports, 36½in. wide.
(Christie's)   £14,500 $23,200

A brass-mounted padoukwood campaign chest, mid 19th century, in two parts: the upper section with two short over one deep drawer, 39in. wide.
(Sotheby's)   £2,630 $4,312

A Louis XV/XVI Transitional tulipwood and purplewood banded secrétaire à abattant by Roger Vandercruse, dit Lacroix, with a marble top and drawer in the quarter-veneered shaped frieze, 35in. wide.
(Christie's)   £9,775 $15,835

A Dutch walnut and marquetry secrétaire à abattant, late 19th/early 20th century, decorated overall with meandering floral sprays, birds and flower filled urns, 33in. wide.
(Christie's)   £2,300 $3,726

A North Italian walnut and marquetry bureau, late 18th century, decorated with crossbanding and figurative inlay, 48in. wide.
(Christie's)   £4,830 $7,728

A Regency ormolu-mounted fiddleback-mahogany and Gonçalo-Alvez secretaire bookcase, inlaid with brass and ebony lines, 36¼in. wide.
(Christie's)   £19,550 $32,062

A fine 19th century French kingwood and tulipwood secrétaire cabinet with a pierced brass balustrade and inset red marble top, 29½in. wide. (Anderson & Garland)   £2,800 $4,620

A Regency mahogany secretaire bookcase, the dentil-moulded cornice above a pair of astragal glazed doors, 47in. wide. (Christie's)   £1,725 $2,760

Renaissance Revival walnut and parcel-gilt secretary, third quarter 19th century, moulded top over a drawer and fall-front enclosing a fitted writing compartment, 38¾in. wide. (Skinner) £1,104 $1,840

BUYER BEWARE
Technically something has to be over a hundred years old to qualify as antique, but this alone won't necessarily increase the value of an otherwise mundane item. More important now are factors such as quality of manufacture, timber, colour and size. For some time now small, delicate late Victorian and Edwardian copies of George III furniture have regularly been outperforming the originals at auction, and just because something is 'antique' doesn't make poor repairs any more acceptable.
    Cheffins Grain & Comins

A Regency mahogany breakfront secrétaire bookcase, the lower section with a secrétaire-drawer enclosing a fitted satinwood and ebony interior, 56½in. wide. (Christie's)   £40,000 $66,400

A late Georgian mahogany secrétaire bookcase, the adjustable shelving enclosed by pair of 13-pane doors, 3ft 8in. wide. (Russell Baldwin & Bright)   £5,300 $8,745

A Hepplewhite period mahogany secrétaire chest on chest, the moulded cornice above three short and three long graduated drawers. (Woolley & Wallis) £6,800 $10,948

A George III satinwood secrétaire cabinet, inlaid overall with boxwood and ebonised lines and banded in amaranth, 34½in. wide. (Christie's)   £49,000 $81,340

A Regency mahogany secrétaire bookcase, crossbanded with ebony stringing, moulded cornice, two astragal glazed doors, 43in. wide. (Andrew Hartley) £1,500 $2,475

George III mahogany
secretary/bookcase, rectangular
moulded cornice over a pair of
glazed mullioned doors in the
Rococo taste, 49¼in. wide.
(Skinner)   £1,552 $2,587

A George III carved and figured
mahogany bureau bookcase last
quarter 18th century, in three parts,
straight bracket feet, 43in. wide.
(Sotheby's)   £5,865 $9,775

A George III mahogany secrétaire
bookcase, the moulded cornice
above twin arched glazed doors,
137.5cm. wide.
(Wintertons)   £1,250 $2,062

A Georgian mahogany secrétaire
bookcase, the dentil cornice above
twin lancet glazed doors, on
bracket feet, width 114cm., possibly
matched. (Bristol)   £1,800 $2,970

A Regency mahogany and
ebonised breakfront secrétaire
bookcase, the pediment above a
pair of geometrically-glazed doors
enclosing three adjustable shelves,
35½in. wide.
(Christie's)   £6,900 $11,454

An early Victorian mahogany
secrétaire bookcase, the canted
cornice above plain frieze and pair
of glazed doors, 120cm. wide.
(Phillips)   £1,700 $2,720

Antique American Hepplewhite two-
part secretary in cherry, upper
section with two tambour doors
under scrolled pediment, 42in.
wide. (Eldred's)   £1,733 $2,860

A pair of Victorian mahogany
secrétaire bookcases, circa 1860,
the arched moulded cornice above
a pair of glazed cupboard doors
with foliate moulded frames, 51in.
wide. (Christie's) £8,500 $13,600

A French walnut secrétaire à
abattant, mid 19th century, with
frieze drawer and fall front
enclosing a fitted interior of drawers
and a central arcade, 38½in. wide.
(Christie's)   £2,070 $3,312

A George III mahogany sofa, on square moulded and beaded legs headed by later pierced ogee brackets, joined by pierced quatrefoil stretchers, 79in. wide. (Christie's)   £10,350 $17,181

A George IV rosewood daybed, after a design by George Smith, with scrolled padded ends, the back carved with acanthus and lion's head, the ends carved with scrolling foliage. (Christie's)   £5,750 $9,545

An early Victorian mahogany sofa, heavily reeded overall, the padded rectangular shaped back, sides, buttoned seat-cushion and pair of bolsters covered in close nailed dark red leather, the toprail centred by a fan and foliate motif flanked on each side by S-scrolls, 80in. wide. (Christie's)   £4,600 $7,498

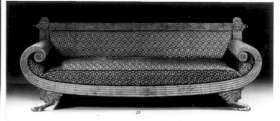

A Biedermeier ebony-inlaid bird's-eye maple and birch sofa, first half 19th century, with a reeded frame, the corners of the back with inlaid anthemions, the curved front seat-rail continuing to inwardly-scrolled arms with inlaid foliate medallions, 99in. wide. (Christie's)   £5,175 $8,590

A George II mahogany settee, attributed to Wright and Elrick, the arms with scrolled supports with C-scroll and acanthus terminals, on cabriole legs headed by clasped acanthus, 73in. wide. (Christie's)   £26,450 $43,378

A George II mahogany sofa, attributed to William Hallett, on cabriole legs headed by a pendant-hung shell and gadrooned angle-brackets, on claw feet below a circular collar, 66½in. wide. (Christie's)   £17,250 $28,290

A poplar and oak Windsor settee, branded by S. Budd, Pennsylvania, 1770–1800, the moulded crest continuing to baluster and ring-turned arm supports and terminating in knuckle grips with carved volutes, 77½in. wide. (Christie's)   £6,555 $10,925

A giltwood sofa, part 18th century, the bowed padded back with husk-trail frame centred by a ribbon-tied bow above a serpentine seat, the arms with serpentine husk-trail supports, 86in. wide. (Christie's)   £3,450 $5,727

A Regency brass-inlaid rosewood sofa, the arms carved with scrolling acanthus leaves and with a sunken foliate-inlaid panel, 88in. wide. (Christie's) £6,900 $11,316

An Irish Regency mahogany daybed, the back with a gadrooned border, the front outlined by an eagle's head and neck to one end and a fish tail to the other. (Christie's) £23,000 $38,180

One of a matched pair of North European mahogany sofas, second quarter 19th century, each with an arched back, outscrolled arms, padded seat and bolsters, the arms carved with a foliate cornucopia issuing fruits above the bolection-moulded seat-rail, 78in. and 78¾in. wide.
(Christie's) (Two) £7,360 $12,217

A Louis XVI giltwood duchesse brisée, in two sections, the channelled back and end-section with a twisting ribbon, with raised centre flanked by leaf finials. (Christie's) £3,450 $5,727

One of a pair of George III mahogany sofas, on acanthus-wrapped cabriole legs and scrolled feet with sunk leather and brass castors, 68in. wide. (Christie's) £10,350 $16,974

A giltwood hump-back sepentine sofa, 19th century, of large size, with a channelled frame and scroll arm terminals and cabriole legs terminating in scroll feet, re-gilt, 112in. wide. (Christie's) £1,725 $2,795

A Regency ormolu-mounted rosewood and ebonised sofa, in the manner of George Bullock, the sides of the back with reeded uprights, the front of the arms each with a foliage anthemion mount, above a plain seat-rail, 80in. wide. (Christie's) £11,500 $18,860

A pair of carved parcelgilt sofas, Italian, circa 1880, each with padded back beneath a scrolled rail carved with foliage and centred by a stylised shell, the padded arms, terminating in rosettes, scrolls and anthemia, 152cm. wide. (Sotheby's) £11,500 $18,975

Stickley Brothers settle, attributed, nine vertical slats, three vertical side slats, 65¼in. (Skinner) £1,242 £2,070

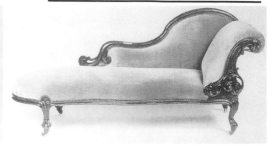

A Victorian mahogany chaise longue, with carved scrolled back and front, on knopped cabriole supports with castors, width 120cm. (Bristol) £680 $1,088

Louis XV Provincial brass mounted bench, late 18th/19th century, with hinged rectangular seat, downscrolled arms with spindle galley, 71in. wide. (Skinner) £1,071 $1,725

Federal mahogany carved square-back upholstered sofa, probably New Hampshire, circa 1815, the straight crest continuing to shaped sides with carved arms, 78½in. wide. (Skinner) £1,464 $2,415

Fine Victorian carved walnut double chair back chaise longue, the pierced and buttoned back above an overstuffed seat, shaped frieze and floral carved cabriole supports. (Lawrences) £1,450 $2,335

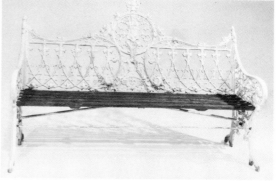

A Coalbrookdale cast iron garden bench of Gothic pattern, the pierced arched tracery back centred with an armorial shield, 60in. wide. (Andrew Hartley) £1,700 $2,720

An Edwardian mahogany sofa, the buttoned back and sprung seat green damask upholstered, on cabriole supports with leaf carving and brass castors, 142cm. wide. (Bristol) £540 $886

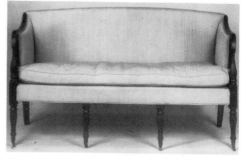

Antique American Sheraton sofa, in mahogany with four ribbed front legs and two rear legs. Cut down from a larger size, 5ft. long. (Eldred's) £619 $990

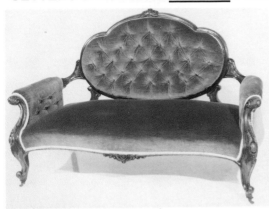

A Victorian carved walnut framed sofa, the oval padded back with arched crest, padded arms on scrolled supports, on cabriole front legs, 16in. wide. (Andrew Hartley) £660 $1,056

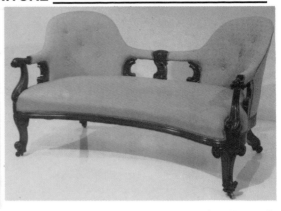

A rosewood framed double backed sofa with scroll carved centre splat, scrolled arms on shaped supports, on flower carved front supports. (Andrew Hartley) £1,100 $1,760

A Knole sofa, early 20th century, upholstered in gilt damask, the rectangular back and sides with acorn shaped finial above a squab cushion, on brass castors, 61½in. wide. (Christie's) £805 $1,288

Cast iron garden settee, John McLean maker, New York, the three-panel pierced back joined to the scrolled arms on the rectangular seat with Gothic valance, painted black, 46in. wide. (Skinner) £522 $862

A George II carved mahogany diminutive camelback sofa, probably 19th century, the shaped back above an overupholstered serpentine-fronted seat flanked by outscrolled arms on shell and leaf-carved knees, 4ft.9in. wide. (Sotheby's) £3,858 $6,325

A Victorian rosewood framed settee with string and marquetry inlay, the serpentine padded back and incurving arms on pierced foliate splats each centred by a marquetry panel depicting a basket of fruit, 59in. wide. (Andrew Hartley) £1,400 $2,240

A Victorian oak and parcel-gilt sofa, with outswept padded arms with scroll-carved arm terminals decorated with imbricated discs and a stylised anthemion, the legs carved with roundels, fluting and stiff-leaf ornament. (Christie's)   £2,875 $4,658

A George III mahogany sofa, the serpentine buttoned padded back, scrolled arms, squab cushion and five loose cushions covered in pale green and yellow cotton, on square legs joined by stretchers, 97in. wide. (Christie's)   £14,375 $23,862

A carved giltwood tête-à-tête sofa, French, of oval form, each section with a padded seat and back within moulded uprights carved with scrolls, divided by acanthus carved arms, on eight cabriole legs, 170cm. wide. (Sotheby's)   £18,400 $30,360

Allessandro Mendini for Alchimia, 'Kandissi' sofa, 1979, walnut veneered wood and painted blue, yellow, pink, white, green, black, blue, upholstered seat, back and rear panel covered in blue, purple, brown, beige and cream fabric, 80in. wide. (Sotheby's)   £12,650 $20,493

A large giltwood canapé, Italian, circa 1870, the padded back within a border of scrolling foliage centred by a coat of arms within a broken pediment, the padded armrests terminating in bold scrolls, 230cm. (Sotheby's)   £8,625 $14,231

A walnut and parcel-gilt day bed, Victorian, circa 1860, with a stuffed arm, padded seat and a loose cushion on gadrooned carved legs and brass carpet castors stamped: *Collinson Patent*, 6ft. 10¾in. long. (Sotheby's)   £3,450 $5,762

A George III giltwood settee, possibly by Thomas Chippendale, the back with a rockwork and C-scroll cresting, the C-scroll arched apron with blind-trellis ground and rockwork border, 93in. wide.
(Christie's)   £40,000 $66,400

A pair of William IV rosewood daybeds, the toprail centred by an eagle-head cresting issuing carved foliage, the ends of the toprail also carved with foliage, the head-end carved with lotus leaves, 85in. wide.
(Christie's)   £11,500 $18,745

A Victorian walnut conversation settee, surmounted by a carved finial, above a padded back and seat, on cabriole legs headed with paterae, 60in. diameter.
(Christie's)   £3,450 $5,520

An important red and brown painted cut-decorated and carved pine bench, New Mexico, circa 1780, the projecting stiles with shaped tops centring a moulded geometrically-shaped crest with five diamond-form splats below. (Sotheby's)   £16,836 $27,600

A Swedish Gustav IV green and cream-painted canapé, early 19th century, the pierced sides with acanthus-carved turned uprights, and fluted supports headed by Egyptian masks above a stiff-leaf carved rail, 72in. wide. (Christie's)   £2,760 $4,471

A Regency mahogany sofa, with a reeded frame carved with paterae, the scrolled top-rail centred with a scallop shell above a padded back, with padded outswept arms, padded seat and bolster cushions, 81in. wide. (Christie's)   £6,325 $10,246

A Regency rosewood scroll end sofa, decorated with scrolling brackets, raised on splay legs and brass paw feet fitted castors, 88in. long.
(Anderson & Garland)   £900 $1,485

Italian Renaissance walnut and marquetry cassapanca, rectangular back over hinged seat, scrolled arms, shaped moulded base, 70½in. long.
(Skinner)   £828 $1,380

Classical mahogany carved veneer sofa, New England, 1820–40, the veneered cylindrical crest ends in leaf carved volutes above an upholstered seat and rolled veneered seat rail on leaf carved supports ending in carved paw feet, 92in. wide.
(Skinner)   £988 $1,610

A William IV style settee with raised camel back and scroll arms, the tapering turned legs mounted with ormolu water leaves upholstered in coral embossed heavy cotton loose weave fabric. (Dee Atkinson & Harrison)   £1,800 $2,970

Carved mahogany and bird's-eye maple veneer Grecian sofa, 1805–20, Middle Atlantic States, with scrolled and reeded arm and foot, continuing to a similar reeded seat rail with inlaid dies, 75in. long.
(Skinner)   £2,257 $3,680

Victorian child-size sofa, in walnut with carved grape and leaf design, 58in. long.
(Eldred's)   £154 $247

Antique American Mammy's bench, in yellow paint with stencilled decoration, unusual long length of 5ft.
(Eldred's)   £466 $770

J.M. Young settle, uneven arm, four side slats, fourteen vertical back slats, paper label, 34½in. high. 81½in. wide, 31½in. (Christie's)   £1,311 $2,185

A French mahogany chaise longue in the Empire taste, the overscrolled back with squab cushion and forward scrolled foot-rest, parts early 19th century, 66in. long. (Christie's)   £2,530 $4,048

A Victorian walnut framed sofa, the padded deep buttoned back with a channelled arched and foliate scroll-carved cresting, curved ends and a serpentine seat, 81in. wide. (Christie's)   £805 $1,288

An Edwardian French walnut framed sofa, the rectangular back and sides with upholstered panels enclosed within moulded and flower carved frame, 187cm. across. (Phillips)   £2,000 $3,200

Arts and Crafts settle, uneven arm, fifteen vertical back slats, five side slats, original dark brown finish, 75½in. wide. (Skinner)   £1,518 $2,530

A Louis Philippe mahogany meridienne, with a reeded frame, downswept back between outswept ends with foliate carved terminals, 65in. wide. (Christie's)   £2,070 $3,312

Modern Louis XVI style green painted and upholstered armchair and ottoman, with Neoclassical-style print cotton in greens, blues, and beige, 37in. high. (Skinner)   £759 $1,265

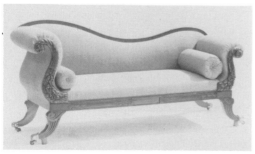

A Regency carved mahogany settee, with damage, 83in. wide. (Dockree's)   £850 $1,402

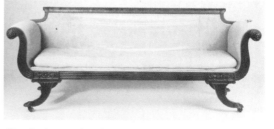

Classical carved mahogany veneer sofa, attributed to the workshop of Duncan Phyfe, New York City, 1815–25, the rolled single panelled crest, above scrolled and reeded arms punctuated with carved rosettes, 85in. long. (Skinner)   £2,822 $4,600

A walnut chaise longue, Victorian, circa 1850, with buttoned back and side above an upholstered seat on turned feet and ceramic castors.
(Sotheby's) £1,035 $1,728

A William IV rosewood framed scroll-end chaise longue, the low curved end with moulded S and leaf scroll back panel, 76in. long.
(Canterbury) £1,400 $2,240

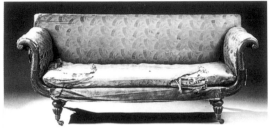

A mahogany sofa, George IV, circa 1825, with a padded back and scrolling ends, with moulded and patera incised frame above lobed turned tapering legs, 6ft.10¾in. wide. (Sotheby's) £3,680 $6,146

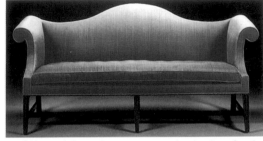

A Chippendale mahogany serpentine-back sofa, the serpentine upholstered back with outward scrolling arms above an over-upholstered seat, 80in. wide.
(Christie's) £3,312 $5,520

A rare Federal grain-painted and parcel-gilt recamier, Baltimore or Philadelphia, circa 1810, the reverse-scrolling armrest joined by a turned crest centring two horizontal stayrails, 6ft.6in. long.
(Sotheby's) £5,963 $9,775

A Chippendale mahogany camelback sofa, Philadelphia, circa 1780, the serpentine crest with outscrolled arms on downswept supports centring a loose fitted cushion, 7ft.8in. long.
(Sotheby's) £47,700 $79,500

A Federal carved mahogany sofa, the scrolled crest in three tablet reserves centring a bow-tied sheaf of wheat flanked by similarly tied straw above an upholstered canted back and arms with downscrolling reeded arms on ring and baluster-turned arm supports, 78½in. wide. (Christie's) £2,070 $3,450

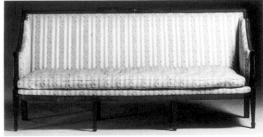

A very fine Federal carved mahogany sofa, attributed to Slover and Taylor, New York, circa 1790, the horizontal moulded crest with projecting spandrel-and leaf-carved tablet, flanked by peaked downswept crossbanded arms, 6ft.7in. long.
(Sotheby's) £6,900 $11,500

A William IV rosewood chaise longue, decorated with foliate carvings, the shaped padded back with outswept padded end above a squab bolster cushion, 78in. long. (Christie's) £2,875 $4,600

A mahogany and upholstered settee, Regency, circa 1810, with a reeded frame, on turned tapering legs now, with ceramic castors, 6ft. wide. (Sotheby's) £3,680 $6,146

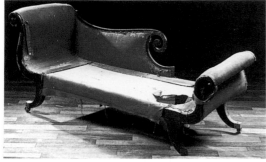

An ebonised chaise longue, Regency, circa 1820, with a scroll back, arm and foot, on sabre legs and castors, 6ft.7½in. long. (Sotheby's) £977 $1,632

A Regency ebonised sofa, decorated with gilt lines, with a downscrolled toprail and rounded padded sides, 84in. long. (Christie's) £1,495 $2,392

A Federal Windsor settee, New England, 1810–1820, the bowed crestrail above four bamboo-turned spindles centring three medallions over eighteen bamboo-turned spindles above downscrolling arms, 66in. wide. (Christie's) £2,208 $3,680

A Regency rosewood scroll ended and scrolled back three seater sofa, having a rectangular section cresting with decorative box stringing, supported on four sabre legs terminating in brass castors, 210cm. (Locke & England) £1,200 $1,980

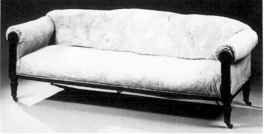

An unusual mahogany and parcel-gilt chaise-longue, probably Austrian, scrolled ends, each with a hinged cover enclosing small counters and glasses, 218cm. wide. (Sotheby's) £13,225 $21,556

An ebonised and upholstered sofa, Victorian, mid-19th century, with anthemion-carved and fluted arm facings, on turned feet, 7ft.2½In. wide. (Sotheby's) £517 $863

A Regency mahogany and inlaid sideboard, in the Sheraton manner, the serpentine shaped top with crossbanding and boxwood stringing. (Phillips) £2,300 $3,680

An early 19th century Scottish mahogany breakfront sideboard, the raised back with sliding compartments, 79½ in. wide. (Andrew Hartley) £2,500 $4,200

A Regency mahogany breakfront sideboard, with ebony string inlay and brass lion mask ring handles, 73in. wide. (Andrew Hartley) £2,700 $4,536

A Beaverman oak sideboard, the adzed rectangular top above three frieze drawers and three fielded panel doors enclosing shelves, 50in. wide. (Christie's) £460 $690

Large early Victorian Renaissance style walnut and burl-walnut sideboard, mid-19th century, with mirrored superstructure, 84½in. long. (Skinner) £2,857 $4,600

A George III mahogany sideboard, with raised stage and turned brass rail, the frieze ebony lined and with two pull-out doors, 187.5cm. wide. (Phillips) £2,900 $4,640

A small Regency figured mahogany pedestal sideboard, the central gallery with raised and rosette moulded back with a single drawer under, 54in. wide. (Dee Atkinson & Harrison) £2,800 $4,620

A mid 19th century mahogany sideboard, the serpentine ledge back enclosed within a leafy scroll carved frame, with central vine cartouche, 232cm. wide. (Phillips) £2,100 $3,360

A Victorian mahogany three tier buffet, the rectangular moulded edge top, base with frieze drawer with remains of paper trade label for *Wilkie & Cockran*, 4ft.5in. (Woolley & Wallis) £1,000 $1,600

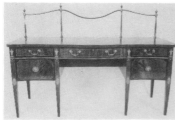

A George III mahogany and inlaid serpentine sideboard, the crossbanded top with boxwood lining and brass rail above a central drawer. 191cm. wide. (Phillips) £2,900 $4,640

Louis XV walnut buffet, rectangular top with rounded corners over a pair of drawers above a pair of cabinet doors, 49½in. wide. (Skinner) £1,794 $2,990

A Victorian mahogany reverse breakfront side cabinet, the rectangular shaped top with three frieze drawers, 54in. wide. (Christie's) £1,150 $1,840

A William IV mahogany pedestal sideboard, the shaped superstructure with shell, lotus and scroll mouldings, 72in. wide.
(Peter Francis)   £800 $1,280

A George III mahogany sideboard, inlaid overall with boxwood lines, the demi-lune top with a band of radiating segments, 78in. wide.
(Christie's)   £8,625 $14,058

Federal mahogany inlaid sideboard, Massachusetts, circa 1810, with shaped top outlined in inlay above a conforming case, 71½in. wide.
(Skinner)   £13,405 $21,850

An early 19th century mahogany sideboard, the top with raised back and plate rest grooves, the front with three drawers to the front with three drawers to the frieze, 7ft.10in.
(Woolley & Wallis) £1,800 $2,988

A Victorian inlaid rosewood sideboard base, the superstructure lacking, 60½in.
(Dockree's)   £460 $736

A Regency mahogany pedestal sideboard, inlaid with boxwood and ebonised lines, the rectangular top containing a frieze drawer, 183cm. wide. (Phillips)   £2,000 $3,280

American mahogany Sheraton/Empire sideboard, with two drawers above case, with two long drawers flanked by two wine drawers, 51½in. long.
(Eldred's)   £1,200 $1,980

A Jacobean style carved oak late 19th century sideboard, 72in. wide.
(Dockree's)   £850 $1,360

Classical carved mahogany and cherry veneer sideboard, Middle Atlantic States, 1840–45, 40in. wide. (Skinner) £1,581 $2,530

A George III mahogany breakfront sideboard of D shape, with string inlay, central frieze drawer over arched apron, 60½in. wide.
(Andrew Hartley)   £4,000 $6,720

Arts and Crafts sideboard, original colour, (replaced drawer bottoms), 54in. wide. (Skinner) £138 $230

A George III mahogany serpentine sideboard, the rectangular top with serpentine-shaped front above a frieze drawer and arch, 68in. wide.
(Christie's)   £29,900 $49,634

A late Georgian mahogany and ebony inlaid stepped bow fronted sideboard, the raised back with three drawers and bowed ends, 82in. wide.
(Andrew Hartley) £1,800 $2,880

An Edwardian mahogany pedestal sideboard, in the manner of William Kent, stamped *Waring and Gillows Ltd,* the panelled back above serpentine top, 250cm. wide.
(Phillips) £6,000 $9,600

A 19th century sideboard of Sheraton design in mahogany with satinwood cross-banding, on six squared tapering legs, 5ft.10in. wide. (Russell Baldwin & Bright)
£1,700 $2,805

A Federal figured maple and pine huntboard, probably Southern, circa 1800, the rectangular top above a frieze drawer flanked by cupboard doors, 5ft.10in. wide.
(Sotheby's) £5,612 $9,200

A George III mahogany serpentine sideboard, banded overall with fruitwood lines and inlaid with fruitwood and ebonised lines, 76¼in. wide.
(Christie's) £10,350 $16,974

A Victorian burr walnut breakfront credenza ornately decorated with inset French porcelain painted panels of flowers and figures, 72in. wide. (Anderson & Garland)
£4,600 $7,590

19th century mahogany, satinwood banded and boxwood and ebony line inlaid bowfronted sideboard with inlaid fan corners, 45in.
(Ewbank) £1,200 $1,980

A William IV mahogany pedestal sideboard, carved with rocaille flames and pendants with gadrooned mouldings, 61in. wide.
(Christie's) £3,220 $5,216

A mahogany bowfront sideboard, early 19th century, fitted with a central drawer above an arched kneehole, 48in.wide.
(Christie's) £1,610 $2,608

A Regency mahogany sideboard with low raised back, fitted with four cross-banded drawers and cupboard, 6ft. wide.
(Russell Baldwin & Bright)
£3,200 $5,280

A thuya, ebony and gilt-bronze credenza, Victorian, circa 1870, in the Etruscan style, the shaped black-veneered top within a cast beaded border, 177.2cm. wide.
(Sotheby's) £4,600 $7,590

A fine and rare Classical marble and ormolu-mounted figured mahogany sideboard, New York City, circa 1815, the concave fronted rectangular top 6ft. wide.
(Sotheby's) £11,224 $18,400

A Regency bronze-mounted fiddleback-mahogany and mahogany pedestal sideboard, in the manner of Thomas Hope, on a concave-fronted plinth base, 97in. wide. (Christie's) £11,500 $19,090

A George IV mahogany pedestal sideboard of breakfront outline, the raised back centred with a foliate and gadrooned scroll cresting, 81in. wide. (Christie's) £2.990 $4.784

A very fine Federal inlaid mahogany sideboard attributed to John Shaw, Annapolis, Maryland, circa 1800, 6ft. wide.
(Sotheby's) £33,321 $54,625

A George IV mahogany sideboard, possibly Irish, of broken outline, the raised top fitted with two stepped knife boxes, each with pierced brass galleries, 90½in. wide.
(Christie's) £4,140 $6,624

A William IV ebonised-inlaid mahogany sideboard, inlaid overall with lines, the everted breakfront top with brass gallery, plate-rack and three veneered panels, 95¾in. wide. (Christie's) £23,000 $38,180

A 19th century Dutch mahogany and marquetry bowfront sideboard, decorated with foliate scrolls, vases of flowers and putti, 154cm. wide.
(Phillips) £3,200 $5,248

A mahogany breakfront sideboard, George III, circa 1790, with satinwood banded top above frieze drawer, 4ft.1in. wide.
(Sotheby's) £1,610 $2,689

An Edward Barnsley walnut sideboard, the rectangular top above two short and three long drawers, flanked by two fielded cupboard doors, stringing decoration, 5ft. wide, 1947.
(Christie's) £3,220 $4,830

A mid-19th century mahogany sideboard, the raised back with foliate S-scrolls and palmettes, 139cm. wide.
(Bearne's) £1,200 $1,980

19th century mahogany, banded and boxwood and ebony line inlaid bowfronted sideboard, with a central drawer flanked by a drawer and cupboard on each side, 67in.
(Ewbank) £1,900 $3,135

A Regency oak and brown-oak side cabinet, the rectangular grey and white-veined marble top above a foliate blind fretwork frieze, 95in. wide. (Christie's) £3,910 $6,412

A George III mahogany bow fronted sideboard with marquetry inlaid urn design top, fitted central drawer flanked by a pair of deep drawers, 5ft6in. (Russell Baldwin & Bright) £2,950 $4,868

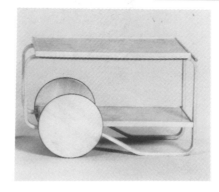

Arts and Crafts plantstand, original finish, 29½in. high.
(Skinner) £241 $402

Alvar Aalto for Finmar, tea trolley (No.98), designed 1935–36, birch, laminated frame, black rubber tyres, 35½in. long.
(Sotheby's) £2,185 $3,539

Arts and Crafts drink stand, original finish, 21½in. wide.
(Skinner) £276 $460

A rosewood and marquetry casket on stand, Charles X, circa 1830, the upper part of sarcophagus form, the hinged top with marquetry foliage, 64cm. wide.
(Sotheby's) £3,450 $5,692

A pair of gilt-bronze and parquetry pedestals, French, circa 1890, in the manner of Riesener, each with a white marble top above a tapering body, 125cm. high.
(Sotheby's) £9,200 $15,180

A mahogany boot rack, part 19th century, the arched top rail with pegs protruding from either side and brass carrying handle, 27¾in. wide. (Christie's) £575 $920

A bentwood hall stand, the arched top flanked by S-shaped bentwood hooks, above slatted projecting shelf and single frieze drawer, 35½in. wide. (Christie's) £345 $517

A large mahogany cheval linen airer, George IV, circa 1825, the two turned and graduated tiers with tapered rectanguar supports, 6ft. wide. (Sotheby's) £1,840 $3,073

Federal mahogany reading stand with canterbury, Albany, New York, early 19th century, the stand above a ring-turned tapering post on a rectangular shaped canterbury, 22¼in. wide.
(Skinner) £1,905 $3,105

Arts and Crafts plantstand, cut-out design, original finish, 30¼in. high. (Skinner) £155 $258

A pair of Colonial padouk tripod torchères, mid-18th century, each with a rosewood hexagonal top with pierced brass gallery, supported by three C-scrolls, 20in. total diameter. (Christie's) £34,500 $57,270

Gustav Stickley magazine stand, no. 72, three shelves, paper label, original finish, 22in. wide. (Skinner) £2,277 $3,795

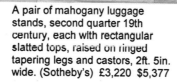

Aesthetic Movement ebonised, polychrome incised, and parcel-gilt pedestal, New York, circa 1878, Kimbel and Cabus, octagonal top, shaped support, stepped plinth base, 37½in. high. (Skinner) £586 $977

A pair of mahogany luggage stands, second quarter 19th century, each with rectangular slatted tops, raised on ringed tapering legs and castors, 2ft. 5in. wide. (Sotheby's) £3,220 $5,377

A Wardle pottery stickstand, tubeline decorated with stylised flowers and foliage on sinuous stems, in shades of brown and yellow, 56cm. high. (Christie's) £460 $690

An Arts and Crafts oak umbrella stand with close-nailed copper decoration, with original drip-pan, 18in. wide. (Christie's) £126 $189

A brass-bound hardwood jardinière, 19th century, of oval shape, with slatted sides, on rectangular splayed legs, 26in. wide. (Christie's) £414 $662

Grain painted pine stand, New England, early 19th century, the top with shaped corners above a single drawer and square tapering legs, 18in. wide. (Skinner) £1,058 $1,725

A verre-eglomisé plinth, circa 1850, the rectangular hinged top painted with flowers above a similarly panelled door, 53cm. wide. (Sotheby's)   £1,495 $2,437

A draughtsman's easel, 19th century, with an adjustable leather stand inset with the points of the compass, 92cm. wide. (Sotheby's)   £4,025 $6,561

An early Victorian walnut folio stand, the pierced ratcheted hinged sides on ring-turned supports and tapering end standards, 31½in. wide. (Christie's) £2,875 $4,658

A mahogany easel, carved all over in the rococo style and headed by a cartouche of C scrolls, acanthus and diapered fretwork, 202cm. (Tennants)   £1,600 $2,560

A pair of brown oak, bamboo and polychrome-decorated jardinières, 2nd half 20th century, of Regency style, each with later tin liner and moulded pentagonal top, 34in. high. (Christie's)   £16,100 $26,243

A French mahogany guéridon, late 19th century, the circular top inset with a mottled rouge marble, on downswept supports, 12½in. diameter. (Christie's) £1,495 $2,392

A mahogany jardinière, late 19th century, decorated with lines and satinwood crossbanding, with a lift-out copper bucket with swing handle, 18½in. high. (Christie's)   £1,092 $1,769

A pair of Chinese mahogany parquetry torchères, circa 1900, each with mother-of-pearl panels birds, flowers and insects, on a parquetry ground, 104cm. high. (Sotheby's)   £2,300 $3,749

A pair of George III mahogany urns and pedestals, each with a lead-lined urn with fluted frieze, ormolu satyr-mask handles and a pinched socle, 19½in. wide. (Christie's)   £84,000 $137,760

A mahogany cutlery stand, late 19th/early 20th century, with two hinged tops between a pierced carrying handle with a rounded end, 21in. wide.
(Christie's)　　£862　$1,379

An Anglo-Indian gold and green-decorated and carved ivory plinth, late 18th/early 19th century, the square stepped top above a foliage-carved pinched neck, 17¾in. square.
(Christie's)　£10,350　$16,974

A French mahogany floor standing jardinière, circa 1880, of rectangular form, the panels with brass beading and twin handles, 23in. high.
(Christie's)　　£1,495　$2,392

A Roman giltwood vase stand, late 18th/early 19th century, the oval moulded top above a fluted frieze and the stand with a scantily draped youth supporting on his head grape-vines, 40½in. high.
(Christie's)　　£8,970　$14,890

A pair of parcel-gilt and green-painted torchères, triangular tapering shaft with foliate clasps, on three panelled and scrolling triangular supports, 38½in. high.
(Christie's)　　£4,600　$7,636

A good Federal black and orange painted pine splayed leg one drawer stand, probably Pennsylvania, circa 1800, the rectangular top above a thumb-moulded frieze drawer, 21¼in. wide. (Sotheby's)　£4,209　$6,900

A patinated iron umbrella stand, mid 20th century, with two hippopotamus feet fitted with circular drip pans and bound with copper piping.
(Christie's)　　£1,265　$2,049

A Regency white-painted and parcel gilt jardinière, the oval well with later metal liner and blind-trellis frieze, possibly European, 22in. wide. (Christie's) £21,850 $35,834

A mahogany walking stick stand, early 20th century, the rectangular base, with drip pan, supporting a turned column with acorn finial, 33in. high.
(Christie's)　　£2,070　$3,312

A walnut and parcel-gilt decorated
X-frame stool, late 19th/early 20th
century, the channelled frame with
beast mask terminals joined by
ring-turned armrests.
(Christie's)   £632 $1,011

A late Regency simulated
rosewood music chair, decorated
with reeded mouldings, the top rail
inlaid with floral brass designs.
(Christie's)   £690 $1,104

A 19th century pouffé, of circular
form, the top worked with gros point
flowers, 67cm. wide.
(Sotheby's)   £1,092 $1,780

A small painted stool, French, early
19th century, the hinged top in the
form of four volumes, 43cm. wide.
(Sotheby's)   £2,300 $3,749

A pair of George II mahogany
stools, each with scrolled
rectangular sides and padded seat,
on cabriole legs headed by scrolling
acanthus, 48in. wide.
(Christie's)   £52,100 $85,444

A walnut-framed stool in the 18th
century manner with leather-
covered drop-in seat, 52.5cm. wide.
(Bearne's)   £1,350 $2,227

A Victorian mahogany footstool,
upholstered in close nailed
buttoned red leather, with hinged
ratcheted supports, 25in. wide,
18in. (Christie's) £862 $1,379

A walnut stool, the square seat
upholstered in 17th century
needlework, with a later tasselled
fringe, on baluster turned legs,
16in. wide. (Christie's) £747 $1,195

A Regency simulated-rosewood
stool, in the manner of Gillows, the
padded scrolled seat above an X-
shaped support joined by a ring-
turned baluster stretcher, 20½in.
wide. (Christie's) £2,875 $4,686

A classical carved mahogany window-seat, School of Duncan Phyfe (1768–1854), New York City, 1810–1820, the rectangular slip-seat flanked by raised double klismos-type splat ends, 46in. wide. (Christie's) £8,970 $14,950

A gilt and ebonised stool, in the manner of Thomas Hope, the stylised panther masks with ring handles, 39in. wide. (Christie's) £1,495 $2,422

A fine and rare Federal carved mahogany bow-fronted window bench, attributed to Duncan Phyfe or one of his contemporaries, New York, circa 1810, 40in. long. (Sotheby's) £12,777 $20,700

A Victorian oak and upholstered stool, the rectangular upholstered seat above a pierced shaped frieze, 20in. wide. (Christie's) £230 $368

A pair of Victorian yew-wood stools, circa 1840, the needlework seats on ring turned legs. (Bonhams) £500 $800

A Louis XVI style giltwood stool, the square padded seat above beaded and stop-fluted rails, 16in. wide. (Christie's) £437 $699

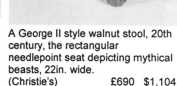

An early 18th century walnut stool, with a slip-in needlework seat on cabriole legs with scroll knees. (Phillips) £1,000 $1,640

An oval walnut stool, on scroll capped and plain turned splay legs to pad feet, 21in. (partly early 18th century). (Woolley & Wallis) £3,000 $4,830

A George II style walnut stool, 20th century, the rectangular needlepoint seat depicting mythical beasts, 22in. wide. (Christie's) £690 $1,104

A fine and rare yellow painted poplar footstool, probably Pennsylvania, late 18th/19th century, the rectangular moulded top with shallow heart-carved decoration, width 11¼in.
(Sotheby's) £2,306 $3,737

A pair of brass stools, each with a padded velvet cushion flanked by four lion heads clasping rings on a folding base, 72cm. wide.
(Sotheby's) £8,050 $13,121

A pair of late Biedermeier beechwood and birch stools, each with a padded saddle seat and ball finials, on sabre legs, 20in. wide.
(Christie's) £3,220 $5,216

A George IV oak and brown oak stool, designed by A.W.N. Pugin, made by Morel and Seddon, the drop-in seat with its original covering of red repp with central embroidered floral motif, 17¼in. square.
(Christie's) £26,450 $43,907

A Provincial walnut and rootwood stool, 18th/19th century, the rounded rectangular dished seat on three branch legs, 19in. high.
(Christie's) £3,450 $5,727

A pair of Charles X bronze-mounted mahogany stools, the sides with outscrolled ends terminating in ram's masks and joined by a turned baluster, 27in. wide. (Christie's) £6,900 $11,454

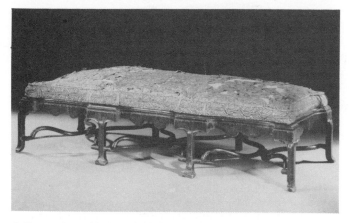

A Queen Anne black and gilt-japanned long stool, possibly by Philip Guibert, the rectangular padded drop-in-seat with eared corners and triple concave cut front, 79½in. wide.
(Christie's)   £51,000 $83,640

A pair of George III white-painted and parcel-gilt window seats, attributed to Gillows, each with waved and outscrolled arm-supports and serpentine seat, 58in. wide. (Christie's) £18,400 $30,176

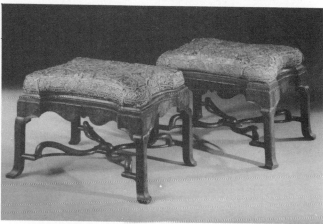

A brass and red velvet throne-stool, circa 1870, in Gothic style, the padded seat and armrests held by a double x-shaped frame.
(Sotheby's)   £7,130 $11,764

A pair of Queen Anne black and gilt-japanned stools, possibly by Philip Guibert, the stool decorated overall with foliage, with a waved apron and square legs joined by a waved X-shaped stretcher, 28½in. wide.
(Christie's)   £117,000 $191,880

A pair of George IV rosewood stools, in the manner of Gillows, each with a dished rectangular padded seat, on channelled X-frame scrolled supports, 20¼in. wide. (Christie's)   £16,100 $26,404

A Regency mahogany stool, the square caned seat flanked by cylindrical sides with a patera to each end, 20½in. wide.
(Christie's)   £8,625 $14,317

An Art Deco figured walnut-veneered dining room suite comprising: a dining table with decagonal ends, 280cm, a bow-front sideboard, a side table, a side table with one drawer, and a set of eight dining chairs including two armchairs. (Bearne's) (Twelve)   £3,600 $5,760

A suite of Continental walnut seat-furniture, second half 19th century, comprising a two-seat sofa, an armchair and two side chairs, each with padded back and seat covered in green and pink cut-velvet, with green and red twisted silk rope fringing and green tasselled apron on ring-turned tapering legs, 60in. wide. (Christie's)   £3,220 $5,345

An Art Deco rosewood and walnut dining suite, comprising: a dining table, 66in. wide, a matching sideboard, and a set of six matching side chairs, including two carvers. (Christie's)   £4,600 $6,900

An Art Deco cream leather lounge suite, sofa with square padded back above padded seat, flanked by rounded armrest, with rosewood panel fronts, on block feet, 83in. wide, and two matching armchairs. (Christie's) £1,610 $2,415

A late Victorian ebonised and inlaid salon suite comprising a lady's and gentleman's chair, six side chairs and a converted piano stool, all with line-inlaid stylised foliate oval centred top-rails, all on turned line-inlaid legs. (Christie's) £1,035 $1,656

Three-piece suite of Biedermeier-style fruitwood and inlay seating furniture, late 19th century, comprising a settee and two armchairs each with shaped back and vertical splats, striped silk upholstery, raised on sabre legs, 67in. long. (Skinner) £2,242 $3,737

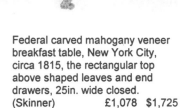

An early Victorian rosewood breakfast table, the circular tilt top with a moulded edge, on a bulbous faceted pedestal, 51in. wide.
(Christie's)   £2,300 $3,680

A George III mahogany and fiddleback-mahogany small breakfast table, the circular tilt-top with reeded edge above a ring-turned baluster shaft, 37¼in. diameter.
(Christie's)   £2,645 $4,390

Federal carved mahogany veneer breakfast table, New York City, circa 1815, the rectangular top above shaped leaves and end drawers, 25in. wide closed.
(Skinner)   £1,078 $1,725

A Victorian rosewood oval breakfast table of shaped outline, the well figured top with moulded edge and plain apron, 60in.
(Canterbury)   £2,600 $4,160

A George III mahogany breakfast table, the rounded rectangular twin-flap top above a frieze-drawer, above a concave-fronted undertier, 39in. wide.
(Christie's)   £9,200 $15,272

A Regency rosewood breakfast-table, geometric tilt-top inlaid with boxwood banding and geometrical patterns and stars, 47in. diam.
(Christie's)   £5,520 $8,997

Classical carved mahogany veneer breakfast table, New York, 1820–30, the rectangular leaves with rounded ends fall above straight veneered skirts, 22¼in. wide.
(Skinner)   £1,438 $2,300

Federal mahogany inlaid breakfast table, attributed to William Whitehead, New York City, 1792–1800, the line-inlaid top with hinged leaves and stringing, 32in. wide.
(Skinner)   £84,062 $134,500

An amboyna breakfast table, George IV, circa 1825, attributed to Gillows, the circular tilt top with a gadrooned border, 4ft.½in. diameter.
(Sotheby's)   £14,950 $24,966

An early 19th century mahogany card table, the D shaped folding top with beaded edged frieze, 35in. wide.
(Andrew Hartley)   £1,275 $2,142

A Victorian walnut folding card table with amboyna banding and string and marquetry inlay, 36in. wide.
(Andrew Hartley)   £1,300 $2,184

A William IV figured mahogany oblong fold over combination tea and card table with swivel top, width 26in.
(H. C. Chapman)   £700 $1,155

An early 18th century Dutch walnut turnover top card table, parquetry work surface with card and counter recesses, 85cm. wide.
(Locke & England) £2,200 $3,630

A Chippendale figured walnut games table, Philadelphia, circa 1780, the hinged rectangular top above a frieze drawer and moulded apron, 32in. wide.
(Sotheby's)   £2,105 $3,450

A kingwood and gilt-bronze envelope card table by Somani, Paris, circa 1890, the segmentally hinged top above a frieze drawer, 58cm. wide.
(Sotheby's)   £4,025 $6,641

A 19th century ebonised and boullework inlaid foldover card table, the serpentine top with central boullework panel, on square section cabriole legs, 89cm. wide.
(Phillips)   £1,400 $2,240

An 18th century red walnut metamorphic games, tea and reading table with triple fold-over top on carved cabriole legs, 2ft.7in. wide. (Russell Baldwin & Bright)
£1,650 $2,722

An Anglo-Colonial brass inlaid hard/rosewood card table, early 19th century, the hinged top decorated with cut floral designs and lines, 36½in. wide.
(Christie's)   £4,830 $7,728

A good Federal brass-mounted carved and figured mahogany lyre-base games table, Boston, Massachusetts, circa 1815, 35¼in. wide.
(Sotheby's)   £7,716 $12,650

A Dutch walnut, burr-walnut and marquetry card table, 18th century and later, the hinged rounded eared rectangular top inlaid with a central vase issuing scrolling flowers and foliage, 29¼in. wide.
(Christie's)   £2,300 $3,818

A George III mahogany revolving work/games table, the moulded rectangular double-hinged top enclosing to one side a compartmentalised interior, 27¼in. wide. (Christie's) £4,025 $6,681

An Edwardian rosewood, marquetry and bone inlaid envelope card table, decorated with meandering floral trails, urns and lines, 23in. wide. (Christie's) £1,955 $3,128

A pair of brass-inlaid scarlet-veneered and ebonised serpentine card tables, late 19th century, inlaid première and contra-partie, with panels of meandering foliage, 36in. wide. (Christie's)   £4,370 $6,992

A walnut card-table, the eared rectangular folding top inlaid with feather banding enclosing a grey suede-lined interior, 33¼in. wide.
(Christie's)   £6,325 $10,499

An early 19th century Sheraton style mahogany and rosewood crossbanded demi-lune card table, plain frieze with satinwood crossbanding and oval inlaid paterae, 92cm. wide.
(Wintertons)   £1,350 $2,160

A mahogany card table, 19th century, decorated with lines, the crossbanded rectangular hinged top enclosing a gilt tooled tan leather writing surface, 33¾in. wide.
(Christie's)   £2,530 $4,099

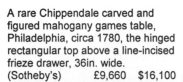

A rare Chippendale carved and figured mahogany games table, Philadelphia, circa 1780, the hinged rectangular top above a line-incised frieze drawer, 36in. wide.
(Sotheby's)   £9,660 $16,100

A rare Chippendale carved and figured mahogany games table, Massachusetts, circa 1770, the hinged oblong chip-carved top with outset corners, depth open 33in.
(Sotheby's)   £12,420 $20,700

A mahogany, kingwood, marquetry and gilt-bronze card table, French, circa 1890, the rectangular shaped folding top within a moulded cast border, 80cm. wide.
(Sotheby's)   £3,680 $6,072

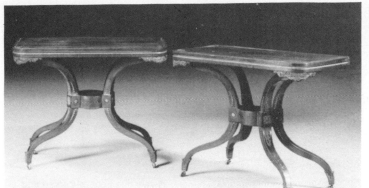

A pair of Regency brass-inlaid and brass-mounted rosewood and parcel-gilt scissor-action card tables, each with a rounded rectangular hinged top, 36¼in. wide. (Christie's)   £18,400 $30,544

A George II red walnut envelope table, the moulded triangular three-flap swivel top above a plain frieze, possibly Irish, 29¼in. diameter.
(Christie's)   £18,400 $30,544

An Irish George II mahogany card table, the rounded eared rectangular hinged top enclosing four oval counter-wells, four circular candle-stands and a green baize-lined playing surface, 37½in. wide.
(Christie's)   £9,200 $15,272

An Edwardian satinwood and polychrome painted envelope card table, decorated with lines, rosewood crossbanding and ribbon-tied floral trails and swags, 25¾in. wide closed.
(Christie's)   £3,680 $5,888

A very fine Federal inlaid mahogany bowfront card table, Massachusetts, circa 1805, the shaped hinged line-inlaid top above a conformingly-shaped conch-shell-inlaid frieze.
(Sotheby's)   £8,418 $13,800

Federal mahogany and flame birch veneer inlaid card table, North Shore, Massachusetts, early 19th century, the edge of the top outlined in banding above the veneered skirt, 34¾in. wide.
(Skinner)   £2,822 $4,600

William IV rosewood folding card table with swivel top, on reeded tapering and foliage carved column with platform base and four scroll and foliage feet, 36in.
(Ewbank)   £720 $1,188

A George III mahogany and satinwood-banded card table, on square tapering boxwood lined legs, headed by chequer banded panels, 38½in. wide.
(Christie's)   £1,380 $2,208

A Classical carved mahogany card-table, New York, 19th century, the lobed hinged top above a conforming apron over a water-leaf-carved support, 36½in. wide.
(Christie's)   £1,173 $1,955

A Biedermeier ebonised and parcel-gilt and Chinese Export lacquer triple-flap games table, early 19th century, the lacquer top mid-18th century, 31in. wide.
(Christie's)   £8,625 $14,317

A very fine Federal carved and figured satinwood and mahogany trick-leg card table attributed to Duncan Phyfe or one of his contemporaries, New York, circa 1815, 35in. deep, open.
(Sotheby's)   £17,250 $28,750

A William IV rosewood card table, lotus and acanthus-carved stem with reeded base, concave-sided platform, 91cm wide.
(Bearne's)   £650 $1,040

One of a pair of Regency rosewood card tables, circa 1810, the crossbanded and boxwood inlaid hinged top above an inlaid frieze with applied gilt-metal and ebonised band, 36in. wide.
(Christie's) (Two) £13,000 $20,800

A Federal inlaid mahogany serpentine-front card-table, mid-Atlantic States, 1790–1810, the serpentine hinged top with banded edge above a conforming veneered frame, 36in. wide.
(Christie's)   £3,105 $5,175

A Chippendale mahogany card-table, Philadelphia, 1760–1770, the rectangular moulded hinged top above a conforming frame, on cabriole legs, 32¼in. wide (open). (Christie's)   £3,105 $5,175

A Regency rosewood and brass marquetry card table, the rounded rectangular swivel top above a shaped frieze, 92cm. wide. (Phillips)   £3,600 $5,904

A 19th century Continental mahogany folding card table, the oblong top inlaid in various woods with ebony banding, 30in. wide. (Andrew Hartley)   £850 $1,360

A Federal inlaid mahogany card-table, probably Virginia, 1790-1810, the hinged demi-lune top above a conforming case with line-inlaid edges, 36in. wide. (Christie's)   £41,100 $68,500

A Classical carved mahogany card-table, New York, 19th century, the rectangular hinged top with canted corners above a conforming apron over four double-baluster supports, 36½in. deep (open). (Christie's)   £1,242 $2,070

An important Federal satinwood-inlaid and figured mahogany demilune games table, labelled *John Seymour & Son, Creek Square, Boston, Massachusetts,* 1794-96, 36in. wide. (Sotheby's)   £334,259 $541,500

A good Federal flame birch-inlaid and figured mahogany serpentine-front games table, Northern Coastal New England, circa 1815, 35in. wide. (Sotheby's)   £3,194 $5,175

A 19th century rosewood card table, the fold over moulded top with cross-banding raised on baluster turned and carved column, 3ft.11in. (Russell, Baldwin & Bright)   £1,220 $2,025

A George IV rosewood and parcel-gilt card-table, the rounded rectangular folding top enclosing a green baize-lined interior, 35¾in. wide. (Christie's)   £2,070 $3,374

A Regency brass-mounted rosewood centre table, the circular top above a frieze and faceted splayed shaft, on a concave-sided triangular base, 47¾in. diameter.
(Christie's)   £5,750 $9,372

Painted cherry and pine table, south eastern New England, 18th century, the rectangular top above a valanced apron, 24½in. wide.
(Skinner)   £9,344 $14,950

Classical carved mahogany veneer centre table, possibly Boston, circa 1840, the circular top with rounded edge on conforming veneered apron, 40½in. diameter.
(Skinner)   £1,222 $1,955

A French kingwood crossbanded and gilt-metal mounted circular bijouterie table, 19th century, the lobed hinged top enclosing an interior with a dish decorated with a roundel in gilt of Louis XIV, 26½in. diameter.
(Christie's)   £3,450 $5,520

A micromosaic, pietre dure and walnut centre table, Italian, circa 1870, the octagonal top inset with various marbles in the form of petals, centred by a veduta of Saint Peter's, 101cm. wide.
(Sotheby's)   £17,250 $28,462

A Regency ormolu-mounted and brass-inlaid rosewood centre table, inlaid overall with boxwood and ebonised lines and banded in fruitwood, 23½in. wide.
(Christie's)   £8,050 $13,363

A gilt-bronze and malachite centre table, Paris, circa 1890, with a rectangular top within a foliate cast border above a frieze drawer, 70cm. wide.
(Sotheby's)   £21,850 $36,052

A pair of giltwood centre tables, one George II, the other of later date, with later moulded rectangular pèche marble top, 39½in. wide.
(Christie's)   £7,475 $12,408

An Art Deco walnut centre table, the circular top above four brushing slides, on four uprights, 30in. wide.
(Christie's)   £517 $775

A French marquetry centre table, 19th century, the top with D-shaped ends and decorated with rinceaux scrolls with flowers, 53in. wide. (Christie's) £1,380 $2,208

A black marble pietre dure and giltwood centre table, the circular top centred by violets and within a band of summer flowers, 77cm. diameter.
(Sotheby's) £20,700 $34,155

A fine carved walnut and gilt-bronze centre table by Millet, Paris, circa 1880, the rectangular rouge marble top within a border cast with flower heads, 129cm. wide.
(Sotheby's) £95,000 $156,750

A George II gilt-gesso centre table, decorated overall with scrolling acanthus on a pounced ground, the dished rectangular top with acanthus and strapwork, 29½in. wide. (Christie's) £31,050 $51,543

A Chinese Export brass-inlaid padouk centre table, late 18th/early 19th century, the reeded circular top inlaid with geometrical brass patterns, with inset panels of pink and grey marble, 45¼in. diameter. (Christie's) £25,300 $41,998

A George III polychrome-decorated and parcel-gilt centre table, the canted rectangular top decorated with a central roundel with doves drinking from a fountain, 29in. high. (Christie's) £2,530 $4,124

An attractive Edwardian inlaid satinwood bowfront centre table, circa 1910, the shaped top inlaid with a diamond of husks and flowerheads, 28¾in. wide. (Christie's) £3,400 $5,440

A Regency giltwood and specimen-marble centre table, the later circular specimen marble top supported by a winged dolphin, 36½in. diameter. (Christie's) £9,200 $15,272

An Irish George II mahogany and Chinese black and gold-lacquer centre table, the moulded rectangular top decorated with a Chinese landscape with figures and birds, 26½in. wide. (Christie's) £51,000 $84,660

A giltwood and marble centre table French, in Régence style, the verde antico marble top above a frieze with carved rosettes, 182cm. wide.
(Sotheby's)   £35,600 $58,740

A Victorian walnut centre table, for displaying cold meats, inset rouge fossilised marble.
(Woolley & Wallis) £700 $1,162

A marble and giltwood centre table, the rectangular green variegated marble top with a moulded giltwood edge supported by four gilt dolphin figures, 80in. wide.
(Christie's)   £2,070 $3,105

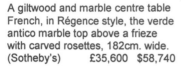

A gilt-bronze and porcelain centre table, Napoleon III, circa 1870, the top with a dished centre painted with a lady at her toilet attended by a gentleman, 80cm. diameter.
(Sotheby's)   £26,450 $43,642

A Tuscan walnut centre table, late 16th/early 17th century, the hexagonal removeable triple-plank top on a tripartite base, each shaped part with an eagle claw foot, 45in. diameter.
(Christie's)   £23,000 $38,180

A 19th century mahogany centre table with applied gilt metal mounts, moulded circular black marble top, 32in. wide.
(Andrew Hartley)   £5,600 $9,408

A rare ebonised and gilt-bronze centre table by Diehl, Paris, circa 1865, the onyx and marble-banded circular top within a moulded border, 124cm. diameter.
(Sotheby's)   £17,250 $28,118

A good Victorian rosewood and marquetry circular centre table, the walnut and marquetry top with central floral garland, 54in. diameter.
(Canterbury)   £7,000 $11,200

An Irish William IV brass-mounted giltwood centre table, the rounded rectangular red leather-lined top crossbanded in ebony, 46¼in. wide.
(Christie's)   £23,000 $37,720

A Continental rococo carved and figured walnut centre table, Portuguese, mid-18th century, the rectangular top above three thumb-moulded frieze drawers, top 8ft. 1in. wide. (Sotheby's)   £5,679 $9,200

An Edwardian rosewood octagonal centre table, satinwood strung with foliate inlay, on four square section tapering legs, 90cm. wide. (Wintertons)   £580 $957

A pair of rosewood centre tables, inlaid overall with fruitwood lines, each with a rectangular top crossbanded in satinwood, incorporating early 19th century parts, 28in. wide. (Christie's)   £9,775 $16,031

A George IV rosewood centre table, the circular tilt-top banded in burr-elm and with gadrooned edge, above a plain frieze, 28in. diam. (Christie's)   £17,250 $28,290

A pietre dure micromosaic and walnut centre table by Orlandi Aristide, Rome, dated 1897, the shaped top inset with a patchwork of sample marbles, 113cm. wide. (Sotheby's)   £16,675 $27,514

A Regency brass-mounted and inlaid rosewood centre table, the circular hinged tilt-top with three foliage motifs, above a plain frieze with three ebony-inlaid patera panels, 53½in. diameter. (Christie's)   £17,250 $28,290

A Regency rosewood, simulated-bamboo, red and gilt-japanned and parcel-gilt centre table, the octagonal crossbanded top above a plain frieze, 51½in. diameter. (Christie's)   £13,800 $22,632

A German pewter-inlaid rosewood, specimen marble and parcel-gilt centre table, second quarter 19th century, inlaid overall with lines, 59¾in. wide. (Christie's)   £5,750 $9,545

A George IV oak, brown-oak and parcel-gilt centre table, the circular radiating veneered tilt-top above a plain frieze with beaded edge, 51½in. diameter. (Christie's)   £9,200 $15,088

An oak rectangular console table, Victorian, circa 1860, profusely carved in the Kent style, with foliage and a central mask on cabriole legs, 4ft.5½in. high.
(Sotheby's) £1,725 $2,881

A good giltwood console table, the later chinoiserie decorated rectangular top depicting figures and a pavilion in a watery landscape, basically early 18th century, 47¼in. wide.
(Christie's) £3,200 $5,120

An Irish George II mahogany console table, the rounded rectangular moulded top above a plain frieze and an acanthus-scrolled carved shaped apron centred by a scallop-shell, 41½in. wide.
(Christie's) £24,150 $40,089

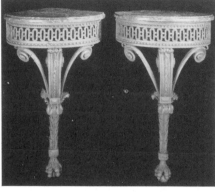

Whimsical carved ebonised oak console table, late 19th century, serpentine Carrara marble top, the base carved as mermaids atop dolphins, 27½in.
(Skinner) £1,500 $2,415

A pair of carved and stained demi-lune corner consoles, each with a variegated marble top and a bead and pierced stylised guilloche frieze, 18½in. wide.
(Christie's) £2,185 $3,540

A Victorian walnut serpentine console table and mirror, decorated with foliate-carved C-scrolls, on carved cabriole legs, 52in. wide.
(Christie's) £5,750 $9,200

A George II carved giltwood console in the manner of Matthias Lock, surmounted by a serpentine siena marble top, the pierced apron with a bearded mask, the top 130 x 68cm. (Phillips) £90,000 $147,600

A late 18th century painted and parcel gilt console table, with later rectangular white marble top, the frieze with a band of waterleaf and lambrequin, possibly Piedmont, 112cm. wide.
(Phillips) £1,600 $2,624

One of a pair of North German giltwood console tables, late 17th/early 18th century, probably Hannover, each with a rectangular dished top with a central female figure holding drapery, 31in. wide.
(Christie's) (Two) £20,700 $34,362

An oak extending dining table, parts first half 19th century, the circular acanthus-lapetted and foliate collared column, with incurved quadripartite base, 59in. diameter. (Christie's) £2,760 $4,416

Classical carved and veneered mahogany extension dining table, New York City, circa 1840, circular top with moulded edge, 48in. diameter, together with seven leaves. (Skinner) £4,485 $7,475

An early 19th century mahogany dining table, the round moulded edge tilt top on turned baluster column, 47in. wide. (Dreweatt Neate) £580 $957

Louis XVI style brass mounted mahogany extension dining table, late 19th/20th century, circular top with drop leaves, raised on six circular tapering legs ending in casters, 43¼in. wide. (Skinner) £5,520 $9,200

A Victorian mahogany oval extending dining table, the rounded top with moulded edge above a plain frieze, 93¼in. extended. (Christie's) £1,265 $2,024

Gustav Stickley dressing table, no. 907, paper label, Gustav Stickley red mark, 48in. wide.
(Skinner) £1,380 $2,300

A fine satinwood-veneered Holland and Sons dressing table, with pierced arcaded brass gallery, the five drawers about an arch, 54in.
(David Lay) £520 $832

A marquetry dressing table, 19th century, in two sections, inlaid in various woods and with geometric patterns, flowers and foliage, 41in.
(Christie's) £8,050 $13,122

A Victorian walnut pedestal dressing table with oblong mirror on scrolled supports, eight pedestal drawers flanking a lower central frieze drawer, 59in. wide.
(Andrew Hartley) £1,150 $1,932

Painted and decorated dressing table, New England, early 19th century, the shaped back splash with gold and green stencilled decoration above a green and mustard gold grained surface, 32¼in. wide.
(Skinner) £863 $1,380

Federal mahogany carved and mahogany veneer brass inlaid dressing table, probably New York State, circa 1825, the cockbeaded rectangular mirror on scrolled acanthus leaf carved supports, 36¼in. wide.
(Skinner) £1,045 $1,725

A French table à toilette, veneered in kingwood and tulipwood, moulded cabriole legs, 24.5cm.
(Woolley & Wallis) £1,750 $2,818

A late George III mahogany and line-inlaid enclosed dressing chest, with twin hinged flaps opening to a multiple compartmented interior with central ratcheted mirror, 30in. wide. (Christie's) £1,035 $1,656

A Classical mahogany dressing-table, probably New York, Mid-19th century, in two sections: the upper section with an arched mirror and conforming frame, 29½in. wide.
(Christie's) £1,932 $3,220

Queen Anne style oak dressing table, rectangular moulded top over a frieze with three drawers, shaped apron, 32¼in. long.
(Skinner)   £607 $978

An Edwardian gentleman's mahogany dressing table crossbanded with string inlay, brass towel rail to the side, 21in. wide.
(Andrew Hartley)   £1,400 $2,352

A Regency mahogany gentleman's dressing chest, the divided folding top enclosing mirror and compartments, 71cm wide.
(Phillips)   £1,650 $2,640

Painted and decorated dressing table, New Hampshire or Massachusetts, early 19th century, the shaped splashboard above a table top with a single drawer below, 34½in. wide.
(Skinner)   £697 $1,150

Eldred Wheeler Queen Anne-style lowboy, in tiger maple, top with moulded edge and inset slate, one long drawer over three narrow drawers, 31½in. wide.
(Eldred's)   £1,100 $1,760

A walnut and floral marquetry kneehole dressing table/writing desk, split hinged top inlaid with vases of flowers, late18th century English, 26in. wide.
(Andrew Hartley)   £1,600 $2,640

Queen Anne walnut dressing table, probably Rhode Island, circa 1760, the overhanging top with moulded edge and shaped corners, 31in. wide. (Skinner)   £9,758 $16,100

A Cotswold School walnut dressing chest, with rectangular swing-plate mirror above rectangular top, above a bank of two short and three long drawers, 33½in. wide.
(Christie's)   £747 $1,120

Gustav Stickley vanity and chair, no. 914, original finish, (chair missing stretcher), 36in. wide.
(Skinner)   £2,932 $4,887

Antique American Sheraton drop-leaf table, in tiger maple with turned legs, top 36 x 19in. plus two 11in. drop leaves. (Eldred's) £688 $1,100

Antique American Sheraton drop-leaf two-part dining table, with shaped ends and turned legs, 21in. drop leaves, top 46 x 20½in. (Eldred's) £1,238 $1,980

Classical carved mahogany inlaid breakfast table, New York, 1820–30, the top with brass inlay in outline and stamped brass on the edge of the shaped leaves, 39in. wide. (Skinner) £1,481 $2,415

A Queen Anne carved and figured walnut drop-leaf dining table, Pennsylvania, 1730–50, the rectangular top centring a shaped apron, width open 4ft.6½in. (Sotheby's) £1,578 $2,587

A Sheraton style oval mahogany and satinwood crossbanded drop-leaf Pembroke table, fitted single end drawer, on square tapering block legs, oval 82cm. (Wintertons) £750 $1,238

A Chippendale carved mahogany drop-leaf table, Newport, 1780–1800, the rectangular top with hinged leaves, on stop-fluted Marlborough legs, 40½in. wide. (Christie's) £19,320 $32,200

A Victorian burr walnut oval Sutherland table, on turned columns with cabriole supports, 104cm. wide. (Bristol) £600 $960

Classical carved mahogany veneer breakfast table, New York, 1820–25, the shaped drop leaves with reeded edge above four spiral-carved supports, 25¹/₃in. wide. (Skinner) £1,199 $1,955

American drop-leaf table, 18th century, in cherry, with carved reeded legs, 39in. long, leaves 13in. (Eldred's) £300 $495

Chippendale walnut drop leaf dining table, possibly Pennsylvania, late 18th century, with shaped skirt and moulded Marlborough legs, 15½in. wide. (Skinner)　£318　$518

A mid Victorian burr walnut Sutherland table, the moulded edge drop flap top of undulating outline on four moulded and carved cabriole legs, 35½in. wide. (Dreweatt Neate)　£1,550　$2,557

Antique American Sheraton drop-leaf table, mahogany, turned and ribbed legs, top 42 x 18in. with two 14½in. drop leaves with rounded corners. (Eldred's)　£258　$412

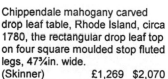

Chippendale mahogany carved drop leaf table, Rhode Island, circa 1780, the rectangular drop leaf top on four square moulded stop fluted legs, 47¾in. wide. (Skinner)　£1,269　$2,070

Antique American butterfly table, in walnut, single drawer, turned legs and box stretcher, top 24 x 11in. with two 11in. leaves. (Eldred's)　£550　$880

A Chippendale carved mahogany drop-leaf table, Pennsylvania, circa 1760, the oblong top flanked by rectangular leaves, width open 45in. (Sotheby's)　£4,560　$7,475

Small Queen Anne cherry dining table, New England, circa 1760, the circular overhanging drop-leaf top above a valanced apron, 35in. diameter. (Skinner)　£25,788　$42,550

A mahogany drop-leaf table, early 19th century, the rounded rectangular top with a moulded edge, a pair of cock-beaded drawers to the frieze, 55in. wide. (Christie's)　£1,265　$2,024

A Federal figured maple drop-leaf table, New England, circa 1810, the oblong top with shaped leaves above a frieze drawer, 39in. wide. open. (Sotheby's)　£2,415　$4,025

An early 19th century mahogany drum table, the leather inset top with narrow banded edge, eight alphabetically lettered drawers, 108cm. diameter.
(Bristol)   £4,600 $7,360

A George IV oak drum-top library table with four real and four false drawers to the frieze, 104cm.
(Bearne's)   £1,550 $2,480

A late Georgian mahogany rent table, the octagonal top having green leather inset writing surface over eight drawers with satinwood banding, 4ft. diameter. (Russell Baldwin & Bright) £5,000 $8,250

A Regency mahogany drum table, the octagonal moulded top with green leather-lined writing surface above four ash-lined frieze drawers and four simulated frieze drawers, 41½in. diameter.
(Christie's)   £9,200 $15,088

A George IV mahogany small drum table, the moulded circular top above a frieze drawer and five simulated frieze drawers, on a reeded flared shaft, 23in. diameter.
(Christie's)   £6,325 $10,120

A Regency ebony-inlaid satinwood and ebonised drum table, the circular top with foliate-inlaid border with calamander crossbanding, above four hinged mahogany-lined drawers, 47¼in. wide.
(Christie's)   £27,600 $45,816

A Regency mahogany drum table, inlaid overall with ebonised lines, the crossbanded top with pale-cream and gilt-tooled leather, 47½in. diameter.
(Christie's)   £3,000 $4,800

A George III rosewood and marquetry library drum table, by Thomas Chippendale, crossbanded overall, the circular revolving green leather-lined top with moulded edge, 56¾in. diameter.
(Christie's) £320,500 $525,620

A mahogany drum table, 19th century, the circular red-leather lined top above four drawers and four simulated drawers, 47in. diameter.
(Christie's)   £2,500 $4,000

500

A Jacobean Country gateleg table in walnut with oval top, small drawer and twist-turned supports, 3ft.8in. x 4ft.9in. open, the top probably of later date.
(Russell Baldwin & Bright)
£1,500 $2,400

A walnut gateleg table, late 17th century, the oval top above compound baluster supports with moulded oblong stretchers, width open 5ft. 9½in.
(Sotheby's)   £6,670 $11,139

Victorian walnut Sutherland table with two shaped drop flaps, raised on foliate pierced supports, 36½in.
(G.A. Key)   £700 $1,120

A late 17th century/early 18th century oak gateleg table, on baluster turned legs joined by square stretchers, 160cm. wide.
(Bearne's)   £1,600 $2,640

A William and Mary style miniature oak drop-leaf oval gateleg table, the shaped top above a plain frieze, width extended 26in.
(Sotheby's)   £1,052 $1.725

A late 17th/early 18th century oak gateleg table with oval top, frieze drawer and on baluster and ball-turned legs, 121cm. wide.
(Bearnes)   £620 $992

An early 18th century oak gateleg table with rectangular top on baluster turned and squared legs and stretchers, 2ft.6in x 3ft.4in.
(Russell Baldwin & Bright)
£3,300 $5,280

A Heals oak drop-leaf table, the oval top on ring-turned uprights joined by square stretchers on shaped feet, 55in. wide.
(Christie's)   £218 $327

An Edwardian satinwood Sutherland table, crossbanded with string inlay, moulded edged shape oblong top, 24in. wide.
(Andrew Hartley)   £840 $1,344

Federal mahogany carved and mahogany veneer two-part banquet table, Massachusetts, circa 1825, the D-shaped tops with reeded edges and rectangular drop leaves, 75in. long. (Skinner) £1,045 $1,725

Federal cherry and bird's-eye maple two-part dining table, New England, 1820–25, the two rectangular ends each with a hinged drop-leaf, 82in. wide. (Skinner) £1,045 $1,725

An oak refectory table, the cleated end planked top with canted corners an arcaded thumb carved frieze, 7ft.3in. long. (Woolley & Wallis) £2,300 $3,818

A late Regency mahogany hunting table, the top of demi-lune form with drop flap ends and reeded edge, 183cm. wide. (Phillips) £5,000 $8,000

A 19th century plain walnut extending dining table, on turned fluted supports with brass castors, with one leaf, overall length 222.5cm. (Bristol) £1,700 $2,805

A late Victorian oak extending dining table, including five extra leaves, the circular top when closed above a plain frieze, on ring-turned reeded tapering legs, 190in. fully extended. (Christie's) £4,025 $6,520

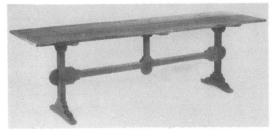

Oak and pine table, probably New England, 18th century, the rectangular top on three chamfered cleats and two shaped legs resting on trestle feet and joined by a shaped medial stretcher, 92½in. wide. (Skinner) £5,390 $8,625

An early 19th century circular mahogany extending dining table, with boxwood and ebony stringing, on a large bulbous reeded baluster and acanthus leaf and reed stage, 248cm. long. (Tennants) £2,000 $3,200

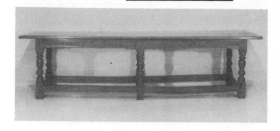

An oak side table with plank top, fluted frieze, six baluster turned legs, 120in. long, 17th century and later. (Andrew Hartley) £3,000 $5,040

A Victorian mahogany extending dining table, two extra legs added, 72½in. long, 53in. wide. (Dockree's) £950 $1,520

Federal cherry drop-leaf dining table, New England, 1820s, the rectangular leaves and straight skirt above spiral carved tapering legs, 45in. wide. (Skinner) £296 $488

A fine and rare classical carved and figured mahogany two-pedestal dining table, Anthony Quervelle, Philadelphia, circa 1825, in two parts, 8ft. long open. (Sotheby's) £11,358 $18,400

A late George III mahogany extending dining table, the reeded edge top with rounded corners, turned fluted legs on brass caps and castors (two extra leaves), 87in. extended. (Dreweatt Neate) £5,400 $8,910

A late Victorian mahogany extending dining table, 87in. long, 45in. wide. (Dockree's) £1,050 $1,680

George III mahogany two-pedestal dining table, early 19th century, top with reeded edge, turned support, moulded tripartite base ending in brass paw feet, 48in. wide. (Skinner) £2,070 $3,450

A late 19th century mahogany extending dining table, rounded ends, moulded edge, plain frieze, carried on carved cabriole legs, elaborate shoulders, ball and claw feet, 243 x 136cm. (Locke & England) £1,400 $2,310

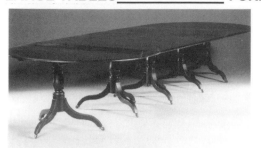

A Regency Provincial mahogany five-pedestal dining table, comprising two semi-circular tilt-top end-sections, three tilt-top central pedestals and a narrow leaf, 13ft.2in. long, fully extended.
(Christie's) £13,800 $22,908

An early 19th century mahogany concertina action extending dining table with reeded edge to the rounded rectangular top and on tapering ring-turned legs, 293cm. including four extra leaves.
(Bearne's) £4,600 $7,590

A William IV mahogany extending dining table, including three extra leaves, the rounded rectangular top with a moulded edge, on ring-turned reeded tapering legs, 94in. long. (Christie's) £7,475 $12,109

A Regency mahogany extending dining table, the round cornered crossbanded top with reeded edge raised on four detachable reeded baluster legs, 210cm. long. (Tennants) £3,500 $5,600

A late Regency mahogany extending dining table by Gillows, including four extra leaves, the rounded rectangular top on ring-turned reeded tapering legs, 130in. extended. (Christie's) £6,900 $11,040

A Victorian mahogany extending dining table, including two extra leaves, with a moulded edge and a later plain frieze, 110in. fully extended.
(Christie's) £4,025 $6,440

A William IV mahogany triple pedestal extending dining table, comprising two D-ends, a central section and two extra leaves, on tapering columns with stylised lotus and roundel decoration, 130in. fully extended. (Christie's) £19,550 $31,280

A late Classical mahogany veneered dining-table, American, 1835–1850, in three parts, the two ends each with a semicircular top with a single hinged rectangular drop-leaf above a comforming veneered apron, 45½in. wide. (Christie's) £3,450 $5,750

A Victorian walnut circular library table, the leather-lined top above a panelled frieze, on turned reeded and fluted tapering legs, 72in. diam. (Christie's)   £1,552 $2,483

A George IV mahogany library table, the eared rectangular green leather-lined top above a panelled frieze with three mahogany-lined drawers to each side, 81¼in. wide. (Christie's)   £17,250 $28,635

A late George III mahogany library table, the top inset with a panel of tooled leather, the frieze with a hinged dummy drawer fall to either side, 58½in. wide. (Christie's)   £2,760 $4,471

A William IV mahogany library table, the rectangular top inset with gilt tooled tan leather-lined writing surface above a frieze, 48in. wide. (Christie's)   £3,450 $5,589

Regency satinwood, calamander, part ebonised, and parcel-gilt circular library table, circa 1810, 28½in. high, 42in. diameter. (Skinner)   £4,485 $7,475

Gustav Stickley library table, worn original finish and leather, 30in. high, 40in. diameter. (Skinner)   £828 $1,380

A George IV mahogany library table, the top crossbanded in rosewood above a pair of frieze drawers opposing false drawers, 42in. wide. (Dreweatt Neate) £3,200 $5,280

A Regency ebony-inlaid mahogany and ebonised library table, the rectangular twin-flapped top with removable book-stops, 59½in. wide open. (Christie's) £7,475 $12,408

A mid-Victorian Gothic Revival oak library table, the octagonal top with green leather surface, above deep apron and four frieze drawers, 56½in. wide. (Christie's)   £862 $1,379

An Aesthetic carved maple library-table, stamped *Herter Brothers.* (Christie's)   £15,180 $25,300

Gustav Stickley desk, centre drawer flanked by two side drawers, original worn finish, 50in. deep. (Skinner)   £448 $748

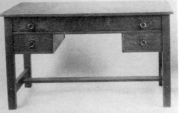

Lifetime library table, no. 929, original finish, 50in. wide. (Skinner)   £759 $1,265

Gustav Stickley hexagonal table, stacking stretcher-form, work to top, original finish on base, 46¾in. wide. (Skinner) £1,380 $2,300

A Swiss walnut and marquetry occasional table, early 19th century, the shaped top inlaid with an oval medallion depicting mountain goats and an eagle, 25½in. wide. (Christie's) £517 $827

Classical carved mahogany veneer table, Philadelphia, circa 1827, the rectangular top with moulded edge above a cockbeaded frieze with a single central working drawer, 45¼in. wide. (Skinner) £1,581 $2,530

Painted oval table, New England, 18th century, the pine top overhangs a stretcher base table with splayed vase and ring-turned legs, 30¼in. wide. (Skinner) £2,751 $4,485

A 19th century rosewood boudoir table, kidney shaped with string and marquetry inlay, 23in. wide. (Andrew Hartley) £1,450 $2,393

THE ART OF HOUSE CLEARANCE

If you have decided to employ auctioneers for the purpose of house clearance, ask them to make an initial appraisal before getting to grips with the task of shifting the unsaleable.

Their daily involvement in the marketplace equips them to earmark and assess those pieces of furniture and other personal property which others might dismiss as valueless. The 'art' of house clearance is not a misnomer, and it is wise to consult those best practised in the skill.

Amersham Auction Rooms

A mahogany and kingwood drinks table, Victorian, circa 1880, opening to reveal a raising glass tray, 96cm. wide. (Sotheby's) £6,900 $11,385

A George III rectangular mahogany reading table, the gun barrel turned adjustable pillar with screw action stop, 20½in. (Dreweatt Neate) £700 $1,155

A Victorian mahogany 33in. tripod table. (Dockree's) £150 $248

A 19th century rosewood wine table with circular top, faceted tapering stem with scrolled brackets, 18in. wide. (Andrew Hartley) £520 $874

A 19th century Chinese padouk wood table, the top with scrolled ends terminating in carved dragon heads, 46in. wide. (Andrew Hartley) £680 $1,142

A good Regency inlaid mahogany reading table, the adjustable top on a ring-turned column, 42cm. wide. (Bristol) £820 $1,353

Paint decorated papier mâché and pine tilt-top stand, attributed to Litchfield Mfg. Co., Litchfield, Connecticut, mid-19th century, 17in. diameter. (Skinner) £1,603 $2,645

A good William IV rosewood bed reading table, the veneered rectangular top with a lidded compartment and a pair of flaps on easels 35in. (Woolley & Wallis) £1,000 $1,660

A Regency mahogany reading table with adjustable square top on baluster turned column and reeded tripod base, 15 x 17in. (Russell, Baldwin & Bright) £800 $1,320

A fine George II style occasional table with circular pietra-dura top on tapering moulded and carved pillar support, 15½in. diameter. (Dee Atkinson & Harrison) £2,400 $3,960

A Victorian campaign mahogany folding table, the central butler's tray with raised sides and pierced carrying handles, on an X framed stand, 83½in. extended. (Dreweatt Neate) £1,100 $1,793

An early Victorian rosewood occasional table, with moulded edged canted square top on collared and lobed baluster stem, 15½in. wide. (Andrew Hartley) £1,100 $1,848

A J & J Kohn bentwood occasional table designed by Joseph Hoffman, circa 1905, the circular top with fabric surface, 24in. wide. (Christie's) £575 $863

A Hille bird's-eye maple occasional table, the rectangular top with fluted edge and inset with black glass top, 33½in. wide. (Christie's) £552 $828

Queen Anne maple and pine table, New England, late 18th century, with a scrubbed top above a straight skirt with beaded edge. 28 x 28½in. (Skinner) £1,552 $2,530

A George III mahogany painting-table, the moulded rectangular hinged top above a fitted interior, above a fitted drawer and a further drawer, 24¾in. wide. (Christie's) £805 $1,312

A George II yew-wood architect's table, the rounded rectangular crossbanded moulded top, inlaid with boxwood and ebonised lines, on a ratcheted support, 36in. wide. (Christie's) £4,025 $6,681

A red stained pine pedestal table, Cimmarron, New Mexico, circa 1860, in two parts, the oval top rotating above a tapering urn-form support on four shaped cabriole legs, 32in. wide. (Sotheby's) £1,122 $1,840

Italian Neoclassical mahogany, parcel-gilt and marble gueridon, early 19th century, circular Carrara marble top over a plain frieze, 24½in. diameter. (Skinner) £3,105 $5,175

A chess table with glazed cover, the rectangular moulded top with an inlaid chess board beneath a detachable glazed cover, 2ft.5½in. wide. (Sotheby's) £1,380 $2,305

Queen Anne painted pine table, New England, 18th century, the oval top overhangs a painted base with straight moulded skirt, 26¼in. high. (Skinner) £9,172 $14,950

A Paul Kiss wrought iron and marble gueridon, the circular marble top supported on hammered wrought iron base, with inswept uprights, 20in. wide.
(Christie's)   £2,760 $4,140

A mahogany octagonal tip-top table George III, circa 1790, crossbanded with satinwood, upon a reeded stem, 2ft.4in. wide.
(Sotheby's)   £4,370 $7,298

A George III mahogany tripod table, the dished circular moulded tilt-top above a bird-cage support and spirally-fluted column, 19¾in. diam.
(Christie's)   £5,750 $9,545

An Empire burr-elm and ormolu-mounted vide-poche, early 19th century, the rectangular well top with a thin leaf band above a single mahogany lined frieze drawer, 1ft. 7½in. wide.
(Sotheby's)   £13,800 $23,046

A matched pair of mahogany and brass-mounted oval guéridons, late 20th century, each with a pierced three-quarter gallery and marble top, 18¾in. wide.
(Christie's)   £1,150 $1,863

A mahogany circular tripod table, the dished tilt-top with ribbon and rosette border, on a stop-fluted and acanthus-clasped ring-turned baluster support, 29½in. diameter.
(Christie's)   £4,600 $7,498

George III mahogany tilt-top tripod table, third quarter 18th century, oval moulded top raised on a plain and fluted standard, 33½in. wide.
(Skinner)   £759 $1,265

A mahogany tray top table, William IV, circa 1835, the panelled and moulded oblong top on a turned tapering stem, 2ft.7in. wide.
(Sotheby's)   £3,220 $5,377

A kingwood and marquetry table ambulante, French, late 19th century, in Louis XV style, the mottled red marble top within a shaped and moulded border, 1ft. 6in. wide.
(Sotheby's)   £2,070 $3,457

A George II mahogany draughtsman or architect's desk, with a double ratcheted elevating top with later rest, having a frieze compartment with pen drawer to the side, the top 106 x 59cm. (Phillips) £4,000 $6,560

A Victorian painted cast-iron and oak lectern, third quarter 19th century, the rectangular moulded top with a ledge, 28in. high. (Sotheby's) £351 $575

A kingwood table, Louis-Philippe, the serpentine top inset with an oval panel of painted porcelain, 1ft.7½in. wide. (Sotheby's) £1,610 $2,689

A Victorian yew wood and parquetry inlaid circular occasional table, circa 1840, the circular top inlaid with various exotic woods above a band frieze, 17½in. diameter. (Christie's) £680 $1,088

A pair of Edwardian satinwood and rosewood occasional tables, each banded overall in boxwood and ebony lines, the oval crossbanded galleried top centred by an oval fan motif, 24¼in. wide. (Christie's) £4,025 $6,681

A George II mahogany, brass and mother-of-pearl inlaid supper table attributed to Frederick Hintz, the decagonal lobed dished snap top with raised centre and cinquefoil centre, 70cm. diameter. (Phillips) £85,000 $139,400

An antique fruitwood pillar table with octagonal top, 15in. diameter. (Russell Baldwin & Bright) £1,520 $2,508

A mahogany and inlaid bijouterie table, the hinged rectangular top with an oval glass panel, 74cm. wide. (Tennants) £2,200 $3,520

A George IV mahogany coaching-table, by Hindley and Sons, with hinged X-frame support joined by a baluster stretcher and rounded eared folding top, 36in. wide open. (Christie's) £4,370 $7,254

A walnut draw leaf table, French, 16th/17th century, upon nine columnar supports with a double cruciform flat stretcher, 4ft. 1in. wide. (Sotheby's) £12,650 $21,125

A Victorian mahogany and marquetry octagonal table, the top veneered with radiating stellar, geometric and lozenge designs, 29in. wide. (Christie's) £2,070 $3,312

Painted Queen Anne black walnut and pine table, Pennsylvania, 1760–1800, the removeable plank three-board pine top above two thumb-moulded drawers, 48½in. wide. (Skinner) £1,509 $2,415

A 19th century rosewood and parcel gilt specimen marble top pedestal table, the circular moulded top with a radiating design in coloured marbles, 68cm. diameter. (Phillips) £2,700 $4,428

George III mahogany bird cage tripod table. (Christopher Matthews) £2,500 $4,125

A 19th century rosewood and marquetry inlaid two tier occasional table with shaped top and undertier, on cabriole supports having ormolu mounts, 2ft.2in. wide. (Russell Baldwin & Bright) £470 $775

A William and Mary cherrywood chamber-table, on compressed ball and block-turned legs on bun feet, 30½in. wide. (Christie's) £3,450 $5,750

A French rosewood display table, 19th century, applied with ormolu mounts, the rectangular glazed hinged top enclosing a fabric lined interior, 32in. wide. (Christie's) £2,070 $3,312

A Russian gilt-bronze and malachite guéridon, 19th century, the frieze with swans, swags and garlands, 60cm. diameter. (Sotheby's) £23,000 $37,490

A Sheraton mahogany and box strung oval Pembroke table, the frieze drawer opposed by a dummy, 87cm. wide. (Bristol) £480 $792

A George III mahogany Pembroke table, crossbanded with string inlay, rounded oblong top, 35½in. wide. (Andrew Hartley) £800 $1,320

A George III mahogany Pembroke table, crossbanded with string inlay, oval top, frieze drawer with brass handles, 30in. wide. (Andrew Hartley) £2,600 $4,368

A Federal inlaid mahogany Pembroke table, Eastern Connecticut or Rhode Island, 1795–1810, the rectangular moulded bowed top with line-inlay enclosed by hinged shaped leaves, 33in. wide. (Christie's) £6,900 $11,500

A George III satinwood, kingwood crossbanded and harewood inlaid Pembroke table, the quarter veneered hinged top centred by an oval medallion with a frieze below and a dummy drawer to the reverse, on square chamfered legs terminating in castors, 103cm. wide. (Phillips) £2,800 $4,592

A late 19th century mahogany Pembroke table with inlaid top having husk pendant decoration on turned tapering supports, 3ft.6in. max. wide. (Russell Baldwin & Bright) £1,300 $2,145

A George III palisander and kingwood crossbanded Pembroke table, circa 1790, the top with rounded rectangular above an end frieze drawer, 32in. long. (Christie's) £1,200 $1,920

A George III mahogany Pembroke table with rounded oblong top, frieze drawer, square tapering supports, 30in. wide. (Andrew Hartley) £1,000 $1,600

A George III mahogany Pembroke table, circa 1775, the crossbanded top centrally inlaid with an oval, the serpentine leaves with outset corners, 35½in. wide open. (Christie's) £3,000 $4,800

A Chippendale mahogany Pembroke table, Philadelphia, 1780–1790, the rectangular top with hinged shaped leaves above a conforming frame fitted with one drawer, 37in. wide (open). (Christie's) £3,450 $5,750

A Regency mahogany Pembroke table, in the manner of Gillows, decorated with reeded mouldings, on a ring-turned reeded tapering legs, 31in. wide. (Christie's) £2,760 $4,416

Chippendale mahogany Pembroke table, New England, late 18th century, old refinish, (restored), 19in. wide. (Skinner) £1,340 $2,185

A George III mahogany and marquetry serpentine Pembroke table, crossbanded to the top in rosewood, on square tapering fluted legs headed by later pierced angle-brackets,38½in. wide open. (Christie's) £12,650 $20,999

A George III mahogany Pembroke table, decorated with tulipwood crossbanding and lines, on square tapering legs, 38½in. wide. (Christie's) £3,680 $5,962

A George III satinwood Pembroke table, inlaid overall with boxwood and fruitwood lines and crossbanded in amaranth, 36in. wide, open. (Christie's) £6,900 $11,454

A George III mahogany Pembroke table, the oval twin-flap top above a frieze drawer, on square tapering legs, 40in. wide. (Christie's) £2,070 $3,374

A black japanned Pembroke table, Chinese export, circa 1820, the shaped top painted with figures and birds above a small drop panel, 79cm. wide. (Sotheby's) £2,300 $3,749

A small satinwood and tulipwood crossbanded Pembroke table, the oval hinged top above a single end frieze drawer on square section tapered legs and castors, 30½in. open. (Christie's) £2,000 $3,200

A German ormolu-mounted mahogany side table, the semi-circular later Breccia marble top above a panelled beaded frieze, 47¼in. wide.
(Christie's)   £10,350 $17,181

A side table, the rectangular moulded edge top in hardwood, the frieze drawer veneered in rosewood, 3ft.10½in.
(Woolley & Wallis)   £650 $1,079

A pair of George II gilt-gesso side tables, attributed to Benjamin Goodison, each with a pounced ground, the rectangular top with re-entrant corners and gadrooned edge, 59¾in. wide.
(Christie's)   £936,500 $1,535,860

A good Classical stencil-decorated and parcel-gilt marble top mahogany pier table, possibly the firm of Joseph Meeks & Sons, New York, circa 1820, 39in. wide.
(Sotheby's)   £5,261 $8,625

A George III mahogany marble-top pier-table, mid-18th century, the rectangular marble top with moulded edge and cusped corners above a conforming frame with a gadrooned apron, 37½in. wide.
(Christie's)   £8,970 $14,950

A Federal inlaid mahogany marble-top pier-table, the demi-lune marble top above a conforming case fitted with one large line-inlaid drawer flanked by two similar sham drawers, 38½in. wide.
(Christie's)   £6,900 $11,500

A fine and rare Classical stencil-decorated marble top carved mahogany pier table, School of Anthony Quervelle, Philadelphia, circa 1825, 43in. wide.
(Sotheby's)   £5,261 $8,625

A Regency style mahogany pier table, the inset marble top with brass bound edge above frieze drawer, 87cm. wide.
(Phillips)   £1,650 $2,640

A pair of Roman giltwood pier tables, last quarter 18th century, each with a later brown and grey striated alabaster top, 51in. wide.
(Christie's)   £45,500 $74,620

An adzed oak serving table by Robert Thompson of Kilburn, on four faceted and turned supports joined by an undershelf, 54in. wide. (Andrew Hartley)   £1,100 $1,848

A mahogany serving table, the rectangular top with moulded edge above a fluted frieze and twin panelled drawers, 153cm. (Phillips)   £680 $1,088

A Regency mahogany, ebony inlaid and ebonised serving table, surmounted by a brass curtain rail with central lyre and anthemion, 199cm. wide. (Phillips)   £21,000 $34,440

An 18th century oak side table, the rectangular top with curved corners over two short and one long drawer, 34in. wide. (Dee Atkinson & Harrison)   £1,000 $1,650

A rare Federal carved and figured mahogany serving table, labelled *Duncan Phyfe and Sons, New York* circa 1820, the rectangular top above two short drawers and one long drawer, 34½in. wide. (Sotheby's)   £6,664 $10,925

A Dutch marquetry inlaid walnut side table, the serpentine top with outset corners, re-constructed using early 18th century marquetry panels, 27½in. wide. (Christie's)   £2,600 $4,160

A George III mahogany serving table, the rectangular diagonally-banded top above a fluted frieze interspersed with oval paterae, 66¼in. wide. (Christie's)   £21,850 $35,834

Limbert server, no. 1404, brand mark, original finish, 40in. wide. (Skinner)   £1,518 $2,530

A William IV mahogany serving table, the rectangular top on cabriole legs with scroll and foliate trailing inlay, the top 160 x 74cm. (Phillips)   £2,200 $3,608

A Scottish William IV mahogany side table, the later rectangular grey fossil marble top above a panelled frieze, on lappeted cabriole legs, 51½in. wide.
(Christie's)   £5,750 $9,372

A walnut veneered and elm side table with feather stringing to the crossbanded rectangular top, 74cm wide, early 17th century and later.
(Bearne's)   £680 $1,122

A Neapolitan giltwood side table, first half 18th century, the shaped and waved verde antico marble top above a pierced apron with foliate scrolls and flowers, 61in. wide.
(Christie's)   £10,350 $17,181

A George II joined oak side table, circa 1730, the rectangular top with moulded edge above a single frieze drawer, 25¼in. wide.
(Bonhams)   £2,700 $4,320

A pair of Regency mahogany, bronzed and parcel-gilt side tables, each with a rectangular white marble top, supported by a naturalistically carved eagle, 44¼in. wide.
(Christie's)   £34,500 $56,580

A George II walnut side table, the associated rectangular padouk top above a moulded frieze, on acanthus-wrapped cabriole legs, 32in. wide.
(Christie's)   £5,750 $9,372

A Swedish giltwood side table, early 19th century, the inset later rectangular black granite top on a foliate and egg-and-dart stepped frieze, 31in. wide.
(Christie's)   £1,495 $2,482

A George III sabicu, satinwood and marquetry serpentine side table, inlaid overall with boxwood and ebony lines, the rectangular top diagonally-banded in tulipwood, 50in. wide.
(Christie's)   £13,800 $22,632

A black japanned side-table, Chinese, circa 1850, with a hinged rectangular top inset with a panel with figures in a landscape, 55cm. wide. (Sotheby's) £1,610 $2,656

A mahogany sofa table, early 19th century, the rounded rectangular top decorated with satinwood crossbanding, on a concave sided platform, 60in. wide.
(Christie's)   £4,600 $7,452

Regency brass-inlaid rosewood sofa table, first quarter 19th century, rectangular top with rounded flaps above a pair of frieze drawers, 56½in. (extended).
(Skinner)   £2,143 $3,450

A late George III mahogany and line-inlaid sofa table, the rounded rectangular twin-hinged top with two frieze drawers opposed by dummy drawers, 61in. wide.
(Christie's)   £1,495 $2,392

A Regency rosewood and satinwood crossbanded sofa table, circa 1820, the top with rounded rectangular leaves above a central frieze drawer with a 'U' shaped support, 59¼in. wide.
(Christie's)   £2,400 $3,840

A Regency rosewood sofa table, inlaid overall with boxwood, the rounded rectangular twin-flap top above a pair of mahogany-lined frieze drawers, 58in. wide open.
(Christie's)   £4,600 $7,498

A French rosewood and kingwood sofa table, late 19th century, the serpentine twin flap top above a frieze drawer, on faceted bulbous end standards, 42in. wide.
(Christie's)   £1,092 $1,742

A George III mahogany sofa table, the rounded rectangular twin-flap top crossbanded and inlaid with boxwood and ebony lines, 58¾in. wide.
(Christie's)   £16,100 $26,404

A Regency ormolu-mounted and brass-inlaid rosewood, bronzed and parcel-gilt sofa table, the rounded rectangular twin-flap top inlaid with foliage angles, 65½in. wide open.
(Christie's)   £32,200 $53,452

A George III rosewood sofa table, inlaid with boxwood and ebonised lines, the rounded rectangular crossbanded twin-flap top banded in satinwood, 61¼in. wide.
(Christie's)   £23,000 $38,180

A George III mahogany tilt top table, the round top on ring and wrythen turned column, 30½in. (Dreweatt Neate)   £2,000 $3,260

Chippendale mahogany tilt-top tea table, Deerfield, Massachusetts, late 18th century, the serpentine moulded top above a turned pedestal on cabriole leg base, 30½in. wide. (Skinner) £669 $1,092

A George III mahogany folding tea table with moulded edged serpentine top and frieze drawer, 33½in. wide. (Andrew Hartley)   £1,600 $2,560

A George III mahogany tea table with rectangular fold-over top on leafage carved cabriole legs and ball and claw feet, 2ft.8½in. wide. (Russell Baldwin & Bright)   £1,420 $2,343

Chippendale mahogany carved tilt-top tea table, probably Pennsylvania, circa 1770, on a birdcage support and vase and ring turned post, 29¾in. diameter. (Skinner)   £1,269 $2,070

A Chippendale mahogany tilt-top tea-table, Philadelphia, 1760–80, the circular dished top tilting and turning above a bird-cage support, 33in. diameter. (Christie's)   £26,220 $43,700

Federal mahogany inlaid card table, Massachusetts, early 19th century, the rectangular top with ovolo corners above a skirt, 34in. wide. (Skinner)   £1,834 $2,990

The Penrose Family Queen Anne carved and figured walnut pie-crust tilt-top tea table, Philadelphia, 1740–1750. (Sotheby's)   £29,814 $48,875

A George II mahogany supper table, the circular tilt-top with thumbnail rim, raised on turned baluster pedestal, 92cm. diameter. (Phillips)   £2,000 $3,200

A George III mahogany tea table, of small size, the hinged rectangular top with rounded angles, 24in. wide.
(George Kidner)   £1,100 $1,826

A George II mahogany table, circa 1755, the shaped and moulded tip-top carved with shells, on fluted turned tapering stem, diameter 2ft. 11in. (Sotheby's) £1,840 $3,073

A George II mahogany single gateleg tea table, the one-piece top above deep frieze with bulbous angles and single drawer, 84cm. wide. (Bristol)   £1,000 $1,640

A Queen Anne oak tray-top tea table, circa 1790, the rectangular moulded with a gallery, above a plain frieze, 29¾in. wide.
(Sotheby's)   £4,209 $6,900

A mahogany tripod table with oval piecrust tip-up top, 70cm. wide, basically 18th century,
(Bearne's)   £1,300 $2,145

A Queen Anne maple and birch tray-top tea-table, New England, 1740–60, the rectangular tray top with concave moulded edges above an applied moulding, 30¼in. wide. (Christie's)   £11,040 $18,400

A Queen Anne walnut tray-top tea table, Goddard-Townsend School Newport, Rhode Island, 1750–70 the rectangular top within a beaded convex moulding, 31in. wide.
(Sotheby's)   £29,325 $48,875

A rare Queen Anne carved and figured walnut piecrust tea table, Philadelphia, 1740–55, the shaped circular top tilting and revolving above a birdcage support.
(Sotheby's)   £14,490 $24,150

A Chippendale mahogany tea-table, Philadelphia, 1760–1780, the circular dished top tilting and turning above a birdcage support, 36in. diameter.
(Christie's)   £5,520 $9,200

A Federal figured mahogany work table, Boston, Massachusetts, circa 1815, the square top with outset corners, 23¾in. wide. (Sotheby's) £2,455 $4,025

A Victorian walnut work table, the burr veneered octagonal hinged top revealing a fitted interior, 18in. (Woolley & Wallis) £680 $1,095

A 19th century Milanese ebonised and ivory inlaid workbox, the hinged lid opening onto a satin lined interior. (David Lay) £600 $966

A William IV marquetry circular work table, the hinged top with amboyna stylised foliate marquetry, enclosing a frieze compartment, 58cm. diameter. (Phillips) £2,200 $3,608

Classical mahogany veneer and grained drop-leaf sewing table, circa 1840, stencil labelled _J. & J. W. Meeks Makers No. 4 Vesey St. New York_, on the inside of the drawer, 26½in. wide. (Skinner) £697 $1,150

An Edwardian satinwood, mahogany, boxwood and harewood-inlaid octagonal work table, the shaped chequer-banded top with raised edge and central hinged section, 22in. wide. (Christie's) £1,035 $1,656

A Federal figured mahogany two-drawer work table, Massachusetts, circa 1810, the rectangular top with ring-turned outset corners above two cockbeaded drawers, 20½in. wide. (Sotheby's) £1,775 $2,875

A Victorian rosewood and inlaid work/games table, the serpentine shaped top with chequerboard inlay flanked by floral panels, 21½in. wide. (Christie's) £517 $827

A late 19th century mahogany Continental work table, the crossbanded hinged top with canted corners enclosing central well and lidded compartments, 22in. (Dreweatt Neate) £680 $1,108

A Victorian mahogany pedestal workbox, on turned column with lion paw supports, 42.5cm. wide. (Bristol) £400 $640

Late Empire three-drawer work table, 19th century, in mahogany with mahogany veneers, carved pedestal legs and paw feet, 22½in. wide. (Eldred's) £1,400 $2,310

A Victorian walnut octagonal sewing table, 16½in. diameter. (Dockree's) £390 $643

Classical mahogany carved and mahogany veneer work table, Massachusetts, circa 1825, the rectangular top with rounded drop leaves above two cockbeaded graduated drawers, 20in. wide. (Skinner) £575 $920

Federal mahogany veneer sewing table, New England, the mahogany top with hinged drop leaves has a reeded edge, 18½in. wide. (Skinner) £697 $1,150

Federal mahogany astragal-end carved and mahogany veneered work table, New York, circa 1815–20, the rectangular top flanked by hinged tops above conforming case, 25¼in. wide. (Skinner) £1,437 $2,300

Classical tiger maple work table, New England, circa 1820–30, the rectangular drop leaf above two drawers with convex fronts, 16½in. wide. (Skinner) £934 $1,495

A Regency pollard oak and ebony strung drop flap work table, containing a drawer and sliding well below, on a U-shaped stretcher, 73cm. wide. (Phillips) £1,700 $2,788

A William IV rosewood work table, with a hinged cavetto moulded lid and bowed sides with brass ring carrying handles, 46cm. wide. (Phillips) £1,300 $2,132

A William IV rosewood work table, circa 1835, the hinged rectangular top above a pair of drawers and a sliding work basket, 28¾in. leaves open. (Christie's)   £950 $1,520

A thuya work table, Austrian, the top with scrolled sides headed by ebonised eagles heads, 57cm. wide. (Sotheby's) £12,075 $19,682

A Regency amboyna work table, the rounded twin-flap top above a fitted drawer to the front and a simulated drawer to the reverse, 30¾in. wide.
(Christie's)   £2,530 $4,199

A 19th century French worktable in the Louis XVI style, the walnut hinged lid with musical trophy and scroll marquetry design, 2ft wide. (Russell Baldwin & Bright)
    £1,180 $1,947

A German ormolu-mounted and brass-inlaid mahogany work table, late 18th/early 19th century, the canted rectangular hinged lid with central roundel inlaid with a flowerhead and with satinwood banding, 23in. wide.
(Christie's)   £10,350 $17,181

A ladies Victorian walnut writing/sewing table with floral marquetry, on cheval type base. (Russell Baldwin & Bright)
    £1,100 $1,815

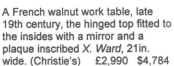

A William IV rosewood work table with foldover oblong top having leather writing surface, 20¾in. wide. (Andrew Hartley)
    £650 $1,092

A French walnut work table, late 19th century, the hinged top fitted to the insides with a mirror and a plaque inscribed *X. Ward*, 21in. wide. (Christie's) £2,990 $4,784

A French mahogany work table, mid 19th century, the hinged dished rectangular top with canted corners crossbanded in rosewood, 22½in. wide. (Christie's) £2,070 $3,312

A Victorian burr walnut oval writing table, with line inlaid decoration, fitted single frieze drawer above carved stretchered supports, 107cm. wide.
(Bristol) £1,700 $2,805

A mahogany writing table, George III, circa 1770, in chinoiserie taste, the leather-inset top with a moulded border above four blind-fret drawers, 111cm. wide. (Sotheby's) £19,550 $31,866

A mahogany writing table, early 20th century, the leather lined rectangular top with three quarter gallery and a foliate-carved edge, 48in. wide.
(Christie's) £1,035 $1,656

A French mahogany writing table, late 19th century, the oval crossbanded top with rounded angles inset with parquetry above a frieze fitted with a drawer, 39½in. wide. (Christie's) £2,185 $3,496

A mid-Victorian Gothic Revival oak writing desk, the chamfered three-quarter gallery above rectangular top, above a pair of frieze drawers, 44in. wide.
(Christie's) £2,242 $3,587

An Edwardian mahogany and marquetry lady's writing table, the shaped leather-lined top with a low superstructure hinged to reveal a stationery compartment, 36in. wide. (Christie's) £1,150 $1,840

Victorian burr walnut writing table by Holland & Sons, London.
(Christopher Matthews)
£1,750 $2,888

An 18th century South German walnut and brassbanded kneehole writing table, of undulating outline, the top inset with a fabric panel and brass border edge, 120cm. wide.
(Phillips) £1,800 $2,952

A Victorian mahogany writing table, the mirrored four-drawer back above a leather inset top, 106cm. wide. (Bristol) £380 $627

A French kingwood and ormolu-mounted bureau plat, in the manner of F. Linke, late 19th century, the undulating top inset with a panel of tooled leather, 53½in. wide.
(Christie's)   £3,450 $5,589

A mahogany desk, Dutch, circa 1820, the upper part with a pierced gallery above an arrangement of six small drawers, 125cm. wide.
(Sotheby's)   £8,280 $13,496

A French brass inlaid mahogany writing table, early 20th century, inlaid with lines, the rectangular top centred with a flower-filled urn, 27¾in. wide.
(Christie's)   £2,530 $4,048

A good Regency rosewood and brass inlaid writing table, circa 1810, the pierced brass galleried rectangular top with square central panel flanked by a pair of hinged compartments, 36¼in. wide.
(Christie's)   £8,000 $12,800

A kingwood, marquetry and giltbronze lady's writing table, Paris, circa 1890, the leather-inset top within a moulded cast border, 115cm. wide.
(Sotheby's)   £6,325 $10,436

A Russian Neo-Classical kingwood, marquetry and parquetry inlaid kidney shape writing table, St. Petersburg, circa 1780, the shaped top with a central circular panel inlaid with a basket of flowers, 38½in. wide.
(Christie's)   £4,000 $6,400

A Regency mahogany pedestal writing table, decorated with lines, the square top lacking a ratcheted hinged surface, 31in. wide.
(Christie's)   £1,955 $3,167

A gilt-bronze mounted mahogany small writing table, French, 19th century, in Louis XV style, the tulipwood banded top of serpentine outline, 2ft. wide.
(Sotheby's)   £2,300 $3,841

A Regency mahogany writing-table, in the manner of Gillows, the rectangular green leather-lined top with re-entrant corners, 36¼in. wide.
(Christie's)   £7,475 $12,259

A Regency brass-mounted and rosewood writing-table, attributed to Gillows, the rounded rectangular top inset with brown tooled leather writing-surface, 48in. wide.
(Christie's)   £26,450 $43,378

A George III mahogany writing table, the moulded rectangular brown leather-lined top above three frieze drawers to the front and reverse, 48¼in. wide.
(Christie's)   £10,350 $16,870

A 19th century mahogany writing table with reeded edged oblong top having central ratcheted slope, 42in. wide.
(Andrew Hartley)   £1,800 $3,024

A William IV rosewood pedestal writing table, the rectangular hinged top enclosing a fitted interior, 24½in. wide.
(Christie's)   £1,380 $2,235

A George III mahogany Pembroke writing table, the rectangular twin-flap top with central sliding panel revealing a green baize-lined ratcheted hinged writing-surface, 40in. wide open.
(Christie's)   £2,070 $3,374

A late Victorian mahogany campaign folding writing table, decorated with lines and crossbanding, the hinged top fitted with two drawers, 24in. wide.
(Christie's)   £1,840 $2,944

A George III mahogany, satinwood and marquetry bonheur du jour, in the manner of John Cobb, inlaid overall with floral sprays of roses and pearwood and ebonised lines, 37in. wide.
(Christie's)   £5,175 $8,435

A Chinese Export padouk harlequin table, mid-18th century, the rounded rectangular treble-hinged top, enclosing a plain surface, a games table and a writing table.
(Christie's)   £58,700 $97,442

A Regency brass-mounted partridgewood writing table, in the manner of John McLean, the rounded rectangular green leather-lined top with three-quarter pierced Greek-key gallery, 51½in. wide.
(Christie's)   £45,500 $74,620

A Dutch mahogany and marquetry upright chest, 19th century, inlaid with classical urns, shell spandrels and ribbon tied swags, 40½in.wide. (Christie's)　　£3,450　$5,589

A late 18th/early 19th century Dutch mahogany and marquetry tall chest, containing six long drawers inlaid with floral garlands, 97cm. wide. (Phillips)　　　　£1,900　$3,116

Chippendale maple tall chest, southern New England, late 18th century, the cornice moulding above six thumb-moulded drawers, 37in. wide. (Skinner) £2,998 $4,887

Chippendale carved tiger maple tall chest, Rhode Island, late 18th century, the cornice includes dentil moulding above a case of seven graduated drawers, 38in. wide. (Skinner)　　£17,250　$27,600

Two nearly identical Federal inlaid cherrywood and maple tall chests of drawers, Pennsylvania, circa 1800, each with an overhanging cove moulding above a diamond-inlaid frieze, approximately 5ft.6in. high. (Sotheby's)　　£10,522　$17,250

A George III mahogany tallboy, the rectangular cavetto and dentilled cornice above a plain frieze and a pair of panelled doors, 44½in. wide. (Christie's)　　£5,750　$9,545

A Chippendale figured walnut tall chest of drawers, Pennsylvania, circa 1770, the rectangular overhanging cornice above five short and four graduated thumbmoulded long drawers, 40in. wide. (Sotheby's) £5,324 $8,625

Chippendale painted maple tall chest of drawers, south eastern Massachusetts, circa 1790–1810, the flat moulded cornice above a case of two short drawers and five graduated long drawers, 34¾in. (Skinner)　　　　£3,136　$5,175

A George III mahogany tallboy, the moulded cornice above two short and three long graduated drawers, 43in. wide. (Christie's)　　　　£2,185　$3,496

A William IV rosewood teapoy of bombé form, the hinged lid with foliate finial and leaf carved rim. (Andrew Hartley)   £1,100 $1,848

William IV period mahogany teapoy of rectangular form, the bead moulded cover enclosing a fitted interior, 17½in. (Aylsham)   £880 $1,461

A William IV mahogany teapoy, circa 1835, the canted hinged lid opening to reveal a pair of lidded compartments centred by a recess, 18in. wide. (Christie's) £750 $1,200

A Regency mahogany teapoy, the sarcophagus body with hinged top enclosing lidded compartments, 41cm. wide.
(Bearne's)   £320 $528

An early Victorian solid-rosewood tripod teapoy, the circular domed foliage-carved hinged top enclosing four circular wells, two with pots, 30in. high, 17½in. diameter. (Christie's)   £3,450 $5,520

A George IV mahogany teapoy, the brass-mounted sarcophagus body with interior fitted with lidded compartments, 40cm. wide.
(Bearne's)   £1,000 $1,650

A Regency rosewood and brass-inlaid teapoy, the tapering drum with a hinged moulded lid revealing an interior with two tea caddies and zinc liner, 17in. wide.
(Christie's)   £1,265 $2,024

An early Victorian burr oak-veneered teapoy, the tapering rectangular body with hinged top enclosing two lidded containers, 44.5cm wide.
(Bearne's)   £880 $1,408

A William IV figured mahogany teapoy, the rising top with moulded edge and chamfered corners over shield-shaped crenulations, 17in. wide. (Dee Atkinson & Harrison)
                  £820 $1,312

Ettore Sottsass for Poltronova, wardrobe, 1965, wood, brown ceramic tiles, black handles inset with shiny metal discs behind, 39½in. wide.
(Sotheby's)   £3,105 $5,030

A Victorian pollard oak triple wardrobe, with ebony banding, mirrored door flanked on either side by a marquetry inlaid door, 87in. wide, and a matching pedestal dressing table.
(Andrew Hartley)   £1,600 $2,640

Classical mahogany veneer wardrobe, Middle Atlantic States, 1840, with two recessed panel doors and similar sides, 65in. wide.
(Skinner)   £1,905 $3,105

An 18th century Cuban mahogany clothes press, the cavetto moulded cornice above an interior with sliding trays, 4ft.1in. wide, probably North Country, circa 1770.
(Woolley & Wallis) £3,800 $6,308

A George IV mahogany gentleman's press, delicate ebony stringing, fitted two drawers with fitted three sliding trays, turned feet, 125cm. (Locke & England)
                  £1,100 $1,815

A Heals oak wardrobe, the rectangular top above a pair of fielded panel doors, enclosing hanging space and an open recess, 59in. wide. (Christie's) £517 $775

A Gordon Russell oak wardrobe, the rectangular top above a pair of cupboard doors, two bevelled mirrors attached to the inside, 39¾in. wide.
(Christie's)   £977 $1,465

A William IV mahogany gentleman's wardrobe, the central section with pediment surmounted by anthemion and scroll carving, 244cm. (Phillips) £2,200 $3,520

A fruitwood armoire, Louis XV, Provincial, circa 1760, the double arched top above a pair of doors each with two shaped panels, 4ft.3in. wide.
(Sotheby's)   £1,610 $2,689

An Edwardian mahogany triple wardrobe crossbanded with string inlay, 77in. wide. (Andrew Hartley) £1,000 $1,600

A Colonial hardwood breakfront wardrobe, late 19th century, profusely decorated with foliate carving and fruiting vines, 103in. wide. (Christie's) £2,070 $3,312

Louis XVI Provincial oak armoire, 19th century, moulded cornice over a pair of carved doors, 54in. wide. (Skinner) £1,500 $2,415

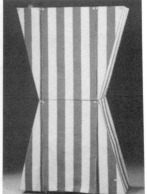

An Arts and Crafts oak dressing cabinet, the rectangular top above a pair of cupboard doors enclosing pull-out swing plate, 42in. wide. (Christie's) £310 $465

A Classical mahogany wardrobe, Baltimore, 1820–1840, in seven sections, the pedimented top set with quarter and demi-anthemions, 78½in. wide. (Christie's) £6,210 $10,350

Elizabeth Garouste and Mattia Bonetti for Gouache, 'Bobine' wardrobe, 1986, blue and white striped cotton over a sycamore structure, adjustable internal shelves, 47¼in. wide. (Sotheby's) £2,300 $3,726

A French Provincial fruitwood armoire, late 18th/early 19th century, decorated with foliate carvings, on short cabriole legs, 65in. wide. (Christie's) £1,265 $2,024

A good George III mahogany breakfront wardrobe, circa 1800, the moulded cornice above a pair of central crossbanded arched panelled doors enclosing six linen slides, 96in. wide. (Christie's) £5,400 $8,640

A George III gentleman's mahogany wardrobe, the detachable moulded cornice with a veneered frieze, on bracket feet, 4ft. 2in. wide. (Woolley & Wallis) £1,800 $2,988

A George III mahogany and line inlaid bowfront corner washstand, with later top covering bowl aperture, 61.5cm. wide. (Bristol) £390 $639

A late Georgian rosewood and mahogany kneehole washstand with shallow raised gallery, having a long drawer over, 32½ wide. (Dee Atkinson & Harrison) £1,200 $1,980

Federal mahogany inlaid chamber stand, Portsmouth, New Hampshire area, circa 1800, the shaped splashboard centring a quarter round shelf, 23in. wide. (Skinner) £3,594 $5,750

A Classical mahogany tambour washstand, New York, 1800–1815, the domed tambour top flanked by reeded stiles sliding to reveal a compartmented interior, 19¼in. wide. (Christie's) £1,932 $3,220

A pair of white painted washstands, George III, circa 1810, the galleried top with splash boards over two graduated basin holes on tapering legs, 3ft.2½in. wide. (Sotheby's) £690 $1,152

A satinwood bowfront corner washstand, late 19th century, decorated with lines and rosewood crossbanding, on downswept legs, 53in. wide. (Christie's) £575 $840

A George III mahogany, satinwood banded and boxwood strung washstand, the dual hinged top enclosing a sliding ratcheted mirror, 45cm. wide. (Phillips) £1,600 $2,624

A George III mahogany bowfront corner washstand, circa 1795, the hinged splash back folding down to a boxwood strung top, above three false drawers and a cupboard door, 27½in. wide. (Christie's) £2,600 $4,160

A George III mahogany enclosed washstand, the twin flap top enclosing part-fitted interior, 60.5cm. wide. (Bristol) £250 $410

A Victorian mahogany whatnot, the moulded rectangular top with three-quarter gallery above two open shelves divided by turned baluster columns, 57cm. wide.
(Phillips)   £1,300 $2,080

A Regency mahogany three-tier whatnot, the moulded rectangular top above two further tiers, the base with a drawer, 17½in. wide.
(Christie's)   £3,220 $5,345

An early 19th century rosewood whatnot, the two veneered rectangular shelves with turned blocks supports, 17.5cm.
(Woolley & Wallis) £1,900 $3,154

A pair of kingwood and inlaid three-tier étagères, mid 19th century, applied with brass mounts and inlaid with floral sprays bordered by walnut crossbanding, 15¼in. wide.
(Christie's)   £1,265 $2,024

An early Victorian mahogany four tier whatnot with bobbin turned supports and a single low drawer.
(David Lay)   £700 $1,127

A Regency mahogany four tier square etagère fitted drawer on turned supports and casters, 1ft.4in. wide. (Russell Baldwin & Bright)   £2,350 $3,877

A Regency mahogany whatnot, inlaid overall with lines, the moulded rectangular top with gilt-tooled embossed leather frieze, 22in. wide.
(Christie's)   £5,520 $9,163

A late George III mahogany whatnot, with a drawer above three concave fronted shelves, 49.5cm. wide. (Bearne's) £1,250 $2,063

A Victorian walnut three-tier whatnot, the shaped tiers joined by ring-turned supports, on turned and tapering legs, 21in. wide.
(Christie's)   £483 $773

A George III mahogany oval wine cooler with crossbanded hinged top enclosing a fitted zinc-lined interior, 66cm wide.
(Bearne's)   £3,600 $5,760

A William IV mahogany cellaret, of sarcophagus form, the hinged lid enclosing divided interior, 68cm. wide. (Phillips)   £720 $1,152

A George III mahogany and brass bound wine cooler, on square tapered legs, brass cappings and castors, 18in. wide.
(George Kidner)   £2,800 $4,600

A George III brass-bound mahogany wine cooler, with later removable brass liner to the interior, the gadrooned rim above three beaded brass bands, 15in. diameter.
(Christie's)   £18,400 $30,544

A mahogany wine cooler, early 19th century, fitted with a lift-out lead-lined interior above a panelled body, 33in. wide.
(Christie's)   £2,185 $3,540

An early 19th century brass bound mahogany bottle carrier, with domed lid revealing fitted interior, brass campaign handles, 17¼in. high. (Andrew Hartley) £620 $1,042

A George III brass-mounted mahogany cellaret, last quarter 18th century, the hinged oval top above a conforming tapering well, 22½in. wide. (Sotheby's) £2,587 $4,312

A William IV mahogany wine cooler, the canted rectangular panelled body with a reeded border, with later tin liner, 30½in. wide. (Christie's) £2,300 $3,680

A Regency mahogany cellaret, the rectangular hinged lid opening to reveal an interior fitted for bottles, 47.5cm. wide.
(Phillips)   £620 $992

A George III brass-bound mahogany cellaret, the cross-banded oval hinged top enclosing a metal liner with handles, 21¾in. wide. (Christie's)   £3,450 $5,623

A George IV plum-pudding mahogany wine cooler, of tapering rectangular form with scrolled ends centred by flowerheads, 38¼in. wide. (Christie's) £4,370 $7,254

A George III mahogany octagonal wine cooler on stand, the brass-bound body with hinged top and drop-ring carrying handles, 46cm. wide. (Bearne's)   £1,450 $2,393

A George III octagonal mahogany wine cooler and stand, bound in brass and with brass handles, the stand on four legs with brass castors, 69cm. high. (Tennants)   £2,500 $4,000

A George III mahogany wine cooler, inlaid overall with boxwood and ebony lines, of oval shape with metal-lined interior, 24¾in. wide. (Christie's)   £6,900 $11,454

A George III mahogany cellaret the rectangular hinged top above a deep body with chamfered angles and brass carrying handles to the sides, 13½in. wide. (Christie's)   £1,265 $2,024

A George III mahogany and brass-bound cellaret, the moulded octangular hinged top enclosing a later brass liner, on a moulded stand, 26in. wide. (Christie's)   £3,105 $5,154

A Scottish George IV mahogany wine-cooler, of sarcophagus form, the stepped moulded top enclosing a lead-lined cellaret with two side shelves, 37½in. wide. (Christie's)   £6,900 $11,454

A George II brass-mounted and banded mahogany wine-cooler, of oval shape with tapering sides and lion-mask ring handles to each end, 26in. wide. (Christie's)   £3,910 $6,490

A lead garden fountain on dolphin supports, 65cm. high, 66cm. wide. (Bearne's) £640 $1,056

A pair of Scottish painted terracotta garden urns, early 20th century, modelled as tree trunks entwined with foliage, on tapering bases with four recesses to the angles, 36½in. high.
(Christie's) £920 $1,472

After the Antique, a large carved figure of The Wild Boar, on stepped rectangular base, 19th century, 32cm. long. (Bearne's) £760 $1,254

A large pair of cast iron garden urns, the bulbous bodies with twin satyr mask handles and foliate banding, on waisted socles, 32in. high.
(Christie's) £4,600 $7,360

A Victorian blue painted cast iron garden urn of Classical form with tongue mounts to rim, partly fluted and partly reeded body and on square footrim and pedestal, 26in. diameter, 52in. high.
(Canterbury) £680 $1,088

Pair of classical-style black painted cast iron urns, early 20th century, of typical form with two handles, classical figures to sides, 32in. high. (Skinner) £1,286 $2,070

A large pair of Italian terracotta garden urns in the classical style, each moulded with ram's heads, 78cm. diameter.
(Bearne's) £1,400 $2,240

A Victorian cast iron conservatory plant stand, comprising six pierced circular trays on a scrolled support, 44½in. wide.
(Andrew Hartley) £420 $693

A pair of Italian figural carved marble throne chairs, late 19th century, each with a square back centred by a medallion carved with a lion. (Sotheby's) £8,280 $13,800

Eyptian Revival marble figural garden ornament, early 19th century, formed as a standing male, 48in. high. (Skinner) £4,643 $7,475

A pair of Italian Provincial carved marble reclining lions, one with its paws resting on a sphere, the other on a shield, 16th/17th century, 34cm. (Bearne's) £900 $1,485

After St. Gaudens, (American 1848–1907), Diana The Huntress, unsigned bronze, 72in. high. (Skinner) £2,046 $3,335

An Italian Rococo style gilt-lead wall ornament, 19th century, cast with a dolphin amidst cattails and carps, 41in. high.
(Sotheby's) £8,970 $14,950

A pair of large lead garden urns of baluster form with square bases, 18th/19th century, 89cm. high.
(Bearne's) £2,900 $4,640

One of a pair of large terracotta campana urns, each with a moulded foliate rim, the bodies modelled with group of putto and with satyr mask handles.
(Christie's) (Two) £2,760 $4,416

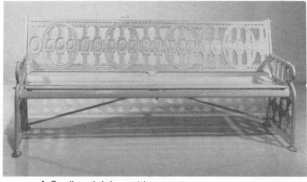

One of a pair of 19th century sandstone garden urns on pedestals, with square bases, 107cm.
(Bearne's) (Two) £360 $594

A Coalbrookdale cast iron seat, with straight crest, the back pierced with oval paterae, scrolled arm terminals and wooden slatted seat, 76½in. wide. (Andrew Hartley) £425 $714

A large white marble garden urn of Classical form 35in. high, and an octagonal pedestal for same, 53in. high overall.
(Canterbury) £1,700 $2,805

A marble figural group, early 20th century, depicting a nude couple in amorous position, 20in. high.
(Sotheby's) £2,070 $3,450

A George III Coade stone keystone, carved with a classical female mask, 12 x 12in.
(Sotheby's) £1,173 $1,955

American School, 20th century, Trumpeting Merman, a fountain, unsigned, cast metal, 22½in. long.
(Skinner) £2,116 $3,450

A lead figural group with infants Pan and Bacchus, 19th century, raised on an associated pedestal carved with masks and foliage, height of figure 36in.
(Sotheby's) £8,280 $13,800

A marble figure of a spaniel, late 19th century, wearing a collar inscribed *JESSIE*, seated beside a basket amidst roses, signed *M. Muldoon & Co. Louisville, Kentucky*, 29in. high.
(Sotheby's) £6,900 $11,500

A large marble urn, first quarter 19th century, in the manner of Thomas Hope, with high arched handles above a reeded ovoid body, 39in. high.
(Sotheby's) £6,555 $10,925

A stone figural group, 18th century, Flemish, with two young frolicking putti, the girl holding a key seated on a cushion beside a puppy, 36in. high. (Sotheby's) £13,110 $21,850

A Chinese cast-iron basin, 18th century, decorated with Chinese symbols and foliage, 38½in. long.
(Sotheby's) £2,070 $3,450

Ferdinand von Miller. (German, 1842–1929), a bronze figure of a young Native American hunter, signed and inscribed *München 1873*, 6ft. 1in. high.
(Sotheby's) £35,160 $58,600

A marble figure of Hercules, 19th century, 46in. high.
(Sotheby's)   £2,932 $4,887

A pair of Continental stone lion's heads, 17th century, 24in. long.
(Sotheby's)   £2,242 $3,737

A marble figure of a bather, signed *R.S. GreenoughRoma889*, the base inscribed *ANIMULA*, 6ft. high.
(Sotheby's)   £9,660 $16,100

A marble figure of young Bacchus, early 20th century, seated on an urn, raised on a square plinth with lion's mask decoration, 4ft. 8in. high. (Sotheby's) £2,415 $4,025

A pair of stone figures of eagles, late 19th century, each standing with wings out-stretched on a square base, 43in. high.
(Sotheby's)   £6,210 $10,350

An Italian lead figure of a seated blackamoor supporting a sundial, the figure 18th century, the dial inscribed *IO VADO E VENGO OGNI GIORNO MA TU ANDRAI SENZA RITORNO*, 5ft. 4in. high.
(Sotheby's)   £12,420 $20,700

A painted cast-iron figural garden fountain, late 19th century, formed as a boy holding a goose, the mouth plumbed for water, 30in. high. (Sotheby's) £1,242 $2,070

A pair of cast-iron pedestal tables, late 19th century, each with a trellis and scroll pierced top cast with the symbols of the zodiac, 31in. wide.
(Sotheby's)   £1,035 $1,725

A painted cast-iron figural wall fountain, late 19th century, by Antoine Durenne Sommevoire, with two putti seated beside an urn.
(Sotheby's)   £4,140 $6,900

A pair of painted metal recumbent lions, 20th century, stamped *J.W. Fiske Ironworks, New York, Made in U.S.A.,* 4ft. 4in. long. (Sotheby's)   £4,485 $7,475

A pair of composition stone sphinxes, 20th century, each reclining on a rectangular base, 45in. long. (Sotheby's)   £2,760 $4,600

A pair of enamelled stone fruit baskets, 21in. high. (Sotheby's)   £3,105 $5,175

A pair of zinc greyhounds, late 19th century, by J.W.Fiske, New York, oxidised grey-blue patina, 41in. long. (Sotheby's)   £6,555 $10,925

A pair of Neoclassical style cast-iron urns, 19th century, of campana form with an everted rim above a classically decorated frieze, 31in. high. (Sotheby's)   £2,760 $4,600

A pair of terracotta urns on pedestals, each of low bulbous form modelled with ram's masks joined by berried oak leaf swags, 34in. high. (Sotheby's)   £3,277 $5,462

A pair of copper corbels, each voluted bracket cast with foliage, 32in. high. (Sotheby's)   £552 $920

A painted stone figure of a lamb, 38in. high. (Sotheby's)   £3,795 $6,325

A lead figure of an eagle on pedestal, circa 1900, overall height 4ft. 4in. (Sotheby's)   £1,897 $3,162

A pair of lead figures of sphinxes, late 19th century, 4ft. 3in. long. (Sotheby's)   £15,180 $25,300

A pair of massive painted cast-iron urns on stands, late 19th century, attributed to J.L. Mott, New York, each waisted vessel with a foliate and floral decorated frieze. (Sotheby's)   £22,770 $37,950

A pair of monumental terracotta urns on pedestals, circa 1910, of campana form, stamped *Galloway*, overall height 7ft. 2¼in. (Sotheby's)   £22,425 $37,375

An opaque white through pale blue cased frill basket with aventurine inclusions, late 19th century, 22cm. high. (Christie's)   £230 $375

An Archimede Seguso macchie ambre verde blown glass basket, designed circa 1952, in clear glass with gold foil inclusions, 9¾in. high. (Sotheby's)   £1,808 $2,875

A Victorian swing handled circular sugar basket, monogrammed and dated amongst pierced scrollwork, E. & J. Barnard, 1858, 17cm. high overall, with blue glass liner and fiddle pattern sugar sifter. (Bearne's)   £260 $429

BEAKERS

A Bohemian opaque pale-blue flared faceted beaker, circa 1845, silvered and gilt with stylised urns linked by foliage scrolls, with lobed cut foot, 4⅝in. high. (Christie's)   £460 $768

Four Lobmeyr flared cylindrical tumblers after designs by Michael Powolny, circa 1914, engraved with circular cartouches of children representing the Four Seasons, 3½in. high. (Christie's)   £1,150 $1,920

A Bohemian waisted opaque yellow beaker, circa 1845, enamelled in white and gilt with stylised foliage scrolls with faceted lower part, 4in. high. (Christie's)   £517 $863

BOWLS

A cameo glass bowl, by Gallé, circa 1900, the grey glass overlaid in red, acid-etched and carved with pendant berries and leafy branches, 10.2cm. diameter. (Christie's)   £633 $1,038

A Barbini inciso cased glass bowl, designed by Alfredo Barbini, designed circa 1960, in clear glass, the interior in brilliant red/orange, 9in. diameter. (Sotheby's)   £1,157 $1,840

A cameo and enamelled glass bowl, by Daum, circa 1910, the grey glass internally mottled with yellow and amethyst towards base and overlaid in mottled yellow, 20cm. diameter. (Christie's)   £2,645 $4,338

A cameo glass bowl, by Gallé, circa 1900, the circular rim pulled at four points, the frosted grey glass internally mottled with yellow and overlaid in blue and brown, 21cm. diameter. (Christie's) £920 $1,509

A Venini blown and applied glass bowl, designed by Napoleone Martinuzzi, circa 1925, in pale blue glass with an applied deep blue trailed band, 7in. high. (Sotheby's) £289 $460

An early 20th century Daum wavy rimmed glass bowl, decorated in enamels with a frieze of orange flowers, on a mottled and frosted pink ground, 12cm. diameter. (Wintertons) £680 $1,122

A cameo and carved glass bowl, by Daum, circa 1910, the lemon glass with pale opalescence and overlaid in tangerine and emerald green, 10.5cm. high. (Christie's) £2,530 $4,149

Steuben crystal engraved bowl, The United States of America, designed by Sidney Waugh, central piece from a series of engraved bowls honouring the individual states, 18in. high. (Du Mouchelles) £12,500 $20,000

A cameo glass bowl, by Gallé, circa 1900, the frosted glass internally mottled with yellow with pale opalescence and overlaid in rust red, 12.5cm. high. (Christie's) £1,610 $2,640

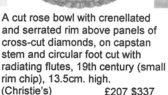

A fine Barovier & Toso oriente glass bowl, designed by Ercole Barovier, circa 1940, the shallow vessel with irregular rim composed of intricate patchwork of woven glass canes, 8in. diameter. (Sotheby's) £6,509 $10,350

A cut rose bowl with crenellated and serrated rim above panels of cross-cut diamonds, on capstan stem and circular foot cut with radiating flutes, 19th century (small rim chip), 13.5cm. high. (Christie's) £207 $337

An Orrefors Ariel glass bowl, designed by Edvin Öhrström, circa 1954, the thick glass walls enclosing a geometric grid pattern of graduated rectangles, 7in. diameter. (Sotheby's) £1,302 $2,070

A Lalique opalescent 'Perruches' glass bowl, the exterior moulded in relief with frieze of budgerigars, 9½in. wide.
(Andrew Hartley)   £1,000 $1,660

Carder Steuben engraved roseline cased bowl, oval centrebowl of roseline cut to alabaster in Grapes pattern, 12½in. long.
(Skinner)   £138 $230

European etched and enamelled centre bowl, colourless body with pulled and crimped gold accented rim, 5¼in. high.
(Skinner)   £103 $172

Tiffany favrile transparent bowl, flared rim on jardinière-form crystal body internally decorated by eight pulled green feather devices, 7¼in. diameter. (Skinner)   £310 $517

Tiffany blue opal pastel bowl, curved sapphire blue and opal dish with crackled iridescence and raised on gold disc foot, 6¼in. diameter. (Skinner)   £586 $977

Brilliant cut glass and silver punch bowl, decorated with four star-cut devices spaced by notched vertical ribbing, star-cut base, 12¼in. diameter. (Skinner)   £621 $1,035

Carder Steuben verre de soie centrebowl, catalogue 2775, with eight pinched apertures around rim of flower arrangement, 8in. diameter. (Skinner)   £172 $287

Daum etched bowl on silvered foot, folded crimped rim on blush-pink shaded to colourless bowl with delicate medial blossoming garland, 3¼in. high. (Skinner)   £328 $546

René Lalique circular bowl, moulded with the 'Dahlia' pattern, of a spreading rosette, within a frosted border, signed, 7in.
(Christie's)   £310 $496

Rare golden amber cut glass ruffled bowl, blank attributed to Union Glass Company of Somerville, Massachusetts, 9¼in. diameter. (Skinner)   £2,070 $3,450

Schneider Le Verre scarab centre bowl, shaped orange glass bowl layered with tortoiseshell brown etched as five beetles, 4½in. high. (Skinner)   £414 $690

A Bohemian glass bowl, the blue glass decorated with scrolling gilt band enamelled and moulded in low relief, 42cm. diameter.
(Christie's)   £288 $465

A cameo glass bowl, by Gallé, circa 1900, the grey glass internally mottled with yellow and overlaid in deep cherry red, 14.7cm. diameter. (Christie's)   £1,093 $1,793

An enamelled cameo glass bowl by Daum, circa 1905, the grey glass internally mottled with chocolate brown and yellow, 12cm. diameter. (Christie's)   £805 $1,320

A Montjoye glass bowl, the frosted blue glass enamelled in shades of blue and white with a swallow and butterfly, 19.5cm. diameter. (Christie's)   £368 $594

Tiffany blue lily pad flower bowl, cobalt blue glass decorated with golden green lily pads and lustrous stretched iridescence, 10in. diameter. (Skinner) £966 $1,610

Bohemian crystal enamelled covered bowl, in the manner of Steinschonau with translucent studio enamels in gold, red, blue, and green foliate elements, 6½in. diameter. (Skinner) £379 $632

A cameo glass box and white metal cover, by Gallé, circa 1900, the yellow glass overlaid in red with flowering cherry blossom branches, 7.6cm. diameter. (Christie's)   £368 $604

Fine and large cranberry circular punch bowl and stand and matching ladle, the cover applied with faceted ball finial, fluted tapering base, circa 1850, (possibly Bohemian), 16in. high. (G.A. Key)   £1,800 $2,880

A Roman pale green glass cast bowl with twenty-six pronounced ribs around the exterior, late 1st century B.C./1st century A.D., 6³/₈in. (Bonhams)   £280 $448

Sèvres crystal Atlas centrebowl, colourless glass with frosted pedestal base of figural Atlas, arms extended supporting the bowl-world, 10¼in. high. (Skinner)   £310 $517

René Lalique opalescent glass Perruches parrot bowl, twenty repeating birds executed in high relief with blue patine enhancing the blossom recessed panels, 9¾in. high. (Skinner)   £1,794 $2,990

An Orrefors glass bowl and stand, designed by Edward Hald, the pale blue glass finely engraved and etched with stylised design of two mermaids each riding a dolphin, 1928, 21.2cm. diameter. (Christie's)   £920 $1,486

An enamelled glass bowl by Daum, circa 1910, the clear glass internally mottled with pink and orange and umber towards base, 15cm. diameter. (Christie's) £805 $1,320

A cameo glass box and cover by Daum, circa 1910, the frosted grey glass internally mottled with yellow and overlaid in orange, yellow and green with amethyst patches, 10cm. diameter.
(Christie's) £1,035 $1,697

Wavecrest mounted covered box, scroll moulded opal glass 'collar' box with handpainted pink flowers top and sides, 6in. high.
(Skinner) £293 $488

An enamelled glass box and cover by Daum, circa 1900, the pale amethyst glass finely etched enamelled and gilded with an allover design of scrolling thistles and briars, 10cm. diameter.
(Christie's) £1,725 $2,829

An enamelled glass box and cover, by Daum, circa 1905, clear glass internally mottled with milky white graduating to mottled yellow and brown towards base, enamelled with two small butterflies, 8cm. high. (Christie's) £2,185 $3,583

An enamelled glass box and cover by Daum, circa 1910, the clear glass internally mottled with yellow and with a band of aubergine towards foot, 8.5cm. diameter.
(Christie's) £1,725 $2,829

A late Georgian burr walnut and brass mounted decanter box, fitted with four glass decanters with stoppers, initials to the lid, 21.5cm. wide. (Wintertons) £400 $640

CANDLESTICKS

A pair of cut table candlestick lustres, the thistle-shaped nozzles with a band of horizontal flutes, late 19th century, 23cm. high.
(Christie's) £633 $1,032

A flat-cut taper stick, the everted waved rim nozzle with band of ovals, above octagonal collar and notched stem, quarter 18th century, 14cm. high.
(Christie's) £518 $844

A pair of Regency ormolu and cut-glass two-light candelabra, each with a lozenge-cut circular shaft surmounted by a reeded band and issuing a central branch terminating in a ball and two scrolling faceted branches, 13¾in. high.
(Christie's) £13,225 $21,953

Pair of Carder Steuben amber candlesticks, circa 1925, amber glass baluster-shaped stems on a wide disc foot, 11¾in. high.
(Skinner) £431 $690

A pair of Stourbridge concentric millefiori candlesticks, each of baluster form with loop handles, the base formed as domed paperweight, 3³⁄₈in. diameter.
(Christie's) £1,153 $1,955

Pair of Steuben engraved wisteria candlesticks, circa 1927, each of dichroic lead glass engraved in the Pillar pattern, reverse-engraved dot on base, 8¼in. high.
(Skinner) £647 $1,035

COMPÔTES

Quezal Art Glass compôte, crimped and ruffled rim on oval bowl raised on pedestal foot of opal white decorated by three broad green leaves, 5½in. high.
(Skinner) £1,449 $2,415

Carder Steuben red-threaded compôte, circa 1925, shallow bowl of colourless glass decorated with a band of red threading, raised on a colourless shaft, 7in. diameter.
(Skinner) £198 $316

A Bohemian white overlay ruby glass comport, the deep rim of the bowl painted with an encircling floral band on a gold ground, 21.5cm. high.
(Bearne's) £680 $1,122

CUPS

One of a set of eight cups and saucers of blue tinted glass, decorated with white dot border.
(Christie's) £300 $460

A cameo glass cup, by Gallé, circa 1890, the clear glass overlaid in honey yellow, acid-etched and carved with four small bees amongst honeycombs, 11.2cm. high. (Christie's) £1,840 $3,018

Tiffany favrile decorated loving cup, large ambergris vasiform with three applied reeded handles spacing three green leaf-forms, 8in. high.
(Skinner) £1,518 $2,530

A Dutch mahogany decanter box in the form of a bureau, 19th century, with simulated roll top above three drawers flanked by ebonised columns, 14in. high.
(Christie's) £2,300 $3,680

A Bohemian blue-flashed and cut spirit service comprising: a pair of fluted decanters and stoppers, ten spirit glasses with fluted bowls and a tray, circa 1900.
(Christie's) £805 $1,312

An Edwardian oak three bottle tantalus with electroplated mounts, the glass decanters with circular stoppers and spirit labels, 40cm.
(Bearne's) £340 $561

Rockwell silver overlaid cocktail set, Czechoslovakian black glass vasiform, decorated with Art Deco floral design repeated on martini glasses of Flambo red and black glass, 11 and 5¼in. high.
(Skinner) £414 $690

An I.V.R. Mazzega fasce orizzontali, glass stoppered decanter, possibly designed by Fulvio Bianconi, circa 1950s, body and stopper in red, blue and green bands, 11½in. high.
(Sotheby's) £2,531 $4,025

A mallet shape glass decanter with globular supports, enamelled in the Beilby manner, circa 1770, 34cm. high. (Bearne's) £760 $1,254

A pair of 'Bristol' blue glass decanters and stoppers, inscribed in gold *Hollands* and *Rum*, 21.5cm. high. (Bearne's) £270 $440

Cranberry cut to clear glass engraved decanter, flattened colourless oval with obverse medallion engraved *Mollies Pony 1869*, 10in. high.
(Skinner) £586 $977

A St. Louis wafer dish and macedoine paperweight base, the crimped rim with a spiral pale red and white band, mid 19th century, 8cm. high. (Christie's) £690 $1,125

A William IV cut glass butter dish comprising a frosted glass barrel with faceted chased lid, 7in. wide. London 1833, 10oz. 19dwt. (Andrew Hartley)   £430 $722

A Victorian cut and part frosted pedestal bonbon dish, with foldover rim, 15cm. diameter. (Bristol)   £40 $65

ÉPERGNES

A white tinged light blue glass épergne, comprising a central ribbed and three curved vases with frilled rims, set in a bowl with upturned 'stalagmite' rim, 45cm. high. (Bearne's)   £420 $693

An early 19th century Old Sheffield plated épergne on four supports with paw feet and gadrooned border, circa 1815, 31cm. high x 54cm. (Christie's) £1,322 $2,115

A cranberry and clear glass épergne, comprising a central trumpet vase surrounded by three similar vases and three barley twist rods, 55.5cm. high. (Bearne's)   £760 $1,254

EWERS

A Stevens and Williams 'Rock Crystal' silver-gilt mounted wine ewer, circa 1900, the mounts marked for Sheffield, 1909, with maker's marks for Walter and Charles Sissons, 12¼in. high. (Christie's)   £4,600 $7,682

Carder Steuben Spanish green ewer, circa 1925, slightly ribbed oval form with flared mouth, applied angled handle, and raised disc foot, 9in. high. (Skinner)   £288 $460

Daum early cameo etched silver mounted ewer, colourless frosted glass oval layered in bright rose-red, deeply etched as convolvulus blossoms, 12in. high. (Skinner)   £2,932 $4,887

Gunnar Cyrén for Orrefors, 'Pop' goblet, 1967, clear and coloured blown glass, 8¼in. high. (Sotheby's) £747 $1,210

A mammoth baluster goblet, circa 1710, the funnel bowl set on a triple annulated knop over a true baluster section enclosing a large tear, 11in. high. (Christie's) £2,530 $4,225

A Bohemian amber-flash goblet, late 19th century, the bell-bowl engraved with two hounds in a landscape, 13¼in. high. (Christie's) £517 $863

An Anglo-Netherlands goblet, late 17th century, the flared funnel bowl with a solid lower part set on a collar, 7½in. high. (Christie's) £1,265 $2,112

Four Steuben engraved wisteria glass goblets, circa 1927, bell-shaped goblets in dichroic leaded glass, engraved in the Pillar pattern, 9in. high. (Skinner) £719 $1,150

A drawn-trumpet goblet, circa 1740, the stem enclosing an elongated tear, on a conical folded foot, 9³/₈in. high. (Christie's) £713 $1,190

A façon de Venise colour-twist serpent-stemmed goblet (Flügelglas), 17th century, The Netherlands, the coiled stem with a central figure-of-eight enclosing brick-red and opaque white threads 7³/₈in. high. (Christie's) £747 $1,247

A Bohemian dated engraved amber-flash spa goblet, dated *1832*, the waisted bowl engraved with oval cartouches of named views of Anna Kappelle, Warmbrunn and Kynaot, 6½in. high. (Christie's) £402 $671

A façon de Venise winged goblet, 17th century, Venice or Low Countries, the flared bowl with opaque combed ornament on a merese, hollow wrythen knopped and slender tapering stem, 7½in. high. (Christie's) £1,150 $1,920

A Venini a canne glass pitcher, designed by Gio Ponti, circa 1952, in clear glass enclosing multi-coloured canes, 9½in. high. (Sotheby's) £2,531 $4,025

A cameo glass jug by Schneider, circa 1922, the grey glass internally mottled with yellow and overlaid in red, graduating to green towards base. (Christie's) £1,610 $2,640

A small enamelled jug by Daum, circa 1905, etched and finely enamelled with stalks of wheat, field poppies, larkspur and slender grasses, 12.2cm. high. (Christie's) £4,025 $6,601

Daum etched and enamelled hops pitcher, early flattened miniature of fiery yellow amber with scrolling stylised decoration, 3in. high. (Skinner) £1,104 $1,840

A miniature enamelled jug by Daum, circa 1910, the clear glass internally mottled with rose white and pink, graduating to green and cobalt blue, 6.2cm. high. (Christie's) £1,495 $2,452

An enamelled glass jug by Daum, circa 1905, the clear glass internally mottled with white and yellow speckled with blue and graduating to yellow, 9.2cm. high. (Christie's) £1,610 $2,640

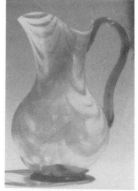

Antique pressed glass pitcher, in diamond and thumbprint pattern, 9½in. high. (Eldred's) £53 $88

A 19th century panel-cut ovoid water jug, with prism-cut neck and wide spout, 19.5cm. (Bristol) £66 $108

American South Jersey blown glass pitcher, in clear with white swag decoration, applied handle, 13½in. high. (Eldred's) £600 $990

A cameo glass coupe, by Gallé, circa 1900, the frosted glass internally mottled with yellow with pale opalescence, 19.5cm. diameter. (Christie's) £1,495 $2,452

A Victorian white opaque and ruby glass edged épergne, the four trumpet shaped vases with clear trailed and crimpled decoration, 21.5cm. high. (Canterbury) £190 $304

A Schneider glass tazza, the clear glass bowl decorated with internal orange mottling graduating to darker tones around the rim, 31cm. diameter. (Christie's) £575 $929

A fine and rare Venini murrina arlequino figure, designed by Fulvio Bianconi, circa 1950, the harlequin's body in blue and white murrina, amidst a lavender ground, 8in. high. (Sotheby's) £15,912 $25,300

Black glass basket, attributed to Steuben, mirror bright black moulded body folded and applied with berry prunts at sides, total height 11½in. (Skinner) £138 $230

A Scandinavian Art Deco white metal and glass decanter and stopper, of lozenge form upon a squared base with lug handle, 18cm. high. (Christie's) £322 $520

A cut-glass preserve jar, cover and stand, second quarter 19th century, each piece cut with bands of diamonds, 7¼in. (Sotheby's) £253 $422

A cameo glass plafonnier, by Gallé, circa 1900, the frosted glass internally mottled with pink towards rim and overlaid in amethyst and blue, 39.5cm. diameter. (Christie's) £2,645 $4,338

A St. Louis blue and white globular carafe, mid-19th century, the clear glass enclosing spiralling blue threads edged in white, 7¼in. high. (Christie's) £517 $863

Joe Colombo for Arnolfo di Cambio 'Biglia' ashtray, designed 1968–69, yellow painted metal over pink tinted glass, moveable clear glass top element, 4¾in. high.
(Sotheby's)   £368 $596

A pair of Victorian glass sweetmeat jars, with turnover petal rims cut with printies and domed cover, 31cm. high. (Bearne's) £370 $592

A pâte sur pâte circular plaque, 6½in. diameter, depicting Dr. Jenner innoculating his son with cowpox liquid, 10¾in.
(Christie's)   £230 $368

A chemist jar and cover, inscribed for toothbrushes, with gilt cover, 19th century, 28cm.
(Tennants)   £650 $1,040

A pair of Barovier & Toso glass figures of jazz musicians, circa 1930, each seated figure in blue powders cased in clear bullicante glass, 6½in. high.
(Sotheby's)   £1,808 $2,875

A façon de Venise serpent-stemmed drinking vessel, 17th century, Low Countries or Venice, the entwined wrythen-moulded serpent stem enclosing opaque threads and with lattimo raspberry-prunt terminals, 5½in. high.
(Christie's)   £920 $1,536

A cameo glass tazza by Schneider, circa 1926, the mottled orange and yellow glass overlaid in orange graduating to mottled amethyst towards foot.
(Christie's)   £2,070 $3,395

A pair of cut-glass preserve jars and covers, late 19th century, each shield-shaped body engraved with swags of flowers and foliage tied with ribbons, 10½in.
(Sotheby's)   £690 $1,152

An Aureliano Toso mezza filigrana glass figure of a rooster, designed by Dino Martens, circa 1954, in blown and applied glass, unsigned, 9¾in. high.
(Sotheby's)   £289 $460

A Saint Louis camomile weight, the flower composed of numerous rows of white recessed petals about a blue, red, yellow and white cane centre, 6.6cm. diameter.
(Christie's)　　　£1,357　$2,300

A Bohemian faceted engraved weight, the translucent amber-flash ground engraved with a lady riding her mare side-saddle in a wooded landscape, 2½in. diameter.
(Christie's)　　　£271　$460

A Saint Louis Marbrie weight, the bright-red loops forming a quatrefoil festoon with a central composite cane in shades of salmon-pink, blue and white, 6.6cm. diameter.
(Christie's)　　　£1,764　$2,990

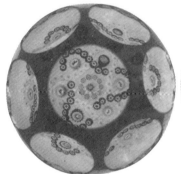

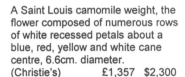

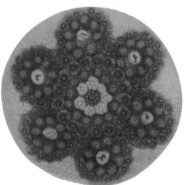

A Baccarat faceted translucent green overlay weight, the clear glass set with two interlocking millefiori trefoil garlands in red and white and green and white, each loop containing a silhouette, 7.9cm diameter. (Christie's) £2,171 $3,680

A Paul Stankard dated 'First' bouquet weight, the clear glass set with three orange St. Anthony's fire flowers, three white bellflowers, two pale-yellow meadow wreaths, engraved AO78/1978, 2¾in. diameter.
(Christie's)　　　£1,221　$2,070

A Baccarat carpet-ground weight, the six alternating blue, salmon-pink and green millefiori panels each enclosing a silhouette cane of animals and a dancer, 7.3cm. diameter.
(Christie's)　　　£8,142　$13,800

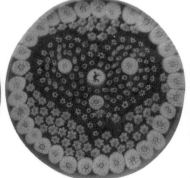

A Clichy three-colour swirl weight, the pink, turquoise and white alternating staves radiating from a central green and white composite cane, 7.3cm. diameter.
(Christie's)　　　£2,035　$3,450

A Paul Ysart dragonfly weight, the insect with long shaded blue body with yellow markings, on a translucent mottled purple ground, 2¾in. diameter.
(Christie's)　　　£577　$978

A Saint Louis heart weight, the clear glass set with a heart composed of red, blue and white florettes central silhouette cane of a devil, 3in. diameter.
(Christie's)　　　£6,785　$11,500

A Baccarat garlanded butterfly weight, the insect with deep-purple body with shaded grey-blue eyes and antennae, multi-coloured marbleised wings, 7.3cm. diameter. (Christie's)   £2,375 $4,025

A Clichy blue-ground sulphide weight, mid-19th century, with Louis Philippe facing to the right, in military uniform, 3in. diameter. (Christie's)   £368 $614

A Saint Louis 'Swan' weight, the clear glass set with a white swan with black eyes and yellow bill with black markings afloat on a pale-blue pond, 3in. diameter. (Christie's)   £10,178 $17,250

A Saint Louis encased blue double overlay upright bouquet weight, the bouquet composed of a deep salmon-pink double clematis flower, flanked by cobalt-blue, yellow and white buds, 6.6cm. diameter. (Christie's)   £4,750 $8,050

A Baccarat pansy weight, mid-19th century, the purple and yellow flower with five petals centred with a pink and white star cane, with three green leaves showing behind, 2½in. diameter. (Christie's)   £402 $671

A Saint Louis encased green double-overlay upright bouquet weight, the bouquet composed of a large central cobalt-blue single clematis flower with yellow centre, flanked by buds, 7.3cm. diameter. (Christie's)   £5,428 $9,200

A Clichy spaced concentric turquoise-ground weight, mid-19th century, with a central pink, green and white rose, surrounded by three circles of pastry mould and other canes, 2¾in. diameter. (Christie's)   £1,380 $2,304

A Clichy faceted double-overlay concentric millefiori mushroom weight, the tuft composed of five rows of tightly packed assorted millefiori canes in shades of green, purple and white, 3in diameter. (Christie's)   £6,446 $10,925

A Baccarat faceted sulphide weight, the clear glass set with a sulphide of a hunter and his dog standing in a wooded landscape, on a translucent ruby-red ground fool, 3½in. diameter. (Christie's)   £2,035 $3,450

A Saint Louis moulded Lizard weight, naturalistically moulded with a coiled lizard enriched with gilding lying on top to a hollow bulbous base, 3¼in. diameter.
(Christie's)   £1,086 $1,840

A Baccarat commemorative signed and dated millefiori weight, the clear glass set with assorted tightly packed brightly coloured large millefiori canes, *Baccarat 21 Avril, 1858*, 2¾in. diameter.
(Christie's)   £7,464 $12,650

A Daum paperweight, the clear glass internally mottled with cream and amber, with gilt aventurine inclusions and a green outline of a shamrock, 10cm diameter.
(Christie's)   £345 $557

Victor Trabucco raspberry and roses magnum paperweight, complementary branches of red berries and white blossoms in crystal clear surround, inscribed *Trabucco 1996*, 3⅜in. diameter.
(Skinner)   £414 $690

A Pairpoint pedestal rose weight, of oviform, the clear glass containing a shaded deep crimson multi-petalled flower, resting on four green leaves, 3¼in. diameter.
(Christie's)   £170 $288

Paul J. Stankard blueberry and spirit paperweight, clusters of pink blossoms, blueberries, and yellow flowers above complex under system, 3¼in. diameter.
(Skinner)   £1,449 $2,415

A Debbie Tarsitano dahlia weight, the clear glass set with a large multi-petalled flower in shades of rust about a yellow stamen and black centre, 3¼in. diameter.
(Christie's)   £950 $1,610

Large millefiori paperweight, modelled as a balustered circular ink well, cover and base decorated with lines of concentric canes in puce, pale blue and green, 5in.
(G.A. Key)   £70 $112

A Baccarat dated scattered millefiori weight, *B 1847* to one cane, with silhouettes of a dog, a cockerel and other animals, 2¾in. diameter.
(Christie's)   £1,380 $2,304

Twelve Carder Steuben engraved celeste blue luncheon plates, circa 1918-32, moulded blue body with engraved border of leaves and dots, variant of the Kensington pattern, 8½in. diameter. (Skinner) £341 $546

Tiffany pastel pink plate, rim of bright pink with opal at reverse and in ten decorative wedge-shaped sections, 8¾in. diameter. (Skinner) £327 $546

Tiffany favrile gold iridescent plate, fourteen-rib card tray form of ambergris with pastel opal colouration and stretched lustre, 7¾in. diameter. (Skinner) £155 $258

SHADES

Leaded glass lamp shade, attributed to Bigelow & Kennard, rose pink slag glass segments with green acorn-shaped leaf-on-vine decorative belt, 16in. diameter. (Skinner) £690 $1,150

Handel overlaid panelled glass hanging shade, massive octagonal conical shade composed of leaded amber slag and tan panels, widest shade diameter 27½in. (Skinner) £1,104 $1,840

American leaded glass ceiling lamp, broad conical glass shade with raised amber slag crown and brickwork shoulder, 26in. diameter. (Skinner) £414 $690

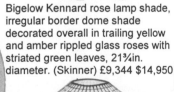

Bigelow Kennard rose lamp shade, irregular border dome shade decorated overall in trailing yellow and amber rippled glass roses with striated green leaves, 21¾in. diameter. (Skinner) £9,344 $14,950

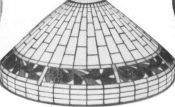

Deux Sirenes, a Lalique frosted glass plafonnier, moulded with two swimming water nymphs, their hair forming streams of bubbles, 39.5cm. (Bonhams) £2,200 $3,520

Bigelow Kennard pine cone leaded glass shade, large conical shade with white opalescent brickwork segments, shade diameter 22in. (Skinner) £1,656 $2,760

Quezal Art Glass mushroom cap lamp shade, cased opal to amber glass with four large pulled and hooked feathers in lime-green colouring, shade diameter 12½in. (Skinner) £862 $1,380

Kew-Blas Art Glass vase, cased ambergris oval vessel with gold iridescent feathers on opal body, 7in. high. (Skinner) £586 $977

A pair of Victorian clear glass lustre vases, frieze of painted alternating portrait and floral medallions on gilded leaf ground, 12¾in. high. (Andrew Hartley)   £620 $1,023

Ernest-Baptiste Leveille silver mounted carved glass vase, elliptical sang-de-boeuf translucent body intaglio decorated with swirling scrolls, 8in. high. (Skinner)   £2,415 $4,025

Dale Chihuly Navajo Horse Blanket glass cylinder, translucent green glass with intricate surface decoration incorporating Native American weaving techniques, 10¼in. high. (Skinner)   £21,390 $35,560

A pair of cut-glass and gilt-bronze urns in the manner of Baccarat, Paris, circa 1900, each of campana form, with diamond-cut body and stem, 44cm. high. (Sotheby's)   £8,050 $13,282

Daum cameo glass scenic vase, raised rim on mottled blue oval body with etched landscape 'painted' in naturalistic vitrified colouration, 5⅝in. high. (Skinner)   £1,656 $2,760

Schlevogt green malachite glass ingrid vase, heavy walled press moulded oval vessel with four panels depicting partially nude women, 9½in. high. (Skinner)   £293 $488

A pair of Continental amber glass vases, one painted with King Charles on horseback, the other with Prince Rupert, 29cm. high. (Bearne's)   £260 $429

Schneider Le Verre Art Deco vase, unusual mottled white body colour layered with swirled orange and brown-green glass etched as stylized blossoms, 15½in. high. (Skinner)   £621 $1,035

Webb Cameo glass tricolour water lily vase, complex oval body composed of transparent ice blue with white layer below etched and carved as pond lilies, 7½in. high. (Skinner) £12,420 $20,700

Mount Washington Royal Flemish vase, raised rim with applied angular handles on bulbous transparent colourless glass, 4½in. high. (Skinner) £1,587 $2,645

A Daum Art Deco vase, the grey glass internally mottled with white and overlaid in blue, 22cm. high. (Christie's) £575 $929

Venini Incalmo 'Colletti' vase, design of Ludovico de Santillana, circa 1961, raised crimson red flared rim with medial dark stripe, 10½in. high. (Skinner) £448 $747

Pair of Bohemian mounted Art Glass vases, tall pigeon blood red oval body with purple iridized surface further enhanced by opal-grey random threading, 23in. (Skinner) £2,346 $3,910

Tiffany heart and vine decorated vase, double bulbed gourd-form amber body with green leaves and amber vines, 5in. high. (Skinner) £1,104 $1,840

Emile Gallé cameo glass fern vase, elongated elliptical body of frosted colourless and fiery golden amber glass layered in chartreuse and dark green, 9¾in. wide. (Skinner) £1,380 $2,300

A Lalique opalescent glass vase, the ovoid body moulded with three bands of running antelope below a slightly everted rim, 17.8cm. high. (Bearne's) £1,350 $2,160

A cameo glass vase, by Gallé, circa 1900, the frosted grey glass internally mottled with apricot and overlaid in white, yellow and green, 9cm. high. (Christie's) £403 $661

A cameo glass vase, by Gallé, circa 1900, acid-etched and carved with stalks of delphinium blossom, buds and leafage, 18cm. high. (Christie's) £1,150 $1,886

A cameo glass vase, by Gallé, circa 1900, the frosted grey glass internally mottled with yellow and overlaid in brown, 12.8cm. high. (Christie's) £1,265 $2,075

A cameo glass vase, by Gallé, circa 1900, the frosted grey glass internally mottled with yellow and overlaid in cherry red, 12cm. high. (Christie's) £1,035 $1,697

An etched, enamelled and gilded glass vase, by Gallé, circa 1890, the clear glass etched with upper and lower band of overlapping daisies and foliage, 29.5cm. high. (Christie's) £2,185 $3,583

An enamelled glass vase, by Daum, circa 1905, the clear glass internally mottled with white graduating to amethyst towards base, 12cm. high. (Christie's) £1,035 $1,697

A cameo glass vase, by Daum, circa 1910, the clear glass internally mottled with amethyst graduating emerald green towards base, 36cm. high. (Christie's) £3,680 $6,035

A cameo glass vase, by Gallé, circa 1900, the frosted yellow glass overlaid in brownish amethyst, 9cm. high. (Christie's) £276 $453

A French glass vase, in the style of Delvaux, enamelled in blue, black and gilt with stylised pendant floral sprays, 30cm. high. (Christie's) £207 $334

A cameo glass vase by Schneider, circa 1920, , the textured glass overlaid in royal blue graduating to aqua green towards rim, 19cm. high. (Christie's) £633 $1,038

A cameo glass vase, by Gallé, circa 1900, the grey glass internally mottled with white and overlaid in green and pink, 13.5cm. high. (Christie's) £1,265 $2,075

A cameo glass vase, by Gallé, circa 1900, the frosted glass internally mottled with yellow towards base, overlaid in amethyst, 9.5cm. high. (Christie's) £483 $792

A carved and cameo glass vase, by Daum, circa 1914, the grey glass overlaid in cobalt blue and etched and finely carved with a profusion of daisies and foliage, 39.5cm. high. (Christie's) £9,775 $16,031

A cameo glass vase, by Daum, circa 1910, the frosted glass internally mottled with orange and overlaid in brown with continuous river view, 16cm. high. (Christie's) £460 $754

A carved and internally decorated cameo glass vase by Burgun, Schverer & Cie., circa 1895, the pink rose sides shading to pale pink with pink flowerheads and shaded green foliage, 17cm. high. (Christie's) £5,520 $9,053

A cameo and enamelled glass vase, by Daum, circa 1910, acid-etched and enamelled in colours with an alpine landscape, 19.5cm. high. (Christie's) £5,980 $9,807

A cameo and carved glass vase, by Gallé, circa 1900, the grey glass overlaid in cream, pale yellow and amethyst, 20cm. high. (Christie's) £1,265 $2,075

A cameo glass vase, by Gallé, 1890, the clear glass overlaid in deep maroon mottled with amethyst and blue, 22cm. high. (Christie's) £4,830 $7,921

Webb cameo glass latticed vase, design attributed to George Woodall, diminutive oval body of deep cobalt blue, 4in. high. (Skinner)   £4,140 $6,900

René Lalique Courlis red-amber vase, broad shouldered oval moulded with stylised sea terns in flight above ocean waves, 6½in. high. (Skinner)   £2,210 $3,680

Vetreria Artistica Aureliano Toso 'Oriente' face vase, by Dino Martens, circa 1954, waisted vessel of brightly coloured glass sections, 11½in. high. (Skinner)   £11,040 $18,400

A carved and cameo glass vase, by Daum, circa 1900, acid-etched and carved with flowering poppies and foliage, 36.2cm. high. (Christie's)   £2,070 $3,395

A pair of Northern French ruby-tinted and polychrome-enamelled vases, third quarter 19th century, the undulating and everted rims with gilt borders, decorated with polychrome flowers, 11½in. high. (Christie's)   £6,900 $11,178

Bohemian applied cased glass vase, striated blue, green, burgundy-red oval cased to opal and lined in turquoise blue, 8¾in. high. (Skinner)   £189 $316

Orrefors Ariel Edvin Ohrstrom feather vase, heavy walled colourless oval vessel internally decorated by vertical trapped air panels, 7½in. high. (Skinner)   £1,518 $2,530

Kosta Art Deco cut and polished vase, large rosebowl sphere of colourless glass with etched surface, 7in. high. (Skinner)   £292 $488

Barovier & Toso Graffito vase, Ercole Barovier, 1969 design, executed on tapered colourless glass cylinder with combed lattimo white outlines, 11in. high. (Skinner)   £828 $1,380

Carder Steuben jade and alabaster handled vase, 2939, classic deep green jade with applied M handles at each shoulder, 10¼in. high. (Skinner) £448 $747

Pair of Sandwich light amethyst pressed tulip vases, with octagonal bases, Barlow 302lb, 10in. high. (Skinner) £1,150 $1,840

An Argentor silvered metal and blue glass vase, the silvered metal base decorated with semi-circular motifs on two sides, 24cm. high. (Christie's) £460 $743

Daum etched Art Deco vase, polished rim on monochromatic topaz coloured bulbous vessel with repeating etched panels of geometric devices, 7¾in. high. (Skinner) £224 $373

Tapio Wirkkala for Iittala, 'Jäävuorl' (Iceberg), designed 1950, manufactured 1952–69, this example 1954, clear mould blown crystal, 7¹⁵/₁₆in. high. (Sotheby's) £2,530 $4,098

Venini Murano Studio fasce verticali vase, Fulvio Bianconi 1952 design with fused stripes of alternating red, blue, and green transparent glass, 10½in. high. (Skinner) £2,484 $4,140

English cameo glass red vase, Thomas Webb & Sons, white layered on flared red oval cameo etched as rose blossoms and buds, 7in. high. (Skinner) £1,104 $1,840

Venini Studio Glass handled vase, design attributed to Napoleone Martinuzzi, broad sphere of transparent teal blue-green colour, 8¼in. high. (Skinner) £586 $977

English swirled satin glass vase, attributed to Stevens and Williams, tooled crimped rim on green shaded to rose body, 7½in. high. (Skinner) £483 $805

A cameo glass vase, by Gallé, circa 1900, acid-etched and carved with sprays of hydrangea and leafy foliage, 24cm. high.
(Christie's)   £1,840 $3,018

An enamelled glass vase by Daum, circa 1910, the frosted grey glass internally mottled with cloudy white graduating to indigo, 10cm. high.
(Christie's)   £1,150 $1,886

A cameo glass vase, by Gallé, circa 1900, the clear glass internally mottled with white and overlaid in amber, 34cm. high.
(Christie's)   £1,955 $3,206

A small enamelled glass vase by Daum, circa 1906, the yellow glass with pale opalescence, etched and enamelled with spray of flowering thistles, 5cm. high.
(Christie's)   £575 $943

A pair of enamelled glass vase, by Daum, circa 1910, the clear glass internally mottled with sky blue with a band of yellow above base, etched and finely enamelled with pink/violet flowers, 9.7cm. high.
(Christie's)   £2,530 $4,149

A cameo glass vase, by Gallé, circa 1900, the frosted grey glass internally mottled with yellow and overlaid in cherry red and pale brown, 21.5cm. high.
(Christie's)   £1,955 $3,206

A large cameo glass vase, by Gallé, circa 1900, the frosted grey glass internally mottled with yellow and overlaid in blue and amethyst, 42cm. high.
(Christie's)   £7,475 $12,259

A small enamelled glass vase by Daum, circa 1910, etched and delicately enamelled with blue cornflowers and stems, heightened in gilt, 6.5cm. high.
(Christie's)   £1,380 $2,263

A cameo and enamelled glass vase by Daum, circa 1910, the grey glass internally streaked with white, yellow and pink with brown towards base, 9cm. high.
(Christie's)   £920 $1,509

An enamelled glass vase by Daum, circa 1910, etched and enamelled with wild poppies and foliage, heightened in gilt, 11.4cm. high. (Christie's)   £1,093 £1,793

An enamelled glass vase by Daum, circa 1905, the clear glass internally mottled with yellow and aubergine, etched and enamelled with sprays of aquilegia and foliage, 17cm. high. (Christie's) £2,875 $4,715

A cameo glass vase by Richard, circa 1922, the mottled pink glass overlaid in river brown with a continuous lakeside view, 33.5cm. high. (Christie's) £518 $850

A 'marqueterie-sur-verre' glass vase, by Gallé, circa 1900, Inlaid with two flowering anemones in white, purple, rust red and yellow, 18cm. high. (Christie's)   £7,130 $11,693

An enamelled glass vase, by Daum, circa 1910, the clear glass Internally mottled with milky white opalescence, etched and finely enamelled with a mother and child walking through a forest, 7.5cm. high. (Christie's)   £2,300 $3,772

A cameo glass vase, by Gallé, circa 1900, the grey glass triple overlaid in yellow, lilac and amethyst, carved with flowering wild tulips, 22cm. high. (Christie's)   £2,875 $4,715

A small enamelled vase by Daum, circa 1905, the clear glass internally striped with yellow and milky white graduating to grassy green towards base, 15cm. high. (Christie's)   £4,025 £6,601

A cameo glass vase, by Gallé, circa 1900, the frosted yellow glass overlaid in deep red, etched and carved with wild roses, buds and leafy stems, 20cm. high. (Christie's)   £5,520 $9,053

A cameo, carved and enamelled glass vase, by Gallé, circa 1890, the pond green glass internally coloured towards rim with burnt red and overlaid in deep amber, 31cm. high. (Christie's) £8,625 $14,145

A Lalique glass vase of tumbler form, moulded with encircling bands of blue tinted daisy like flowers, 14.5cm. high.
(Bearne's)   £500 $825

A pair of French opaque trumpet vases, painted in coloured enamels with iris and other flower sprays, gilt line rims, circa 1870, 30cm. high.
(Christie's)   £3,450 $5,623

A Fratelli Toso nerox glass vase, designed by Ermanno Toso, circa 1965, the waisted vessel in clear glass decorated with patches of crimson and orange, 8'/₈in. high.
(Sotheby's)   £289 $460

A rare Orrefors Edvin glass vase, designed by Edvin Öhrström, dated *1944,* the cylindrical vessel in turquoise blue glass overlaid in purple, 5½in. high.
(Sotheby's)   £13,019 $20,700

A Barovier & Toso intarsio glass vase, designed by Ercole Barovier, circa 1961-63, composed of triangular inlays in bright red, amber, pale lavender and cobalt blue, 6¾in. high.
(Sotheby's)   £4,520 $7,187

A Cenedese glass aquarium vase, circa 1950s, the flaring cylindrical form with thick walls shading from emerald green to pale green, 11½in. high.
(Sotheby's)   £1,736 $2,760

An English cut-glass vase and cover, second half 19th century, raised on a tall domed foot and cut with stylised flowers and fine diamond panels, 21in.
(Sotheby's)   £632 $1,055

A Daum vase, the cased glass internally decorated with maroon graduating to a mottled design of maroon, tangerine and amber, 25cm. high.
(Christie's)   £1,035 $1,672

A pale pink opalescent shouldered vase of flattened form, possibly Moser, the jewelled gilt line rim suspending an enamelled band of lappets, 19th century, 14cm. high.
(Christie's) £633 $1,032

A Lalique baluster glass bottle vase, 'Aras', post 1924, frosted opalescent glass, moulded with exotic birds in branches, 10in.
(Sotheby's) £402 $671

A Gallé vase, the milky white glass overlaid in blue and amethyst, 27.5cm. high.
(Christie's) £2,875 $4,643

A Fratelli Toso applied blown glass vase, circa 1950s, the flattened teardrop form vessel in emerald green glass overlaid with gold foil, 11½in. high.
(Sotheby's) £940 $1,495

Two fine similar Aureliano Toso oriente glass vases, designed by Dino Martens, circa 1952, the thick walls enclosing coloured ground glass powders, 11¼in. high.
(Sotheby's) £18,082 $28,750

An Orrefors Ariel glass vase, designed by Edvin Öhrström, circa 1950, the thick ovoid vessel enclosing a pair of reclining odalisques, in deep cobalt blue and aubergine, 6in. high.
(Sotheby's) £10,849 $17,250

An Archimede Seguso sommerso ribbed glass vase, circa 1960, with thick walls in clear over cranberry and purple, 7¼in. high.
(Christie's) £796 $1,265

A Venini zanfirico fazzeletto vase, designed by Fulvio Bianconi, circa 1949, in clear glass enclosing vertical zanfirico canes, 5½in. high.
(Sotheby's) £1,808 $2,875

A fine Murano murrhine glass wisteria vase, circa 1920, possibly by Vittorio Zecchin for Artisti Barovier, 6¾in. high.
(Sotheby's) £6,148 $9,775

A wine glass, circa 1730, the bell bowl set on an angular knop and multi-annular knop, 7½in. (Sotheby's)   £747 $1,248

A wine glass, circa 1770, the ogee bowl on a faceted stem, engraved with flowers and butterfly, 6in. (Sotheby's)   £345 $576

A wine glass, circa 1770, the part-fluted funnel bowl, set on opaque twist stem and conical foot, 8¾in. (Sotheby's)   £287 $479

A baluster wine glass, circa 1730, with bell bowl, knopped teardrop stem and folded conical foot, 6in. (Sotheby's) £575 $960

A composite-stemmed wine glass, circa 1740, with drawn bell bowl set on an airtwist stem above an annular collar, 6¼in. (Sotheby's)   £517 $863

A wine glass, circa 1720, the trumpet bowl with teared base, set on an inverted baluster and basal knop, 7in. (Sotheby's)   £862 $1,440

A large wine flute, circa 1770, the elongated funnel bowl, with moulded lower part, airtwist stem and conical foot, 8¾in. (Sotheby's)   £460 $768

A Jacobite wine glass, circa 1745, engraved with an heraldic rose and oak leaves, the drawn trumpet bowl on an airtwist stem, 6in. (Sotheby's) £529 $883

A wine glass, circa 1750, the drawn bell bowl engraved with vine, set on an airtwist stem, 6½in. (Sotheby's)   £368 $615

A wine glass, circa 1775, the plain funnel bowl set on a faceted stem and conical foot, 6¼in. (Sotheby's)   £115 $192

A large goblet, circa 1740, the drawn trumpet bowl set on a plain stem with tear, 8¾in. (Sotheby's)   £437 $730

A wine glass, circa 1770, the bell bowl set on an opaque twist stem with central swelling, 6in. (Sotheby's)   £253 $423

A wine glass, circa 1780, the ogee bowl on a faceted stem, engraved with a floral spray, 5½in. (Sotheby's) £345 $576

A wine glass, circa 1720, waisted bell bowl set on a multi-annular knop and inverted baluster, 6¼in. (Sotheby's) £368 $615

A toasting glass, circa 1750, the drawn trumpet bowl set on a plain slender stem and conical foot, 7¾in. (Sotheby's) £138 $230

A baluster wine glass the funnel bowl with solid lower section and single bead inclusion, circa 1730, 15.5cm. high. (Christie's) £345 $562

A fine diamond-point engraved façon de Venise goblet, Dutch, dated 1706, the funnel bowl engraved with a scene of a stag and two hounds, 8⅛in. (Sotheby's) £4,370 $7,298

An airtwist quadruple-knopped wine glass, circa 1750, the bell bowl supported on a quadruple-knopped stem filled with spiral threads, 7⅞in. high. (Christie's) £805 $1,344

An engraved 'cotton' twist wine glass, English, late 18th/19th century, cup with a bust of George Washington or Thomas Jefferson, 6in. high. (Sotheby's) £1,578 $2,587

A 'Tartan Twist' wine glass, circa 1765, the bell bowl on a stem enclosing a translucent green core entwined by an opaque corkscrew twist, 6⅞in. (Christie's) £2,530 $4,225

A wine glass, circa 1750, the pan-top bowl engraved with fruiting vine, set on an airtwist stem, 6½in. (Sotheby's) £437 $730

A goblet, circa 1770, opaque twist stem, engraved with a band of flowers and foliage, 7in. (Sotheby's) £460 $768

A wine glass, circa 1760, the funnel bowl engraved with vine, airtwist stem and conical foot, 6¼in. (Sotheby's) £322 $538

A wine flute, circa 1750, the elongated funnel bowl set on a double knopped airtwist stem, 8½in. (Sotheby's) £57 $95

Malby & Sons, London, 1876, a 12in. diameter terrestrial globe mounted on a three-legged stand, 18½in. high.
(Christie's) £2,530 $4,124

An Indo-Persian 8in. brass celestial globe, engraved with the constellations, on four cast pillar supports and ring-base, 16⅝in. high. (Christie's) £805 $1,312

R. Max Lippold, Leipzig, a rare 12in. diameter terrestrial school globe, mounted on an ebonised wooden four-legged stand, 21½in. high. (Christie's) £1,207 $1,967

F. Siedentopf, Karlsruhe, (c. 1820), a 12in. diameter terrestrial globe with metal axis, graduated brass meridian and hour cycle, mounted on a Biedermeier-style tripod stand. (Christie's) £3,450 $5,623

George Philip & Son Ltd, London, 1918, a 12in. diameter terrestrial time globe made up of twelve coloured printed paper gores. (Christie's) £6,325 $10,309

Replogle, Chicago, (c.1935), a 12in. diameter terrestrial globe, supported by bronze white metal warriors, in the Art Deco manner, 16in. high overall.
(Christie's) £517 $843

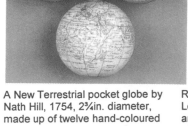

Heinrich Kiepert and Arvid Kempe, Stockholm and Berlin, 1909, a 24in. diameter terrestrial globe, on turned ebonised oak column and base, 41in. high.
(Christie's) £1,092 $1,779

A New Terrestrial pocket globe by Nath Hill, 1754, 2¾in. diameter, made up of twelve hand-coloured engraved paper gores and two polar calottes.
(Christie's) £4,370 $7,123

Ruddiman Johnston & Co. (Ltd), London, (c.1900), made in France, an 8in. diameter terrestrial table globe, mounted on a cast iron stand, 13¾in. high.
(Christie's) £345 $562

Ginn & Heath (c. 1840), a rare 6in. diameter terrestrial Instructional globe, mounted on a steel axis over an iron horizontal plate, 9¼ high. (Christie's)　£3,450　$5,623

George Philip & Son Ltd, London (c.1930), an 8in. diameter terrestrial globe, made up of twelve printed and coloured paper gores, 10¾in. high. (Christie's)　£207　$337

Caley & Son, Norwich, (c.1900), a 5¼in. diameter terrestrial globe on ebonised baluster turned pillar support, 11³/₈in. high. (Christie's)　£287　$468

James Wyld, (1812–1887), London, a 12in. diameter terrestrial globe, showing the United States before the purchase of California, Arizona and Texas, 18½in. high. (Christie's)　£2,185　$3,561

Henri Selves, Paris, a 6¼in. diameter terrestrial table globe, spherical casing of two halves, lined internally with two sets of twelve colour printed gores. (Christie's)　£5,175　$8,435

Lorieux, Paris (c.1900), an 8¼in. diameter Star Globe, made up of twelve printed paper gores with polar calottes, the constellations delineated and labelled, 15in. high. (Christie's)　£2,300　$3,749

Johann Georg Klinger (1764–1806), Nürnberg, a 12in. diameter celestial globe, mounted in a hexagonal four-legged stand, 22in. high. (Christie's)　£3,680　$5,998

Félix Delamarche (fl. 1817–47), Paris, a 2½in. diameter terrestrial pocket globe, made up of twelve hand-coloured engraved paper gores, the equatorial graduated in degrees. (Christie's) £1,725　$2,811

J.G. Klinger, Nürnberg, (c.1850), a 6in. diameter terrestrial table globe, raised on four fruitwood quadrant supports, 10¾in. high. (Christie's)　£1,380　$2,249

W. & A.K. Johnston Ltd, Edinburgh, (c.1925), an 18in. diameter terrestrial library globe, on cast iron splayed tripod stand, 32¼in. high. (Christie's) £1,725 $2,812

Lane, London, 1818, a 2¾in. diameter terrestrial pocket globe, with a 2¾in diameter celestial pocket globe, made up of twelve printed coloured paper gores with two polar calottes. (Christie's) £6,900 $11,247

A decorative brass armillary sphere, unsigned and undated, at the centre a reproduction 3in. diameter terrestrial globe, after the antique, decorated in colours, 24in. high. (Christie's) £1,725 $2,812

Newton, Son & Berry (fl. 1830–38), London, a 3in. diameter terrestrial pocket globe, made up of twelve hand-coloured engraved paper gores, the equatorial graduated in degrees. (Christie's) £2,185 $3,561

L.E. Belot Fils, Brussels, [?]late 19th century, a 3¼in. diameter terrestrial globe, made up of twelve printed coloured paper gores with polar calottes, the oceans marked with major currents. (Christie's) £805 $1,312

An anonymous late 19th century 3in. diameter facsimile terrestrial globe, unsigned and undated, after Matthaus Seutter (1678–1757), Augsburg, made up of twelve coloured printed paper gores. (Christie's) £1,035 $1,687

A 5¼in. long, ovoid wooden case in two halves, covered with two sets of ten coloured printed paper terrestrial globe gores, the prime meridian marked *Longitude du Meridien de Paris,* ungraduated. (Christie's) £977 $1,592

[?]Paul Wolfgang Jenig, (d. 1805), Nürnberg, an 8in. diameter terrestrial table globe, supported by the four turned oak legs joined by stretchers, with circular plate and centrepost, 11½in. high. (Christie's) £2,185 $3,561

A 3in. diameter terrestrial thread case globe, made up of two sets of twelve coloured printed gores pasted over a hollow turned wooden sphere, on an ebonised, turned wooden plinth base. (Christie's) £483 $787

John Newton (1759–1844), London, a 3in. diameter terrestrial pocket globe made up of twelve hand-coloured engraved paper gores, the prime meridian marked *Meridian of London,* ungraduated.
(Christie's) £3,910 $6,373

Thomas Malby & Son (fl. circa 1840–1900), London, a 3in. diameter terrestrial pocket globe, made up of twelve hand finished, coloured printed paper gores, the prime meridian marked *Meridian of Greenwich.*
(Christie's) £2,070 $3,374

A rare mid-18th century brass Ptolemaic Armillary Sphere, signed *Daniel Heckinger fecit a Augusta Vendelicorum [sic]*; circa 1735, the foot composed of four scrolled brackets that straddle a windrose below.
(Christie's) £138,000 $224,940

Newton, Son & Berry (fl. 1830–38), London, 1½in. diameter terrestrial miniature globe, made up of twelve hand-coloured engraved paper gores, the prime meridian marked *Meridian of London,* ungraduated.
(Christie's) £2,530 $4,124

Karl Wilhelm Kummer, (1785–1855), Berlin, an important 15in. diameter terrestrial relief globe, made up of two moulded and painted papier-mâché hemispheres, 21¼in. high.
(Christie's) £4,600 $7,498

Newton, London, a 3in. diameter celestial pocket globe made up of twelve hand-coloured lithographed paper gores, the Colurus Solstitiorum and Colorus Equinoctiorum shown.
(Christie's) £2,300 $3,749

An Indo-Persian 6in. brass celestial globe, engraved with the constellations represented by figures and animals, raised on four cast baluster supports, 10¼in. high.
(Christie's) £517 $843

[?] M.P.S., a 1¾in. diameter terrestrial miniature globe, made up of twelve hand-coloured engraved gores, the equatorial and the ecliptic both ungraduated, the continents coloured in outline.
(Christie's) £3,220 $5,248

An Indo-Persian 4¼in. brass celestial globe, the axis formed as two brass pins, located at the north and south celestial poles, 6in. high.
(Christie's) £1,955 $3,186

A three-colour gold snuff box maker's mark *PM* crowned, French prestige marks including charge mark of E. Brichard, Swiss, late 18th century, 3½in. wide.
(Sotheby's)   £2,990 $4,993

A jewelled gold desk seal, unmarked, late 19th century, formed as an Indian rhinoceros with baroque pearl body and chased gold head and legs, 2¾in. long.
(Sotheby's)   £3,910 $6,530

A gold and enamel 'Turkish Export' snuff box, apparently unmarked, Swiss, circa 1850, the lid decorated in taille d'épargne enamel, 2½in. wide.
(Sotheby's)   £1,725 $2,881

A three-colour gold snuff box, Simon-Achille Léger, Paris, 1819-1838, the lid with raised border of chased flowers, 2½in. wide.
(Sotheby's)   £1,725 $2,881

A French gold-mounted tortoiseshell snuff box, Adrien-Jean-Maximilien Vachette, Paris, 1789, with later baby's head titre, 3⅛in. wide. (Sotheby's) £8,625 $14,404

An 18ct gold vinaigrette, John Linnet, London, 1820, engine-turned body with applied flower and shell thumbpiece, 1⅞in. wide.
(Sotheby's)   £1,725 $2,880

A gold-mounted ivory desk seal, unmarked, English, circa 1840, carved as a hand grasping a baton, the leaf-chased 'cuff' cushion inset with an amethyst matrix, 2½in. high.
(Sotheby's)   £2,760 $4,609

A French gold-mounted tortoiseshell boîte à miniature, Catherine-Adelaïde Dupannoise, veuve Leferre, the lid inset with a miniature of a lady, 3in. wide.
(Sotheby's) £4,140 $6,914

A gold and enamel combined thimble/scent bottle holder, unmarked, English, late 18th century, the tapering body decorated with a broad translucent red enamel band, ¾in.
(Sotheby's)   £3,450 $5,762

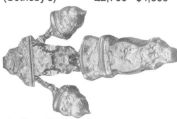

A gilt-metal châtelaine, Birmingham, mid 18th century, the hinged belt clasp decorated with an allegorical figure and a dolphin amidst scrolls, overall length 7⅝in.
(Sotheby's)   £632 $1,055

A gold snuff box, Vienna, circa 1850, stamped overall with sprig-centred discs interspersed with stars, 3⅝in.
(Sotheby's)   £1,725 $2,881

A gilt-metal etui à cire, unmarked, French, circa 1775, the shaped panels decorated with flower entwined poles, 4½in. long.
(Sotheby's)   £345 $576

A silver waiter, presented by Slazengers to Bobby Locke, of shaped circular form on scrolled feet, engraved with seven facsimile signatures, 10½in. diameter.
(Christie's) £850 $1,394

William Dunn Seniors gutty ball line cutter. (Phillips) £39,751 $64,000

A Minton tea pot and cover with dark blue ground applied in white with figures of four golfers and two caddies, 16cm. wide.
(Phillips) £460 $741

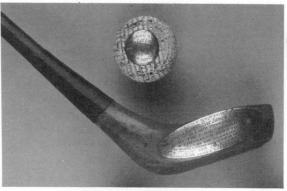

A late Victorian silver vesta case, enamelled with a panel of a golfer at the top of his backswing, the reverse inscribed *Joseph Mescan*, 2¼in. high.
(Christie's) £3,800 $6,232

An important and rare club and ball, the club with a beechwood head the top carved with Edinburgh's Coat of Arms, and an inscribed silver plate, the mesh gutty ball also with two inscribed silver plates.
(Phillips) £2,700 $4,347

A Carltonware beaker, transfer-printed with a golfing scene, 4in. high. (Christie's) £180 $293

A hand-written book, Scraps on Golf, by N. Ferguson Blair, dated *1842*, containing hand-written poems on golf and matches of character dedicated without permission to The Royal Perth Golfing Society.
(Christie's) £11,000 $18,040

A silver salver, of waved circular form, inscribed *Presented to Bobby Locke on the occasion of winning his fourth Open Championship with a record score of 279, St. Andrews, 1957,* 14in. diameter.
(Christie's) £950 $1,558

A life size bronzed resin statue of Jack Nicklaus after the original by Leicester C. Thomas, commissioned in 1988 by the American PGA.
(Wintertons) £2,000 $3,300

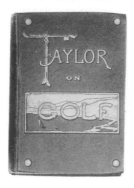

Taylor J.H. – Taylor on Golf, 1st Edition (London) 1902, 328p.p. green cloth gilt. (Phillips) £90 $145

The Golfing Annual…edited by C. Robertson Bauchope (later David S. Duncan), a complete run from volume one to 22, together 22 volumes, 8vo, Horace Cox, 1888–1909. (Sotheby's) £8,280 $13,496

Travis (Walter) The Art of Putting, original printed wrappers, 8vo, Macmillan and Co., 1904. (Sotheby's) £414 $675

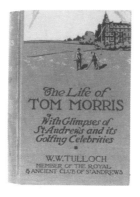

Tulloch (W.W.) The Life of Tom Morris, with Glimpses of St. Andrews and its Golfing Celebrities, first edition, 27 illustrations on 25 plates, 8vo. (Sotheby's) £506 $825

A signed and dated photograph of George Duncan, 1933, framed and glazed, 9 x 7in. (Sotheby's) £276 $450

Kerr. Rev. John – The Golf Book of East Lothian, Edinburgh, small paper edition 1896 (no. 279 of 500 copies), signed by Author, 516pp. plus xxx iv p.p. (Phillips) £520 $837

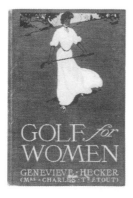

Hecker (Genevieve) Golf for Women, half-title, portrait frontispiece, plates, some double-page, original pictorial cloth gilt, New York, Baker and Taylor Co., circa 1904. (Sotheby's) £310 $496

A pair of Victorian ladies leather golfing boots, circa 1895, in good condition with hammered-in studs. (Sotheby's) £690 $1,104

A signed postcard of Old Tom Morris 1908, inscribed in pencil to the reverse, *signed by (Old) Tom Morris on his 87th birthday at St Andrews,* 5 x 3¹/₈in. (Sotheby's) £1,380 $2,249

A 'Black Diamond' ball mould circa 1920s, by the Worthington Golf Ball Co. (Sotheby's) £230 $375

A John Player's Country Life cigarettes Advertising board circa 1907, the image 10 x 15½in. (Sotheby's) £747 $1,218

A pint tankard, the domed lid with small modelled golfer addressing the ball, Sheffield 1938, 10oz, inscribed *Annual Golf Trophy Won by J.W. Waller at Thrybergh July 1939*. (Phillips) £260 $419

A signed photograph of Harold Hilton, 1910, framed and glazed, 8 x 6in. (Sotheby's) £575 $937

Darwin (Bernard) The Golf Courses of the British Isles, first edition, 64 coloured plates by Harry Rountree, scorecards and press cuttings loosely inserted, bookplate of Samuel Pope, 8vo, Duckworth and Co., 1910. (Sotheby's) £598 $975

A signed photograph of James Braid 1908, framed and glazed, 5½ x 4in. (Sotheby's) £862 $1,405

A signed photograph of Harry Vardon 1920, framed and glazed, 8 x 6in. (Sotheby's) £529 $862

A circular silver medal, one side engraved *Celurca Golf Club, Montrose 1879*, another for the M.E.G.C, another *Glengorse Golf Club won by W.W. Crawford, 71, May 1910*. (Phillips) £500 $800

Clark. R. - Golf, A Royal and Ancient Game, second edition, Edinburgh 1893, 305 p.p. green cloth. (Phillips) £240 $384

A silver cigarette case, of rectangular form, decorated with an oval enamelled panel of a golfer, rubbed and chipped, 2½in. wide. (Christie's) £550 $902

A cast-iron press, possibly for a golf ball mould, 11½in. wide. (Christie's) £600 $978

A Macintyre Burslem claret jug, transfer-printed with a panel of a golfer, with engraved silver plated spout, lid and scrolled handle 10in. high. (Christie's) £600 $984

A Royal Doulton Kingsware pitcher, decorated in relief with Puritan golfers in blues, browns and greens, 9in. high. (Christie's) £500 $820

A Lenox Pottery tyg, with Sterling silver rim, the flared body decorated with panels of a male and female golfer, 6½in. high. (Christie's) £3,000 $4,920

A Royal Doulton Kingsware pitcher, decorated in greens, reds and dark browns, with Puritan golfers in relief, 9½in. high. (Christie's) £480 $787

A cast-metal and bronze figure of a golfer, on the follow through, on naturalistic base, 11½in. high. (Christie's) £280 $459

A Victorian porcelain tobacco jar, with circular detachable top, transfer-printed with panels of golfers, the base inscribed S.F. & Co., 4½in. high. (Christie's) £300 $492

A bronze figure of a golfer, modelled at the top of his back-swing, wearing plus twos, on an oval naturalistic base, 9½in. high. (Christie's) £750 $1,230

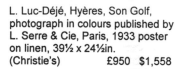

L. Luc-Déjé, Hyères, Son Golf, photograph in colours published by L. Serre & Cie, Paris, 1933 poster on linen, 39½ x 24½in. (Christie's) £950 $1,558

A Royal Doulton Seriesware punch bowl, with flared shaped rim, painted with Puritan golfers, inscribed *All fools are not knaves, but all knaves are fools*, 10in. diameter. (Christie's) £220 $361

A late Victorian silver vesta case, of rectangular form, decorated with an enamelled panel of a golfer, 2⅛in. high. (Christie's) £3,200 $5,248

A George Golf Club scratch medal of shield shape dated *1892* with crossed clubs, and a mesh gutty ball, engraved *For Monthly Competition*. (Phillips) £300 $483

Two Dutch kolf club heads, made from lead alloy, one with patterning to the face and top, 3½in. wide. (Christie's) £700 $1,148

An Attl Engineering Corp. Union City N.J. golf ball compression tester circa 1930, in working condition. (Sotheby's) £1,150 $1,874

Norman Fraser, Golf in Canada's Evergreen Playground, Vancouver Island, colour lithograph, 37 x 24½in. (Christie's) £450 $738

A Royal Doulton Seriesware teapot, painted with Puritan golfers and inscribed *Every dog has his day, every man his hour*, 6½in. high. (Christie's) £400 $656

Photographic print of Harry Vardon, by George Bedlam, signed in pencil in the margin *Harry Vardon*. (Christie's) £380 $623

A fine Allan Robertson feather golf ball, 1843, 4½cm.
(Sotheby's)   £6,325 $10,310

An A1 27½ mesh-patterned gutty golf ball, the cover chipped.
(Christie's)   £260 $426

A feathery golf ball signed *Allan*, some hack marks but distinctly signed. (Phillips) £6,000 $9,660

A feather-filled golf ball, circa 1840, possibly re-painted.
(Christie's)   £1,500 $2,460

An 'Eclipse' Patent golf ball circa 1877, in used condition.
(Sotheby's)   £1,207 $1,967

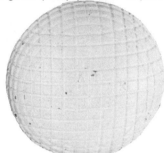

An A1 black, 27½ mesh-patterned gutty golf ball, in mint condition.
(Christie's)   £500 $820

A feather-filled golf ball, circa 1840, inscribed in ink *Presented by W. Muir-Smith, 1904*, the cover possibly re-painted.
(Christie's)   £2,000 $3,280

An exceptionally rare Henry's Rifled ball circa 1903, invented by Alexander Henry of Edinburgh. Patent No. 4360 with stamp to both poles. (Sotheby's) £29,900 $48,737

A feather-filled golf ball, stamped W. & J. Gourlay, in good condition with three small scuffs and a small hole to the cover.
(Christie's)   £2,800 $4,592

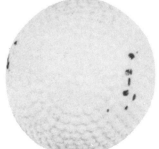

A Springvale 27½ bramble gutty ball circa 1900, by Hutchison Main & Co. Glasgow.
(Sotheby's)   £460 $750

A red hand hammered gutty ball circa 1855, with what is known as the Forgan patterning.
(Sotheby's)   £7,475 $12,184

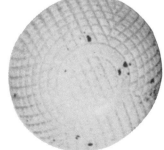

An Ocobo 27½ golf ball circa 1890, by the Silvertown Rubber Co., in pristine condition.
(Sotheby's)   £598 $975

The Challenger Bramble-pattern golf ball. (Christie's) £200 $328

A smooth-moulded gutta-percha ball, the cover dented. (Christie's) £1.100 $1,804

A smooth Silvertown gutty golf ball. (Christie's) £820 $1,345

A hand hammered gutta percha golf ball circa 1860. (Sotheby's) £345 $562

A rare J.P. Cochrane of Edinburgh bramble pattern World ball, circa 1910. (Sotheby's) £4,600 $7,498

A rare F.H. Ayres Vaile golf ball circa 1900. (Sotheby's) £1,380 $2,249

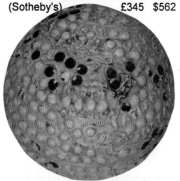

An extremely rare Terrestrial Globe bramble on 'Map of the World' ball, some paint lacking but condition very good. (Phillips) £5,500 $8,800

A splendid Dunlop V bramble golf ball, circa 1914, in its original paper within its own hessian sack. (Sotheby's) £1,207 $1,967

A black hand hammered gutty ball circa 1855, with what is known as the Forgan patterning. (Sotheby's) £1,840 $2,999

A feather-filled golf ball, by Allan Robertson, in mint condition, stamped *Allan,* and numbered in ink *49.* (Christie's) £7,500 $12,300

A red-painted Silvertown mesh-patterned gutty golf ball, in near mint condition. (Christie's) £880 $1,443

A fine Allan 29 feather ball, circa 1840, by Allan Robertson of St. Andrews, approximately 1¾in. (Sotheby's) £4,830 $7,873

A Fred Saunders, Highgate, patent straight line putter, circa 1920, with U.S. patent no. 364265. (Sotheby's) £402 $655

A Simplex Torpedo headed patent putter, patent no. 9514 1897. (Sotheby's) £862 $1,405

A James Gourlay Carnoustie very deep smooth faced mashie, circa 1900, with hickory shaft in good condition. (Sotheby's) £437 $712

A Tom Morris baffing spoon, the head stamped with a horn insert and lead back weight. (Phillips) £1,250 $2,012

A 'Nigger' putter by Charles Gibson of Westward Ho, with a 7 inches long hosel and slightly offset face. (Phillips) £100 $161

A McEwan of Musselburgh, long nosed driver, circa 1860, in golden beech, with hickory shaft. (Sotheby's) £862 $1,405

Maker unknown, general iron circa 1865, with hosel seam exposed, hickory shaft and cork grip. (Sotheby's) £299 $487

A rare aluminium putter by G.S. Sprague and Co., Boston, patented 1904, a two sided example, the head with a ball and socket joint enabling a left or right handed player to use the club. (Phillips) £1,750 $2,818

A play club with horn insert and a lead back weight, some damage to the toe, in golden beechwood, the head stamped. (Phillips) £460 $741

An Urquhart's patent adjustable iron, the face stamped Urquhart, the head stamped U No.231, the hozel similarly stamped. (Christie's) £780 $1,279

A transitional long nosed spoon by Fryer of Edinburgh, some damage to the toe, with horn insert and three circular lead back weights. (Phillips) £220 $354

A Ping Echo steel-shafted putter, the head stamped Made in USA, Phoenix, Arizona, Karsten & Company, the sole stamped Slazenger. (Christie's) £280 $459

A Mammoth niblick by Spalding, circa 1930, with hickory shaft, in good condition.
(Sotheby's)   £506 $825

A 'Brown' mashie-niblick rake iron by Winton of Montrose, circa 1905.
(Sotheby's)   £1,380 $2,249

A very rare Park Patent 'PETO' rut iron, circa 1880, with original greenheart shaft, in good condition.
(Sotheby's)   £747 $1,218

A long nosed putter with horn insert and lead back weight, the head stamped *Patrick*, with leather grip.
(Phillips)   £720 $1,159

A Ping 1A putter, by Karsten, circa 1962, with the Scottsdale Arizona address in good condition.
(Sotheby's)   £575 $937

A rut niblick by an unknown maker circa 1895, with hickory shaft, in good condition but with later grip.
(Sotheby's)   £195 $318

A long nosed baffy with horn insert and lead back weight, the head stamped *Mc Donald* and in large letters *R.A.*
(Phillips)   £1,650 $2,656

An aluminium Huntly putter, the front of the top of the shaft unit with a deep groove to accommodate the player's thumbs.
(Phillips)   £70 $113

A beechwood brassie with a lofted face with a leather face insert and lead back weight, the head stamped *T. Morris*, some repairs.
(Phillips)   £550 $880

A fine McEwan unused long spoon club head, circa 1875, in golden beech with long spoon annotated in ink to sole.
(Sotheby's)   £1,035 $1,687

A roller head putter (although this club was advertised as being a general club with which all shots could be played).
(Phillips)   £1,400 $2,254

A David Strath long nosed long spoon circa 1860, with lemon wood shaft and beech head, in good condition.
(Sotheby's)   £5,750 $9,372

A blade putter, circa 1860.
(Christie's)   £240 $394

A smooth-faced lofter, circa 1865.
(Christie's)   £120 $197

A smooth-faced cleek, circa 1860.
(Christie's)   £130 $213

A left handed scared-head long-
nosed playclub, by John Jackson of
Perth, the tapering shaft with paper
label, with suede grip.
(Christie's)   £9,000 $14,760

A Ping Anser putter, circa 1968,
with the Phoenix address and Gary
Player's autograph stamped on the
sole. (Sotheby's)   £1,150 $1,875

A smooth-faced rut-iron, by Carrick,
Musselburgh, the head stamped
Carrick, with a cross, circa 1850.
(Christie's)   £1,200 $1,968

The Royal Perth rut-iron, a
blacksmith made rut-iron early/mid
19th century, with small rounded
dished head, the hickory shaft with
suede grip, the hozel 4½in. long.
(Christie's)   £5,000 $8,200

The Royal Perth putter, a rare
metal-headed blade putter,
late18th/early 19th century, with
fruitwood shaft and well-knopped
hozel, inscribed in ink, probably
Simon Cossar, the hozel 6¼in.
long. (Christie's) £95,000 $155,800

The Royal Perth heavy iron, a rare
blacksmith made cut-off nose track
iron, late 18th/early 19th century,
with dished and rounded face and
long knopped hozel, hozel 4½in
long. (Christie's) £40,000 $65,600

A presentation putter with lead back
weight and horn insert, the head
carved with a Maltese Cross and
crossed clubs and balls, near mint
condition. (Phillips) £6,200 $9,982

A Gassiat putter, circa 1925,
manufactured by Gibson of
Kinghorn with persimmon head,
hickory shaft.
(Sotheby's)   £391 $637

A McEwan of Musselburgh long
nosed driver, circa 1865, with
beech head and hickory shaft, in
good condition.
(Sotheby's)   £1,725 $2,812

A cylinder-headed putter, the shaft reduced, with later grip. (Christie's) £320 $525

A mammoth niblick, by Cochranes Limited of Edinburgh, with dotted face. (Christie's) £550 $902

A steel-shafted whole-in-one adjustable iron, patent No. 467398. (Christie's) £110 $180

A long-nosed scared-head playclub, by Hugh Philp of St. Andrews, the sole with ram's horn inset. (Christie's) £7,500 $12,300

A rare left handed one piece transitional bulger, with horn insert and lead back weight, the head stamped *Dunn & Son*. (Phillips) £1,300 $2,093

A socket-headed putter, the head stamped *J.Hughes, Dunstanton*, the stained shaft with later leather grip. (Christie's) £130 $213

The Royal Perth light iron, a rare blacksmith made cut-off nose track iron, late 18th/early 19th century, with slightly dished face and well-knopped hozel 4in. long. (Christie's) £72,000 $118,080

A long-nosed scared-head playclub, by John Jackson of Perth, the head stamped *Jackson*, the face with hooped nose and slightly concave face, circa 1850. (Christie's) £7,200 $11,808

A Ping Echo One putter, by the Karsten company, the inset stamped *Phoenix, Ariz. 85029 Pat Pend*, the sole stamped *Slazenger, Jack Nicklaus.* (Christie's) £780 $1,279

A smooth-faced cleek, by Condie of St. Andrews, the shaft stamped *W. Anderson, St. Andrews.* (Christie's) £150 $240

A very lofted play club, stamped *Jackson* with a horn insert and lead back weight. (Phillips) £2,300 $3,703

A Spalding model G spring-faced iron, the shaft stamped *A.G.Spalding & Bros,* with white kid grip. (Christie's) £450 $738

A long-nosed scared-head putter, by McEwan of Musselburgh, the head stamped *McEwan,* circa 1870. (Christie's) £1,250 $2,050

A long-nosed scared-head driver, by John Jackson of Perth, the shaft indistinctly stamped *.dol..,* circa 1850. (Christie's) £7,200 $11,808

A long-nosed scared-head putter, by James Anderson of St. Andrews, the head stamped *J. Anderson,* circa 1880. (Christie's) £900 $1,476

A long-nosed scared-head putter, by James Wilson of St. Andrews, the head stamped *J. Wilson,* with greenheart shaft, circa 1850. Christie's) £2,000 $3,280

A Transitional scared-head driver, by Joe Anderson of Perth, the head stamped *Joe Anderson Special,* the shaft stamped *R. Forgan & Son, St. Andrews.* £550 $902

A long-nosed scared-head playclub, by McEwan of Musselburgh, the head stamped *McEwan,* the sole with ram's horn inset. (Christie's) £2,800 $4,592

A child's scared-head long-nosed playclub, by Hugh Philp of St. Andrews, the tapering hickory shaft with suede leather grip and with cross stringing. (Christie's) £2,800 $4,592

A Transitional scared-head putter, by Tom Morris of St. Andrews, the sole with ram's horn inset, the back with two later brass screws to the lead weighting. (Christie's) £700 $1,148

A long-nosed scared-head playclub, by Willie Park of Musselburgh, the head stamped *Wm. Park,* the tapering hickory shaft with suede grip. (Christie's) £9,000 $14,760

A scared-head bulger driver, by George G. Bussey & Co., London, the head stamped *George Bussey & Co.,* with Bussey Patent grip. (Christie's) £240 $394

A Turner's patent wood and aluminium-headed driver, the head stamped *Turners,* the sole stamped *Turners Patent,* Oxford Model. (Christie's) £600 $984

An Urquhart's patent adjustable iron, the face stamped *Urquhart,* the head stamped No.3029, the shaft with red leather grip. (Christie's) £820 $1,345

A smooth-faced mid-iron, by Tom Morris of St. Andrews, the head stamped *T. Morris, St. Andrews*.
(Christie's)   £650 $1,066

A long nosed play club, the head stamped *A. Patrick*, with horn insert and lead back weight.
(Phillips)   £650 $1,047

A putter with horn insert and lead back weight, the head stamped *Anderson, Perth*.
(Phillips)   £260 $419

A Transitional scared-head driver, by J. Murray, the head stamped *J. Murray*, the shaft similarly stamped, re-gripped.
(Christie's)   £350 $574

A long-nosed scared-head playclub, by Tom Morris of St. Andrews, the head stamped *T. Morris*, circa 1875.
(Christie's)   £2,000 $3,280

A scared-head bulger brassie, by F.H. Ayres, the head stamped *F.H.Ayres*, the shaft similarly stamped, circa 1885.
(Christie's)   £200 $328

A large long-nosed scared-head putter, by Robert Munro, with greenheart shaft, the sole with rams horn inset, set with four pins, the head 6½in. long.
(Christie's)   £1,100 $1,804

A Ping Echo putter, by the Karsten Company, the head stamped *Phoenix Arizona 85029 Patent Pending*, the sole stamped *Slazenger, Jack Nicklaus*.
(Christie's)   £320 $525

A Transitional scared-head presentation putter, by Robert Forgan of St. Andrews, with silver metal presentation band, inscribed *Rev. T.D. Miller, from R. Forgan*.
(Christie's)   £1,900 $3,116

A long-nosed scared-head playclub, by John Jackson of Perth, the head stamped *Jackson,* the sole with ram's horn inset.
(Christie's)   £6,500 $10,660

A long-nosed scared-head baffing spoon, by John Jackson of Perth, the head stamped *Jackson*, with well-curved lofted face, circa 1850.
(Christie's)   £2,700 $4,428

A smooth-faced iron with oval face, by Tom Stewart of St. Andrews, the head stamped *T. Morris, St. Andrews, Patent 3059*.
(Christie's)   £160 $262

An American Victor VV-IV oak-cased table gramophone with integral speaker, Victrola 4 sound pick-up, and front doors for volume regulation, circa 1910.
(Auction Team Köln) £113 $181

A small tin Induphon 138 gramophone by the Industria Fabrik, Berlin, lithographed in red-brown to imitate wood, Odeon sound pick-up and Steidinger motor, 1923.
(Auction Team Köln) £188 $301

A Pathé Concert gramophone with integral wooden speaker, original sound pick-up, two-speeds, circa 1910.
(Auction Team Köln) £293 $469

An Academy circular cabinet gramophone, in mahogany case with simulated inlay, 31½in. high.
(Christie's) £345 $552

An early Bang & Olufsen table gramophone,110v, with ammeter and speed regulator, in mahogany case, circa 1930.
(Auction Team Köln) £125 $201

A Dulcephone horn gramophone, No. B78192, with mahogany Music Master horn, Dulcephone soundbox on straight tapered tone-arm, the horn 21¼in. diam., circa 1914.
(Christie's) £920 $1,472

An undocumented gramophone with brass horn, most parts original and in working order.
(Auction Team Köln) £335 $536

An American tinpalte Columbia gramophone with integral speaker and original soundbox.
(Auction Team Köln) £380 $609

A horn gramophone, possibly by HMV, with decorative convolvulus horn.
(Auction Team Köln) £377 $603

A Bing Kiddyphone round lithographed tinplate toy gramophone, with two 15cm. discs, 1925.
(Auction Team Köln)   £167 $267

A Columbia Type BKT Graphophone (New Leader), with tone-arm, black back-bracket and maroon flower horn, 17in. diameter.
(Christie's)   £1,495 $2,392

A Pigmyphone toy gramophone by Bing Bros, Nürnberg, with fairytale motifs on the base.
(Auction Team Köln)   £251 $401

A Pooley Model 1500 walnut-cased standard gramophone, with undocumented wind-up record player and Atwater Kent Model 20 radio, circa 1925.
(Auction Team Köln)   £335 $536

A coin-operated gramophone with Polyphon 'Expression' soundbox on gooseneck tone-arm with lifting lever operated by coin mechanism, 27½in. diameter.
(Christie's)   £977 $1,563

An undocumented redwood and nickel mounted horn gramophone, with eight brass columns to the corners, and a Swiss Sonata sound box.
(Auction Team Köln)
£1,591 $2,546

A Monarch gramophone by the Gramophone and Typewriter Co., England, with light wood case and brass horn, 1903.
(Auction Team Köln) £523 $837

An H.M.V. 203 Re-entrant gramophone in mahogany case, on leafage carved turned and squared supports, 2ft4in. wide.
(Russell Baldwin & Bright)
£6,000 $9,900

An undocumented tin gramophone with Columbia sound pick-up, with built in speaker, circa 1925.
(Auction Team Köln) £138 $221

Saint Nicholas the Wonder-Worker, Russia, possibly 16th century, traditionally painted in sombre colours, shown shoulder length, 9½ x 6¾in. (Christie's) £1,610 $2,640

Russian icon depicting the Dormition of the Virgin, early 19th century, with Christ and the Apostles receiving her soul, with metal base, 14½ x 19in. (Skinner) £345 $575

Russian icon of St. John the Baptist, late 18th/early 19th century, including life scenes of the saint, 12½ x 10¼in. (Skinner) £517 $862

The Old Testament Trinity, Russia, circa 1500, the oklad with unrecorded maker's Cyrillic initials ID, Galich, 1768, the three angels seated at Abraham's table, with his house and the oak of Mambre in the background, 12¼ x 10¼in. (Christie's) £4,600 $7,544

A Tabletka of Christ teaching in the Temple and Christ and the Woman of Samaria, Russia, Novgorod School, circa 1500, the front with Christ with his right hand raised, between two elders, 24.8 x 22.5cm. overall.(Christie's) £23,000 $37,720

The Birth of the Mother Of God, Russia, in Palekh style, circa 1800, St. Anna on a couch attended by three handmaidens, in the foreground the Mother of God attended by two servants, 35.8 x 30.4cm. (Christie's) £2,415 $3,960

Saint George the Victorious, Russia, possibly 16th century, the saint mounted on a white charger lancing the serpent below, in a mountainous background, 33.5 x 27.6cm. (Christie's) £2,990 $4,903

Mother of God of the Sign, Russia, 17th century, the Mother of God with her arms upraised, Christ Emmanuel in a roundel on her breast, 34.3 x 30.4cm. (Christie's) £1,150 $1,886

The Presentation in the Temple, Russia, possibly 16th century, the Mother of God and St. Joseph stand on the left facing St. Simeon holding the Christ Child, 13½ x 11¼in. (Christie's) £13,800 $22,632

Russian icon of a bishop saint, early 19th century, in a landscape with monastery beyond, gilt floral borders, 12 x 10½in. (Skinner) £357 $575

Saint Nicholas, North Russia, 17th century, shown half length holding a book of Gospels in his left hand, his right hand raised in blessing, 12¼ x 10in. (Christie's) £2,530 $4,149

Christ Enthroned, Russia, 17th century, traditionally painted in sombre colours, 34¼ x 22¾in. (Christie's) £2,070 $3,394

Mother of God Bogoliubskaia, Russia, late 16th century, shown full length holding a scroll, on the right the Patriarch of Moscow stands above a group of kneeling supplicants, 25.5 x 19.4cm. (Christie's) £5,175 $8,487

Triyptych of Sts. Alexander Nevskii and Mary Magdalen, Russia, 1855, the oklad marked with the initials of Fedor Verkhovtsev, St. Petersburg, 1857, 10¼ x 11½in. (Christie's) £5,175 $8,487

Christ Pantocrator, Russia, early 20th century, on gilt ground with scroll decoration within shaped pan-Slavic border of scrolls and geometric motifs, 53.5 x 44cm. (Christie's) £1,610 $2,640

Mother of God of Iaroslavl, Russia, 18th century, the Mother of God tenderly holds the Christ Child against her left shoulder, He rests His head against her cheek, 15.5 x 12.2cm. (Christie's) £5,980 $9,807

Saint Nicholas the Wonder-Worker, Russia, circa 1800, shown half-length, his right hand raised in blessing, his left holding the Gospels, 31.2 x 27.2cm. (Christie's) £1,495 $2,451

Saint Michael the Archangel, Russia, 17th century, with spread wings holding the book of Gospels in his left hand while blowing his horn, 12½ x 10½in. (Christie's) £2,415 $3,960

A 19th century French brass and bronze inkwell in the form of an eagle surmounting a globe on stand, 9in. high.
(Andrew Hartley)   £420 $706

Tiffany favrile glass and silver inkwell, double-bulbed transparent green-amber glass vessel decorated by dark red pulled feather motif, total height 4½in.
(Skinner)   £1,794 $2,990

A 19th century French brass and coconut shell inkwell, satirically modelled as a seated Louis Philippe in barbarian dress holding a hatchet, 7in. high.
(Andrew Hartley)   £390 $655

An American Mogul-style gold, enamel and jewel-mounted inkwell, Tiffany & Co., New York and Paris, circa 1900, the round glass body with raised bosses, 3¾in. high.
(Sotheby's)   £31,568 $51,750

A 19th century French bronzed metal inkwell modelled as a setter's head 6¼in. wide.
(Andrew Hartley)   £300 $504

An American silver and favrile glass inkwell, Tiffany & Co., New York, 1902–07, (the glass circa 1897), the bombé body of rich cobalt blue glass decorated with iridescent silver-blue pulled feathering, 5¾in. high. (Sotheby's)   £9,821 $16,100

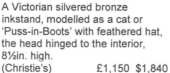

A Victorian carved oak desk stand with standing figures besides inkwell and cupboard with hinged door, 9in. high, inscribed *G.H. Stokes, 1845*. (Russell Baldwin & Bright)   £480 $792

A Victorian silvered bronze inkstand, modelled as a cat or 'Puss-in-Boots' with feathered hat, the head hinged to the interior, 8½in. high.
(Christie's)   £1,150 $1,840

A 19th century Continental gilt metal inkwell, modelled as a seated bear with glass eyes and hinged head holding a tree stump pen holder, 4in. high.
(Andrew Hartley)   £160 $269

A four case gyobu ground inro, signed *Kajikawa Saku* and *Kao*, Edo period, decorated with a cockerel in gold takamakie, 3⁷/₈in. high. (Christie's) £3,220 $5,249

A wooden tonkotsu, ojime and netsuke, the netsuke signed *Mitsukoni*, Edo period, 19th century, the tonkotsu inlaid in aogai and stag antler, 3in. (Christie's) £2,990 $4,874

A four case Shibayama inro, late 19th century, gold panel with a woman with an umbrella beneath a weeping cherry tree, 4⁷/₈in. high. (Christie's) £5,750 $9,373

A three-case lacquer inro, signed *Jokasai*, Edo period (19th century), decorated in gold, silver and iroe hiramakie depicting the warrior Soga Juro's brother mounted on a horse, 2¾in. long. (Christie's) £3,450 $5,796

A four-case inro with an ivory netsuke, signed *Kanshosai* and sealed *Kan*, Edo period, (19th century), decorated in gold and silver hiramakie, takamakie, togidashi, kirikane, kinpun and iroe takamakie with chaffinches by a meandering stream, 3¼in. long. (Christie's) £5,175 $8,694

A large single case inro, signed *Deme Mankon kizamu Kajikawa Saku*, Edo period, 19th century, carved in the round in the form of a mask of Hannya wrapped around a bell, 4⁷/₈in. high. (Christie's) £4,025 $6,561

A single case inro, late 18th/early 19th century, carved in the round in the form of a Nembutsu oni carrying a gong, 4½in. high. (Christie's) £2,875 $4,686

A four-case black and gold lacquered inro, signed *Shiomi Masanari*, Edo period (18th century), decorated in a pale and dark gold and brown takamakie on a roiro and kinpun ground, 8.1cm. high. (Christie's) £1,380 $2,318

A four case brown lacquer ishimeji ground inro, 18th century, decorated in gold and iroe takamakie and inlaid with mother-of-pearl, 3⁵/₈in. long. (Christie's) £1,495 $2,437

A Phywe Wimshurst machine, with black painted cast iron frame and two conical Leyden jars, circa 1910, 30 x 37 x 25cm.
(Auction Team Köln) £137 $221

A filament lamp Enigma encoding machine developed by Arthur Scherbius, Berlin for 22 billion code combinations, 1940.
(Auction Team Köln)
£8,374 $13,399

An Edwardian gilt brass barograph by Thomas Armstrong & Brother Ltd, Manchester & Liverpool, with combined mercury thermometer, 44.5cm. (Bearne's) £700 $1,155

A lacquered-brass compound monocular microscope, signed on the horseshoe stand *J. Swift & Son London*, with rack and pinion coarse and micrometer fine focusing, 14½in. high.
(Christie's) £230 $368

An 18th century brass octagonal compass sundial, signed *Butterfield A Paris,* the horizontal plate engraved with hours for latitudes 52°, 51°, 48°, 46° and 43°, 2⁷/₈in. wide. (Christie's) £782 $1,245

A 19th century hour glass, with turned mahogany ends and side supports, 20.5cm. high.
(Phillips) £460 $754

An early 19th century lacquered-brass Culpeper-type microscope, unsigned, the body-tube with rack and pinion focusing, sprung stage and slide holder, 13¼in. high.
(Christie's) £575 $916

An ornamental lathe with tambour top by Holtzapffel & Deyerlein, No. 489, the semi-circular top pivoting on the double mahogany frame, 42in. wide overall.
(Christie's) £2,185 $3,496

A rare early 18th century magnet, the brass suspension clamp signed *Lenoir 1807,* the iron magnet with tie-strip encased with mahogany shields, 6½in. long.
(Christie's) £782 $1,245

A late 18th century gilt-metal and agate etui in the rococo style, 10.5cm. (Bearne's) £490 $808

A brass Culpeper microscope, circa 1790, on wooden base, signed *Joh. Rider, Belfast,* 39cm. high, with slides, in velvet case with accessories.
(Auction Team Köln)

£1,508 $2,412

An early 20th century barograph by John Trotter, Glasgow, with seven section steel chamber, in an oak case, 35.5cm.
(Bearne's) £480 $792

A rare 19th century French lacquered-brass compound monocular microscope, signed on the folding tripod stand *Pixii, à Paris,* in mahogany case, 12¼in. wide. (Christie's) £3,450 $5,494

A mahogany saw-vice with lead-faced jaws with ogival underside and urn-shaped stem with turned clamping handle, 18½in. high. (Christie's) £207 $331

A rare 19th century lacquered-brass 2³/₈in. refracting telescope, signed *Ross, London,* the 28³/₈in. long body tube in two sections which screw together.
(Christie's) £2,070 $3,296

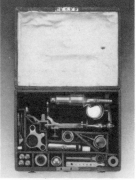

A Nema NEue MAschine Type T-D encoding machine, with ten barrels and low serial number TD195, built on the Enigma principle, 1947.
(Auction Team Köln)
£1,005 $1,608

An unusual 19th century brass telescopic apparatus, signed *Luis Schopper Leipzig No. 150,* the telescope with rack and pinion focusing, 12¾in. long closed.
(Christie's) £322 $513

A rare late 18th century lacquered-brass compound and simple microscope compendium, signed on the tripod stand *Martin London,* in fitted fishskin-covered case, 12in. wide. (Christie's) £10,350 $16,482

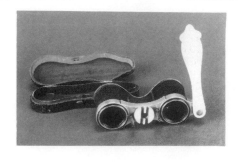

An 18th century waywiser, signed on the brass dial *T. Heath Fecit,* the dial engraved for miles, furlongs and poles. (Christie's) £782 $1,245

A rare 19th century pair of silver telescopic opera glasses, signed on the eyepiece surrounds *Lunette Bautain,* in original silk-lined shaped leather-covered case, 4⁷/₈in. wide. (Christie's) £1,725 $2,747

A 19th century aneroid barometer, the oxidised-brass case with suspension loop and silvered dial, signed *R. & J. Beck Ltd., 68 Cornhill, London,* 5⁷/₈. long. (Christie's) £207 $330

A 19th century lacquered-brass compound binocular microscope, unsigned, body tubes mounted on a Ross-type arm, with prism, 18in. high. (Christie's) £1,035 $1,648

A late 18th century lacquered-brass and silvered compass sundial, signed on the hour ring *Harris & Co., 50 Holborn, London,* with folding gnomon, 5⁷/₈in. wide. (Christie's) £1,610 $2,564

An 18th century brass Cuff-type compound monocular microscope, signed on the eared stage *Thomas Ribright London fecit,* 17in. high. (Christie's) £1,610 $2,564

A late 18th century brass theodolite, signed on the horizontal circle *Wellington, Crown Court, Soho, London,* 11in. high. (Christie's) £1,610 $2,564

A 19th century demonstration concave mirror, with moulded ebonised frame and brass mounts, raised on a baluster-turned support, 13¾in. high; and another demonstration mirror, 13¼in. high. (Christie's) £483 $769

A late 18th century lacquered-brass 4in. reflecting telescope, signed on the back plate of the 23¾in. long body-tube *J. Dolland Londini Fecit.* (Christie's) £3,220 $5,128

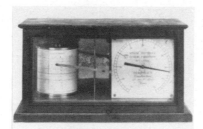

An Edwardian period boudoir table thermometer, signed on the ivorine dial *O. Comitti & Son, London,* 10⅝in. high.
(Christie's)   £288 $459

A late 19th century electric barograph, signed and engraved on the silvered dial *Diligeon & Cie.* the lacquered-brass base plate mounted with the electric mechanism, 15½in. wide.
(Christie's)   £414 $659

An unusual [?] 17th century fruitwood simple microscope, the magnifying lens supported by three baluster-turned columns from the base, 4in. high fully closed.
(Christie's)   £633 $1,008

A late 17th century Nuremberg-pattern bronze nesting weight master cup, the handle moulded in the form of two serpents supported by a pair of twin-tailed mermaids, 10¾in. high with handle raised.
(Christie's)   £2,990 $4,762

A late 16th century gilt-brass table compass and calendar dial, signed on the volvelle on the underside *V. Klieber 1585,* 2¾in. square.
(Christie's)   £1,150 $1,831

A late 18th century lacquered-brass Jones Most Improved-pattern compound monocular microscope, signed on the folding tripod stand *Smith Royal Exchange London,* 11¾in. wide.
(Christie's)   £1,840 $2,930

A late 17th/early 18th century French ivory dyptich dial, signed on the cover *C. Blovd A Dieppe,* the cover further engraved with a horizontal dial, 4¼in. long.
(Christie's)   £1,955 $3,113

An early 18th century part-set of English boxwood Napier's Bones, unsigned, with broad rod for cubes and squares, and nine (of ten), multiplier rods, 3⅝in. wide, and an abacus in cased case, 7in.
(Christie's)   £3,680 $5,860

A late 19th century lacquered-brass compound monocular microscope, with a collection of slides, in thirteen drawers, in a walnut case, 24¼in. high. (Christie's)   £2,300 $3,663

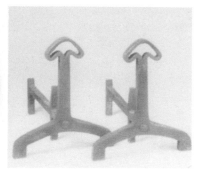

A Victorian cast iron architectural fire grate cover, 19th century, in the form of the front of a quoined town house, 17¼in. long.
(Sotheby's)　　£1,193　$1,955

Cast iron medallion portrait of George Washington, in contemporary wood frame, 26½in. high. (Skinner)　£353　$575

Rare Gustav Stickley andirons, attributed, early form, unsigned, 16in. high.
(Skinner)　　£6,555　$10,925

Cast iron and glass aquarium, probably J.W. Fiske & Co., New York, last quarter 19th century, the shell and foliate decorated octagonal tank centring a rockery-form fountain, 47¾in. high.
(Skinner)　　£2,046　$3,335

A pair of black-painted cast-iron hitching post finials, American, 19th century, each of horsehead form with articulated and moulded head and mane and bit in mouth, 14in. high. (Christie's)　£2,208　$3,680

A polychrome-painted cast metal cigar store indian, stamped Wm. Demuth (1835–1911) & Company, New York City, late 19th century, 70½in. high.
(Christie's)　　£6,900　$11,500

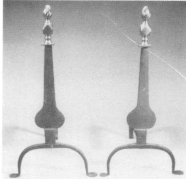

A wrought iron fire grate, probably late 18th century, the rectangular basket with part writhen rails, flanked by brand dog standards, 35½in. wide.
(Christie's)　　£1,380　$2,208

A cast-iron figure of a perched owl, American, late 19th/early 20th century, cast in two pieces, the swell-bodied figure with prominent wing and feather detail, 19½in. high overall. (Sotheby's) £1,333 $2,185

Pair of brass and wrought iron flame and chamfered ball-top knife blade andirons, American, third quarter 18th century, 23in. high.
(Skinner)　　£1,340　$2,185

A George III style steel and cast iron firegrate, early 20th century, the three railed basket of U-section with double urn finials, 36in. wide. (Christie's) £1,955 $3,128

Cast iron and glass aquarium, J.W. Fiske & Co., New York, circa 1875, foliate decorated octagonal form tank with shaped skirt, 28in. diameter. (Skinner) £1,269 $2,070

A French cast iron child's bed, 19th century, with foliate cast shell-capped uprights and floral-carved spandrels, 55½in. wide. (Christie's) £633 $1,013

A Coalbrookdale cast-iron corner hall stand with pierced wheel and leafage decoration, fitted six pegs and bowfront base, 6ft. 3in. high. (Russell Baldwin & Bright) £780 $1,287

A pair of cast-iron duck andirons, American, 20th century, hollow cast and mounted on wrought-iron guards, 17in. long. (Sotheby's) £702 $1,150

Cast iron horse's head hitching post, 19th century, painted black, 59in. high. (Eldred's) £300 $495

A very decorative early cast iron Magic Franklin stove by Cox, Warren, Morrison & Co., Troy, NY, 1854. (Auction Team Köln) £176 $281

A pair of painted cast-iron 'Dr. Owl' andirons, American, 20th century, each cast in the half-round with inset yellow and black glass eyes, 21½in. high. (Sotheby's) £1,263 $2,070

Wrought iron snake-form holder, 19th century, with ball joint a caliper form clamp, 20¼in. high. (Skinner) £1,552 $2,530

A 19th century carved ivory group of a male entertainer with a drum, a dancing monkey at his feet, 6½in. high. (Andrew Hartley) £170 $280

A pair of carved ivory candlesticks, South German or Austrian, 19th century, the nozzles with cabochon scrolls and entwined serpent heads, 8½in. (Christie's) £2,875 $4,600

A 19th century ivory tusk vase, inlaid with mother of pearl depicting birds on a flowering branch, with silver mounts, 13½in. high. (Andrew Hartley) £600 $1,010

Two German carved ivory figures of itinerant musicians, late 18th or early 19th century, each shown playing bagpipes, 7in. high. (Christie's) £1,495 £2,392

Oriental carved ivory figural group of two gentlemen seated at a table with a pomegranate, raised on a panelled ivory base and teak wood stand, 11in. long. (Du Mouchelles) £625 $1,000

A miniature carved ivory phrenological head, unsigned, the cranium with incised numbers and divisions showing the areas of the sentiments, 3¼in. high. (Christie's) £1,840 $2,944

An ivory okimono, signed *Ikkosai*, Edo period, 19th century, of three monkeys carved in an affectionate family group. (Christie's) £2,070 $3,374

A German carved ivory figure of Napoleon, mid 19th century, standing in full uniform, with orders to his chest, 11½in. high. (Christie's) £4,025 $6,440

A 19th century Continental carved ivory group of a patriarchal gnome-like figure lecturing two similar squatting figures, 10cm. long. (Bearne's) £460 $759

A Continental carved ivory model of
a mythical winged beast, on
rectangular base, now mounted as
a candle stick, 15¼in. high.
(George Kidner) £25,000 $41,500

A carved skeleton in coffin, opening
to a black fabric-lined interior
containing a jointed and articulated
skeleton, 6¾in. long.
(Sotheby's)   £5,612 $9,200

A Japanese carved ivory figure of a
lady carrying a samisen and a rose,
signed *Nobyakito*, Meiji, 20cm.
(Bearne's)   £640 $1,058

A miniature carved ivory
phrenological head, signed
LEVESLEY, the cranium with
incised numbers and divisions
showing the areas of the
sentiments, 3¾in. high.
(Christie's)   £1,955 $3,128

A carved ivory snuff bottle,
Qianlong seal mark and possibly of
the period, carved as twin boys
representing the spirits of mirth and
harmony, 3in. high.
(Christie's)   £3,680 $5,998

A Tokyo School ivory study of
Bodhisattva, signed on base, late
19th/early 20th century, 10.5cm.
(Bearne's)   £390 $644

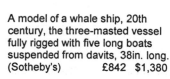

Fine French Second Empire silk
purse with ivory portrait miniature,
early 19th century, the cover and
back with a portico and memorial
urn in a floral landscape, 8¼in.
long. (Skinner)   £276 $460

A Japanese articulated ivory model
of a crayfish, second half 19th
century, naturalistically carved and
modelled with moving tail, legs and
antennae, 12⅜in. long.
(Sotheby's)   £3,335 $5,569

A model of a whale ship, 20th
century, the three-masted vessel
fully rigged with five long boats
suspended from davits, 38in. long.
(Sotheby's)   £842 $1,380

A fine white jade carving of a recumbent elephant, Qianlong, the reclining beast carved with its head sharply turned to the left, 5½in. wide.
(Christie's)   £23,000 $37,490

A Chinese spinach-green jade rectangular censer and domed cover, with Buddhist lion finial, upright handles with attached loose rings, 9in. high.
(Christie's)   £690 $1,118

A fine pale grey jade archaistic libration vessel, probably Song dynasty, delicately carved around the exterior with a wide band of geometric motifs between two confronted dragons, 6¾in. wide.
(Christie's)   £25,300 $41,239

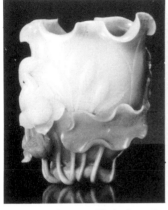

A white and caramel jade 'Lotus' vase, late Qing dynasty, crisply carved as a closed lotus leaf forming the vessel, the rim irregularly everted, 6in. high.
(Christie's)   £2,530 $4,124

A brown-flecked white jade tripod censer and cover, 17th century, applied at the side and rim with two rectangular handles, 6in. wide.
(Christie's)   £2,300 $3,749

A small jadeite vase and cover, 19th century, carved and pierced with a grapevine and a chrysanthemum branch flanking either side, 4in. high.
(Christie's)   £2,875 $4,686

A finely carved archaistic spinach jade double 'hero' vase, Qianlong four-character mark and of the period, the cylindrical vases deeply carved with chilong clambering on the sides, 4⅞in. high.
(Christie's)   £6,325 $10,310

A large Mughal-style chloromelanite vase and cover, 19th century, the sides carved and pierced with an upright serrated leaf, 13½in. high.
(Christie's)   £9,775 $15,933

A celadon jade 'Rock & Monkey' boulder, 17th/early 18th century, carved as a mountain landscape with a pine tree at one side and a peach tree at the other, 5in. high.
(Christie's)   £2,070 $3,374

A citrine mounted shaped oval brooch, the single oval citrine within a textured foliate and scroll frame.
(Bearne's)   £250 $413

A dragonfly brooch set twenty nine diamonds & two rubies with blue enamel wings.
(Russell, Baldwin & Bright)
                                £1,700 $2,720

An oval carved agate cameo brooch depicting a lady writing, within a scroll frame.
(Bearne's)   £420 $672

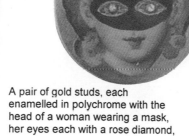

An enamelled and diamond set flower brooch, circa 1900, in the design of a pansy, the leaves and petals with green violet enamel, 2¼in. long.
(Sotheby's)   £2,185 $3,649

A pair of gold studs, each enamelled in polychrome with the head of a woman wearing a mask, her eyes each with a rose diamond, late 19th century.
(Tennants)   £420 $672

An Edwardian brooch/pendant, set with pearls and diamonds, with detachable brooch mount.
(Wintertons)   £720 $1,180

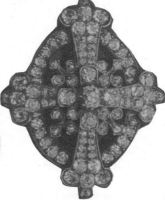

A modern ruby and diamond flower-head brooch with circular rubies and circular brilliant-cut diamonds pavé-set. (Bearne's) £700 $1,155

A pair of coral relief pendant earrings, each carved with the portrait of a young woman.
(Bearne's)   £310 $511

A 19th century gold, silver and diamond oval silver brooch with cross motif, pavé set with old mine brilliant-cut stones.
(Bearne's)   £1,800 $2,970

A diamond mounted leaf brooch with baguette and marquise mounted diamonds, stamped *14K*. (Bearne's) £920 $1,518

A 19th century gold, baroque pearl and seed-pearl bird of paradise brooch, with central baroque pearl body and textured gold feathers. (Bearne's) £950 $1,568

A French enamelled gold stick-pin with Arab horse and rider motif. (Bearne's) £350 $578

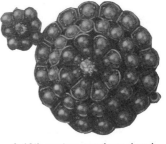

A late 19th century enamelled gold and diamond mounted swallow brooch, the outstretched wings and tail with blue enamelled feathers. (Bearne's) £700 $1,155

An Edwardian sapphire and pearl bar brooch, together with reverse intaglio crystal pendant. (George Kidner) £190 $313

Art Nouveau enamel and gem-set duck pin, designed as a bird in flight with pale golden-green basse taille enamel body, the wings edged with a row of channel-set square-cut rubies and bead-set round diamonds. (Skinner) £2,515 $4,025

Gold and ruby cat brooch, the body designed with prong-set round rubies, twisted 19ct. yellow gold wire face and tail, signed *Tiffany & Co.* (Skinner) £1,581 $2,530

Diamond and enamel fish pin, the pierced body decorated with blue-green enamel scales and yellow-orange fins, diamond-set mouth, ruby eye, 18ct. yellow gold mount. (Skinner) £395 $632

A 19th century seed-pearl and diamond brooch with hair slide fitment, in original fitted case, by Hunt & Roskell. (Bearne's) £450 $742

Sapphire and diamond butterfly brooch, the pierced platinum-topped wings set with round diamonds and sapphires, approximate total diamond weight 3.30cts. (Skinner) £1,797 $2,875

A pair of dress cuff links, each with a pair of opals mounted in gold, 16cm. (Tennants) £900 $1,440

A modern 18ct gold cluster ring set with centre oval blue sapphire surrounded by brilliant cut diamonds and baguette cut diamonds to shoulders. (Wintertons) £500 $825

Gold slide bracelet, the quatrefoil slide with seed pearl accents, black enamel tracery, and fox-tail tassels, 14ct. yellow gold mesh bracelet. (Skinner) £466 $747

A gold-coloured metal brooch in the form of a horse's head, 47mm. long. (Bearne's) £440 $704

South Sea pearl necklace, comprising a strand of graduated baroque cultured pearls, 14ct. yellow gold reeded barrel clasp set with a row of round diamonds, 15in. long. (Skinner) £2,587 $4,140

Antique gold and enamel portrait brooch, the oval porcelain plaque painted with a scene of doves and putti, surrounded by a bow and flower motif frame in multicolour enamel. (Skinner) £1,222 $1,955

Victorian gold bracelet, the hinged bangle design in 18ct. yellow gold with wolf's head terminals, diamond eye accents. (Skinner) £1,150 $1,840

Gold and ruby bow brooch, the large triple-loop bow fastened with two rows of prong-set round rubies, 14ct. yellow gold. (Skinner) £719 $1,150

A black opal mounted oval brooch with a single pear-shaped black opal in an openwork frame. (Bearne's) £550 $908

Tourmaline and diamond brooch, designed as two horse heads, one of carved pink tourmaline, the other with pavé bead-set round diamonds. (Skinner) £1,868 $2,990

Victorian gold and diamond locket pendant, the shield shape decorated with five prong-set old mine-cut diamonds, 18ct. bicolour gold. (Skinner) £611 $977

Ruby and diamond bee brooch, set with faceted oval rubies and round diamonds, the wings and head set en tremblant, 18ct. gold mount. (Skinner) £1,868 $2,990

Emerald and diamond brooch, a modified kite-shape step-cut emerald weighing approximately 5.25cts., surrounded by diamonds set in a platinum and 18ct gold mount. (Skinner) £18,750 $30,000

Antique diamond and pearl floral spray brooch, the central flowerhead mounted en tremblant, set with round and rose-cut diamonds. (Skinner) £359 $575

A Chinese export lacquer tea caddy, early 19th century, decorated overall in gilt with foliage to the cover and reserves of flower baskets to the sides, 7½in. wide. (Christie's) £2,875 $4,605

A lacquer okimono, late 19th century, of a Noh actor in the role of Shojo, standing with a dragon on his back. (Christie's) £2,070 $3,374

A Chinese lacquer sewing box, 19th century, with red decoration on a black ground, fitted compartments and numerous ivory items, separate black lacquer base, 13in. wide. (Eldred's) £412 $660

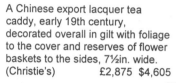

A gold lacquer kodansu with two doors and a drawer, late 19th century, the top doors, drawer, back and sides decorated in kinji, takamakie and aogai with numerous open and closed fans, 5½in. high. (Christie's) £3,220 $5,249

A small suzuribako, late 19th century, the cover decorated in togidashi with fuyo and ominaeshi on a sparse black and e-nashiji ground, 6⁹/₁₆in. high. (Christie's) £2,070 $3,374

An elaborately decorated kodansu with signatures after well-known artists, Koremitsu, Naomitsu, Tashiyuki Kizamu, Toshima saku, Ryozan and others, Edo Period (19th century). (Christie's) £10,350 $16,870

A leaf-tea caddy in the form of a covered jar, late 19th century, one of the two main panels shows a Ranryo dancer 6½in. high. (Christie's) £11,500 $18,745

A fundame ground kogo, 19th century, modelled as a duck, decorated in gold, silver and iroe hiramakie, 5¼in wide. (Christie's) £1,955 $3,187

A roironuri ground suzuribako, Edo period, finely decorated in gold and iroe takamakie with a bouquet of chrysanthemums and ashi, 7¾in. wide. (Christie's) £2,875 $4,686

An early Victorian brass oil lamp, the spherical opaque shade and Hinks & Sons patent burner and reservoir on a neo-classical style fluted urn shaped base, 19¼in. high. (Christie's) £1,035 $1,656

A pair of German patent bronze oil lamps, Wild & Wesson, late 19th century, in the neo-classical taste, the boat-shaped reservoirs cast with masks and scrolls, 21¾in. high. (Christie's) £5,370 $8,592

A cameo glass lamp, by Gallé, circa 1900, the frosted grey glass internally mottled with yellow towards rims and overlaid in amethyst, 36.5cm. high. (Christie's) £5,175 $8,487

A pair of French gilt bronze mounted opaline oil lamps, late 19th century, with fret-work burners above waisted necks and tapering bodies, 19½in. high. (Christie's) £2,760 $4,416

A pair of Regency bronze argand lamps, the reservoirs of inverted trumpet-shape, cast with fluted ornament, with bands of egg and dart, 16¹/₈in. high. (Christie's) £1,840 $2,944

A pair of Chinese porcelain models of hens, circa 1900, later gilt bronze mounted and adapted as table lamps, 15in. excluding fitment. (Christie's) £1,380 $2,208

Jefferson reverse-painted table lamp, frosted domed shade with landscape design, signed, copper finished two-socket metal base, 19½in. high. (Eldred's) £653 $1,045

An American gilt and bronze patinated colza table lamp, by B. Gardiner N. York, mid 19th century, the urn reservoir with scroll handles to the neck, 17¾in. high. (Christie's) £1,150 $1,840

A pair of English brass colza oil lamps, mid 19th century, the campana-shaped reservoirs with lobed undersides with gadrooned everted rims, 17in. high. (Christie's) £2,185 $3,583

Tiffany bronze and leaded glass spreading daffodil lamp, domed shade of yellow, green, amber, and opal white glass segments, 20in. high. (Skinner) £13,110 $21,850

Leaded glass floral table lamp, shade of caramel amber slag glass segments in brickwork progression, 25in. high. (Skinner) £517 $862

Tiffany Studios bronze desk lamp, dark patina on spun bronze dome shade with silver colour reflective interior, 18in. high.
(Skinner) £1,173 $1,955

Duffner & Kimberly 'Colonial No. 501' table lamp, leaded mosaic dome shade composed of pink, lavender, amber, yellow, and green glass segments, 21½in. high. (Skinner) £2,415 $4,025

Mount Washington Burmese fluid lamp, late 1890s decorated parlour lamp with fine pink to yellow Burmese glass handpainted and enamelled with Egyptian decoration, 20in. high.
(Skinner) £6,210 $10,350

Handel etched and enamel painted parrot lamp, shade composed of four tapered curved panels, two etched and enamelled with brilliant orange parrots, 28in. high.
(Skinner) £2,415 $4,025

Tiffany bronze and favrile arrowroot lamp, diminutive conical leaded glass shade with twelve repeating green leaf-root elements, 21in. high.
(Skinner) £11,040 $18,400

Handel overlaid Goldenrod lamp, seven amber slag glass bent panels framed with metal overlay to depict field flowers, 22in. high.
(Skinner) £2,000 $3,335

Etched metal and green slag glass lamp, attributed to Riviere Studios, beaded metal framework in grapevine pattern on shade, 21in. high. (Skinner) £759 $1,265

Double painted scenic table lamp, painted on exterior in monochromatic winter scene, 23in. high. (Skinner)   £690 $1,150

Fine Goldscheider lamp base, finely detailed figure of a woman decorated in colours on a bluish white ground, 18½in. high. (Skinner)   £966 $1,610

Overlaid slag glass panel lamp, octagonal metalwork shade with eight bent amber slag panels 20in. high. (Skinner)   £345 $575

Important Rookwood Pottery sea green glaze lamp, 1901, decorated by Kataro Shirayamadani, electroplated copper floral sprays over lotus blossoms, shade by Tiffany Studios, overall height 17¾in. (Skinner) £20,010 $33,350

A Sitzendorf porcelain table lamp, with three scroll feet, applied overall with roses and foliage, 43cm high. (Bearne's)   £360 $576

Handel leaded glass harp desk lamp, bronzed metal base with adjustable swivel socket fitted with six sided panelled amber slag glass shade, 19in. high. (Skinner)   £897 $1,495

Leaded glass acorn border lamp, domed shade attributed to Tiffany Studios, composed of mottled green, blue opalescent amber rippled glass segments, 25in. high. (Skinner)   £4,485 $7,475

Tiffany bronze and favrile damascene single student lamp, original dark patina on Manhattan single-post model, 24in. high. (Skinner)   £2,760 $4,600

Tiffany bronze and favrile glass 'Harvard' lamp, octagonal leaded glass shade of dichroic and blue-green, amber rectangular segments, 26½in. high. (Skinner)   £8,280 $13,800

Bigelow Kennard and Grueby pottery table lamp, leaded glass shade in sunflower blossom configuration, on green matte glaze Grueby pottery base, total height 23in. (Skinner)   £5,520 $9,200

Art and Crafts slag glass lamp, original finish, 21½in. high. (Skinner)   £517 $862

G. Argy-Rousseau pâte de verre veilleuse, oval moulded glass shade of mottled grey-lavender decorated by three repeating red-centred purple blossoms, total height 8¼in. (Skinner)   £3,174 $5,290

A cameo and carved glass lamp, by Daum, circa 1910, the double domed shade resting on three wrought-iron arms above tapering cylindrical stem and domed circular foot, 31.5cm. high. (Christie's)   £5,750 $9,430

A pair of George IV bronze colza-oil lamps, in the manner of Thomas Messenger, each of rhyton horn form, with a tusked boar's mask holding a foliate and turned lamp, 11in. high. (Christie's)   £5,750 $9,545

Austrian Art Glass and green metal desk lamp, closed top teardrop opal glass shade of green iridescent Loetz-type papillon surface, 17in. high. (Skinner)   £897 $1,495

Handel scenic landscape table lamp, domed shade of Teroma-textured glass reverse painted as mountainous scenic view, 20½in. high. (Skinner) £2,415 $4,025

Quezal Art glass and figural desk lamp, bronze lion reclining on faceted weighted pedestal foot supporting offset curved lamp shaft, 13in. high. (Skinner) £621 $1,035

Tiffany ten-light lily lamp, rare original etched silver finish on bronze base with curved drop stems, 21½in. high. (Skinner)   £3,967 $6,612

A cameo glass lamp, by Daum, circa 1900, the frosted grey glass internally mottled with yellow and overlaid in cherry red and green, 43cm. high.
(Christie's)　　£6,325　$10,373

Art glass and brass desk lamp, angular adjustable gilt metal drop socket lamp base fitted with frosted blue glass shade, 15in. high.
(Skinner)　　£172　$287

An enamelled glass lamp, by Daum, circa 1910, the clear glass internally mottled with yellow and orange, acid-etched and finely enamelled, 38cm. high.
(Christie's)　　£9,200　$15,088

Exceptional Grueby Pottery lamp with Tiffany Studios Crocus Shade, base with five leaf-forms under a rich, leathery, matte green glaze, 20in. high.
(Skinner)　　£22,770　$37,950

Ettore Sottsass for Stilnovo, 'Valigia' table lamp, designed 1977, black and red metal, black rubber, 14½in. high.
(Sotheby's)　　£575　$931

A pair of pressed colourless glass whale oil lamps, probably Sandwich, Massachusetts, mid 19th century, the lamps in the Bulls eye pattern with pewter tops, 9in. high.
(Sotheby's)　　£702　$1,150

An Art Deco oyster wood table lamp, second quarter 20th century, the domed shade above a bulbous and tapering column, 22¾in. high.
(Christie's)　　£1,725　$2,760

A pair of candle holders in neo-classical style, the leaf cast nozzles with glass storm shades, on fossil marble socles, 1ft. 6½in. high.
(Sotheby's)　　£1,840　$3,073

A fine plique à jour lamp shade, Meiji period, decorated with a spray of flowers, foliage and scrolling clouds, 19¹/₈in. high.
(Christie's)　　£6,900　$11,247

Handel Tam-o'-Shanter table lamp, converted fluid lamp with glass shade obverse painted with green stylised leaf motif, sanded interior, 19in. high. (Skinner)   £327 $546

Fine Fulper Pottery leaded glass lamp, cat's eye flambé glaze, fitted with amber and red slag glass, 18½in. high. (Skinner)   £4,830 $8,050

Pittsburgh scenic table lamp, domed yellow glass shade painted on surface with rough-textured green full-length trees, 18in. high. (Skinner)   £483 $805

Tiffany bronze tulip lamp on turtleback base, domed leaded glass shade with multicoloured upright tulip blossoms and buds, 23in. high. (Skinner)   £20,700 $34,500

Tiffany Studios bronze and leaded favrile glass double student lamp, dark patina on wiretwist decorated central font between double post frame, 29in. high. (Skinner)   £6,555 $10,925

Wilkinson leaded mosaic water lily table lamp, broad tuck-under domed glass mosaic shade composed as pink and white pond lilies, 30in. high. (Skinner)   £4,485 $7,475

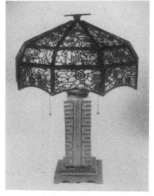

Handel reverse painted basketweave wild rose lamp, domed glass shade moulded with vertical ribs and horizontal ridges, impressed *Handel*, 22in. high. (Skinner)   £1,311 $2,185

Etched metal and glass shade on pottery lamp base, possibly the work of Riviere Studios, nine-sided geometric panel lamp with green slag glass segments, 21in. high. (Skinner)   £759 $1,265

Tiffany gilt bronze and gold linenfold glass table lamp, large model #1952 sixteen-sided shade of favrile-fabrique golden amber glass, 27in. high. (Skinner)   £5,865 $9,775

Handel reverse painted harbour scenic boudoir lamp, domed glass shade, painted on interior with tall sailing ships in port, 14½in. high. (Skinner)   £1,449 $2,415

Reverse painted pond lily lamp, smooth domed glass shade with three repeating motifs of water lily blossoms, 23½in. high. (Skinner)   £1,104 $1,840

Handel reverse painted boudoir lamp, tuck-under dome shade with pond lilies and cat-o' nine-tails on blue background, 13½in. high. (Skinner)   £1,104 $1,840

Tiffany bronze and favrile glass pansy lamp, domed shade with repeating clusters of multicoloured blossoms, on dark bronze three-socket ribbed cushion base, 22in. high. (Skinner) £13,800 $23,000

Tiffany gilt bronze counterbalance dragonfly desk lamp, mounted with cased favrile glass with gold damascene iridescent surface engraved with five intaglio dragonflies, total height 14in. (Skinner)   £3,450 $5,750

Pittsburgh reverse painted lamp, conical textured glass shade painted orange and fuchsia inside with green and black Arts and Crafts geometric motif, 19in. high. (Skinner)   £517 $862

Bradley and Hubbard owl lamp, six-sided shade of bent panel slag glass inserts in brickwork frame raised on metal base with three owl shaft, 12in. high. (Skinner)   £414 $690

Tiffany Studios bronze adjustable fancy student lamp, elaborate single-post arrangement with burner and font embellished by beading, 21in. high. (Skinner)   £2,760 $4,600

Handel reverse painted black bird of paradise lamp, textured glass dome shade decorated by two pairs of long-tailed brightly coloured birds, 24½in. high. (Skinner)   £6,900 $11,500

An ormolu and glass ovoid lantern, early 20th century, the reeded frame with cone terminal and berried floral swags, 14¼in. high. (Christie's)   £805 $1,288

A gilt-bronze hall lantern, French, circa 1890, of cylindrical form, hung with cast swags of flowers and fruit, 88cm. high.
(Sotheby's)   £5,175 $8,538

A brass hall lantern, probably Dutch, late 19th century, of square section with canted angles, the panels with pierced foliate tracery, 16in. high. (Christie's) £805 $1,288

A French ormolu and glass lantern, late 19th or early 20th century, of faceted polygonal form, the tubular framework with pierced floral bosses, shell and caryatid crestings, 28in. high.
(Christie's)   £5,520 $8,832

One of a pair of Louis XV style gilt bronze pentagonal hall lanterns, 20th century, the serpentine sides with arched foliate crestings, with scroll suspension to the corona, 35in. high.
(Christie's) (Two) £5,520 $8,832

A Continental polychrome wrought iron lantern, late 19th century, of rectangular form, inset with glazed panels, the crestings modelled with male masks, 33in. high. approximately.
(Christie's)   £5,750 $9,200

A gilt and bronze patinated brass gas lantern, late 19th century, of tapering rectangular form with Greek key frieze and pierced foliate crestings, 38in. high.
(Christie's)   £2,300 $3,680

A gilt and wrought iron hall lantern, second half 19th century, of tapering hexagonal form with embossed and pierced foliate friezes, 33½in. high.
(Christie's)   £2,530 $4,048

An early Victorian japanned metal and brass mounted hall lantern, of hexagonal outline, later re-decorated in the chinoiserie taste, 24½in. high.
(Christie's)   £1,955 $3,128

A gilt-bronze hall lantern, French, circa 1890, of hexagonal form, with serpentine sections, 84cm. high. (Sotheby's)   £4,600 $7,590

A Victorian brass hall lantern, circa 1870, of cylindrical form, the frame pierced with friezes of foliate ornament, 46in. high. (Christie's)   £3,450 $5,520

A Regency brass hall lantern, circa 1820, of square tapering form, the angles applied with laurel garlanded bearded mask crestings, 12½in. high. (Christie's)   £862 $1,379

A Victorian brass rectangular hall lantern, the bevelled glass panels with star-burst facets, the tubular frame, suspending a twin light fitting, 27in. high. (Christie's)   £460 $736

A pair of Louis XVI style gilt bronze cylindrical hall lanterns, 20th century, each with pierced balustrade frieze and tasselled beaded swags, with flowerhead finials, 36in. high. (Christie's)   £4,370 $6,992

A Victorian frosted glass and brass hanging storm lantern, the shade of campana-shape, cut with a continuous band of Greek key pattern, 10¾in. diameter. (Christie's)   £920 $1,472

A Victorian brass hall lantern, by Farraday & Son, of pentagonal serpentine, the glazing bars applied with bellflower pendants and floral swag mounts, 38¾in. high. (Christie's)   £5,520 $8,832

A patinated and gilt bronze hall lantern, 20th century, the tapering cylindrical glazed frame with a boldly cast pierced cresting flanking cartouches, 50in. high. (Christie's)   £2,990 $4,784

A French wrought brass hall lantern, late 19th century, of inverted bombé outline, inset with frosted glass panels below embossed rocaille crestings, 29½in. high. (Christie's)   £632 $1,011

Dunhill, a 9ct. gold cased Rollagas pocket lighter, with Fabergé style 'nugget' finish, London, 1967. (Bonhams) £300 $480

Dunhill, a silver plated 'Sylph' paper knife lighter, the lighter/handle with fine barley finish, London, circa 1954.(Bonhams) £140 $224

Dunhill, a silver and maki-e 'Bijou Unique' pocket lighter with iroe-hira maki-e, mura nishiji and aogai decoration depicting a hare running down a hillside in the night, London, 1929. (Bonhams) £350 $560

Art Metal Work, a Ronson 'Bar Tender' Touch Tip lighter, comprising a combined lighter and cigarette box in a chrome plated and brown enamelled 'bar' behind which stands a black, enamelled barman, American, 1930s. (Bonhams) £350 $560

Dunhill, a white metal watch lighter, with French control marks, plain finish and watch set into hinged, drop down front, the watch with white face, French, circa 1920s. (Bonhams) £800 $1,280

An undocumented wooden-cased inductor table lighter, surmounted by two hand-painted brass figures of Moors in Turkish costume, a spark passing between the figures on use, circa 1890. (Auction Team Köln) £837 $1,340

Dunhill, a 9ct. gold lady's wafer 'Unique' lighter, stamped *Asprey & Co. Ltd New Bond St* on the base, with wavy line finish, London, 1932. (Bonhams) £340 $544

Dunhill, a silver plated Unique lighter, with circular pipe tamper to snuffer, Swiss, circa 1926. (Bonhams) £110 $176

Parker, a white metal Beacon, marked *925*, with plain finish, Swiss,1930s. (Bonhams) £90 $144

A marble bust of a Roman emperor, 20th century, on a waisted square section plinth, 33in. high.
(Christie's)　　£6,325　$10,120

A large marble double portrait bust by Leon Morice, titled *V.F. Cavaroc, 10 Rue de la Paix, Paris, Noces d' Argent, 16 Octobre 1922*.
(Academy Auctioneers)
　　　　　　　　　　£360　$576

A French sculpted white marble bust of a lady, 19th or early 20th century, her hair tied back with a band, on an integral socle, 25in. high. (Christie's) £1,725　$2,760

A pair of malachite and gilt-bronze pedestals, modern, each with a square top above a Corinthian capital, 115cm. high.
(Sotheby's)　　£9,200　$15,180

A sculpted white marble group of Cupid and Psyche, 19th century, after the model by Antonio Canova (1757–1822), 31¼in. wide.
(Christie's)　　£2,875　$4,658

A pair of gilt metal mounted onyx pedestals, early 20th century, with square platforms and plain cylindrical columns with laurel collars and pierced foliate banding, 42¾in. high.
(Christie's)　　　　£1,495　$2,392

A white marble bust of Napoleon after Denis-Antoine Chaudet, early 19th century, head and shoulders, wearing a laurel wreath in his hair, 26in. high.
(Sotheby's)　　£2,875　$4,801

A 19th century marble bust of The Duke of Wellington by M A Edwards, raised on turned socle, 13in. high.
(Andrew Hartley)　　£360　$594

A white marble bust of a Roman Emperor, B.F.Hardenberg, early 19th century, head and shoulders, 30½in. high.
(Sotheby's)　　£10,925　$18,245

Unusual black marble mosaic decorated ink stand of heart shape, fitted with a pen tray and with lead crystal covered ink well, 19th century, 12½in.
(G..A. Key)   £140 $224

A white marble bust of Milton, 19th century, 12¼in. high.
(Christie's)   £322 $515

A Roman marble relief fragment, 2nd/3rd century A.D., carved with seven lines of funerary inscription, mounted on a wood frame, 16in. long. (Sotheby's)   £982 $1,610

A French sculpted white marble bust of a laughing youth, second half 18th century, portrayed with unkempt hair and head to sinister, 15½in. high overall.
(Christie's)   £1,265 $2,024

A pair of mid-19th century marble busts by Wales of Leeds, Milton and Shakespeare, 16in. high.
(Dee Atkinson & Harrison)
                    £1,500 $2,475

A 19th century white marble bust of curly haired child, 16in. high.
(Dee Atkinson & Harrison)
                    £1,500 $2,475

A white marble bust of Bacchus, Italian, 18th century, head and shoulders, draped in a lion skin, 26in. high.
(Sotheby's)   £4,140 $6,914

A portrait bust of a young man, Broome, Philadelphia, signed, with curling hair and a drape across his right shoulder, 18½in. high.
(Sotheby's)   £2,280 $3,737

A marble bust of a Roman emperor, 20th century, on a waisted square section plinth, 31½in. high.
(Christie's)   £4,140 $6,624

A large Lyth's Patent ship's lantern, by G.W. Lyth, Stockholm, lacking burner.
(Auction Team Köln) £84 $134

A whaleboat compass in a wood box, D. Barker, New Bedford, 19th century, the box with chamfered sliding lid and finger holes containing the compass, 5½ x 7in.
(Sotheby's)   £315 $517

A Tyfon Patent ship's siren by Kockums MLK Workshop, Malmö, Sweden, brass air-pump with attached signal horn, on wooden plinth. (Auction Team Köln)
£209 $334

Illuminated brass binnacle, with rectangular wooden base and iron compensating balls, 49in. high, 25in. wide.
(Eldred's)   £1,203 $1,925

Rare ship's iron-bound oak bucket, 18th century, with whalebone pins securing handle to body, 12½in. diameter. (Eldred's) £309 $495

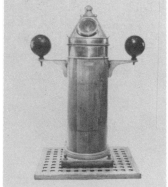

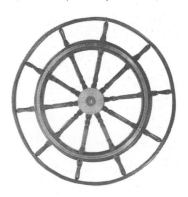

Ship's binnacle, label of Kevin & Wilfrid O. White, compass by Ritchie, with compensating balls, 52in. high, together with a wooden grate on which it stands.
(Eldred's)   £1,031 $1,650

An early complete diver's set by Siebe Gorman & Co., London, withbrass mounted copper helmet and lead plated diver's boots, 35cm. helmet diameter.
(Auction Team Köln) £2,931 $4,689

A large red-painted wooden ship's wheel with ten turned spokes and brass hub and brass-mounted inner ring, circa 1850, 190cm. diameter.
(Auction Team Köln) £355 $569

A 19th century mahogany domestic medicine cabinet, the rear with 'poison' compartment containing two (of five) original bottles, the slide secured by secret brass catch, each drawer with ivory pull, 37cm. high. (Christie's)   £2,530 $4,048

An unusual surgical saw, stamped *D.R.G.M.*, the blade with double-row serrations, with folding articulated handle, 13in. long opened. (Christie's)   £322 $515

A fine tracheotomy set, by S. Maw, Son & Thompson, London, with ivory-handled silver vertebrated tracheotomy tubes with canulae, 7¼in. wide.
(Christie's)   £575 $840

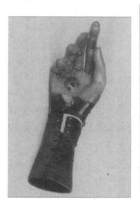

A carved wood articulated hand, with brass mounting for implements, with leather hinged forearm and tieholes, 11¾in. long. (Christie's)   £460 $736

Equipment, books and documents from the estate of the brothers Reinhold and Frederick Wappler, pioneers in X-ray development and the use of electrical equipment for surgery. (Auction Team Köln)

£5,682 $9,379

A late 19th century black-enamelled brass ear trumpet, of bell shape, with tapering extension piece with vulcanite end, detachable, with suspension cord, 19in. long.
(Christie's)   £345 $552

A fine late 19th century electro-medical coil, unsigned, the burnished-iron magnet with adjustable sector, the quadrant stamped 0-60, in a mahogany case, 13¾in. wide, with glazed door. (Christie's)   £460 $736

A 19th century rosewood homeo-pathic chest, by Ashton & Parsons...London, the hinged top fitted with bottles, etc, 29cm. (Bristol)   £410 $656

A [?] surgical stitching instrument, unsigned, circa 1890, constructed of burnished steel with nickel-plated brass fittings, ebony handle, 4in. long closed. (Christie's) £149 $238

618

A 19th century breast aspirator, the glass bowl with lacquered-brass mounts, the valve stamped *Mathieu*, an ivory nipple shield, 1¾in. diameter, and two others. (Christie's) £460 $736

A late 19th century cupping set, unsigned, probably French, comprising five glass cups with nickel-plated brass valve attachments, syringe and a circular twelve-blade scarificator, 11¼in. wide. (Christie's) £920 $1,472

A 19th century pewter enema apparatus, with nozzle, pump action and fruitwood handle, the base 12in. long, a French pewter pairing pot, and a pewter flask with screw-on top, 3¼in. high. (Christie's) £483 $773

A fine mahogany homeopathic domestic medicine case, cross-banded with box and kingwood, the lid decorated with an elongated star in ebony and fruitwood, 21¾in. wide. (Christie's) £1,725 $2,760

A 17th century iron dental elevator, an 18th century iron dental probe, and a [17th century] iron dental chisel, stamped *Joseph Gibbs*, bone handle, 3½in. long. (Christie's) £1,840 $2,944

A fine 19th century part set of surgeon's instruments, by Charrière, others by Mariaud, Joyant, and Bonnet, 20¼in. wide. (Christie's) £4,370 $6,992

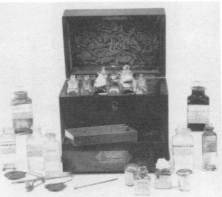

A composition, leather and fabric corset, with straps and buckles, 29.5cm. high. (Christie's) £28 $45

A 19th century mahogany domestic medicine chest, the lid rising to reveal plush lined compartments containing 16 bottles, 9¾in. wide. (Christie's) £977 $1,563

A 19th century mahogany pharmacy chest, of six small and four large drawers, each with glass pull-handles and decorative labels, 25¾in. high. (Christie's) £437 $699

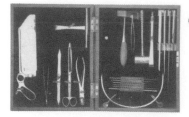

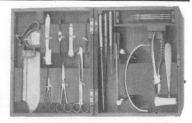

An American military-pattern post-mortem set, by The Surgical Manufacturing Company, in plush-lined brass-bound mahogany case, 14in. wide.
(Christie's) £690 $1,104

A 19th century steel Ségalas-pattern lithotrite, signed *CHARRIERE A PARIS 00*, with rack and pinion closing mechanism, calibrated 5-15, 9in. long.
(Christie's) £230 $368

A nickel-plated anad steel post-mortem set, by John Bell & Croyden, Arnold & Son Wigmore Street, London, W.1., mahogany case, 14in. wide.
(Christie's) £322 $515

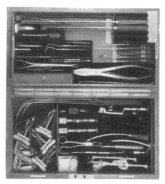

A silver drinking beaker, arranged so as to concertina and be contained in a plush-lined leather-covered drum-shaped case, 2⅝in. diameter. (Christie's) £138 $221

A rare late 18th century burnished iron fleam, unsigned, with sprung arm, finger grip and trigger guard, the three double-sided blades with threaded shanks, 3¾in. wide.
(Christie's) £253 $405

A fine reproduction porcelain leech jar, the blue ground decorated in gilt with cover, 14½in. high.
(Christie's) £460 $736

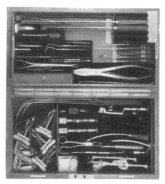

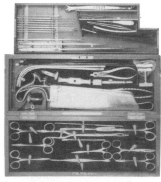

A late 19th century field surgeon's part operating set, by Down Bros., with two Liston knives, forceps, trocar and cannulae and other items, in mahogany case, 18in. wide. (Christie's) £1,150 $1,840

A coloured wax model of the nerves, arteries, veins and muscles of the head, by Lehrmittelwerke Berlin, with sheet of coded parts, 10 x 7½in. (Christie's) £299 $478

A field surgeon's part set of instruments, by Evans & Wormull, containing a bone saw, finger saw, forceps, and other items, in plush-lined mahogany case, 17¾in. wide.
(Christie's) £1,150 $1,840

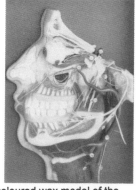

A beechwood and ebony stethoscope, signed *G.F. THACKRAY LEEDS,* 12¼in. long.
(Christie's) £1,265 $2,024

A pharmacist's mahogany cabinet, of twenty drawers, each labelled, with glass pulls, 48in. wide.
(Christie's) £483 $772

An exhibition-standard part-constrictor, signed *ROBERT & COLLIN,* with herringbone-patterned ivory handle with gilt ferrules, 12in.
(Christie's) £322 $515

An 18th century iron and brass trepanning brace, unsigned, with quick-release action and 19th century attachment, 12½in. long. (Christie's) £391 $626

A Chinese doctor's ivory anatomical model of a young woman, with finely carved hair coloured in black, both wrists with bracelets, and wearing shoes, 9¾in. long. (Christie's) £747 $1,195

A silver double-measure folding medicine spoon, the pierced centre section modelled with the form of a closely draped standing female, 2¾in. long. (Christie's) £138 $221

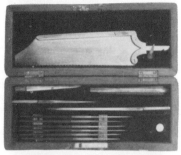

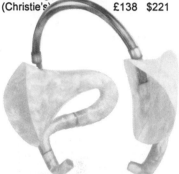

A lacquered-brass scarificator, unsigned, with twelve blades, trigger and release catch, in leatherette-covered card case, 2⅞in. (Christie's) £172 $275

A 19th century part post-mortem set, signed *W.B. HILLIARD GLASGOW,* containing a chequer grip ebony universal handle, saw, Liston knife and other items, 9¼in. wide. (Christie's) £437 $699

A simulated tortoiseshell and mother-of-pearl aurolese phone, unsigned, with adjustable head band and earpieces. (Christie's) £253 $405

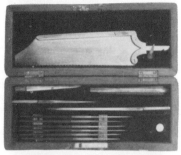

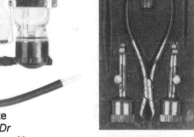

A 19th century ophthalmological set, including horn-handled eyelid retractor, silver syringe with two needles, 6½in. wide. (Christie's) £460 $736

A French, glass and bakelite inhaler, signed *SPIRO DU Dr JULIAN,,* the glass container with bakelite base, reversible sand-glass and bakelite cap, in cardboard case, 6½in. long. (Christie's) £287 $459

An ivory-handled brass and steel trephine, with two heads, and forceps signed *WEISS,* in plush-lined part case, 7⅛in. long. (Christie's) £517 $827

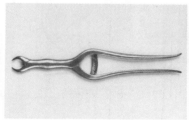

A burnished-steel pair of pincers, signed *SALLES St MARTIN PARIS,* with ratchet grip and concealed spring, 14⅛in. long. (Christie's) £28 $45

A fine 19th century cupping part set, by Savigny & Co, in the original brass-bound plush-lined mahogany case, 10¼in. wide. (Christie's) £1,380 $2,208

A 19th century steel Civiale-pattern lithotrite, signed *CHARRIERE A PARIS ½,* with brass collar to allow the moving rod to travel freely or be screwed, 15in. long. (Christie's) £345 $552

A panbone cradle having a shaped hood and scalloped sides, the whole, mounted on shaped rockers, 4¾in. high x 6in. long. (Sotheby's)   £1,562 $2,500

A North Italian miniature walnut commode, fitted with three drawers with bone inlaid fronts, top and sides, 26cm. wide. (Tennants)   £450 $720

A Spanish rosewood miniature table, 18th/19th century, the rectangular top with ripple-moulded edge above a ripple-moulded frieze with raised panel drawer, 18¾in. wide. (Christie's)   £3,450 $5,727

Miniature Georgian-style oak chest of drawers, 19th century, with three crossbanded drawers, ivory pulls and ivory teardrop escutcheons, on ivory bracket feet, 7¾in. long. (Skinner)   £251 $402

A William and Mary painted pine child's chest of drawers, the rectangular top above three small drawers on ball feet, 13¼in. high. (Sotheby's)   £2,750 $4,400

Victorian mahogany miniature chest of drawers, three graduating drawers, on bracket feet, 12in. high. (Skinner)   £232 $374

Miniature Empire-style gilt-metal mounted secrétaire à abattant, with drawer to top over drop front revealing interior drawers and mirror, 7½in. wide. (Skinner)   £323 $517

A Victorian mahogany miniature bed, with panelled head and footboards between ring-turned uprights, on similar legs, 21½in. long. (Christie's)   £437 $708

An Empire miniature marble-top mahogany dressing table, first half 19th century, the arched mirror plate pivoting between posts, 14¼in. (Sotheby's) £1,193 $1,955

A silvered composition girandole, late 19th century,the oval plate bordered by marginal plates within a foliate decorated frame, 28in. wide. (Christie's) £977 $1,563

A George II Irish silver dressing-table mirror, Thomas Walker, Dublin, 1734, oblong with incurved sides and on two lion sejant feet, 33in. high.
(Christie's) £29,900 $49,933

A silver plated brass table mirror, early 20th century, the bevelled oval plate between twin bobbin standards on splayed feet, 23in. high. (Christie's) £1,495 $2,392

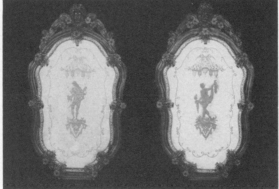

A late 17th century hanging wall mirror, with rectangular plate within a walnut cushion moulded frame, 37cm. x 63cm.
(Tennants) £4,000 $6,400

A pair of Venetian cut glass mirrors, each with a cartouche shaped plate engraved with classical figures, 20½in. wide.
(Christie's) £3,450 $5,520

An Edwardian mahogany cheval mirror, the bevelled plate with arched surmount on square section supports, 75in. high.
(Andrew Hartley) £875 $1,470

A late Victorian brass table mirror, the bevelled oval plate with a ropetwist border, within a pierced triform frame, stamped *MARION, LONDON*, 18in. high.
(Christie's) £977 $1,563

A French champlevé enamel mounted onyx table mirror, late 19th century, the shaped bevelled plate within a cartouche shaped double border, 21¾in. high.
(Christie's) £1,840 $2,944

A brass mirror frame, 20th century, the ovolo moulded cast surround surmounted by a ringed wreath wrapped cartouche, 52in. wide.
(Christie's) £1,610 $2,576

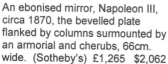

An ebonised mirror, Napoleon III, circa 1870, the bevelled plate flanked by columns surmounted by an armorial and cherubs, 66cm. wide. (Sotheby's) £1,265 $2,062

A George II carved pine and giltwood overmantel mirror, 18th century, the pierced C-scroll and leaf-form cartouche above a tri-partite frame, patches to leaf tips, 4ft.9in. wide.
(Sotheby's) £2,280 $3,737

A Regency mahogany cheval mirror, the rectangular plate between ring turned and finialled supports, 79cm. wide.
(Tennants) £1,400 $2,240

An Edwardian satinwood, mahogany and floral marquetry cheval mirror, decorated with lines, floral borders and bellflower swags, 31in. wide.
(Christie's) £2,300 $3,680

Pair of 19th century French champlevé enamelled frames, the inner borders with flowers on a pale blue ground, 12½in. high.
(Ewbank) £480 $792

An 18th century Dutch East Indies rosewood and marquetry dressing table bureau, the whole inlaid into the solid with sprays of flowers, butterflies and boxwood stringings, 22½in. wide.
(Canterbury) £1,100 $1,760

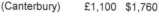

A painted and gilt pier mirror in the manner of William Kent, with broken pediment and frieze with projecting shell and foliate scrolls and vines, 179cm. x 121cm.
(Phillips) £5,800 $9,512

An Art Nouveau wall mirror, the copper frame decorated with a sun motif, flowering plants and a peacock, 56 x 81cm.
(Bearne's) £620 $992

A George II giltwood girandole, the later shaped rectangular bevelled plate, within a gadrooned slip, the outer frame with pierced acanthus and foliate scrolls, 51in. x 32in.
(Christie's) £10,350 $16,974

A George IV mahogany cheval mirror, the rounded rectangular plate between rectangular spreading supports, on hipped downswept reeded legs, 23¼in. wide. (Christie's) £1,840 $2,999

A Swedish giltwood overmantel mirror, second quarter 19th century, the oval plate in a moulded frame with a pierced C-scrolled and acanthus cresting, 36¼in. x 59½in. (Christie's) £1,725 $2,863

A Queen Anne red lacquer miniature bureau/toilet mirror on stand, part 18th century, the shaped plate within a deep moulded frame held by waved supports, 21¾in. wide. (Christie's) £1,400 $2,240

A pair of George III giltwood two-light girandoles, each with two later shaped plates in acanthus and C-scroll frames, with pierced pagoda-shaped acanthus-carved cresting, 42½in. high. (Christie's) £17,250 $28,290

A pair of Queen Anne giltwood and mirror-bordered pier glasses, each with a shaped arched central plate engraved with a vase of flowers, 75¼ x 36½in. and 71 x 36¾in. (Christie's) £31,050 $50,922

A Dutch fruitwood mirror, third quarter 17th century, the associated rectangular plate within a frame carved with flowers, acorns, corn and thistles, 48½in. x 37½in. (Christie's) £9,200 $15,272

A William and Mary raised-work and white-metal thread dressing mirror, the later rectangular plate in a later gilded slip, 24¾ x 21¾in. (Christie's) £4,600 $7,544

A George II parcel-gilt sand-decorated mirror, of rectangular form with square outset corners centring shells, 27in. wide. (Sotheby's) £1,578 $2,587

An enamel and gilt-bronze toilet mirror, French, circa 1890, with a shaped bevelled plate flanked by scrolls, 52cm. wide. (Sotheby's) £2,760 $4,554

A grained wall mirror, George II, circa 1740, with a broken scroll swan neck pediment and scallop cresting, 5ft.4in.
(Sotheby's)   £21,850 $36,490

A fine and rare Classical giltwood and part-ebonized overmantel mirror, New York, circa 1825, with a wing-spread eagle finial on a rocky crag, 4ft.8in. wide.
(Sotheby's)   £5,612 $9,200

A marble and giltwood diminutive Bilbao mirror, Spanish or Portuguese, circa 1800, surmounted by an urn issuing a spray of leaves and flowers, 29in. high. (Sotheby's) £3,277 $5,462

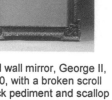

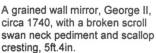

An Italian carved giltwood pier-glass Piedmontese, third quarter 18th century, the scrolled and shaped frame surmounted by a laurel wreath cresting supporting trophies, 3ft. 11in. wide.
(Sotheby's)   £19,550 $32,649

A giltwood mirror, in late 17th century style, the arched oblong plate within a frame carved with fruit, shells, putti, birds, masks, 5ft.6½in.
(Sotheby's)   £8,050 $13,443

A parcel-gilt simulated mahogany wall mirror, Italian, circa 1820, with a divided upright plate surmounted by a pediment of military trophies, 7ft.7½in. high.
(Sotheby's)   £3,450 $5,762

A George III mahogany toilet mirror, circa 1760, the later bevelled oblong plate above a slope fronted base and drawer, 1ft. 7½in. wide.
(Sotheby's)   £1,840 $3,073

A rare pair of Classical giltwood convex two-light mirrors first quarter 19th century, each surmounted by a finial in the form of a sea serpent, 37½in. high.
(Sotheby's)   £20,010 $33,350

A satin birch and marquetry easel dressing mirror, Art Nouveau, circa 1900, the cartouche plate within a shaped frame inlaid with ribbon tied fruit and foliage, 2ft. 4½in. high.
(Sotheby's)   £115 $192

A walnut mirror, circa 1735, the later oblong plate within a beaded, outstepped frame, 3ft. 2in. high. (Sotheby's)   £1,610 $2,689

A carved wood overmantel, George I, circa 1720, the bell flower cresting and key pattern with the sides of trailing oak leaves, 4ft.9½ x 5ft.5¼in.
(Sotheby's)   £14,950 $24,966

A mahogany cheval glass, Edwardian, circa 1910, strung with boxwood, in a trestle frame, 2ft. 4in. wide. (Sotheby's) £2,300 $3,841

Federal giltwood looking glass, bearing the label *Parker and Clover looking Glass and Picture Frame Makers 180 Fulton St. New York*, 29¹/₈in. high.
(Skinner)   £1,765 $2,875

A pair of Sitzendorf flower-encrusted oval mirror frames, late 19th century, in the Meissen style, each surmounted with two cherubs holding a garland of roses, 13in.
(Sotheby's)   £287 $479

A classical carved mahogany cheval glass, New York, 1810–20, the spiral and ring-turned rectangular reeded frame with rosette-carved corner blocks, 33¼in. wide.
(Christie's)   £10,350 $17,250

A carved and gilded wall mirror, 19th century, the cartouche shaped frame carved with rococo scroll and rocaille work, 3ft. 3in. high.
(Sotheby's)   £690 $1,152

A George III giltwood mirror, circa 1760, the oval mirror plate within a conforming rocaille and C-scrolled foliate frame, 27in. wide.
(Christie's)   £3,450 $5,750

A Venetian wall mirror, the octagonal bevelled edge upright plate with an edged floral mirrored border, 2ft. 10in. high.
(Sotheby's)   £253 $423

Classical gilt gesso girandole mirror, America or England, circa 1810–20, the crest with an eagle flanked by acanthus leaves, 35in. high. (Skinner)   £3,234 $5,175

An early George III giltwood overmantel mirror, the later rectangular bevelled plate within a slight C-scroll border with columns to each side, 55 x 65in. (Christie's)   £20,700 $34,362

A giltwood mirror, early 20th century, the rectangular plate within a moulded frame decorated with foliate carvings on pounced ground, 22in. wide. (Christie's) £632 $1,011

A fine gilt-bronze and champlevé enamel toilet mirror by Giroux, Paris, circa 1870, the oval bevelled plate within a border worked with arabesques, 60cm. high. (Sotheby's)   £7,475 $12,334

A Chinese Export reverse-painted mirror picture, the border mid-18th century, the later cartouche-shaped central plate in a border with a scene of three Chinese figures seated in an extensive river landscape, 23in. x 20¾in. (Christie's)   £8,050 $13,363

A Florentine style carved giltwood wall mirror, 19th century, the rectangular bevelled plate within a pierced acanthus and shell-carved frame, 39in. high. (Christie's)   £1,150 $1,840

A German giltwood and gilt gesso mirror, 19th century, the oval plate within a moulded frame decorated with acanthus leaves and vitruvian scroll mouldings, 43½in. wide. (Christie's)   £3,450 $5,589

A George I giltwood mirror, the later rectangular plate within a foliate slip, the scrolling broken pediment with pounced ground, 48in. x 25in. (Christie's)   £3,220 $5,248

An American ormolu mirror, attributed to Edward F. Caldwell, New York, late 19th/early20th century, the oval plate within a guilloche and beaded frame, 31 x 46¼in. (Christie's)   £11,500 $19,090

628

A marble and giltwood Bilbao mirror, Spanish or Portuguese, circa 1800, surround centring an oil-painted panel depicting a bucolic scene, 55¼in. high.
(Sotheby's)   £11,730 $19,550

A pair of William IV mahogany toilet mirrors, of large size, each with a rectangular swing plate with a scroll carved cresting, 38in. wide.
(Christie's)   £1,840 $2,980

An Edwardian mahogany and inlaid cheval mirror, decorated with lines, satinwood crossbanding and ribbon-tied bellflower swags, 36½in. wide. (Christie's)   £2,185 $3,496

A George IV giltwood, gilt-composition and ebonised mirror, the later rectangular plate within a reeded slip flanked by oak-leaf columns, 46¼in. x 30in.
(Christie's)   £3,680 $5,998

A pair of giltwood mirrors, of George III style, one early Victorian, the other of later date, each with a central shaped plate surrounded by further small reserves with an asymmetrical frame, 75½ x 36in.
(Christie's)   £13,800 $22,908

A gilt-brass repoussé, tortoiseshell and thuyawood veneered mirror, the rectangular plate within a moulded frame decorated with gilt brass foliate panels, 28in. wide.
(Christie's)   £2,530 $4,099

A Regency mahogany toilet mirror, decorated with lines and tulipwood crossbanding, the bevelled plate with arched top surmounted by finials, 23in. wide.
(Christie's)   £598 $969

A George II mahogany and parcel-gilt mirror, the rectangular plate within a foliate-carved slip and eared egg-and-dart moulding, possibly Irish, 57¼in. x 32in.
(Christie's)   £4,830 $7,873

A Federal ivory-mounted mahogany shaving mirror, Pennsylvania, circa 1810, with flaring reeded stiles surmounted by urn-form finials, 24½ in. wide.
(Sotheby's)   £631 $1,035

An Adam style shield shaped gilt-wood wall mirror, with bevelled plate, crested with an urn and scrollwork, 39 x 23in.
(Dee Atkinson & Harrison)
£620 $1,023

Victorian giltwood and gesso overmantel, the arched plate within overlapping leaf surround surmounted by a foliate scroll and shell cresting, 7in. x 5ft. 11in.
(Lots Road Galleries) £740 $1,221

An early 19th century convex mirror, with ebonised reeded slip to the gilded ball decorated moulded frame, 3ft.8in. overall height.
(Woolley & Wallis) £800 $1,328

Classical carved mahogany and mahogany veneer cylinder top dressing mirror, 19th century, the cylinder top opens to reveal four drawers, 19in. wide.
(Skinner) £976 $1,610

A 19th century gilt wood and gesso overmantel mirror, the frieze with classical scene in low relief depicting figures and a chariot, 52¼in. wide.
(Andrew Hartley) £1,550 $2,604

Dresden porcelain mirrored three-light wall sconce, 20th century, shaped mirror plate and frame elaborately modelled with putti and foliage, 33in.
(Skinner) £393 $633

A William and Mary oyster veneered walnut mirror, the rectangular plate within cushion moulded frame, 71cm. wide. x 110cm. high.
(Phillips) £2,200 $3,520

A Regency gilt wood and composition overmantel mirror, the pierced surmount with central foliate motif, 46in. wide.
(Andrew Hartley) £1,100 $1,848

A 19th century Continental wall mirror, parcel gilt, having central mask surmount flanked by griffins and urns, 4ft. wide.
(Russell, Baldwin & Bright)
£880 $1,452

A 19th century Venetian glass mirror, canted oblong plate surrounded by polychrome enamelled scrolling foliate panels, 48in. high.
(Andrew Hartley)   £2,900 $4,872

Federal mahogany inlaid dressing glass, Massachusetts or New Hampshire, circa 1815–25, the block vase and ring-turned posts and stretcher support a rectangular mirror, 27¼in. wide.
(Skinner)   £139 $230

A George III wall mirror with shaped plate, the heavily carved gilt frame decorated with foliage and flowerheads, 48 x 32in.
(Dee Atkinson & Harrison)
                          £2,700 $4,455

A Victorian mahogany cheval mirror, the arched plate within a moulded frame, on moulded and faceted tapering uprights, 63½in. high.
(Andrew Hartley) £1,300 $2,145

Federal gilt gesso overmantel mirror, possibly Boston, Massachusetts, circa 1820, the rectangular frame with central frieze of a shell and grape vines, 56in. wide. (Skinner)   £2,858 $4,715

A mahogany and ebony inlaid cheval mirror, early 19th century, the bevelled rectangular plate within a reeded slip and inlaid frame support, 45½in. high.
(Christie's)   £977 $1,563

A Regency convex mirror, with an inner reeded ebonised strip and leaf gesso inner border, a black and gilt cable outer border, the carved scallop shell surmount on a rocky base, 22in. diameter x 28in. high.
(Woolley & Wallis)   £550 $913

A Florentine carved giltwood frame mirror, the rectangular glass to a ribbon tied foliage bud carved inner frame, 31in. x 3ft.3½in.
(Woolley & Wallis) £1,500 $2,415

An Irish Regency wall mirror, the oval plate in glass studded moulded frame with alternating gilt and ebonised banding, 29½ x 23in.
(Andrew Hartley)   £700 $1,120

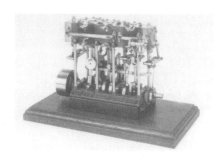

A Stuart S 50 D horizontal two-cylinder steam engine motor with regulator and manometer, wood-clad cylinders, 47mm. external diameter.
(Auction Team Köln) £670 $1,072

A brass vertical steam engine, possibly by Weeden, USA, complete with burner and chimney, 14.5cm. diameter, 31cm. high, circa 1900.
(Auction Team Köln) £293 $469

A well engineered model Stuart triple expansion vertical reversing marine engine, with blacked steel clad cylinders, display base, 7¼in. x 9in. (Christie's) £1,495 $2,381

A well engineered and presented model of a Return Tube Marine Boiler as originally built by Plenty and South, the copper boiler with fire tubes, drum diameter 10½in.
(Christie's) £920 $1,465

A large workshop stationary engine, with 14cm. diameter boiler, complete with spirit burner, circa 1920, 50cm. long.
(Auction Team Köln) £460 $736

A well engineered model of a single cylinder overtype scotch crank driven stationary engine of circa 1840, built by A. Mount, finished in green and polished brightwork, 11 x 10in. (Christie's) £575 $916

A well engineered 1½in. scale model of the Allchin single cylinder two speed four shaft General Purpose Traction Engine Reg. No. NU 7483 'Royal Chester', in red, maroon and black, black and yellow lining. (Christie's) £1,898 $3,023

A two-cylinder model Stuart D 110 ship's steam engine, combined with an English wood-clad descaling engine.
(Auction Team Köln) £921 $1,473

A model Stuart Beam counterbalance steam engine motor, with regulator and water pump, 400mm. high.
(Auction Team Köln) £837 $1,340

A Stuart No. 1 ship's steam engine motor, on round wooden base, circa 1960, 180mm. high.
(Auction Team Köln) £251 $402

A Stuart Beam balancing-steam engine, complete with Stuart boiler, wood-clad, with 19 steam tubes, 650mm. long.
(Auction Team Köln)
£1,005 $1,608

A full size Heinrici motor hot air engine, with twin 41cm. flywheels, one with cast-in belt wheel.
(Bearne's) £900 $1,485

A well presented model of a single cylinder overcrank pumping engine originally built by Wicks Hargreave & Co. circa 1840, mounted on a simulated tiled floor.
(Christie's) £506 $806

An exhibition standard 4½in. scale model of the Burrell single cylinder three shaft two speed traction engine Reg. No. WTE 615 Harvey, built by A. Howarth, finished in green, maroon, red, black, 46 x 68in. (Christie's) £13,800 $21,977

A vertical stationary steam engine, possibly Märklin, on cast painted base, single cylinder driving fly wheel and water pump, complete with dummy governor.
(Andrew Hartley) £240 $396

A vertical steam engine, with centre four-spoke flywheel, cylinder with eccentric piston rod, 52cm. high.
(Bearne's) £600 $990

A well engineered 1/5th scale working model of a 9-cylinder Gnome-Rhone rotary aero engine, built by R.C. Lowe, mounted on a metal demonstration stand, 11¾ x 12in. (Christie's) £3,220 $5,128

A stationary Doll engine with 7cm. diameter boiler, circa 1914, 27cm. high.
(Auction Team Köln) £209 $335

Clipper ship model, hand carved and painted wood, rigged with canvas sails, 50in. long. (Skinner) £682 $1,092

Cased plank-on-frame model of the American frigate U.S.S. Constitution, copper-sheathed hull below waterline, cannons rigged to bulwark, model length 39in. (Eldred's) £2,818 $4,510

Early model of a three-masted schooner, rigged with a full suit of sails, bread and butter laminated hull with varnish finish, length 44in. (Eldred's) £653 $1,045

A scale shipyard model of a Gato class submarine USS Lionfish, 1/8in. scale approximately 77in. long, two piece grey black fibreglass hull, fully fitted with motor and electrics, built by Ralph Ingram of Exmouth Devon. (Wallis & Wallis) £600 $960

A Fleetscale Models 1/128 scale HMS Repulse battle cruiser, approximately 74½in. long, 9in. beam, fibreglass maroon and grey hull and superstructure, four engines, virtually ready to run, with radio control unit. (Wallis & Wallis) £700 $1,120

A painted pine model of the 'Shenandoah', American, 20th century, the wood hull with four masts fitted with rigging, 43½in. long. (Sotheby's) £646 $1,035

Cased shadowbox model of a three-masted schooner, with lighthouse in background, 19 x 31in. (Eldred's) £859 $1,375

Cased plank-on-frame model of the Swedish tall ship 'Vasa', outfitted with extensive cast fittings and cannon, in an oak display case, 45in. long. (Eldred's) £2,000 $3,300

Cased ship model opium clipper 'Rose', built in Swansea, Massachusetts, 1836, 44in. long. (Skinner) £1,221 $1,955

Model of the American whaleship 'Calendar', 19th century, Eagle and 'Calendar' on well-executed sternboard, five whaleboats, deck with tryworks, hatches, winch, wheel and cabin, model length 49in. (Eldred's) £1,650 $2,640

Builder's laminated half model of a schooner, 19th century, 46½in. long. (Skinner) £1,365 $2,185

Well-made model of the paddlewheel steamboat 'Mount Washington', 45in. long. (Eldred's) £1,169 $1,870

Cased model of the American frigate 'Essex', copper-sheathed hull from waterline down, deck carries rigged cannon, hatches, companionway, etc. Full-standing and running rigging, mounted into a glass case, model length 32in. (Eldred's) £894 $1,430

Carved and painted model of the fisherman schooner 'Bluenose', 1/20th scale, red, black, and white paint, fully rigged with cotton sails, 80in. long. (Skinner) £790 $1,265

Wooden model of a double-ended boat, 19th century, incomplete, planked hull and original green and white paint, possibly Norwegian, 43in. long. (Eldred's) £309 $495

A good ship builder's half block model of the single screw steamer Rappahannock by Alexander Stephen & Sons Ship Builders and Engineers Glasgow, length of case 102in. (David Lay) £2,500 $4,025

A fully detailed exhibition model of R.M.S. 'Queen Mary', of painted wood and metal construction and finished in Cunard colours, 165cm. long. (Bearne's) £860 $1,419

Cased model of the Belknap class cruiser CG18 'Worden', outfitted with all appropriate armament, radar, towers, etc. Model length 33in. Mahogany case. (Eldred's) £619 $990

A large scale model of the Royal Yacht 'Britannia', the exhibition model finished in authentic colours and having well detailed decking, 178cm. overall. (Bearne's) £2,000 $3,300

Cased plank-on-frame model of the British Royal yacht 'Royal Caroline', planked hull carries many pieces of decoration, rigged with standing and running cords, mounted in free-standing mahogany inlaid case, 36in. long. (Eldred's) £2,131 $3,410

Cased model of the American clipper ship 'Flying Cloud', painted black with copper sheathed hull below waterline. Free standing glass mahogany case, 37in. long. (Eldred's) £1,925 $3,080

Cased model of the primitive steam yacht 'Champion', mahogany cabin with brass portholes, doors, railings, etc, hull painted black above waterline and green below, inlaid case. Model length 22in. (Eldred's) £756 $1,210

Finely executed model of an American whaleboat, interior fully outfitted with gear, finely inlaid mahogany case with brass trim, 15in. long. (Eldred's) £412 $660

A finely engineered 3½in. gauge model of the B.R. 2-6-2 locomotive and tender No. 5670 'Boadicea', with brazed superheated copper boiler with water and pressure gauges, 10¾ x 47in. (Christie's) £1,725 $2,747

An exhibition standard 5in. gauge of the Great Western Railway Manor Class 4-6-0 locomotive and tender No. 7800 'Torquay Manor', finished in GWR green livery, 14 x 65¼in. (Christie's) £4,830 $7,692

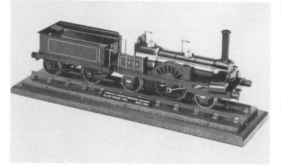

The LNWR Allan 2-2-2 locomotive and tender No. 1876, of circa 1846, 13¼in. long. (Christie's) £483 $769

A 5in. gauge model of the SR (ex LB & SCR) Class W 0-6-0 (Terrier) side tank locomotive No. 9 built by A.G.D. Payne, finished in Stroudley livery, 12¼ x 28in. (Christie's) £805 $1,282

Hornby Dublo EDG7 tank goods set with Southern N2 tank locomotive coal truck (No 2594 to bunker), goods van, brake van, track and controller, boxed with packing and instructions. (Andrew Hartley) £720 $1,188

Argentinian clockwork No. 2 Special Goods Train Set: FCO No. 2 special tank locomotive painted in lined green, FCO open wagon, cattle truck, brake van, Royal Daylight tank wagon, and a circle of track, in original train set box, circa 1936. (Christie's) £253 $402

A finely engineered 3½in. gauge model of the B.R. 4-6-2 Pacific locomotive and tender No. 35201 'Pamela', with brazed superheated copper boiler with water and pressure gauges, finished in green and black with orange lining, 11 x 53in. (Christie's) £3,680 $5,860

An exhibition standard 5in. gauge model of the B.R. (ex LNER) Class B1 4-6-0 locomotive and tender No. 61003 'Gazelle', built by Aubrey Bentley to the design of M. Evans, finished in finely lined B.R. black livery and lining, 14 x 65½in. (Christie's) £7,475 $11,904

Märklin 40cm. bogie CIWL sleeping car, 'Mitropa' 1333/1G, painted in teak with white roof and detailed interior, circa 1928. (Christie's) £1,150 $1,828

Märklin electric German 4-6-0 locomotive and accessories: DR230 Cat. Ref. GR70/12920 painted in lined black with late smoke deflectors, circa 1939, a DC rectifier switch 13374N, and other accessories. (Christie's) £437 $695

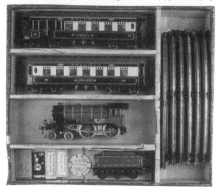

Argentinian market electric Passenger Pullman Train Set: E220 special electric locomotive the 'Bramham Moor' and FCO No. 2 special tender, both painted in lined green, No. 2 special Pullman's 'Lorraine' and brake end 'Verona', and a circle of track, in original train set box, circa 1935.
(Christie's) £2,185 $3,474

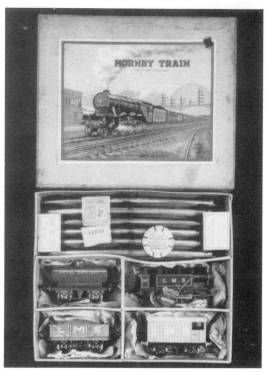

Hornby Series electric locomotive, accessories and a steam locomotive: E36 GW4-4-2 tank locomotive No. 2221, a No. 2E turntable, and a quantity of track, mostly in original boxes, wagon, accessories, and a Bowman 4-4-0 steam locomotive in lined green, in original wooden box, circa 1935.
(Christie's) £552 $877

Hornby Series electric tank goods set, accessories and track: E120 LMS Tank Locomotive No. 2115, B Wagons and a circle of track with fuse wire and other accessories, a T20 transformer, buffer stops and a quantity of track, all in original boxes, circa 1940.
(Christie's) £690 $1,097

Hornby Series E220 special electric GWR 'County of Bedford' locomotive No. 3821 and No. 2 special tender, painted in lined green, circa 1938.
(Christie's) £1,380 $2,194

Märklin bogie Passenger van, eight-wheel 16cm. baggage guards van 1846/0, with guards look-out, hinged roof and detailed interior, painted in lined brown, circa 1909. (Christie's) £1,495 $2,377

Bing gauge I electric American outline locomotive and tender, 4-4-0 Pennsylvania railroad locomotive in lined black, body in cast-iron, tender lithographed, circa 1924. (Christie's) £862 $1,370

Märklin 40cm. 'Mitropa' dining car (Speisewagen) painted in lined red, Cat. Ref. 1932/1G, with hinged roof and detailed interior, circa 1928. (Christie's) £1,610 $2,560

Märklin 40cm. bogie baggage car No. 19341, painted in green, black and brown roof, circa 1929, and a quantity of electric track, one point and crossover. (Christie's) £368 $585

Märklin early Great Northern bogie dining car, 17cm. eight-wheel dining car 1842, painted in gold lined brown with hinged clerestorey roof and detailed interior, circa 1904. (Christie's) £977 $1,553

French Hornby electric goods train set 'Le Bourguignon' OBBN: OBB eight-wheel SNCF locomotive BB8051, lithographed in green and red, refrigerator van STEF, an open wagon with tarpaulin, transformer, circle of track, and instructions, all in original box, circa 1960. (Christie's) £345 $548

A well detailed 7mm. fine-scale two rail electric model of the LMS Fowler Class 4F 0-6-0 locomotive and tender No. 4515 with internal guide bars and valve rods and external details including fluted coupling rods, brake and sanding gear, finished in black, 3¾in. x 14¼in. (Christie's) £460 $731

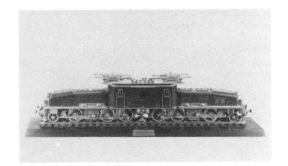

A Hehr replica electric 20 volt DC 1'B'B1 Crocodile articulated electric locomotive, CCS 12920/79, painted in brown, 1979-1985. (Christie's) £1,380 $2,194

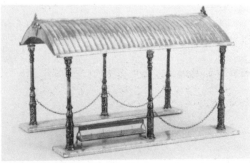

Station canopy with supports: 37cm. double-platform canopy 02059, with six ornate pillars and a seat, circa 1925. (Christie's) £483 $768

Trix Trains A4 4-6-2 locomotive and tender 'Merlin', finished in BR green, boxed.
(Andrew Hartley)   £50 $82

Trix Trains AH Peppercorn A1 locomotive, finished in LNER green, boxed.
(Andrew Hartley)   £55 $91

Bassett-Lowke electric 2-6-0 locomotive and tender: Great Western 'Mogul' No. 4331 painted in lined green with *Great* - garter - *Western* on tender, circa 1930. (Christie's)   £575 $914

Bassett-Lowke electric 'Flying Scotsman': 4-6-2 No. 60103 and eight-wheel tender, lithographed in British Railways dark green with tangerine lining, in original box, circa 1959. (Christie's)   £977 $1,553

A finely engineered 5in. gauge model of the BR class 9 4-6-2 locomotive and tender No. 70025 'Western Star' built by R. E. Day, finished in finely lined BR livery and lining, 14½ x 73½in., Dexion trolley, firing shovel, flue brushes. (Christie's)   £6,325 $10,073

A collection of well detailed 5in. gauge freight stock, including two twin bogie three plank open wagons, a twin bogie bolster, a four plank four wheel coal wagon, a four wheel box van with sliding doors and a four wheel guard's van. (Christie's)   £2,300 $3,663

A finely engineered 5in. gauge model of the GWR King Class locomotive and tender No. 6009 'King Charles II' built by W.S. Baker, finished in finely lined GWR livery and lining, firing irons, Dexion trolley, 15 x 72½in. (Christie's)   £8,625 $13,735

A recently completed 5in. gauge 'Speedy' No. 1510 painted B.R. black, designed by L.B.S.C. and modelled on an ex G.W.R. 1500 class 0-6-0 tank locomotive with outside cylinders with piston valves and Walschaerts gear, length 90cm. long. (Bearne's)   £2,100 $3,465

The LMS Duchess class 4-6-2 locomotive and tender No. 6245 'City of London' in LMS red/gold livery, 21⁵/₈in. long. (Christie's)   £460 $733

Hornby Dublo Bristol Castle locomotive, finished in BR green, boxed. (Andrew Hartley)   £90 $148

Trix Trains 4472 Flying Scotsman locomotive, finished in LNER green with second tender, boxed. (Andrew Hartley) £140 $231

Hornby Dublo Silver King locomotive and tender, finished in BR green, boxed. (Andrew Hartley) £110 $181

Hornby Series electric 'Princess Elizabeth' LMS locomotive No. 6201 and six-wheel tender, painted in lined lake, in original fitted presentation box, circa 1938. (Christie's) £1,265 $2,011

A Bassett-Lowke electric 4-6-2 A3 Flying Scotsman locomotive, finished in lined BR green, slight paint damage to tender, boxed. (Andrew Hartley) £620 $1,023

A Bassett-Lowke electric 0-6-0 LMS tank locomotive, finished in black with LMS to tank, M8 to cab, boxed. (Andrew Hartley) £250 $412

A Bassett-Lowke clockwork 4-6-2 LNER 'Flying Scotsman' No. 4472 and eight-wheel tender, lithographed in lined green, circa 1939. (Christie's) £437 $695

A 5in. gauge industrial type 0-4-0 saddle tank locomotive 'Ann of Holland', built to the drawings of J.H.E. Rodgers, 1945, with outside cylinders, Walschaerts valve gear, cab operated drain cocks and hand water pump. (Bearne's) £1,350 $2,228

A 5in. gauge 0-6-0T locomotive 'Twin Sisters', by Austen-Walton, castings by Kennion, painted in L.M.S. livery No. 11665, outside cylinders with Walschaerts valve gear, length of engine 80cm. (Bearne's) £2,000 $3,300

A Bassett-Lowke Enterprise 4-4-0 live steam locomotive, spirit fired boiler with twin outside cylinder, finished in black, lined red, boxed. (Andrew Hartley) £220 $363

A Märklin O gauge Mitropa restaurant car, four-axle, with celluloid windows, four opening doors and internal lights, 1934, 24.5cm. long. (Auction Team Köln £113 $181

A Dinah mechanical bank by John Harper & Co. Willenhall, version with long arms, 17cm. high, 1911. (Auction Team Köln) £270 $432

A mechanical Calamity Bank (Football) by J. & E. Stevens, Cromwell CT, cast iron, 18cm. wide, post 1905. (Auction Team Köln) £418 $688

Cast iron 'State Bank' still bank, by Kenton, circa 1900, 8in. high. (Eldred's) £241 $385

A cast iron Tammany Bank mechanical bank by J. & E. Stevens, USA, the figure with grey trousers and brown jacket, 1873, 15cm. high. (Auction Team Köln) £230 $368

Stevens cast iron mechanical bank, 19th century, 'Eagle & Eaglets', 8in. long. (Eldred's) £100 $165

A Pascall Type 2 red-brown and gold lithographed mechanical bank, made in Germany for the English confectionery company, 14.5cm. high. (Auction Team Köln) £105 $167

A Kilgore Mfg Co. 'Owl, Slot In Book' bank, cast-iron owl standing on log with book under wing, 5⁷/₈in. high. (Christie's) £253 $273

A Shephard Hardware Co., USA Jolly Nigger mechanical bank, cast-iron, circa 1882, 17.5cm. high. (Auction Team Köln) £146 $234

A J & E Stevens Paddy & the Pig bank, cast-iron, Irishman with pig held between legs, 7¹/₈in. base length. (Christie's) £276 $439

A Swiss Nicole Frères musical box with 12 cylinders playing 4 overtures, the rosewood case with floral and scroll inlay and kingwood banding, 22in. (Russell Baldwin & Bright) £4,600 $7,590

An automaton musical picture of a forge, of painted lithographed card, framed and glazed, 24¾ x 32¼in. (Christie's) £2,875 $4,600

A rare Longue Marche musical box playing six airs on sublime harmony combs, with quadruple-spring motor, 30in. wide. (Christie's) £3,450 $5,520

A Victorian Swiss musical box with cylinder playing 12 airs in an upright walnut cabinet with interior drawer and glazed door, cabinet 16in. wide. (Russell Baldwin & Bright) £760 $1,254

Rosewood cylinder music box, late 19th century, rectangular case inlaid with a lute, medallion and floral centre with banding about, 20½in. wide. (Du Mouchelles) £875 $1,400

A late 19th century Swiss bells in sight cylinder musical box, the 28cm. crank-wound cylinder playing ten airs, 60cm. (Bearne's) £640 $1,024

A musical box by P.V.F., No. 5607, playing six light airs, accompanied by six engine-turned bells, 20¼in. wide. (Christie's) £1,725 $2,760

Schiaparelli 'Shocking', a clockwork display carousel music box of card construction, the silvered turntable fitted with four miniature clear glass bottles of torso form, height of display 4¼in. (Bonhams) £320 $512

A Forte Piano musical box, playing four airs by Donizetti, Grasset and Strauss, the bedplate stamped Lee, in re-finished case, 14½in. wide. (Christie's) £1,380 $2,208

A fine ivory netsuke, signed *Tomotada,* Edo period, 18th century, of a wolf, seated and holding down a frightened crab, 1¹³/₁₆in. long.
(Christie's)   £19,550 $31,867

An ivory netsuke, with signature *Masatada,* Edo period, 18th century, of a finely detailed, standing and grazing horse, 3⁹/₁₆in. long. (Christie's)   £2,185 $3,562

A fine ivory netsuke, signed *Tomotada,* Edo period (18th century), of a goat steadying a branch of loquat fruit to eat it, 1⁷/₈in. long.
(Christie's)   £16,100 $26,243

A wood netsuke, signed *Ikkosai to,* Edo period, 19th century, of the poet Kakimoto no Hitomaro seated and holding a poem card, 1¾in. high. (Christie's)   £1,840 $2,999

An ivory netsuke, Edo period, 18th century, of a tall standing figure holding a peach and grimacing. (Christie's)   £1,725 $2,812

An ivory netsuke, signed *Masatsugu,* Edo period (19th century), of a finely rendered monkey, seated scratching his left leg, eyes inlaid in light and dark horn, age crack, 1¼in. high.
(Christie's)   £8,970 $15,070

A fine ivory netsuke, signed *Tomotada,* Edo period, 18th century, of a wolf, seated and holding down a turtle with his paws, 1¾in. long.
(Christie's)   £10,350 $16,871

A coral and kinko netsuke, signed *Someya Chomin* on an inlaid gold plaque, Meiji period, late 19th century, the coral enclosed in a hinged mount of silver and two colours of gold, 2³/₈in. high. (Christie's)   £9,200 $14,996

A wood netsuke, signed *Masateru,* Edo period, 19th century, of two rats coiled together, eyes inlaid in horn, 1¼in. long.
(Christie's)   £1,610 $2,624

A marine ivory netsuke, Edo period, 18th century, of a karashishi carved as ball, holding in his mouth a small ball, 1¾in. diameter.
(Christie's) £3,220 $5,249

A wood netsuke, signed *Tanaka Minko,* Tsu School, Edo period (18th Century), of an octopus and a monkey standing and embracing on an awabi shell, eyes inlaid, 5.4cm. high. (Christie's) £2,645 $4,444

A wood netsuke, signed *Shunko,* Edo period, 19th century, of a monkey sitting on a toad with a turtle on a leash, 2³⁄₈in. long.
(Christie's) £2,760 $4,499

An ivory netsuke in the form of a mokkugyo, unsigned, Edo period, 19th century, the face carved with a star constellation, approx. 4.4cm. diam. (Christie's) £977 $1,593

An ivory netsuke, Edo period, 18th century, of a tall standing figure of Kakkio with his son tucked into the front of his kimono.
(Christie's) £4,140 $6,748

A wood netsuke, Edo period, 19th century, carved as a group of nine noh masks including Okame, Hyottoko, and Hannya, 1½in. wide.
(Christie's) £862 $1,405

An ivory, wood, silver and stone netsuke, signed *Tokoku,* with seal Ryubai, Meiji period, 19th century, of a priest showing a cat to a young boy, 2in. high.
(Christie's) £6,670 $10,872

A wood netsuke, Edo period, 18th century, of a karako standing on a backgammon board, 1¹¹⁄₁₆in. high.
(Christie's) £1,610 $2,624

A wood netsuke of Daruma, signed *Shumin,* Meiji period, 19th century, seated in meditation, part of his robe covering his head, 1⁷⁄₁₆in. high. (Christie's) £1,380 $2,249

The Postal, an American type wheel machine, 1902. (Auction Team Köln) £711 $1,138

A cast iron Jupiter No 1 pencil sharpener by Guhl & Harbeck, Hamburg, lacking shavings holder. (Auction Team Köln)   £117 $187

An Archimedes Model C German drum calculator, brass, by Reinhold Pöthig, Saxony, with result slide, 1912. (Auction Team Köln) £669 $1,071

An American Merritt pointer upstrike typewriter, the carriage lifting for better legibility, 1889. (Auction Team Köln) £711 £1,138

A rare small Virotyp pocket model of the French Kavalleristen Viry pointer typewriter, with two original brochures and leather case, 1914. (Auction Team Köln)   £460 $736

An Austria (Badenia) nine row brass drum calculator by Math. Bäuerle, St. Georgen, Black Forest, lacking six keys. (Auction Team Köln) £196 $314

A Jowei German rotary pencil sharpener, in original condition, with original shavings container. (Auction Team Köln) £125 $201

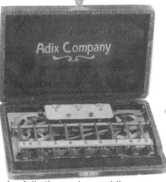

An Adix three-place adding machine with latch drive and nine keys, by Pallweber & Bordt, Mannheim, 1903. (Auction Team Köln) £544 $870

The Sampo, the first Swedish typewriter from Ernst Martin, of which only 1158 were produced, with even rarer original tin case, 1894. (Auction Team Köln £5,862 $9,379

A US Automatic rotary pencil sharpener, with original metal case for shavings. (Auction Team Köln) £251 $402

An Abbott Automatic Check Perforator, an early American cheque writer, 1891. (Auction Team Köln)   £313 $502

An Odell's Typewriter, an early model of the decorative American pointer machine, still with traces of the gold-green index mount of the original models, 1890. (Auction Team Köln) £586 $937

An English chain drive No. 1 Roneo Addressing Machine, for stamped metal plates, 1920.
(Auction Team Köln)   £87 $140

An attractive British Belknap Addressor by the Rapid Addressing Machine Co., to US Patent of 24 August 1897.
(Auction Team Köln)   £104 $167

A Tim Unitas Model 1 drum adding machine by Ludwig Spitz & Co., Berlin, low serial number 900, tin cover with French inscriptions.
(Auction Team Köln) £1,381 $2,210

A Trinks System Brunsviga Model MJR adding machine with special keying-in display, key-in handle with ivory grip, with 9, 10 or 15 place function, 1919.
(Auction Team Köln) £229 $367

A Edison Mimeograph Duplicator No. 61, with wax stencils, very early model, circa 1890.
(Auction Team Köln)   £117 $187

An Archimedes Model DE a D version of the four-function drum calculating machine by Reinhold Pöthing, with manual and electric drive, nine row keyboard, circa 1927.
(Auction Team Köln) £376 $602

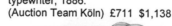

An Addo rare original version of the popular Swedish 10 row adding machine with direct display, with original base and case, 1920.
(Auction Team Köln) £586 $937

The Improved Hall Typewriter, an improved version of the American index typewriter, which was arguably the first practical portable typewriter, 1886.
(Auction Team Köln) £711 $1,138

A Virotyp, small pocket edition of the the French pointer typewriter by Kavalleristen Viry, 1914.
(Auction Team Köln) £334 $535

A cast iron Courant pencil sharpener, with original shavings drawer and table clamp, circa 1920.
(Auction Team Köln)   £158 $254

A German KUM tin toy pencil sharpener by Jos. Eckert, Fürth, Bavaria, with original box, 9.5cm. high, circa 1955.
(Auction Team Köln)   £75 $120

A very early cast iron pencil sharpener, with table clamp, with razor type blade, circa 1850.
(Auction Team Köln)   £108 $173

An early magic lantern by L. Aubert, with original lens, for 6.5cm. glass strips, lacking burner, 32 cm. high. (Auction Team Köln) £754 $1,206

A bronzed brass mounted hardwood Megalétoscopia Privilegiata by Carlo Ponti, Venice, 1862, for curved photographic plates, with five original photographs. (Auction Team Köln) £3,101 $4,962

A Talkie Jecktor by the Movie Jecktor Co., New York, painted tin body, for broad paper strips which can be laid and projected alternately to achieve a cinematographic effect, with built-in gramophone for 17.5cm. discs, 1920. (Auction Team Köln) £837 $1,340

A coin operated stereo viewer for 9 x 18cm. stereocards, with light and key, with 18 cards of young ladies in various poses and stages of undress. (Auction Team Köln) £560 $895

Pair of decorative opera glasses, the porcelain barrels decorated with panels of stylised garden flowers on white reserves, fitted with mother of pearl eye pieces, 3½in. (G.A. Key) £180 $288

A gilt mounted miniature Dagron-Stanhope magic lantern with Stanhope miniature nude photograph entitled *La belle esclave*, 1870-80, 20mm. high. (Auction Team Köln) £732 $1,172

A Plank brass magic lantern, on wood base, for round discs with feed for strips, with two discs and 8 strips. (Auction Team Köln) £837 $1,340

An unusual British mahogany and brass mounted viewer, with adjustable optics and focusing and brown leather bellows and mirrored light well, circa 1885. (Auction Team Köln) £502 $804

A Stéréoscope Vérascope Richard, French stereo viewer by Jules Richard, Paris, for 50 glass slides, with hardwood case, circa 1910. (Auction Team Köln) £326 $602

A red Tri-ang Comet child's pedal car, 68cm. long, circa 1940. (Auction Team Köln) £183 $294

A rare Porsche adult's pedal car with chain drive to the rear wheels, 2.1m. long, circa 1952. (Auction Team Köln) £523 $837

A Pee Wee pedal car, unattributed, possibly by Tri-ang, England, 81cm. long, circa 1935. (Auction Team Köln) £117 $187

A VW Cabrio pedal car, by Tri-ang, black painted tinplate coachwork, lacking windscreen, 85cm. long, circa 1980. (Auction Team Köln) £158 $254

A one-off Mercedes SSK pedal car, with wood and pressed steel body on a metal chassis, leather seats, 145cm. long, 1926. (Auction Team Köln) £1,758 $2,813

A Ferrari child's pedal car, by Giordani, Italy, lacks radiator grille, windscreen and upholstery, 112cm. long, 1955. (Auction Team Köln) £293 $468

A Tri-ang Ford Zephyr pedal car, by Lines Bros. England, lacks handbrake, 104cm. long, circa 1950. (Auction Team Köln) £104 $167

A Willi's Jeep pedal car, unattributed, perhaps home-made, thick sheet-steel construction on a welded t-profile chassis, 117cm. long. (Auction Team Köln) £83 $133

A US3541 Army Jeep by Tri-ang, tin, with plastic upholstery, with petrol tank and spare wheel, 100cm. long, circa 1960. (Auction Team Köln) £158 $254

Pilot, a maki-e piston filler, with 'volcanic' finish, gold plated fittings and over/under fed warranted nib, Japanese, 1940s. (Bonhams) £420 $672

Parker, a gold plated 61 Cumulus, with medium nib, English, 1970s. (Bonhams) £80 $128

Sheaffer, a white metal Fred Force 10 pen, with cable twist design and inlaid medium nib French/American, 1980s. (Bonhams) £220 $352

Pelikan, a tortoiseshell No. 520, with gold plated cap and turning knob and with Pelikan nib, German, circa 1955. (Bonhams) £160 $256

Mont Blanc, a rolled gold No. 232, with No. 2 nib, German, circa 1936. (Bonhams) £700 $1,120

Conklin, a light jade Endura Senior, with 18ct. Endura nib, American, 1920s. (Bonhams) £360 $576

Parker, a ring top Vest Pocket Duofold pen set with white metal overlay, with 18ct. French Parker nib and Art Deco pattern, Continental, 1930s.
(Bonhams) £500 $800

Parker, a limited edition Norman Rockwell Commemorative pearl and black Duofold Centennial Pen No. 3149/5000, English, 1996, with reproduction Rockwell advertisements in a folder, leather presentation box. (Bonhams) £480 $768

Kaweco, a black safety pen with Toledo work overlay, the body decorated with rampant dragons in oval surrounds, German, circa 1920.
(Bonhams) £1,000 $1,600

Parker, a burgundy and black Duofold, with Parker Duofold nib, English, 1941–45. (Bonhams) £90 $144

Parker, a red Lucky Curve Duofold Senior, with Duofold Pen nib, American, circa 1926.
(Bonhams) £170 $272

Waterman, a 402 Barleycorn, with replaced nib, London, 1902. (Bonhams) £200 $320

Parker, a mandarin yellow Lucky Curve Duofold Senior pen and Junior pencil, the pen with Duofold nib, Danish, circa 1928. £380 $608

Mont Blanc, a limited edition Imperial Dragon No. 189/888, the clip marked 750, with stylised dragon clip and nib, German 1994. (Bonhams) £2,600 $4,160

Waterman's, a 9ct. gold fine Barley lever-filler, with No. 2 nib, London 1939. (Bonhams) £320 $512

Waterman, a turquoise Patrician, with Patrician nib, American, circa 1930. (Bonhams) £650 $1,040

Mont Blanc, an octagonal 2M safety pen with white metal overlay, the cap marked 900S, with each facet having a fine barley design panel, with No. 2 nib, German, 1920s. (Bonhams) £1,300 $2,080

Parker, a red and black mottled taper cap eyedropper, the barrel reading 'Geo. S. Parker Fountain Pen Pat. June 30.91Jan.9.94.' with 'Lucky Curve' and Lucky Curve nib, American, circa 1900.
(Bonhams) £480 $768

J. Whytwarth, a 9ct. gold overlaid safety pen, with alternating panels of plain and hatched design and medium Whytwarth nib, English, 1920s.
(Bonhams) £380 $608

Waterman, an onyx Patrician, with Patrician nib, American, circa 1930. (Bonhams) £420 $672

The King, a gold plated 12 safety pen, with alternating columns of floral and plain finish and with 'The King' nib, probably Italian, 1920s. (Bonhams) £110 $176

Waterman, a 552½ 'filigree', the cap and barrel marked *14ct.* with No. 2 New York nib, American, 1920s. (Bonhams) £500 $800

Waterman, a 412PSF 'filigree', lacks nib, American, 1920s. (Bonhams) £140 $224

Waterman, a pearl and black Partician, with Patrician nib, American, circa 1930. (Bonhams) £750 $1,200

Parker, an 18ct. gold Fine Barley 61 ballpen, with 18ct. gold clip, London, 1973.
(Bonhams) £280 $448

Parker, a black streamlined Duofold Senior, with No. 27 Duofold Pen nib and original price band, Canadian, circa 1929. (Bonhams) £80 $128

Sheaffer & Levanger, a transparent Mediterranean blue Connoisseur ballpen, American, 1996. (Bonhams) £100 $160

Conklin, a gold plated filigree ring-top crescent-filler, with Conklin nib, American, 1920s.
(Bonhams) £110 $176

Mont Blanc, a limited edition Oscar Wilde pencil No. 09371/12,000, German, 1994. (Bonhams) £170 $272

Mont Blanc, an eight-sided No. 10 pencil, marked *585,* German, circa 1930. (Bonhams) £620 $992

Waterman's, a black 'Smallest Pen in the World' eyedropper, with clip, American, circa 1910. (Bonhams) £1,200 $1,920

Omas, a limited edition Marconi '95 QSL, No. O22/340, marked *750,* with Omas nib, Italian, 1995. (Bonhams) £1,700 $2,720

Inkograph Co., a black Mickey Mouse pen, the barrel transfer decorated with a picture of Mickey and with cap topped by Mickey head, with Mickey nib, American, circa 1935. (Bonhams) £260 $416

Sheaffer & Levanger, a transparent Mediterranean blue Connoisseur ballpen with engraved Sheaffer/Levager nib, American, 1996. (Bonhams) £200 $320

Pilot, a maki-e piston filter, with 'scalloped togidashi' lacquer where the upper layers of the dark brown lacquer have been removed revealing the underlying brick red and black layers, with warranted nib, Japanese, 1940s. (Bonhams) £380 $608

Dunhill Namiki, a maki-e lacquer balance, the barrel decorated with a kingfisher skimming over a rocky pool, with No. 3 Dunhill namiki nib and five character, red seal signature, Japanese, 1930s.
(Bonhams) £520 $832

Waterman's, a limited edition Signé Boucheron No. 0770/3741, with gold filigree over blue barrel and blue lacquer inlaid into clip, with medium inlaid nib, French, 1996. (Bonhams) £700 $1,120

Mont Blanc, a No. 6F safety pen with Toledo work overlay, the overlay with panels of elegantly sinuous foliate and floral designs, Mont Blanc 'M' nib, German, circa 1920s. (Bonhams) £4,000 $6,400

Waterman's, a rose ripple 94, with No. 4 Ideal nib, American, circa 1928. (Bonhams) £320 $512

Waterman's, a 452½ LEC hand engraved Vine, with No. 2 nib, American, 1920s. (Bonhams) £200 $320

J. Paillard, a white metal basket weave filigree red ripple 'Semper' safety pen, with replaced steel nib and replaced feed, French, 1920s. (Bonhams) £200 $320

Omas, a limited edition Galileo Galilei, No. 0585/1343, with pearl and black body and two-colour 18ct. Omas nib, Italian, 1993. (Bonhams) £500 $800

Waterman, an 0518 SF Filigree, with No. 8 Ideal nib, American, circa 1912, extremely rare.
(Bonhams) £2,700 $4,320

Parker, a red Lucky Curve Duofold Special, with Duofold Pen nib, American, circa 1926.
(Bonhams) £180 $288

Parker, a Mandarin yellow Lucky Curve Duofold Junior, with Duofold Pen nib, American, circa 1927.
(Bonhams) £200 $320

Parker, a gold plated and mother-of-pearl No. 15 eyedropper, corrugated abalone and mother-of-pearl covered barrel, with twin foliate design barrel bands, American, 1908–1915. (Bonhams) £2,400 $3,840

Waterman's, an 0544 filigree safety pen and a basketweave pencil, with No. 2 nib, American, circa 1920. (Bonhams) £500 $800

Omas, a limited edition Tassili No. 1073/1500, with 18ct. brushed gold nib and the cap decorated with prehistoric cave paintings, Italian, 1996.
(Bonhams) £275 $440

Waterman's, a 554 LEC 'Basketweave' pen set, the pen marked 14K, with 14K clip and 4 nib and matching propelling pencil, American, 1920s.
(Bonhams) £1,000 $1,600

Conway Stewart, a No. 58 cracked ice, with Duro nib, English, 1950s. (Bonhams) £70 $112

Parker, a limited edtion mandarin yellow Centennial Duofold No. 8794/10,000, with Duofold Arrow nib, American, 1995. (Bonhams) £270 $432

Parker/Osmia, a jade green Duofold Senior, with Parker/Osmia imprint and broad italic Parker Duofold nib, German, 1920s. (Bonhams) £150 $240

Montblanc, a red and black mottled hard rubber 6 EF lever-filler, with 6 nib, German, 1920s.
(Bonhams) £2,200 $8,000

Wahl Eversharp, a black and bumble bee yellow ringtop lever-filler, with Wahl Pen 2 nib, American, circa 1929. (Bonhams) £300 $480

Progress, an onyx marble Progress lever filler, with enamelled tudor rose cap top decal and warranted nib, English, 1930s. (Bonhams) £70 $112

Aurora, a limited edition Colombo '92 No. 0766/1492, with gold plated cap head engraved 1492–1992 and with 18ct. Aurora nib, Italian, 1992.
(Bonhams) £800 $1,280

Waterman, a 552½ 'The King' pen set, marked 14ct. with No. 2 nib, American, 1920s.
(Bonhams) £580 $928

Dunhill Namiki, a maki-e lacquer balance, the barrel decorated with two crane in flights, executed in iroe-hira and mura nashiji maki-e, with No. 3 Dunhill Namiki nib, Japanese, 1930s.
(Bonhams) £550 $880

Montblanc, a limited edition Prince Regent 271/888, marked '750' on the filigree overlay, and set with diamonds and rubies in the cap, German, 1995.
(Bonhams) £2,400 $3,840

T.B. Ford, an electric blue enamelled Ford pen, with Ford nib, English, early 1930s. (Bonhams) £600 $960

Sheaffer, a pearl and black Senior Lifetime Flat-Top, with Lifetime nib, American, circa 1926.
(Bonhams)   £90 $144

Omas, a limited edition FAO 50 rollerball, with forest green body, the cap band reading *1945–1995 FAO*, Italian, 1995. (Bonhams)   £90 $144

Mont Blanc, a black Rouge Et Noir No. 4 BB, with No. 4 Simplo nib, German, circa 1910.
(Bonhams)   £500 $800

Conklin, a burgundy and black marbled 14-sided Nozac, with Cushion Point nib, American, circa 1932.
(Bonhams)   £160 $256

Conklin, a black and white 'Zebra' striped lever-filler, with two Toledo nib, American, circa 1932.
(Bonhams)   £350 $560

Parker, a limited edition World War II commemorative orange Duofold Centennial Pen No. 0881/1945, **English, 1995.** (Bonhams)   £280 $448

Montblanc, a black hard rubber 8 safety pen, with Simplo 8 nib, (later) decorative cap band and monkey clip, German, 1920s. (Bonhams)   £650 $1,040

Conklin, a black chased hard rubber 75 crescent-filler, with 7 Toledo nib, American, circa 1918.
(Bonhams)   £400 $640

Conklin, a black chased 30 Crescent Filler, with 18ct. Conklin No. 3 nib, American, circa 1918.
(Bonhams)   £60 $96

Montblanc, a limited edition Octavian No. 1964/4810, with two-colour 4810 nib, German, 1993.
(Bonhams)   £1,300 $2,080

Mont Blanc, a limited edtion Semiramis No. 4273/4810, with stylised filigree overlay with red enamel highlights and engraved nib, German, 1996.
(Bonhams)   £1,000 $1,600

Pelikan, a 'Toledo' T111, the gold plated silver barrel decorated with hand engraved pelicans, and with engraved clip and replaced nib, German, 1937-39.
(Bonhams)   £1,100 $1,760

Montblanc, a gold plated 0-size baby safety pen set, the pen with '0' nib and alternating panels of plain and floral decoration and matching pencil, Italian, 1920s.
(Bonhams)   £2,200 $3,520

Omas, a Silver Pearl celluloid coloured double pen, with scissor mechanism, two pump filling reservoirs allowing the user to write with two different colours of ink, original nibs, Italian, circa 1945.
(Bonhams)   £3,500 $5,600

Parker, a transparent, red and black brickwork prototype Vacumatic, with 'Parker Vacumatic' barrel imprint and oblique tin nib, American, 1930s.
(Bonhams)   £1,600 $2,560

John Dunhill, a black Two-Pen, with black pen with engraved spiral decoration, D.D. Zerollo clip and two John Dunhill nibs, Italian, circa 1930.
(Bonhams)   £1,000 $1,600

Montblanc, a 1497 Meisterstück Solitaire pen and 1647 ballpen, both marked *750*, the pen with two-colour 4810 nib, German, modern.
(Bonhams)   £1,600 $2,560

Mont Blanc, a limited edition Lorenzo de Medici No. 1530/4810, marked *925*, with octagonal engraved overlay and two-colour 4810 nib, German, 1992.
(Bonhams)   £2,550 $4,080

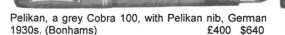

Pelikan, a grey Cobra 100, with Pelikan nib, German 1930s. (Bonhams)   £400 $640

Mont Blanc, a black 20L safety, with No. 2 nib, German, circa 1935. (Bonhams)   £210 $336

A 17th century pewter tankard of tapered form with incised line, 8¼in. high.
(Andrew Hartley)   £430 $710

A Liberty & Co. pewter bowl, decorated with four turquoise enamel mounts, 22cm. diameter.
(Bearne's)   £430 $770

An unusual Liberty Tudric pewter mantle clock, in the style of C F A Voysey, cast in relief with three stylised doves, 34cm. high.
(Christie's)   £3,680 $5,520

A W.M.F. silvered metal centrepiece, the circular clear glass bowl supported on foliate stem cast in relief with a scantily clad maiden, 53.5cm. high.
(Christie's)   £322 $520

Five early 19th century Irish pewter 'Haystack' measures, half noggin to a quart, the quart stamped *Dublin*, 3in. to 7¾in.
(Woolley & Wallis)   £960 $1,545

A Liberty pewter teaset, designed by Archibald Knox, cast in relief with stylised honesty, comprising: teapot and hinged cover, hot-water pot and cover, milk-jug and sugar basin. (Christie's)   £690 $10,135

Antique American pewter lighthouse coffee pot with banded decoration, mark of Roswell Gleason of Dorchester, MA (1822-1871. 11in. high.
(Eldred's)   £213 $352

Pewter coffee pot and pewter cream and sugar.
(Remmey)   £25 $40

A rare and important pewter flagon, Johann Christopher Heyne, Lancaster, Pennsylvania, 1715–81, on three cherubic mask feet, 11½in. high. (Sotheby's) £88,755 $145,500

Antique American pewter teapot, by E. Smith, base repaired, 7½in. high. (Eldred's) £53 $88

Kayserzinn pewter basket, floral relief decoration, signed, 9in. high, 11½in. wide. (Skinner) £189 $316

Antique American pewter conical-form teapot, with incised lines, stamped *Morey & Ober 2 Boston*, 7in. high. (Eldred's) £66 $110

A rare pewter flask, Johann Christopher Heyne, Lancaster, Pennsylvania, 1715–81, the removable thimble-sized lid threaded above a circular line-incised vessel.
(Sotheby's) £6,314 $10,350

A pair of Liberty & Co. pewter candlesticks, each with spreading circular drip pan on tapering column and flared base, 24cm.
(Bearne's) £300 $495

A rare pewter chalice attributed to Johann Christopher Heyne, Lancaster, Pennsylvania, 1715–81, the moulded rim above a tapering body, 8¾in. high.
(Sotheby's) £25,254 $41,400

English pewter charger, London, late 18th/early 19th century, marks untraced, 16½in. diameter.
(Eldred's) £120 $198

Pair of antique American pewter push-up candlesticks, in baluster form, unmarked, 8½in. high.
(Eldred's) £193 $319

A Liberty Tudric pewter biscuit box and cover, square section modelled in relief with stylised flowers, with blue enamel roundels, 11cm. high.
(Christie's) £747 $1,120

Framed photograph, Abraham Lincoln, taken on June 3, 1860 by Alexander Hesler of Chicago. (Eldred's) £500 $825

William Edward Kilburn, portrait of a gentleman seated by a table reading a book, 1850s, stereoscopic daguerreotype, hand-tinted with gilt highlights, black card surround. (Christie's) £690 $1,124

An original photograph showing Mussolini in military uniform presenting a medal to a soldier, 9¼ x 7in. (H. C. Chapman) £60 $99

Julia Margaret Cameron (1815-79), May Prinsep as Beatrice Cenci, 1870, albumen print, 12⅞ x 10¾in., mounted on modern card, titled *May Prinsep* in pencil on mount. (Christie's) £5,750 $9,372

Roger Fenton, 'The Council of War, held on the morning of the taking of the Mamelon', 1855, salt print, 7¼ x 6¼in., mounted on card. (Christie's) £460 $749

Full-length portrait of a Japanese man and woman, circa 1860s, ambrotype, 3¼ x 2½in., in original balsa-wood case. (Christie's) £517 $842

Brassaï, Matisse in his studio, 1939, printed later, gelatin silver print, image size 14¼ x 10¼in., signed in ink in margin. (Christie's) £3,450 $5,623

Jacques-Henri Lartigue (1894-1986), The rabbit has arrived; 1911; Descent of the rabbit, 1911, the latter printed circa 1960s, two gelatin silver prints, 4¾ x 3⅜in. and 6¾ x 9½in., (Christie's) £9,200 $14,996

Bill Brandt, Ellison Place, Jarrow, circa 1939, printed 1975, gelatin silver print, 13 x 10½in. mounted on card, signed in ink on mount. (Christie's) £1,265 $2,062

Guglielmo Pluschow, male nudes, late 19th century, albumen print, 8¹⁵/₁₆ x 6⁵/₈in.
(Christie's) £437 $712

Anonymous, school portrait with eight girls and a teacher, 1850s quarter-plate daguerreotype, gilt-metal surround, in folding case.
(Christie's) £299 $487

William Ellis, portrait of a man, 1856, salt print, possibly from a waxed paper negative, untrimmed, 9 x 7³/₈in.
(Christie's) £7,820 $12,746

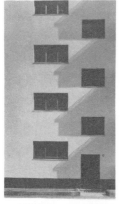

Werner Mantz (1901-83), Apartment house, Kalkerfeld, Cologne, 1928, gelatin silver print, 15¼ x 8¾in., signed and dated *W. Mantz, 1928* on verso, matted.
(Christie's) £26,450 $43,113

David Octavius Hill and Robert Adamson, group at Bonaly Towers, the home of Lord Cockburn, including Lord Cockburn, Miss & Mrs. Cockburn, John Henning and D. O. Hill, mid 1840s, calotype, 6¹/₈ x 8¹/₈in. (Christie's) £1,150 $1,874

Yakov Khalip, 'Landing of the SSSR – B6 Airship, Moscow', 1936-37, printed later, gelatin silver print, 11⁷/₈ x 8in., signed, titled and dated in blue pencil in Russian.
(Christie's) £805 $1,312

Bill Brandt (1906-84), 'Pre-War London, Ride in a Hansom Cab', circa 1935, printed circa 1948, gelatin silver print, 9 x 7⁵/₈in., titled in ink by the photographer on verso.
(Christie's) £4,830 $7,872

William Ellis, 'Sodra a Betsimisaraka bearer', 1854 or 1856, salt print, 13¾ x 11¾in.
(Christie's) £6,325 $10,309

Frank Meadow Sutcliff, 'Sunshine & Showers', late 19th century, carbon print, 11¾ x 9⁵/₈in., numbered *8* in the negative, mounted on card, signed and titled on verso.
(Christie's) £483 $787

Oscar Gustaf Rejlander (1813-75), Charity, circa 1854, albumen print, 7¾ x 6in., arched top, mounted on blue card with two other albumen prints, matted.
(Christie's)   £4,025 $6,561

Robert Frank (b. 1924), Urinal, Piazza Cremitani, Padua, circa 1949, gelatin silver print, 10³/8 x 12⁷/8in., signed in ink in margin, matted. (Christie's) £3,680 $5,998

Antoine Claudet, young girl, seated and holding a hoop, 1850s, sixth-plate daguerreotype, gilt-metal mount, in folding morocco case.
(Christie's)   £460 $750

Lewis Carroll (Charles Lutwidge Dodgson) Portrait of Henry Kitchin seated on a sofa, 1860s-70s, albumen print mounted as a cabinet card. (Christie's)   £1,150 $1,874

Frank Meadow Sutcliffe, 'In Puris Naturalibus', late 19th century, carbon print, 9 x 11½in., signed in pencil on recto, original oak frame.
(Christie's)   £1,265 $2,061

Lev Borodulin, Divers, 1960s, printed later, gelatin silver print, 11⁷/8 x 7⁷/8in. signed, titled and dated in Russian in ink.
(Christie's)   £1,610 $2,624

Brassaï [Gyula Halasz] (1899-1984), Bal des Quatre Saisons, Paris, circa 1932, glossy gelatin silver print, 8½ x 7in., photographer's ink credit stamp on verso.
(Christie's)   £19,550 $31,866

Daniel Farson, 'John Deakin', 1960s, gelatin silver print, 7 x 7in., titled in ink, annotated in pencil and with photographer's ink credit stamp. (Christie's)   £299 $373

Arnold Genthe and Ruth Harriet Louise, Greta Garbo, circa 1925, two toned gelatin silver prints, each approximately 12 x 9½in., the former inscribed and the latter with ink credit stamp.
(Christie's)   £1,610 $2,624

Maull & Polyblank, Professor Owen, 1856, albumen print, 7⅞ x 5¾in., arched top, mounted on card within gilt border. (Christie's)   £517 $842

Gambier Bolton, 'Indian Rhinoceros', circa 1880s-90s, carbon print, 10 x 12in., untrimmed, titled, numbered 307.
(Christie's)   £2,300 $3,749

Anonymous, Portrait of a young Asian girl, July 1850, quarter-plate daguerreotype, mounted as oval in passe-partout with black surround and gilt border.
(Christie's)   £575 $937

David Octavius Hill and Robert Adamson, Miss Mary Schetky, 1840s, calotype, 7⅞ x 5¾in., incorrectly identified *Mrs. Rigby* in pencil on verso.
(Christie's)   £1,092 $1,780

Gustave Le Gray (1820-82), The Great Wave, Sète, 1856-69, albumen print from two negatives, 13³/₈in. x 16³/₈in., photographer's red facsimile signature stamp on recto, mounted on card.
(Christie's)   £47,700 $77,781

Heinrich Kuhn(1866-1944), Portrait of a seaman, 1897, gum-bichromate print, 15¼ x 11¼in., signed and dated in pencil on recto, inscribed *Holzkohle* (charcoal) in pencil on verso.
(Christie's)   £977 $1,592

Anonymous, 'Manille – Jeune fille Mestiza (métis.)', circa 1870s, albumen print, 10½ x 8¼in., arched corners, mounted on card, titled in ink on mount, matted.
(Christie's)   £1,380 $2,249

John Dillwyn Llewelyn, Rhubarb leaves and basket under a hornbeam hedge, circa 1850-52, calotype, 6³/₈ x 8in.
(Christie's)   £2,070 $3,374

Horst P. Horst (b. 1906), Noel Coward, Paris, 1934, printed later, gelatin silver print, image size 17¾ x 13⁷/₈in., photographer's blindstamp in margin, matted, framed. (Christie's) £1,035 $1,687

Unusual upright piano with panelled front and engraved ironwork hinges, made in Arts and Crafts style by Oskar Dawson & Son of Haslemere in 1932, with matching piano stool on octagonal legs. (Ewbank) £1,150 $1,897

Italian Rococo-style polychrome decorated hammer dulcimer, late 19th century, shaped top raised on cabriole legs, scenes of Venice and floral devices, 47in. wide. (Skinner) £897 $1,495

A Steinway & Sons ebonised baby grand piano, serial number 429699L with a piano bench.
(Sotheby's) £9,120 $14,950

A Steinway grand pianoforte, 7 octaves, overstrung, in ebonised case on fluted turned legs, 6ft.2in. long, circa 1889. (George Kidner) £5,100 $8,415

A Baldwin model SD-10 concert grand piano, commissioned for Liberace, circa 1965, the brushed satin finish ebonised case with lucite lid, now raised on Art Deco style chromed-steel supports, 108in. long. (Christie's) £10,350 $15,525

Early 19th century mahogany spinet, inlaid with ebonised stringing, the keyboard crested with brass inlaid panels, flanked by two fret work pierced panels, by John Broadwood & Sons, London, circa 1820, 66in. (G.A. Key) £480 $768

An EWC phonograph by the Excelsior Werke Cologne, export edition for the British market, with aluminium horn, cover and eight cylinders, 1903.
(Auction Team Köln) £230 $368

An Edison Standard Phonograph Model B, oak-cased, with original speaker, 1905.
(Auction Team Köln) £355 $569

An Edison Home-Phonograph Model B cylinder player, with eleven section tin convolvulus horn internally painted with a rose motif, 1905.
(Auction Team Köln) £795 $1,273

A 24½in. Polyphon with twin combs, coin mechanism with manual over-ride and typical walnut case, 60½in. high, with approximately seventy-three discs.
(Christie's) £5,750 $9,200

A 14⅛in. table Polyphon with bells, with twin combs, two banks of six bells with on/off lever, walnut case, with nine discs.
(Christie's) £3,220 $5,152

A 22in. upright Polyphon with sixteen-note glockenspiel, two combs and conventional walnut case, 56in. high.
(Christie's) £5,520 $8,832

A Pathé No. 1 phonograph with original case and aluminium horn, with 11 original cylinder boxes, circa 1903.
(Auction Team Köln) £418 $669

A Nympho phonograph, with non-spindle cylinder player, cast metal plate in the form of a nymph, green and gold painted, 1905.
(Auction Team Köln) £754 $1,206

An unattributed Puck phonograph, with cast iron lyre base and aluminium horn, circa 1900.
(Auction Team Köln) £334 $535

Cheret, Jules, Halle aux Chapeaux, lithograph in colours, 1892, printed by Chaix, Paris, backed on japan. (Christie's)   £1,495 $2,392

Anonymous, Relojes Union, lithograph in colours, circa 1925, 39½ x 28in. (Christie's) £322 $515

Cheret, Jules, Taverne Olympia, lithograph in colours, 1899, printed by Chaix, Paris, 48 x 34in. (Christie's)   £1,725 $2,846

Grasset, Eugene (1841-1917), Salon des Cent, lithograph in colours, 1894, printed by G. de Malherbe, Paris, backed on linen, 23½ x 16in. (Christie's)   £862 $1,379

Bovard, Fortune (1875-1947), Schuster & Co., lithograph in colours, 1916, printed by J.E. Wolfensberger, Zürich, backed on japan, 48 x 33in. (Christie's)   £460 $736

Baumberger, Otto (1889-1961), Kinderschuhe Capitol, lithograph in colours, 1923, printed by Wolfsberg, Zürich, backed on old linen, 50 x 35½in. (Christie's)   £368 $589

Anonymous, Münchener Tierpark, Hellabrunn, lithograph in colours, 1938, printed by Th. Wengeler, Schöneberg, 33 x 23in. (Christie's)   £253 $405

Womrath, Andrew K (1869-?), XXVe Exposition, Salon des Cent, lithograph in colours, 1897, backed on linen, 21 x 15½in. (Christie's)   £345 $552

Zietara, Valentin (1883-1935), Hosen-Zeit bei Loden Frey, lithograph in colours, 1930, printed by Dr. C. Wolf & Sohn, 47 x 32½in. (Christie's)   £460 $736

Cheret, Jules, Saxoleine, lithograph in colours, 1892, printed by Chaix, Paris, backed on old linen, framed, 48 x 34in. (Christie's)   £575 $920

Anonymous, Tabonuco Pectoral, lithograph in colours,, circa 1920, printed by A. Trüb y Cia., Aarau, 37 x 25in. (Christie's) £1,265 $2,024

Matejko, Theo, Lilie, lithograph in colours, circa 1920, printed by WEAG, Wien, 49 x 37in. (Christie's)   £517 $853

Cheret, Jules, La Diaphane, lithograph in colours, 1890, printed by Chaix, Paris, backed on linen, 16 x 34in. (Christie's)   £460 $736

Cheret, Jules, Folies Bergere, Fleur de Lotus, lithograph in colours, 1893, printed by Chaix, Paris, backed on old linen, framed, 48 x 34in. (Christie's)   £1,725 $2,760

Thoren, M. de, F. Pinet, lithograph in colours, circa 1900, printed by Kossuth & Cie., Paris, backed on linen, 50½ x 36in. (Christie's)   £253 $405

Schnackenberg, Walter (1880-1961) Lena Amsel, lithograph in colours, 1918, printed by O. Consée, Munich, 49 x 34in. (Christie's)   £1,610 $2,576

Mucha, Alphonse, Moravian Teachers' Choir, lithograph in colours, 1911, printed by V. Neubet, Praha, 43 x 32in.
(Christie's)   £2,300 $3,795

Anonymous, Exposition Franco-Britannique, Londres, 1908, lithograph in colours, 1908, printed by Benrose & Sons, Ltd., London, 42 x 30in. (Christie's) £862 $1,422

Prusakov, Nikolai(1900-1952), Borisov, Grigori (1899-1942), Two Worlds, lithograph in colours, circa 1927, 49 x 37in.
(Christie's)   £1,610 $2,656

Schlatter, Ernst Emil (1883-1954), Elektr.Strassenbahnen im Kanton Zug, lithograph in colours, 1914, printed by J.C.Müller, Zürich, backed on japan, 40 x 27½in.
(Christie's)   £575 $920

Noury, Gaston (1866-?), Les Corsets Le Furet, lithograph in colours, circa 1910, printed by Atlas, Paris, backed on old linen, 54½ x 39in.
(Christie's)   £805 $1,328

Anonymous, Concours Luna, lithograph in colours, circa 1910, printed by Société des Affiches Artistiques, Geneva, backed on linen, 66 x 44in.
(Christie's)   £517 $827

Stenberg, Vladimir & George (1899-1982, 1900-1933), Sea Hawk, lithograph in colours, 1927, printed by Sovkino, Moscow, 39½ x 28in.
(Christie's)   £1,610 $2,656

Chagall, Marc (1887-1985), Kunsthalle Basel, lithograph in colours, 1956, printed by Wassermann, Basel, 50 x 35½in.
(Christie's)   £1,380 $2,277

Kirschner, Z., Maria Tafelmeyer Damenkonfektion, lithograph in colours, 1927, printed by Oscar Consée, Munich, 47 x 34½in.
(Christie's)   £517 $827

Urech, Rudolph (1888-1951), Quodlibet Maskenball, lithograph in colours, circa 1928, printed by W. Wassermann.
(Christie's) £414 $683

Mich, (Michel Liebeaux 1881-1923), Boulogne S. Mer, lithograph in colours, circa 1900, printed by E. Dauvissat, Paris, backed on linen, 42 x 29in. (Christie's) £149 $245

Benda, G.K. (Georges Kugelmann), Mistinguett, lithograph in colours, 1913, printed by Philippe G. Dreyfus, Paris, 63 x 48in.
(Christie's) £1,035 $1,707

Blott, Georges, Ville de Perpignan, lithograph in colours, 1989, printed by P. Vercasson & Cie., Paris, backed on linen, 59½ x 43in.
(Christie's) £1,380 $2,208

Cappiello, Leonetto, Gramophone J'Accuse, lithograph in colours, circa 1910, printed by Vercasson, Paris, 94 x 63in.
(Christie's) £2,645 $4,365

Handschin, Hans (1899-1948), Flims, lithograph in colours, circa 1934, printed by Wassermann & Co., Graphische, Basel, 39½ x 27½in. (Christie's) £437 $699

Misti, (Ferdinand Mifliez), Bougie à 5 Trous, lithograph in colours, circa 1900, printed by H. Laas, E. Pécaud & Cie., Paris, 55 x 39in.
(Christie's) £747 $1,230

Hohlwein, Ludwig, Zoo Berlin, lithograph in colours, circa 1930, printed by Herm. Sonntag & Co. Munich, 23½ x 16½in.
(Christie's) £414 $662

Anonymous, Championnat de Lutte, 1906, lithograph in colours, 1906, printed by Cercle des Arts Industriels, 63 x 45in.
(Christie's) £460 $760

Dufrene, Maurice (1876-1955), Rayon des Soieries, lithograph in colours, 1930, printed by Chaix, Paris, backed on linen, framed, 47 x 31in. (Christie's) £920 $1,472

Steglitz, Lehmann, Luna Park, lithograph in colours, circa 1920, printed Weylandt, Berlin, 28 x 37½in. (Christie's) £287 $459

Herdt, Hans Rudi, Münchner-Kindl-Keller, lithograph in colours, 1913, printed by Hollerbaum & Schmidt, Berlin, 47 x 36in. (Christie's) £920 $1,518

Bakst, Leon (1866-1924) Caryathis, lithograph in colours, circa 1919, printed by H. Cachoin, Paris, 90 x 54in. (Christie's) £6,900 $11,385

Dellepiane, David (1866-1932), Exposition Internationale d'Electricité, Marseille, lithograph in colours, 1908, printed by Moullot, Paris, 43½ x 63in. (Christie's) £4,025 $6,640

Mucha, Alphonse, Chocolat Idéal, lithograph in colours, 1897, printed by F. Champenois, Paris, backed on linen, 33½ x 22½in. (Christie's) £4,370 $6,992

Baumberger, Otto, Baumann, lithograph in colours, 1919, printed by Jmentor Verlag, Zürich, backed on old linen, 49½ x 34½in. (Christie's) £299 $478

Anonymous, Pathé Baby, lithograph in colours, circa 1925, printed by A. Trüb y Cia., Aarau, 27½ x 39in. (Christie's) £1,840 $2,944

Ellis, Clifford & Rosemary, River, Trolleybus, lithograph in colours, 1932, printed by the Baynard Press, London, 40 x 25in. (Christie's) £368 $589

Cappiello, Leonetto, France, lithograph in colours, 1937, printed by Edimo, Paris, 39½ x 24½in. (Christie's) £690 $1,104

Bernhard, Lucian (1883-1972), Cords, lithograph in colours, 1912, printed by Hollerbaum & Schmidt, Berlin, 27½ x 37½in. (Christie's) £437 $699

Vertes, Marcel (1895-1961), Simone Frévalles, lithograph in colours, 1923, printed by L'Affiche d'Art, Paris, 48½ x 32½in. (Christie's) £172 $283

London Hippodrome, Houdini, photography and letter press in colours, 1904, printed by David Allen & Sons Ltd., London, backed on card, 30 x 20in. (Christie's) £8,970 $14,352

Ehmcke, Fritz Hellmut (1878-1965), Pianoforte Fabrik Thein, lithograph in colours, 1902, printed by Hollerbaum & Schmidt, Berlin, 32½ x 43½in. (Christie's) £805 $1,328

Anonymous, 'Who is She?', lithograph in colours, circa 1930, printed by Stafford & Co., Nottingham, with nine others mainly for Gilbert & Sullivan operas, 30 x 20in. (Christie's) £345 $552

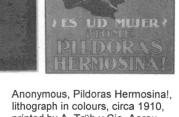

Hohlwein, Ludwig, Riquet, Mammut-Kakao, lithograph in colours, 1928, printed by Emil Gerasch GmbH, Leipzig, 44 x 29in. (Christie's) £1,150 $1,840

Oppenheim, Louis, (1879-?), AEG, lithograph in colours, circa 1920, printed by Arnold Weylandt, Berlin, 28½ x 37½in. (Christie's) £862 $1,379

Anonymous, Pildoras Hermosina!, lithograph in colours, circa 1910, printed by A. Trüb y Cia, Aarau, 39½ x 27½in. (Christie's) £1,150 $1,897

Nagel, Günther, Süßwasserfisch, offset lithograph in colours, 1933, printed by Joh. Wilh. Ehrlich, Fürth,, 28 x 19in. (Christie's) £460 $736

Lucas, Charles E, Cabaret des Arts, lithograph in colours, circa 1900, backed on linen, 57 x 43in. (Christie's) £575 $920

Riemer, Durch Fisch Gesund und Frisch, lithograph in colours, 1931, printed by Otto Holzhauser, Berlin, 46 x 33in. (Christie's) £299 $478

Klimsch, K., Engelhorn's Allgemeine Roman-Bibliothek, lithograph in colours, circa 1910, printed by Union Deutsche Verlagsgesellschaft, Stuttgart, backed on linen, 29½ x 20in. (Christie's) £517 $827

Loupot, Charles (1892-1962), St. Raphael, lithograph in colours, printed by Affiches Gaillard, Paris, on four sheets, backed on linen, framed 42½ x 42½in. (Christie's) £575 $920

Cheret, Jules, Grands Magasins du Louvre, Étrennes, lithograph in colours, 1896, printed by Chaix, Paris, backed on old linen, framed, 47½ x 34in. (Christie's) £1,610 $2,576

Naegele, Otto Ludwig (1880-1952), Saison Gemälde Ausstellung, lithograph in colours, 1908, printed by J.G. Velisch, Munich, 47 x 35in. (Christie's) £460 $736

Hohlwein, Ludwig, Rosenthal Porzellan-Ausstellung, lithograph in colours, 1910, printed by Fritz Maison, Munich, 42½ x 31in. (Christie's) £368 $589

Chagall, Marc (1887-1985), Metropolitan Opera, lithograph in colours, 1966, printed by Mourlot, Paris, backed on linen, framed, 40 x 25½in. (Christie's) £575 $920

Wolff, Willy, Arche Noah, lithograph in colours, 1928, printed by Leudruck, 47 x 33in. (Christie's) £322 $515

Anonymous, Rodex, Coats of Fine Quality, offset lithograph in colours, circa 1930, printed by Forman, 19 x 13in. (Christie's) £552 $883

Gut, W, Philips Radio, lithograph in colours, circa 1955, printed by Maurer, Zürich, 36 x 25in. (Christie's) £287 $459

Karner, Theodor, Frances-Metz Tänze, lithograph in colours, 1914, printed by Albert Ebner, Munich, 39½ x 27½in. (Christie's) £517 $827

Heudflass, Werner von, Persil für alle Wäsche, lithograph in colours, 1932, printed by Henkel & Cie., Düsseldorf, on two sheets, 48 x 33in. (Christie's) £322 $515

Cheret, Jules (1892-1985), Madame Sans-Gêne, lithograph in colours, 1894, printed by Chaix, Paris, backed on linen, 49 x 34½in. (Christie's) £460 $736

Baylac, Lucien (1851-1913), Electricine, lithograph in colours, 1895, printed by Chaix, Paris, backed on linen, 48½in. x 34in. (Christie's) £345 $552

Anonymous, Bayerische Volkspartei, lithograph in colours, 1919, printed by Art Anstalt, Munich, 39½ x 29½in. (Christie's) £414 $662

Maier, Johann Baptiste (Ibe, Hans), Kieler Herbst Woche, lithograph in colours, 1921, printed by C. Schaidt, Kiel, 36½ x 24in. (Christie's) £368 $589

Anonymous, Pathé-Baby, lithograph in colours, circa 1923, printed by A. Trüb y Cia., Aarau, 39 x 27½in. (Christie's) £1,092 $1,747

Anonymous, Les Troubadours Eureka, lithograph in colours, circa, 1900, printed by Finot, Paris, 30½ x 46in. (Christie's) £195 $320

Anonymous, Chocolat Suchard, lithograph in colours, circa 1910, vertical and horizontal fold marks, 61 x 41in. (Christie's) £920 $1,518

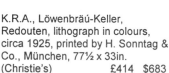

K.R.A., Löwenbräu-Keller, Redouten, lithograph in colours, circa 1925, printed by H. Sonntag & Co., München, 77½ x 33in. (Christie's) £414 $683

Cleaver, Ralph, Richmond Royal Horse Show, lithograph in colours, 1906, 2 letterpress sheets, 1959, printed by J.H. Broad & Co., Surrey and Gale & Polden Ltd., London, on three sheets, 110 x 40in. (Christie's) £51 $81

Cocteau, Jean (1889-1963), Théatre de Monte-Carlo, Ballet Russe, lithographs in colours, 1911, printed by Eugène Verneau & Henri Chachoin, Paris, each 36 x 23in. (Christie's) £8,050 $13,282

Martin, G, Crême Soleil, lithograph in colours, circa 1920, printed by Wall, Paris, backed on linen, 46 x 30in. (Christie's) £57 $94

Hohlwein, Ludwig, Engleder und Finkenzeller Bürobedarf, lithograph in colours, 1925, printed by Dr. C. Wolf u. Sohn, Munich, 35½ x 49in. (Christie's) £402 $643

Metlicovitz, Leopoldo, Concordia, lithograph in colours, 1905, printed by G.Ricordi & C., Milano, 80 x 54½in. (Christie's) £632 $1,042

Anonymous, Les Avants, lithograph in colours, circa 1910, printed by Muller & Trüb, Lausanne, 40 x 27in. (Christie's) £1,840 $2,944

Larramet, H Z, Monol, lithograph in colours, circa 1910, printed by B. Chapellier, Jne., Paris, 47 x 62in. (Christie's) £345 $570

Börmel, Saison-Ausverkauf, lithograph in colours, circa 1930, printed by S. Malz GmbH, Berlin, 47 x 31in. (Christie's) £345 $552

Anonymous, Azerbaijan, lithograph in colours, minor defects, 40 x 25in. (Christie's) £172 $283

Grun, Jules-Alexandre (1868-1934), Excelsior, lithograph in colours, circa 1900, printed by CH. Verneau, Paris, 55 x 86in. (Christie's) £2,530 $4,175

Mucha, Alphonse, La Dame Aux Camelias, lithograph in colours, 1896, printed by F. Champenois, Paris, 82½ x 30in. (Christie's) £12,075 $19,923

Kreibig, Erwin von (1904-1961), Pariser Luft, lithograph in colours, 1929, printed by opb, Munich, 55x 33in. (Christie's) £517 $827

Herdt, Hans Rudi (1883-1918), Den Berliner Börsen-Courier, lithograph in colours, 1913, printed by Hollerbaum & Schmidt, Berlin, 27½ x 38in. (Christie's) £460 $760

Anonymous, Chocolat Suchard, Grand Prix Paris 1900, lithograph in colours, 61 x 42in. (Christie's) £1,380 $2,277

Bouisset, Firmin, Chocolat Menier, lithograph in colours, 1893, printed by Camis, Paris, 51½ x 39in. (Christie's) £1,840 $3,036

Mucha, Alphonse, Figaro Illustré, lithograph in colours, 1896, front cover of magazine with contents, 16 x 12½in. (Christie's) £506 $810

Thal, A. R. Martin Legeay, lithograph in colours, circa 1950, printed by Paul-Martial, Paris, 23½ x 15½in. (Christie's) £253 $417

Gray, H. (Henri Boulanger), Pétrole Stella, lithograph in colours, 1897, printed by Courmont Frères, Paris, 51 x 39in. (Christie's) £1,840 $3,036

Hohlwein, Ludwig, Franck Spezial, lithograph in colours, circa 1925, minor repaired tears in the margins, 46½ x 35in. (Christie's) £920 $1,518

Cappiello, Leonetto, Poulain-Orange, lithograph in colours, 1911, printed by P. Vercasson & Cie., Paris, 62 x 42in. (Christie's) £862 $1,422

Anonymous, Les Lutteurs de Stamboul, lithograph in colours, circa 1895, printed by Nouvelles Affiches Artistique, Paris, 43 x 31½in. (Christie's) £184 $303

Keimel, Hermann (1889-1948), Cherubin Palast, Carneval 1926, lithograph in colours, 1926, printed by M. Kragl, München, 49 x 37½in. (Christie's) £1,955 $3,225

Anonymous, Lux, lithograph in colours, circa 1930, printed by Gebr. Fretz A.G., Zürich, backed on linen, 50 x 35½in. (Christie's) £253 $405

Baumberger, Otto, Doelker, lithograph in colours, 1923, printed by Wolfsberg, Zürich, 50 x 35½in. (Christie's) £1,380 $2,277

Anonymous, La Femme Fatale, lithograph in colours, circa 1900, printed by Emile Levy, Paris, 51½ x 36½in. (Christie's) £57 $94

Anonymous, Radio Lot, lithograph in colours, circa 1930, printed by A. Trüb y Cia., Aarau, 47 x 35in. (Christie's) £920 $1,472

Rassenfosse, Armand A L (1862-1934), Salon des Cent, from Les Maitres de L'Affiche, lithograph in colours, 1896, printed by Chaix, Paris, 15 x 11in. (Christie's) £1,265 $2,087

Anonymous, Torino-Concorso Ippico Nazionale, lithograph in colours, circa 1930, printed by G. Ricordi & Cia., Milan, backed on linen, 39½ x 39in. (Christie's) £862 $1,379

Metlicovitz, Leopoldo (1868-1944), Exposition Internationale, Turin, 1911, lithograph in colours, 1911, printed by G. Ricordi & Co., Milan, 39 x 27½in. (Christie's) £1,035 $1,707

Anonymous, Pildoras Anti-Anémicas, lithograph in colours, circa 1910, printed by A. Trüb y Cia., Aarau, 27 x 19cm. (Christie's) £632 $1,042

Don, Jean (1900-1985), Jane Marny, lithograph in colours, 1930, printed by H. Chachoin, Paris, backed on linen, 62½ x 47in. (Christie's) £322 $515

Redon, Georges (1869-1943), A La Place Clichy, Blanc, lithograph in colours, 1900, printed by Chaix, Paris, 62 x 42½in. (Christie's) £862 $1,422

Soubie, Roger (1898-1984), Tempete sur le Mont-Blanc, lithograph in colours, circa 1930, printed by Delattre, Paris, backed on linen, 61 x 46in. (Christie's) £747 $1,230

Cavre, Lucien, Première Traversée de la Méditerranée, Un Français, Roland Garros, lithograph in colours, 1913, printed by La Publicité Synchronisée, Paris, 14½ x 11in. (Christie's) £460 $760

Dorival, Georges (1879-1968), Exposition de la Locomotion Aerienne, 4eme , lithograph in colours, 1910, printed by Atelier Geo Dorival, Paris, 30 x 22in. (Christie's) £805 $1,328

Ashley, KLM, lithograph in colours, circa 1955, printed by The Baynard Press, vertical and horizontal fold marks, 40 x 27½in. (Christie's) £51 $84

Göderström, Populäre Luftfahrten, lithograph in colours, circa 1910, printed by Hans Lindenstaedt, Charlottenburg, backed on japan, 27 x 37½in. (Christie's) £1,150 $1.840

Harald, 2e Grande Semaine d'Aviation de la Champagne, Reims, lithograph in colours, 1910, printed by Harald, Paris, 64 x 47in. (Christie's) £1,035 $1,707

Diem, Carl, Gordon-Bennett Fahren, lithograph in colours, 1912, printed by Emil Hochdanz, Stuttgart, 39½ x 29in. (Christie's) £1,092 $1,747

Walther, Jean (1910-), Douglas DC-3, lithograph in colours, circa 1935, monor defects, small losses at the edges, 24 x 29½in. (Christie's) £690 $1,138

Anonymous, Luposta, Danzig, lithograph in colours, 1932, printed by A.W. Kafemann, Danzig, 26 x 19in. (Christie's) £1,265 $2,024

Peckham, C, Imperial Airways, England-Egypt-India, lithograph in colours, 1934, backed on linen, 30 x 20in. (Christie's)   £747 $1,230

Jan Transports Aériens, Maicon, lithograph in colours, circa 1910, **printed by de L'Eclaireur de Nice,** minor defects, backed on linen, 11½ x 16in. (Christie's) £250 $400

Lessieux et Carry, Circuit d'Anjou, Angers, lithograph in colours, 1912, printed by Editions Nationales, Paris, backed on linen, 62 x 46½in. (Christie's)   £3,450 $5,520

Koworsky, N, ABA, offset lithograph in colours, 1945, printed by Esselte, Stockholm, repaired tears, backed on linen, 39 x 25in. (Christie's)   £450 $720

Anonymous, Pau-Aviation, lithograph in colours, circa 1910, printed by Garet & Haristoy, backed on linen, 31 x 46½in. (Christie's)   £1,035 $1,707

Andersen, I.B., DDL Danish Air Lines, lithograph in colours, 1945, printed by Andreasen & Lachmann, backed on japan, 39½ x 24½in. (Christie's)   £299 $478

Glass, Franz Paul (1886-1964), Fördert den Luftsport, lithograph in colours, 1933, printed by Cromolith Kunstanstalt, Munich, 34 x 23½in. (Christie's)   £287 $459

Anonymous, Lucerne, First Swiss Airship-station, lithograph and photography in colours, circa 1930, printed by Orell Füssli, Zürich, backed on japan, 27 x 38½in. (Christie's)   £747 $1,230

Anonymous, Dijon-Aviation, lithograph in colours, 1910, printed by G. Gerin, Paris, backed on linen, 62 x 46in. (Christie's)   £2,760 $4,416

Cappiello, Leonetto, Cognac Albert Robin, lithograph in colours, circa 1910, printed by Vercasson, Paris, 62 x 47in. (Christie's) £920 $1,472

Erdt, Hans Rudi, Müller Extra, lithograph in colours, 1908, printed by Hollerbaum & Schmidt, Berlin, 46 x 34in. (Christie's) £632 $1,011

Cappiello, Leonetto (1875-1942), Cinzano, lithograph in colours, circa 1910, printed by Ortega, Valencia, 55 x 37½in.
(Christie's) £2,875 $4,600

Gipkens, Julius E.F. (1883-circa 1969), Kupferberg Gold, lithograph in colours, 1913, printed by Hollerbaum & Schmidt, 34 x 23in. (Christie's) £575 $920

Anonymous, Guinness As Usual, Guinness Is Good For You, lithograph in colours, 1941, printed by Sanders Phillips & Co., Ltd., London, generally in excellent condition, framed, 29½ x 19½in. (Christie's) £437 $700

Gilroy, John (1898-?), My Goodness, My Guinness, lithograph in colours, 1952, printed by John Waddington Ltd., Leeds, backed on linen, 60 x 40in. (Christie's) £690 $1,104

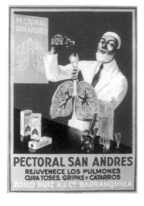

Anonymous, Pectoral San Andres, lithograph in colours, circa 1925, printed by A. Trüb y Cia., Aarau, 39½ x 27½in. (Christie's) £1,380 $2,208

Anonymous, Guinness after work, offset lithograph in colours, 1961, printed by John Waddington Ltd., Leeds, minor creasing, 30 x 20in. (Christie's) £368 $588

Tamagno, Francisco, L'Absinthe Oxygénée, lithograph in colours, circa 1895, printed by Camis, Paris, backed on linen, 51 x 37½in. (Christie's) £2,990 $4,784

Cappiello, Leonetto, Cognac Monnet, lithograph in colours, 1927, printed by Devambez, Paris, 78 x 50in. (Christie's) £2,300 $3,795

Anonymous, Stade Anis, lithograph in colours 1921, printed by Wetterwald Frères, backed on linen, 23½ x 31½in. (Christie's) £322 $515

Cappiello, Leonetto, Vermouth Martini, lithograph in colours, circa 1925, printed by Teatrale Torinese, Turin, backed on linen, 38½ x 27in. (Christie's) £632 $1,011

Gilroy, John (1898-?), 'Lovely Day For A Guinness', lithograph in colours, 1954, printed by John Waddington Ltd., Leeds, 60 x 40in. (Christie's) £460 $760

Dryden, Ernst (Ernst Deutsch 1883-1938), Kupferberg Riesling, lithograph in colours, 1912, printed by Hollerbaum & Schmidt, 23 x 34½in. (Christie's) £747 $1,195

Gilroy, John, Guinness Time, lithograph in colours, circa 1929, printed by Mills & Rockleys (Production) Ltd., Ipswich, 30 x 20in. (Christie's) £414 $683

Biscaretti, Carlo di Ruffia (1879-1959) Anisetta Evangelisti, lithograph in colours, 1925, printed by Doyen, Turin, 55 x 39½in. (Christie's) £977 $1,563

Gipkens, Julius E.F., Kupferberg Gold, lithograph in colours, 1912, printed by Hollerbaum & Schmidt, Berlin, 27½ x 37½in. (Christie's) £517 $827

Hohlwein, Ludwig (1874-1949), Wilhelm Mozer, lithograph in colours, 1909, printed by Schuh & Co., München, 49 x 36in. (Christie's) £805 $1,328

Barnum & Bailey Greatest Show On Earth, Ecuyers Debout, lithograph in colours, circa 1890, printed by The Strobridge Litho. Co., New York, backed on linen, 30 x 39in. (Christie's) £667 $1,067

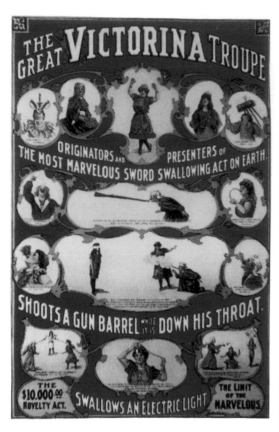

The Great Victorina Troupe, The Most Marvelous Sword Swallowing Act On Earth, lithograph in colours, circa 1915, printed by The Donaldson Litho. Co., Newport, backed on linen, 40½ x 27in. (Christie's) £552 $883

Anonymous, Barnum and Bailey, lithograph in colours, 1899, printed by The Strobridge Litho Co., New York, 30 x 40in. (Christie's) £747 $1,230

Die Barnum & Bailey, Männlicher jockeys, lithograph in colours, circa 1910, printed by The Strobridge Litho. Co., New York, backed on linen, 29½ x 19½in. (Christie's) £552 $883

Cole Bros. Circus, Miss Jean Allen, lithograph in colours, circa 1900, printed by Erie Litho. & PTG. Co., Erie, backed on linen, 28 x 41in. (Christie's) £805 $883

Hockney, David, Parade, lithograph in colours, 1981, printed by Petersburg Press, 38 x 24in. (Christie's) £414 $683

Ringling Bros and Barnum & Bailey Circus, The Otari Troupe, lithograph in colours, circa 1920, printed by Erie Litho. & PTG. Co., backed on linen, 27½ x 40in. (Christie's)   £1,092 $1,747

Barnum & Bailey Greatest Show on Earth, Desperate Struggle For The Lead, lithograph in colours, circa 1895, printed by The Strobridge Lith. Co., New York, backed on linen, 29 x 37½in.
(Christie's)   £632 $1,011

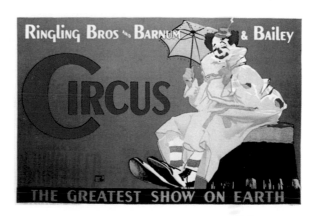

Ringling Bros. And Barnum & Bailey, Circus, lithograph in colours, 1942, backed on linen, 27 x 41in. (Christie's)   £575 $920

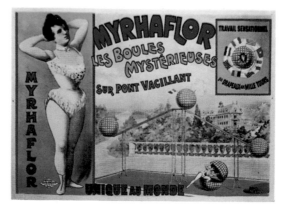

Ringling Bros. And Barnum & Bailey Combined Circus, Antalek Troupe, lithograph in colours, circa 1900, printed by Erie Litho. & PTG. Co., Erie, slight staining, backed on linen, 53 x 20in. (Christie's)   £402 $643

Myrhaflor, Les Boules Mysterieuses, lithograph in colours, circa 1910, printed by Louis Galice, Paris, faint vertical and horizontal fold marks, backed on linen, 29½ x 41in. (Christie's)   £700 $1,120

Perot, Roger (1908-1976), Cycles Peugot, lithograph in colours, 1931, printed by Hachard & Cie., Paris, on linen, 47 x 31½in.
(Christie's) £460 $760

Cappiello, Leonetto, Pneu Velo Baudou 'La Sirène', lithograph in colours, circa 1920, printed by Vercasson, Paris, 63 x 47in.
(Christie's) £1,840 $3,036

Tichon, Charles, Cyclistes!!! Attention, lithograph in colours, circa 1910, printed by Kossuth, Paris, 49 x 36in.
(Christie's) £253 $417

Thiriet, Henri, Dayton Cycles, lithograph in colours, 1900, printed by Courmont, Freres, Paris, tears and losses, slight staining and surface dirt, 63 x 94in.
(Christie's) £400 $640

Anonymous, Pneu Vélo Michelin, lithograph in colours, circa 1900, printed by Chaix, Paris, 48 x 32in.
(Christie's) £805 $1,288

Favre, G. Peugeot, lithograph in colours, circa 1930, printed by Affiches Gaillard, Paris, 46 x 31in.
(Christie's) £402 $663

Weber-Brauns, A., Victoria Motorräder, lithograph in colours, 1928, printed by C. Naumanns, Frankfurt am Main, 33 x 23in..
(Christie's) £460 $736

Bresster, Henriette, Humber Cycles, lithograph in colours, circa 1905, printed by Caby & Chardin, Paris, backed on linen, 59½ x 41½in.
(Christie's) £552 $883

Montaut, Ernest (1879-1936), Pneu Hutchinson, lithograph in colours, circa 1905, printed by C.H. Wall & Cie., Paris, backed on linen, 54 x 38½in. (Christie's) £747 $1,195

Le-Queux, Emile, Manufacture Gle., De Caoutchouc, lithograph in colours, circa 1900, printed by R. Carvin, Paris, 27 x 18in.
(Christie's) £322 $530

Mich (Michel Liebeaux, 1881-1923), Circuit Français Peugeot, lithograph in colours, circa 1910, printed by L. Revon & Cie., Paris, 47 x 63in.
(Christie's) £747 $1,230

Bonnar?, A., Cycles Papillon, lithograph in colours, circa 1900, printed by H.Laas, Paris, 47 x 31in.
(Christie's) £276 $455

Anonymous, Opcl, lithograph in colours, circa 1900, printed by Grimme & Hempel, Leipzig, backed on japan, 32 x 19½in.
(Christie's) £253 $405

Anonymous, Raleigh, lithograph in colours, circa 1930, printed by J. Howitt & Son Ltd., Nottingham, backed on japan, 19½ x 29½.
(Christie's) £632 $1,011

Misti (Ferdinand Mifliez, 1865-1923), Triumph Cycles, Coventry, lithograph in colours, 1907, printed by Jombart Frères, Asnières, 46 x 31½in. (Christie's) £632 $1,042

Anonymous, The Raily's Cycling Act, lithograph in colours, circa 1930, printed by Marci, Bruxelles, vertical and horizontal fold marks, backed on linen, 47 x 33½in.
(Christie's) £400 $640

Misti, (Ferdinand Mifliez 1865-1923), Cycles et Automobiles Le Clément, lithograph in colours, circa 1910, printed by Chambrelent, Paris, backed on linen, 47 x 63in.
(Christie's) £690 $1,104

Tichon, Charles, Acatene Metropole, lithograph in colours, circa 1900, printed by Kossuth, Paris, generally in excellent condition, backed on linen, 53 x 38½in. (Christie's) £1,200 $1,920

Anonymous, Porsche, offset lithograph in colours, 1952, 23½ x 17in. (Christie's) £747 $1,195

Jangma, Jacob, Blom en van der A, lithograph in colours, circa 1935, 25 x 33½in. (Christie's) £483 $773

Anonymous, Mercedes Benz, offset lithograph in colours, circa 1955, 33 x 23in. (Christie's) £977 $1,563

HAM, Geo (Georges Hamel), 5eme. Grand Prix Automobile, Monaco, lithograph in colours, 1933, printed by Monégasque, Monte-Carlo, 47 x 31½in. (Christie's) £2,300 $3,795

Cegrelles, Josep, (1885-1969), Autodromo Nacional, lithograph in colours, 1923, printed by Rieusset, Barcelona, 33½ x 46in. (Christie's) £2,990 $4,784

Carpanetto, G., Fabrica Italiana Di Automobili, lithograph in colours, 1899, printed by L. Simondetti, Torino, 76½ x 43in. (Christie's) £6,670 $11,000

Leupin, Herbert (1916-), Dauphine, lithograph in colours, 1957, printed by Hug & Söhne A.G. Zürich, 50 x 35½in. (Christie's) £517 $853

Barbey, Maurice, Amilcar, lithograph in colours, 1932, printed by H. Chachoin, Paris, 46 x 61in. (Christie's) £805 $1,328

De Grineau, Bryan, R.A.C., lithograph in colours, 1933, printed by Temple Press Ltd., London, 30 x 20in. (Christie's) £345 $570

K., E., Internat. Automobil Ausstellung, Frankfurt, lithograph in colours, 1904, printed by Kornsand & Co., Frankfurt, 39 x 29½in. (Christie's) £1,955 $3,225

Bric, G, Grand Prix de l'A.C.F., Dieppe, lithograph in colours, 1908, printed by Chapellier Jne, Paris, 47 x 63½in. (Christie's) £1,380 $2,275

Vincent, René (1879-1936), Bugatti, lithograph in colours, 1930, printed by Joseph Charles, Paris, backed on linen, 55 x 39½in. (Christie's)   £6,325 $10,120

Ham, Geo (Georges Hamel (1900-1972) Monaco 7e Grand Prix Automobile, lithograph in colours, 1935, printed by Monégasque, Monte Carlo, backed on linen, 47 x 31½in. (Christie's) £4,370 $6,992

O'Galop (Marius Rossillon, 1867-1946), Vinot-Deguingand, lithograph in colours, circa 1910, printed by O'Galop-Sonnet, Paris, backed on linen, 93 x 124in. (Christie's)   £690 $1,138

Lacaze, Julien (1886-1971), Route des Alpes et du Jura, PLM, lithograph in colours, circa 1930, printed by McCorquodale & Co. Ltd., London, 39 x 24½in. (Christie's)   £632 $1,011

Anonymous, Dunlop Fort '90', lithograph in colours, circa 1935, printed by J.C., Paris, 59 x 39in. (Christie's)   £805 $1,328

M. S., Cabanne-Nirouet, lithograph in colours, circa 1910, printed by Ch. Wall & Cie., Paris, 39½ x 55in. (Christie's)   £575 $948

Mink, M., Rolandur, lithograph in colours, 1914, printed by J.C. Konig & Ebhardt, Hannover, 41 x 26½in. (Christie's)   £690 $1,104

Hook, Sandy (Georges Taboureau), L. Blériot, lithograph in colours, circa 1905, printed by Tourangelle, Tours, backed on linen, 51 x 39in. (Christie's) £1,150 $1,840

Anonymous, Riley, For Magnificent Motoring, offset lithograph in colours, circa 1950, printed by The Nuffield Press Limited, 25 x 35in. (Christie's) £460 $760

Montaut, Ernest (1897-1936), Le Pneu Michelin, lithograph in colours, 1905, printed by L.Revon, Paris, backed on linen, 63 x 47½in. (Christie's) £2,415 $3,984

Arthur, Peugot, lithograph in colours, circa 1935, printed by Affiche Adalta, Geneve, restored tears and losses, backed on japan, 50 x 35½in. (Christie's) £1,000 $1,600

Elzingre, Edouard (1880-1966), Automobiles Martini, lithograph in colours, circa 1915, printed by Affiches Atar, Geneva, backed on japan, 41 x 56in. (Christie's) £1,610 $2,576

HAM, Geo (Georges Hamel 1900-1972), A.C.F., lithograph in colours, 1938, printed by P.A. Chavane et Cie., Paris, minor defects, 16 x 11½in. (Christie's) £400 $640

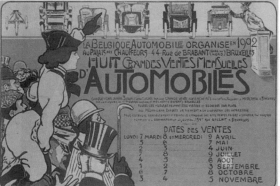

Chab, Renault, offset lithograph in colours, circa 1950, printed by Georges Lang, Paris, 38½ x 31in. (Christie's) £632 $1,042

Gaudy, Georges (1872-) d'Automobiles, lithograph in colours, 1902, printed by Louis Vogels, Bruxelles, 22 x 33½in. (Christie's) £460 $760

Ferracci, Steve McQueen, Le Mans, offset lithograph in colours, 1971, printed by Lalande-Courbet, backed on linen, 62 x 45½in. (Christie's) £1,955 $3,128

Baumberger, Otto (1889-1961), Zurich, lithograph in colours, 1916, printed by J.E. Wolfensberger, Zürich, 50 x 35½in.
(Christie's)　　　　£977　$1,612

Anonymous, Red Star Line, Antwerpen-New York, Belgenland, lithograph in colours, 1923, 42 x 25½in. (Christie's)　£667 $1,100

Raymond, Chargeurs Réunis, offset lithograph in colours, circa 1955, printed by Affiches Gaillard, Paris, backed on linen, 39½ x 24½in.
(Christie's)　　　　£402　$663

Anchor Line, Londonderry & New York, lithograph in colours, circa 1925, printed by Alf Cooke, Ltd., Leeds, vertical and horizontal fold marks with corresponding defects, 39½ x 24½in.
(Christie's)　　　　£368　$607

Hook, Sandy (Georges Taboureau 1879-1960), Cie.Gle. Transatlantique, Par 'Ville D'Alger', lithograph in colours, circa 1936, printed by Editions Atlantique, 38½ x 24in.
(Christie's)　　　　£322　$530

Anonymous, Aberdeen & Commonwealth Line, England To Australia, lithograph in colours, circa 1935, printed by Gibbs & Gibbs, London, nicks, tears and creases in the margins, 40 x 25in.
(Christie's)　　　　£517　$853

Shoesmith, Kenneth Denton (1890-1939), Royal Mail, West Indies, lithograph in colours, 1939, printed by The Baynard Press, London, backed on linen, 40 x 25in.
(Christie's)　　　　£172　$283

D'Alesi, Hugo F (1849-1906) Cie. De Navigation Mixte, PLM, lithograph in colours, circa 1905, printed by F. Hugo D'Alesi, Paris, 41½ x 29in.
(Christie's)　　　　£598　$986

Longmate, England to Australia, Aberdeen & Commonwealth Line, lithograph in colours, circa 1930, printed by Gibbs & Gibbs Ltd., London, 40 x 24½in.
(Christie's)　　　　£598　$986

Hook, Sandy (Georges Taboureau), Les Messageries Maritimes, Paul Lecat, lithograph in colours, circa 1920, printed by Reunies, Paris, 41 x 29in. (Christie's)　£402　$663

Sebille, Albert, Brésil-Plata, lithograph in colours, circa 1930, printed by Omer Henry, Paris, backed on japan, 31 x 23in. (Christie's)　£460　$760

Anonymous, Brighton Railway For Isle Of Wight, lithograph in colours, circa 1910, printed by Waterlow & Sons Ltd., London, 39½ x 24½in. (Christie's)　£862　$1,422

Hook, Sandy, (Georges Taboureau 1879-1960), Cie. Gle. Transatlantique, lithograph in colours, circa 1920, printed by F. Champenois, Paris, backed on linen, 40 x 28½in. (Christie's)　£437　$699

McDowell, William, Shaw Savill Lines, Dominion Monarch, lithograph in colours, circa 1939, nicks tears and creases in the margins, 40 x 25in. (Christie's)　£517　$853

Rosenvigne, Odin, Royal Line Fastest To Canada, Royal Edward, lithograph in colours, circa 1905, printed by Turner & Dunnett, Liverpool, backed on thick paper, 40 x 24½in. (Christie's)　£345　$570

Kück, Über Bremen an die Nordsee, Norddeutscher Lloyd Bremen, lithograph in colours, 1934, printed by Wilm. Jöntzen, Bremen, 48½ x 32½in. (Christie's)　£747　$1,195

Anonymous, Compagnie De Navigation Mixte, Djurjura, lithograph in colours, circa 1905, printed by Moullot, Marseille, 44 x 28in. (Christie's)　£747　$1,230

Fuss, Albert, Weihnachts- und Sylvesterfahrt, Hamburg-Amerika Linie, lithograph in colours, 1936, printed by Mühlmeister & Johler, Hamburg, 47 x 32½in. (Christie's)　£345　$552

Anonymous, White Star To New York, lithograph in colours, 1931, restored losses and tears, backed on linen, 39 x 24in.
(Christie's)　　　£977　$1,612

Anonymous, Ligne Allan au Canada, lithograph in colours, circa 1905, vertical and horizontal fold marks with corresponding defects, 24 x 40in. (Christie's)　£598　$986

Thomas, Walter, Cunard White Star, Queen Elizabeth, lithograph in colours, circa 1948, backed on linen, 39 x 23in.
(Christie's)　　　£667　$1,100

Yorke, P.H., Aberdeen & Commonwealth Line, Australia, lithograph in colours, circa 1935, printed by Howard, Jones, Roberts & Leete Ltd., London, 39½ x 24in.
(Christie's)　　　£483　$796

Anonymous, S.S. Ulysses (Blue Funnel Line) lithograph in colours, circa 1925, vertical and horizontal fold marks, new left and right hand margins, 40½ x 60in.
(Christie's)　　£1,092　$1,800

Rosenvigne, Odin, Cunard Canadian Service, Ascania, lithograph in colours, circa 1911, printed by Turner & Dunnett, Liverpool, 40 x 24½in.
(Christie's)　　　£575　$948

Waters, E. J., Shaw Savill & Albion Line, Captain Cook, lithograph in colours, circa 1939, 40 x 25in.
(Christie's)　　　£552　$910

Rosenvinge, Odin, lithograph in colours, circa 1930, backed on linen, 30 x 40in.
(Christie's)　　£1,092　$1,747

Tonelli, J., Cie de Navigation Paquet, lithograph in colours, 1952, losses, creases and stains, 39 x 24in. (Christie's)　　£218　$360

Anonymous, Cunard, lithograph in colours, circa 1935, losses in upper image, other losses, tears and creases, 39 x 25in.
(Christie's)   £460 $760

Wilkinson, Norman R. I., Cheshire Lines, Holidays In The Isle Of Man, lithograph in colours, circa 1930, printed by David Allen & Sons Ltd., London, 40 x 50in.
(Christie's)   £575 $948

Brun, A., Cie. des Messageries Maritimes, Touraine, lithograph in colours, 1900, printed by E. Marx, Paris, backed on linen, 47 x 31½in.
(Christie's)   £575 $920

Anonymous, Red Star Line, Antwerpen Amerika, lithograph in colours, 1909, printed by O. De Rycker, Bruxelles, restored losses, backed on linen, 33 x 20½in.
(Christie's)   £460 $760

Cassiers, Henri (1858-1944), Port Scene, offset lithograph in colours generally in excellent condition, 21 x 25in. (Christie's)   £287 $473

Hook, Sandy (Georges Taboureau) Chargeurs Réunis, lithograph in colours, circa 1930, printed by Affiches Gaillard, Paris, central horizontal fold, 39½ x 24½in.
(Christie's)   £747 $1,230

Cassandre, A.M. (Adolphe Mouron 1901-1968) Normandie, lithograph in colours, 1935, printed by Alliance Graphique, Paris, 39 x 24½in.
(Christie's)   £7,475 $11,960

Pears, Charles (1873-1958), Innavigable, lithograph in colours, circa 1925, printed by John Waddington Ltd., Leeds, backed on linen, 40 x 60in.
(Christie's)   £437 $699

Hamilton, E., Canadian Pacific, Canada & USA, lithograph in colours, circa 1925, minor repaired tear, backed on linen, 40 x 24in.
(Christie's)   £862 $1,422

Sysimetsä, Ilmari (1912-1955), XV Olympiakisat Helsingissä, offset lithograph in colours, 1952, printed by OY Tilgman, 39½in. x 24½in. (Christie's) £690 $1.104

Hertz, Walter (1909-), Olympic Games, London 1948, lithograph in colours, 1947, printed by McCorquodale & Co., Ltd., London, 30 x 20in. (Christie's) £1,955 $3,225

Orsi (1889-1947), Jeux Olympiques Paris 1924, lithograph in colours, 1924, printed by Phogor, Paris, backed on linen, 47½ x 31½in. (Christie's) £2,760 $4,416

Hohlwein, Ludwig (1874-1949), Deutschland 1936, IV Olympische Winterspiele, lithograph in colours, 1936, printed by Reichsbahnzentrale für den deutschen Reutschen Reiseverkehr, Berlin, 40 x 25½in. (Christie's) £1.725 $2.760

Nunez, Pati, Games of the XXV Olympiad, Barcelona 1992, offset lithograph in colours, 1992, minor defects, generally in excellent condition, 27½ x 19½in. (Christie's) £50 $82

Droit, Jean (1884-1961), Jeux Olympiques, Paris 1924, lithograph in colours, 1924, printed by Hachard & Cie., Paris, backed on linen, 47 x 31½in. (Christie's) £2,990 $4,784

Cappiello, Leonetto, Cachou
Lajaunie, lithograph in colours,
1920, printed by Devambes, Paris,
backed on linen, 58½ x 39½in.
(Christie's)   £1,150 $1.840

Kügler, W.G., Da Capo, lithograph
in colours, 1914, printed by Leutert
& Schneidewind AG, Dresden, 47½
x 35½in. (Christie's) £345 $552

Leroi, Otto, Salem Gold, lithograph
in colours, 1912, backed on japan,
35 x 23½in.
(Christie's)   £690 $1,104

Anonymous, MOB Railway
Switzerland, lithograph in colours,
circa 1920, printed by Muller &
Trub, Aarau, 28½ x 19½in.
(Christie's)   £402 $643

Langenberg, Echte Florida
Zigaretten, lithograph in colours,
1926, printed by J.J. Weber,
Leipzig, 23½x 35½in.
(Christie's)   £253 $405

Anonymous, Cigarettes Postillon,
lithograph in colours, circa 1920,
printed by J. Aberle & Co., Berlin,
29 x 19in. (Christie's) £115 $190

Matejko, Theo (1896-1946), Caid
Zigaretten, lithograph in colours,
1928, printed by Eckert,
Schönberg, 47 x 33½in.
(Christie's)   £368 $589

Anonymous, Da Capo, lithograph in
colours, 1917, printed by J. Aberle
& Co., Berlin, 48 x 36in.
(Christie's)   £322 $515

Price, Nick, Camel Filters,
lithograph in colours, 1975, printed
by Chabrillac, Paris, backed on
linen, 68 x 47in.
(Christie's)   £667 $1,067

Anonymous, Australia, offset lithograph in colours, circa 1950, printed by McLaren & Co., Melbourne, 39½ x 25in. (Christie's) £632 $1,011

De Faria, Candido Aragonese (atelier 1849-1911) Cachat's-Majestic, lithograph in colours, circa1910, printed by Atelier Faria, Paris, 47 x 62in. (Christie's) £1,610 $2,655

Mucha, Alphonse (1860-1939), Monaco. Monte-Carlo, lithograph in colours, 1897, printed by F. Champenois, Paris, on japan, 43 x 29in. (Christie's) £2,990 $4,784

Lambert, Alfred, (1902-?), Roker and Seaburn, British Railways, lithograph in colours, circa 1953, printed by Jordison & Co. Ltd., London, 40 x 25in. (Christie's) £690 $1,104

Anonymous, Grand Hotel Rimini, lithograph in colours, circa 1910, printed by A. Trüb & Co., Aarau, 35 x 55in. (Christie's) £1,380 $2,277

Laubi, Hugo (1888-1959), St. Moritz, lithograph in colours, 1953, printed by Gebr. Fretz A.G., Zürich, 40½ x 25½in. (Christie's) £402 $663

Anonymous, Paris in London, lithograph in colours, 1902, printed by Gale & Poldon, London, backed on linen, 36 x 24in. (Christie's) £345 $552

Anonymous, Hotel Astoria, Nice, lithograph in colours, circa 1910, 23½ x 31½in. (Christie's) £920 $1,518

Earl, Robert(?), The Drakensberg, Union of South Africa, lithograph in colours, circa 1930, printed by E.P. Herald, Port Elizabeth, 40 x 25in. (Christie's) £632 $1,011

Barnes, Desmond (1921-), New Brighton, British Railways, lithograph in colours, circa 1955, printed by London Lithographic Co., 39½ x 25in. (Christie's) £322 $530

Gorbatoff, C., Austria via Harwich, LNER, lithograph in colours, circa 1935, printed by the Haycock Press, London, 40 x 50in. (Christie's) £598 $957

Anonymous, London At Its Brightest, London Transport, lithograph in colours, 1934, printed by Waterlow & Sons Ltd., 40 x 25in. (Christie's) £402 $663

Henry ,Paul, Donegal, Ireland For Holidays, LMS, lithograph in colours, circa 1926, printed by John Horn, limited, London, 40 x 25in. (Christie's) £1,150 $1,897

Forsyth, Gordon Mitchell (1879-1952), Harrogate, LNER, lithograph in colours, 1939, printed by Waterlow & Sons Ltd., London, 40 x 50in. (Christie's) £690 $1,104

Bland, G.H., Killarney, Great Southern Rys., lithograph in colours, circa 1930, printed by Helys Limited, Dublin, 40 x 24in. (Christie's) £437 $721

José Maria Morell (1899-1949), Playas de Cataluña, lithograph in colours, 1945, printed by I.G., Vilado S.L., Barcelona, 39 x 25in. (Christie's) £230 $368

Henry, Paul, (1876-1958), Come to Ulster for a Better Holiday, lithograph in colours, circa 1930, printed by S.C. Allen & Co. Ltd., London, 40 x 50in. (Christie's) £805 $1,288

Smithson Broadhead, W, This Is Torquay, GWR, lithograph in colours, circa 1936, printed by W.E.Berry, Ltd., 40 x 25in. (Christie's) £805 $1,328

Newbould, Frank (1887-1950), East
Coast Frolics, LNER, lithograph in
colours, 1933, printed by Chorley &
Pickersgill Ltd., Leeds, 39½ x 25in.
(Christie's)   £517 $853

Purvis, Tom (1888-1959), East
Coast, LNER, lithograph in colours,
circa 1930, printed by J.G. Hudson
& Co. Ltd., London, 40 x 50in.
(Christie's)   £805 $1,288

Ayling, George, Folkestone,
Southern Railway, lithograph in
colours, 1926, printed by
McCorquodale & Co., Ltd., London,
40 x 25in. (Christie's) £414 $683

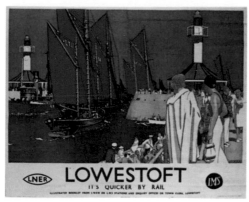

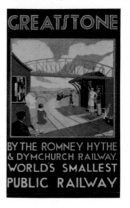

Wilkinson, Norman R.I. (1878-
1971), Come To Britain For Fishing,
lithograph in colours, circa 1955,
printed by W.S. Cowell Ltd.,
London, 30 x 20in.
(Christie's)   £414 $683

Shoesmith, Kenneth Denton (1890-
1939), Lowestoft, LNER, LMS,
lithograph in colours, circa 1940,
printed by Jarrold & Sons Ltd.,
London, 40 x 50in.
(Christie's)   £1,092 $1,800

Cramer Roberts, N., Greatstone,
World's Smallest Public Railway,
lithograph in colours, circa 1930,
printed by Vincent Brooks Day &
Son Ltd., London, 39½ x 25in.
(Christie's)   £322 $530

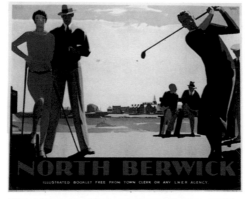

Tittensor, H., York, The Shambles,
LNER, lithograph in colours, circa
1938, printed by Ben Johnson &
Company Limited., York, 40 x 25in.
(Christie's)   £368 $607

Johnson, Andrew, North Berwick,
LNER, lithograph in colours, circa
1935, printed by David Allen &
Sons, Ltd., London, 40 x 50in.
(Christie's)   £6,900 $11,385

H.S., Clacton-On-Sea, British
Railways, lithograph in colours,
circa 1950, printed by Jordison &
Co., Ltd., London, 40 x 25in.
(Christie's)   £632 $1,042

Virenque, E. Aix les Bains, PLM, lithograph in colours, 1920, backed on linen, 41½ x 29½in. (Christie's) £402 $643

Linford, Alan Carr (1926-), Oxford, lithograph in colours, circa 1955, printed by Waterlow & Sons Ltd., London, 40 x 50in. (Christie's) £690 $1,104

Ponty, Max, Plages de France, lithograph in colours, circa 1936, 39½ x 24½in. (Christie's) £184 $294

Purvis, Tom, Continent Via Harwich, LNER, lithograph in colours, circa 1930, printed by the Dangerfield Printing Co., Ltd., London, 40 x 25in. (Christie's) £460 $760

Newbould, Frank, Eastern Scotland, Royal Deeside, LNER, LMS, lithograph in colours, circa 1930, printed by Haycock Press, London, 40 x 50in. (Christie's) £920 $1,518

Bee, John, Somerset, GWR, lithograph in colours, circa 1939, printed by J.Weiner Ltd., London, 40 x 25in. (Christie's) £287 $473

Anonymous, Blarney Castle, Co Cork, Great Southern Rys., lithograph in colours, circa 1930, printed by Helys Ltd., Dublin, 40 x 24in. (Christie's) £402 $663

Purvis, Tom, Yorkshire Coast, LNER, lithograph in colours, circa 1930, printed by The Dangerfield Printing Co., London, 40 x 25in. (Christie's) £322 $530

Buckle, Claude, Ross-on-Wye, GWR, lithograph in colours, circa 1938, printed by the Dangerfield Printing Co., Ltd., London, 40 x 24½in. (Christie's) £747 $1,230

Dorival, Georges S, Chamonix-Mont-Blanc, PLM, lithograph in colours, 1921, printed by Cornille & Serre, Paris, 42½ x 31in. (Christie's) £253 $405

Johnson, Andrew, Farm Collection And Delivery Services, LNER, lithograph in colours, circa 1928, printed by The Dangerfield Printing Co., Ltd., London, 40 x 50in. (Christie's) £690 $1,138

Ayling, George (1887-?), The Matlocks, lithograph in colours, circa 1930, 33 x 25in. (Christie's) £230 $380

Higgins, Reginald Edward (1877-1933), The Continent Via Harwich, LNER, lithograph in colours, circa 1925, printed by Jarrold & Sons., Ltd., London, 40 x 25in. (Christie's) £230 $380

Dickens, Blackpool, British Railways, lithograph in colours, circa 1955, printed by Jordison & Co., London, 39½ x 50in. (Christie's) £1,955 $3,225

Sharland, Edward (Attributed to), Final Tie Manchester City v. Bolton Wanderers, Great Northern Railway, lithograph in colours, 1904, printed by Petty & Sons, 40 x 25in. (Christie's) £7,475 $11,960

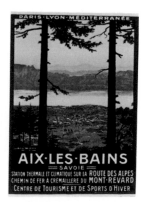

Ernst, Otto (1884-1967), Vallée de Joux, lithograph in colours, circa 1930, printed by A. Trüb & Cie., Aarau, 39½ x 27½in. (Christie's) £575 $948

Buckle, Claude, Bath, British Railways, lithograph in colours, circa 1955, printed by Jordison & Co., Ltd., London, 40 x 50in. (Christie's) £517 $853

Dorival, Georges S (1879-1968), Aix-Les-Bains, PLM, lithograph in colours, 1913, printed by F. Champenois, Paris, on linen, 42½ x 31in. (Christie's) £287 $459

TO VISIT BRITAIN'S LANDMARKS

JEZREEL'S TEMPLE, GILLINGHAM KENT   TRISTRAM HILLIER
YOU CAN BE SURE OF SHELL

BRITISH ARMY CEREMONIAL

Hillier, Tristram Paul (1905-1983), You Can Be Sure of Shell, Jezreel's Temple, Gillingham, Kent, lithograph in colours 1936, printed by the Baynard Press, 30 x 45in. (Christie's) £460 $736

Clark, Christopher (1875-1942), British Army Ceremonial, British Railways, lithograph in, circa 1955, printed by Jordison & Co., Ltd., London, 40 x 50in. (Christie's) £1,150 $1,897

MARIENBAD
BOHÈME
LA PERLE DES VILLES D'EAUX

HOTEL ESPLANADE

CRUDEN BAY

BY EAST COAST ROUTE

S, P, Marienbad, Hotel Esplanade, lithograph in colours, circa 1930, printed by A. Trüb & Cie., Lausanne, 39½ x 27in. (Christie's) £3,220 $5,313

Purvis, Tom, Cruden Bay, LNER, lithograph in colours, circa 1925, printed by S.C. Allen & Co. Ltd., London, 40 x 50in. (Christie's) £7,475 $11,960

DRESDEN VIA HARWICH

THESE MEN USE SHELL

YOU CAN BE SURE OF SHELL

Taylor, Fred (1875-1963), Dresden via Harwich LNER, offset lithograph in colours, circa 1935, printed by John Waddington Ltd., London, 40 x 50in. (Christie's) £460 $736

Armstrong, John (1893-1973), You Can Be Sure of Shell, lithograph in colours, 1939, printed by Waterlow & Sons, London, 30 x 45in. (Christie's) £517 $827

WWII Merchant Navy Comforts
poster, with the title 'From ship to
shop' and depicts a butcher holding
a side of meat, 20 x 30in.
(Bosleys)   £70 $111

WWII Merchant Navy Comforts
poster, by Pellet, depicts a troop
ship returning to harbour, 20 x 30in.
(Bosleys)   £40 $64

WWII Navy Comforts poster, a
large poster by Marc Stane, depicts
a smiling merchant seaman with
woollen hat and scarf, 40 x 20in.
(Bosleys)   £55 $88

WWII Merchant Navy Comforts
poster, by Vernon, depicting a
merchant seaman high in the crows
nest with the text 'If This
Man...does not keep his eyes
skinned you may lose 6,000 tons of
sugar', 20 x 30in.(Bosleys) £40 $64

United States Marine Corps
Recruiting Poster, an inter-war
period colourful example depicting
a Sergeant of the Corps wearing
full dress and holding a rifle, 35 x
28in.
(Bosleys)   £65 $104

Coloured poster depicting Red
Cross and text, 'Think of the
Wounded! Give more for your flag
on Red Cross & St. John Flag Day',
approximately 8 x 12in.
(Bosleys)   £30 $48

WWII Merchant Navy Comforts
poster, the poster is with the title
On the Arctic Front, and depicts four
members of crew scraping ice from
the deck and a gun.
(Bosleys)   £70 $111

WWII Merchant Navy Comforts
poster, by Ellis Silas, bears the title
'On the Atlantic Front' and depicts a
merchant ship rolling in a swell at
steam, 20 x 30in.
(Bosleys)   £85 $136

WWII Merchant Navy Comforts
poster, by Charles Wood, depicting
the text 'North Africa' an Officer
wearing uniform with North African
locals in the background, 20 x 30in.
(Bosleys)   £50 $80

T, W., Kandersteg, lithograph in colours, circa 1950, printed by Wolfsberg, Zürich, 40 x 25in. (Christie's) £483 $796

F. Tamagno. Chamonix, Mont-Blanc, PLM Sports d'Hiver Concours, Emile Pecaud & Cie circa 1900, 40 x 28in. (Graves Son & Pilcher) £2,300 $3,795

Cachoud, F., Le Mont-Blanc, lithograph in colours, circa 1925, printed by Chaix, Paris, 42 x 30½in. (Christie's) £632 $1,011

Anonymous, Nordwestschweizerisches, lithograph in colours, 1935, printed by Wassermann, Basel, minor folds, 28 x 20in. (Christie's) £632 $1,011

Thoni, Hans (1906-1980), Wengen, photomontage and lithography in colours, 1936, printed by Kunstanstalt Brügger A.G., Meiringen, minor defects, 39½ x 27½in. (Christie's) £500 $800

Anonymous, Championnat International, Villars-Chesières-Bretaye, lithograph in colours, 1938, printed by Wassermann & Co., Basle, generally in excellent condition, 50 x 35½in. (Christie's) £1,150 $1,840

Reb, Henry, Mont-Revard, PLM, lithograph in colours, 1935, printed by Lafayette, Paris, backed on linen, 39½ x 24½in. (Christie's) £414 $662

Muret, Albert (1874-1955), Chemin-de-Fer, Martigny-Orsières, lithograph in colours, 1913, printed by Sonor, Genève, 39½ x 27½in. (Christie's) £1,380 $2,208

Coulon, Eric de (1888-1956), Alpes & Jura, lithograph in colours, circa 1935, printed by Le Novateur, Paris, 39 x 24in. (Christie's) £805 $1,328

Italian School, circa 1790, Grand Duke Ferdinand III of Tuscany, facing left in blue coat with orange collar, 54mm. diameter.
(Christie's) £1,495 $2,392

John Downman ARA (1750-1824), Sarah Hussey Delaval, Countess of Tyrconnel, facing left in pale grey riding habit, oval, 3¼in. high.
(Christie's) £51,000 $86,700

Jeremiah Meyer RA (1735-1789), Lady Dorothy Frankland, full face in a lace-bordered white dress with pnk surcoat, oval, 3in. high.
(Christie's) £8,625 $13,800

George Engleheart (1750-1829), Mrs William Hayley, née Mary Welford, facing right in her bridal gown, signed and dated *1809*, oval, 79mm. high.
(Christie's) £11,500 $18,400

George Engleheart (1750-1829), Captain Richard Gregory of the Coldstream Guards, facing right in scarlet coat, signed and dated on reverse *1791*, oval, 60mm. high.
(Christie's) £12,650 $20,240

Richard Cosway RA (1742-1821), Lady Murray of Elibank, facing right in lace-bordered white dress with pearls at corsage, oval, 74mm. high,
(Christie's) £11,500 $18,400

Christian Friedrich Zincke (1683/4-1767), John Elwood, facing left in blue velvet coat and white lace cravat, enamel on copper, oval, 1¾in. high.
(Christie's) £1,035 $1,656

Richard Gibson (1615-1690), Elizabeth Capell, Countess of Carnarvon, facing right in low-cut dress with yellow bodice, signed and dated *1657*, oval, 79mm. high.
(Christie's) £18,975 $32,250

David des Granges (1611/13- circa 1675), a Gentleman, facing left in gilt-studded armour and white lawn collar, signed with initials, on vellum, oval, 54mm. high.
(Christie's) £7,475 $11,960

George Engleheart (1750-1829), a young Lady, in profile to the right, in lace-bordered white dress, oval, 41mm. high.
(Christie's)   £6,900 $11,040

Jean-Baptiste Sambat (circa 1760-1827), a young Lady, full face in embroidered-edged white muslin tunic, signed, 60mm. diameter.
(Christie's)   £1,610 $2,576

Henry Spicer (1743-1804), an Infantry Officer, facing right in scarlet coat with yellow facings and lapels, enamel, oval, 2½in. high.
(Christie's)   £1,495 $2,392

Charles-Joseph de la Celle, Chevalier de Chateaubourg,(1758-1837), a Gentleman called W Chapman, facing left in black coat, signed and dated 1825, oval, 88mm. high.
(Christie's)   £1,035 $1,656

Andrew Robertson (1777-1845), 'The Miniature', Mrs Wadham Wyndham and her sister Miss Slade admiring a miniature, rectangular, 6¼ x 5in.
(Christie's)   £5,175 $8,280

Monsieur de Verquelle (fl. circa 1819-1826), a young Gentleman, facing right in brown coat with white waistcoat and knotted cravat, signed and dated 1819, 77mm. diameter.
(Christie's)   £4,025 $6,440

George Engleheart (1750-1829), a Naval Officer, probably of the east India Company, facing right in a blue coat, signed with initial, oval, 74mm. high.
(Christie's)   £5,520 $8,832

Richard Cosway RA (1742-1821), James Lowther, 1st Earl of Lonsdale, facing right in scarlet coat with blue lapels, oval, 1¾in. high. (Christie's) £4,600 $7,360

Noah Seaman (fl.1724-1741), a young Gentleman, facing right in plum-coloured coat and frilled cravat, signed and dated 1734 , enamel on copper, oval, 41mm. high. (Christie's) £1,092 $1,747

N. Freese (fl. circa 1794-1814), a young Lady, facing left in white dress with embroidered cutaway pointed collar, oval, 68mm. high.
(Christie's)   £1,380 $2,208

French School, circa 1780/1785, a bare breasted young Lady, facing left in frill-bordered white shift, 56mm. diameter.
(Christie's)   £920 $1,472

Andrew Plimer (1763-1837), a young Boy, facing left in red coat and white shirt with frilled collar, oval, 68mm. high,
(Christie's)   £1,265 $2,024

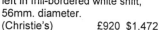

Nathaniel Hone RA (1718-1784), Mary Wilkes, facing right in a blue silk day-gown with lace-bordered white underslip, signed and dated *1753*, enamel on copper, oval, 48mm. high.
(Christie's)   £5,175 $8,280

Jean François Strasbaux (fl. circa 1801-1824), a young Singer, facing right in low-cut classical muslin chemise with jewelled clasp at sleeve, signed and dated *1812*, octagonal, 66 x 65mm.
(Christie's)   £1,955 $3,128

Nathaniel Hone RA (1718-1784), Margaret Woffington, facing right in open yellowy/green day-gown, signed with monogram and dated *1750*, enamel on copper, oval, 46mm. high.
(Christie's)   £6,325 $10,120

Adam Buck (1759-1833), a young Officer of the 50th Regiment of Foot, facing left in scarlet coat with black facings, signed and dated *1802*, oval, 71mm. high
(Christie's)   £6,900 $11,040

Carl-Christian Kanz (1758- after 1818), a young Lady, facing left in mauve-edged transparent muslin dress, signed, enamel on copper, 65mm. diameter.
(Christie's)   £1,265 $2,024

Christian Friedrich Zincke (1683/4-1767), a Gentleman, facing left in moss coloured velvet coat and white lace cravat, enamel on copper, oval, 1¾in. high.
(Christie's)   £1,150 $1,840

James Scouler (circa 1740-1812), a self-portrait of the Artist, in profile to the right, in blue coat and waistcoat, oval, 124mm. high. (Christie's)   £10,925 $17,480

Jean-Etienne Liotard (1702-1789), a double portrait of Charles Edward Stuart and Prince Henry Benedict Stuart, rectangular, 52 x 71mm. (Christie's)   £13,800 $22,080

Attributed to Edward Miles (1752-1828), a young Boy, facing right in blue coat and white shirt with large frilled collar, oval, 1¾in. high. (Christie's)   £1,495 $2,392

Andreas Henry Groth (fl. circa 1739-1753), Elizabeth Riveley, facing right in white dress with blue laced bodice, signed with initial and dated *1753*, enamel, oval, 46mm high. (Christie's) £3,220 $5,152

John Smart (1742/43-1811), Miss Isobel Page, facing right in pearl-bordered white dress, signed with initials and dated *1776*, oval, 43mm. high. (Christie's)   £8,625 $13,800

Nathaniel Horne RA (1718-1784), a young Gentleman, facing right in silver-bordered plum-coloured coat, signed with monogram and dated *1751*, enamel, oval, 41mm. high. (Christie's)   £2,530 $4,048

Circle of William Prewett, circa 1735, King George II, facing right in gilt-studded armour, enamel on copper, oval, 2¼in. high. (Christie's)   £4,600 $7,360

Moritz Michael Daffinger (1790-1849), Princess Esterházy, facing left in long-sleeved blue riding habit, signed, oval, 93mm.high. (Christie's)   £32,200 $54,740

Thomas Hazlehurst (circa 1740-circa 1821), a young Boy, facing left in blue coat, white shirt and frilled collar, signed with initials, oval, 53mm. (Christie's)   £2,875 $4,600

Heinrich Friedrich Füger (1751-1818), Francis II (1768-1835), Holy Roman Emperor, as a boy, facing left in white uniform, oval, 81mm. high. (Christie's) £8,625 $13,800

John Faber (circa 1650-1721), Queen Mary II (1662-1694) facing left in gem-set ermine-edged cloak, plumbago on vellum, oval, 92mm. high. (Christie's) £1,610 $2,576

Jeremiah Meyer RA (1735-1789), Ann Chambers, née Radcliffe (1741-1825), facing left in white dress with fichu, oval, 91mm. high. (Christie's) £25,300 $43,000

John Smart (1742/43-1811), a young Gentleman, facing right in gold-bordered scarlet coat with gold buttons, signed and dated 1779, 35mm. high.
(Christie's) £15,525 $24,840

Pierre-Louis Bouvier (1765-1836), Empress Joséphine, facing right in a low-cut gold-figured white satin dress with pleated collar, signed and dated {18}12, oval, 41mm. high. (Christie's) £6,900 $11,040

Christian Friedrich Zincke (1683/4-1767), Trevor Hill, 1st Viscount Hillsborough, facing left in blue velvet coat, enamel of copper, oval, 1¾in.high.
(Christie's) £1,840 $2,944

Dutch School, circa 1650-60, a young Lady, facing left in low-cut blue dress with white underslip, oil on copper, oval, 54mm. high.
(Christie's) £1,840 $2,944

Louis Sicard (1743-1825), Jean-Nicolas Brodelet, facing left in olive green coat, signed and dated 1785, oval, 42mm. high.
(Christie's) £1,725 $2,760

Peter Paillou (fl. 1774-1780/84), an Officer called Captain Henry Dundas Beatson, facing left in gold-bordered blue coat, oval, 73mm. high. (Christie's) £1,035 $1,656

Nathaniel Plimer (1757-1822), a young Lady, facing right in blue riding habit, oval, 3in. high. (Christie's) £6,900 $11,040

George Engleheart (1750-1829), a young Lady, facing right in lace-bordered white dress, rectangular, 73 x 51mm., gilt metal frame. (Christie's) £2,185 $3,496

Richard Cosway RA (1742-1821), General Gale, facing right in pale grey coat, oval, 2in. high. (Christie's) £2,185 $3,496

Nathaniel Plimer (1757-1822), a Gentleman, facing left in blue coat with gold buttons, signed and dated *1787*, oval, 2¾in. high. (Christie's) £1,840 $2,944

John Cox Dillman Engleheart (1782/84-1862), Miss Alison Farrow, facing right in lace-bordered pale pink dress, signed and dated 1814, rectangular, 84 x 65mm. (Christie's) £3,680 $5,888

George Engleheart (1750-1829), a Gentleman, facing left in scarlet coat, white waistcoat and frilled cravat, oval, 41mm. high. (Christie's) £3,450 $5,520

Franciszek Smiadecki (fl. circa 1664), a young Gentleman, facing right in black coat with white lawn collar, oil on card, oval, 62mm. high. (Christie's) £4,370 $6,992

Samuel Collins (1735-1768), Elizabeth Moore as a young girl, facing right in lace-bordered mauve dress, oval, 36mm. high. (Christie's) £1,955 $3,128

Christian Friedrich Zincke (1683/4-1767), Thomas, 4th Duke of Leeds, facing left in gold bordered brown velvet coat, enamel, oval, 46mm. high. (Christie's) £4,830 $7,728

John Smart Junior (1776-1809), a Boy, facing left in black coat and waistcoat, signed and dated *1806*, oval, 68mm. high. (Christie's) £3,220 $5,152

Marie-Thérèse de Noireterre (1760-1819), a young Gentleman, facing left in double-breasted dark grey coat, 59mm. diameter. (Christie's) £4,370 $6,992

Henry Burch (b. 1763), a young Child, facing left in white dress with yellow sash, oval, 2½in. high. (Christie's) £920 $1,472

Johann Heinrich von Hurter (1734-1799), Queen Charlotte, facing left in gold-bordered pale grey dress with fichu, signed and dated *1782*, enamel on copper, oval, 52mm. high. (Christie's) £16,100 $25,760

John Thomas Barber Beaumont (1774-1841), a Child, facing left in blue dress and black bonnet, holding a dove in his arms, signed and dated *1797*, oval, 67mm. high. (Christie's) £1,495 $2,392

Horace Hone ARA (1754/56-1825), Mrs Caulfield of Levitstown, facing left in white dress with ruched neckline, signed and dated *1791*, oval, 71mm. high. (Christie's) £9,775 $15,640

Charles Robertson (circa 1760-1821), a Gentleman, facing left in brown coat, white and red waistcoat, oval, 61mm. high. (Christie's) £1,035 $1,656

George Engleheart (1750-1829), a young Lady, facing left in low-cut white dress wwith frilled underslip, oval, 53mm. (Christie's) £1,265 $2,024

Christian Friedrich Zincke (1683/4-1767), a young Gentleman facing left in white shirt, enamel on copper, oval, 46mm. high. (Christie's) £5,750 $8,400

Currier and Ives (Publishers) 'Trotting Cracks' on the Snow, hand coloured lithograph with tint stone, with touches of gum arabic, 1858, after Louis Maurer, image 423 x 710mm. (Sotheby's) £1,929 $3,162

N. Currier (Publishers), The Road, - Winter, hand coloured lithograph, with touches of gum arabic, 1853, on stone by O. Knirsch, framed, image 442 x 662mm. (Sotheby's) £4,209 $6,900

Currier and Ives, Publishers (Active 1857–1907) Across the Continent. *Westward the Course of Empire Takes its Way.* by James Merritt Ives and Fannie F. Palmer), lithographed with hand-colouring and touches of gum arabic, 1868, on wove paper, 25 x 33⁷/₈in. (Christie's) £11,040 $18,400

Nathaniel Currier, Publisher, *Tacony and Mac: Hunting Park Course Phila., June 2nd 1853*, by Louis Maurer, lithograph with hand-colouring, 1853, and Currier and Ives, Publishers, *Won by a Neck*, by John Cameron, lithograph with hand colouring, 1869, on wove paper. (Christie's) £1,380 $2,300

Currier and Ives (Publishers), The Life of a Fireman, the New Era, Steam and Muscle, hand coloured lithograph, with touches of gum arabic, 1861, Charles Parsons del., image 434 x 653mm. (Sotheby's) £1,122 $1,840

Currier and Ives (Publishers), A Midnight Race on the Mississippi, hand coloured lithograph, with touches of gum arabic, 1860, on stone by Frances F. Palmer, after the sketch by H.D. Manning, image 463 x 706mm. (Sotheby's) £4,910 $8,050

Currier and Ives (Publishers) The Farmyard in Winter, hand coloured lithograph, with touches of gum arabic, 1861, after the painting by George H. Durrie, image 413 x 597mm. (Sotheby's)   £3,156 $5,175

C. Matter (lithographer), bird's eye view of New York and Brooklyn, hand coloured lithograph, with touches of gum arabic, circa 1852, printed by I. Schaerer, image 526 x 723mm. (Sotheby's)   £2,806 $4,600

Caltin's North American Indian Portfolio. *Hunting scenes and Amusements of the Rocky Mountains and Prairies of America,* five lithographs with hand-colouring, 1844, on smooth, wove paper, four mounted, published by G. Catlin, London, approximately 12 x 17⁵/₈in.
(Christie's)   £4,830 $8,050

Currier and Ives, Publisher, *The Champion Pacer Johnston,* by John Cameron, lithograph in colours, 1884, on wove paper, with margins, staining, *Queen of the Turf. Maud S. Driven by W.W. Blair,* by Scott Leighton) – lithograph in colours, 1880.
(Christie's)   £1,173 $1,955

McKenney and Hall (Publisher) Hunting the Buffaloe; and War Dance of the Sauks and Foxes, two hand coloured lithographs, published by E.C. Biddle, Philadelphia, in wove paper, image 231 x 390mm. (Sotheby's)   £1,754 $2,875

Currier and Ives (Publishers), The Life of a Fireman, The Metropolitan System, hand coloured lithograph, with touches of gum arabic, with the signature of John Cameron in the stone, image 431 x 665mm. (Sotheby's)   £1,754 $2,875

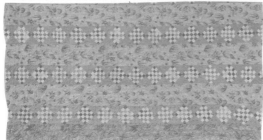

An American pillar pattern quilt, early 19th century, the bands of cotton chintz alternating with pillars pieced with postage stamp diamonds, all in tones of tan, brown, green, red and ochre, 92½ x 91¼in. (Sotheby's) £912 $1,495

Pieced and embroidered occupational quilt, Stamford, New York, dated 1885, Irish chain design worked in red on a white ground with red, white, purple and green embroidery, 96 x 79in. (Skinner) £976 $1,610

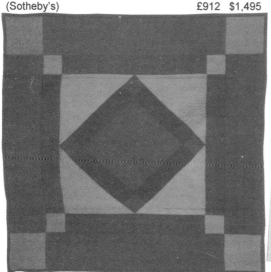

A fine pieced all-wool Amish quilt, probably Lancaster County, Pennsylvania, late 19th/early 20th century, composed of navy blue, hunter green and maroon patches in the Diamond in the Square pattern, 76 x 80in. (Sotheby's) £4,209 $6,900

A fine pieced red, yellow and green flower basket quilt, American, mid 19th century, the appliqued cotton patches in a flower basket and blossom pattern mounted on a white cotton ground, approximately 88 x 88in. (Sotheby's) £1,403 $2,300

Appliqué quilt, America, second half 19th century, Rose of Sharon and heart design with scrolling foliate border, 84 x 82½in. (Skinner) £503 $805

A pieced cotton pinwheel quilt, American, probably Pennsylvania, early 20th century, composed of vividly coloured red, yellow, white, green and navy blue patches, 68 x 68in. (Sotheby's) £1,403 $2,300

A pieced polished cotton Amish crib quilt, Holmes County, Ohio, 1915–25, Fox and Geese pattern, 35 x 43in. (Sotheby's) £1,753 $2,875

A fine and rare pieced and appliquéd and embroidered crazy quilt: The Return, comprised of fifty-six squares made from patches of variously coloured and embroidered silk, damask and velvet patches, approximately 80 x 68in. (Sotheby's) £3,858 $6,325

A fine pieced wool and cotton Amish quilt, probably Mifflin County, Pennsylvania, late 19th/early 20th century, composed of slate blue, dusty rose, olive green, and black patches arranged in a variation of the Nine Patch pattern, 80 x 84in. (Sotheby's) £5,612 $9,200

An unusual pieced and appliqued and reverse appliqued cotton quilt, American, early 20th century, composed of bright blue and white patches in an Eye Dazzler pattern of stars and circles, 76 x 84in. (Sotheby's) £1,227 $2,012

A pieced and appliqued cotton quilt, American, mid-19th century, composed of red, white and slate blue patches arranged in a variation of the Princess Feather pattern, 78 x 68in. (Sotheby's) £701 $1,150

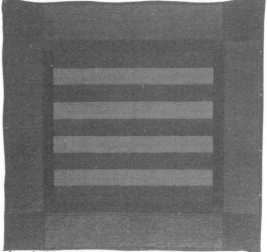

An Amish pieced bar quilt, Lancaster County, Pennsylvania, late 19th/early 20th century, the central square comprising nine alternating bars of grape and dark brown, stitched with pineapples and feathers, 77¼ x 74in. (Sotheby's) £2,280 $3,737

A Marconi Type 297 5-valve standard radio, 1935-38. (Auction Team Köln) £54 $87

A Nora PN20 3-valve battery operated radio with integral coil, in wooden case, 1926. (Auction Team Köln) £837 $1,339

A Radiola 18 gramophone with 7-valve radio and electric record player, American, circa 1928. (Auction Team Köln) £377 $603

An HMV Model 801 Concert Autoradiogram in walnut cabinet of irregular hexagon form with three speakers and counterbalanced Florentine-bronze-finished pick-up arm, 40½in. wide, circa 1938. (Christie's) £552 $883

A very early de Forest Spherical Double-Wing Audion radio tube, circa 1906. (Auction Team Köln) £837 $1,340

Philippe Charbonneaux for Teléavia, television p111, 1950s, dark purple and cream wood and metal, brass, purple tinted plastic front, 54½in. high. (Sotheby's) £1,955 $3,167

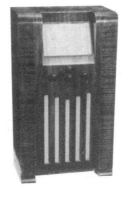

A Philco Radio Model 90 superhet American 7-valve receiver of cathedral form. (Auction Team Köln) £209 $334

A Centrum Type G.U. 66, Sandinavian standard radio with unusual European dial, 6-valve. (Auction Team Köln) £179 $287

An Ekco type AC74 receiver in black bakelite cabinet with chromium plated trim, circa 1933. (Academy Auctioneers) £240 $384

The Beatles, a rare British EMI promotional poster for an album Sgt Peppers Lonely Hearts Club Band, 1967, 17¾ x 24¾in. framed. (Christie's)   £862 $1,379

Ringo Starr, signed colour 8 x 10, half-length, in recent years. (Vennett-Smith)   £45 $72

Jim Morrison, a piece of paper signed and inscribed in black ballpoint pen *cheers Stan J Morrison*, 2¾ x 4¼in. with a black and white photograph of subject. (Christie's)   £747 $1,195

A T-shirt signed by Oasis, in blue cotton with logo and red and white stripes, signed in black marker by all members of the band. (Sotheby's)   £437 $699

Jimi Hendrix, a stage shirt of psychedelic patterned cotton, two coloured photographs of Hendrix wearing the shirt in Paris, 1967. (Christie's)   £3,910 $6,256

John Lennon's jacket 1970s, in two-tone denim with check panels to sleeves, shoulders and collar. (Sotheby's)   £13,800 $22,080

The Rolling Stones, signed 7 x 9.5 magazine photo, by all five individually, overmounted in black and ivory. (Vennett-Smith)   £350 $560

Elvis Presley, signed colour 4 x 6 postcard, head and shoulders in T-shirt. (Vennett-Smith) £450 $720

Elvis Presley, a single record 'Baby Let's Play House/ I'm Left, You're Right, She's Gone', 1955, Sun Records, the slip sleeve with rare signatures and inscriptions in blue ballpoint pen on both sides. (Christie's)   £4,830 $7,728

A promotional shop display The Beatles, circa 1963/4, the hardboard display with black and white photograph of the group and their printed facsimile signatures, 40 x 30in. (Christie's) £207 $331

The Rolling Stones, an E.P. record The Rolling Stones, 1964, Decca Records, the sleeve signed on the reverse in different coloured inks by all five members of the group. (Christie's) £402 $643

The Who, a promotional poster 'The Who Maximum R & B', Marquee Club, London, circa 1964, 22½ x 15¼in. (Christie's) £437 $699

Jimi Hendrix, a page from a autograph album signed in red biro by Jimi Hendrix, 3 x 3½in. in common mount with a colour photograph. (Christie's) £690 $1,104

The Spice Girls, a life-size cardboard cut-out standee of the group made for the Pepsi promotion, signed in different coloured felt pens by all five Spice Girls, 70 x 67in. (Christie's) £253 $405

A 'Beatles Come To Town' film poster, 1964, U.S. one-sheet, in red and white 104.1 x 68.6cm., 41 x 27in., linen backed. (Sotheby's) £575 $920

The Travelling Wilburys, a colour publicity photograph of subjects signed in black felt pen by George Harrison, Bob Dylan, Roy Orbison, Tom Petty and Jeff Lynne, 9½ x 7½in. framed. (Christie's) £1,380 $2,208

The Rolling Stones and others, a rare early concert poster Return Visit Of The Sensational Everly Brothers, Bo Diddley, Rolling Stones and others, Gaumont, Bradford, Saturday, 19th October, 1963. (Christie's) £1,265 $2,024

Queen, a Queen News Of The World promotional shop display stand for the album News Of The World, 1977, made of moulded silver plastic in two parts, with record rack attached to front, 54in. high. (Christie's) £747 $1,195

Bruce Springsteen, signed colour 8 x 10, half-length holding guitar, slightly in darker portion.
(Vennett-Smith) £70 $120

A rare early concert poster Brian Epstein Presents The Beatles Christmas Show, featuring The Beatles, Billy J. Kramer and The Dakotas, The Fourmost and others, Finsbury Park Astoria, 1963-1964, 30 x 40in.
(Christie's) £3,680 $5,888

The Beatles, The Beatles Book Monthly Calendar for 1964, complete, featuring various photos, some colour.
(Vennett-Smith) £45 $72

Buddy Holly And The Crickets, a piece of paper signed in blue ballpoint pen by Buddy Holly, Joe Mauldin, Jerry Allison and Norman Petty, 3 x 3½in. framed.
(Christie's) £977 $1,563

A Gold sales award for the album 'Elvis – Aloha From Hawaii Via Satellite' American, 1970s, presented to Elvis Presley for sales of more than $1,000,000.
(Sotheby's) £6,210 $9,936

John Lennon's green corduroy jacket, 1966, labelled *Craft Of Canada*, round-necked with stud fastening to front and cuffs, with photograph of John wearing the jacket. (Sotheby's) £9,200 $14,720

An autographed Beatles concert programme, 1963, signed on the front in blue ink, with corresponding concert ticket for Odeon Theatre, Weston-super-Mare, 24th July.
(Sotheby's) £690 $1,104

Elvis Presley, a rare page of lyrics in Elvis Presley's hand for 'Never Leave Me', circa 1959, the words and music credited by Presley to Gordon Jenkins, the foot of the page signed and inscribed *Could be a good one, Elvis*, 11 x 8in.
(Christie's) £3,680 $5,888

John Lennon, In His Own Write, 1964, London: Jonathan Cape, 4to. front end paper signed in blue ballpoint pen *John Lennon*.
(Christie's) £552 $883

Boyzone, signed colour 8 x 10in., by all five.
(Vennett-Smith) £42 $67

Madonna, signed 10 x 8in., three quarter length seated in black fishnet tights.
(Vennett-Smith) £160 $257

Paul McCartney, signed colour 5½ x 8in., 1997, full-length with guitar.
(Vennett-Smith) £130 $211

The Spice Girls, signed colour, 8 x 10in., by all five, first names only, showing them all in bikinis and basque.
(Vennett-Smith) £270 $435

The Rolling Stones, signed and inscribed 6 x4in., by Mick Jagger, Brian Jones, Bill Wyman, Keith Richard and Charlie Watts individually.
(Vennett-Smith) £390 $628

The Beatles, signed front cover of concert programme, by all four individually, inscribed by McCartney with the additional words The Beatles.
(Vennett-Smith) £810 $1,304

The Beatles, early signed piece, by John Lennon and Ringo Starr, affixed to the reverse of an early 6 x 8in. publicity photo.
(Vennett-Smith) £310 $505

Bob Dylan, signed 8 x 10in. half length holding snooker cue.
(Vennett-Smith) £240 $386

Michael Jackson, signed colour 5 x 7in., full-length, performing on stage.
(Vennett-Smith) £105 $169

George Harrison, signed 8 x 10in., head and shoulders, to lower white border. (Vennett-Smith) £180 $293

Bob Dylan, signed LP record sleeve, to front cover, *Bob Dylan*, record still present. (Vennett-Smith) £380 $619

Spice Girls, signed colour 8 x 10in., by all five, first names only. (Vennett-Smith) £160 $257

The Beatles, ephemera, Fan Club Newsletter No. 4 (Xmas 1964), handbill for Pop's Alive at the Prince of Wales Theatre, 8 x 10in. press still, 1963 Fan Club magazines. (Vennett-Smith) £420 $685

The Rolling Stones, signed colour 10 x 8in., by Mick Jagger, Brian Jones, Keith Richard, Bill Wyman and Charlie Watts. (Vennett-Smith) £305 $491

The Beatles, a 5½ x 12in. colour handbill, for The Beatles at The Odeon, Leeds, 3rd November 1963, with booking form attached to base. (Vennett-Smith) £380 $619

The Who, signed colour 8 x 10in. by Roger Daltrey, Pete Townsend and John Entwhistle, in recent years. (Vennett-Smith) £80 $130

Paul McCartney, signed CD, 'This One', disc still present, signed to plastic casing. (Vennett-Smith) £160 $257

Stevie Wonder, signed and inscribed 8 x 10in., half-length at keyboard. (Vennett-Smith) £80 $128

Whitney Houston, signed 8 x 10, head and shoulders from The Bodyguard.
(Vennett-Smith)   £45 $72

John Lennon's acetate recording of 'Power Boogie' by Elephant's Memory, 1972, the 10inch disc inscribed by John *more voices add sax's on boogie riff (top voice?)*.
(Sotheby's)   £828 $1,325

Abba, signed and inscribed 8 x 10, by all four individually, composite image. (Vennett-Smith) £140 $224

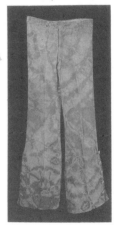

Tina Turner's Versace dress in black mesh with diamante studs, diagonal neckline, single shoulder strap with designer's motif, by Gianni Versace, size 39½.
(Sotheby's)   £4,830 $7,728

Marc Bolan, a stage waistcoat of black and silver leather, the cap-sleeve top lined in black and pink art silk, circa 1976; with corresponding still of Bolan on stage in 1976.
(Christie's)   £1,150 $1,840

A pair of Mick Jagger's velvet trousers, late 1960s/early 70s, grey and pink tie-dyed, waist with star and heart-shaped bead fasteners.
(Sotheby's)   £1,725 $2,760

Buddy Holly And The Crickets, a page from an autograph book signed in black ballpoint pen by Buddy Holly, Joe Mauldin and Jerry Allison, 6¹/₈ x 5³/₈in, 19 x 10in.
(Christie's)   £414 $662

Madonna, a black lace bustier, in common mount with a black and white head and shoulders publicity photograph of subject signed and inscribed in gold felt pen *Love Madonna*, 8¾ x 6½in.
(Christie's)   £1,150 $1,840

Elvis Presley, a black and white German publicity postcard, circa 1959, signed by subject in blue ballpoint pen *Elvis Presley*, 5½ x 3½in. framed.
(Christie's)   £437 $699

716

The Rolling Stones, signed 10 x 8in. by Mick Jagger, Keith Richard, Brian Jones, Bill Wyman and Charlie Watts, some creasing affecting Richard signature.
(Vennett-Smith)   £360 $587

Ian Gillan/Deep Purple, an overstrung, underdamped upright piano by Crowley, England, in a mahogany case, owned and used by Ian Gillan in the 1970s.
(Christie's)   £230 $368

Buddy Holly, signed piece, 3 x 4, rushed example, together with unsigned postcard.
(Vennett-Smith)   £310 $496

The baseball costume worn by Madonna in 'A League of Their Own', 1992, comprising pale pink, dress, front with *City Of Rockford Peaches* patch.
(Sotheby's)   £4,600 $7,360

Two promotional posters for the album Never Mind The Bollocks, Here's The Sex Pistols, 1978, 59 x 36in. and 39½ x 26in.; and corresponding banner, 39 x 7in.
(Christie's)   £368 $588

Elvis Presley's black leather motorcycle jacket, 1960s, labelled *Kennedy's Under-Grad Shop*, red lining. (Sotheby's) £6,440 $10,304

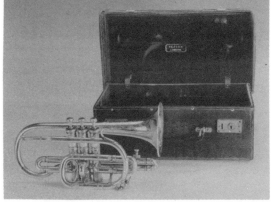

Jimi Hendrix, a page from an autograph book signed in black felt pen by subject, 4 x 5⅛in.
(Christie's)   £402 $643

A Besson & Co. cornet played by Derek Watkins on several Beatles' recordings, including 'Strawberry Fields Forever' 1967/8.
(Sotheby's)   £4,140 $6,624

A pair of red and silver glitter platform boots, by Shelly, each with three stars to the front, belonging to Geri Halliwell.
(Sotheby's)   £1,380 $2,208

A fine modern Heriz carpet, the ivory field with overall design of bold polychrome hooked palmettes, 12ft. 7in. x 9ft. 8in. (Christie's) £1,840 $2,981

A wool hooked rug, American, 19th century, worked in brown, green, cream, crimson, salmon and yellow in a floral and geometric design, 94 x 120in. (Christie's) £4,485 $7,475

A fine Tabriz carpet, the light blue field with angular palmette vine around a stepped and indented ivory medallion, 11ft.10in. x 8ft. 4in. (Christie's) £1,840 $2,981

A fine Mahal carpet, the shaded brick-red field with various polychrome palmettes, angular flowering vine, floral sprays and serrated leaves, 17ft. x 10ft. 9in. (Christie's) £862 $1,396

An unusual American pictorial hooked rug, late 19th/early 20th century, worked in tones of blue, green, pink, brown and cream with a mountain lion, 30 x 42in. (Sotheby's) £2,455 $4,025

A fine Tabriz carpet, the shaded terracotta field with overall design of meandering vine issuing various polychrome serrated palmettes and leafy sprays, 11ft. 5in. x 7ft. 5in. (Christie's) £632 $1,024

An antique Heriz carpet, the brick-red field with angular flowering vine around large hooked and stepped shaded indigo medallion with bold hooked palmette pendants, 12ft. 4in. x 10ft. 8in. (Christie's) £2,760 $4,471

A fine antique Karabagh carpet, the shaded raspberry-red field with various polychrome angular and floral panels, floral sprays and stylised floral vases, 11ft. 2in. x 8ft. 2in. (Christie's) £2,760 $4,471

MONEY MAKER

The current value of oriental rugs suggests that they are seriously undervalued, especially when you consider the amount of time it would take to hand-knot such an item.

A good time to purchase is when they are semi-antique, i.e. pre-1940, as any decent examples are sure to appreciate in value.

The same is true for large Chinese carpets, which, having regard to their size and quality, often sell for low hundreds and are extremely cheap for what they are.

Dockree's

A Qum rug, the ivory field with repeating rows of botehs amongst flowers and foliage, within a floral border, 140 x 204cm.
(Bearne's) £580 $928

A fine Bakhtiari carpet of garden design, the field with polychrome large lozenge medallions containing multicoloured radiating flowerheads, 13ft. 9in. x 10ft. 11in.
(Christie's) £5,750 $9,315

A fine antique Tabriz carpet, the field with Safavid design of meandering vine lattice with multicoloured shaped panels,13ft. 7in. x 10ft. 2in.
(Christie's) £10,350 $16,767

A fine Kerman carpet, the shaded medium blue field with overall design of polychrome stylised floral vases, 14ft. 4in. x 9ft. 10in.
(Christie's) £2,300 $3,726

An American pictorial hooked rug, 20th century, worked in tones of green, blue, violet and brown fabric with the figures of two foxes resting near a lake side, 33½ x 55½in.
(Sotheby's) £2,630 $4,312

A fine antique Heriz carpet, the light rust field with angular polychrome palmette and leafy vine around large medallion with bold hooked palmette pendants, 12ft. 7in. x 9ft.
(Christie's) £2,300 $3,726

A fine antique Bakshaish carpet, the shaded light aubergine field with overall design of stylised polychrome angular palmettes linked by angular vine, 11ft.4in. x 10ft.2in.
(Christie's) £11,500 $18,630

A fine Isfahan carpet, the ivory field with overall design of meandering leafy vine connecting various polychrome large palmettes and fleur-de-lys, 14ft. 11in. x 10ft. 5in.
(Christie's) £2,990 $4,844

A fine antique Serapi carpet, the dusky-pink field with angular floral vine around large shaded indigo hooked and stepped medallion with bold palmette pendants, 11ft. 8in. x 10ft. 1in.
(Christie's) £2,875 $4,657

Sarouk rug, West Persia, early 20th century, lobed circular medallion and delicate flowering vines on the rust field, black flowerhead border, 4ft.10in. x 3ft.4in.
(Skinner) £1,653 $2,645

Shahsavan bagface, Northwest Persia, last quarter 19th century, 2ft.5in. x 2ft.2in.
(Skinner) £2,084 $3,335

Qashqai kelim, Southwest Persia, late 19th/early 20th century two large stepped diamond medallions flanked by triangles, on the red field, 9ft.8in. x 5ft.3in.
(Skinner) £3,953 $6,325

Uzbek flatweave saddlebags, Central Asia, early 20th century, diamond lattice with hooked polygons in navy blue, gold ivory, and dark blue-green on the red field, 5ft.4in. x 2ft.8in.
(Skinner) £305 $488

An American pictorial hooked rug, late 19th/early 20th century, worked in red, yellow, black and blue fabric with the figure of an ocean liner under steam, 30½ x 64in.
(Sotheby's) £3,157 $5,175

Northwest Persia kelim saddlebags, late 19th century, small cross and 'S' motifs on zig-zag vertical bands in navy blue, red, ivory, gold, and blue-green, 4ft. x 1ft.8in.
(Skinner) £575 $920

Kuba rug, Northwest Caucasus, late 19th century, central 'vase' medallion flanked by two serrated diamond medallions, on the midnight blue field, 6ft. x 4ft.
(Skinner) £1,185 $1,897

Yarn and cloth hooked rug, New England, first half 19th century, the scrolling vine border centres a reserve of a stylised potted plant, 49 x 48in.
(Skinner) £1,255 $2,070

A Chinese rug, the deep indigo field regularly interspersed with coral red bats amongst stylised clouds, framed by simple linear borders, 8ft.2in. x 5ft.
(Phillips) £2,100 $3,444

Yomud Ensi, West Turkestan, last quarter 19th century, staggered diamond motifs, on the abrashed aubergine-brown field, 5ft.4in. x 4ft.4in. (Skinner)   £790 $1,265

A Tabriz silk Prayer rug, North West Persia, the abrashed ice blue field having a pair of columns and a hanging lamp beneath the ivory stepped mihrab, 5ft.3in. x 4ft. (Phillips)   £1,700 $2,788

Northwest Persian rug, second quarter 20th century, overall design with floral groups, circular flowering vines, and paired serrated leaves, on the midnight blue field, 5ft. x 3ft.8in.
(Skinner)   £719 $1,150

Bessarbian Kelim, Southeast Persia, late 19th/early 20th century, central group of summer blossoms, surrounded by a sky blue lobed circular frame on the black field, 8ft. x 7ft.4in. (Skinner)   £575 $920

Ersari Chuval, West Turkestan, early 20th century, nine chuval guls in midnight and navy blue, red, ivory, gold, and blue-green on the aubergine field, 4ft.2in. x 3ft.2in. (Skinner)   £467 $747

Kurd bagface, Northwest Persia, last quarter 19th century, diamond lattice with hooked diamonds in midnight and royal, red, apricot, aubergine, and blue-green, 2ft.6in. x 2ft. (Skinner)   £647 $1,035

TOP TIP

Cleaning antiques, like restoration, is a vexed subject - to clean or not to clean, that is the question, as in many cases connoisseurs prefer to purchase items in their original condition and may even pay more for the privilege.

This is certainly so with rugs and textiles. They are best left in their original state to avoid overcleaning.

This advice from Woolley & Wallis was borne out in one of their recent sales, when a carpet, originally from New Wardour Castle, Wiltshire, sold for £86,000. Dating from the late 19th century and measuring 22 x 15ft, it was made by the Manchester firm of Ziegler, who were much engaged in trade with Persia and produced high quality carpets for Europe's grander houses.

This example had been in the same family for many years and at some stage had had two holes cut in it, one for a foot bell push and another for an electric point. In addition, there was a worn patch where the family dog used to sleep at night. The vendors were actually considering cutting it in two, when it was spotted during an insurance valuation.

The vendors attended the sale, but the wife, who was eight months pregnant, had to leave when the bidding reached £50,000, as she feared the excitement might result in an unexpected arrival in the saleroom!

Woolley & Wallis

A Heriz design rug, the ivory field with angular vines issuing flowers centred by a large medallion framed by madder spandrels, 115 x 91in.
(Christie's) £600 $960

Floral hooked rug, America, late 19th/early 20th century, the striated and scrolling leaf border centres a field of repeating geometric and leaf design, 61 x 61in.
(Skinner) £1,533 $2,530

A late 19th century Melayer, West Persia, rug with blue medallion on cream and brick field, 56 x 77½in.
(Dreweatt Neate) £300 $495

Qum Rug, Central Persia, mid 20th century, circular medallion, matching spandrels and blossoming vines on the sky blue field, ivory border, 5ft. 4in. x 3ft. 7in.
(Skinner) £647 $1,035

A fine American pictorial hooked rug, circa 1930, depicting a village scene with houses, horses, chickens and a man fishing, 9 x12ft.
(Sotheby's) £4,209 $6,900

Lillihan Rug, northwest Persia, early 20th century, square medallion, 'cloudbands' and floral sprays on the midnight blue field, red border, 5ft. 8in. x 3ft. 9in.
(Skinner) £467 $748

Maslinghan rug, Northwest Persia, early 20th century, elongated lightning medallion and columns of rosettes, 7ft.2in. x 4ft.6in.
(Skinner) £846 $1,380

A fine Aubusson rug, the strawberry pink field centred by a floral medallion enclosing a celadon panel with central bouquet and butterflies, 6ft.6in. x 6ft.3in.
(Phillips) £6,200 $10,168

Kashan rug, west central Persia, early 20th century, lobed circular medallion, matching spandrels and flowering vines, 6ft.8in. x 4ft.6in.
(Skinner) £714 $1,150

Khamseh rug, Southwest Persia, early 20th century, four stepped diamond medallions flanked by half-medallions, 7ft. 2in. x 4ft.
(Skinner) £341 $546

An American pictorial hooked rug, first half 20th century, worked in red, brown, blue and cream fabrics, 32 x 18in.
(Sotheby's) £1,122 $1,840

Hamadan rug, Northwest Persia, early 20th century, two stepped diamond medallions surrounded by bird and serrated leaf motifs, 6ft. x 3ft.2in. (Skinner) £599 $977

Bergama rug, West Anatolia, last quarter 19th century, one large and four smaller square medallions surrounded by star-in-octagon motifs, 6ft.6in. x 4ft.6in.
(Skinner) £209 $345

An American pictorial hooked rug depicting a bird on a branch and a butterfly, first half 20th century, worked with a bird on a fruit tree branch and a butterfly, 28½ x 20¼in. (Sotheby's) £701 $1,150

Kurd rug, Northwest Persia, late 19th century, three square medallions surrounded by serrated triangles and hooked diamonds, 7ft. 2in. x 4ft. 5in.
(Skinner) £348 $575

An Agra rug, North India, the deep indigo field having a lattice of floral vines, centred by an 'Ardebil' medallion, 8ft.10in. x 5ft.11in.
(Phillips) £3,400 $5,576

An American pictorial hooked rug, first half 20th century, worked in lavender, black red, yellow and green fabrics, 36 x 19in.
(Sotheby's) £420 $690

Shirvan Kelim, East Caucasus, last quarter 19th century, horizontal bands of hexagons and S motifs, 10ft. x 5ft. 9in.
(Skinner) £459 $748

A sampler by M A Cartwright 1837 finely embroidered in coloured silks, the central field with alphabets in cross stitch and Algerian eye with the verse *Next unto God...*, 17½ x 19¾in. (Christie's) £1,955 $3,125

Needlework sampler, *Paulina F. Freeman Aged 9 Years August 31, 1820*, upper panel of alphabets and pious verse, 16⅝ x 17⅛in. (Skinner) £917 $1,495

Needlework sampler, *Mary Greenleaf born in July the 16 1786*, Newburyport area, Massachusetts, upper panel of alphabets and pious verse, 21⅛ x 16¼in. (Skinner) £6,702 $10,925

A fine needlework sampler, signed *Catherine Leatherbury, Philadelphia, Pennsylvania, dated 1827*, worked with a pious verse within a rectangular reserve below a landscape, 20½ x 21in. (Sotheby's) £5,261 $8,625

A fine needlework sampler, signed *Elizabeth Masson*, English or Scottish, *dated March 24, 1835*, executed in a variety of vivid green, brown, blue, yellow and rose silk stitches on a linen ground, 16 x 19¼in. (Sotheby's) £5,612 $9,200

A fine needlework sampler, signed *Susanna Leatherbury*, Philadelphia, Pennsylvania, dated *1825*, at centre a pious verse within a rectangular reserve below a landscape scene, 17¼ x 17½in. (Sotheby's) £2,455 $4,025

Needlework sampler, *Margaret Craigs sampler done in the 10th year of her age, 1837*, the upper panel with a basket of fruit flanked by various motifs, 22 x 20½in. (Skinner) £683 $1,093

A sampler by Sophia Tabitha Hogson 1789 worked in freshly coloured silks in shades of pink, blue, green and yellow in cross stitch, 16½ x 15¾in. (Christie's) £632 $1,011

Needlework sampler, *Haverhill Auguft 29 Betsey Gage Plummer Born AD 1782 this wrought in the 14 year of her age...*, Massachusetts, 19⅜ x 15¾in. (Skinner) £6,702 $10,925

A sampler by Eleanor Linzey 1833 worked predominantly in cross stitch in shades of brown, yellow, ivory and green silks, 16¾ x 19¾in. (Christie's) £483 $773

Needlework sampler, *Lucy Deweys sampler wrought in the eleventh year of her age 1794*, upper panel of a flowering vine with bow, 15½ x 17in. (Skinner) £1,269 $2,070

Needlework sampler, *Harriet French AE7 at Miss Hammonds School Boston,* upper panel of alphabets and pious verse, 11⅞in. x 11³⁄₈in. (Skinner) £705 $1,150

A fine needlework sampler, Rebecca Elizabeth Loomer, probably Pennsylvania, dated *1851*, worked with a pious verse above a red cottage, 21 x 19in. (Sotheby's) £1,403 $2,300

An unusual sampler by Elizabeth Herbert 1789, embroidered in coloured silks in shades of black, brown and green, with the verse *Learning is better than riches…*, 14 x 17in. (Christie's) £897 $1,435

A needlework sampler, signed *Augusta Marsh, Massachusetts*, dated *1822*, worked with a boy and a girl standing in the doorway of a white house, 16¼ x 16¾in. (Sotheby's) £2,630 $4,312

A sampler by Margaret Leslie 1827 worked in brightly coloured wools with silk highlights, the central band with various spot motifs including a butterfly, peacock and rabbits, 14½ x 19in. (Christie's) £460 $736

Needlework sampler, *Mary Jowett Work*, probably Pennsylvania, circa 1830's, upper panel of fruit and foliate devices, pious verse and Adam and Eve, 25 x 24in. (Skinner) £1,623 $2,645

A sampler by Christine 1804 worked in brightly coloured silks against a wool ground in cross stitch, the upper third with alphabets and numerals, 13½ x 18¾in. (Christie's) £552 $883

An Edwardian silver and porcelain scent bottle, Birmingham 1904, realistically modelled as a strawberry, with screw-off top, 2¼in. long. (Bonhams) £350 $560

Lucretia Vanderbilt 'Lucretia Vanderbilt', the bottle of cobalt blue glass and disc form with butterfly stopper, 4¾in. high. (Bonhams) £900 $1,440

A 19th century French silver-gilt and blue glass scent bottle, decorated with gilt foliate motifs within scroll and lattice work, 3¼in. high. (Bonhams) £240 $384

Baccarat for Plassard 'De Fleur en Fleur', a clear panel form bottle swollen above the base, 4¼in. high. (Bonhams) £130 $208

A pair of silver mounted glass dressing table scent bottles, Birmingham 1885, maker's mark of 'H & A', the mounts pierced with foliate scroll and lattice motif, 5¼in. high. (Bonhams) £600 $960

A late 19th century French parcel-gilt and opaque blue glass scent bottle, circa 1860–80, the pierced mounts chased with floral motifs within oval cartouches, 3⅝in. high. (Bonhams) £650 $1,040

A silver and porcelain scent bottle, Birmingham 1913, David Loebl, depicting a scene from Shakespeare's 'Hamlet', with screw-off top, 2½in. high. (Bonhams) £220 $352

A late Victorian silver scent bottle, Birmingham 1892, maker's mark of Hilliard & Thomason, shaped pointed oval form, with part fluted and foliate scroll decoration, 3¼in. high. (Bonhams) £190 $304

A late 19th century Continental red and white foiled glass scent bottle, probably Venetian, egg form, with electroplated screw-off knop top, 2⅝in. (Bonhams) £100 $160

A late 19th century French brass and opaque blue glass scent bottle, circa 1880s, compressed circular form, set with cameos of various ladies, 3³/₈in. high. (Bonhams) £360 $576

Lubin 'Enigma', 1921, designed by Julien Viard, the clear bottle and stopper of pyramidal panel form intaglio moulded and heightened in gilt with a sphinx and pillar, 3½in. high. (Bonhams) £1,300 $2,080

An early 19th century Bohemian telescopic cut-glass clear scent bottle circa 1830, circular form, with brass mounts, the screw-off top with dependent loop, 2³/₈in. (Bonhams) £420 $672

A mid Victorian silver-gilt and cobalt blue glass scent bottle, London 1864, Abraham Brounett, retailed by Asprey, mounts engraved with Gothic beaded scrolls, foliate decoration and entwined decoration, 3¼in. high. (Bonhams) £450 $720

A pair of late Victorian silver mounted clear cut-glass dressing table scent bottles, Birmingham 1885, John Grinsell & Sons, with mullet motif within lozenges, with cut-glass shoulders, 5¼in. high. (Bonhams) £380 $608

A late 19th century novelty scent bottle, circa 1880s, probably French, cover modelled as a silver-gilt chick set with ruby eyes, peering out of a pink guilloche enamelled broken egg, 1³/₈in. high. (Bonhams) £420 $672

A 19th century novelty scent bottle, modelled as a bird's egg, with brass screw-off top, fitted in a brass nest with padlock, height of bottle 2³/₈in. (Bonhams) £220 $352

Depinoix for L. T. Piver 'Mascarade', 1927, the cinnabar bottle and domical stopper intaglio moulded and gilt with spiral motifs, 3½in. high. (Bonhams) £560 $896

J. Grossmith and Son 'Phul-Nan', a clear bottle of oval section, sealed with original contents and paper label in presentation carton, 4½in. high. (Bonhams) £30 $48

A late Victorian silver and ruby red overlay glass scent bottle, Birmingham 1897, Hilliard & Thomason, icicle form, with lozenge decoration, 5⁷/₈in. high. (Bonhams) £280 $448

Lentheric three miniatures 'Pink Party', 'Risque Tout' and 'Shanghai', all of upright panel form and with rectangular stopper, 2¼in. high. (Bonhams) £60 $96

A late Victorian silver and porcelain scent bottle, London 1884, Charles May, painted with trailing flowering branches with burgundy and pale pink flowers, 5¹/₈in. long. (Bonhams) £320 $512

A 19th century, Continental enamel scent bottle, probably Swiss, flowerhead form, each petal coloured black, white and pale blue alternatively with follate decoration, 1⁵/₈in. long. (Bonhams) £300 $480

Baccarat for Guerlain 'Coque d' Or', the cobalt blue glass gilt and modelled in the form of a bow tie with button stopper titled in black, 3¹/₈in. high. (Bonhams) £180 $288

A late 19th century/ early 20th century silver novely scent bottle, modelled as a monkey nut, the hinged cover opening out to reveal a screw-off top, 1¾in. long. (Bonhams) £260 $416

Colgate's handkerchief extract 'Lily of the Valley', cylindrical bottle, sealed with original contents and presentation carton 3¾in. high. (Bonhams) £45 $72

Baccarat for Guerlain 'Vega', the small bottle horizontally ribbed and with ball stopper, 3¹/₈in: (Bonhams) £720 $1,152

A Czech ruby glass bottle with clear stopper, acid cut and gilt with a berry and leaf design, the bottle of facet cut pyramidal form, 6½in. high. (Bonhams) £110 $176

A mid Victorian silver scent bottle/vinaigrette, London 1874, S. Mordan & Co. Ltd, plain cornucopia form, one end with screw-off top, 4¼in. long. (Bonhams) £300 $480

A Schuco monkey novelty perfume bottle, the removable head fitted with a small internal glass flask, 3½in. high. (Bonhams) £150 $240

De Vigny 'Le Golliwogg,' a frosted bottle and enamelled stopper with black fur hair, the latter with facial detail in orange and white, 3½in. high. (Bonhams) £350 $560

A late Victorian silver scent bottle, Birmingham 1893, maker's mark *H & A,* tear drop form, embossed with part fluting and foliate scrolls, 4½in. high. (Bonhams)   £320 $512

A mid Victorian silver and opaque cream glass novelty scent bottle, Birmingham 1865, modelled as a stylised eagle's head, 7⅛in. (Bonhams)   £2,400 $3,840

A 19th century German pale blue glass scent bottle, circa 1860–80, icicle form, painted with gilt girdle with lattice decoration, 5½in. high. (Bonhams)   £400 $640

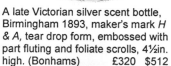

A late 19th century silver and ruby flash glass scent bottle, circa 1860–80, with ovoid and star motifs, the hinged cover embossed with foliate scrolls, 3¼in. high. (Bonhams)   £240 $384

Du Barry 'Blue Lagoon', circa 1919, designed by Julien Viard, an enamelled and clear glass bottle with figural stopper, 4¼in. high. (Bonhams)   £520 $832

Lalique for Coty 'Ambre Antique', a frosted and sienna-stained bottle, intaglio moulded with a frieze of four classically draped maidens holding flora, 6⅛in. high. (Bonhams)   £400 $640

Lalique for Worth 'Dans la Nuit', a large clear and cobalt blue stained cologne bottle of spherical form moulded in relief with a mass of stars polished clear against the matt blue reserves, 10in. high. (Bonhams)   £620 $992

'Le Val Creaux', 1930, a black glass bottle of slim panel form moulded at each side with a coral design, 3½in. high. (Bonhams)   £280 $448

Giraud 'Soiree', 1920s, a clear and frosted bottle moulded in low relief with title, 3¾in. high. (Bonhams)   £680 $1,088

A late 19th century Bohemian blue flash glass dressing table scent bottle, baluster form, with ovoid and lattice decoration, 6¾in. high. (Bonhams)   £280 $448

Baccarat for Guerlain 'Coque D' Or' or 'Dawaesk', the cobalt blue bottle modelled in the form of a bow tie, domical stopper, 3in. high. (Bonhams)   £140 $224

An interesting clear bottle of compressed bell form with figural blue stopper modelled as a pierrot, possibly Du Barry, 5¼in. high. (Bonhams)   £180 $288

Thomas Webb cameo glass yellow cologne, white over yellow sphere intricately etched as decumbent fuchsia, total height, 4¾in. (Skinner) £586 $977

René Lalique Epines dresser jar, sepia patine on colourless moulded thorny bramble motif on round bottle, 3½in. high. (Skinner) £276 $460

Webb cameo glass square blue cologne, four panels of etched blossoms on squared amber bottle with screw-on silver cover, total height 5in. (Skinner) £310 $517

An enamelled glass scent bottle and stopper by Daum, circa 1905, etched and enamelled in colours with wild violets and leaves, 9.5cm. high. (Christie's) 1,610 $2,640

A pair of carved and etched glass scent bottles and stoppers, by Gallé, circa 1880, clear glass etched and carved, with gilt detailing, 14cm. high. (Christie's) £1,380 $2,263

An Apsley Pellatt sulphide scent bottle and stopper, cut with a rectangular panel containing a profile bust sulphide of the Duke of Wellington, circa 1820, 12cm. high. (Christie's) £805 $1,312

Thomas Webb cameo glass yellow cologne, brilliant red oval bottle layered in white cameo etched on blossoming leafy vines, 5½in. high. (Skinner) £897 $1,495

A pair of large uranium green square section scent bottles and stoppers, moulded in relief *The Crown Perfumery Company London*, late 19th century, 53.5cm. high. (Christie's) £460 $749

René Lalique Le Jade perfume, flattened snuff bottle form with moulded jungle bird decoration, 3¼in. high. (Skinner) £1,311 $2,185

Carder Steuben gold aurene cologne, eight-lobed bottle with tapered conforming stopper, total height 6½in. (Skinner) £483 $805

Baccarat for Guerlain 'Mitsouko', a clear panel form bottle with scroll moulded shoulders and open scroll stopper, 4¾in. high. (Bonhams)   £120 $192

A cut glass scent bottle, the glass with central star motifs surrounded by pierced scroll, flower head and lattice work, 5¾in. high, London 1912. (Andrew Hartley) £420 $693

An enamelled glass scent bottle and stopper, by Gallé, circa 1890, enamelled with two lobed reserves containing a medieval Persian warrior on horseback, 15cm. high. (Christie's)   £5,750 $9,430

René Lalique Bouchon Cassis perfume, vertically ribbed colourless barrel-form bottle with integrated tiara stopper, 4¾in. high. (Skinner)   £4,312 $7,187

An extremely rare Kelsterbach porcelain and gilt-metal mounted scent bottle and stopper, circa 1760–1765, modelled by Vogelmann, 3½in. (Sotheby's)   £1,840 $3,073

An amber tint and cut Apsley Pellatt sulphide scent bottle and silver stopper, cut with a square panel enclosing a sulphide of Princess Charlotte, second quarter 19th century, 7.5cm. high. (Christie's)   £150 $244

A pair of late 18th century blue glass scent bottles, probably Bristol, circa 1760, painted in the chinoiserie style with gilt exotic birds, floral decoration and rustic scene, height of box 2⅛in. (Bonhams)   £700 $1,120

Lalique for Molinard 'Madrigal', a limited edition, the ovoid body moulded with a frieze of classically draped maidens above a short stem circular foot. (Bonhams)   £650 $1,040

Potter and Moore 'OLoo', a black glass bottle modelled in the form of a seated dog with screw twist head stopper, 3in. high.
(Bonhams)   £85 $136

Mury – Jasmin, clear cylindrical bottle with black button stopper, in original open flowerhead amber silk display case, 3in. high.
(Bonhams)   £260 $416

Baccarat for L. Plassard 'Une Femme Passa', a frosted bottle of slender baluster form moulded in low relief with a network of dense foliage, 4¾in. high.
(Bonhams)   £3,000 $4,800

Lancome 'Tropiques' limited edition 1945, designed by Georges Delhomme, the panel form bottle moulded and detailed in gilt with a zephyr, 4in. high.
(Bonhams)   £1,250 $2,000

Rosine 'Chez Poiret', a domical clear bottle with emerald green stopper, 2½in. high.
(Bonhams)   £130 $208

René Lalique 'Belle Saison', a frosted and sienna stained bottle and stopper moulded at one side with a central profile portrait of a young woman, 4in. high.
(Bonhams)   £700 $1,120

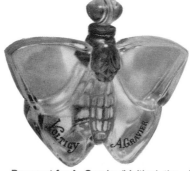

A fine and early 19th century French gold and black enamel scent bottle, depicting cupid holding a butterfly in one hand and a bow in the other, 3½in. high.
(Bonhams)   £2,200 $3,520

Baccarat for A. Gravier 'Voltigy', the bottle and stopper modelled in the form of a butterfly with wings displayed, in fitted cream silk box, 3⁵⁄₈in. high.
(Bonhams)   £5,800 $9,280

Lanvin, a green glazed ceramic counter display bottle of turret shape, labelled with numerous Lanvin perfume advertising posters, cork plug stopper, 10⁵⁄₈in. high.
(Bonhams)   £260 $416

Lucien Lelong 'Opening Night', the clear small bottle of compressed and fluted vase shape, 4½in. high. (Bonhams) £90 $144

Rosine 'Aladin', a grey metal bottle of arched panel form cast in relief with rearing horses, 2½in. high. (Bonhams) £500 $800

Richard Hudnut 'Lily of the Valley', circa 1894, a frosted panel form cologne bottle, sealed but with contents evaporated, 7in. high. (Bonhams) £90 $144

A pair of late 19th century French clear glass scent bottles fitted in a gilt-metal mounted mother-of-pearl case, height overall 5⅛in. (Bonhams) £350 $560

Rosine 'Le Bosquet de Apollon', 1923, the clear bottle of cigar case form with gilt metal half cover embossed with a young woman's head, 3½in. high. (Bonhams) £1,600 $2,560

Jean Patou 'My Own' cocktail range, circa 1930, the panel form bottle with arched shoulders and cabochon stopper, 4¼in. high. (Bonhams) £280 $448

Louis Chalon for Roger et Gallet 'Bouquet Nouveau', a green glass panel form bottle, decorated with an Art Nouveau design, 4¼in. high. (Bonhams) £380 $608

Vantine 'Hi Yang', 1920, a clear and frosted bottle modelled in the form of seated partially robed oriental, 2⅞in. high. (Bonhams) £520 $832

A late Victorian silver-gilt and enamel opera glass scent bottle, inscribed *S. Mordan & Co. Makers*, decorated with white flowers, 2¾in. high. (Bonhams) £380 $608

A 19th century scrimshaw whale's tooth, engraved American flags, eagle, cannon, vase of flowers and three sailing ships, 7½in. long. (Anderson & Garland) £420 $693

A fine scrimshawed and engraved porpoise jaw, probably American, mid 19th century, engraved in red, black and blue ink with both shipping and town scenes, 15in. long. (Sotheby's) £4,560 $7,475

An unusual pin-pricked and engraved scrimshawed sperm whale tooth, initialled *T.M.*, probably American, mid 19th century, 6½in. high. (Sotheby's) £842 $1,380

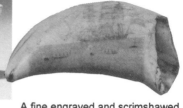

Important American scrimshaw sperm whale's tooth, engraved decoration of a whaling scene, signed lower centre *S. Eaton at sea Feb. 4th 1832*, 8in. long. (Eldred's) £6,187 $9,900

A fine and rare engraved scrimshawed erotic sperm whale tooth, probably American, mid 19th century, the obverse engraved with the figure of a reclining nude, 6½in. high. (Sotheby's) £31,567 $51,750

A fine engraved and scrimshawed sperm whale's tooth, probably American, mid 19th century, the obverse engraved with a whaling scene, 7in. long. (Sotheby's) £4,209 $6,900

A fine pair of relief-carved sperm whale teeth, probably English, early 19th century, the first carved with the figure of a British sailor standing on a pile of rope, 5¼in. and 5½in, high. (Sotheby's) £3,332 $5,462

Important pair of large scrimshaw whale's teeth, 19th century, with inlaid mother of pearl decoration, each tooth decorated with two whaleships, one above the other, 7½in. and 8in. (Eldred's) £6,187 $9,900

A pair of engraved scrimshawed sperm whale teeth, probably American, third quarter 19th century, the first engraved with the allegorical figure of Liberty, 4¼in. high. (Sotheby's) £1,754 $2,875

A very fine engraved and scrimshawed sperm whale tooth, probably American, dated 1873, the obverse engraved with two whale ships and men pursuing whales in longboats, dated *1873,* 7in. long. (Sotheby's) £1,263 $2,070

Engraved whale's tooth, early 20th century, decorated with a reserve of a whaling scene, flanked by various whaling implements, rope border, 9¼in. long. (Skinner) £1,690 $2,760

A fine engraved and scrimshawed sperm whale's tooth: Outward Bound, probably American, mid 19th century, the obverse engraved with a whale ship leaving port, 6½in. high. (Sotheby's) £2,455 $4,025

An American Singer chainstitch child's sewing machine. (Auction Team Köln) £15 $23

An Original Express chainstitch sewing machine by Guhl & Harbeck, circa 1875, complete. (Auction Team Köln) £158 $254

An American New England chain stitch machine, circa 1872. (Auction Team Köln) £142 $227

A French Hurtu No. P12 standard swing shuttle machine, with original table and wooden cover, circa 1895. (Auction Team Köln) $158 $254

A small chain-stitch sewing machine, probably a Newton, Wilson 'Matchless', with parallel action needle arm, gilt and red decoration, wood baseboard and case, 7½in. wide. (Christie's) £2,875 $4,600

A standard, folding Stoewer swing shuttle machine by the famous German typewriter and car manufacturers Stoewer, circa 1912. (Auction Team Köln) £96 $154

A small chainstitch sewing machine, probably a Newton, Wilson 'matchless', with parallel action needle arm, 7½in. wide. (Christie's) £2,875 $4,600

An American Florence long shuttle machine with shuttle and well preserved decoration, circa 1868. (Auction Team Köln)
£2,931 $4,690

A rare Russian MPZ child's sewing machine, a copy of a Singer machine by Pensa, Kazakhstan, circa 1920, with original wood cover. (Auction Team Köln) £146 $234

An unusual carved wood and shell work frame, third quarter 19th century, the oval frame composed of a wood puzzle carving and mollusc shells, dated *1864*, 8in. x 6in. (Sotheby's) £280 $460

A fine sailor's valentine: *For my sister*, probably American, late 19th century, in a folding octagonal wood box composed of pink, green and brown shells, 9¼in. diameter. (Sotheby's) £772 $1,265

An unusual sailor's valentine inscribed *Naval Review at Spithead*, dated *1895*, having a shellwork heartshaped frame surrounding a glass enclosed diorama, 8¾in. x 7¾in. (Sotheby's) £842 $1,380

SHIBAYAMA

A Japanese ivory Shibayama bezique marker, decorated with foliage birds and insects, 9cm. (Bearne's) £250 $412

A pair of Shibayama style vases and ivory stands, Meiji period (19th century), of trumpet form decorated in various coloured inlays on a kinji ground with butterflies and dragonfly, 6¾in. high including base. (Christie's) £6,000 $10,080

A Shibayama-style box and cover modelled as a bijin seated on a caparisoned elephant, Meiji period (19th century), the elephant bejewelled in ivory and various coloured inlays on a rich kinji ground, 22cm. long. (Christie's) £27,600 $46,368

A Shibayama silver mounted ivory box, the lid realistically decorated with a fish breaking water, Meiji, 31cm. (Bearne's) £860 $1,419

A Shibayama ivory tusk vase of curved cylindrical form, inlaid with various coloured hardstones and mother-of-pearl, late Meiji, 35.5cm. (Bearne's) £1,300 $2,145

A Shibayama wood elephant, bearing an ivory finial on its back, decorated with tortoiseshell, ivory and coloured glass, signed, Meiji, 17cm. (Bearne's) £500 $829

A painted metal barbershop trade sign, *Shave for a Penny, Let Blood for Nothing, Teeth Drawn With a Touch*, 32½ x 26½in.
(Sotheby's) £421 $690

Painted and decorated two-sided tavern sign, *Thompson Hotel, Vernon Stiles 1831,* in gilt letters flanking a scene with men in a carriage, 44¼in. high x 66in. wide.
(Skinner) £10,583 $17,250

The Stephens Pen, 8 -colour offset poster in contemporary frame, 50 x 76cm., circa 1920.
(Auction Team Köln) £334 $535

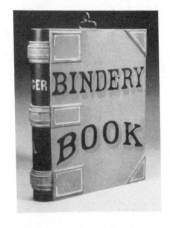

Carved gilt-wood and metal watch trade sign, America, late 19th/early 20th century, 22⅝in. high.
(Skinner) £625 $1,000

Painted tin 'Book Bindery' trade sign, America, late 19th/early 20th century, 19¼in. high.
(Skinner) £359 $575

A cast metal tobacconist's gypsy cigar and cigarette lighter, probably New York, late 19th century, the half length figure of a gypsy girl with cigarette in mouth, 31in. high.
(Sotheby's) £3,157 $5,175

European double-sided tavern sign, marked *Wadworth's* with a landscape scene of a stag, late 19th century,48½ x 31in.
(Eldred's) £412 $660

A Coca Cola display with Coca Cola calendar for 1954, six pages, and enamel sign, convex, with stamped bottle and writing, 40.5cm. diameter, 1954.
(Auction Team Köln) £146 $234

A rare carved and painted pine trade sign: Captain Ahab, American, late 19th/early 20th century, overall height 32¾in.
(Sotheby's) £16,134 $26,450

An American Arts and Crafts silver basket, John O. Bellis, San Francisco, circa 1910, in basketweave of silver strips, 41oz. 15dwt, 9in. high.
(Sotheby's)   £2,630 $4,312

A pair of Edwardian fruit baskets, the pierced trellis sides embossed with floral festoons, 9in. wide, London 1902, 24oz. 19dwt.
(Andrew Hartley)   £620 $1,042

A George III silver basket, William Plummer, London 1771, the body pierced with scalework, latticework, scrolls and foliage, 15½in. long, 39oz. (Christie's) £2,990 $4,904

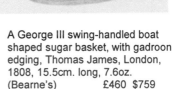

A George III swing-handled boat-shaped sugar basket with thread edging, vacant panels and bright cut decoration, 12.5 cm. long, Henry Chawner, London 1792, 5oz.
(Bearne's)   £340 $561

A pair of Victorian bon bon baskets, moulded foliate rims and swing loop handles, 5½in. wide, maker's mark for Elkington & Co, Birmingham 1896, 15oz 1dwt.
(Andrew Hartley)   £500 $825

A George III swing-handled boat shaped sugar basket, with gadroon edging, Thomas James, London, 1808, 15.5cm. long, 7.6oz.
(Bearne's)   £460 $759

A Russian parcel gilt cake basket, of woven form, with similarly decorated tubular swing handle, by Stefan Wakera, St. Petersburg, 1889, 20oz., 27.5cm.
(Tennants)   £1,100 $1,760

A George III basket of oval form with a pierced swing handle and a ropework rim, by S. Herbert & Co., 1765, 32cm. wide, 20.5oz.
(Christie's)   £1,955 $3,128

English Classical Revival cake basket, London 1920, raised on pierced and engraved foot with beaded border, marked by Crichton Bros., London and New York, 13in. long, approximately 25 troy oz.
(Skinner)   £786 $1,265

One of a set of four Victorian beakers of tapering form with skirted bases, by Edward Pairpoint, 1868, 9.75cm. high, 23oz. (Christie's)   (Four) £2,070 $3,457

A George III beaker, the tapering body decorated with three reeded girdles, the base inscribed *Charles Phelps*, 9.2cm. high, London, 1788, 7.1oz. (Bearne's)   £500 $800

A late 18th century beaker with a spreading circular pedestal base and a flared bowl, Jersey, last quarter of 18th century, 9cm. high, 3oz. (Christie's)   £977 $1,632

A fine Dutch silver-gilt beaker stamped *O*, the tapered cylindrical body finely engraved with three ovals depicting Joseph's Dream, 6in. high, 7oz 12dwt. (Sotheby's)   £34,500 $57,615

A German silver-gilt rummer beaker, Isack de Voeghelaer, Emden, circa 1600, the conical bowl engraved with monster's head scrolls and tassels at the rim, 3in. high, 3oz. (Sotheby's)   £10,925 $18,245

A German parcel-gilt silver beaker, Dreslau, 1737-1745, maker's mark *PMG* in a heart, shaped oval and on a domed spreading foot, 5¾in. high, 7oz. (Christie's)   £1,265 $2,113

A James II silver beaker, John Duck, London, 1681, the sides chased and engraved with a broad band of flower heads and foliage, 3½in. high, 3oz. (Christie's)   £1,840 $3,073

An Elizabeth I silver beaker, maker's mark *W1*, London, 1599, tapered cylindrical, engraved with a band of formal foliage and three scrolling pendants, 5½in. high, 6oz 18dwt.(Sotheby's) £11,500 $19,205

A fine Charles II silver-gilt beaker, maker's mark *TH* crowned above a pellet, London, 1674, 4in. high, 15oz 2dwt. (Sotheby's)   £34,500 $57,615

American silver footed bowl, J.& I. Cox, New York, 1817–35, panelled octagonal form, Rococo-style feet, engraved decoration and monogram, 3¹/₈in. high., approximately 17 troy oz. (Skinner) £172 $287

An Edward VII Art Nouveau circular rose bowl, decorated with flowers and scrolling foliage, Mappin & Webb, Sheffield 1902, 21cm. diameter, 19.5oz. (Bearne's) £280 $462

An American silver two-handled punch bowl, Gorham Mfg. Co., Providence, RI, circa 1903, applied with grapevine stemming from twisted branch handles, 149oz. length over handles 19in. (Sotheby's) £3,858 $6,325

A Victorian circular rose bowl with gadroon edging chased with flowers, scrolls and vacant panels, 21cm. diameter, William Hutton & Sons, Sheffield 1900, 551gm. (Bearne's) £240 $396

A Victorian half fluted rose bowl, with moulded rim over a band of embossed ribbon festoons, 9in. wide, London 1897, 19oz. 18dwt. (Andrew Hartley) £340 $544

Ball, Black & Co. two handled Sterling bowl, third quarter 19th century, on tapered foot, with open wire work handles, 7⁵/₈in. diameter, approximately 23 troy oz. (Skinner) £456 $748

An Edward VII pierced oval fruit bowl decorated with scrolling foliage, 37.5cm. long, George Maudsley Jackson & David Landsborough Fullerton, London 1903, 1019gm. (Bearne's) £520 $858

Gorham Sterling centre bowl, circa 1901, the wide shaped and pierced edge with an elegant design of swirling oak leaves and acorns, 14¼in. diameter, approximately 56 troy oz. (Skinner) £714 $1,150

A Victorian circular punch bowl with reeded and fluted lower body, on a similarly decorated spreading base, 29.5cm. diameter, Charles Stuart Harris, London, 1895, 35.65oz. (Bearne's) £380 $608

A Victorian silver-gilt strawberry bowl and cover, John S. Hunt, London, 1845, the openwork body and detachable cover pierced and chased with fruiting vines, 7½in. high, 37oz.
(Christie's)   £4,025 $6,722

An American silver punch bowl, George W. Shiebler & Co., New York, circa 1905, raised on four cast grapevine feet, 113ozs., 14½in. diameter.
(Sotheby's)   £3,508 $5,750

The City of Exeter and Exeter Cycling Club trophy; a large, late Victorian rose bowl, embossed with festoons of fruit and swirl fluting, 1900, 44cm. diameter, 139.5oz.
(Christie's)   £4,370 $6,992

An American silver monteith, Gorham Mfg. Co., Providence, RI, late 19th century, in the 17th century English style, 12½in. diameter.
(Sotheby's)   £2,630 $4,312

An Art Nouveau circular rose bowl, the plain bowl on a square base, 25cm. diameter, West & Son, London 1905, 1972gm.
(Bearne's)   £460 $759

A Victorian circular punch bowl of semi-fluted form with raised foliate decoration and ribbon tied swags, 24cm. diameter, John Marriott Wintle, London 1894, 819gm.
(Bearne's)   £280 $462

A silver and mixed-metal sugar bowl, Tiffany & Co., New York, circa 1880, the spot-hammered surface applied with silver, gold and copper leaves, dragonfly and butterfly, 3½in. wide, gross weight 5oz. (Christie's)   £1,518 $2,530

An American silver covered sugar bowl, Joseph Richardson Sr., Philadelphia, circa 1748, of hemispherical form with moulded borders, 9oz. 4 dwt., 4⅜in. diam.
(Sotheby's)   £12,627 $20,700

A silver ice bowl, Gorham, Providence, 1870, body and foot formed as blocks of ice, chased with frost and hung with cast icicles, 11¼in. long, 28oz.
(Christie's)   £4,830 $8,050

Important Frank G. Hale box, enamelled ship signed *Hale*, box with hammered finish signed *F.G. Hale*, 4½in. wide.
(Skinner)   £1,656 $2,760

A Continental silver rectangular box, the base embossed with a scene of a girl crowning a boy with a garland, 2in., import marks for London 1912.
(Woolley & Wallis)   £70 $112

An Edwardian trinket box, shagreen and silver mounted, the cartouche shape body with anthemion and fleur de lis mounts, 4¾in., George Fox III, London 1909.
(Woolley & Wallis) £1,350 £2,174

A modern circular cigarette 'tin' with a push-in circular cover and engine turned decoration, by Asprey & Co, Birmingham 1925, 7cm. high, 6oz.
(Christie's)   £299 $478

CANDELABRUM

Austrian sugar box, mid to late 19th century, rectangular with central repoussé banding of human masks and foliage, 800 fine, maker's mark, 19 troy oz. (Skinner) £679 $1,093

A silver-plated biscuit box, presented by Abraham Lincoln, 1863, with classical bacchic reliefs, the cover with a relief of Silenus, 44oz. 2dwt., 6½in. high.
(Sotheby's)   £2,806 $4,600

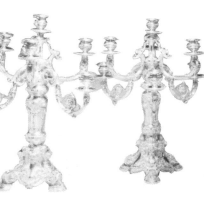

A pair of George III silver candlesticks and a pair of silver-plated three-light candelabra branches, John Scofield, London, 1785, 12½in. high, the candlesticks 38oz. (Christie's)   £4,600 $7,682

A large five-light silver candelabrum, Omar Ramsden, London, 1923, the spool-shaped base on eight pad feet, 32in. high, the branches 101oz.
(Christie's)   £15,525 $25,927

A pair of American silver seven-light candelabra, Gorham Mfg. Co., Providence, RI, circa 1908, in Renaissance taste, decorated with lion masks, 401oz., 23³/₈in. high.
(Sotheby's)   £20,344 $33,350

A pair of Victorian silver plated candlesticks with urn shaped nozzle, knopped baluster stem and square base with anthemion borders, 10in. high.
(Andrew Hartley) £190 $319

A pair of modern Corinthian column table candlesticks, the stepped square bases and detachable nozzles, 30cm. high, London 1962, weighted. (Bearne's) £380 $627

A pair of Georgian silver table candlesticks, Dublin, mid-18th century, each shaped square base with a shell at each corner, 50oz., 10¾in. high.
(Sotheby's) £3,858 $6,325

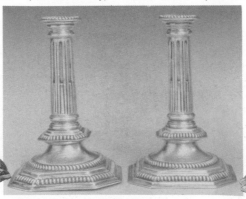

A pair of Victorian table candlesticks, square bases, tapering stems and detachable nozzles, 33cm. high, Walker and Hall, Sheffield 1900, weighted.
(Bearne's) £1,100 $1,815

A pair of Victorian cast candlesticks, the lobed detachable drip trays with flower and leaf panels, London 1872, 10oz. 6dwt.
(Andrew Hartley) £500 $825

A pair of late Edward VII Corinthian column table candlesticks, stepped square bases, 26cm. high, Hawksworth, Eyre and Co., Sheffield 1907, weighted.
(Bearne's) £1,050 $1,680

A pair of Victorian silver table candlesticks, London, 1898, in George II style, each shaped square base fluted at the corners, 7¼in. high.
(Sotheby's) £702 $1,150

A pair of William III candlesticks, the stopped fluted stems with gadrooning to the candleholders and the low drip pans, 8in. possibly Richard Syng, London 1695, 19.5oz.
(Woolley & Wallis) £5,400 $8,694

A pair of Irish table candlesticks, with spirally fluted inverted tapering and knopped stems, by Robert Holmes, Dublin, circa 1755, 42oz., 28cm.
(Tennants) £1,200 $1,920

An Edwardian vase shape sugar caster, the part swirl fluted body with embossed ribbon tied garlands, 8in. high. Maker James Jay, Chester 1902, 6oz.
(Woolley & Wallis)   £230 $368

Four George I silver casters, three with maker's mark of Anthony Nelme, London, two 1726, and one with maker's mark of Gabriel Sleath, 6¼in. high, 29oz.
(Christie's)   £4,600 $7,682

Rooster-form silver spice shaker, probably northern Europe, wings hinged for movement, lid rendered as rooster's head, 7in. high, approximately 11 troy oz.
(Skinner)   £500 $805

A set of three Queen Anne silver casters, John Fawdery I, London, 1712, Britannia standard, baluster with applied girdles and spreading feet, 5¼in. high, 15oz.
(Sotheby's)   £3,450 $5,762

Three George II silver casters, Samuel Wood, London, two 1749 and one 1753, with moulded borders and pierced detachable domed covers, 17cm. high, 17oz.
(Christie's)   £1,322 $2,208

A pair of American silver casters, Dominick & Haff, New York, 1879, realistically formed as seated pugs wearing collars, 5oz. 6dwt., 2¾in. high. (Sotheby's) £2,981 $4,887

CENTREPIECES

A George III silver épergne, James Young and Orlando Jackson, London, 1773, on four scrolled legs with lion's head and paw feet, 114oz., 10dwts., 21in. wide.
(Sotheby's)   £26,306 $43,125

A centrepiece, with two foliate branches springing from a similar stem, by Matthew Boulton, Birmingham, approximately 1828, 105oz, 39cm.
(Tennants)   £3,520 $5,808

The Morse George III six-light candelabrum centrepiece, Paul Storr, London 1813, shaped triangular base on three shell feet, 20¼in. high, 362oz.
(Christie's)   £84,000 $137,760

Silver ecclesiastical chalice, on spreading repoussé foot with foliate edge, knopped stem with central applied foliate band, 9½in., approximately 20 troy oz.
(Skinner)   £714 $1,150

Gold-washed silver ecclesiastical chalice, raised on panelled flared foot with two panels stamped with designs of wheat and grapes, 9in. high, approximately 18 troy oz.
(Skinner)   £500 $805

French silver-gilt chalice, late 19th century, maker's mark *Chevron Frères*, hexafoil base with stamped gothic-style detailing and three painted porcelain plaques, 9⁷/₈in.
(Skinner)   £929 $1,495

CHAMBERSTICKS

A George I silver chamberstick, David Green, London, 1719, the vase-shaped socket with openwork stem, 19.5cm. long, 265gr.
(Christie's)   £1,725 $2,881

A pair of George IV chamber sticks, of circular form, with ivory side handles, and one snuffer, by Samuel Webster II, 1828.
(Tennants)   £1,500 $2,400

A George III chamberstick and snuffer with a shaped circular base, decorated with gadrooning by William Burwash, 1816, 15cm. diameter, 14.5oz.
(Christie's)   £1,035 $1,728

An American silver and enamel chamber candlestick, Gorham Mfg. Co., Providence, RI, 1893, of shaded cloisonné enamel, height to top of snuffer 5in.
(Sotheby's)   £1,929 $3,162

An early Victorian taperstick on a domed and foliate base with a scroll handle, by H. Wilkinson & Co, Sheffield 1838, 9cm. high overall, loaded. (Christie's)   £299 $478

An early Victorian taperstick with a petal shaped foot, embossed foliate motifs and a detachable conical snuffer, by H. Wilkinson & Co, Sheffield 1842, loaded, 10.25cm. high. (Christie's)   £250 $400

A rare early Irish chocolate pot maker's mark *?R* below a fleur-de-lis, Dublin, 1694, the tapered cylindrical body engraved with armorials, 8¾in. high., 28oz 3dwt all in. (Sotheby's) £24,150 $40,330

A late 18th century French Provincial pot of baluster form on three feet with chased shell caps, probably circa 1780, 24.5cm. high, 32oz. (Christie's) £1,495 $2,392

A late Victorian chocolate pot on three curved feet with a large, turned wooden handle and a faceted spout with a drop, by Joshua Vander, 1900, 26.5cm. high, 27.25oz. (Christie's) £977 $1,563

CHRISTENING CUPS

A late 18th century christening cup with a campana shaped bowl and two s-scroll handles, Guernsey, circa 1775, 6.25cm. high, 2.25oz. (Christie's) £862 $1,440

A late 18th century two-handled christening cup with a campana shaped bowl, unascribed, Guernsey, last quarter of the 18th century, 6.25cm. high, 3oz. (Christie's) £1,035 $1,656

A Victorian silver-gilt christening mug, decorated with foliate bands, Charles Fox, Sheffield 1870, 11.5in. high. (Bearne's) £240 $396

CIGARETTE CASES

A Russian metalware oblong cigarette case of plain oblong form decorated on the cover with the portrait of a hound, 1908-17, 11cm. long. (Christie's) £207 $331

A parcel-gilt silver cigarette case, Tiffany & Co., New York, 1878–1891, in the Japanese taste, shaped rectangular, the surface spot-hammered, 5¼in. long. 6oz. 10dwt. (Christie's) £1,794 $2,990

Russian cloisonné enamel cigarette box, late 19th century, the enamelling of foliage, birds and butterflies on gold-washed stippled ground, 4 x 3in., approximately 5 troy oz. (Skinner) £786 $1,265

Tiffany & Co. silver and cut glass claret jug, late 19th/early 20th century, tall glass body with flared base cut with diagonal ribbing, approximately 10¾in. high.
(Skinner)   £322 $518

A Victorian claret jug with beaded and engraved silver mount and ovoid body, W. & C. Sissons, Sheffield 1870, 18cm. high.
(Christie's)   £1,265 $2,024

A late Victorian parcel-gilt mounted cut-glass claret jug, the mount with a domed cover, ornate scroll handle and a bearded mask spout, Charles Edwards, 1882, 30.25cm. high.
(Christie's)   £1,610 $2,689

A Victorian vase-shaped hot water or claret jug, decorated in the Neo-Classical manner with engraving, bead borders and chased stiff leaves, R. Martin & E.Hall 1876, 32cm. high, 28oz.
(Christie's)   £1,035 $1,656

A pair of modern mounted cut-glass claret jugs with angular handles and oviform bodies, by Hukin & Hukin, Birmingham 1913, 19.5cm. high.
(Christie's)   £1,150 $1,840

A silver-mounted cut-glass exposition claret jug, Tiffany & Co., New York, 1893, for the World's Columbian Exposition, 1893, baluster, on a circular base, 13¼in. high. (Christie's) £9,660 $16,100

A William IV silver-gilt mounted faceted glass claret jug, Robert Garrard, London 1835, with decanter label pierced for *Madeira*, Charles Rawlins & William Summers, London 1835.
(Bearne's)   £2,800 $4,620

A pair of Victorian silver-mounted crystal claret jugs, Charles Edwards, London 1887, chased with stylised foliage on a matted ground, 13¼in. high.
(Christie's)   £10,580 $17,351

A Victorian glass claret jug, the ovoid body with cut decoration of a trellis of stars and hatched work on the foliage fruiting neck, 10½in. W & C Sissons, Sheffield 1889.
(Woolley & Wallis) £1,250 $2,000

A Tiffany silver-coloured metal bottle stand, monogrammed above a frieze of putti amongst fruiting vines on four vine pattern supports, 19.5cm. diameter.
(Bearne's)   £200 $330

A pair of George III coasters, of cylindrical form, with slightly flared rims and reeded lower edge, with turned wooden centres, 1797, 14cm.
(Tennants)   £1,250 $2,000

A pair of large diameter Low Countries wine coasters with reeded borders and arcaded lattice-work sides, probably Dutch/Belgian, first half 19th century, 15.5cm. diameter. (Christie's) £575 $840

A pair of William IV wine coasters with everting, fruiting vine borders and turned wooden bases, H. Wilkinson & Co, Sheffield, 1835, 19cm. diameter.
(Christie's)   £1,955 $3,128

A set of four George III silver coasters, Robert Hennell, London, 1792, with pierced gallery sides and turned wood base, 4¾in. diameter.
(Christie's)   £5,520 $9,218

A pair of late period Old Sheffield plated wine coasters, with turned wooden bases, plain concave sides and broad overhanging rims of fruiting vines, circa 1840, 23cm. diamater. (Christie's)   £230 $368

A pair of George III wine coasters, with a narrow engraved frieze of trailing foliage, between pricked borders, by George Ashworth, Ellis, Hawksworth & Best, Sheffield, 1811, 13.5cm. diameter.
(Christie's) £1,495 $2,497

A pair of Victorian, electroplated wine coasters with cast openwork fruiting vine sides, by Elkington & Co, 16cm. diameter.
(Christie's)   £575 $840

A pair of early period Old Sheffield plated wine coasters with bead borders, the sides pierced with slots, circa 1785, turned wooden bases, 14cm. diameter.
(Christie's)   £437 $699

A Queen Anne Irish coffee pot, the curved tapering spout issuing from a tear drop moulding, 9¾in. high. David King, Dublin 1704, 28¾in. all in.
(Woolley & Wallis) £12,000 $19,200

A George II silver coffee pot, Edward Feline, London 1727, plain tapering cylindrical and on moulded feet, 7½in. high, 18½oz. gross.
(Christie's)   £2,530 $4,149

A George IV coffee pot in the early George III manner, a domed cover and embossed swirling floral designs and two cartouches, by Charles Fox (II) 1824, 31cm. high, 34oz. (Christie's)   £1,380 $2,208

A George III silver coffee jug, John Scofield, London 1794, the lower part of the body chased with flutes, 11¼in. high, 23oz. gross.
(Christie's)   £2,070 $3,395

A café au lait set in George II style, the tapering bodies with hinged bun covers with urn finials, 9in. high, London 1961, 46oz. (all in)
(Woolley & Wallis)   £660 $1,050

A George III coffee pot of baluster form with partly swirl-fluted decoration, by Francis Crump, 1765, 28.25cm. high, 31oz.
(Christie's)   £1,035 $1,728

A George II small coffee pot of tapering form with a tucked-in base, a domed cover and knop finial, by Richard Bayley, 1745, 21cm. high, 18oz. (Christie's)   £1,840 $2,944

A modern coffee pot with a hexagonal baluster body and pedestal foot, Birmingham 1915, 34oz. (Christie's) £230 $384

A late George II coffee pot of baluster form with a spreading circular base, by Thomas Whipham, 1756, 25cm. high, 27.25oz.
(Christie's)   £1,955 $3,265

A George II coffeepot of tapering cylindrical form with engraved decoration, 25cm. high, Elizabeth Godfrey, London 1743, 32.6oz.
(Bearne's)   £750 $1,238

A late George II coffee pot, the baluster shape body engraved with a contemporary armorial, 9¼in. high, John Swift, London 1756, 20.5oz.
(Woolley & Wallis) £1,250 $2,012

American repoussé silver coffee pot, A.E. Warner, chased floral pattern, goat head finial on handle, 9in. high, approximately 23 troy oz.
(Skinner)   £448 $747

TOP TIP

Collectors can often be very reticent about how much they paid for something. On the other hand, they certainly don't want their children or beneficiaries sending their prize possessions off to the charity shop after their demise just because they don't know any better.

It's a good idea, therefore, to keep receipts, photographs and even catalogues in a safe place where they may easily be found.

Ewbank

A George III coffee jug of semi-reeded form with gadroon and scroll edging, on four paw feet, 19cm. high, maker's mark *J. A.* London 1814, 24.7oz.
(Bearne's)   £240 $384

A George II coffee pot of slightly tapering form embossed and chased with flowers, scrolls and dolphins, Newcastle 1750, 31oz. all in, by Isaac Cookson.
(Russell, Baldwin & Bright)   £1,000 $1,660

A George III silver coffee pot, Crispin Fuller, London 1801, the body bright-cut engraved with flowers, foliage, swags and scrolls, 11in. high, 25oz. gross.
(Christie's)   £1,380 $2,263

A Victorian coffee pot of pear shape, floral and scroll embossed and chased with vacant cartouches, Edinburgh, 1853, 28oz.
(Russell Baldwin & Bright)   £640 $1,056

A George II silver coffee pot, Thomas Mason, London, 1737, the tapering cylindrical body engraved with a rampant lion, 23oz. gross, 9¼in. high.
(Sotheby's)   £2,280 $3,737

A George III oviform coffee pot with a detachable cover and urn finial, by William Frisbee, 1801, 23cm. high, 24oz. (Christie's) £575 $877

A George II coffee pot of plain tapering cylindrical form, engraved with armorials, John Webb, Exeter 1724, 25cm. high, 26.5oz. (Bearne's) £3,700 $5,920

A Wiiliam IV coffee pot, of tapered form, with domed cover, the spout and handle with scrolled leafy mounts, by Michael Starkey, 1830, 26oz. (Tennants) £500 $800

A silver coffee biggin with stand and burner, Gorham Mfg. Co., Providence, 1871, the pot pear-shaped, the lower body engraved with Greek key, 16¼in. high, gross weight 64oz. 10dwt. (Christie's) £1,932 $3,220

A modern coffee pot of tapering circular form with a cushion domed cover, together with a matching hot water jug, by Toye, Kenning & Spencer, Birmingham 1973, 23.5cm. high, 47oz. (Christie's) £747 $1,203

A George III silver coffee pot, London, 1764, maker's mark *WC*, probably that of William Chawner, baluster form, on a spreading circular foot chased with a gadrooned band, 12in. high, gross weight 30oz. 10dwt. (Christie's) £1,869 $2,990

Fessenden coin silver coffee pot, Boston, mid-20th century, baluster-form fruit finial, beaded borders, engraved scroll and leaf cartouches, pot 9⁷/₈in. high., approximately 21 troy oz. (Skinner) £276 $460

Edward VII silver coffee server, London, 1910–11, SG maker, flared cylindrical form, lined, ivory finial and handle, 8in. high, approximately 48 troy oz. (Skinner) £517 $862

Fine William IV silver coffee pot, well chased and embossed with floral and foliate designs, 9½in. tall, London 1834 by Rebecca Emes and Edward Barnard, 30oz. (Aylsham) £360 $598

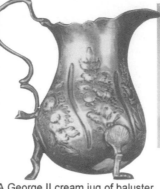

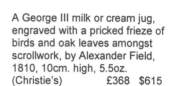

A Victorian Irish cream/milk jug on four cast mask and leaf feet, Jas. Le Bas, Dublin 1868, 12.5cm. high, 14oz. (Christie's)   £517 $827

A George II cream jug of baluster form on three feet, embossed with wrythen fluting and flowers, 1757, 9.75cm. high, 3oz. (Christie's)   £149 $249

A George III milk or cream jug, engraved with a pricked frieze of birds and oak leaves amongst scrollwork, by Alexander Field, 1810, 10cm. high, 5.5oz. (Christie's)   £368 $615

A George II silver-gilt cast cream jug, the oviform body on three anthemion mask feet with a dolphin scroll handle and waisted neck, possibly by Benjamin West, 1737, 12.5cm. high, 7oz. (Christie's)   £1,150 $1,840

A George II cow creamer, the hinged cover chased with a border of flowers and applied with a fly, by John Schuppe, 1757, 14.5cm. long, 5oz. (Christie's)   £5,980 $9,987

A George II sparrow beak cream jug of baluster form with a scroll handle and reeded circular, spreading foot, by Benjamin Cartwright (I) 1742, 8.75cm. high, 2oz. (Christie's)   £747 $1,247

A George III cream jug, with a punch beaded rim and chased flowers and c-scrolls on a matt ground, by Thomas Shepard, 1771, 11cm. high, 2oz. (Christie's)   £207 $346

Krider repoussé sterling Aesthetic design creamer, Peter L. Krider Co., Philadelphia, 1850–60, chased floral decoration, 6³/₈in. high, approx. 13 troy oz. (Skinner)   £359 $575

A George III cream jug of circular outline with an engraved, squat baluster body, initialled, 1802, 11cm. high, 3.5oz. (Christie's)   £368 $615

Late Victorian oval plated cruet with pierced decoration, wave formed gadrooned top border, raised on claw and ball feet.
(G.A. Key)   £85 $141

A rare Queen Anne cruet frame with a tapering stem, ring handle and circular guard rings, by Thomas Fockingham, 1708, 23cm. high, 24oz. (Christie's) £575 $840

An Old Sheffield plated cruet frame, fitted with six cut-glass stoppered bottles, a mounted cut-glass caster and a mustard pot with a Victorian silver spoon, 21cm. high, circa 1840. (Christie's)   £345 $552

A George III silver egg cruet, Henry Chawner, London 1792, the shaped square form on four stud feet, 7½in. high, 15oz.
(Christie's)   £2,070 $3,395

A pair of Victorian breakfast cruet sets of quatrefoil outline with embossed decoration to simulate wickerwork, by Robert Hennell 1858, 13.5cm. long, 13oz. weighable silver.
(Christie's)   £1,265 $2,024

A Victorian cruet stand comprising six glass cruets on oblong stand with reeded loop handle, 7in. wide, London 1880, 17oz. 5dwt.
(Andrew Hartley)   £600 $1,008

A Victorian large silver cruet frame, Edward I, Edward II, James & William Barnard, London 1838, the frame on four eagle's mask, acanthus and claw-and-ball feet, 15¼in. high, 110oz.
(Christie's)   £37,800 $61,992

A late Victorian cruet frame in the George IV style fitted with three mounted and three stoppered cut-glass bottles, and a matching spoon, by Atkin Bros, Sheffield 1900, 18cm. high overall, 24oz weighable silver.
(Christie's)   £862 $1,379

An American silver cruet stand, Gorham Mfg. Co., Providence, RI, circa 1870, the rim applied with four triangular panels with male and female heads and garlands, 38oz. without bottles, 13½in. high.
(Sotheby's)   £1,754 $2,875

Chinese silver handled cup, circa 1840, raised figural and dragon motif, dragon handle, marked *Onnsing* on base, 5in. high, 11.8 troy oz. (Eldred's) £894 $1,430

A George III two-handled campana shaped cup, with reeded girdle and scroll handles, John Payne, London 1762, 13cm. high, 11.4oz. (Bearne's) £260 $429

A George II two handled cup, with moulded lipped rim, 4¾in. high, Newcastle 1757, maker's mark for John Langlands I, 7oz. 18dwt. (Andrew Hartley) £240 $403

A Queen Anne two-handled cup and cover, engraved with crest above reeded girdle 21.5cm. high, Pentecost Symonds, Exeter 1708, 770gm., 24.7oz. (Bearne's) £1,200 $1,980

A silver presentation loving cup, Whiting Mfg. Co., New York, circa 1894, flaring baluster on a circular base applied with a band of seashells and kelp at intervals, 10½in. high, 84oz.10dwt. (Christie's) £2,898 $4,830

A silver-mounted cut-glass loving cup, Tiffany & Co., New York, circa 1890, the cut-glass body with S-scrolls and flower sprays at intervals, 9in. high. (Christie's) £2,208 $3,680

An American silver three-handled cup, Dominick & Haff, New York, 1901, of campana form with a girdle of scrolling flowers, 90oz., 10dwt., 11¼in. high. (Sotheby's) £2,280 $3,737

An American silver three-handled loving cup, Gorham Mfg. Co., Providence, RI, 1908, Martelé, .9584 standard, vase-shaped, 79oz., 15 dwt., 11¼in. high. (Sotheby's) £7,015 $11,500

Two-handled Sterling trophy cup, Black Starr & Frost, engraved to one side *1937 Washington Handicap...*, 11½in. high, approximately 50 troy oz. (Skinner) £429 $690

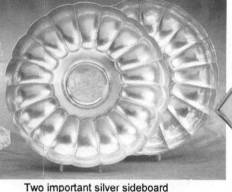

A pair of early 19th century Old Sheffield plated soufflé dishes, of circular form, with foliate loop handles, 9¼in. wide.
(Andrew Hartley) £300 $495

Georg Jensen silver dish with serving spoon, 1933–44, lightly hammered finish, *Dessin* over *JR*, 4in. high. (Skinner) £448 $748

Pair of George III silver covered entrée dishes, 1798–99, John Schofield maker, cut-corners shaped rectangular form, gadrooned border on dish, 10¼in. long. approximately 99 troy oz. (Skinner) £3,450 $5,750

A pair of Victorian shaped circular entrée dishes and covers with highly chased shell and acanthus edging, 33cm. diameter, E.E. J & W Barnard, London 1843, 113.6oz. (Bearne's) £1,500 $2,475

Two important silver sideboard dishes one probably Francis Garthorne, 1691, the other maker's mark *H.?* date letter overstruck by Garthorne, circa 1675, both London, 17in. diameter, 116oz 17dwt.(Sotheby's) £56,500 $94,355

A pair of English silver shell-form dishes, bearing marks for John Crouch I and Thomas Hannam, London, 1804, 7oz., 4in. long. (Sotheby's) £351 $575

A James I silver dish, London, 1607, maker's mark a trefoil slipped, in shaped cartouche, the dish pierced and engraved with strapwork, scrolls and oval lobes, ·9½in. diameter, 11oz.
(Christie's) £20,700 $34,569

An American silver covered casserole dish on lampstand, New York, circa 1845, bombé circular chased with rococo ornament, by Tiffany & Co., circa 1870, 80oz., length over handles 13in.
(Sotheby's) £1,403 $2,300

An American Exhibition silver and other metals sideboard dish, Tiffany & Co., New York, circa 1876, engraved and etched the head and shoulders of a pensive 16th century woman, 136oz., 8dwt. gross, 20in. diameter.
(Sotheby's) £45,140 $74,000

A Victorian silver-gilt mounted cut-glass travelling dressing table set, Frances Douglas, London 1863, in a brass bound amboyna case. (Bearne's)   £2,400 $3,960

A modern travelling dressing case in cream simulated hide, containing four brushes, comb, hand mirror, three toilet water bottles, and four boxes, by Goldsmiths & Silversmiths Co 1948-52, 6oz weighable silver. (Christie's)   £690 $1,104

A modern ladies crocodile skin dressing case, containing rose coloured 9ct., gold items, maker's mark *HW, 1923*, retailed by Asprey & Co. 12.5 oz. approx. weighable silver. (Christie's) £1,265 $2,024

EWERS

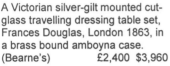

A Victorian ewer, the girdled body chased with bands of vitruvian scrolls, 10¼in. high, mark for John James Keith, London 1844, 16oz. 14dwt. (Andrew Hartley) £270 $454

A German silver ewer and basin, Friedrich Ernst Dassdorf, Augsburg, 1808, the partly-fluted vase-shaped ewer on a spreading circular foot, the ewer 10¾in. high, gross 31oz. (Christie's)   £1,610 $2,689

A 19th century Portuguese white metal wine ewer of inverted baluster form with foliate spout, flying scroll handle, 11in. high, 1219gm. (Andrew Hartley)   £600 $1,008

A William IV silver ewer, Paul Storr, London 1836, of ascos form, the matted body applied with two scrolls and fruiting vine scroll handle, 8¾in. high, 32oz. (Christie's)   £16,100 $26,404

A Victorian ewer, decorated with a row of beads, the angular handle terminating in a female mask, crested, by Frederick Elkington, 1873, 19.5cm. high, 27oz. (Christie's)   £1,725 $2,881

A Victorian claret ewer, in the manner of Dr Christopher Dresser, the glass of angled bellied shape with star cut base, by E. Hutton, 1884, 24cm. to thumbpiece. (Tennants)   £760 $1,216

An early 18th century Provincial trefid spoon, the stem pricked with initials *E.S/T.S.* and dated *1724*, George Trowbridge, Exeter 1711. (Bearne's)   £300 $495

An early 18th century Provincial trefid spoon, Henry Muston, Exeter, 1710, with traces of later gilding. (Bearne's)   £300 $495

An apostle spoon with gilt St. Jude terminal, Exeter, circa 1660.
(Woolley & Wallis)   £1,000 $1,610

Possibly Peter Elliot of Dartmouth, Exeter 1714, a dog nose spoon, with rat tail bowl.
(Woolley & Wallis)   £340 $547

Set of Durgin gold washed sterling flatware, Empire pattern, engraved monogram, approx. 79 troy oz. weighable silver. (Skinner)   £503 $805

Gorham sterling flatware service in chest on stand, Versailles pattern, approx. 457 troy oz. weighable silver, chest 21½in. wide. (Skinner)   £5,750 $9,200

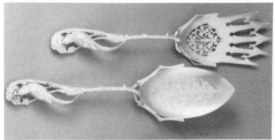

A pair of American silver servers, Whiting Mfg. Co., New York, circa 1875–1880, a fork with a gilt openwork tines, the spoon with gilt bowl and chased foliate centre, 7oz., 10in. long.
(Sotheby's)   £2,105 $3,450

A William & Mary engraved trefid spoon with a shaped and cleft terminal and a ribbed rat-tail, flanked by an engraved leaf motif, probably by Thomas Issod, 1689, 20cm. long.1oz. (Christie's)   £632 $1,055

Possibly Thomas Mansell of Guernsey, circa 1700, a trefid spoon with beaded rat tail bowl.
(Woolley & Wallis)   £1,350 $2,174

Gorham enamel, Sterling, and gold washed ice cream slicer, late 19th century, champlevé blue, yellow, and brown stylised floral pattern handle, engraved Aesthetic design on blade, inscription on reverse, 12⅝in. long, approximately 5 troy oz.
(Skinner)   £828 $1,380

Joseph Collier of Plymouth, overstriking another, Exeter 1718, a Hanoverian rat tail basting spoon.
(Woolley & Wallis)   £800 $1,288

Thomas Furlong of Exeter (probably), circa 1700, a trefid spoon. (Woolley & Wallis)   £400 $644

Gorham silver ladle, circa 1855, Saxon stag pattern, gold washed bowl, 12¾in. long, approx. 6 troy oz. (Skinner) £1,078 $1,725

Ball, Black & Co. sterling fruit ladle, 1860s, caryatid finial, gold washed scalloped and pierced bowl, 8¾in. long, approx. 4 troy oz. (Skinner) £683 $1,093

Stieff flatware service, late 19th/early 20th century, in a floral repoussé pattern, monogrammed to back, with storage box, 59 pieces approximately 67 troy oz. weighable silver. (Skinner) £714 $1,150

Hester Bateman silver spoon, London, 1785, round end back-tipped pattern, engraved monogram, approximately 1 troy oz. (Skinner) £190 $316

A Queen Anne silver basting spoon William Mathew I, London, 1704, Britannia standard, with oval bowl, engraved with a bird holding horseshoe crest, 16in. long, 5oz 13dwt. (Sotheby's) £8,625 $14,404

Dominick & Haff sterling soup ladle, no. 10 pattern, a chrysanthemum design, engraved name, 11⁷/₈in. long, approx. 6 troy oz. (Skinner) £108 $173

A 17th century lion sejant affronté spoon, John Quick, Barnstaple, circa 1620, pricked on the bowl reverse *AR MT 1664*, 6¾in., 1oz 3dwt. (Sotheby's) £3,220 $5,380

A Provincial silver child's trefid spoon, William Webb, Winchester, circa 1680, inscribed *ES/AH/1691*, 5in. long, 10dwt. (Sotheby's) £1,035 $1,728

Whiting serving spoon, possibly for oysters, carved ivory handle dyed ochre, gold-washed oval-form bowl with design of scrolling kelp and pierced edge, 9¹/₈in. long. (Skinner) £357 $575

An Edward VII fiddle pattern part table service, comprising: nine tablespoons, five dessert spoons, ten table forks, and eight dessert forks, James William Benson, London 1905/6/7, together with two matching tablespoons and two teaspoons, 67.5oz. (Bearne's) £520 $832

George III silver fish slice, fiddle pattern with star and stylised foliate pierced blade, London, 1818, by Godbehere and Bult. (G.A. Key) £170 $272

Ball, Black & Co., sterling punch ladle, 1860s, caryatid finial on spiral handle, gold washed bowl, monogram, 14⁵/₈in. long., approx. 6 troy oz. (Skinner) £396 $633

American silver serving spoon, possibly Gorham, circa 1865, squirrel finial, cylindrical handle, gold washed bowl, 11³/₈in. long, approx. 4 troy oz. (Skinner) £467 $748

Tiffany sterling stuffing spoon, chrysanthemum pattern, monogram and date, 1893, 12³/₈in. long, approx. 8 troy oz. (Skinner) £395 $633

English mother-of-pearl handled fruit set, Sheffield, 1927, with twelve forks and knives, in velvet fitted wooden box, three-tined forks 5³/₈in. long, knives 6³/₈in. long. (Skinner) £393 $633

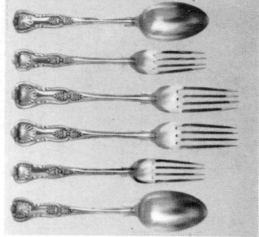

An Edward VII Kings pattern part table service, comprising: six table forks, six dessert forks and six dessert spoons, Jackson and Fullerton, London 1905/6, 46.0oz. (Bearne's) £380 $608

A Dutch silver-gilt spoon, maker's mark three pellets, Hoorn, date letter M probably for 1675, the stem notched and with engraved foliage below bird finial, length 7½in., 45gr. (Sotheby's) £805 $1,344

Gorham Sterling ice spoon, 1869, pierced and gold washed bowl, with three dimensional polar bear, crossed harpoons handle, 11¹/₈in. long, approximately 3 troy oz. (Skinner) £2,587 $4,312

Gorham Sterling punch ladle, old Baronial pattern, wide bowl with tripartite shaping, marked with patent year 1898, monogrammed, approximately 12in. long, 8 troy oz. (Skinner) £179 $288

A James I seal top spoon, maker's mark a crescent enclosing a mullet, London, 1617, the gilt lobed and foliate seal with plain nimbus, 6½in. long, 1oz 8dwt. (Sotheby's) £1,150 $1,920

A pair of George III goblets with beaded pedestals and vase-shaped bowls, crested, probably by John Carter, (II) 1775, 15.5cm. high, 17oz. (Christie's) £1,840 $3,073

A moulded coconut goblet with a polished bowl, three strapwork mounts and a pedestal circular foot, probably late 18th century, possibly colonial, 10.25cm. high. (Christie's) £575 $960

A pair of George III silver wine goblets, John Scofield, London 1794, engraved overall with horizontal lines and stylised borders, 6¾in. high, 17oz. (Christie's) £1,380 $2,263

INKSTANDS

An Old Sheffield plated ink stand with cut glass oval bottle, on serpentine oval galleried base with gadrooned rim, 6¼in. wide. (Andrew Hartley) £80 $132

A fine Victorian silver gilt circular inkstand, the glass well with foliage engraved pendants and hatched panels, 10in. diameter. Maker Samuel Whitford, London 1855, 18oz. (Woolley & Wallis) £1,150 $1,840

A Victorian ink well of circular form, the hinged lid revealing glass liner, the body with embossed strap work on flared and reeded base, 4in. wide. London 1894. (Andrew Hartley) £170 $280

A George III silver-gilt inkstand, William Pitts and Joseph Preedy, London 1794, the base with gallery rim, fitted with three bottle holders, 14½in. long, 102oz. (Christie's) £13,800 $22,632

Early 20th century silver inkstand, square shaped with gadrooned edge, the central fixed silver ink well with plain hinged lid, Birmingham 1920, 14oz. free. (Aylsham) £210 $349

An Edwardian inkstand of shaped oblong form with a moulded border and pad feet, by Charles Stuart Harris, 1901, 28 cm. long, 32oz. weighable silver. (Christie's) £1,265 $2,024

Liberty & Co., silver hot water jug of tapering cylindrical baluster form to a spreading flat circular foot, 7½in. high, Birmingham 1911, 13½ oz. all in. (G.A. Key)   £280 $448

A George III hot milk jug of bellied form with a reeded girdle, by Solomon Hougham, 1809, 10.5cm. high, 6.75oz. (Christie's)   £230 $384

A George III baluster hot water jug with lignum vitae scroll handle, Newcastle 1769, 29oz, maker John Langlands. (Dee Atkinson & Harrison)   £2,000 $3,300

TRICKS OF THE TRADE

There are few more disheartening sights than an attractive but perhaps not very valuable piece of silver plate where the plate is badly worn. Is it worth going to the expense of having it replated?

If in doubt, temporary results can be achieved by careful use of this method. Place the item in your almost exhausted silver dip. The silver nitrate in the dip will plate on to the exposed metal - but the process must be carefully watched.

Whitworths

A pair of William IV hot water jugs or ewers, the lower bodies embossed with a calyx of stiff leaves, by Messrs Barnard, 1834, 30.5cm. high, 63.5oz. (Christie's)   £2,875 $4,810

Victorian wine jug with beaded borders, the ovoid body with a band of reeding above scrolling foliage ands two cartouches, London 1865, 12in. high, 17½oz. (Ewbank)   £620 $1,029

A late George III oval helmet shape milk jug, the ogee body with shield cartouches, Robert Jones, London 1798, 4.5oz. (Woolley & Wallis)   £230 $370

A George III hot water jug of compressed circular form with a helmet shaped rim and an ivory scroll handle, Benjamin (II) and James Smith (III), 1808, 23oz. (Christie's)   £667 $1,067

A George III argyle, cylindrical with a water jacket, a long slender spout and a cane insulated scroll handle, I.N, 1771, 12cm. high, 11oz. (Christie's)   £1,667 $2,784

A Victorian model of an open parasol, with turned handle, 4in. long, Sheffield 1899.
(Andrew Hartley)   £130 $218

A George III cream pail, with reeded bands and a flared lip, Thomas Daniel & John Wall, London 1781, 3oz.
(Woolley & Wallis)   £660 $1,062

An electro-plated cocktail shaker in the form of a bell, by Asprey & Co., 28.5cm. high, and another very similar plated example by Hukin & Heath. (Christie's)   £345 $552

Austrian owl-form cookie jar, 20th century, silver plated head and collar, glass eyes, clear glass jar, 9⁷/₈in. (Skinner)   £655 $1,092

A small gilt-silver crouching bear, Han dynasty, the animal cast hunched and supported on its forelegs, 2³/₈in. high.
(Christie's)   £11,500 $18,745

A Victorian silver mounted cut-glass biscuitière, with swing handle and detachable cover with turned finial, 18.5cm. high, James Deakin and Sons, Sheffield 1898.
(Bearne's)   £220 $363

A George II brandy saucepan of baluster form with a turned wooden handle, by Thornas Cooke II & Richard Gurney, 1751, 13cm. diameter, 14.5oz.
(Christie's)   £1,322 $2,115

A late 19th century Elkington electrotype circular wall plaque decorated in high relief with classical female figures.
(Bearne's)   £360 $576

A Hukin & Heath electroplated letter rack, designed by Dr Christopher Dresser, arched quarter-circular form on bun feet, 13cm. high.
(Christie's)   £575 $862

A George III silver cased corkscrew by Samuel Pemberton.
(Russell, Baldwin & Bright)
£540 $896

A set of thirty six gaming tokens commemorating the coronation of Charles I and his marriage to Henrietta Maria, 1in. wide.
(Andrew Hartley)   £800 $1,344

An American silver dinner bell, Tiffany & Co., New York, 1851–1869, the bell with a die-rolled band of moresque ornament around the bottom, 10oz., 6½in. high.
(Sotheby's)   £1,403 $2,300

A George III Old English pattern silver gilt dessert service George Smith & William Fearn, London, 1790, the grape scissors Eley & Fearn, London, 1814, 63 pieces.
(Sotheby's)   £9,200 $15,364

A Victorian model of a dancing girl, her arms raised, on circular base decorated with floral garlands, 37cm. high, makers mark S.S. London 1873, 41oz.
(Bearne's)   £1,350 $2,228

A silver koro, late 19th/early 20th century, in the form of two quails, the feathers finely detailed, 5½in. high. (Christie's)   £4,600 $7,498

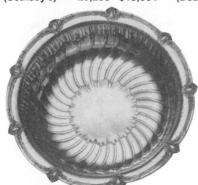

A French silver large basin, D. Roussel, late 19th/early 20th century, the swirled, lobed body centred by gadrooned borders, 64oz., 17½in. long.
(Sotheby's)   £1,333 $2,185

A Russian silver gilt and green onyx photo frame, the central blue enamelled panel applied with marcasite and gem stones, 5¾ x 3½in. in original case.
(Andrew Hartley)   £2,600 $4,368

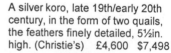

An Elkington & Co replica 'Ladies Wimbledon Trophy', the copper electro-type relief with central boss of Temperance, 47.5cm. diameter.
(Bristol)   £310 $511

A good George II mug of baluster form with a scroll handle and spreading foot, crested by Ayme Videau, 1734, 11.75cm. high, 13oz.
(Christie's)   £1,610 $2,689

A Queen Anne mug of tapering form with an S-scroll handle and a skirted base, by Robert Cooper, 1711, 10¾in. high, 10oz.
(Christie's)   £862 $1,379

American silver mug, marked for Tiffany, Young & Ellis, with chased floral and acanthus decoration, mid-19th century, 4½in. high., 5 troy oz.
(Eldred's)   £300 $495

A George II silver mug, Gurney & Cook, London, 1748, baluster body engraved with armorials, 4¾in. high, 13oz 16dwt.
(Sotheby's)   £1,092 $1,824

A mid 18th century mounted serpentine mug, the upper and lower mount engraved with stiff leaf borders, probably German, circa 1730, 11.5cm. high.
(Christie's)   £1,840 $2,944

William Parry of Plymouth, Exeter 1750, a baluster mug, gilt lined, engraved with a crest, 10.5oz.
(Woolley & Wallis) £1,350 $2,174

A Queen Anne silver mug, John Elston, Exeter, 1704, Britannia Standard, the lower part of the body chased with flutes, 4¼in. high, 7oz.
(Christie's)   £2,530 $4,225

A Victorian mug of cylindrical form with leaf capped scroll handle and engraved floral decoration, 12cm. high, Robert Hennell, London 1872, 12.9oz. (Bearne's) £220 $352

A George III mug of baluster form with a leaf capped scroll handle and spreading foot, by an unascribed pair of makers, W.F. I.K., (incuse) 1767, 12.5cm. high, 11.5oz.
(Christie's)   £747 $1,247

Fine George IV silver mustard pot, well engraved with floral and foliate designs, plus replacement blue glass liner and silver spoon, London, 1822, probably by Edward Farrell, 2in. high, 3in. diameter. (G.A. Key) £240 $384

A rare, George II mustard pot of plain drum form with a flat cover, by Edward Wakelin, 1759, (blue glass liner), 7cm. high, 5oz. weighable silver. (Christie's) £1,552 $2,592

An early Victorian pierced drum mustard pot with a blue glass liner, by Messrs. Barnard, 1837, 8cm. high, 5oz. weighable silver, (Christie's) £402 $643

18th century Irish silver mustard pot in Adam style on circular beaded base, bright cut strapwork curved handle plus blue glass liner, 4½in. high, Dublin, circa 1780, by J Keating. (G.A. Key) £430 $688

An early Victorian drum mustard pot with an openwork thumbpiece and sides, crested by Charles Fox, 1836, 7cm. high. (Christie's) £275 $440

An early 19th century Dutch mustard pot of navette form with pierced sides, by Hendrick Smits, Amsterdam 1801, 8.25cm. high, 3oz weighable silver. (Christie's) £437 $699

Victorian silver mustard pot of cylindrical design with wavy spreading base, trellis pierced sides, pierced thumbpiece plus blue glass liner, 2¾in. high, London, 1855. (G.A. Key) £200 $320

A Victorian barrel shaped mustard pot with a scroll handle, by Charles Thomas and George Fox, 1858, green glass liner, 7.5cm. high. (Christie's) £300 $480

A Victorian engraved mustard pot with an octagonal body and tapering tented cover, by C. Reily and G. Storer, 1844. (Christie's) £220 $352

Gorham silver medallion water pitcher, 1886, baluster form, three-dimensional stag heads on either side of body, 7¾in., approximately 21 troy oz. (Skinner) £1,720 $2,875

A silver and mixed-metal pitcher, Tiffany & Co., New York, circa 1880, the spot-hammered surface applied with butterflies amid branches, 8in. high, gross weight 30oz. (Christie's) £15,180 $25,300

An American silver large water pitcher, R & W. Wilson, Philadelphia, circa 1840, modelled as a tree trunk, applied with grapevine, 68oz., 14in high. (Sotheby's) £3,508 $5,750

A silver Aesthetic Movement pitcher, Tiffany & Co., New York, circa 1880, the surface repoussé with flowers and leaves against a punched ground, 7¼in. high, 22oz.10dwt.
(Christie's) £2,208 $3,680

A silver Arts and Crafts pitcher, Shreve & Co., San Francisco, circa 1905, the body spot-hammered with angular wooden handle, riveted at joins, 6in. high. gross weight 25oz.
(Christie's) £1,173 $1,955

Verrerie de Sèvres etched, enamelled, and silver mounted pitcher, colourless bottle etched overall and with coloured violet blossoms, 9in. high.
(Skinner) £379 $632

A silver Rococo Revival pitcher, Gorham Mfg. Co., Providence, circa 1855, the body, handle and spout chased and repoussé with lotus plants against a punched ground, 10in. high, 36oz. 10dwt.
(Christie's) £1,656 $2,760

Gorham & Co. pitcher, third quarter 19th century, the handle accented with fruiting vines and topped by a finely modelled putto with a cup in his outstretched hand, 11⅝in., approximately 29 troy oz.
(Skinner) £1,143 $1,840

A silver chrysanthemum pitcher, Tiffany & Co., NY, 1902–1907, globular with reeding and raised on four square feet with chrysanthemum joins, 9in. high, 42oz. 10dwt.
(Christie's) £3,450 $5,750

Reed & Barton repoussé Sterling water pitcher, early 20th century, baluster form, chased floral decoration, 9in. high, approximately 20 troy oz. (Skinner) £759 $1,265

Sterling silver water pitcher, by Gorham, hand-hammered finish with chased leaf and butterfly decoration, 8½in. high. (Eldred's) £825 $1,320

Coin silver water pitcher, Fletcher & Gardiner, Philadelphia, 1811–25, baluster form with applied foliate banding, 9¼in. high. 32 troy oz. (Skinner) £934 $1,495

Redlich & Co. Sterling repoussé pitcher, 20th century, baluster form on tapered foot with ruffled edge, ruffled edge spout, monogrammed, 9¼in. high, approximately 36 troy oz. (Skinner) £1,429 $2,300

A silver and mixed metal japanesque pitcher, Whiting Mfg. Co., New York, circa 1882, spot-hammered body with a frog and insects with copper bodies amid lotus flowers, 9in. high. gross weight 30oz. 10dwt. (Christie's) £10,350 $17,250

A silver repoussé pitcher, Samuel Kirk & Son Co., Baltimore, circa 1903–1907, the body, neck and handle overall chased and repoussé with flowers and leaves, 7in. high, 18oz. (Christie's) £759 $1,265

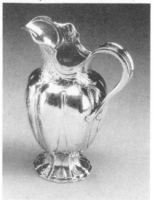

Jarvie sterling water pitcher, hand raised hammer textured baluster form, engraved monogram, 8³/₁₆in. high., approx. 29 troy oz. (Skinner) £647 $1,035

A silver classical pitcher, Hugh Wishart, New York, circa 1815, the sides engraved with cartouches within foliage, 10¼in. high. 33oz. (Christie's) £3,795 $6,325

A silver Art Nouveau pitcher, Gorham Mfg. Co., Providence, 1897, martelé, baluster with undulating circular base, 11¾in. high, 52oz. 10dwt. (Christie's) £9,660 $16,100

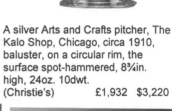

Frank Smith Sterling water pitcher, retailed by Bailey, Banks, and Biddle Co., panelled baluster-form, chased decoration, monogram, 10in. high, approximately 35 troy oz. (Skinner)   £1,587 $2,645

A silver Rococo Revival pitcher, John C. Moore Co., circa 1850, the body repoussé and chased with swans amid cattails and lilies, 9¾in. high., 26oz. (Christie's)   £2,622 $4,370

A silver Arts and Crafts pitcher, The Kalo Shop, Chicago, circa 1910, baluster, on a circular rim, the surface spot-hammered, 8¾in. high, 24oz. 10dwt. (Christie's)   £1,932 $3,220

A silver Rococo Revival presentation pitcher of Southern interest, Gale & Hughes, New York, 1849, the body with repoussé rococo and C-scroll cartouches, 11in. high., 26oz. 10dwt. (Christie's)   £1,035 $1,725

A silver and mixed-metal pitcher, Whiting Mfg. Co., New York, circa 1880, the spot-hammered surface applied on one side with copper carp and diving kingfisher, 7¾in. high, gross weight 29oz.10dwt. (Christie's)   £11,040 $18,400

Reed & Barton Sterling water pitcher, early 20th century, panelled baluster form, applied and engraved Colonial Revival design, 10³/₈in., approximately 34 troy oz. (Skinner)   £577 $862

A silver classical pitcher, probably Boston, circa 1815, vase form, with gadrooned footrim and rim, engraved eagle crest, 9in. high. 29oz. 10dwt. (Christie's)   £1,518 $2,530

A silver Arts and Crafts pitcher, Kalo Shops, Park Ridge, Illinois, circa 1910, vase form, the circular body faceted with angular handle, 9in. high, 28oz. (Christie's)   £2,622 $4,370

A silver Arts and Crafts pitcher, Gorham Mfg. Co., Providence, circa 1907, the rim with applied grapevine border, with handle formed as grapevine, 9¼in. high. 39oz. (Christie's)   £2,415 $4,025

An unusual pail-form silver pitcher, Barbour Silver Co. for International Silver Co., Connecticut, circa 1905, pail-form, with repoussé grapevine cartouche, 10½in. high, 20oz. 10dwt. (Christie's)　£1,518　$2,530

A silver Art Nouveau pitcher, Tiffany & Co., New York, 1891–1902, the body etched with palm leaves, the curved handle acanthus-capped, 6½in. 16oz. (Christie's)　£1,104　$1,840

A silver Rococo Revival pitcher, Ball, Tompkins & Black, New York, circa 1850, the body with repoussé entwining grapevines against a punched ground, 12½in. high, 34oz. (Christie's)　£2,435　$4,025

A large and unusual silver Art Nouveau pitcher, Gorham Mfg. Co. Providence, circa 1897, martelé, body repoussé and chased with peacock feathers and scrolls, 17½in. high. 126oz. (Christie's)　£11,730　$19,550

A silver Rococo Revival pitcher of Southern interest, maker's mark of Adolph Himmel, New Orleans, circa 1855, the body with Rococo repoussé foliage and vacant cartouches, 8¼in. high, 29oz. (Christie's)　£3,312　$5,520

An important silver Arts and Crafts pitcher, Stone Associates, Gardner, Massachusetts, 1926, the lower body repoussé and chased with crocus sprays above band of Aries zodiac signs, 11in. high, 33oz. (Christie's)　£4,140　$6,900

A silver classical pitcher, John Curry, Philadelphia, circa 1820, circular rim and neck applied with band of shells alternating with acanthus leaves, 10in. high. 35oz. (Christie's)　£966　$1,610

An important silver and mixed metal pitcher, Tiffany & Co., New York, circa 1880, the base spreading to imitate water, 9in. high, gross weight 35oz. 10dwt. (Christie's)　£27,600　$46,000

Haddock, Lincoln & Foss silver water pitcher, Boston, circa 1865, hand-raised baluster form, engraved arabesque and floral decoration, 10½in. high, approx. 36 troy oz. (Skinner)　£934　$1,495

A George III silver large oval platter, Robert Sharp, London, 1802, the border engraved with an armorial, 65oz., 20^{1}/8in. long.
(Sotheby's)   £1,578 $2,587

One of a rare pair of Charles II dinner plates of plain circular form with an incised, reeded border, by Francis Leake, 1677, 22.5oz.
(Christie's) (Two) £3,910 $6,530

An Old Sheffield plate, (late period) meat dish, with two tucked-in silver inserts, one engraved with an armorial, circa 1825, 57cm. long.
(Christie's)   £414 $691

Set of twelve Gorham Sterling service plates,1929, bas relief Italian Renaissance border design, 10¾in. diameter, approximately 250 total troy oz.
(Skinner)   £4,657 $7,762

A set of twelve George III silver dinner plates, Thomas Whipham, London, 1766, each shaped border engraved with two crests within a gadrooned rim, 161oz., 9½in. long.
(Sotheby's)   £4,209 $6,900

Set of twelve Gorham Sterling plates, date marked *1927*, with Greek key border and monogram to rim, 10¼in. diameter. approximately 184 troy oz.
(Skinner)   £2,679 $4,313

A set of thirteen George III silver dinner plates, Frederick Kandler, London, 1764, each circular and with gadrooned rim, engraved with a coat-of-arms within a rococo cartouche, 9½in. diameter, 254oz.
(Christie's)   £6,440 $10,755

A set of twelve George III silver soup plates, maker's mark *WS*, London, 1811, each shaped border engraved with an armorial below a bishop's mitre, 200oz., 9½in. long.
(Sotheby's)   £6,664 $10,925

One of a set of six George II dinner plates of shaped circular outline with a gadrooned border and armorials, by Edward Wakelin, 1759, 24.5cm. diameter, 101oz.
(Christie's) (Six) £3,220 $5,152

A Charles II Provincial silver porringer, Mark Gill, York 1676, the body flat-chased with flowers and dragonflies and engraved, 2½in. high, 3oz.
(Christie's)   £4,025 $6,601

A George I silver porringer, Joseph Clare, London 1715, with wirework scroll handles and stamped with a band of stylised foliage, 1¾in. high, 1oz. (Christie's)   £862 $1,414

A George III silver porringer, William & James Priest, London, 1771, cylindrical, later inscribed above ropework girdle, 4in. high.
(Sotheby's)   £690 $1,152

An important Charles II silver porringer and cover, unmarked, circa 1660, attributed to the workshop of Christian van Vianen, chased overall with auricular scrolls and grotesque fish masks, 7½in. high, 26oz.
(Christie's)   £71,900 $120,073

An American silver porringer, Samuel Vernon, Newport, Rhode Island, circa 1730, the double-arched keyhole handle engraved with contemporary initials G above D*M, 10oz, 5¼in. diameter.
(Sotheby's)   £2,932 $4,887

A rare Commonwealth Provincial silver porringer and cover, John Thomason, York, 1659, the plain body with straight sides, caryatid handles and spreading skirt foot, 5¼in. high, 17oz 12dwt.
(Sotheby's)   £25,300 $42,251

A Charles II silver porringer, London, 1678, maker's mark TC, the sides chased with flowers, foliage, a lion and a unicorn, 3½in. high, 6oz.
(Christie's)   £2,875 $4,801

A Commonwealth silver porringer and cover, maker's mark HN, London 1659, the detachable cover with spreading foot, 4¼in. high, 8oz. (Christie's) £4,600 $7,544

An important William and Mary two-handled silver porringer and cover, London, 1690, maker's mark of ID a dagger between, 8½in. high, 48oz.
(Christie's)   £41,100 $68,637

Pair of English George III footed salts, London 1771, possibly Robert and David Hennell, gadrooned bodies with small engraved mottoed crest within cartouche, 1¾in., approximately 6 troy oz. total. (Skinner) £339 $546

A pair of George III salts of oblong basin form with part fluting and borders of gadrooning, by Paul Storr, 1819, 11cm. long, 11oz. (Christie's) £1,092 $1,824

A set of five Old Sheffield plated salts of rounded oblong form, with reeded edge to flared rim, 3¾in. wide. (Andrew Hartley) £100 $168

A George I silver trencher salt, **James** Rood, London, 1718, Britannia standard, octagonal, hand holding palm crested and initialled *D*/*N*, 3in. long, 1oz 13dwt. (Sotheby's) £230 $384

Pair of Ball, Black & Co., sterling open salts, 1860s, the bowl supported by three lions rampant, monogram, 3¹/₈in. high, 3⁹/₁₆in. diameter, approx. 10 troy oz. (Skinner) £503 $805

A pair of late 19th/early 20th century German novelty salts in the form of swans, swimming, with glass liners, 6cm. high, 3oz. weighable silver. (Christie's) £207 $331

A set of four George III rectangular salts with gadroon and shell decorated rim, 4¼in. long, London 1811, 14oz. 3dwt. (Andrew Hartley) £500 $840

A pair of Victorian salts in the form of scallop shells supported by dolphins, 2¾in. wide, maker's mark *HH*, London 1875, 2oz 10dwt. (Andrew Hartley) £130 $215

A fine pair of large oval sauceboats, in mid 18th century style, engraved with a crest to a wavy fret edge, William Comyns, London 1913, 30oz. (Woolley & Wallis) £740 $1,191

A George III Irish sauce boat of plain bellied form on three fluted pad feet, by Charles Townsend, Dublin 1772, 19.5cm. long, 11.25oz. (Christie's) £977 $1,632

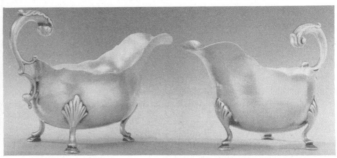

A George III sauce boat with beaded edge, leaf-capped triple scroll handle and three pad feet, Matthew West, Dublin 1787, 20cm. long, 9.3oz. (Bearne's) £700 $1,155

A pair of late 18th century Irish Provincial sauceboats, the oval bodies with a fret edge, leaf capped flying scroll handles, Stephen Walsh, Cork, circa 1780, 15oz. (Woolley & Wallis) £2,400 $3,840

Two pairs of George II silver sauce boats, Thomas Heming, London 1756, each helmet shaped on shaped oval base, two 23cm. long and two 21cm. long, 68oz. (Christie's) £27,600 $45,264

A rare George II single lipped sauceboat of plain circular form with a low spreading foot and s-scroll handle, by John Gamon, 1735, 10cm. diameter, 6oz. (Christie's) £2,070 $3,457

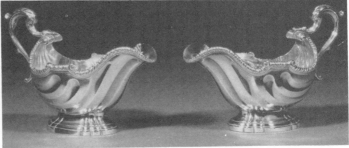

One of a pair of late 19th century German sauceboats, heavily shaped and embossed in the rocaille manner, circa 1900, 20cm. long, 22oz. (Christie's) £632 $1,011

A pair of George II silver sauceboats and a pair of George II silver sauce ladles, Edward Wakelin, London, 1749, the ladles, London, 1759, with unidentified maker's mark WF in script, the sauceboats 8¼in. long, 39oz. (Christie's) £15,525 $25,927

A small, George III brandy saucepan with a bellied circular bowl, a lip spout with a drop and a turned hardwood handle, by William Garrard, 1736, 7.25cm. diameter of bowl, 2.75oz.
(Christie's)   £1,150 $1,921

An Irish George II brandy warming pan by Robert Calderwood, of baluster form with turned ebony handle at right angle to spout, 9in. wide, Dublin 1737, 8oz. 17dwt.
(Andrew Hartley)   £1,300 $2,184

A George III brandy saucepan, the ogee body with a beaded edge, probably John Beldon, London 1776, 6oz.
(Woolley & Wallis)   £460 $740

SNUFF BOXES

A Louis XV silver-mounted white ground enamel snuff box, the mounts Paris, probably 1755, the asymmetrical cartouches on the cover with a shepherd and shepherdess and a chinoiserie group of children, 8.5cm. long.
(Christie's)   £1,092 $1,791

A Meissen gold-mounted royal portrait rectangular snuff-box, circa 1750-55, the interior finely stippled with a bust-length portrait of Augustus III by Johann Heinrici, in armour, 3½in. wide.
(Christie's)   £16,100 $26,887

A diamond-set gold mounted agate snuff box, English or German, circa 1730, cartouche shaped, the brown agate hinged cover with diamond-set floral thumbpiece, 2½in. long.
(Christie's)   £7,475 $12,259

A gold-mounted hardstone snuff box, unmarked, English, mid 18th century, of cartouche form with tapering sides, 2⅛in. wide.
(Sotheby's)   £3,105 $5,185

A 19th century Continental tortoiseshell circular snuff box, the lid with central medallion inlaid in a floral pattern in gold and silver, 3¼in. wide.
(Andrew Hartley)   £210 $346

An agate snuff box with two-colour gold mounts, German/English, circa 1760 and later, the striated brown hardstone panels in cagework mounts, 2⅝in.
(Sotheby's)   £4,255 $7,106

Coin inlaid silver tankard, late 19th century, the body engraved and inlaid with coins of the same type dating from 1669 to 1674, base engraved *October 25, 1893*, 7in. high. (Skinner)   £2,500 $4,025

A George II crested tankard by Isaac Cookson, with scrolled thumb piece, scrolled handle with shell terminal, 6½in. high, Newcastle 1736, 18oz. 13dwt. (Andrew Hartley)   £900 $1,512

A George III tankard of tapering form with a domed cover, skirted base, by Thomas Ollivant, (of Manchester), 1792, 21cm. high, 27oz. (Christie's)   £1,265 $2,024

A George III baluster tankard with a spreading foot and large, double scroll handle, by Thomas Wallis (I), 1768, 20cm. high, 24oz. (Christie's)   £1,150 $1,921

A George III large tankard of baluster form with a moulded girdle, by James Stamp and John Baker (I), 1768, 26.5cm. high, 53oz. (Christie's)   £2,875 $4,600

A Scandinavian silver tankard, maker's ?K, circa 1720, probably Norwegian, the body chased with flowers and foliage, 8¼in. high, 31oz. (Christie's) £4,370 $7,298

A George III small tankard, two beads of incised reeding an a leaf capped scroll handle, by Henry Chawner, 1786, 11.75cm., 17oz. (Christie's)   £920 $1,536

A William III silver tankard, Pierre Harache, London, 1699, Britannia standard, the slight tapering body engraved with the monogram *PJ* in a foliate wreath, 6½in., 27oz 7dwt. (Sotheby's)   £34,500 $57,615

A George II baluster tankard with a domed cover, double scroll handle, by Humphrey Payne, 1745, 19cm. high, 24.5oz. (Christie's)   £1,495 $2,497

Three-piece coin silver tea set, John I. Monell and Charles M. Williams, New York, circa 1825, comprising teapot, covered two-handled sugar and creamer, basket of flowers finials above a chased scrolling leaf lid, teapot 10³/₈in. high, 74 troy oz. (Skinner)   £1,340 $2,185

Anglo/Indian four-piece coffee and tea service, the bodies featuring stamped depictions of Indian scenes, open sugar and creamer, all pieces marked *Orr Silver 22*, coffeepot approximately 10in. high., approximately 104 troy oz. total. (Skinner)   £1,643 $2,645

Three-piece coin silver tea set, Joseph T. Rice, Albany, New York, 1813-53, comprising a teapot, a two handled covered sugar and a creamer, the basket of flower finial above a domed lid with foliate chasing , teapot 9⁵/₈in. high, 98 troy oz. (Skinner) £1,552 $2,530

An Art Deco style modern four-piece tea service, maker's mark of S & W, Sheffield, 1948, together with a modern two handled tea tray, oblong with incurved corners, by Z. Barraclough & Sons, Sheffield, 1931, 57 x 35cm, 156oz. (Christie's)   £2,070 $3,312

A four piece tea and coffee set, comprising a coffee pot, with spout of oblong section upon an oblong foot with ball feet, a tea pot upon ball feet, a milk jug and a sugar bowl, by Th's Wallis, 1807/9, 52oz. (Tennants)   £1,850 $2,960

An American silver five-piece tea and coffee service, Samuel Williamson, Philadelphia, Pennsylvania, circa 1810, comprising: teapot, coffee pot, two-handled sugar bowl and cover, milk jug and waste bowl, 92oz. gross, 4¾in. to 11¼in. high. (Sotheby's)   £9,821 $16,100

An American silver four-piece tea service, A.G. Shultz & Co., Baltimore, Maryland, circa 1900, comprising: teapot, kettle on lamp-stand, two handled sugar bowl and cover and milk jug, each of pear form and chased with buildings and figures, 142oz., 7¼in. to 12½in. high. (Sotheby's)   £3,332 $5,462

Five-piece repoussé Sterling coffee and tea set, ovoid baluster-form, beaded rim, chased floral decoration, composition handles and finials, coffee and tea pots, creamer, open sugar bowl, shaped edge waiter, approximately 95 troy oz. (Skinner) £577 $862

A four piece Edwardian teaset, the circular bombé teapot with foliate cast finial on domed lid, the whole profusely embossed with scrolling foliage, 11in. wide, London 1903/4, 68oz. 19dwt.
(Andrew Hartley)   £1,100 $1,848

Henning Koppel for Georg Jensen, tea and coffee service (No.1017), designed 1952, comprising: teapot, coffee pot, milk jug and sugar bowl, silver coloured metal, teak. (Sotheby's)   £5,980 $9,687

A French silver five-piece tea service, each piece of circular form, decorated with shells on a reeded girdle, the spreading circular bases and covers with gadroon edging, 2074gm. (Bearne's)   £550 $880

A Victorian three-piece bachelor's or afternoon tea set, the globular bodies chased with a broad band of finches amongst foliage and two shaped quatrefoil cartouches, the teapot with a frog finial, by John S. Hunt, 1884/8, 17oz. (Christie's)   £402 $643

An Art Deco three-piece tea service of panelled octagonal form, monogrammed and with angular handles on spreading bases, maker's mark *J.W. & Co.* London 1936, 33.7oz. (Bearne's)   £420 $672

Four-piece Sterling silver tea set, by Gorham, with an oval silver plated footed waiter, engraved with family inscription, consists of a teapot, creamer, sugar, and waste, teapot 7½in. high, 63oz.(Eldred's) £825 $1,320

English George III tea caddy, London, 1771, maker possibly John Harvey, cylindrical, bright cut engraved borders and circular cartouche to centre, 4in. diameter, approximately 3 troy oz. (Skinner)   £1,714 $2,760

Two George I silver tea caddies, one with maker's mark of Anthony Nelme, London, 1725, Britannia Standard, the other unmarked, circa 1725, 4¼in. high, 27oz. (Christie's)   £9,200 $15,364

A square tea caddy, in mid 18th century style, the ogee body embossed with shells, scrolls and beaded panel corners, 4½in. high. S Walton Smith, Birmingham 1888, 11oz. (Woolley & Wallis)   £800 $1,280

A silver tea caddy, John McMullin, Philadelphia, 1790–1810, the plain body with dentillated rims, one side engraved with a coat-of-arms, 6½in. high, gross weight 16oz. (Christie's)   £1,656 $2,760

Fine Victorian silver tea caddy, the vase shaped body well chased and embossed with floral and foliate decoration, London, 1889, by William Comyns, 4½in. high, 9 oz. (G.A. Key)   £510 $816

A Victorian tea caddy of semi-reeded oval form with hinged cover and ebony finial, 15cm. high, Mappin and Webb, Sheffield 1890, 11.96oz. (Bearne's)   £240 $384

A George II silver tea caddy, John Farnell, London, 1727, oval, engraved with armorials within a baroque cartouche, 5in. high, 8oz 6dwt. (Sotheby's) £2,645 $4,417

A set of three George III silver tea caddies, Paul Storr, London 1795, plain oblong with cut corners, in ebony veneered and silver mounted case, the case 12in. long, 62oz. (Christie's)   £36,700 $60,188

Hester Bateman silver tea caddy, 1789–90, ovoid form, engraved crest and stylized bands around body, 5⅝in. high, approximately 9 troy oz. (Skinner) £2,070 $3,450

An early Victorian kettle, the plain body with a foliate scroll handle and fruit finial, T.J. & N. Creswick, Sheffield 1842, (the finial 1841), 36cm. high, 60oz.
(Christie's)   £1,035 $1,656

A modern tea kettle on stand with burner, in the George II manner, kettle embossed and chased with shells, scrolls and two vacant rocaille cartouches, D. & J. Welby, 1914, 35cm. high, 74oz.
(Christie's)   £1,012 $1,619

A George II silver tea kettle, stand and lamp, William Paradise, London 1731, the stand on three shell and scroll feet and with pierced apron, 13½in. high, 59oz. gross. (Christie's) £4,140 $6,790

Jones, Ball & Poor kettle on stand, Boston, mid-19th century, ovoid body chased and embossed with florals, 9¼in. high, approximately 24 troy oz. (Skinner) £536 $863

Attractive large Victorian silver plated spirit kettle of tapering baluster form, the kettle and base having milk glass handles, 14in. high. (G.A. Key)   £260 $416

An Elkington electroplated large oval tea kettle on stand, with engraved crest above motto, with burner, 38.5cm. high overall.
(Bearne's)   £240 $396

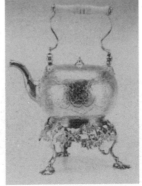

A late 19th century American silver hexagonal tea kettle on stand, with swing handle and burner, stamped *Sterling, Howard & Co, New York 1893*, 31in. high, 1082gm.
(Bearne's)   £230 $380

A George II tea kettle on stand, of spherical form embossed and chased with flowers and scrolls engraved crest, London 1730, 58oz. all in, by Gabriel Smith.
(Russell, Baldwin & Bright)
          £2,000 $3,320

A small travelling tea kettle and folding stand, with spirit burner for same, designed by Christopher Dresser and manufactured by Hukin & Heath, 9in. high.
(Canterbury)   £210 $346

A George III teapot with a panelled body, domed cover and straight spout, bright-engraved with two shield cartouches, by Urquhart & Hart, 1792, 14.5oz.
(Christie's)   £437 $715

A George III teapot of part fluted circular form with a flared rim and an angular handle, crested, probably by William Bennett, 1806, 20oz. (Christie's)   £368 $589

A George III small saffron teapot, of hemispherical form with reeded borders, and c-scroll handle, probably by Henry Nutting, 1806, 10.25cm. diameter, 10oz.
(Christie's)   £483 $807

An octagonal teapot, in early 18th century Oriental style, with two cartouches, Robert Garrard, London 1872, 23.5oz.
(Woolley & Wallis)   £600 $966

A George II teapot, the inverted pear shape body with chased rocaille scroll and foliage scalework to the top, Richard Gurney & Co., London 1748, 18oz.
(Woolley & Wallis)   £1,750 $2,817

A George IV teapot of compressed circular form, highly decorated with acanthus and with laurel girdle, 12cm. high, Rebecca Emes and Edward Barnard, London 1820, 24.4oz. (Bearne's)   £500 $800

A Victorian bachelor's teapot, the squat pear shape body engraved with a band of foliage and bellflowers, swan neck spout, Henry Wilkinson, London 1870, 6½oz. all in.
(Woolley & Wallis)   £320 $512

A George II Provincial silver-gilt bullet teapot with a spreading foot, flush-fitting, hinged cover and ivory handle, John Webber, Exeter 1732, 11.75cm. high, 14oz.
(Christie's)   £598 $957

German hallmarked silver teapot, 19th century, panelled rectangular-form, chased exotic and classical decoration, 6^{15}/16in. high, approx. 25 troy oz. (Skinner)   £305 $489

A George III oval teapot and stand, the body with bright cut decorated shaped cartouches by Cornelius Brand, stand by John Crouch 1st and Thomas Hannam, London 1789, 21oz.
(Woolley & Wallis)   £950 $1,530

A George I Irish silver teapot, apparently without maker's mark, Dublin, 1714, octagonal and later initialled *MP* below a baron's coronet and moulded girdle, 4¼in. high, 404gr, all in.
(Sotheby's)   £23,000 $38,410

A Victorian shaped oval teapot, decorated with bands of bright-cut floral decoration, 28cm. long, Richard Martin & Ebenezer Hall, London 1889, 520gm., 16.7oz., together with a matching teapot stand, 2oz. (Bearne's) £300 $495

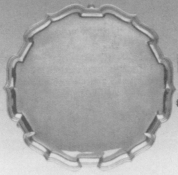

A Victorian large circular salver engraved with a coat of arms, scrolls and scallops, on four leafage scroll feet, London 1843, 17in. diameter, 75oz., R & S Garrard. (Russell, Baldwin & Bright)
£1,520 $2,523

A George VI shaped circular salver with reeded edging, on three pad feet, Mappin & Webb, Sheffield 1944, 47.5cm. diameter, 85.4oz. (Bearne's)   £650 $1,073

A Victorian crested waiter with chased scrolling foliate centre and shell and scroll border, 9½in. wide, London 1851, 13oz 10dwt. (Andrew Hartley)   £150 $248

A large George III salver of circular outline with a chased border of repeating bluebell drops between two rows of beading, by Richard Rugg, 1777, 38cm. diameter, 53oz. (Christie's)   £2,530 $4,048

A late 19th century electroplated two-handled shaped rectangular tea tray, engraved with shells, scrolls, flowers, foliage and scalework, 80cm. over handles. (Bearne's)   £410 $676

A large silver salver, with pie-crust border, the centre engraved with the Gunners Crest and inscribed *Presented to Mr Joseph E. Shaw*, 1908–1933, engraved with all the directors, players and staff, 15¾in. diam. (Christie's)   £5,175 $8,539

A Victorian shaped circular salver with gadroon shell and acanthus edging on four volute feet, 38.5cm. diameter, George Howson, London 1900, 48.8oz. (Bearne's)   £480 $768

A George II silver salver, Griffith Edwards, London, 1735, later chased with rococo ornament within moulded Bath border, 6¼in. diameter, 6¼in., 8oz 10dwt. (Sotheby's)   £517 $863

A George III shaped circular salver within a shell and scroll border on three volute feet, 31cm. diameter, William Peaston, London 1752, 32oz. (Bearne's)   £700 $1,159

An American silver tureen and cover, Gorham Mfg. Co., Providence, RI., 1884, the oval base on four Indian-inspired feet, 69oz. 10dwt. width over handles 14in. (Sotheby's) £4,911 $8,050

A Christofle plate two-handled tureen and cover, crested above a motto, with bead edging, 18cm. high, together with a matching oval sauce boat on stand, 27cm. wide. (Bearne's) £280 $448

Tiffany sterling covered tureen, 1854–55, oval form, geometric and egg and dart border, cast bull head handles, 16³⁄₈in. long, approx. 79 troy oz. (Skinner) £5,031 $8,050

A pair of Sheffield plated sauce tureens and covers, circa 1820–30, fitted with a stepped domed cover with gadrooned rims, length over handles 8½in. (Sotheby's) £561 $920

A pair of George III silver sauce tureens and covers, Simon Harris, London, 1811, oval and on four acanthus-capped scroll and rosette feet, 7½in. long, 63oz. (Christie's) £3,450 $5,762

An American silver soup tureen and cover, S. Kirk & Sons, Baltimore, 1861–68, of boat form, embossed on both sides with a stag hunt, 93oz., 10 dwt., 13¼in. long. (Sotheby's) £4,209 $6,900

One of a pair of George IV Sheffield Plate oval sauce tureens, foliage borders, on foliate cartouche appliqué legs on claw and ball feet, 8¼in. (Woolley & Wallis) £600 $960

A pair of Sheffield Plate oblong sauce tureens and covers with gadroon edging and lion mask drop ring handles, 16cm. long. (Bearne's) £320 $528

A George III silver soup-tureen, Henry Nutting, London, 1807, plain oval and on spreading foot, 15in. long, 79oz. (Christie's) £4,370 $7,298

A 19th century electroplated samovar, 20in. overall.
(Dockree's)   £270 $432

A pair of 19th century French electro-plated cast urns, on square pedestal bases with two boar mask handles, mark of I. Oudry & Co, circa 1870.
(Christie's)   £1,667 $2,667

An American silver tea urn on stand, probably by Gorham Mfg. Co., Providence, RI, circa 1865, of footed baluster form, 86oz., 2dwt., 19¾in. high.
(Sotheby's)   £1,929 $3,162

A late Victorian tea urn in Regency style, with rosette swag engraving to the globular body, 12½in., William Suckling & Son of Birmingham, circa 1890.
(Woolley & Wallis)   £240 $386

A George III small vase shaped tea urn with twin reeded loop handles, a pedestal foot, and a matching rising domed cover with acorn finial, the cover by James Young, 36cm. high, 50.5oz.
(Christie's)   £1,725 $2,760

Victorian Irish two-handled covered urn, crowned *W* maker's mark, chased and embossed with chinoiserie-style figures and foliage, 13in. high, approximately 65 troy oz. (Skinner)   £1,071 $1,725

VASES

Tiffany sterling vase, 1914, double handled egg shape on foliage feet, chased decoration, 9¾in. high, approx. 54½ troy oz.
(Skinner)   £1,509 $2,415

Tiffany & Co. horn-shaped vase, 1875-91, the end with single ball support, the front raised on two splayed legs with paw feet, 11in., approximately 21 troy oz.
(Skinner)   £1,071 $1,725

An American(?) silver coloured metal baluster vase, decorated in repoussé and engraved rococo scrolling foliate and shell motifs, 700g, 33cm.
(Bristol)   £370 $607

The Billiard Player, silver, rounded rectangular, the front enamelled with a billiard player readying to pot a ball, George Heath, London 1888, 5cm. (Christie's)   £862 $1,379

Diamond set Match, gold, the front applied with a facsimile match, the head set with a diamond, probably American, late nineteenth century, 5.2cm. (Christie's)   £460 $759

Tom Cannon, silver, the front enamelled with an oval study of a jockey, Tom Cannon, Birmingham 1881, 3.7cm. (Christie's)   £690 $1,138

Hunters Taking a Stream, silver, rectangular, the front with an angled panel enamelled with a scene of two huntsmen jumping a stream, J.M.B., Chester 1902, 5.4cm. (Christie's)   £500 $800

An Oarswoman, silver, of rectangular box-type, the front enamelled with a standing lady holding an oar, Sampson Mordan, London 1889, 5.7cm. (Christie's)   £1,035 $1,707

Upstairs, Downstairs, silver, the front enamelled with a scene featuring a gentleman's advances being mildly resisted by a maid, French, late nineteenth century, 4.8cm. (Christie's)   £920 $1,518

Girl with Flowers, silver, the cover decorated with an enamelled study of a girl holding flowers, Continental, late nineteenth century, 4.3cm. (Christie's)   £632 $1,042

Girl and Owl, silver, the front with an enamelled scene of a girl in a wooded landscape, an owl in flight in the foreground, American, late nineteenth century, 6.2cm. (Christie's)   £437 $721

A Cricketer, silver-plated, rectangular, the front enamelled with a cricketer taking a swing, surrounded by engraved foliage, probably English, late nineteenth century, 4.2cm.
(Christie's) £437 $721

Gold and Agate Horseshoe, the front inset with panels of gold in quartz, unmarked, probably American, late nineteenth century, 5.5cm. (Christie's) £1,955 $3,225

A Concealed Nude, silver, the exterior plain, double hinged to reveal an enamelled study of a standing lady disrobing herself, German, late nineteenth century, 5.7cm. (Christie's) £977 $1,612

Nude on Shoreline, silver vesta case, rounded rectangular, the front enamelled with a reclining nude female seated on a shoreline, waves and skyline beyond, London import marks, 5cm.
(Christie's) £862 $1,405

A Punch and Judy Tent, silver vesta case, rectangular with a pointed dome, the front enamelled with a seaside Punch and Judy tent, featuring Mr. Punch, the Sea Captain, Toby the Dog and a drummer, Sampson Mordan, London 1887, 5.4cm.
(Christie's) £8,050 $13,120

Nude by a Lake, silver, rounded rectangular, the front enamelled to one side with a rectangular study of a nude female standing beside a lake amidst extensive foliage, probably German, late 19th century, 4.5cm. (Christie's) £500 $800

The Kill, the front enamelled with a scene depicting the conclusion of the Hunt, a huntsman holding aloft a fox, Sampson Mordan, Chester 1903, 5.7cm.
(Christie's) £2,070 $3,415

A Female Head and Shoulders, silver, rectangular, the front enamelled with a female head and shoulders study, she in a blue dress, J.M.B., Birmingham 1893, 4.6cm. (Christie's) £500 $800

Vintage Car, gold, the front die-stamped with a study of a vintage car, the headlights set with rubies, the radiator set with a diamond, American, 6cm.
(Christie's) £920 $1,518

A Railway Ticket, silver, the front enamelled with a First Class return ticket from Monte Carlo to Nice, French, late nineteenth century, 5.7cm. (Christie's) £1,150 $1,897

Pony and Trap combination case, silver, of oval form, the base incorporating two penknives, George Heath, London 1891, retailed by Tiffany, 7cm. (Christie's) £1,380 $2,277

A Single Huntsman, silver, the front enamelled with a single huntsman and horse, Frederick Edmunds, London 1892, 4.6cm. (Christie's) £805 $1,328

Hunting Dogs Taking a Fence, silver, rectangular, the front enamelled, the reverse engraved with entwined initials, Sampson Mordan, London 1897, 5.7cm. (Christie's) £3,220 $5,310

A Billiard Room, silver, circular, the front cast with a scene of two players in a billiard hall, Birmingham 1906, 4cm. diameter. (Christie's) £517 $853

A Yachting Race, silver, the cover enamelled with a scene of two yachts in full sail about to pass a buoy, Sampson Mordan and Co., London 1890, 5.7cm. (Christie's) £1,495 $2,466

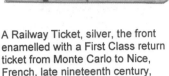

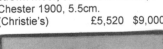

The Grouse Moor, silver vesta case rectangular, the front decorated with an enamelled scene of a grouse hunt featuring two guns, a dog and a beater in a heather strewn moor, J. Millward Banks, Chester 1900, 5.5cm. (Christie's) £5,520 $9,000

A Sentry Box, silver, the front enamelled with a standing sentry, Sampson Mordan and Co, London 1903, 7.3cm. (Christie's) £2,760 $4,554

A Coaching Scene, silver, rectangular, the front enamelled with a coach and horses drawing up outside the entrance to a house, the reverse engraved with initials, probably Sampson Mordan and Co, London 1903, 5.7cm. (Christie's) £1,610 $2,576

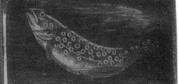

A La Mer, gold, the cover with an enamelled scene of children playing on the seashore, French, late nineteenth century, 4.8cm. (Christie's) £920 $1,518

A Hand of Cards, silver, circular, the front decorated with a raised hand holding a hand of cards, J.F., Birmingham 1907, 4cm. diameter. (Christie's) £552 $910

A Hooked Trout, silver, rectangular, the front enamelled with a fish, still underwater but hooked, J. Millward Banks, Chester 1900, 5.5cm. (Christie's) £2,990 $4,933

Combination vesta and marker, the cover set with numbered markers, possibly for scoring bezique, the base acting as a vesta case, John Millward Banks, 6.3cm.
(Christie's)   £1,380 $2,277

A Fish, silver, realistically stamped and chased to resemble a fish, S Blanckensee and Son Ltd, Birmingham 1891, 6.5cm.
(Christie's)   £517 $853

Amorous Ladies, silver rectangular box-type, the cover enamelled with two ladies exchanging a kiss, Austro-Hungarian, late nineteenth century, 4.4cm.
(Christie's)   £1,840 $3,036

Female Head and Shoulders study, the front enamelled with a woman in a pink dress, H. W & Co., Birmingham 1914, 4.5cm.
(Christie's)   £500 $800

A Football and Rugby Ball, both silver and both chased and engraved to resemble the above, H.W. Ltd., Birmingham marks, the rugby ball 5.5cm.
(Christie's)   £977 $1,612

Seagoing Yacht, silver rectangular, the front enamelled with a yacht in full sail, W.H.S., Birmingham 1897, 3.2cm. (Christie's)   £575 $948

A stamped and addressed envelope, silver, the front enamelled with a postmarked stamp and the name and address, the reverse with a formed simulated flap, C.E.S., Birmingham 1897, 4cm. (Christie's)   £1,265 $2,087

Nude Seated On Rock, silver, the front enamelled with a nude female seated on a rock, American, late nineteenth century, 6cm.
(Christie's)   £920 $1,518

Bagpipe Players, silver, the front enamelled with a study of four bagpipe players standing in a barren landscape, Sampson & Mordan and Co., London 1895, 4.5cm. (Christie's) £1,610 $2,656

A Pig, 9ct gold, formed as a seated pig, one side engraved with an inscription and date, Continental, import marks for London 1905, 4.9cm. (Christie's)   £920 $1,518

Reclining Nude on Shoreline, silver, rectangular, the front enamelled with a nude female reclining on a shoreline, a diaphanous veil covering her lower body, maker's mark rubbed, Birmingham 1887, 4cm. (Christie's)   £500 $800

Swimmers, silver, circular, the front cast with a scene of two swimmers and a pool, Birmingham 1906, 4cm. diameter.
(Christie's)   £575 $948

A Bulldog, silver of rounded rectangular form, the front enamelled with a bulldog's head, Sampson Mordan, London 1887, 5cm. (Christie's)   £437 $721

A Hunting Scene, silver, curved rectangular, the front enamelled with an extensive hunting scene, London import marks, 5cm. (Christie's)   £632 $1,042

Two Coquettes, the front enamelled with two outlandishly attired ladies, Austro-Hungarian, late nineteenth century, 5.5cm. (Christie's)   £460 $760

G.W.R. 'Cornish Express', silver, the front part enamelled with a study of a locomotive in full steam and the phrase, _G.W.R. Cornish Express_, Read and Morris, Birmingham 1918, 5.4cm. (Christie's)   £1,495 $2,466

Lady seated at a Spinning Wheel, silver, the front enamelled with a scene of a woman in traditional costume seated at a spinning wheel, Continental, late nineteenth century, 6.3cm. (Christie's)   £575 $948

Cover of Punch, of rectangular book form, the cover inset with an enamelled plaque depicting the front cover of Punch magazine, Louis Dee, London 1881, 5.2cm. (Christie's)   £977 $1,612

A Landed Fish, silver, rectangular, the front part-enamelled with a fish lying on a grassy and rocky riverbank, George Heath, London 1887, 4.8cm. (Christie's)   £517 $853

An engine-turned case, 9ct gold, engine-turned overall, the front with applied silver initials to one corner, Deakin and Francis, Birmingham 1924, 5.6cm. (Christie's)   £253 $417

For Ever, 15ct gold, the front engraved and set with diamonds, the front hinged to reveal a concealed photograph frame, B.H.J., Birmingham 1901, 4.2cm. (Christie's)   £690 $1,138

A Jockey, the front enamelled with a half study of a jockey, black and white jersey and black cap, Sampson Mordan, London 1889, 4.4cm. (Christie's) £1,035 $1,707

A Bee, silver, rectangular, the front enamelled with a bee in flight, M.B .& Co., Birmingham 1905, 4.7cm. (Christie's)   £402 $663

A Standing Nude, the front enamelled with a standing female nude in a wooded lakeland setting, probably London 1908, 5cm. (Christie's)   £920 $1,518

Horse, Rider and Snaffle, silver, the front enamelled with a horse and rider jumping a representation of a full cheek snaffle, George Heath, London 1891, 5cm. (Christie's)   £575 $948

Man Stealing into Bedroom, silver, rectangular with sloping cover, the front enamelled with a scene of a man climbing through a bedroom window, French, late nineteenth century, 4.9cm. (Christie's)   £862 $1,422

The Queen of Hearts, silver, one side enamelled with the Queen of Hearts playing card, Sampson Mordan and Co, London 1891, 4.4cm. (Christie's)   £1,265 $2,087

A Lady and Her Beau, the front enamelled with a lady being assisted to cross a stream by a young man, French, late nineteenth century, 4.7cm. (Christie's)   £575 $948

Silver vestacase, the front enamelled with a panel depicting an athlete, probably a runner, *Well Done Albert* engraved beneath, J. Gloster Ltd., Birmingham 1913, 5cm. (Christie's)   £747 $1,232

A Rolls Royce Radiator Grille, 9ct gold, the front engine-turned and engraved with the Rolls Royce badge, maker's mark rubbed, Birmingham 1914, 5.2cm. (Christie's)   £1,610 $2,656

A George IV rectangular vinaigrette, engine turned with reeded sides, hinged cover, 1¼in. William Edwards, London 1821.
(Woolley & Wallis)   £240 $384

A watch style George IV vinaigrette, silver gilt with engine turning and chased foliage borders, Joseph Willmore, 1in. diameter. Birmingham 1821.
(Woolley & Wallis)   £260 $416

A George III rectangular vinaigrette with rounded corners and bright cut engraving, Matthew Linwood, 1¾in. Birmingham 1803.
(Woolley & Wallis) £1,250 $2,000

WAX JACKS

An Edwardian wax jack, with gadroon borders, Stokes & Ireland Ltd, London 1904, with extinguisher, Jas Dixon & Son, Sheffield circa 1905, 4.5oz.
(Woolley & Wallis)   £255 $408

A George IV silver wax jack, Samuel Siervent, London 1828, on three claw-and-ball feet and with openwork base pierced with flowers and foliage, 17cm. high, 6oz.
(Christie's)   £1,725 $2,881

A rare Old Sheffield plated wax jack on an oval base with an oval openwork frame and a wax winding mechanism, complete with snuffer and chain, 15cm. high, circa 1785.
(Christie's)   £632 $1,036

WINE COOLERS

A middle period Old Sheffield plated wine cooler, with two lug handles, two reeded bands and a detachable rim and liner, circa 1800, 20cm. high.
(Christie's)   £1,092 $1,824

Pair of Sheffield plate wine coolers, circa 1900, claw feet, lion heads with loose rings, gadroon edge, 6½in. high.
(Du Mouchelles)   £375 $600

An electro-plated wine cooler with an embossed, flared and pierced rim, a plated body with two goat mask handles, 28cm. high.
(Christie's)   £517 $827

A George III wine funnel with thread edging, 14.5cm. high, maker's mark W.A. London 1908, 240gm.
(Bearne's) £310 $511

A George IV wine funnel with a part fluted bowl, shell tang and a gadrooned rim, by R. Emes & E. Barnard, 1822, 14cm. long, 4oz.
(Christie's) £805 $1,296

An early Victorian wine funnel with a tapering spout, a thistle shaped bowl and a shell thumbpiece, crested, by Messrs Barnard, 1838, 16.5cm. high, 6.5oz.
(Christie's) £920 $1,472

A George III wine funnel, crested above reeded lower body, the detachable strainer with gadroon edging, William Burwash, London 1814, 15cm. long, 7oz.
(Bearne's) £600 $990

A late Victorian wine funnel with a detachable strainer and straight spout, by Atkin Bros., Sheffield, 1897, 13cm. high, 5oz.
(Christie's) £345 $552

A George III wine funnel with bead borders and a shaped tang, crested, by Hester Bateman, 1790, 12.25cm. high, 2.5oz.
(Christie's) £1,035 $1,728

WINE TASTERS

A French silver wine taster, Pierre Carreau II, Tours, 1782, entwined serpent handle, 2¾in. diameter, 3oz 6dwt. (Sotheby's) £920 $1,536

A Charles II silver wine taster, indistinct maker's mark, circa 1665, the side chased with stylised foliage, 5¼in. wide, 2oz.
(Christie's) £1,265 $2,075

A French silver wine taster, Louis Nicolas Dehors d'Orléans, circa 1770, reeded strap handle, 2½in. diameter, 2½in., 1oz 13dwt.
(Sotheby's) £575 $960

Lainey Keogh bear, dressed in luxurious Tibetan stole, hand woven lotus belt complete with hand-made gold tassel. (Christie's) £74 $121

An Alpha Farnell teddy bear, with pale blond mohair, black stitched nose, mouth and claws, cream felt pads and label, 18in. tall, 1930s. (Christie's)   £368 $604

A Chiltern teddy bear, with golden mohair, large clear and black glass eyes painted on reverse, pronounced square snout, 25in. tall, 1930s. (Christie's)   £161 $264

A Steiff teddy bear, with golden curly mohair, black boot button eyes, pronounced clipped snout, black stitched nose, mouth and claws, 20in. tall, circa 1910. (Christie's)   £8,050 $13,202

A Steiff teddy bear, with golden mohair, black boot button eyes, swivel head, long jointed shaped limbs, pale felt pads, card lined feet and hump, 16in. tall, circa 1908. (Christie's)   £2,760 $4,526

'Sotheby', a fine Steiff teddy bear, with golden mohair, brown and black glass eyes, 18in. tall, circa 1920, sold with his passport, issued 1988, listing his travels. (Christie's)   £7,705 $12,636

A Steiff teddy bear with rich golden mohair, brown and black glass eyes, swivel head, jointed shaped limbs, felt pads, hump and button in ear, 18in. tall, circa 1920. (Christie's)   £3,450 $5,658

A fine musical Jopi teddy bear, with dark brown tipped silver white mohair, cream felt pads and operative concertina musical movement to tummy, 22in. tall circa 1920. (Christie's) £8,855 $14,522

A fine cinnamon Steiff teddy bear, with black boot button eyes, swivel head, jointed shaped limbs, cream felt pads, hump and button in ear, 16in. tall, (Christie's)   £4,600 $7,544

TEDDY BEARS

A Steiff centre seam teddy bear, with golden mohair, black boot button eyes, black stitched nose, mouth and claws, 16in. circa 1908
(Christie's)   £2,530 $4,149

An early 20th century light golden mohair teddy bear, possibly Steiff, having black boot button eyes, shaved snout with black vertically stitched nose, 51cm.
(Bearne's)   £2,800 $4,480

'Henry Bruin', a Steiff teddy bear, with brown mohair, brown and black glass eyes, pronounced clipped snout, jointed shaped limbs, growler, hump, 19in. tall, 1930s.
(Christie's)   £977 $1,602

A Steiff centre seam teddy bear, with golden mohair, black boot button eyes, pronounced clipped snout, black stitched nose, mouth and claws, 16in. tall, circa 1910.
(Christie's)   £2,300 $3,772

A musical teddy bear, with pink mohair, large clear and black glass eye, swivel head, jointed shaped limbs, concertina musical movement in tummy, 15in. tall, 1920s, probably Helvetic.
(Christie's)   £368 $604

A fine Steiff teddy bear with rich golden mohair, large black boot button eyes, large shaped paws and 'spoon' shaped card lined feet, hump and button in ear, 26in. tall, circa 1910.
(Christie's)   £9,200 $15,088

A Merrythought teddy bear, with golden mohair, deep amber and black glass eyes, pronounced clipped snout, swivel head and jointed limbs, 17in. tall, 1930s.
(Christie's)   £218 $358

A white Steiff teddy bear, with brown and black glass eyes, pronounced snout, beige stitched nose, mouth and claws, hump and button in ear, 20in. tall, 1920s.
(Christie's)   £2,990 $4,904

A large Hermann teddy bear, with pale blond man-made plush, large amber and black glass eyes, clipped plush cut muzzle, inner ears and pads, 42in. tall, 1960s.
(Christie's)   £69 $113

A Steiff teddy bear, with beige curly mohair, brown and black eyes, jointed limbs, felt pads and growler, 25in. tall, 1950s, German. (Christie's)   £1,035 $1,645

A fine Chiltern teddy bear, with golden mohair, deep amber and black eyes, square snout, jointed limbs, original ribbon and card swing tag, 27in. tall, 1950s. (Christie's)   £1,035 $1,645

A Chad Valley teddy bear, with golden mohair, deep amber and black glass eyes, jointed limbs and brown felt pads, 16in. tall, 1950s. (Christie's)   £437 $695

A Chad Valley teddy bear, with golden mohair, black stitched 'button' nose, swivel head, jointed limbs and brown cloth pads, 11in. tall, 1960s. (Christie's) £184 $292

An unusually large Farnell teddy bear, with golden mohair, central facial seam, black stitched nose, mouth and claws, swivel head and large wood lined feet, 47in. tall, 1930s. (Christie's)   £920 $1,462

A German teddy bear, with golden mohair, amber and black eyes, clipped cream plush cut muzzle, swivel head and jointed limbs, 18in. tall, 1930s. (Christie's) £276 $439

An American teddy bear, with golden mohair, clear and black glass eyes, black horizontally stitched nose, jointed limbs, felt pads and hump, 14in. tall, 1920s. (Christie's)   £368 $585

'Winston', a white Steiff centre seam teddy bear, with black boot button eyes, elongated jointed shaped limbs, cream felt pads, hump and black button in ear, 20in. tall, circa 1905. (Christie's)   £5,175 $8,228

A dark golden plush covered teddy bear, with deep amber and black glass eyes, swivel head and jointed shaped limbs, card lined feet and felt pads, 20in. tall. (Christie's)   £483 $768

A Chad Valley teddy bear, with golden curly mohair, amber and black plastic eye, black stitched mouth, swivel head and jointed limbs, 28in. tall, 1950s.
(Christie's)   £483 $767

A Chiltern teddy bear, with pale golden mohair, deep amber and black eyes, tip of snout clipped, swivel head and jointed limbs, 24in. tall, 1950s.
(Christie's)   £632 $1,005

A cinnamon plush covered teddy bear, with deep amber and black glass eyes, black stitched nose and mouth, jointed limbs, cream cloth pads and growler, 22in. tall, 1930s.
(Christie's)   £276 $439

A Chad Valley teddy bear, with golden mohair, deep amber and black eyes, pronounced clipped snout, swivel head, jointed limbs, label to left foot and button in left ear, 20in. tall, 1930s.
(Christie's)   £517 $822

A Farnell teddy bear, with golden mohair, clear and black eyes, swivel head, jointed shaped limbs, webbed paw claws and hump, 20in. tall, 1920s.
(Christie's)   £2,990 $4,754

A Steiff centre seam teddy bear, with golden mohair, black boot button eyes, black stitched nose, mouth and claws, swivel head, jointed limbs and hump, 19in. tall, circa 1908.
(Christie's)   £1,265 $2,011

A Schuco 'Yes/No' teddy bear, with pale beige mohair, brown and black glass eyes, jointed limbs, original collar and bell and tail operating head movement, 8½in. tall, 1930s.
(Christie's)   £977 $1,553

A Steiff teddy bear, with golden mohair, brown and black glass eyes, pronounced clipped snout, hump, growler and button in ear, 19in. tall, circa 1920s.
(Christie's)   £1,092 $1,758

A Strunz teddy bear, with pale golden mohair, black boot button eyes, pronounced clipped snout, cream felt pads and slight hump, 14in. tall, circa 1910.
(Christie's)   £437 $695

A fine Steiff teddy bear, with dark golden mohair, black boot button eyes, black stitched nose, mouth and claws, swivel head, felt pads and hump, 14in. tall, circa 1910. (Christie's)   £3,680 $5,851

A Chiltern teddy bear, with golden curly mohair, large clear and black eyes, black stitched nose, jointed limbs, and card lined feet, 26in. tall, 1930s. (Christie's)   £747 $1,188

A Steiff teddy bear, with golden mohair, black shoe button eyes, pronounced clipped snout, swivel head and jointed limbs, 12in. tall, circa 1908.
(Christie's)   £1,035 $1,646

A Merrythought pink Bingie bear cub, with pink and white artificial silk plush, black stitched nose, mouth and claws, label stitched to inner right leg, 6½in. tall, circa 1931. (Christie's)   £253 $402

A Pedigree teddy bear, with golden mohair, orange and black plastic eyes, hard moulded nose, jointed limbs and squeaker, 21in. tall, 1950s. (Christie's)   £184 $292

A Chiltern musical teddy bear with golden mohair, deep amber and black eyes, swivel head, jointed limbs and fixed key-wind movement to back, 15in. tall, 1950s. (Christie's)   £368 $585

A Chad Valley teddy bear, with golden mohair, deep amber and black eyes, pronounced clipped snout, swivel head and jointed shaped limbs, 23in. tall, 1930s. (Christie's)   £805 $1,280

'Johann', a white Steiff centre seam teddy bear, with large black boot button eyes, beige stitched nose, mouth and claws, swivel head and large 'spoon' shaped feet, hump and button in ear, 24in. tall, circa 1908. (Christie's) £6,900 $10,971

A Chiltern teddy bear, with golden mohair, large deep amber and black eyes, swivel head and jointed limbs, velvet pads and card lined feet, 27in. tall, 1930s. (Christie's)   £690 $1,097

'Clifford', a Steiff centre seam teddy bear, with blonde mohair, black boot button eyes, pronounced clipped snout, growler, hump and button in ear, 16in. tall, circa 1908. (Christie's) £3,220 $5,119

A white Steiff teddy bear, with black boot button eyes, clipped snout, elongated jointed shaped limbs, cream felt pads and hump, 13in. tall, circa 1910. (Christie's) £2,300 $3,657

A rare black Steiff centre seam teddy bear, with black shoe button eyes backed with red felt, jointed shaped limbs, cream pads, hump and button in ear, 21in. tall, circa 1912. (Christie's) £10,925 $17,370

A Steiff teddy bear with golden mohair, black shoe button eyes, pronounced clipped snout, black horizontally stitched nose, black stitched mouth and claws, 11in. tall, circa 1910. (Christie's) £1,265 $2,024

A Farnell teddy bear, with golden mohair, large clear and black glass eyes, pronounced clipped nose, growler and webbed claw paws, with photograph of original owner, circa 1916, 26in. tall. (Christie's) £1,725 $2,743

A Chad Valley Magna teddy bear, with rich golden mohair, clear and black eyes painted on reverse, black stitched mouth and claws, swivel head and jointed limbs, 21in. tall, late 1930s. (Christie's) £299 $475

A white plush covered teddy bear, with black boot button eyes, pronounced snout, swivel head and jointed shaped limbs, felt pads and hump, 22in. tall, circa 1910. (Christie's) £862 $1,370

A fine Steiff teddy bear, with golden mohair, brown and black glass eyes, stitched nose, mouth and claws, growler, hump and button in ear with yellow label intact, 16in. tall, 1930s. (Christie's) £3,335 $5,302

A Merrythought teddy bear with golden mohair, deep amber and black eye, clipped snout, black stitched nose and mouth, 19in. high, circa 1950. (Christie's) £276 $441

An Ericsson skeleton telephone, with later attached number board. (Auction Team Köln) £418 $670

A two-line telephone switchboard, with day/night switch, and Siemens & Halske W28 receiver with hanging arm, circa 1915, modified in the 1940s. (Auction Team Köln) £334 $535

A Model OBO5 desk telephone with front dial and Austrian receiver. (Auction Team Köln) £335 $536

An L.M. Ericsson skeleton telephone with arrester and connection rose, original receiver with speech key. (Auction Team Köln) £712 $1,138

A ZBSA 19 desk telephone by NTT, with external alarm. (Auction Team Köln) £159 $254

An alabaster System Bailleux wall telephone, with key, circa 1900. (Auction Team Köln) £670 $1,072

A Western Electric portable telephone for the Massachusetts State Police, the mahogany case with crank inductor and hand receiver, 1924. (Auction Team Köln) £146 $234

A Western Electric Company telephone, early American wall model, with tin speaking tube, 1910, with wooden resistance decade with hard rubber plate. (Auction Team Köln) £117 $187

A rare L.M. Ericsson field telephone, with speech key and folding receiver guard, in wooden case, circa 1915. (Auction Team Köln) £92 $147

A French terracotta bust of a gentleman, 19th century, in the manner of Antoine Coysevox, the figure dressed in 18th century costume, 29½in. high.
(Christie's) £2,760 $4,416

A terracotta verniciata bust of St. John the Baptist, circa 1580, Della Robbia workshop, modelled as a youth, slightly to the right, wearing a Roman cobalt-blue mantle, 13½in. high. (Christie's) £10,350 $17,284

A French terracotta bust of a boy, 19th century, after a model by Houdon, on a waisted circular socle, 19½in. high.
(Christie's) £1,261 $2,024

A terracotta coloured plaster bust of Jean-Baptiste Poquelin Molière, after an 18th century model by Caffieri, 27in. high.
(Christie's) £747 $1,195

A pair of Austrian polychrome terracotta figures of itinerant children, circa 1890, in Iberian traditional costume, on naturalistic bases, 25in. high.
(Christie's) £2,875 $4,600

A terracotta coloured plaster bust of Jean de la Fontaine, 19th century, after an 18th century model by Caffieri, 30in. high.
(Christie's) £747 $1,195

A French terracotta statuette of a gentleman, 19th century, possibly after Philippe Parmentier, the figure shown standing with tricorn hat under one arm, 30½in. high.
(Christie's) £2,070 $3,312

A pair of Continental terracotta blackamoor figures modelled as two street urchins, 66cm. high.
(Wintertons) £1,700 $2,805

An Austrian painted terracotta tobacco box, late 19th century, modelled as a dog's head, 7½in. high. (Christie's) £690 $1,104

A silk on silk needlework picture, designed and painted by Samuel Folwell (1764–1813), Philadelphia, possibly wrought by Eleanor Genge Hatch, circa 1810, 20 x 27in. sight.
(Christie's)　£13,110　$21,850

German veterans silk embroidered standard, double sided panel brightly embroidered to one side with an Imperial Eagle, with wings outstretched.
(Bosleys)　£650　$1,037

A fine embroidered picture, anonymous, attributed to the Folwell School, Philadelphia, early 19th century, worked in green, gold, blue and white silk threads, 19½ x 23½in.(Sotheby's) £14,030 $23,000

A Charles II wool and silk raised-work picture, worked in polychrome wools and silks, on an ivory silk ground, in a later concave-moulded and beaded giltwood frame, 15¾ x 19½in.
(Christie's)　£12,650　$20,746

A George III oval needlework picture, worked with coloured silks on a dark ground, 60cm., in contemporary giltwood frame.
(Bearne's)　£1,100　$1,815

An extremely fine, rare and important silk embroidered picture: The Tree of Life, Morris Family, Philadelphia, late 18th century, 13½ x 18in.
(Sotheby's)　£175,985　$288,500

Silk needlework memorial, *By Elizabeth Shute 11 years old*, early 19th century, ink highlights, eglomisé matt, framed, 15¼ x 15in.
(Skinner)　£705　$1,150

The Royal Gloucestershire Hussars Regimental guidon, a very fine post 1953 double sided example. Each face of scarlet cloth bearing a gold embroidered regimental device.
(Bosleys)　£460　$733

A William and Mary needlepoint and silver-embroidered picture, circa 1690, depicting William and Mary beneath a double-arched arcade, 14½ x 22½in. overall.
(Sotheby's)　£1,754　$2,875

Navajo rug, circa 1930, 3ft.6in. x 6ft.2in., with repeated diamond motif in shades of brown.
(Eldred's) £366 $605

An Antwerp mythological tapestry, first half 17th century, woven in wools and silks, depicting a soldier in Roman armour 125½ x 187in.
(Christie's) £28,750 $47,725

American Indian rug, Two Gray Hills, 6ft.11in. x 4ft.5in., with spirit line. (Eldred's) £1,266 $2,090

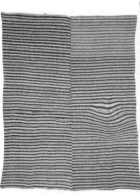

An early Southwest wearing blanket, possibly New Mexico, Rio Grande area, circa 1800–1850, wool, woven in a classic style.
(Sotheby's) £11,224 $18,400

A Brussels mythological tapestry, second half 17th century, woven in wools and silks, depicting the Birth of Adonis, 82¾ x 104in.
(Christie's) £9,200 $15,272

A Queen Anne needlework panel of a shepherd and a shepherdess, early 18th century, the figures with their flock in a pastoral landscape, 28½ x 22½in. overall.
(Sotheby's) £1,929 $3,162

An early 19th century embroidered silk picture depicting a Biblical scene, 17¾ x 14½in. gilt frame.
(Andrew Hartley) £270 $454

An Aubusson pastoral tapestry, French, late 19th century, woven with a scène galante after Boucher, 215cm. wide, 183cm. high.
(Sotheby's) £3,450 $5,692

A Charles II needlework picture of a Biblical narrative, third quarter 17th century, depicting the narrative of Christ and the Woman at the Well, 24 x 19½in. overall.
(Sotheby's) £1,052 $1,725

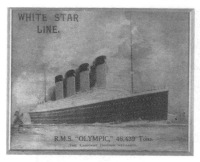

James S Mann, White Star Line RMS Olympic 46,439 Tons The Largest British Steamer, chromo-lithographic showcard, printed by T Forman & Sons Nottingham, 37 x 47cm., framed, circa 1910. (Onslow's) £660 $1,036

Marshall (Logan) Ed.Sinking of The Titanic and Great Sea Disasters, 1st ed, plates and engravings, photographic and decorative boards, 1912. (Onslow's) £50 $79

White Star Triple-Screw Steamers 'Olympic' 45,000 Tons and 'Titanic' 45,000 Tons The Largest Steamers In The World, a monochrome cutaway section by G F Morrell, 24 x 112cm. unfolded. (Onslow's) £800 $1,256

A mahogany dining chair with arm rests and removable cane seat panel, the underside of the chair stamped *White Star line*, repairs and restorations. (Onslow's) £480 $754

Souvenir In Affectionate Remembrance of the Captain Mates Crew and Passengers of the Worlds Largest Liner SS Titanic, decorated paper napkin with vignette of ship and the last hymn, 37cm. square. (Onslow's) £95 $149

A bronze Carpathia Medal, named to Joseph Blakely, *Presented to the Captain Officers and Crew of the RMS Carpathia in Recognition of Gallant & Heroic Services from the Survivors of TSS Titanic April 15th 1912*. (Onslow's) £4,000 $6,280

A Marconigram sent from the Carpathia by Mrs W Bucknell, First Class Survivor to L Pecorini via PO Box 46 Rome *Both Saved Mother* and sent at 7-45am on 18th April 1912. (Onslow's) £1,000 $1,570

Shipping Casualties (Loss of The Steamship Titanic) Report of a Formal Investigation Into The circumstances, pub by HMSO, blue wrappers, 1912. (Onslow's) £750 $1,177

In Memoriam Wallace Hartley The Musician Hero of The Titanic Which Foundered April 14th 1912, printed with vignette of Hartley, the ship and the hymn Nearer My God To Thee, 10 x 15cm. (Onslow's) £140 $220

Hood (A G) Ed. Souvenir Number of The Shipbuilder, The White Star Triple-Screw Atlantic Liners Olympic and Titanic, Mid Summer 1911. (Onslow's)   £1,200 $1,884

Norman Wilkinson, Cunard Line Royal Mail Four-Screw Steamers Lusitania and Mauretania Finest Fastest & Largest Steamers In The World, colour lithographic showcard, 34 x 50cm. (Onslow's)   £550 $864

Mowbray (Jay Henry) Sinking of the Titanic The Most Appalling Ocean Horror, memorial edition, pub by The Minter Company Pennsylvania, plates, blue cloth with plate to cover. (Onslow's)   £95 $150

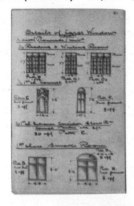

A Harland & Wolff manuscript notebook entitled Particulars of Oceanic Steam Navigation Co SS 'Olympic' May 1911, official Number 131346, rubber stamped *Harland & Wolff Ship Builders & Engineers Belfast* and dated in ink *31/5/11*. (Onslow's) £5,000 $7,850

A sterling silver mug inscribed *To Captain Rostron As A Token of Grateful Appreciation of His Kindness on the Carpathia after the sinking of the Titanic April 15th 1912 from John B Thayer Jr*, 6.5cm. high. (Onslow's)   £4,200 $6,594

Account of Wages for Steward James Witter Titanic, date of engagement 10th April date of discharge 15th April 1912 [the men's pay stopped as the waters closed over Titanic's rudder]; with a signed copy of Walter Lord's book A Night To Remember. (Onslow's)   £1,450 $2,276

Lord (Walter) A Night To Remember, 1st English ed, plates, dj, 1956, fine copy. (Onslow's)   £35 $55

The Titanic Her First and Last Voyage, Carlton China jug, 6½cm. high, repaired. (Onslow's)   £200 $314

An In Memoriam sheet for the Greatest Sea Disaster of Modern Times, printed with five different songs. (Onslow's)   £35 $55

White Star Line 'Olympic' & 'Titanic' Largest Steamers In The World, a publicity booklet entitled Notes and Illustrations of the First and Second Class Passenger Accommodation on the New White Star Line Triple-Screw Royal Mail Steamers 'Olympic' & 'Titanic'.
(Onslow's)   £5,800 $9,106

White Star Line white linen bedspread, ornately decorated with monogram, 215 x 160cm., laundered and starched.
(Onslow's)   £600 $942

SS Titanic Section Plan & Section Scale 1/32 to 1ft rubber stamped *Harland & Wolff Ltd Shipbuilders & Engineers Belfast* and dated in ink *1/5/12*, 71 x 81cm., framed.
(Onslow's)   £1,400 $2,198

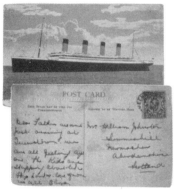

White Star Liner RMS Titanic, colour art postcard No 1830, from Eliza Johnston to Mr William Johnston, Newmachar, Aberdeenshire *Dear Father, We have just arrived at Queenstown We are all feeling A1......*
(Onslows)   £3,000 $4,710

In Memory of the Captain Crew and Passengers Who Lost Their Lives by the Wreck of the Titanic, printed paper napkin with vignette of the ship, 39cm. square.
(Onslow's)   £90 $141

Titanic, a fine real photograph, sent by Joe Boxhall, fourth Officer of the Titanic, published Southampton 5th April 1912.
(Vennett-Smith)   £2,100 $3,423

The Journal of Commerce Report of the British Official Enquiry into The Circumstances Attending The Loss of the RMS Titanic, reprinted from The Journal of Commerce, July 1912. (Onslow's) £420 $659

A copper two handled wine cooler or ice bucket by Elkington & Co, stamped *White Star Line Restaurant*, 23cm. diameter.
(Onslow's)   £600 $942

Royal Opera Covent Garden, programme to the Dramatic and Operatic Matinee in Aid of The Titanic Disaster fund, Tuesday May 14th 1912. (Onslow's) £210 $329

TITANIC

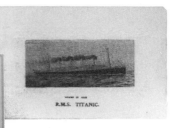

Captain E J Smith, signed
certificate of discharge to Samuel
Taylor Boatswain on the Britannic,
date of discharge 4th August 1893,
signed by Captain Smith; and
another for the Adriatic, dated 1889.
(Onslow's)   £1,150 $1,805

The Sphere Titanic Supplement,
12pp, April 27th 1912; and another
similar The Graphic, April 27th
1912. (Onslow's)   £280 $440

Titanic, embroidered silk, by
Stevens, with yellow and black
funnels and two flags, scalloped
border, rare.
(Vennett-Smith)   £760 $1,216

The key and brass identity tag to
the Chart Room on RMS Titanic,
the mortice lock key attached to the
rectangular shaped brass tag with
brass ring, the tag stamped on one
side Chart Room.
(Onslow's)   £12,000 $18,840

A relic from the RMS Titanic,
comprising a pair of ivory and brass
opera glasses in case, inscribed,
together with a framed manuscript
letter and a volume 'Nicholls's
Seamanship Guide'.
(Andrew Hartley)   £2,000 $3,300

Everett (Marshall) Ed. Wreck and
Sinking of the Titanic The Ocean's
Greatest Disaster, memorial edition,
plates, bound in green cloth, artists
mono photographic plates to cover,
1912.
(Onslow's)   £170 $267

A White Star Line green and gold
decorated soup bowl by Stonier &
Co Liverpool Registered No
589223, with OSNC monogram,
24cm. diameter.
(Onslow's)   £500 $785

Russell (Thomas H) Ed. Sinking of
the Titanic World's Greatest Sea
Disaster, 1st ed, plates, bound in
red cloth, monochrome plate of the
ship sinking.
(Onslow's)   £260 $408

A White Star Line circular cut glass
crystal fruit bowl, engraved with
company burgee, 21cm. diameter.
(Onslow's)   £850 $1,334

A late Victorian painted cast iron and metal coal box of tapered rectangular form with slightly domed and hinged cover, pierced foliate handles, 19¼in. high. (Christie's) £345 $552

A pair of French tôle peinte oil lamps, early 19th century, the red ground heightened in gilt with foliate motifs, 13in. high. (Christie's) £3,450 $5,658

A Ralph Cahoon antique tea bin decorated with a gentleman toasting a lady, oil on wood, 24⅛in. high. (Skinner) £1,552 $2,530

A pair of japanned metal tea canisters with domed tops and covers, each painted black and emblazoned with coats-of-arms, 17¼in. high. (Christie's) £483 $782

Pair of tôle chestnut covered urns, on stepped feet, with serpentine handles, the tapered cover with octagonal gilt finials, paint decorated with foliage in gold and sienna on black ground, 12in. high. (Skinner) £1,438 $2,300

A pair of Regency style black tôle peinte chesnut urns, of ovoid form, decorated with gilt flower sprays, 12½in. (Christie's) £750 $1,200

Pair of tin candle sconces, with chimneyed demi-lune top above elongated body, single candle bobèche, 13½ x 3in. (Skinner) £383 $632

A pair of tôle peinte cache pots and liners, early 19th century, each of flaring square section, gilt with trophies, 7¾in. high. (Sotheby's) £1,104 $1,840

A 19th century five-section treen spice tower. (Academy Auctioneers) £145 $232

An early pair of wrought iron scissors. (Tony Murland) £16 $26

A pair of farriers' pliers, 10 x 2in., beautifully proportioned and decorated and dated *1706*.
(Tony Murland)   £3,450 $5,727

A wrought iron wrench, Wynn & Co. Patent. (Tony Murland)   £45 $75

An 18th century rosewood and brass bevel, dated 1776.
(Tony Murland)   £390 $647

A 31 x 8in., late 17th century/early 18th century, anvil.
(Tony Murland)   £380 $631

A pair of primitive 11in. scissors, probably 18th century.
(Tony Murland)   £36 $60

A 19th century French clogmakers' knife, cleverly carved walnut handle in the form of a booted leg. Small brass pins form eyelets on the boot. Complete with bench vice.
(Tony Murland)   £320 $531

The Grebe Patented adjustable wrench by Carrington. Wrenches are often named after birds.
(Tony Murland)   £45 $75

A rare 2ft two-fold mastmakers' boxwood rule with slide by Samson Aston, 1833-1870. There is a scale for the length of gun deck which suggests a date pre 1850.
(Tony Murland)   £1,350 $2,160

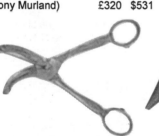

A delightful pair of orchid secateurs with decorated handles and an ingenious device for gently gripping the cut stem to avoid damage.
(Tony Murland)   £15 $25

A 16th/17th century, 13 x 10in. stake anvil. Classic early form, the hexagonal stake thickens at the bottom to form an elegant buttress.
(Tony Murland)   £180 $299

An early 19th century, Continental stirrup adze, smith's stamp and initials *PM* on the blade.
(Tony Murland)   £85 $141

A pair of 18th century scissors. Good for age.
(Tony Murland)   £2 $3

An 18th century wrought iron besaigue, shorter than normal at 38in., smith's stamp in the form of initials. (Tony Murland) £60 $100

A 31 x 8in. 16/17th century French anvil, early style. Museum quality.
(Tony Murland)   £320 $531

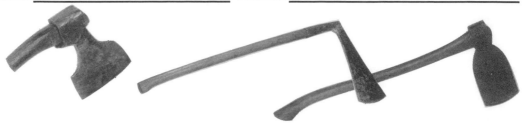

A rare type of 17th century felling axe. (Tony Murland) £190 $315

An 18th century French axe, 15 x 5in. (Tony Murland) £85 $141

A No.2 blocking axe by Gilpin. (Tony Murland) £30 $50

A medieval axe head personifying the days of combat and tyranny. (Tony Murland) £55 $91

A bearded side axe, 5½in. blade. (Tony Murland) £60 $100

A coopers' bowl adze, 9¼in. edge and smith's marks. (Tony Murland) £50 $83

A 3½lb. Brades bearded side axe, 5¾in. blade. (Tony Murland) £120 $199

An 18th century decorated axe, 4½in. blade, probably early replaced handle. (Tony Murland) £125 $207

An all purpose Turkish axe with important decoration on the blade. (Tony Murland) £40 $66

A 13in. American broad axe by Yerkes & Plumb, found in a barn in Kansas. (Tony Murland) £105 $174

A fine American side axe by A. Chaney & Co., Ogdensburg, 11in. blade, most unusual scalloped head. (Tony Murland) £150 $249

A French coachbuilders' side axe, some worm to original handle. (Tony Murland) £50 $83

A quality 14in. socketed side axe head. (Tony Murland) £170 $282

An early socketed axe, 6in. blade. (Tony Murland) £90 $149

An 18th century European side axe head. (Tony Murland) £180 $299

A flamboyant shipwrights' masting axe, 11¾ x 5¼in., by Ward & Payne. (Tony Murland) £75 $125

A bearded side axe by Melhuish, London, 6in. blade. (Tony Murland)   £81 $134

A miners' axe, the handle marked with property marks. (Tony Murland)   £35 $58

A good French coopers' side axe with 8½in. blade, by C. Baudin. (Tony Murland)   £82 $136

A vine cutting tool stamped *Alier Toule*. (Tony Murland) £60 $100

An early foresters' axe with original hickory handle. (Tony Murland)   £45 $75

Clogmakers' axe with a rare shape, reminiscent of medieval times. (Tony Murland)   £75 $125

An embossed, double bitted axe head by Dorpian. (Tony Murland)   £110 $183

A small sugar axe. (Tony Murland) £35 $58

A fine side axe by Simmons, offset hickory handle, 9¼in. blade. (Tony Murland)   £125 $207

A carpenters' socketed paring axe with double bevel, heart design on the blade. (Tony Murland) £65 $108

A vining axe from the north-east of France, marked *Souillet A Pont Dain*. (Tony Murland)   £80 $133

A heavy felling axe from Brittany. (Tony Murland)   £60 $100

A 13in. American side axe with offset hickory handle. (Tony Murland)   £65 $108

An early beheading axe, 9¾in. socket and 8in. blade, pitted but rare. (Tony Murland) £125 $207

A rare plated beech brace with
brass revolving handle and head.
(Tony Murland)   £320 $697

A good Cuban mahogany
archimedian drill.
(Tony Murland) £35 $58

A Continental bevel gear drill,
rosewood fittings.
(Tony Murland)   £90 $149

A fine ebony bowdrill with bow.
(Tony Murland)   £100 $166

A little used French pianomakers'
fruitwood brace with brass baluster
by Mattheau, Paris.
(Tony Murland)   £160 $266

An extremely decorative lignum
vitae bowdrill and bow with box of
bits. (Tony Murland) £135 $224

A brass framed ebony brace,
Holtzapffel.
(Tony Murland)   £720 $1,195

A smaller than normal two bar iron
cage head brace, late 18th/early
19th century.
(Tony Murland)   £50 $83

A beech plated brace by
Mathieson, Glasgow.
(Tony Murland)   £80 $133

A quality European fruitwood
pianomakers' brace marked
Gust Monch.
(Tony Murland)   £100 $166

An early French chairmakers' elm
brace and scarce breast plate, also
a brace blank.
(Tony Murland)   £80 $133

A Robert Marples boxwood and
brass framed brace. Boxwood is
the most rare of all fillings and this
is the only example known.
(Tony Murland)   £2,000 $3,320

A unique plated brace by Frederick
Edmunds, with the never before
seen ring pad mechanism stamped
Edmunds Patent.
(Tony Murland)   £200 $332

An extremely rare breast drill by
Mathieson with the Mathieson
Patent spring lock device, the first
breast drill incorporating this lock.
(Tony Murland)   £85 $151

An extremely rare beech filled
Ultimatum, featuring double ring
pad and the 67, Spring Lane screw
cap, 1854-55.
(Tony Murland)   £420 $697

A fine Pilkington plated brace.
(Tony Murland) £510 $847

An early Scandinavian breast
auger. (Tony Murland) £35 $58

A breech coopers' brace with 3
pads. (Tony Murland) £100 $166

An unusual French brass oil can.
(Tony Murland)   £70 $116

A 4in. miniature copper oil can by
Kayes, stamped *Meccano* on the
base. (Tony Murland) £100 $166

A steel oil can, brass plaque, *Derby
Station*. (Tony Murland) £72 $120

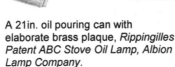

An incredibly rare oil can with
plunger.
(Tony Murland)   £160 $266

A 21in. oil pouring can with
elaborate brass plaque, *Rippingilles
Patent ABC Stove Oil Lamp, Albion
Lamp Company*.
(Tony Murland)   £155 $257

A rare oil can by Garrett & Saveall,
Engineers, Maidstone.
(Tony Murland)   £72 $120

An early 19th century copper glue
pot, 6½in. diameter.
(Tony Murland)   £85 $141

An elegant steel oil can marked
Griffiths & Browett, 1902,
Birmingham.
(Tony Murland)   £100 $166

A 4in. copper glue pot, engraved
E.T. (Tony Murland)   £50 $80

A Stenhau patented brass oil
pourer. (Tony Murland)£130 $216

An early copper spraying can.
(Tony Murland)   £40 $66

A Helix school ink pourer.
(Tony Murland) £30 $50

A copper glue pot, interesting
integral stand.
(Tony Murland)   £80 $133

A 6in. Kayes conical oil can.
(Tony Murland)   £20 $32

A brass oil pourer, attractive style.
(Tony Murland)   £120 $199

An 18th century masons' escutcheon chisel.
(Tony Murland)   £20 $33

A most unusual pair of turning gouges by Addis.
(Tony Murland)   £60 $100

A 2in. sash pocket chisel by Marples. (Tony Murland) £15 $25

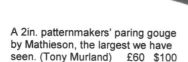

A swan neck chisel by Ibbotson, boxwood handle.
(Tony Murland)   £72 $120

2 oval handled mortise chisels with rope carved handles.
(Tony Murland)   £60 $100

A fine virtually unused 1^{15}/$_{16}$in. bevel edged paring chisel by James Howarth. (Tony Murland) £55 $91

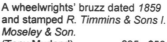

A 2in. patternmakers' paring gouge by Mathieson, the largest we have seen. (Tony Murland)   £60 $100

A wheelwrights' bruzz dated *1859* and stamped *R. Timmins & Sons I. Moseley & Son.*
(Tony Murland)   £35 $58

A 3½in. shipwrights' slick by Watts, New York.
(Tony Murland)   £130 $216

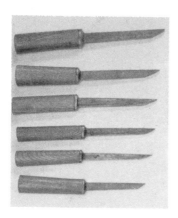

6 good oval handled mortise chisels by Marples.
(Tony Murland)   £70 $116

A complete set of 10 mortise chisels by I.Sorby, Sheffield, ^{1}/$_8$ to ¾in. with oval beech handles in almost unused condition, in hanging workshop cabinet.
(Tony Murland)   £235 $390

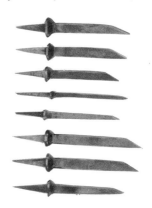

8 graduated mortise chisels. Unhandled and unamed.
(Tony Murland)   £60 $100

5 straight patternmakers' gouges by Marples. (Tony Murland) £50 $83

A set of 22 carving chisels by Herring in the original fitted case.
(Tony Murland)   £360 $598

A set of 12 quality Marples carving chisels in the original oak case.
(Tony Murland)   £180 $299

(Tool Shop Auctions)

DIVIDERS & CALIPERS_____ TOOLS _____

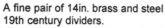

A pair of 8in. decorated 18th century French dividers. It is unusual to find them this small. (Tony Murland)   £240 $398

A fine pair of 14in. brass and steel 19th century dividers. (Tony Murland)   £112 $186

A magnificent pair of 22in. late 17th/early 18th century Dutch dividers decorated with a multitude of Cupid's bows and ovolos. (Tony Murland)   £380 $631

A pair of wrought rion wheelwrights' calipers. Classic 18th century hinge arrangement, 13in. tall. (Tony Murland)   £160 $256

A pair of 4¼in. early 19th century dancing-master calipers with detailed boots and seductive frilly garters. (Tony Murland) £180 $299

An early pair of double ended calipers. (Tony Murland)   £130 $216

EEL & FISH SPEARS

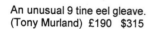

An unusual 9 tine eel gleave. (Tony Murland) £190 $315

A 21¾in. long 5 tine eel gleave. Pitted. (Tony Murland) £110 $183

An early 5 tine eel gleave. (Tony Murland)   £100 $166

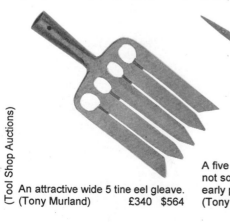

An attractive wide 5 tine eel gleave. (Tony Murland)   £340 $564

A five tine eel gleave. This spear is not socketed and is therefore a very early piece. (Tony Murland)   £250 $415

An early five pronged fish spear. (Tony Murland)   £70 $116

A watchmakers' hammer.
(Tony Murland) £40 $66

An 18th century claw hammer with typical decorative twisted and turned iron handle.
(Tony Murland)   £80 $133

A 19th century double headed veneer hammer.
(Tony Murland)   £50 $83

A strange repoussé hammer with elaborately turned ebony handle.
(Tony Murland)   £85 $141

A very rare coachmakers' hammer and gouge combination.
(Tony Murland)   £65 $107

A small diamondcutters' hammer, boxwood handle.
(Tony Murland)   £50 $83

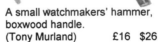

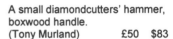

A rare D. Kimberley & Sons Patent combination claw hammer and tool handle, 9 tools in the hollow handle.
(Tony Murland)   £100 $160

A small watchmakers' hammer, boxwood handle.
(Tony Murland)   £16 $26

An unusual iron combination hammer and chisel for opening wine crates, stamped *Peatling & Cawdron - Vintners.*
(Tony Murland)   £20 $32

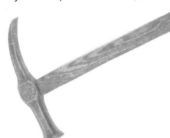

A boatbuilders' copper riveting hammer.
(Tony Murland)   £48 $80

An 18th century French veneer hammer, museum quality.
(Tony Murland)   £1,220 $2,025

A classic French hammer with solid ebony handle.
(Tony Murland)   £78 $129

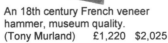

An early farriers' hammer with delightful 'rabbit's ear' claws.
(Tony Murland)   £85 $141

A 19th century watchmakers' hammer, ebony handle.
(Tony Murland)   £65 $107

A rare double claw hammer stamped *Double Claw Patent, Nov. 1902.* (Tony Murland) £135 $224

An early boxwood marking gauge.
(Tony Murland)   £45 $75

A brass headed ebony cutting gauge.
(Tony Murland)   £60 $100

A brass stemmed ebony mortise gauge. (Tony Murland) £80 $133

A combined mortise, slitting gauge. Patent 10785.
(Tony Murland)   £75 $125

A boxwood and brass mortise gauge. (Tony Murland) £55 $91

A brass framed mortise gauge, heavy brass head.
(Tony Murland)   £58 $92

A rare rosewood and brass mortise gauge with rack and pinion adjustment through the face of the stock. (Tony Murland) £100 $160

An extremely scarce rosewood and brass mortise gauge with rack and pinion adjustment.
(Tony Murland)   £110 $183

A hardly used brass stemmed ebony stock mortise gauge by J.&.H. Harrison, Newcastle.
(Tony Murland)   £42 $67

An unusual brass and mahogany slitting gauge.
(Tony Murland)   £15 $25

A solid brass craftsman made dovetail gauge.
(Tony Murland)   £55 $91

A brass expanding dovetail gauge Pat. No. 29191.
(Tony Murland)   £42 $70

A rosewood cutting gauge.
(Tony Murland)   £25 $41

An ebony and brass cutting gauge.
(Tony Murland)   £55 $91

An ebony, brass stemmed mortise gauge. (Tony Murland)   £25 $41

815

A superb 16¾in. dovetailed
Mathieson plane.
(Tony Murland) £630 $1,045

A very rare 27½in. beech jointer by
I. Sym. Round top iron and wedge.
(Tony Murland) £430 $714

A 4in. beech brass fronted
bullnose, Eastwood.
(Tony Murland) £40 $66

An important iron panel plane by
Slater, 12½in. long. overstuffed
rosewood infill with particularly
stylish front bun and rear handle.
(Tony Murland) £460 $764

An early Spiers smoothing plane
with screwed sides, tapered iron.
(Tony Murland) £95 $158

A rare and important 6½ x 2¹/₁₆in.
block plane by Spiers, the brass
lever cap swivels on a pin running
through the body of the plane.
(Tony Murland) £1,220 $2,025

A very rare Preston No. 1355C
bullnose, side fenced, rabbet and
chamfer plane. The side fence
adjusts for ³/₁₆in. to 1in. rabbets and
is operated by the milled head
screw. (Tony Murland) £485 $805

An important patented block plane
by Joseph Fenn, parallel sided
beech adjustable smoothing plane,
7 x 2½in., stamped *J. Fenn
Registered 12 Nov. 1844.*
(Tony Murland) £800 $1,328

A possibly unique combined plough
and fillister by Kimberley, Pat. No.
2848, the body of the plane
stamped *Highest Award 3 Gold
Medals.* (Tony Murland) £560 $930

A Stanley 196 circular rabbet plane,
nickel plating 90% but dull.
(Tony Murland) £500 $830

A pre war Norris A2 dovetailed
smoother, rosewood infill, good
parallel iron by Marples.
(Tony Murland) £370 $614

A 17½in. Spiers panel plane with
original Sorby parallel iron.
(Tony Murland) £206 $342

A Stanley 4½H.
(Tony Murland) £640 $1,062

A Preston beech rebate plane,
3½in. long. (Tony Murland) £25 $42

A fine Stanley No.2C smoothing
plane. (Tony Murland) £250 $400

A Stanley No.10¼in.
carriagemakers' rabbet plane with
tilting handles.
(Tony Murland)   £270 $448

A very important iron Vergatthobel,
3¾ x 1¾in., brazed construction
with protruding toe returning to form
a scroll. (Tony Murland) £350 $581

A pre war Norris A6 dovetailed
smoothing plane with rosewood
infill, good parallel iron.
(Tony Murland)   £600 $996

An early 19th century gunmetal 2¼
x 1⁵/₈in. flat bottom cellomakers'
plane, German steel sole with the
blade retained by a knurled nut
similar to those examples by Norris
and Preston.
(Tony Murland)   £100 $166

A late 16th, early 17th century
European musical Instrument
makers' plane, front tote repaired
with smith-made rivets, with a band
of decoration around the top.
(Tony Murland)   £550 $913

A classically shaped 16th/17th
century violinmakers' plane from
Europe, 19th century toothing iron,
brazed construction, 6 x 1⁷/₈in.
(Tony Murland)   £450 $747

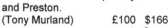

A ¾in. dovetail rebate by Spiers in
a mahogany box.
(Tony Murland) £70 $116

A Stanley 85 scraper plane, original
blade, remains of trade label.
(Tony Murland)   £420 $697

A steel soled gunmetal smoothing
plane, rosewood infill, by Slater.
(Tony Murland)   £350 $581

A ¾in. rebate plane, dovetailed with rosewood infill, by Spiers of Ayr. (Tony Murland) £60 $100

An early 9¼ x 2¾in. Spiers dovetail mitre plane, rosewood infill. Some superficial pitting. (Tony Murland) £220 $365

A 10in. ovolo by Robert Wooding. (Tony Murland) £470 $780

A Defiance No.9 circular plane with the original Defiance cap iron and blade marked _Bailey Tool Co., Woonsocket RI._ (Tony Murland) £210 $349

A 10½in. hollow, Robert Wooding. Stamp. (Tony Murland) £490 $813

A panel raising plane in bird's-eye maple by The N. E. Toolworks, Groton, Connecticut. (Tony Murland) £140 $232

A unique Stanley prototype block plane, 7⅞ x 2¼in., low angle block plane with no mouth adjustment black japanning to the inside of the body. (Tony Murland) £5,150 $8,549

A steel soled gunmetal parallel sided smoothing plane, 2¾ x 9in. overall, by Mathieson, with solid rosewood infill and closed handle, unmentioned in any Mathieson catalogue. (Tony Murland) £885 $1,469

A significant crown moulding plane by Iennion, 1738-1757, 13¾ x 4¼in. Found in Pennsylvania, this plane displays the classic handle and wedge shape of the 18th century East Coast American made cornice planes. (Tony Murland) £720 $1,195

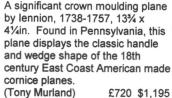

A 5½in, coachmaker's wedge stemmed beech plough with reduced compass skate. (Tony Murland) £200 $360

A majestic D router in hornbeam. (Tony Murland) £45 $75

A tremendous quality 22in. afrormosia tri plane. Extremely attractive figured wood,19th century. (Tony Murland) £50 $83

A steel soled gunmetal smoothing plane by T. J. Gardner, with rosewood infill.
(Tony Murland)   £320 $531

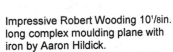

Impressive Robert Wooding 10¹/₈in. long complex moulding plane with iron by Aaron Hildick.
(Tony Murland)   £1,200 $1,992

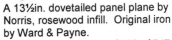

A 13½in. dovetailed panel plane by Norris, rosewood infill. Original iron by Ward & Payne.
(Tony Murland)   £450 $747

A fine complex cornice plane, G. Nurse & Co.
(Tony Murland)   £370 $614

A rare 20½in. dovetailed Norris A1 jointer, rosewood infill.
(Tony Murland)   £1,580 $2,623

An Iron smoothing plane by Holtzapffel, 8¾ x 2¾in. rosewood infill and brass lever cap, tapered iron probably not original.
(Tony Murland)   £530 $880

A significant yellow birch crown moulding plane by Cesar Chelor, 13¹/₈ x 4³/₈in., stamped *Ce:Chelor Living In Wrenthem*. 18th century American.
(Tony Murland)   £8,400 $13,944

A Millers patent adjustable plough plane, the fence and fillister bottom missing otherwise complete with gunmetal fence, shortened spur to rosewood handle.
(Tony Murland)   £440 $730

A rosewood handled centre wheel plough plane with ivory tips by The Ohio Tool Company.
(Tony Murland)   £6,050 $10,043

An important English dovetailed steel panel plane, 14 x 2⁵/₈in., by Robert Towell, sole protrudes at the front and the back, front overstuffed with rosewood.
(Tony Murland)   £880 $1,461

A tremendously rare Smiths' plane by Holtzapffel & Deyerlein, London (pre 1826). This is only one of five known examples actually marked *Holtzapffel*.
(Tony Murland)   £1,150 $1,909

An extremely rare, 7 x 2³/₈in., Norris A16 smoothing plane with original iron, annealed iron body and rosewood infill.
(Tony Murland)   £900 $1,494

A Stanley No. 2 brass plumb bob.
(Tony Murland) £100 $166

A primitive 18th century, 2in., iron plumb bob.(Tony Murland) £35 $58

A No. 11, 6in. brass plumb bob.
(Tony Murland) £135 $224

A lovely 7½in. steel tipped brass plumb bob, with early rope knurling
(Tony Murland) £50 $83

An attractive 2in. brass plumb bob with knurled decoration to the finial, the shoulder and the base, and punched decoration to the waist.
(Tony Murland) £30 $50

A pretty, steel tipped brass plumb bob, 3½in.
(Tony Murland) £45 $75

A 5½in. brass plumb bob with reversible point.
(Tony Murland) £45 $75

A heavy 5in. steel tipped onion bob.
(Tony Murland) £60 $100

A magnificent 6½in. steel tipped plumb bob.
(Tony Murland) £240 $398

An early spherical brass plumb bob with steel pin and finial, 9in. overall.
(Tony Murland) £100 $166

A very decorative, 10½ steel tipped brass plumb bob, late nineteenth early twentieth century.
(Tony Murland) £220 $365

A large 6in. steel tipped brass plumb bob.
(Tony Murland) £100 $166

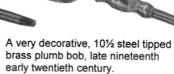

An elegant 8in. steel tipped plumb bob with pretty finial, historically clockmakers'.
(Tony Murland) £230 $382

A tremendous brass plumb square, 15in. wide with exotic fretworked plumb bobs forming the central design, probably 18th century.
(Tony Murland) £390 $647

An unusual brass plumb bob with elongated brass neck and knurled finial. Steel tipped, 5in. overall.
(Tony Murland) £60 $100

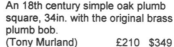

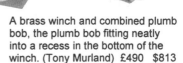

An early 5½in. steel tipped brass plumb bob with contemporaneous bronze reel.
(Tony Murland) £50 $83

An 18th century simple oak plumb square, 34in. with the original brass plumb bob.
(Tony Murland) £210 $349

A brass winch and combined plumb bob, the plumb bob fitting neatly into a recess in the bottom of the winch. (Tony Murland) £490 $813

An exotic brass hacksaw with horn handle. (Tony Murland) £80 $133

A late 18th/19th century hacksaw. (Tony Murland) £45 $75

A miniature 19th century 6in. hacksaw. (Tony Murland) £35 $58

A 14in. brass back Henry Disston tenon saw with applewood handle. (Tony Murland) £60 $100

An elegant mahogany bowsaw, boxwood handles. (Tony Murland) £50 $83

A 16in. Spear & Jackson brass back saw. (Tony Murland) £25 $42

A most unusual 18th century hacksaw, fruitwood handle. (Tony Murland) £60 $100

An important early 28in. compass saw by Hill late Howel. (Tony Murland) £65 $108

An early, shapely hacksaw with boxwood handle. (Tony Murland) £35 $58

An iron hacksaw, 24in. overall. Classic eighteenth century form and construction. (Tony Murland) £75 $125

An eighteenth century, 17½in., surgeons' bone saw, blackwood handle, classic early features. (Tony Murland) £90 $149

An 18th century armourers' saw, lovely ram's horn locking nut and original blade. (Tony Murland) £380 $631

An extremely scarce Shaker flushing saw, 7in., the handle reflecting the elegance of this style. Found in New England. (Tony Murland) £190 $315

An incredibly rare example of a double handled stairsaw in Brazilian rosewood. (Tony Murland) £200 $332

A 7¼in. ivory handled dovetail saw; this intriguing miniature saw, with its curved handle is almost certainly French 19th century. (Tony Murland) £190 $315

A well made Cuban mahogany stairsaw. (Tony Murland) £50 $83

A superb 6in. dovetail saw by Cooker Grayson & Co. (Tony Murland) £130 $216

A 26in. rip saw by Fletcher, Chelsea. (Tony Murland) £28 $46

Dinky Hawker Hurricane Mk IIc in light grey and dark green camouflage, in original bubble pack. (Wallis & Wallis) £95 $152

Dinky A6M5 Zero-Sen Fighter in a metallic turquoise with red dot markings, in original bubble pack. (Wallis & Wallis) £85 $136

Dinky Messerschmitt BF 109E, in light brown and green spotted camouflage, in original bubble pack. (Wallis & Wallis) £110 $176

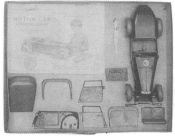

A scarce Meccano No 1 constructor car, in the form of a No3 road racer, black body and tinplate wheel hubs, red seats, windscreen and wheelarches, original box. (Wallis & Wallis) £300 $480

A scarce Chad Valley early 1930s pantechnicon, clockwork powered in tinplate litho, printed in green, cream panelled sides. (Wallis & Wallis) £245 $392

French Dinky Supertoys Super G Constellation Lockheed, in silver Air France livery, F-B HBX registration, boxed. (Wallis & Wallis) £80 $128

A rare Dinky Stripey the Magic Mini in white with red, white blue and yellow chevron stripes, complete in original box with display insert. (Wallis & Wallis) £260 $416

A scarce Britains Lambretta scooter (9685), in grey with blue side panels, and two riders in casual dress both with white helmets, in original box. (Wallis & Wallis) £130 $208

Dinky Bedford TK Crash tender, in white and dark green, Top Rank Motorway Service livery, complete with line and hook, boxed. (Wallis & Wallis) £65 $104

Dinky Military Recovery tractor in matt olive green, complete with line and hook, boxed. (Wallis & Wallis) £45 $72

Dinky horse box in maroon BR livery, Express Horse Box Hire Service etc. to sides, boxed. (Wallis & Wallis) £95 $152

A scarce Hornby No. 5 Speedboat Viking, 17in. long, blue tinplate hull pressed portholes to midships sides, cutaway lower aft deck with cockpit, in original box and packing. (Wallis & Wallis) £360 $576

A rare early 1950s Japanese tinplate Flashy Ray Gun by Nomura, automatic rifle style with battery operated action, in original box. (Wallis & Wallis) £80 $128

Dinky Spitfire Mk II in green and light brown camouflage, with battery pack, in original bubble pack. (Wallis & Wallis) £85 $136

Dinky Missile Erector vehicle with Corporal missile and launching platform, in matt olive green, complete with missile, boxed. (Wallis & Wallis) £140 $224

A rare pre war tinplate farm tractor and trailer by Gunthermann, 9¼ overall when joined, tractor in yellow with red and black litho detail.
(Wallis & Wallis) £70 $112

A Louis Marx Japanese made battery operated BOAC VC 10 airliner, in plastic and tinplate 13½in. wingspan, in original picture lid box. (Wallis & Wallis) £85 $136

A scarce Wells & Co tinplate ambulance, 6½in. long, painted in cream with black chassis, simple litho print detailing, red cross to roof.
(Wallis & Wallis) £230 $368

A rare tinplate saloon car by Johann Distler Nuremberg, 10in. long, painted in yellow and black, with orange black litho print detailing, battery powered headlights and rear number plate box, 1922.
(Wallis & Wallis) £310 $496

Dinky ABC TV mobile control room, in light blue grey and red livery, complete with camera, cables and cameraman, boxed.
(Wallis & Wallis) £140 $224

A 1960s Schuco Elektro construction fire engine, chassis cab unit finished in red with bright trim, remote cord to steering and power control unit and flexi cord to battery box.
(Wallis & Wallis) £460 $736

A late 1920s Lehmann clockwork clown in two wheel cart pulled by a donkey, in pressed and litho finished tinplate.
(Wallis & Wallis) £200 $320

A scarce Merit toys space pilot 3 colour super sonic gun, with high frequency resonator, black plastic body, red muzzle.
(Wallis & Wallis) £40 $64

A Schuco mid 1960s Elektro aircraft Radiant, in Lufthansa livery, silver, blue and white litho printed, battery powered.
(Wallis & Wallis) £160 $256

An Arnold lithographed wind-up military jeep, with three sitting figures, 1948, 17cm. long. (Auction Team Köln)£75 $120

A Märklin Mercedes 300SL, 1952, 1992 Jubilee model in original box with original key and certificate, clockwork, 34cm. long. (Auction Team Köln) £251 $402

A Delage Racer by Jouets de Paris, tinplate with wind-up mechanism, 1930, 45cm. long. (Auction Team Köln)£1,005 $1,608

A Jouets Français Richard-Brasier model car, a one-off tin car, hand-finished and hand-painted, with original clockwork mechanism, circa 1905, 38cm. long. (Auction Team Köln)
£6,280 $10,000

An 'automatic' model rowing boat, possibly by the Scientific Toy Mfg. Co., wooden hull, with French clockwork mechanism, the composition rower with original clothing, circa 1910, 57cm. long. (Auction Team Köln) £2,303 $3,684

A Schuco tinplate Electro-Constructions fire engine, battery-powered, with adjustable extending ladder, 1956, 29cm. long. (Auction Team Köln)
£1,172 $1,875

A Hy-Que wise monkey, battery-powered tinplate toy by Nomura, Japan, with vinyl hands and face, circa 1958, 42cm. high. (Auction Team Köln) £92 $147

Child's painted wooden horse, on wooden base with wheels, original painted decoration and leather fittings, 19th century, 28½in. long. (Eldred's) £825 $1,320

A lithographed tinplate singing bird automaton by Georg Köhler, Nürnberg, which sings, flaps its wings, turns its head and opens its beak, wind-up mechanism. (Auction Team Köln)£293 $469

A Ca-Ju clockwork Sportmodell two-seat Coupé with dickey seat, red and black cast phenolic resin (bakelite), with operating steering, horn and indicators, in original box, 8in. long, late 1930s. (Christie's) £322 $572

Articulated sheet metal figure of a man, 19th century, 13¼in. high. (Skinner) £318 $518

A Greppert & Kelch (Gundka-Werke) 507/8 clockwork 'Cylon' motorcycle and sidecar, lithographed tinplate red motor-cycle, rider dressed in orange, 6¾in. long, 1920s. (Christie's) £552 $877

Painted wood horse-drawn baby vehicle, early 20th century, blue seat and base with red striping, rubber rimmed spoked rear wheels. (Skinner) £418 $690

A French Peugeot Six kit car, tinplate with brass and aluminium fittings, rubber tyres and plastic upholstery, 37cm. long. (Auction Team Köln) £523 $837

A Jouets de Paris Hispano Suiza, large clockwork tinplate toy, with electric lights, forward and reverse movement, 1927, 50cm. long. (Auction Team Köln) £3,475 $5,560

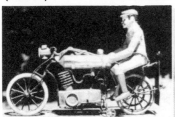

A handmade clockwork tin motorcycle pacer by Jouets Français, with brass headlights and tank, circa 1910-14, 13in. long. (Auction Team Köln) £3,140 $5,024

A Schuco battery-operated pale green Elektro Synchromatic 5700 painted tinplate Packard Convertible, in original box, plastic and tinplate 5550 Nautico, in original box and Varianto Lasto 3042 truck. (Christie's) £368 $585

A lithographed tinplate Technofix 'Man and Woman' wind-up toy, the linked carts shaking and the figures moving as if quarrelling, circa 1925. (Auction Team Köln) £439 $703

A Chad Valley Bonzo, velvet covered with painted facial features, swivel head, jointed limbs, card lined feet and original collar with button attached, 7in. tall, 1930s. (Christie's) £437 $699

A Tipp & Co. clockwork Fire Brigade turntable ladder truck, lithographed in red with yellow and black lining, with operating bell and four crew, 10in. long, 1930s. (Christie's) £402 $639

A Steiff kangaroo, with beige and cream mohair with airbrushed markings, black stitched nose, mouth and claws, swivel head and grey felt inner ears, 25in. tall, 1950s. (Christie's) £230 $366

A carved wooden rocking horse on bow rocker with glass eyes, original tail and remains of original tack, 67in. long. (Christie's) £632 $1,011

A battery-powered lithographed tinplate Space Patrol toy by Modern Toys, Japan, circa 1960. (Auction Team Köln) £79 $127

Hide-covered rocking horse, convertible to a horse on wheels, base painted red and blue, 19th century, 64in. long. (Eldred's) £550 $880

A late 19th century French automaton in the form of a bulldog with natural hide body, glass eyes, nodding head with growler and fibre and leather collar, on casters, 70cm. (Bearne's)   £350 $578

Red or Dead bear, dressed in scarlet satin body suit edged with black net ruff, black net lace stockings, a glittering mask and a diamante choker.
(Christie's)   £345 $566

A Dinky 514 Guy 'Slumberland' van, in original box.
(Christie's)   £437 $699

A Japanese machine robot by Horikawa dating to the 1950s-1960s approximately, 12in. tall, tinplate battery powered walking with swinging arms, in original box.
(Wallis & Wallis)   £110 $176

A rare set of Steiff skittles, comprising king bear, in red felt tail coat, 10in. tall, also a rabbit, elephant, cat, pig, monkey, and dog, each on turned wooden base, circa 1905, 8in. tall.
(Christie's)   £3,220 $5,119

A Saalheimer & Strauss mouse with saxophone, steam-driven lithographed tinplate model, circa 1925.
(Auction Team Köln) £921 $1,473

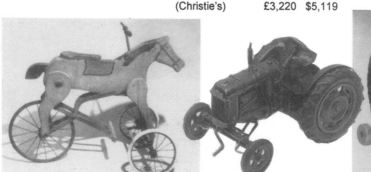

Child's riding horse, early 20th century, replaced wheels, some wear, 30in. high., 40in. long.
(Eldred's)   £100 $165

A rare Chad Valley Fordson E27N tractor, in dark blue with orange wheel hubs and Firestone rubber tyres, clockwork action. (Wallis & Wallis)   £170 $272

A Steiff bear on wheels, with dark brown mohair, cream mohair cut muzzle, brown stitched nose and mouth, pull-cord growler, 22in. long, 1930s. (Christie's)   £632 $1,036

A Louis Vuitton shoe trunk, of natural cow hide with brass rivets, the lid with a handle, the interior base lined in red felt, 22 x 14 x 14in, 1904.
(Christie's)   £1,265 $2,024

A pair of Louis Vuitton large suitcases each in L.V. material, with leather trimming, 31 x 21 x 10in., together with a Louis Vuitton, L.V. holdall. (David Lay)   £700 $1,127

A Louis Vuitton trunk, covered in LV monogram fabric, bound in leather and brass and with wooden banding, 23½ x 19 x 15in.
(Christie's)   £3,220 $5,152

A Louis Vuitton case, covered in LV fabric and bound in leather and brass, the interior with straps, 19½ x 14½ x 5½in.
(Christie's)   £632 $1,011

A Louis Vuitton dressing case of navy blue morocco leather, stamped *M.D.* beneath the handle, lined in navy blue leather and fitted with bottles, flasks, boxes and a mirror, 18½ x 12 x 5½in.
(Christie's)   £632 $1,011

A Louis Vuitton cabin trunk, covered in LV fabric and bound in leather and brass with wooden banding, monogrammed at either end *M.L.*, 110 x 55 x 33cm., 1931, lacks strap and tray.
(Christie's)   £1,092 $1,747

A brown leather, crocodile-skin mounted cosmetic case, with mauve cotton lining, silver topped bottles and boxes, mirror and manicure set, circa 1930, 45cm. wide.
(Auction Team Köln) £46 $74

A Louis Vuitton trunk, covered in LV fabric and bound in leather and brass with wooden banding, monogrammed at either end, 35½ x 21 x 13in.
(Christie's)   £2,530 $4,048

An American silver dressing case with silver fittings, Tiffany & Co., New York, circa 1925, 77oz. weighable, 18 pieces, 15¾in. long.
(Sotheby's)   £1,754 $2,875

A dressing case of dark brown crocodile leather, with foul weather cover monogrammed *L.D.G*, interior fitted with ivory-backed brushes, mirror manicure set, flasks, travel clock and writing case, 20 x 14 x 8½in.   (Christie's)   £690 $1,104

A Goyard trunk, covered in fabric with a basket weave motif, bound in leather and brass with wooden banding, fitted with a tray, 35 x 20½ x 13in.
(Christie's)   £747 $1,195

A barrister's wig in its original oval metal case finished in black with gold banding, circa 1900-1910, 10in. long. 7in. wide.
(H. C. Chapman)   £140 $232

A Louis Vuitton hat trunk, covered in LV fabric, lined in cream and red striped fabric and fitted with two webbed trays, 25½ x 24½ x 24½in, 1910. (Christie's)   £3,450 $5,520

A Louis Vuitton trunk, covered in LV fabric and bound in black painted leather and brass, with wooden banding, 24 x 20½ x 16in., 1911.
(Christie's)   £2,530 $4,040

A fine and very rare incised and gilt-lacquered leather travelling pannier, Liao dynasty, incised through a black lacquer layer and gold-filled on four sides, 16½ x 20½in.
(Christie's)   £20,700 $33,741

A Goyard wardrobe trunk, covered in fabric with a basket weave motif and bound in leather and brass, the interior lined in gold fabric, 34 x 19½ x 10½in.
(Christie's)   £414 $662

A Louis Vuitton trunk, covered in LV fabric, the interior fitted with three trays, two with compartments, 35 x 19½ x 19in.
(Christie's)   £3,220 $5,152

A Louis Vuitton toiletry case, of scarlet morocco leather, with fall front, the interior fitted with crystal bottles with domed silver gilt lids, 20½ x 11 x 6in.
(Christie's)   £1,500 $2,400

A Louis Vuitton hatbox, covered in chequered canvas and bound in leather and brass with a leather handle, 16½ x 15 x 13½in.
(Christie's)   £1,035 $1,656

A W.M.F. silvered metal tray, the centre cast in low relief with a couple preparing to kiss surrounded by a swirling pierced linear design, 28cm. diameter.
(Christie's) £184 $297

A late Victorian papier mâché tray, the black ground inset with mother-of-pearl Greek key and foliate bands, 30½in. wide, upon a later black painted faux-bamboo wooden stand. (Christie's) £402 $643

A small gold lacquer tray, signed *Yasushige*, Meiji period, decorated in hiramakie, takamakie, togidashi and kirikane on a kinji ground, 5in. long. (Christie's) £1,610 $2,624

A Gallé marquetry tray, of rectangular form, inlaid in various woods with a pendant leafy oak branch with acorns, 36cm. diameter. (Christie's) £483 $780

A Secessionist style silvered metal and pottery tray, of oval outline, the dish printed in shades of pink, brown and yellow, with two scroll handles, 65cm. diameter.
(Christie's) £322 $520

A mid late Regency papier mâché tray by Clay, of rectangular form with canted angles, the black ground painted with a vase of flowers, 30½ x 21in.
(Christie's) £3,680 $5,888

A Victorian mahogany butler's tray on stand, 19th century, of rectangular form with a serpentine front and three-sided wood gallery, 29½in. long.
(Sotheby's) £1,193 $1,955

A mahogany butler's tray on X-frame stand, 19th century, the oval tray with hinged sides pierced with carrying handles, the tray 35¼in. wide. (Christie's) £2,530 $4,099

A George III mahogany butler's tray-on-stand, the lift off tray with an undulating gallery, pierced with carrying handles, 27¼in. wide.
(Christie's) £690 $1,104

A Regency tôle ware tea tray, of canted rectangular shape, the angled gallery borders japanned in scarlet and gilded, 76cm. wide.
(Tennants) £8,500 $13,600

A serpentine mahogany tray-on-stand, the tray with a pierced baluster turned gallery, the stand with lapetted club legs, 30½in. wide. (Christie's) £1,380 $2,208

A Continental tôle peinte large rectangular tray, 19th century, finely painted with a wood cutter smoking his pipe, 30¹/8in. long.
(Sotheby's) £491 $805

A Hammond No. 12 American type-shuttle machine with Ideal keyboard, with wooden case and instructions, 1893.
(Auction Team Köln) £313 $502

An Active Export model of the German three-row type-wheel machine, with stationary carriage which presaged the golf-ball machines of the 1960s, 1913.
(Auction Team Köln) £418 $669

An Imperial Model B three-row British typebar machine with round keyboard and double shift keys, 1914.
(Auction Team Köln) £293 $468

A silver Bennett American portable typebar machine, for the coat pocket!, with silver paper panel and cover, 1907.
(Auction Team Köln) £293 $469

A French Virotype pointer typewriter by Kavalleristen Viry, with table base, 1914.
(Auction Team Köln) £293 $468

The Thaler Keyboard, an American practice keyboard for linotype operators, with 26-page original manual, original dispatch note and box, 1923.
(Auction Team Köln) £50 $80

A Salter Standard No. 10 three-row overstrike version, with round porcelain keys, of the popular British typebar machine, 1908.
(Auction Team Köln) £627 $1,004

A Columbia No 2 typewriter designed by the New York clockmaker Charles Spiro, with large type wheel for large and small characters, the first typewriter with porportional type, 1884.
(Auction Team Köln) £2,638 $4,220

A decorative American Odell's Typewriter No 4 pointer machine, with large and small type, in original wooden case, 1889.
(Auction Team Köln) £1,172 $1,875

A Hammond Multiplex American type shuttle machine with Universal keyboard and normal and cyrillic lettering, 1913.
(Auction Team Köln) £137 $220

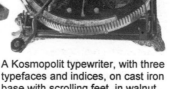

A Kosmopolit typewriter, with three typefaces and indices, on cast iron base with scrolling feet, in walnut case. (Christie's) £6,325 $10,120

A Courier typewriter, Austrian version of the Oliver No. 3, 1903.
(Auction Team Köln) £108 $173

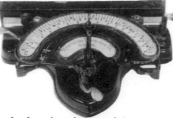

An American Index pointer typewriter with semi-circular dial, lacking platen, 1893.
(Auction Team Köln) £460 $738

An American Index pointer typewriter, lacking platen, 1893.
(Auction Team Köln) £230 $368

A Clavier Ecolier Navarre practice keyboard with spring keys, French, circa 1920.
(Auction Team Köln) £125 $201

A German Rofa Model IV typebar machine with straight three-row Universal keyboard and vertical typebars, Scandinavian keyboard, 1923.
(Auction Team Köln) £314 $502

A rare Titania braille typewriter by Mix & Genest, Berlin.
(Auction Team Köln) £460 $736

A rare Adler No. 8 dual script bumper typewriter for 180 characters, with interchangeable typebasket for 90 characters, 1903.
(Auction Team Köln) £356 $570

A Standard Folding typewriter, the first portable machine, with folding carriage, inspiration for the Corona Folding, 1907.
(Auction Team Köln) £293 $469

A rare version of the Odell No. 5, with maker's details in cast metal on the head and base, *America Co., Momence Ill.,* 1889.
(Auction Team Köln) £1,005 $1,608

A Remington No. 7 upstrike machine with cursive script and shift, as well as Gorin tabulator, rare in Europe, 1896.
(Auction Team Köln) £251 $402

A Mignon No. 4 export model for the French market, with poster type cylinder and original wooden case, 1923.
(Auction Team Köln) £272 $435

An American Rem-Sho upstrike machine with copper case, 1896.
(Auction Team Köln) £920 $1,473

A rare Franklin No. 9 version of the decorative American typebar machine with round Ideal keyboard, with tin case, 1898.
(Auction Team Köln) £502 $804

A Rofa Model IV German typebar machine with straight three-row keyboard, with tin case, 1923. (Auction Team Köln) £272 $435

The Crown, 1894, the first model of the famous American pointer typewriter by Byron A. Brooks, New York, with three row type wheel, and straight front.(Auction Team Köln) £6,280 $10,049

A Moya No. 2 Visible typewriter, with three-row keyboard, oxidised brass top-plate and metal cover. (Christie's) £805 $1,288

A Hammond Model 1a typewriter with typical thick Model 1 piano keys and round Ideal keyboard, in original wooden case. circa 1888. (Auction Team Köln) £1,089 $1,742

A French Typo version of the famous British Imperial Visible Model B typewriter, with Ideal keyboard and shifts to both sides, 1914. (Auction Team Köln) £335 $536

A Mercedes Model 4 German standard typewriter with four row Hebrew keyboard and corresponding left to right carriage return, 1924. (Auction Team Köln) $398 $636

An early Crandall model of rhe popular American typesleeve machine, the square keys with glass covers, with original case, 1879. (Auction Team Köln) £4,606 $7,370

A Typo Visible, the French version of the popular British Imperial Visible Model B, with French Ideal keyboard and shift keys to both sides, 1914. (Auction Team Köln) £460 $736

A Lambert typewriter, by The Gramophone & Typewriter Ltd., with blue and gilt lining, in leather carrying case. (Christie's) £632 $1,011

A rare Helios Klimax foreign language model of the Berlin type-cylinder machine, with two-row keyboard, 1914. (Auction Team Köln)£1,004 $1,607

A Merritt American pointer typewriter with upstrike action, the carriage swivels up for better legibility, 1889. (Auction Team Köln) £335 $536

A very rare German Rico No. 1-A tin toy typewriter by Richard Koch & Co. Nürnberg, with interesting type segment mechanism, circa 1932. (Auction Team Köln) £293 $469

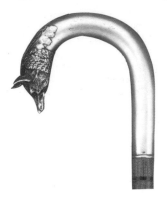

An ivory mounted malacca walking stick, the handle modelled as a snarling dog's head in wing collar with inset ebonised eyes, incised horn collar, ivory ferrule, 34¼in. (Christie's) £747 $1,195

A silver mounted bamboo walking stick, the crooked handle with tip modelled as an oak-leaf crested fox's head mounted with garnet eyes, 37¼in. (Christie's) £747 $1,195

An ivory handled walking stick, early 20th century, the grip amusingly modelled as a smiling moon-faced man, with rosewood shaft and gold collar. (Christie's) £552 $883

An ivory handled walking stick, late 19th/early 20th century, the L-shaped grip carved with a lion's head and extending paw. (Christie's) £1,092 $1,747

A Victorian ivory handled automaton walking stick, late 19th century, a button to the white metal studded collar, operating the articulated eyes and jaw. (Christie's) £4,830 $7,728

An ivory handled walking stick, early 20th century, the grip carved with a horse's head, with white metal collar and tapering hardwood shaft. (Christie's) £1,610 $2,576

An ivory handled walking stick, late 19th or early 20th century, the grip carved as a dog's head with inset glass eyes. (Christie's) £575 $840

A silver mounted walking stick, the handle modelled as a jaguar's head with open jaw and mounted with garnet eyes, upper shaft applied with silver trellis decoration, 34¾in. (Christie's) £977 $1,563

An ivory handled walking stick, late 19th or early 20th century, the grip carved as a snarling dog's head, with inset glass eyes. (Christie's) £805 $1,288

An ivory mounted malacca walking stick, the tapered handle relief-carved to one side with a scene of Adonis snatching Cupid's bow, the reverse showing Venus, 32⅝in. (Christie's)   £414 $662

A silver mounted stained walking stick, the tapered handle inset to the top with a domed rose quartz, above bands of foliate geometric and floral swagged decoration, 32⅝in. (Christie's)   £517 $827

A fine and rare carved ivory and panbone cane, initialled *J.L.*, 19th century, having a whale ivory handle in the form of a fist, 38in. long. (Sotheby's)   £842 $1,380

A fine carved whale ivory and panbone cane, mid-19th century, having a fluted and faceted whale ivory handle fitted with a base metal disc, 32¼in. long. (Sotheby's)   £666 $1,092

An Austrian enamelled-gilt mounted bamboo walking stick, second quarter 19th century, the handle modelled as a miniature sedan chair with two mirror-inset windows about a similar door, 33⅜in. (Christie's)   £517 $827

A fine carved whale ivory and panbone cane, 19th century, having a faceted and baluster-turned whale ivory knob handle continuing to a panbone shaft carved with diamonds and spirals, 33in. long. (Sotheby's)   £772 $1,265

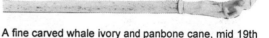

A fine carved whale ivory and panbone cane, mid 19th century, having a whale ivory fist handle continuing to a panbone barley shaft, 36in. long. (Sotheby's)   £1,333 $2,185

A fine carved whale ivory and panbone cane, mid 19th century, the handle carved from whale ivory in the from of a Chinese gentleman, 35½in. long. (Sotheby's)   £631 $1,035

A narwhal tusk walking stick, the naturally tapered and writhen tusk with floral decorated silver top cap, 36¼in. (Christie's)   £2,012 $3,219

A Venetian brass and white metal mounted gondolier's tall cane, mid-19th century, the handle mounted with a stylised lion's mask to the tip, multi-collared shaft with eyelet, decorated with brass studs overall, 38¼in. (Christie's)   £517 $827

An Anglo Indian ivory mounted walking stick, the upper shaft extending to handle modelled as a stylised prowling lion, 36½in. (Christie's)   £322 $515

A hardstone walking stick, the L–shaped handle with diamond lozenge, upon multi-coloured shaft of various hardstones, 34½in. (Christie's)   £350 $560

A carved wood walking stick, the L–shaped handle decorated with figures on horseback to either side, extending to faux bamboo shaft, 34½in. (Christie's)   £460 $736

An ebonised wood mounted marine ivory walking stick, the T-shaped bi-coloured handle on writhen tapering shaft, 36½in. (Christie's)   £483 $773

Ship-form carved wood and zinc weather vane, attributed to Frank Adams, Martha's Vineyard, Massachusetts, circa 1930, 37¾in. long. (Skinner)   £1,128 $1,840

Horse and sulky gilt moulded copper weather vane, attributed to J.W. Fiske & Co., late 19th century, *St Julian* model fine verdigris, areas of gilt, 45¼in. long. (Skinner)   £17,638 $28,750

A moulded copper horse and rider weathervane, American, third quarter 19th century, the flattened full-bodied form with applied tail and rider, 18¾in. long. (Sotheby's)   £5,612 $9,200

Rooster gilt cast zinc and sheet copper weather vane, J. Howard, Bridgewater, Massachusetts, late 19th century, traces of gilt, verdigris surface, 25in. long. (Skinner)   £1,904 $3,105

A fine moulded copper and zinc cow weathervane, American, 19th century, the swell-bodied form with cast zinc head, weathered to a verdigris; mounted on a rod in a black metal base, 33 x 19in. (Sotheby's)   £5,612 $9,200

A fine moulded and gilded copper horse and rider weathervane, American, third quarter 19th century, moulded in the full round, the copper horse with cast zinc rider, mounted on a rod, 27in. long. (Sotheby's)   £14,030 $23,000

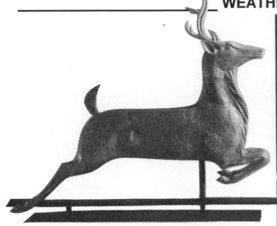

A fine moulded and gilded copper and zinc leaping stag weathervane, late 19th century, the swell-bodied form with cast zinc head and antlers, front legs extended, overall height 23½in.
(Sotheby's)   £4,910 $8,050

A fine moulded and gilded copper leaping horse weathervane, A.L. Jewell & Co., Waltham, Mass., third quarter 19th century, the swell-bodied figure of a leaping horse with applied mane and tail mounted on an orb, 35½in. long. (Sotheby's)   £28,060 $46,000

A fine and rare painted and gilded pine rooster, probably Maine, late 18th/early 19th century, with elaborately and finely carved feather and wing detail and arching tail, 32in. long.
(Sotheby's)   £9,821 $16,100

Eagle gilt moulded copper weather vane, A.L. Jewell & Co., Waltham, Massachusetts, 1855–67, areas of verdigris, 25½in. long. (Skinner)   £2,293 $3,738

Eagle and quill moulded copper weather vane, America, late 19th century, fine verdigris, remnants of old weathered gold paint, 45in. long.
(Skinner)   £1,622 $2,645

A fine moulded copper and zinc horse weathervane, American, third quarter 19th century, with cast-zinc forequarters and a sheet-copper tail, 35½in. long.
(Sotheby's)   £14,030 $23,000

Jumping horse gilt moulded and applied copper weathervane, probably A.L. Jewell & Co., Waltham, Massachusetts, second half 19th century, old painted surface, 36½in. long.
(Skinner)   £13,939 $23,000

Bull moulded and applied copper weathervane, possibly A.L. Jewell & Co., Waltham, Massachusetts, last quarter 19th century, fine verdigris, 42in. long.
(Skinner)   £20,909 $34,500

A carved and painted pine rooster weathervane, American, third quarter, 19th century, the plump robust form carved from three thickness of wood, 20in. high. (Sotheby's)   £2,104 $3,450

A fine moulded and gilded copper horse weathervane, American, late 19th century, with moulded mane and flowing tail, 36in. long.
(Sotheby's)   £16,134 $26,450

Running horse gilt moulded zinc weathervane, America, late 19th century, 19in. high, 31in. long.
(Skinner)   £1,725 $2,760

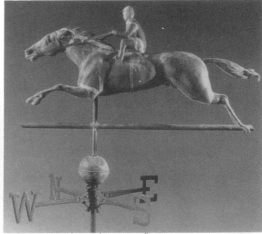

A moulded copper and cast zinc horse and rider weathervane, American, late 19th/early 20th century, the stylised full-bodied form of a horse and rider with cast zinc head, 34in. long.
(Sotheby's)   £2,806 $4,600

Cabinet card photo of Annie Oakley, holding a shot gun, posing with her rifles and medals. Captioned, reverse with a bio of Annie Oakley.
(Christie's)   £2,898 $4,830

A group of flag fragments from a Model 1872 Cavalry guidon silk flag, found in Sitting Bull's camp.
(Christie's)   £1,794 $2,990

An early 20th century top hat style Stetson hat, constructed of a satin brim and felt band, marked with the Stetson crest, together with the original box.
(Christie's)   £138 $230

Lela Cody, Cody Fameux Tireur, lithograph in colour, 1895, linen backed. Cody would shoot the small resin spheres surrounding his wife Lela, on horseback, 71in. long.
(Christie's)   £1,932 $3,220

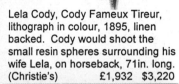

A Levi denim banner, circa 1930s, which may be one of the oldest Levi denim banners, depicting Levi's trademark of horses pulling pants apart, 28 x 64½in.
(Christie's)   £1,035 $1,725

Hollywood Silversmith Western, a silver and gold tone clock with diamond and circle shaped numbers, the frame engraved with floral motifs.
(Christie's)   £207 $345

A Samuel S. Hart brand Queen of Hearts Faro playing card, signed at the bottom margin: *J.W. Hardin July 4, 1895.* This card was shot three times during a shooting exhibition sponsored by Hardin, on July 4th, 1895. (Christie's)   £3,312 $5,520

Texas style spurs, by K & Co., a pair of early 20th century single mounted one piece iron spurs, the heel bands nickel overlaid with Crockett's attractive bull head image, overall spur length 6½in.
(Christie's)   £1,380 $2,300

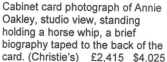

Cabinet card photograph of Annie Oakley, studio view, standing holding a horse whip, a brief biography taped to the back of the card. (Christie's) £2,415 $4,025

A Colt .44 cal. model 1873 single action army revolver, serial no. 98216, large blade fore-sight and frame mounted rear sight, hard rubber grips, butt strap marked *Ben Wheeler/Caldwell Kansas.*, 5¹/8in. barrel. (Christie's) £7,590 $12,650

Thirty-two different examples of 1870 and 1880 barbed wire, each example mounted with a plaque on a wooden display case, 32 x 43in. (Christie's) £1,104 $1,840

Cabinet card photograph of Buffalo Bill, standing dressed in his signature suit.
(Christie's) £1,035 $1,725

A pair of gauntlets made of hide with the top panels adorned with contour beading, against a blue background.
(Christie's) £1,035 $1,725

Cabinet card photo of William F. Cody, standing, with rifle by his side. Captioned at bottom of photo. (Christie's) £1,380 $2,300

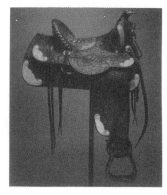

On the Frontier, lithograph in colours, 1901, printed by Armitage and Ibbetson, England, linen backed, 86in. high.
(Christie's) £4,485 $7,475

A pair of early 20th century brown leather chaps, hallmarked *H.H. Heiser Maker Denver Colo.* on the end of the billet, elaborately adorned with nickel plated brass studs. (Christie's) £1,380 $2,300

A circa 1936 black leather saddle, hallmarked *N. Porter Phoenix* with the longhorn motif, the leather completely tooled in a foliage design. (Christie's) £2,200 $3,680

A circa mid twentieth century Bohlin bit constructed of silver steel, with a ½in. Bohlin ranger set with the original black Bohlin leather belt. (Christie's)   £655 $1,093

Cheyenne split style spurs, attributed to Rex Schnitger, circa 1920s, the heel bands are overlaid in a linear motif, overall length 5½in. (Christie's) £1,380 $2,300

A pair of circa 1920s double mounted iron spurs from Amozoc, Mexico, the heel bands adorned with silver inlay in a snake motif, overall spur length: 7½in. (Christie's)   £2,070 $3,450

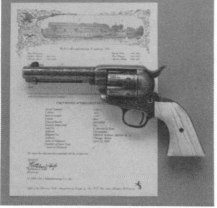

A pair of early 20th century white angora shotgun chaps by Clark, the brown leather belt and tooled in a basket-weave pattern. (Christie's)   £690 $1,150

Rare factory engraved Colt .45 single action army revolver, serial no., 150652, blued and colour case hardened finish. Recoil shield and loading gate engraved with fan patterns, 4¾in. barrel. (Christie's)   £5,520 $9,200

Cabinet card photo of Buffalo Bill, a portrait view of Buffalo Bill. Captioned at bottom of photo. (Christie's)   £655 $1,093

A decorative tin sign with a paper calendar dated 1915, used as a advertisement for Pierson and Hough Saddlery; together with a cardboard calendar dated 1936. (Christie's)   £262 $437

A Levi's denim jacket that won second place in Levi Strauss's oldest jacket contest, circa 1910-1920s. (Christie's) £2,415 $4,025

A beaded hide handbag in the form of a horseshoe with contour beading against a blue and green background. (Christie's)   £1,242 $2,070

Tim Mccoy's Real Wild West Show, lithograph in colour, 1920s, linen backed, 20 x 26in.
(Christie's)   £879 $1,495

Early 20th century one piece single mounted iron Texas style spurs, attributed to Mc Chesney, the heel bands are styled in a scallop motif, overall length, 6½in.
(Christie's)   £2,760 $4,600

101 Ranch Shows, Auto Polo, lithograph in colours, 1913, printed by Strobridge Lithograph Company, linen backed, 19 x 28in.
(Christie's)   £310 $518

A scalping knife blade found on the Timber Fight Line, worn down from years of use and sharpened on one side, which is typical of the American Indian used knives.
(Christie's)   £2,760 $4,600

A 10ct. gold pin, originally owned by Annie Oakley, an exact replica of Annie Oakley's Stevens Slide Action Rifle, commissioned for her to give to her nieces, 2½in. long.
(Christie's)   £3,795 $6,325

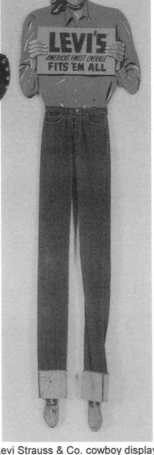

California style spurs by August Buermann, a pair of late 19th century two piece iron spurs, the heel bands silver inlaid and engraved with a card suit motif, overall spur length 6½in.
(Christie's)   £1,035 $1,725

Early 20th century fine grey felt sombrero; the hat band is constructed with contrasting black felt and gold thread to represent the Mexican eagle and snake motif.
(Christie's)   £897 $1,495

A photograph of Captain Myles W Keogh's horse, Comanche, from the 7th Calvary. Keogh's horse was found on the battlefield after the Little Bighorn massacre.
(Christie's)   £1,518 $2,530

Levi Strauss & Co. cowboy display, circa 1930s to 1940s, was used in stores for marketing purposes.
(Christie's)   £1,104 $1,840

Wells Fargo Railroad Safety box, made of wood reinforced with iron straps, used to transport packages, 22 x 38in.
(Christie's)   £2,415 $4,025

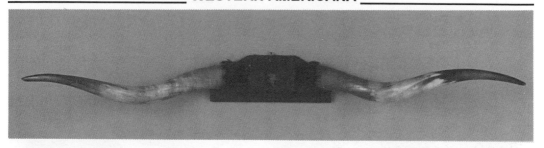

Large Texas longhorns, with a large Texas star, circa late 1880s, with fine patina, six feet long. (Christie's) £2,415 $4,025

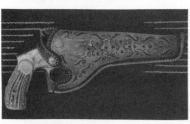

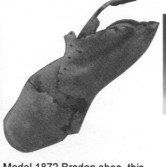

A Smith & Wesson .44 Russian model revolver and a silver mounted holster, nickel plated, with ivory grips, 6½in. barrel. (Christie's) £1,794 $2,990

A Model 1872 Brodan shoe, this shoe was found on the Timber Fight Line. (Christie's) £966 $1,610

A circa 1870s green painted wooden treasure box, hallmarked *Wells Fargo & Co.,* by J.Y. Ayer's, with iron hardware on the corners, and a hand forged iron latch, 20 x 12in. (Christie's) £4,830 $8,050

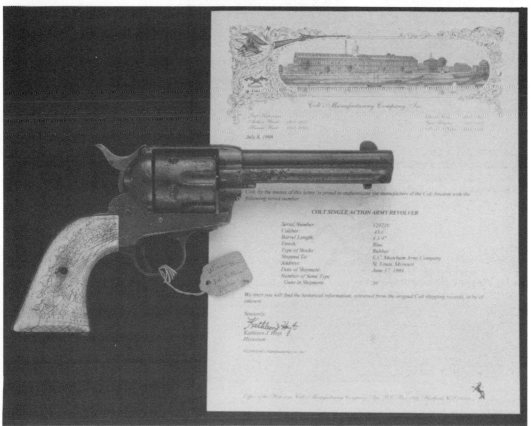

An important historic Colt .45 cal. single action army revolver, two-piece ivory grips with incised decorative motifs, attributed to the legendary Bob Dalton, 4¾in. barrel. (Christie's) £54,300 $90,500

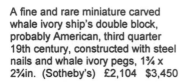

A fine and rare miniature carved whale ivory ship's double block, probably American, third quarter 19th century, constructed with steel nails and whale ivory pegs, 1¾ x 2¾in. (Sotheby's) £2,104 $3,450

A whimsical panbone alphabet set, mid 19th century, the cylindrical panbone container with fitted lid engraved with *ABC* and leafage, 1¾in. high. (Sotheby's) £701 $1,150

A fine panbone and baleen whisk/broom, probably American, mid 19th century, together with a horse hair clothes brush with a turned whale ivory handle, 9½in. long. (Sotheby's) £456 $747

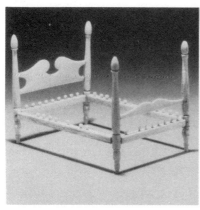

A panbone doll's bed, the four poster bed with shaped head and foot boards, the bed rails with turned heads, 6 x 8½in. (Sotheby's) £351 $575

A whale bone mechanical toy, with the figure of a small cat menacing a smaller bird inside a cage, 5⅜in. high. (Sotheby's) £2,455 $4,025

A fine and rare panbone fruit basket, probably American, mid 19th century, on mahogany base, 5½ x 8in. (Sotheby's) £2,806 $4,600

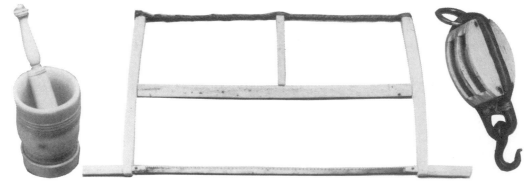

A whale ivory miniature mortar and pestle, probably American, mid 19th century, the mortar and pestle with ring turnings, 2in. high. (Sotheby's) £912 $1,495

A rare panbone cross-cut saw, mid-19th century, with faceted handles fitted with an iron blade, 13½ x 29½in. (Sotheby's) £1,754 $2,875

A rare whalebone ship's double block, probably American, mid 19th century, the block with original canvas covered rope, 5½ x 11in. (Sotheby's) £1,578 $2,587

A fine engraved and scrimshawed whale ivory, baleen and whale teeth watch stand, probably American, third quarter 19th century, 7in. high. (Sotheby's) £9,120 $14,950

A fine carved and turned panbone pounce pot, probably American, mid 19th century, threaded screw base and turned handle, 3½in. high. (Sotheby's) £631 $1,035

A carved whale ivory, panbone and hardwood mechanical sailor and keg toy, the articulated body of the sailor with moving arms and legs pulling a cart, 6¾in. long. (Sotheby's) £1,263 $2,070

A fine and rare panbone whale boat model, probably Azorean, 20th century, a detailed and accurate model of a whaleboat with linen sails, 16 pieces, 14¾in. long. (Sotheby's) £1,734 $2,875

A rare incised whale ivory miniature Bible cover, mid-19th century, with stipple engraved leafage, containing a miniature history of the Bible, 2¼ x 1¾in. (Sotheby's) £701 $1,150

A fine and rare carved panbone birdcage, Anonymous, New London, Connecticut, late 19th century, constructed in the form of an octagonal building with four double columned portals, 25in. high. (Sotheby's) £6,313 $10,350

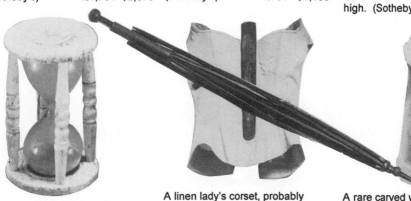

A carved panbone hourglass, the blown glass hour glass mounted in a turned stand with four columnar supports, 4½in. high. (Sotheby's) £455 $747

A linen lady's corset, probably American, mid 19th century, inscribed *Julia A. Hudson No. 7*, with a sterling silver boat pin and an engraved baleen busk. (Sotheby's) £982 $1,610

A rare carved whale ivory pepper pot, probably American, mid 19th century, carved from a single whale's tooth in the form of an 18th century silver shaker, 3¼in. high. (Sotheby's) £1,333 $2,185

A rare panbone rolling pin, probably American, mid 19th century, fashioned entirely from a single length of panbone, 11¾in. long. (Sotheby's) £526 $862

A fine carved whale ivory and panbone jagging wheel, probably American, mid 19th century, the handle carved in the form of a stylized monument, 9¼in. long. (Sotheby's) £842 $1,380

A carved whale ivory and panbone jagging wheel, probably American, mid 19th century, having a turned, incised and tapered whale ivory handle, 8in. long. (Sotheby's) £420 $690

A fine carved whale ivory jagging wheel, probably American, mid 19th century, the handle pierced with hearts, diamonds and a cross, 7½in. long. (Sotheby's) £2,280 $3,737

A rare panbone alphabet set probably American, mid 19th century, a complete set , each tile stained red and inscribed with a letter of the alphabet, 26 pieces, each tile is approximately 1½in. (Sotheby's) £140 $230

A rare set of panbone and ebony dominoes, probably American, late 19th century, comprising approximately twentyeight tiles and a pair of die, 2½ x 7½in. (Sotheby's) £456 $747

A panbone miniature Queen Anne armchair and articulated whalebone doll, the female doll with moving arms and legs and real hair, 6¼in. high. (Sotheby's) £911 $1,495

Man's unusual watch holder, made from two engraved whale's teeth decorated with American ships, watch support in the form of a whalebone anchor with fouled line separates teeth, whalebone base, 8½in. high. (Eldred's) £756 $1,210

A fine and rare inlaid wood and whale ivory sewing stand, probably American, mid 19th century, a three-tiered stand with iron thread holders each topped with a turned whale ivory finial, 17in. high. (Sotheby's) £491 $805

Rare whalebone, whale ivory and mahogany knitting basket, with pierced whalebone splats mounted on a mahogany base, five turned whale ivory feet, 12in. diameter. (Eldred's) £2,544 $4,070

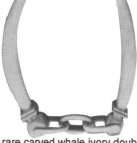

A rare carved whale ivory double bodkin, probably American, mid 19th century, with faceted finials joined by a puzzle carved chain, 4in. long. (Sotheby's) £1,052 $1,725

A fine and rare whale ivory steam engine model, probably American, third quarter 19th century, fully articulated on a walnut base, 8½in. x 12¾in. (Sotheby's) £3,332 $5,462

A fine carved whale ivory jagging wheel, probably American, third quarter 19th century, the tear-drop shaped handle pierced with a flower head, 6in. long.
(Sotheby's) £1,333 $2,185

A carved whale ivory tobacco pipe, probably 20th century, the bowl carved in the form of a woman's head continuing to a panbone stem, 7in. long. (Sotheby's) £245 $402

A fine decorative whale ivory seam creaser, probably American, third quarter 19th century, the handle with a clenched fist and relief carved ropework, 5½in. long.
(Sotheby's) £982 $1,610

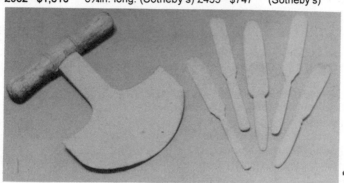

A fine carved whale ivory and coconut shell dipper, third quarter 19th century, the handle with stylized whale ivory columns continuing to a coconut shell bowl, 14½in. long.
(Sotheby's) £982 $1,610

A fine carved and turned panbone seam rubber and needle case, probably American, third quarter 19th century, the turned and incised handle unscrews to a hollow needle case continuing to a shaped wedge, 6¼in. long. (Sotheby's) £455 $747

A rare panbone miniature domino set in a turned whale ivory cylinder box with screw lid, probably American, mid 19th century, comprising twenty-three miniature tiles and a pair of die, 4in. long.
(Sotheby's) £911 $1,495

Extremely rare carved and jointed scrimshaw whalebone doll, first quarter of the 19th century, fully carved with painted carved hair, eyes and mouth, excellent condition, 4¾in. high.
(Eldred's) £1,719 $2,750

A rare panbone food chopper, mid 19th century, fashioned entirely from panbone, having a shaped and incised handle, together with five bone spreaders.
(Sotheby's) £631 $1,035

A fine and rare inlaid panbone, whale ivory and mahogany watch hutch, probably American, mid 19th century, made in the form of a tall case clock, 12in. high.
(Sotheby's) £2,630 $4,312

A pair of turned panbone candlesticks, probably 20th century, the baluster-turned standards with shaped candle cup, 10½in. high.
(Sotheby's) £842 $1,380

A carved and painted wood model of the whaleship 'Morningstar', probably American, late 19th/early 20th century, the fully rigged, three masted whaling vessel with five longboats, 18½in. high x 26in. long.
(Sotheby's) £491 $805

A panbone horse pull-toy, the full-bodied figure of a horse with incised tail and inlaid baleen eyes, 7in. long. (Sotheby's) £631 $1,035

A carved and painted pine coiled rattlesnake, American, late 19th/early 20th century, with incised skin and extended rattler, 12in. high. (Sotheby's) £5,612 $9,200

A treen ladle, the well carved flattened stem with hand finial, the centre part carved with a mask, 19th century, 39cm. (Tennants) £220 $352

An unusual carved and painted primitive man on horseback pull-toy, American, late 19th or early 20th century, 15in. (Sotheby's) £6,313 $10,350

A carved and painted wood large toy figure of a camel, 19th century, possibly American, fitted with leather ears and a rope tail, 23½in. long. (Sotheby's) £175 $287

A Continental polychrome-painted wood figure, late 19th century, modelled as a seated and bewigged gentleman holding a cane, with secret compartment to his back, 31¾in. high. (Christie's) £1,840 $2,944

A white painted composition and wood large bust of George Washington, with a serious jowl, his head inclined slightly to dexter. (Sotheby's) £1,578 $2,587

A carved and painted pine cigar store Indian figure, American, 19th century, the full-length standing figure of an Indian princess wearing a feathered headdress, 69in. high. (Sotheby's) £18,239 $29,900

A carved pine figure of Pan, first half 20th century, shown with one leg raised, the other resting on a conch shell, 54in. high. (Christie's) £1,380 $2,208

Well carved lime wood figure of a saint, his hands tied behind his back around a knarled trunk, 8in. high. (Ewbank) £6,400 $10,560

Paint decorated wood double runner sled, America, late 19th century, decorated with a reserve of a cardinal in a marsh setting. (Skinner) £494 $805

A fine carved and painted pine American eagle, late 19th/early 20th century, with raised wings on a rockwork base, 56in. high. (Sotheby's) £6,664 $10,925

A pair of early 19th century gilt gesso twin branch wall sconces, of ribbon and foliate wreath form, 31in. high. (Dreweatt Neate) £1,300 $2,145

A carved and painted spreadwing eagle, attributed to John Haley Bellamy (1836-1914), Kittery Point, Maine, late 19th century, with upturned neck and articulated eyes, 32in. high, 19½in. wide. (Christie's) £8,280 $13,800

Handpainted and carved 19th century wooden eagle. (Remmey) £625 $1,000

Paint decorated covered turned maple bowl, probably Ohio, first half 19th century, fanciful feather designs in reds and green, 7in. high. (Skinner) £1,603 $2,645

An English painted wood 'Dummy Board', 18th century, painted a s a young gardener resting on a shovel, 66⁵/8in. high. (Sotheby's) £3,508 $5,750

A full carved and painted oak American eagle bowsprit billethead, John Haley Bellamy, Kittery, Maine, circa 1900, 56in. long. (Sotheby's) £7,015 $11,500

Paint decorated carved wood pig, 20th century, with glass eyes, leather ears and metal tail, 20¼in. long. (Skinner) £529 $862

Carved wood lion's head, attributed to Folger of Nantucket, MA. 8in., late 19th century, 8in. high. (Eldred's) £378 $605

Two Fish and a Frog, signed *L.A. Plummer 1904*, polychrome wood carving, 25 x 40¼in. (Skinner) £10,583 $17,250

A rare and important classic New Mexican polychromed wood female bulto of Nuestra Señora de la Rosario, Rafaél Aragón, circa 1850, carved from a single block of wood. (Sotheby's) £18,940 $31,050

A pair of massive Regency giltwood three-light wall appliqués, each with a winged female caryatid figure, 54in. high. (Christie's) £34,500 $56,580

A carved and painted pine owl, American late 19th/early 20th century, with carved feathers and wings, fitted with glass eyes, 18in. high. (Sotheby's) £28,760 $47,150

An amusing painted and lithographed wood toy sailor puppet, probably English, mid 19th century, 15in. high. (Sotheby's) £420 $690

A pair of giltwood and silvered greyhounds, each in the form of a sitting greyhound with a collar, 13½in. wide. (Christie's) £2,300 $3,818

A carved and painted pine bust portrait of a young gentleman, American, late 19th/early 20th century, on a pedestal base, 20½in. high. (Sotheby's) £5,963 $9,775

Paint decorated games board, America, late 19th/early 20th century, the hinged board painted green with red, yellow, blue and black, 19¼ x 19¼in.
(Skinner)   £1,603 $2,645

Carved and painted wood figural carnival mask, America, 19th century, in the form of a black man with hair wig, 14in. high.
(Skinner)   £458 $748

Paint decorated games board, America, late 19th/early 20th century, the board with moulded edge, 18¾ x 18½in.
(Skinner)   £906 $1,495

A rare and early kake hana-ike (hanging flower vase), late 16th/early 17th century, of gnarled wood, perhaps formed from a section of an ancient creeper, 16¹/₈in. (Christie's) £3,220 $5,249

A pair of Italian walnut figurative pricket candlesticks, 17th century and later, each in the form of a kneeling figure holding a turned dish with a spike on a platform, 26in. high.
(Christie's)   £4,370 $7,254

A carved and painted pine Indian Princess cigar store counter top figure, attributed to Samuel Robb, New York, circa 1880, 50in. high.
(Sotheby's)   £17,690 $29,900

A fine and painted pine cigar store Indian counter top figure, New York, third quarter 19th century, 33in. high. (Sotheby's) £17,537 $28,750

A carved and gilded eagle architectural ornament, American, 19th century, the full-bodied figure with carved and articulated head, breast, wings and feet, 41in. wide.
(Christie's)   £2,070 $3,450

Polychrome carved wood chamois, 19th century, on contemporary base, 24½in. high.
(Skinner)   £677 $1,150

A Black Forest carved wood model of a hare, late 19th/early 20th century, shown standing on its haunches amongst foliage, the body hinged at the shoulders, 17½in. high.
(Christie's)   £6,325 $10,120

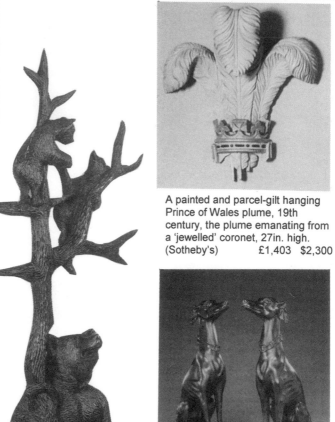

A painted and parcel-gilt hanging Prince of Wales plume, 19th century, the plume emanating from a 'jewelled' coronet, 27in. high.
(Sotheby's)   £1,403 $2,300

Covered wooden firkin, in old grey paint, 19th century, 10in. high.
(Eldred's)   £48 $77

A pair of Regency style ebonised wood models of whippets, circa 1900, each shown seated on their haunches and wearing collars, 30¼in. high.
(Christie's)   £5,060 $8,096

A pair of Charles X giltwood floor standing candlesticks, the tapering uprights carved with foliate and fluted ornament, 42½in. high.
(Christie's)   £1,035 $1,656

A Black Forest carved and stained wood hall stand, circa 1920, modelled as a bear holding a branch with two smaller bears in the upper reaches, 80in. high.
(Christie's)   £4,600 $7,360

Life-size decorative lesser yellowlegs carving by A.E. Crowell, East Harwich, MA.
(Eldred's)   £1,466 $2,420

INDEX

LIST OF ADVERTISERS